Sixth Edition

ACCOUNTING AND FINANCE
for Non-Specialists

Peter Atrill and **Eddie McLaney**

FT Prentice Hall
FINANCIAL TIMES

An imprint of **Pearson Education**

Harlow, England • London • New York • Boston • San Francisco • Toronto • Sydney • Singapore • Hong Kong
Tokyo • Seoul • Taipei • New Delhi • Cape Town • Madrid • Mexico City • Amsterdam • Munich • Paris • Milan

Pearson Education Limited

Edinburgh Gate
Harlow
Essex CM20 2JE
England

and Associated Companies throughout the world

Visit us on the World Wide Web at:
www.pearsoned.co.uk

First published 1995 by Prentice Hall Europe
Second edition published 1997
Third edition published 2001 by Pearson Education Limited
Fourth edition published 2004
Fifth edition published 2006
Sixth edition published 2008

© Pearson Education Limited 2008

ISBN: 978-0-273-71694-5

British Library Cataloguing-in-Publication Data
A catalogue record for this book is available from the British Library

Library of Congress Cataloging-in-Publication Data
Atrill, Peter.
 Accounting and finance for non-specialists / Peter Atrill and Eddie McLaney. — 6th ed.
  p. cm.
 Includes bibliographical references and index.
 ISBN-13: 978-0-273-71694-5 (alk. paper) 1. Accounting. 2. Financial statements. I. McLaney, E. J.
II. Title.
 HF5636.A87 2007
 657—dc22

                                                                    2008007986

10 9 8 7 6 5 4 3 2 1
11 10 09 08

Typeset in 9/12.5pt Stone Serif by 35
Printed and bound in Great Britain by Ashford Colour Press, Gosport, Hants

The publisher's policy is to use paper manufactured from sustainable forests.

ACCOUNTING AND FINANCE
for Non-Specialists

Visit the *Accounting and Finance for Non-Specialists*, sixth edition, MyAccountingLab at **www.myaccountinglab.com** to find valuable **student** learning material including:

- Diagnostic Tests designed to determine your strengths and weaknesses.
- A personalised Study Plan containing practice questions and support materials.
- Key Concept mini-lecture animations.
- Interactive Study Guide containing further activities and exercise material.

PEARSON
Education

We work with leading authors to develop the strongest educational materials in business and finance, bringing cutting-edge thinking and best learning practice to a global market.

Under a range of well-known imprints, including Financial Times Prentice Hall, we craft high quality print and electronic publications that help readers to understand and apply their content, whether studying or at work.

To find out more about the complete range of our publishing, please visit us on the World Wide Web at: **www.pearsoned.co.uk**

Brief contents

Contents

Part 1 FINANCIAL ACCOUNTING

Contents

Part 3 FINANCIAL MANAGEMENT

Supporting resources

Visit **www.pearsoned.co.uk/atrillmclaney** to find valuable online resources:

- Diagnostic Tests designed to determine your strengths and weaknesses.
- A personalised Study Plan containing practice questions and support materials.
- Key Concept mini-lecture animations.
- Interactive Study Guide containing further activities and exercise material.

For instructors:

- Complete, downloadable Instructor's manual.
- PowerPoint slides that can be downloadable and used as OHTs.
- Progress tests, consisting of various questions and exercise material with solutions.
- Tutorial/seminar questions and solutions.
- Solutions to individual chapter exercises.

For more information please contact your local Pearson Education sales representation or visit **www.pearsoned.co.uk/atrillmclaney**.

Preface

This text provides an introduction to accounting and finance. It is aimed primarily at students who are not majoring in accounting or finance but who are, nevertheless, studying introductory-level accounting and finance as part of their course in business, economics, hospitality management, tourism, engineering, or some other area. Students who are majoring in either accounting or finance should, however, find the book a useful introduction to the main principles, which can serve as a foundation for further study. The text does not focus on the technical aspects, but rather examines the basic principles and underlying concepts and the ways in which accounting statements and financial information can be used to improve the quality of decision-making. To reinforce this practical emphasis, there are, throughout the text, numerous illustrative extracts with commentary from company reports, survey data and other sources.

In this sixth edition, we have taken the opportunity to make improvements that have been suggested by both students and lecturers who used the previous edition. We have brought up to date and expanded the number of examples from real life.

Changes brought about as a result of the recent move towards international financial reporting standards mean that the layouts used in previous editions no longer have to be followed by large companies. In this new edition, we have adopted the layouts that now appear to be standard practice.

The text is written in an 'open-learning' style. This means that there are numerous integrated activities, worked examples and questions throughout the text to help you to understand the subject fully. You are encouraged to interact with the material and to check your progress continually. Irrespective of whether you are using the book as part of a taught course or for personal study, we have found that this approach is more 'user-friendly' and makes it easier for you to learn.

We recognise that most of you will not have studied accounting or finance before, and we have therefore tried to write in a concise and accessible style, minimising the use of technical jargon. We have also tried to introduce topics gradually, explaining everything as we go. Where technical terminology is unavoidable we try to provide clear explanations. In addition, you will find all the **key terms** highlighted in the text, and then listed at the end of each chapter with a page reference. All these key terms are also listed alphabetically, with a concise definition, in the glossary at the end of the book (see Appendix A). This should provide a convenient point of reference from which to revise.

A further important consideration in helping you to understand and absorb the topics covered is the design of the text itself. The page layout and colour scheme have been carefully considered to allow for the easy navigation and digestion of material. The layout features a large page format, an open design, and clear signposting of the various features and assessment material. More detail about the nature and use of these features is given in the 'How to use this book' section below; and the main points are also summarised, using example pages from the text, in the guided tour on pp. xviii–xix.

We hope that you find the book both readable and helpful.

How to use this book

We have organised the chapters to reflect what we consider to be a logical sequence and, for this reason, we suggest that you work through the text in the order in which it is presented. We have tried to ensure that earlier chapters do not refer to concepts or terms that are not explained until a later chapter. If you work through the chapters in the 'wrong' order, you will probably encounter concepts and terms that were explained previously.

Irrespective of whether you are using the book as part of a lecture/tutorial-based course or as the basis for a more independent mode of study, we advocate following broadly the same approach.

Integrated assessment material

Interspersed throughout each chapter are numerous **Activities**. You are strongly advised to attempt all of these questions. They are designed to simulate the sort of quick-fire questions that your lecturer might throw at you during a lecture or tutorial. Activities serve two purposes:

- to give you the opportunity to check that you understand what has been covered so far;
- to encourage you to think about the topic just covered, either to see a link between that topic and others with which you are already familiar, or to link the topic just covered to the next.

The answer to each Activity is provided immediately after the question. This answer should be covered up until you have deduced your solution, which can then be compared with the one given.

In each chapter, except for Chapter 1, there is a **self-assessment question**. This is more comprehensive and demanding than most of the Activities, and is designed to give you an opportunity to check and apply your understanding of the core coverage of the chapter. The answer to each of these questions is provided in Appendix B at the end of the book. As with the Activities, it is important that you attempt each question thoroughly before referring to the solution. If you have difficulty with a self-assessment question, you should go over the relevant chapter again.

End-of-chapter assessment material

At the end of each chapter there are four **review questions**. These are short questions requiring a narrative answer or discussion within a tutorial group. They are intended to help you to assess how well you can recall and critically evaluate the core terms and concepts covered in each chapter. Answers to these questions are provided in Appendix C at the end of the book.

At the end of each chapter, except for Chapter 1, there are five **exercises**. These are mostly computational and are designed to reinforce your knowledge and understanding. Exercises are graded as either 'basic' or 'more advanced' according to their level of difficulty. The basic-level questions are fairly straightforward; the more advanced ones can be quite demanding but are capable of being successfully completed if you have worked conscientiously through the chapter and have attempted the basic exercises. Answers to three of the exercises in each chapter are provided in Appendix D at the end of the book. A coloured exercise number identifies these three questions. Here, too, a thorough attempt should be made to answer each exercise before referring to the solution. Answers to the other two exercises are provided in a separate Instructors' Manual.

Guided tour of the book

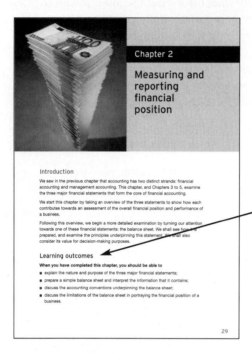

Learning outcomes
Bullet points at the start of each chapter show what you can expect to learn from that chapter, and highlight the core coverage.

Examples
At frequent intervals throughout most chapters, there are numerical examples that give you step-by-step workings to follow through to the solution.

Key terms
The key concepts and techniques in each chapter are highlighted in colour where they are first introduced, with an adjacent icon in the margin to help you refer back to the most important points.

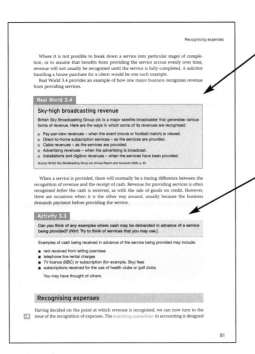

'Real World' illustrations

Integrated throughout the text, these illustrative examples highlight the practical application of accounting concepts and techniques by real businesses, including extracts from company reports and financial statements, survey data and other interesting insights from business.

Activities

These short questions, integrated throughout each chapter, allow you to check your understanding as you progress through the text. They comprise either a narrative question requiring you to review or critically consider topics, or a numerical problem requiring you to deduce a solution. A suggested answer is given immediately after each activity.

Bullet point chapter summary

Each chapter ends with a 'bullet point' summary. This highlights the material covered in the chapter and can be used as a quick reminder of the main issues.

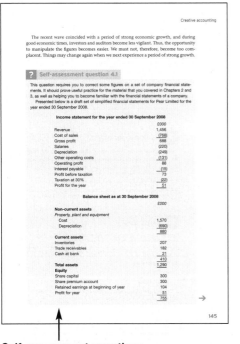

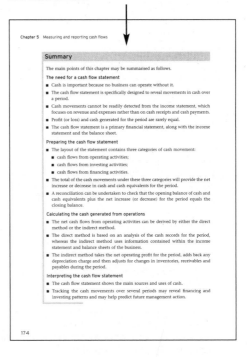

Self-assessment questions

Towards the end of most chapters you will encounter one of these questions, allowing you to attempt a comprehensive question before tackling the end-of-chapter assessment material. To check your understanding and progress, solutions are provided at the end of the book.

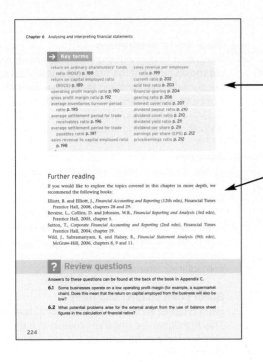

Key terms summary
At the end of each chapter, there is a listing (with page references) of all the key terms, allowing you to easily refer back to the most important points.

Further reading
This section comprises a listing of relevant chapters in other textbooks that you might refer to in order to pursue a topic in more depth or gain an alternative perspective.

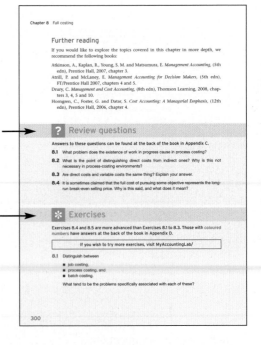

Review questions
These short questions encourage you to review and/or critically discuss your understanding of the main topics covered in each chapter, either individually or in a group. Solutions to these questions can be found at the end of the book.

Exercises
These comprehensive questions appear at the end of most chapters. The more advanced questions are separately identified. Solutions to some of the questions (those with coloured numbers) are provided at the end of the book, enabling you to assess your progress. Solutions to the remaining questions are available online for lecturers only. Additional exercises can be found within MyAccountingLab at **www.pearsoned.co.uk/atrillmclaney.**

Guided Tour – MyAccountingLab

MyAccountingLab puts students in control of their own learning through a suite of study and practice tools tied to the online e-book and other media tools. At the core of **MyAccountingLab** are the following features:

Practice tests

Practice tests for each section of the textbook enable students to test their understanding and identify the areas in which they need to do further work. Lecturers can customise the practice tests or leave students to use the two pre-built tests per chapter.

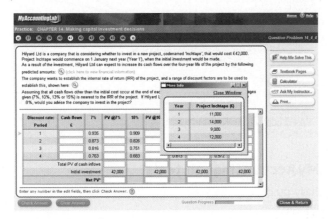

Personalised study plan

Based on a student's performance on a practice test, a personal study plan is generated that shows where further study needs to focus. This study plan consists of a series of additional practice exercises.

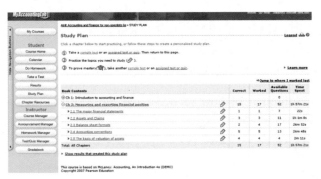

Additional practice exercises

Generated by the student's own performance on a practice test, additional practice exercises are keyed to the textbook and provide extensive practice and link students to the e-book and to other tutorial instruction resources.

Tutorial instruction

Launched from the additional practice exercises, tutorial instruction is provided in the form of solutions to problems, detailed differential feedback, step-by-step explanations, and other media-based explanations, including key concept animations.

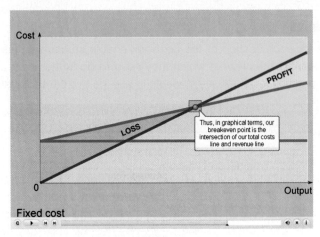

Additional MyAccountingLab tools

1. Interactive study guide.
2. Electronic tutorials.
3. Glossary - key terms from the textbook.
4. Glossary flashcards.
5. Links to the most useful accounting data and information sources on the Internet.

Lecturer Training and Support

We offer lecturers personalised training and support for **MyAccountingLab**. We have a dedicated team of Technology Specialists whose job it is to support lecturers in their use of our media products, including **MyAccountingLab**. To make contact with your Technology Specialist please email **feedback-cw@pearson.com**.

For a visual walkthrough of how to make the most of **MyAccountingLab**, visit **www.MyAcountingLab.com**.

To find details of your local sales representatives go to **www.pearsoned.co.uk/replocater**.

Acknowledgements

We are grateful to the following for permission to reproduce copyright material:

Figure 8.10 from 'Traditional versus activity-based costing', *Activity Based Costing: A Review with Case Studies*, by J. Innes and F. Mitchell, copyright © Elsevier 1990, reproduced with permission; Figure 11.4 'Asset finance provided by members of the Finance and Leasing Association, 2002 to 2006', from *Finance and Leasing Association Review 2007* www.fla.org.uk, reproduced with permission of FLA; and Figure 11.11 from 'Short-term and long-term financing requirements', *Finance for Small Firms: An Eleventh Report*, April 2004 reproduced with permission of the Bank of England.

News International Syndication for Real World 1.2 'The thoughts of Warren Buffet', *The Times*, 26 September 2002; Real World 1.3 'Margin of success for clothing retailers', *The Times*, 20 November 2002; and Real World 4.7 'Dirty laundry: how companies fudge the numbers', *The Times*, 22 September 2002, copyright © NI Syndication Ltd 2002; Millward Brown Optimor for Real World 2.1 'Valuing brands', from *Brandz Top 100 Most Powerful Brands*, reproduced with permission; Tottenham Hotspurs Football & Athletic Co. Ltd for Real World 2.2 'Ditmar is on the team sheet and on the balance sheet', from *Tottenham Hotspur plc Annual Report 2007* reproduced with permission; Marks and Spencer plc for Real World 2.3 'Retailer marks up land and buildings', from *Marks and Spencer plc Annual Report 2006*, and Real World 6.10 from 'Key performance measures of Marks and Spencer plc', from *Marks and Spencer plc Annual Report 2007* reproduced with permission; Greene King plc for Real World 2.6 'Taking stock', from *Greene King plc Annual Report 2007*, reproduced with permission; First Choice for Real World 3.2 'Selling point', from the *First Choice Holidays plc Annual Report 2006*, reproduced with permission; Jarvis plc for Real World 3.3 'Tracking revenue', from *Jarvis plc Annual Report and Accounts 2007*, reproduced with permission; Incisive Media for Real World 3.6 'JJB massages results to boost profits', *Accountancy Age*, 20 October 2005; and Real World 11.16 'Internet FD is in the money after flotation', by David Jetuah, *Accountancy Age*, 2 August 2007, reproduced with permission; Wiley-Blackwell Publishing Ltd for Real World 10.9 'A survey of UK business practice', by G.C. Arnold and P.D. Hatzopoulos, 'The theory-practice gap in capital budgeting: evidence from the United Kingdom', *Journal of Business Finance and Accounting*, June/July 2000, copyright © Wiley-Blackwell Publishing Ltd; Rolls-Royce International Limited for Real World 10.12 'The use of NPV at Rolls-Royce', from *Rolls-Royce plc Annual Report & Accounts 2006*, reproduced with permission; Telegraph Media Group Limited for Real World 11.1 'Ryanair blunted by Buzz takeover', by A. Osborne, *The Daily Telegraph*, 6 August 2004; and Real World 11.15 'From the market to the market', by Harry Wallop, *The Daily Telegraph*, 22 September 2006 copyright © The Telegraph 2004, 2006;

Office for National Statistics for Real World 11.19 'Ownership of UK listed shares', from *Ownership of UK listed shares* from *Financial Statistics, Share Ownership 2006*, Crown copyright material is reproduced with permission of the Controller of Her Majesty's Stationery Office; and REL Consultancy for Real World 12.2 'Working capital not working hard enough!', from *Annual Working Capital Survey*, conducted by REL and CFO Europe www.relconsultancy.com, 29 August 2007, reproduced with permission.

We are grateful to the Financial Times Limited for permission to reprint the following material:

Real World 1.1 'Morrison in uphill battle to integrate Safeway', © *Financial Times*, 26 May 2005; Real World 1.5 'Fair shares?', © *Financial Times*, 11 June 2005; Real World 1.6 'Profit without honour', © *Financial Times*, 29/30 June 2002; Real World 1.7 'Appetite for risks drives industry', © *Financial Times*, 27 June 2007; Real World 3.8 'How the banks assess their customers', © *Financial Times*, 3 October 2007; Real World 4.1 'Monotub Industries in a spin as founder gets Titan for £1', © *Financial Times*, 23 January 2003; Real World 4.8 'Dell to lower writedowns on restated earnings', © *Financial Times*, 30 October 2007; Real World 6.4 'Investing in Bollywood', © *Financial Times*, 26 June 2007; Real World 6.6 'Small companies surprise on lending', © *Financial Times*, 25 April 2003; Real World 7.6 'The tricky question of who pays', © *Financial Times*, 25 July 2007; Real World 9.4 'Watchdog warns on Olympic costs', © *Financial Times*, 20 July 2007; Real World 10.6 'Bond seeks funds in London to min African diamonds', © *Financial Times*, 23 April 2007; Real World 10.7 'A hot topic, but poor returns', © *Financial Times*, 27 August 2005; Real World 10.11 'Satellites need space to earn', © *Financial Times*, 14 July 2003; Real World 11.3 'New appetite develops for Eurobonds', © *Financial Times*, 18 September 2004; Real World 11.13 'Greed and gullibility keep new issues afloat', © *Financial Times*, 8 August 2003; Real World 12.8 'Late payment hits small companies', © *Financial Times*, 29 January 2007; Real World 12.12 'NHS paying bills late in struggle to balance books, say suppliers', © *Financial Times*, 13 February 2007.

In some instances we have been unable to trace the owners of copyright material and we would appreciate any information that would enable us to do so.

Chapter 1

Introduction to accounting and finance

Introduction

Welcome to the world of accounting and finance! In this opening chapter we provide a broad outline of these subjects. We begin by considering the roles of accounting and finance and then go on to identify the main users of financial information. We shall see how both accounting and finance can be valuable tools in helping these users improve the quality of their decisions. In subsequent chapters, we develop this decision-making theme by examining in some detail the kinds of financial reports and methods used to aid decision-making.

For many of you, accounting and finance are not the main focus of your studies and you may well be asking 'Why do I need to study these subjects?' So, after we have considered the key features of accounting and finance, we shall go on to discuss why some understanding of them is likely to be relevant to you.

Learning outcomes

When you have completed this chapter, you should be able to

■ explain the nature and roles of accounting and finance;

■ identify the main users of financial information and discuss their needs;

■ distinguish between financial and management accounting;

■ explain why an understanding of accounting and finance is likely to be relevant to your needs.

What are accounting and finance?

Let us start our study of accounting and finance by trying to understand the purpose of each. Accounting is concerned with collecting, analysing and communicating financial information. This information is useful for those who need to make decisions and plans about businesses, including those who need to control those businesses. For example, the managers of businesses may need accounting information to decide whether to

- develop new products or services (as with a computer manufacturer developing a new range of computers);
- increase or decrease the price or quantity of existing products or services (as with a telecommunications business changing its mobile phone call and text charges);
- borrow money to help finance the business (as with a supermarket wishing to increase the number of stores it owns);
- increase or decrease the operating capacity of the business (as with a beef farming business reviewing the size of its herd); and
- change the methods of purchasing, production or distribution (as with a clothes retailer switching from UK to overseas suppliers).

The information provided should help in identifying and assessing the financial consequences of these sorts of decisions.

Though managers are likely to be important users of accounting information relating to their particular business, they are by no means the only users. There are those outside the business (whom we shall identify later) who may need accounting information to decide whether to

- invest or disinvest in the ownership of the business (for example, buy or sell shares);
- lend money to the business;
- offer credit facilities (for example, a bank to grant an overdraft); and
- enter into contracts for the purchase of products or services.

Sometimes the impression is given that the purpose of accounting is simply to prepare financial reports on a regular basis. While it is true that accountants undertake this kind of work, the preparation of financial reports does not represent an end in itself. The ultimate purpose of the accountant's work is to give people better information on which to base their decisions. This decision-making perspective of accounting dictates the theme of this book and shapes the way in which we deal with each topic.

Finance (or financial management), like accounting, exists to help decision-makers. It is concerned with the ways in which funds for a business are raised and invested. This lies at the very heart of what a business is about. In essence, a business exists to raise funds from investors (owners and lenders) and then to use those funds to make investments (in equipment, premises, inventories and so on) in an attempt to make the business, and its owners, wealthier. It is important that funds are raised in a way that is appropriate to the particular needs of the business, and an understanding of finance should help in identifying

3

- the main forms of finance available;
- the costs and benefits of each form of finance;
- the risks associated with each form of finance; and
- the role of financial markets in supplying finance.

Once the funds are raised, they must be invested in a way that will provide the business with a worthwhile return. An understanding of finance should help in evaluating

- the returns from an investment; and
- the risks associated with an investment.

Businesses tend to raise and invest funds in large amounts for long periods of time. The quality of the investment decisions made can, therefore, have a profound impact on the fortunes of the business.

There is little point in trying to make a sharp distinction between accounting and finance. We have already seen that both are concerned with the financial aspects of decision-making. There is considerable overlap between the two subjects: for example, accounting reports are a major source of information for financing and investment decision-making. In this book, we shall not emphasise the distinctions between accounting and finance.

Who are the users of accounting information?

For accounting information to be useful, the accountant must be clear *for whom* the information is being prepared and *for what purpose* the information will be used. There are likely to be various groups of people (known as 'user groups') with an interest in a particular organisation, in the sense of needing to make decisions about it. For the typical private-sector business, the most important of these groups are shown in Figure 1.1. Take a look at this figure and then try Activity 1.1.

Activity 1.1

Ptarmigan Insurance plc (PI) is a large motor insurance business. Taking the user groups identified in Figure 1.1, suggest, for each group, the sorts of decisions likely to be made about PI and the factors to be taken into account when making these decisions.

Your answer may be as follows:

User group	Decision
Customers	Whether to take further motor policies with PI. This might involve customers seeking to assess PI's ability to continue in business and to meet their needs, particularly in respect of any insurance claims made.

Competitors	How best to compete against PI or, perhaps, whether to leave the market on the grounds that it is not possible to compete profitably with PI. This might involve using PI's performance in various aspects as a 'benchmark' when assessing their own performance. They might also try to assess PI's financial strength and to identify significant changes that may signal PI's future actions (for example, raising funds as a prelude to market expansion).
Employees	Whether to continue in employment with PI and, if so, whether to demand higher rewards for their labour. The future plans, profits and financial strength of the business are likely to be of particular interest to employees when making these decisions.
Government	Whether PI should pay tax and, if so, how much; whether it complies with agreed pricing policies; whether financial support is needed. In making these decisions an assessment of PI's profits, sales revenues and financial strength would be made.
Community representatives	Whether to allow PI to expand its premises and/or whether to provide economic support for the business. PI's ability to continue to provide employment for the community, to use community resources and to help fund environmental improvements are likely to be considered when arriving at such decisions.
Investment analysts	Whether to advise clients to invest in PI. This would involve an assessment of the likely risks and future returns associated with PI.
Suppliers	Whether to continue to supply PI and, if so, whether to supply on credit. This would involve an assessment of PI's ability to pay for any goods and services supplied.
Lenders	Whether to lend money to PI and/or whether to require repayment of any existing loans. PI's ability to pay the interest and to repay the principal sum would be important factors in such decisions.
Managers	Whether PI's performance needs to be improved. Performance to date would be compared with earlier plans or some other 'benchmark' to decide whether action needs to be taken. Managers may also wish to decide whether there should be a change in PI's future direction. This would involve looking at PI's ability to perform and at the opportunities available to it.
Owners	Whether to invest more in PI or to sell all, or part, of the investment currently held. This would involve an assessment of the likely risks and returns associated with PI. Owners may also be involved with decisions on rewarding senior managers. The financial performance of the business would normally be considered when making such a decision.

Although this answer covers many of the key points, you may have identified other decisions and/or other factors to be taken into account by each group.

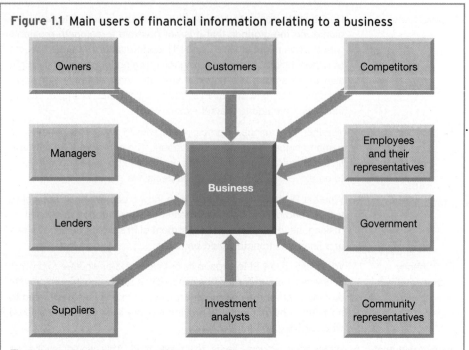

Figure 1.1 Main users of financial information relating to a business

There are several user groups with an interest in the accounting information relating to a business. The majority of these are outside the business but, nevertheless, they have a stake in it. This is not meant to be an exhaustive list of potential users; however, the groups identified are normally the most important.

Accounting as a service

One way of viewing accounting is as a form of service. Accountants provide financial information to their 'clients', who are the various users identified in Figure 1.1. The quality of the service provided is determined by the extent to which the needs of the various user groups have been met. To meet these users' needs, it can be argued that accounting information should possess certain key qualities, or characteristics: relevance, reliability, comparability and understandability.

Relevance

Accounting information must have the ability to influence decisions. Unless this characteristic is present, there is really no point in producing the information. The information may be relevant to the prediction of future events (for example, in predicting how much profit is likely to be earned next year) or relevant in helping to confirm past events (for example, in assessing how much profit was earned last year). The role of accounting in confirming past events is important because users often wish to check the accuracy of earlier predictions that they have made. The accuracy (or inaccuracy) of earlier predictions may then help users to judge the likely accuracy of current predictions. To influence a decision, the information must, of course, be available when the decision is being made: in other words, it must be timely.

Reliability

Accounting information should be free from serious error or bias. Users should feel confident that it represents what it is supposed to represent. Though both relevance and reliability are very important, the problem that we often face in accounting is that information that is highly relevant may not be very reliable, and that which is reliable may not be very relevant.

Activity 1.2

To illustrate this last point, let us assume that a manager has to sell a custom-built machine owned by the business and has recently received a bid for it. This machine is very unusual and there is no ready market for it.

What information would be relevant to the manager when deciding whether to accept the bid? How reliable would that information be?

The manager would probably like to know the current market value of the machine before deciding whether or not to accept the bid. The current market value would be highly relevant to the final decision, but it might not be very reliable because the machine is unique and there is likely to be little information concerning market values.

Where a choice has to be made between providing information that has either more relevance or more reliability, the maximisation of relevance is usually the guiding rule. No matter how reliable the information is, it is useless if it is not relevant. On the other hand, information that is not totally reliable can be useful if it is relevant.

Comparability

This quality will enable users to identify changes in the business over time (for example, the trend in sales revenue over the past five years). It will also help them to evaluate the performance of the business in relation to similar businesses. Comparability is achieved by treating items that are basically the same in the same manner for accounting purposes. Comparability tends also to be enhanced by making clear the policies that have been adopted in measuring and presenting the information.

Understandability

Accounting reports should be expressed as clearly as possible and should be understood by those at whom the information is aimed.

Activity 1.3

Do you think that accounting reports should be understandable to those who have not studied accounting?

It would be very useful if everyone could understand accounting reports, but realistically this is not likely to be the case. Complex financial events and transactions cannot always be reported easily. It is probably best that we regard accounting reports in the same way as we regard a report written in a foreign language. To understand either of these, we need to have had some preparation. Generally speaking, accounting reports assume that the user not only has a reasonable knowledge of business and accounting but is also prepared to invest some time in studying the reports.

Despite the answer to Activity 1.3, the onus is clearly on accountants to provide information in a way that makes it as understandable as possible to non-accountants.

But . . . is it material?

The qualities, or characteristics, that have just been described will help us to decide whether accounting information is potentially useful. If a particular piece of information has these qualities then it may be useful. However, this does not automatically mean that it should be reported to users. We also have to consider whether the information is material, or significant. This means that we should ask whether its omission, or misrepresentation in the accounting reports, would really alter the decisions that users make. Thus, in addition to possessing the characteristics mentioned above, accounting information must also cross the threshold of materiality. If the information is not regarded as material, it should not be included within the reports, as it will merely clutter them up and, perhaps, interfere with the users' ability to interpret the financial results. The type of information and amounts involved will normally determine whether it is material.

Weighing up the costs and benefits

Having read the previous sections you may feel that, when considering a piece of accounting information, provided the four main qualities identified are present and it is material, it should be gathered and made available to users. Unfortunately, there is one more hurdle to jump. Something may still exclude a piece of accounting information from the reports even when it is considered to be useful. Consider Activity 1.4.

Activity 1.4

Suppose an item of information is capable of being provided. It is relevant to a particular decision; it is also reliable, comparable, can be understood by the decision-maker concerned and is material.

Can you think of a practical reason why you might choose not to produce the information?

The reason that you may decide not to produce, or discover, the information is that you judge the cost of doing so to be greater than the potential benefit of having the information. This cost–benefit issue will limit the extent to which accounting information is provided.

In theory, a particular item of accounting information should only be produced if the costs of providing it are less than the benefits, or value, to be derived from its use. In practice, however, these costs and benefits are often difficult to assess.

To illustrate the practical problems, let us suppose that someone has dented and scraped the paint of one of the doors of our car. We wish to have the dent taken out and the door resprayed at a local garage. We know that the nearest garage would charge £250 but believe that other local garages might do the job for a lower price. The only ways of finding out the prices at other garages is to visit them, so that the garages can see the extent of the damage. Visiting the garages will involve using some petrol. Also some of our time will be involved. Is it worth the cost of finding out the price for the job at the various local garages? The answer, as we have seen, is that if the cost of discovering the price is less than the potential benefit, it is worth having that information.

To identify the various prices for the job, there are several points to be considered, including:

■ How many garages shall we visit?
■ What is the cost of petrol necessary to visit each garage?
■ How long will it take to make all the garage visits?
■ How much do we value our time?

The economic benefit of having the information about the prices for the job is probably even harder to assess – remember that we have only contacted one garage so far. The following points need to be considered:

■ What is the cheapest price that we might be quoted for the job?
■ How likely is it that we shall be quoted a price cheaper than £250?

As we can imagine, the answers to these questions may be far from clear. When assessing the value of accounting information we are confronted with similar problems.

Providing accounting information can be very costly; however, the costs are often difficult to quantify. Although the direct, out-of-pocket costs, such as salaries of accounting staff, may be quantifiable, these are only part of the total costs involved. There are also less direct – and less quantifiable – costs, such as the cost of the user's time spent on analysing and interpreting the information contained in reports.

The economic benefit of having accounting information is even harder to assess. It is possible to apply some 'science' to the problem of weighing the costs and benefits, but a lot of subjective judgement is likely to be involved. Whereas no one would seriously advocate that the typical business should produce no accounting information, at the same time no one would advocate that every item of information that could be seen as possessing one or more of the key characteristics should be produced, irrespective of the cost of producing it.

The characteristics that influence the usefulness of accounting information and which have been discussed in this section and the preceding section are set out in Figure 1.2.

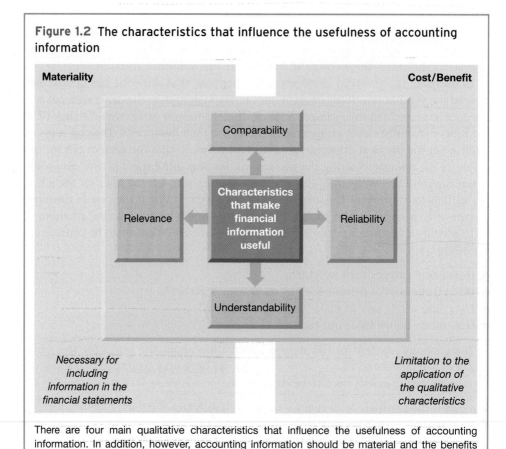

Figure 1.2 The characteristics that influence the usefulness of accounting information

There are four main qualitative characteristics that influence the usefulness of accounting information. In addition, however, accounting information should be material and the benefits of providing the information should outweigh the costs.

Accounting as an information system

We have already seen that accounting can be seen as the provision of a service to 'clients'. Another way of viewing accounting is as a part of the business's total information system. Users, both inside and outside the business, have to make decisions concerning the allocation of scarce resources. To try to ensure that these resources are allocated efficiently, users need financial information on which to base their decisions. It is the role of the accounting system to provide this information.

The accounting information system should have certain features that are common to all information systems within a business. These are:

- identifying and capturing relevant information (in this case financial information);
- recording the information collected in a systematic manner;
- analysing and interpreting the information collected;
- reporting the information in a manner that suits the needs of users.

The relationship between these features is set out in Figure 1.3.

Figure 1.3 The accounting information system

| Information identification | → | Information recording | → | Information analysis | → | Information reporting |

There are four sequential stages of an accounting information system. The first two stages are concerned with preparation, whereas the last two stages are concerned with using the information collected.

Real World 1.1

Blaming the system

When Sir Ken Morrison bought Safeway for £3.35bn in March 2004, he almost doubled the size of his supermarket chain overnight and went from being a regional operator to a national force. His plan was simple enough. He had to sell off some Safeway stores – Morrison has to date sold off 184 stores for an estimated £1.3bn – and convert the remaining 230 Safeway stores into Morrison's. Sir Ken has about another 50 to sell. But, nearly 15 months on, and the integration process is proving harder in practice than it looked on paper. Morrison, once known for its robust performance, has issued four profit warnings in the past 10 months. Each time the retailer has blamed Safeway. Last July, it was because of a faster-than-expected sales decline in Safeway stores. In March – there were two warnings that month – it was the fault of Safeway's accounting systems, which left Morrison with lower supplier incomes. This month's warning was put down to higher-than-expected costs from running parallel store systems. At the time of the first warning last July, Simon Procter, of the stockbrokers Charles Stanley, noted that the news 'has blown all profit forecasts out of the water and visibility is very poor from here on out'. But if it was difficult then to predict where Morrison's profits were heading, it is impossible now. Morrison itself cannot give guidance. 'No one envisaged this,' says Mr Procter. 'When I made that comment about visibility last July, I was thinking on a 12-month time frame, not a two-year one.' Morrison says the complexity of the Safeway deal has put a 'significant strain' on its ability to cope with managing internal accounts. 'This is impacting the ability of the board to forecast likely trends in profitability and the directors are therefore not currently in a position to provide reliable guidance on the level of profitability as a whole,' admits the retailer.

Source: 'Morrison in uphill battle to integrate Safeway', Elizabeth Rigby, FT.com, 26 May 2005.

Given the decision-making emphasis of this book, we shall be concerned primarily with the final two elements of the process: the analysis and reporting of financial information. We shall consider the way in which information is used by, and is useful to, users rather than the way in which it is identified and recorded.

Efficient accounting systems are an essential ingredient of an efficient business. When the accounting systems fail, the results can be disastrous. Real World 1.1 provides an example of a systems failure when two businesses combined and then attempted to integrate their respective systems.

Management and financial accounting

Accounting is usually seen as having two distinct strands. These are:

- Management accounting, which seeks to meet the needs of managers; and
- Financial accounting, which seeks to meet the accounting needs of all of the other users identified earlier in the chapter (see Figure 1.1).

The difference in their targeted users has led to each strand of accounting developing along different lines. The main areas of difference are as follows:

- *Nature of the reports produced*. Financial accounting reports tend to be general-purpose. That is, they contain financial information that will be useful for a broad range of users and decisions rather than being specifically designed for the needs of a particular group or set of decisions. Management accounting reports, on the other hand, are often specific-purpose reports. They are designed either with a particular decision in mind or for a particular manager.
- *Level of detail.* Financial accounting reports provide users with a broad overview of the performance and position of the business for a period. As a result, information is aggregated and detail is often lost. Management accounting reports, however, often provide managers with considerable detail to help them with a particular operational decision.
- *Regulations.* Financial accounting reports, for many businesses, are subject to accounting regulations that try to ensure that they are produced in a standard way. The law and accounting rule makers impose these regulations. As management accounting reports are for internal use only, there are no regulations from external sources concerning them. They can be designed to meet the needs of particular managers.
- *Reporting interval*. For most businesses, financial accounting reports are produced on an annual basis, though large businesses may produce half-yearly reports, and a few produce quarterly ones. Management accounting reports may be produced as frequently as required by managers. In many businesses, managers are provided with certain reports on a monthly, weekly or daily basis, which allows them to check progress frequently. In addition, special-purpose reports will be prepared

when required (for example, to evaluate a proposal to purchase a piece of equipment).

■ *Time orientation.* Financial accounting reports reflect the performance and position of the business for the past period. In essence, they are backward-looking. Management accounting reports, on the other hand, often provide information concerning future performance as well as past performance. It is an oversimplification, however, to suggest that financial accounting reports never incorporate expectations concerning the future. Occasionally, businesses will release projected information to other users in an attempt to raise capital or to fight off unwanted takeover bids. Even preparation of the routine financial accounting reports (which deal with past events) typically requires making some judgements about the future, as we shall see in Chapter 3.

■ *Range and quality of information.* Financial accounting reports concentrate on information that can be quantified in monetary terms. Management accounting also produces such reports, but is also more likely to produce reports that contain information of a non-financial nature, such as physical volume of inventories, number of sales orders received, number of new products launched, physical output per employee and so on. Financial accounting places greater emphasis on the use of objective, verifiable evidence when preparing reports. Management accounting reports may use information that is less objective and verifiable, but nevertheless provide managers with the information they need.

We can see from this that management accounting is less constrained than financial accounting. It may draw from a variety of sources and use information that has varying degrees of reliability. The only real test to be applied when assessing the value of the information produced for managers is whether or not it improves the quality of the decisions made.

The distinctions between management and financial accounting suggest that there are differences between the information needs of managers and those of other users. While differences undoubtedly exist, there is also a good deal of overlap between these needs.

Activity 1.5

We have seen that managers are provided with information that tends to be different from that provided to other users. Does this mean that managers are not interested in the information provided to other users and that others are not interested in management accounting information?

We thought of two points:

■ Managers will, at times, be interested in receiving a historical overview of business operations of the sort provided to other users.
■ Other users would be interested in receiving information relating to the future, such as the planned level of profits and non-financial information such as the state of the sales order book and the extent of product innovations.

The distinction between the two areas of accounting reflects, to some extent, the differences in access to financial information. Managers have much more control over the form and content of information they receive. Other users have to rely on what managers are prepared to provide or what must be provided to satisfy the financial reporting regulations. Though the scope of financial accounting reports has increased over time, fears concerning loss of competitive advantage and user ignorance concerning the reliability of forecast data have led businesses to resist providing other users with the same detailed and wide-ranging information available to managers.

Scope of this book

This book covers both financial accounting and management accounting topics. Broadly speaking, the next five chapters (Part 1, Chapters 2 to 6) are concerned with financial accounting topics, and the following three (Part 2, Chapters 7 to 9) with management accounting topics. The final part of the book (Part 3, Chapters 10 to 12) is concerned with the financial management of the business, that is, the chapters examine issues relating to the financing and investing activities of the business. As we have seen, accounting information is usually vitally important for these kinds of decisions.

Has accounting become too interesting?

In recent years, accounting has become front-page news and is a major talking point among those connected with the world of business. Unfortunately, the attention that accounting has attracted has been for all the wrong reasons. We have seen that investors rely on financial reports to help to keep an eye on both their investment and the managers. However, what if the managers provide misleading financial reports to investors? Recent revelations suggest that the managers of some large companies have been doing just this.

Two of the most notorious cases have been those of

- Enron, an energy-trading business based in Texas, which was accused of entering into complicated financial arrangements in an attempt to obscure losses and to inflate profits and
- WorldCom, a major long-distance telephone operator in the US, which was accused of reclassifying $3.9 billion of expenses so as to falsely inflate the profit figures that the business reported to its owners (shareholders) and to others.

In the wake of these scandals, there was much closer scrutiny by investment analysts and investors of the financial reports that businesses produce. This led to further businesses, in both the US and Europe, being accused of using dubious accounting practices to bolster profits.

Accounting scandals can have a profound effect on all those connected with the business. The Enron scandal, for example, ultimately led to the collapse of the business, which, in turn, resulted in lost jobs and large financial losses for lenders, suppliers and investors. Confidence in the world of business can be badly shaken by such events and this can pose problems for society as a whole. Not surprisingly, therefore, the relevant authorities tend to be severe on those who perpetrate such scandals. In the US, Bernie Ebbers, the former chief executive of WorldCom, received twenty-five years in prison for his part in the fraud.

Various reasons have been put forward to explain this spate of scandals. Some may have been caused by the pressures on managers to meet investors' unrealistic expectations of continually rising profits, others by the greed of unscrupulous executives whose pay is linked to financial performance. However, they may all reflect a particular economic environment.

Real World 1.2 gives some comments suggesting that when all appears to be going well with a business, people can be quite gullible and over-trusting.

Real World 1.2

The thoughts of Warren Buffett

Warren Buffett is one of the world's shrewdest and most successful investors. He believes that the accounting scandals mentioned above were perpetrated during the 'new economy boom' of the late 1990s when confidence was high and exaggerated predictions were being made concerning the future. He states that during that period:

> You had an erosion of accounting standards. You had an erosion, to some extent, of executive behaviour. But during a period when everybody 'believes', people who are inclined to take advantage of other people can get away with a lot.

> He believes that the worst is now over and that the 'dirty laundry' created during this heady period is being washed away and that the washing machine is now in the 'rinse cycle'.

Source: The Times, Business Section, 26 September 2002, p. 25.

Whatever the causes, the result of these accounting scandals has been to undermine the credibility of financial statements and to introduce much stricter regulations concerning the quality of financial information. We shall return to this issue in later chapters when we consider the financial statements.

The changing face of accounting and finance

Over the past twenty-five years, the environment within which businesses operate has become increasingly turbulent and competitive. Various reasons have been identified to explain these changes, including

- the increasing sophistication of customers;
- the development of a global economy where national frontiers become less important;
- rapid changes in technology;
- the deregulation of domestic markets (for example, electricity, water and gas);
- increasing pressure from owners (shareholders) for competitive economic returns; and
- the increasing volatility of financial markets.

This new, more complex, environment has brought new challenges for managers and other users of accounting information. Their needs have changed and both financial accounting and management accounting have had to respond. To meet the changing needs of users there has been a radical review of the kind of information to be reported.

The changing business environment has given added urgency to the search for a clear framework and principles upon which to base financial accounting reports. Various attempts have been made to clarify the purpose of financial accounting reports and to provide a more solid foundation for the development of accounting rules. The frameworks and principles that have been developed try to address fundamental questions such as:

- Who are the users of financial accounting information?
- What kinds of financial accounting reports should be prepared and what should they contain?
- How should items be measured?

In response to criticisms that the financial reports of some businesses are too opaque, accounting rule makers have tried to improve reporting rules to ensure that the accounting policies of businesses are more comparable and more transparent and that they portray economic reality more faithfully. While this has had a generally beneficial effect, the recent accounting scandals have highlighted the limitations of accounting rules in protecting investors and others.

The internationalisation of businesses has created a need for accounting rules to have an international reach. It can no longer be assumed that users of accounting information relating to a particular business are based in the country in which the business operates or are familiar with the accounting rules of that country. Thus, there has been increasing harmonisation of accounting rules across national frontiers.

Management accounting has also changed by becoming more outward-looking in its focus. In the past, information provided to managers has been largely restricted to that collected within the business. However, the attitude and behaviour of customers and rival businesses have now become the object of much information-gathering. Increasingly, successful businesses are those that are able to secure and maintain competitive advantage over their rivals.

To obtain this advantage, businesses have become more 'customer driven' (that is, concerned with satisfying customer needs). This has led to management accounting information that provides details of customers and the market. Such information might include results of surveys of customer satisfaction with the services provided by the business, and of the business's market share. In addition, information about the costs and profits of rival businesses, which can be used as 'benchmarks' by which to gauge competitiveness, is gathered and reported.

To compete successfully, businesses must also find ways of managing costs. The cost base of modern businesses is under continual review and this, in turn, has led to the development of more sophisticated methods of measuring and controlling costs.

How are businesses managed?

We have already seen that the environment in which businesses operate has become increasingly turbulent and competitive. The effect of these environmental changes has been to make the role of managers more complex and demanding. It has meant that managers have had to find new ways to manage their business. This has increasingly led to the introduction of strategic management.

Strategic management is designed to provide a business with a clear sense of purpose and to ensure that appropriate action is taken to achieve that purpose. The action taken should link the internal resources of the business to the external environment of competitors, suppliers, customers and so on. This should be done in such a way that any business strengths, such as having a skilled workforce, are exploited and any weaknesses, such as being short of investment finance, are not exposed. To achieve this requires the development of strategies and plans that take account of the business's strengths and weaknesses, as well as the opportunities offered and threats posed by the external environment. Access to a new, expanding market is an example of an opportunity; the decision of a major competitor to reduce prices is an example of a threat. This topic will be considered in more depth in Chapter 9 when we consider business planning and budgeting.

What is the financial objective of a business?

A business is normally created to enhance the wealth of its owners, and throughout this book we shall assume that this is its main objective. This may come as a surprise, as there are other objectives that a business may pursue that are related to the needs of others associated with the business. For example, a business may seek to provide good working conditions for its employees, or it may seek to conserve the environment for the local community. While a business may pursue these objectives, it is normally set up with a view to increasing the wealth of its owners, and in practice the behaviour of businesses over time appears to be consistent with this objective.

Real World 1.3 provides an example of the way that many clothes retailers pursue the search for profit.

Real World 1.3

From rags to riches

Progress in the search for profit is reported by the accounting information system. If managers find that the reported profits are inadequate, it can be an important driver for change. This change can, in turn, have a profound effect on the working lives of those both inside and outside the business.

Many clothes retailers have been concerned with profit levels in recent years. This has led them to make radical changes to the ways in which they operate. Low inflation and increased competition in the high street have forced the retailers to keep costs under strict control in order to meet their profit objectives. This has been done in various ways, including:

- moving production to cheaper countries and closing inflexible manufacturing offshoots;
- using fewer manufacturers and working more closely with manufacturers in the design of clothes. This has enabled the retailers to add details, such as embroidery or unusual design features, and to command a higher price for relatively little cost;
- improving communication to suppliers of materials and to manufacturers so that design and sourcing decisions can be made faster and more accurately. This has meant that the time to make garments has been reduced from as much as nine months to just a few weeks;
- predicting more accurately what customers want in order to avoid being left with inventories of unwanted items.

The effect of implementing these changes has been to reduce costs, and thereby improve profits, and to have more flexibility in the cost structure so that the clothes retailers are more able to weather a downturn.

Source: Adapted from 'Margin of success for clothing retailers', *The Times*, 20 November 2002, p. 30.

Within a market economy there are strong competitive forces at work that ensure that failure to enhance owners' wealth will not be tolerated for long. Competition for the funds provided by the owners and competition for managers' jobs will normally mean that the owners' interests will prevail. If the managers do not provide the expected increase in ownership wealth, the owners have the power to replace the existing management team with a new team that is more responsive to owners' needs.

Does this mean that the needs of other groups associated with the business (employees, customers, suppliers, the community and so on) are not really important? The answer to this question is certainly no, if the business wishes to survive and prosper over the longer term. Satisfying the needs of other groups will normally be consistent with increasing the wealth of the owners over the longer term.

The importance of customers to a business cannot be overstated. Dissatisfied customers will take their business to another supplier and this will, in turn, lead to a loss of wealth for the owners of the business losing the customers. Real World 1.4 provides an illustration of the way in which one leading business acknowledges the link between customer satisfaction and creating wealth for its owners.

Real World 1.4

Checking out Sainsbury's objectives

J. Sainsbury plc is a leading food retailer, which recognises the importance of customers to increasing the wealth of the owners (shareholders), as follows:

> Our vision is simple; we are here to serve customers well with a choice of great food at fair prices and, by so doing, to provide shareholders with strong, sustainable financial returns.

Source: 'Corporate objectives', in J Sainsbury plc *Annual report and financial statements 2007*, p. 1.

A dissatisfied workforce may result in low productivity, strikes and so forth, which will in turn have an adverse effect on owners' wealth. Similarly, a business that upsets the local community by unacceptable behaviour, such as polluting the environment, may attract bad publicity, resulting in heavy fines and a loss of customers.

Real World 1.5 provides an example of how two businesses responded to potentially damaging allegations.

Real World 1.5

The price of clothes

US clothing and sportswear manufacturers Gap and Nike have much of their clothes produced in Asia where labour tends to be cheap. However, some of the contractors that produce clothes on behalf of the two companies have been accused of unacceptable practices.

Campaigners visited the factories and came up with damaging allegations. The factories were employing minors, they said, and managers were harassing female employees.

Nike and Gap reacted by allowing independent inspectors into the factories. They promised to ensure their contractors obeyed minimum standards of employment. Earlier this year, Nike took the extraordinary step of publishing the names and addresses of all its contractors' factories on the internet. The company said it could not be sure all the abuse had stopped. It said that if campaigners visited its contractors' factories and found examples of continued malpractice, it would take action.

Nike and Gap said the approach made business sense. They needed society's approval if they were to prosper. Nike said it was concerned about the reaction of potential US recruits to the campaigners' allegations. They would not want to work for a company that was constantly in the news because of the allegedly cruel treatment of those who made its products.

Source: 'Fair shares?', Michael Skapinker, FT.com, 11 June 2005.

It is important to recognise that generating wealth for the owners is not the same as seeking to maximise the current year's profit. Wealth creation is a longer-term concept, which relates not only to this year's profit but to that of future years as well. In the short term, corners can be cut and risks taken that improve current profit at the expense of future profit. Real World 1.6 gives some examples of how emphasis on short-term profit can be damaging.

Real World 1.6

Short-term gains, long-term problems

In recent years, many businesses have been criticised for failing to consider the long-term implications of their policies on the wealth of the owners. John Kay argues that some businesses have achieved short-term increases in wealth by sacrificing their longer-term prosperity. He points out that

> The business of Marks and Spencer, the retailer, was unparalleled in reputation but mature. To achieve earnings growth consistent with a glamour rating the company squeezed suppliers, gave less value for money, spent less on stores. In 1998, it achieved the highest (profit) margin on sales in the history of the business. It had also compromised its position to the point where sales and profits plummeted.
>
> Banks and insurance companies have taken staff out of branches and retrained those that remain as sales people. The pharmaceuticals industry has taken advantage of mergers to consolidate its research and development facilities. Energy companies have cut back on exploration.
>
> We know that these actions increased corporate earnings. We do not know what effect they have on the long-run strength of the business – and this is the key point – do the companies themselves know? Some rationalisations will genuinely lead to more productive businesses. Other companies will suffer the fate of Marks and Spencer.

Source: 'Profit without honour', John Kay, *Financial Times Weekend*, 29/30 June 2002.

Balancing risk and return

All decision-making is an attempt to influence future outcomes and financial decision-making is no exception. The only thing certain about the future, however, is that we cannot be sure what is going to happen. There is a risk that things will not turn out as planned, which should be carefully considered in making all financial decisions.

As in other aspects of life, risk and return tend to be related. Evidence shows that returns relate to risk in something like the way shown in Figure 1.4.

This relationship between risk and return has important implications for setting financial objectives for a business. The owners will require a minimum return to induce them to invest at all, but will require an additional return to compensate for taking risks; the higher the risk, the higher the required return. Managers must be aware of this and must strike the appropriate balance between risk and return when setting objectives and when pursuing particular courses of action.

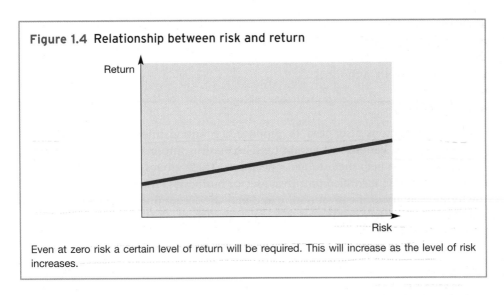

Figure 1.4 Relationship between risk and return

Even at zero risk a certain level of return will be required. This will increase as the level of risk increases.

Real World 1.7 describes how some businesses have been making higher-risk investments in pursuit of higher returns.

Real World 1.7

Appetite for risk drives businesses

Over the last few years, companies from the US and western Europe, joined increasingly by competitors from China and India, have looked to new markets abroad both to source and sell their products.

Driven by intensifying competition at home, companies have been drawn into direct investment in markets that not long ago were considered beyond the pale. But in the drive to increase returns, they have also been forced to accept higher risks.

Over time, the balance between risk and reward changes. For example, companies flooded into Russia early in the decade. But recently returns have fallen, largely due to booming raw materials prices. Meanwhile the apparent risk of investing in Russia has grown significantly.

As the risk/reward calculation has changed in Russia, companies have looked to other countries such as Libya and Vietnam where the rewards may be substantial, and the threats, though high, may be more manageable.

Source: Adapted from 'Appetite for risk drives industry', Stephen Fidler, FT.com, 27 June 2007.

Not-for-profit organisations

Though the focus of this book is accounting as it relates to private-sector businesses, there are many organisations that do not exist mainly for the pursuit of profit. Examples include

- charities;
- clubs and associations;
- universities;
- local government authorities;
- churches;
- trade unions.

Such organisations also need to produce accounting information for decision-making purposes. Various user groups need accounting information about these types of organisation to help them to make decisions. These groups are often the same as, or similar to, those identified for private-sector businesses. They may have a stake in the future viability of the organisation and may use accounting information to check that the wealth of the organisation is being properly controlled and used in a way that is consistent with its objectives.

Real World 1.8 provides an example of the importance of accounting to relief agencies.

Real World 1.8

Accounting for disasters

In the aftermath of the Asian tsunami more than £400m was raised from charitable donations. It was important that his huge amount of money for aid and reconstruction was used as efficiently and effectively as possible. That did not just mean medical staff and engineers. It also meant accountants.

The charity that exerts financial control over aid donations is Mango: Management Accounting for Non-Governmental Organisations (NGOs). It provides accountants in the field and it provides the back-up, such as financial training, and all the other services that should result in really robust financial management in a disaster area.

The world of aid has changed completely as a result of the tsunami. According to Mango's director, Alex Jacobs, 'Accounting is just as important as blankets. Agencies have been aware of this for years. But when you move on to a bigger scale there is more pressure to show the donations are being used appropriately.'

Source: Adapted from 'Tsunami: finding the right figures for disaster relief', Robert Bruce, FT.com, 7 March 2005, and 'The work of Mango: Coping with generous donations', Robert Bruce, FT. com, 27 February 2006.

Why do I need to know anything about accounting and finance?

If you are planning a career in accounting or finance, you will be clear as to why you are now studying these subjects.

If your career plans do not lie in that direction, you may be asking yourself at this point 'Why do I need to study accounting and finance? I don't intend to become an accountant!' Well, from the explanation of what accounting and finance is about, which has broadly been the subject of this chapter, it should be clear that the accounting/finance function within a business is a central part of its management information system. On the basis of information provided by the system, managers make decisions concerning the allocation of resources. These decisions may concern whether to

- continue with certain business operations;
- invest in particular projects; or
- sell particular products.

Such decisions can have a profound effect on all those connected with the business. It is important, therefore, that *all* those who intend to work in a business should have a fairly clear idea of certain important aspects of accounting and finance. These aspects include:

- how accounting reports should be read and interpreted;
- how financial plans are made;
- how investment decisions are made;
- how businesses are financed.

Many, perhaps most, students have a career goal of being a manager within a business – perhaps a personnel manager, production manager, marketing manager or IT manager. If you are one of these students, an understanding of accounting and finance is very important. When you become a manager, even a junior one, it is almost certain that you will have to use financial reports to help you to carry out your management tasks. It is equally certain that it is largely on the basis of financial information and reports that your performance as a manager will be judged.

As a manager, it is likely that you will be expected to help in forward planning for the business. This will often involve the preparation of projected financial statements and setting of financial targets. If you do not understand what the financial statements really mean and the extent to which the financial information is reliable, you will find yourself at a distinct disadvantage to others who know their way round the system. As a manager, you will also be expected to help decide how the limited resources available to the business should be allocated between competing options. This will require an ability to evaluate the costs and benefits of the different options available. Once again, an understanding of accounting and finance is important to carrying out this management task.

This is not to say that you cannot be an effective and successful personnel, production, marketing or IT manager unless you are also a qualified accountant. It does mean, however, that you need to become a bit 'streetwise' in accounting and finance in order to succeed. This book should give you that street wisdom.

Summary

The main points of this chapter may be summarised as follows.

What are accounting and finance?

- Accounting provides financial information to help various user groups make better judgements and decisions.
- Finance is concerned with the financing and investing activities of the business and is also concerned with improving the quality of user decisions.

Who are the users of accounting information?

- For accounting to be useful, it must be clear *for whom* and *for what purpose* the information is needed.
- Owners, managers and lenders are important user groups, but there are several others.

Accounting as a service

- Accounting can be seen as a form of service as it provides financial information for various users, or 'clients'.
- To provide a useful service, accounting information must possess certain qualities: relevance, reliability, comparability and understandability.
- Accounting information must also be material and should be produced only if the cost of providing it is less than the benefits gained.

Accounting as an information system

- Accounting shares the features that are common to all information systems within a business: identification, recording, analysis and reporting of information.

Management and financial accounting

- Accounting has two main strands: management accounting and financial accounting.
- Management accounting seeks to meet the needs of the business's managers and financial accounting seeks to meet the needs of the other user groups.
- These two strands differ in terms of the types of reports produced, the level of reporting detail, the time orientation, the degree of regulation and the range and quality of information provided.

Is accounting too interesting?

- In recent years, there has been a wave of accounting scandals in the US and Europe.
- These occurred during buoyant economic conditions, although other factors may also have played a part.

The changing face of accounting

- Changes in the economic environment have led to changes in the nature and scope of accounting.

■ Financial accounting has improved its framework of rules and there has been greater international harmonisation of accounting rules.

■ Management accounting has become more outward-looking, and new methods for managing costs have emerged.

How are businesses managed?

■ Strategic management has been increasingly adopted to cope with the more complex and more competitive business environment.

■ It is designed to provide a clear sense of purpose and to ensure that any action taken is consistent with this purpose.

What is the financial objective of a business?

■ The key financial objective is to enhance the wealth of the owners. To achieve this objective, the needs of other groups connected with the business, such as employees, cannot be ignored.

■ When setting financial objectives, the right balance must be struck between risk and return.

Why study accounting?

■ Everyone connected with business should be a little 'streetwise' about accounting and finance because they exert such an enormous influence over business operations.

→ Key terms

accounting p. 3
finance p. 3
financial management p. 3
relevance p. 6
reliability p. 6
comparability p. 6

understandability p. 6
materiality p. 8
accounting information system p. 11
management accounting p. 12
financial accounting p. 12
strategic management p. 17

Further reading

If you would like to explore the topics covered in this chapter in more depth, we recommend the following books:

Atrill, P. and McLaney, E., *Management Accounting for Decision Makers* (5th edn), Prentice Hall, 2007, chapter 1.

Elliot, B. and Elliot, J., *Financial Accounting and Reporting* (12th edn), Financial Times Prentice Hall, 2008, chapter 7.

Horngren, C., Bhimani, A., Datar, S. and Foster, G., *Management and Cost Accounting* (4th edn), Prentice Hall, 2007, chapter 1.

McLaney, E., *Business Finance: Theory and Practice* (7th edn), Prentice Hall, 2006, chapters 1 and 2.

? Review questions

Answers to these questions can be found at the back of the book in Appendix C.

1.1 What is the purpose of producing accounting information?

1.2 Identify the main users of accounting information for a university. Do these users differ very much from the users of accounting information for private-sector businesses? Is there a major difference in the ways in which accounting information for a university would be used compared with that for a private-sector business?

1.3 Management accounting has been described as 'the eyes and ears of management'. What do you think this expression means?

1.4 Financial accounting statements tend to reflect past events. In view of this, how can they be of any assistance to a user in making a decision when decisions, by their very nature, can only be made about future actions?

Part 1

FINANCIAL ACCOUNTING

Chapter 2

Measuring and reporting financial position

Introduction

We saw in the previous chapter that accounting has two distinct strands: financial accounting and management accounting. This chapter, and Chapters 3 to 5, examine the three major financial statements that form the core of financial accounting.

We start this chapter by taking an overview of the three statements to show how each contributes towards an assessment of the overall financial position and performance of a business.

Following this overview, we begin a more detailed examination by turning our attention towards one of these financial statements: the balance sheet. We shall see how it is prepared, and examine the principles underpinning this statement. We shall also consider its value for decision-making purposes.

Learning outcomes

When you have completed this chapter, you should be able to

- explain the nature and purpose of the three major financial statements;
- prepare a simple balance sheet and interpret the information that it contains;
- discuss the accounting conventions underpinning the balance sheet;
- discuss the limitations of the balance sheet in portraying the financial position of a business.

Wealth, cash and profit

We saw in Chapter 1 that most people become involved in business ownership to generate wealth, that is, to make themselves better off economically. This is true whether the people concerned are in business on their own account (as sole proprietors) or jointly with others (as partners or shareholders in a company). This concern for wealth generation raises several important, practical questions, such as:

- How can the amount of wealth generated for a particular period be assessed?
- Is generating wealth the same as making a profit?
- Does generating wealth mean having more cash at the end of the period that at the start?
- Is the wealth of the business the same the wealth of the owners?

These are some of the questions that we shall consider in this chapter.

The major financial statements – an overview

The major financial accounting statements aim to provide a picture of the financial position and performance of a business. To achieve this, a business's accounting system will normally produce three particular statements on a regular, recurring basis. These three are concerned with answering the following questions:

- What cash movements (that is, cash in and cash out) took place over a particular period?
- How much wealth (that is, profit) was generated, or lost, by the business over that period? (Profit (or loss) is defined as the increase (or decrease) in wealth arising from trading activities.)
- What is the accumulated wealth of the business at the end of that period and what form does the wealth take?

To address each of these questions, there is a separate financial statement. The financial statements are:

- the cash flow statement
- the income statement (also known as the profit and loss account)
- the balance sheet (also known as the statement of financial position).

When taken together, they provide a picture of the financial health of the business.

Perhaps the best way to introduce these financial statements is to look at an example of a very simple business. From this we shall be able to see the sort of information that each of the statements can provide. It is, however, worth pointing out that, while a simple business is our starting point, the principles that we consider apply equally to the largest and most complex businesses. This means that we shall meet these same principles again in later chapters.

Example 2.1

Paul was unemployed and unable to find a job. He therefore decided to embark on a business venture. Christmas was approaching, and so he decided to buy gift wrapping paper from a local supplier and to sell it on the corner of his local high street. He felt that the price of wrapping paper in the high street shops was excessive. This provided him with a useful business opportunity.

He began the venture with £40 in cash. On Monday, Paul's first day of trading, he bought wrapping paper for £40 and sold three-quarters of it for £45 cash.

What cash movements took place during Monday?

For Monday, a cash flow statement showing the cash movements for the day can be prepared as follows:

Cash flow statement for Monday

	£
Cash introduced by Paul	40
Cash from sales of wrapping paper	45
Cash paid to buy wrapping paper	(40)
Closing balance of cash	45

The statement shows that Paul placed £40 cash into the business. The business received £45 cash from customers, but paid £40 cash to buy the wrapping paper. This left £45 of cash by Monday evening. Note that we are taking the standard approach found in financial statements of showing figures to be deducted (in this case the £40 paid out) in brackets. We shall take this approach consistently throughout the chapters dealing with financial statements.

How much wealth (that is, profit) was generated by the business during Monday?

An *income statement (profit and loss account)* can be prepared to show the wealth (profit) generated on Monday. The wealth generated will represent the difference between the value of the sales made and the cost of the goods (that is, wrapping paper) sold.

Income statement (profit and loss account)
for Monday

	£
Sales revenue	45
Cost of goods sold (¾ of £40)	(30)
Profit	15

Note that it is only the cost of the wrapping paper *sold* that is matched against (and deducted from) the sales revenue in order to find the profit. It is not the whole of the cost of wrapping paper acquired. Any unsold inventories (in this case $\frac{1}{4}$ of £40 = £10) will be charged against the future sales revenue that it generates.

What is the accumulated wealth at Monday evening?

To establish the accumulated wealth at the end of Monday's trading, we can draw up a *balance sheet (statement of financial position)*. This will list the resources held at the end of that day.

Balance sheet (statement of financial position)
as at Monday evening

	£
Cash (closing balance)	45
Inventories of goods for resale (¹/₄ of £40)	10
Total assets	55
Equity	55

Note the terms 'assets' and 'equity' that appear in the above balance sheet. 'Assets' are business resources (things of value to the business) and include cash and inventories. 'Equity' is the word used in accounting for the investment or stake of the owner(s) (in this case Paul) in the business. Both of these terms will be discussed in some detail a little later in this chapter.

We can see from the financial statements in Example 2.1 that each statement provides part of a picture portraying the financial performance and position of the business. We begin by showing the cash movements. Cash is a vital resource that is necessary for any business to function effectively. Cash is required to meet debts that may become due and to acquire other resources (such as inventories). Cash has been described as the 'lifeblood' of a business, and movements in cash are usually given close scrutiny by users of financial statements.

However, it is clear that reporting cash movements alone would not be enough to portray the financial health of the business. The changes in cash over time do not tell us how much profit was generated. The income statement provides us with information concerning this aspect of performance. For example, we saw that during Monday the cash balance increased by £5, but the profit generated, as shown in the income statement, was £15. The cash balance did not increase by the amount of the profit made because part of the wealth generated (£10) was held in the form of inventories.

A balance sheet can be drawn up as at the end of Monday's trading, which should provide an insight into the total wealth of the business. Cash is only one form in which wealth can be held. In the case of this business, wealth is also held in the form of inventories (also known as stock). Hence, when drawing up the balance sheet, both forms of wealth held will be listed. In the case of a large business, there may be many other forms in which wealth will be held, such as land and buildings, equipment, motor vehicles and so on.

Let us now continue with our example.

Example 2.1 (continued)

On Tuesday, Paul bought more wrapping paper for £20 cash. He managed to sell all of the new inventories and all of the earlier inventories, for a total of £48.
The cash flow statement for Tuesday will be as follows:

Cash flow statement for Tuesday

	£
Opening balance (from Monday evening)	45
Cash from sales of wrapping paper	48
Cash paid to buy wrapping paper	(20)
Closing balance	73

The income statement for Tuesday will be as follows:

Income statement for Tuesday

	£
Sales revenue	48
Cost of goods sold (£20 + £10)	(30)
Profit	18

The balance sheet as at Tuesday evening will be:

Balance sheet as at Tuesday evening

	£
Cash (closing balance)	73
Inventories	–
Total assets	73
Equity	73

We can see that the total business resources (wealth) had increased to £73 by Tuesday evening. This represents an increase of £18 (that is, £73 less £55) over Monday's figure – which, of course, is the amount of profit made during Tuesday as shown on the income statement.

Activity 2.1

On Wednesday, Paul bought more wrapping paper for £46 cash. However, it was raining hard for much of the day and sales were slow. After Paul had sold half of his total inventories for £32, he decided to stop trading until Thursday morning.
Have a go at drawing up the three financial statements for Paul's business for Wednesday.

Cash flow statement for Wednesday

	£
Opening balance (from the Tuesday evening)	73
Cash from sales of wrapping paper	32
Cash paid to buy wrapping paper	(46)
Closing balance	59

Income statement for Wednesday

	£
Sales revenue	32
Cost of goods sold (¹/₂ of £46)	(23)
Profit	9

Balance sheet as at Wednesday evening

	£
Cash (closing balance)	59
Inventories (¹/₂ of £46)	23
Total assets	82
Equity	82

Note that the total business wealth had increased by £9 (that is, the amount of Wednesday's profit) even though the cash balance had declined. This is because the business is holding more of its wealth in the form of inventories rather than cash, compared with the position on Tuesday evening.

We can see that the income statement and cash flow statement are both concerned with measuring flows (of wealth and cash respectively) during a particular period (for example, a particular day, a particular month or a particular year). The balance sheet, however, is concerned with the financial position at a particular moment in time.

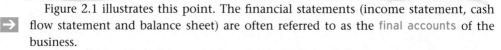

Figure 2.1 illustrates this point. The financial statements (income statement, cash flow statement and balance sheet) are often referred to as the final accounts of the business.

For external users (that is virtually all except the managers of the business concerned), these statements are normally backward-looking because they are based on information concerning past events and transactions. This can be useful in providing feedback on past performance, and in identifying trends that provide clues to future performance. However, the statements can also be prepared using projected data to help assess likely future profits, cash flows and so on. The financial statements are normally prepared on a projected basis for internal decision-making purposes only, as we shall see in Chapter 9. Managers are usually reluctant to publish these projected statements for external users, as they may reveal valuable information to competitors.

Now that we have an overview of the financial statements, we shall consider each statement in more detail. We shall go straight on to look at the balance sheet. Chapter 3 looks at the income statement; Chapter 5 goes into more detail on the cash flow

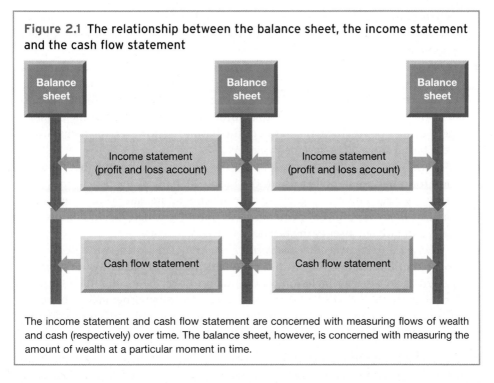

Figure 2.1 The relationship between the balance sheet, the income statement and the cash flow statement

The income statement and cash flow statement are concerned with measuring flows of wealth and cash (respectively) over time. The balance sheet, however, is concerned with measuring the amount of wealth at a particular moment in time.

statement. (Chapter 4 considers the balance sheets and income statements of limited companies.)

The balance sheet

The purpose of the balance sheet is simply to set out the financial position of a business at a particular moment in time (hence its alternative name, *statement of financial position*). We saw above that the balance sheet will reveal the forms in which the wealth of the business is held and how much wealth is held in each form. We can, however, be more specific about the nature of the balance sheet by saying that it sets out the assets of the business on the one hand, and the claims against the business on the other. Before looking at the balance sheet in more detail, we need to be clear about what these terms mean.

Assets

An asset is essentially a resource held by the business. For a particular item to be treated as an asset for accounting purposes it should have the following characteristics:

■ *A probable future benefit must exist.* This simply means that the item must be expected to have some future monetary value. This value can arise through its use within the business or through its hire or sale. Thus, an obsolete piece of equipment that could be sold for scrap would still be considered an asset, whereas an obsolete piece of equipment that could not be sold for scrap would not be regarded as one.

■ *The business must have an exclusive right to control the benefit.* Unless the business has exclusive rights over the resource it cannot be regarded as an asset. Thus, for a business offering holidays on barges, the canal system may be a very valuable resource, but as the business will not be able to control the access of others to the canal system, it cannot be regarded as an asset of the business. (However, the barges owned by the business would be regarded as assets.)

■ *The benefit must arise from some past transaction or event.* This means that the transaction (or other event) giving rise to the business's right to the benefit must have already occurred, and not be going to arise at some future date. Thus an agreement by a business to buy a piece of equipment at some future date would not mean the item is currently an asset of the business.

■ *The asset must be capable of measurement in monetary terms.* Unless the item can be measured in monetary terms, with a reasonable degree of reliability, it will not be regarded as an asset for inclusion on the balance sheet. Thus, the title of a magazine (for example *Hello!* or *Vogue*) that was created by its publisher may be extremely valuable to that publishing business, but this value is usually difficult to quantify. It will not, therefore, be treated as an asset.

Note that all four of these conditions must apply. If one of them does not apply, the item will not be treated as an asset for accounting purposes, and will not appear on the balance sheet.

We can see that these conditions strictly limit the kind of items that may be referred to as 'assets' in the balance sheet. Certainly not all resources exploited by a business will be assets of the business for accounting purposes. Some, like the canal system or the magazine title *Hello!*, may well be assets in a broader sense, but not for accounting purposes. Once an asset has been acquired by a business, it will continue to be considered an asset until the benefits are exhausted or the business disposes of it in some way.

Activity 2.2

Indicate which of the following items could appear as an asset on the balance sheet of a business. Explain your reasoning in each case.

1 £1,000 owing to the business by a customer who is unable to pay.
2 The purchase of a patent from an inventor that gives the business the right to produce a new product. Production of the new product is expected to increase profits over the period during which the patent is held.
3 The business hiring a new marketing director who is confidently expected to increase profits by over 30 per cent during the next three years.
4 The purchase of a machine that will save the business £10,000 each year. It is currently being used by the business but it has been acquired on credit and is not yet paid for.

Your answer should be along the following lines:

1 Under normal circumstances a business would expect a customer to pay the amount owed. Such an amount is therefore typically shown as an asset under the heading 'trade receivables' (or 'debtors'). However, in this particular case the customer is unable to pay, which means that the item is incapable of providing future benefits, and the £1,000 owing would not be regarded as an asset. Debts that are not paid are referred to as 'bad debts'.
2 The purchase of the patent would meet all of the conditions set out above and would therefore be regarded as an asset.
3 The hiring of a new marketing director would not be considered as the acquisition of an asset. One argument against its classification as an asset is that the business does not have exclusive rights of control over the director. (Nevertheless, it may have an exclusive right to the services that the director provides.) Perhaps a stronger argument is that the value of the director cannot be measured in monetary terms with any degree of reliability.
4 The machine would be considered an asset even though it is not yet paid for. Once the business has agreed to buy the machine, and has accepted it, the machine is legally owned by the business (and, therefore, under its control) even though payment is still outstanding. (The amount outstanding would be shown as a claim, as we shall see below.)

The sorts of items that often appear as assets in the balance sheet of a business include:

- property
- plant and equipment
- fixtures and fittings
- patents and trademarks
- trade receivables
- loans made by the business.

Activity 2.3

Can you think of any other items that might appear as assets in the balance sheet of a business?

You may be able to think of a number of other items. Two that we have met so far, because they were the only types of asset that were held by Paul's wrapping-paper business (in Example 2.1), are inventories and cash at bank.

Note that an asset does not have to be a physical item – it may also be a non-physical right to certain benefits. Assets that have a physical substance and can be touched are referred to as tangible assets. Assets that have no physical substance but which, nevertheless, provide expected future benefits (such as patents) are referred to as intangible assets.

Claims

A claim is an obligation on the part of the business to provide cash, or some other form of benefit, to an outside party. A claim will normally arise as a result of the outside party providing funds in the form of assets for use by the business. There are essentially two types of claim against a business:

■ **Equity.** This represents the claim of the owner(s) against the business. This claim is sometimes referred to as the *owner's capital*. Some find it hard to understand how the owner can have a claim against the business, particularly when we consider the example of a sole-proprietor-type business where the owner *is*, in effect, the business. However, for accounting purposes, a clear distinction is made between the business (whatever its size) and the owner(s). The business is viewed as being quite separate from the owner and this is equally true for a sole proprietor like Paul, the wrapping-paper seller in Example 2.1, or a large company like Marks and Spencer plc. It is seen as a separate entity with its own separate existence and when financial statements are prepared, they relate to the business rather than to the owner(s). This means that the balance sheet should reflect the financial position of the business as a separate entity. Viewed from this perspective, any funds contributed by the owner will be seen as coming from outside the business and will appear as a claim against the business in its balance sheet.

As we have just seen, the business and the owner are separate for accounting purposes, irrespective of the type of business concerned. It is also true that the operation of the equity section of the balance sheet is broadly the same irrespective of the type of business concerned. As we shall see in Chapter 4, with limited companies the owner's claim figure must be analysed according to how each part of it first arose. For example, companies must make a distinction between that part of the owner's claim that arose from retained profits and that part that arose from the owners putting in cash, usually by buying shares in the company.

■ **Liabilities.** Liabilities represent the claims of all individuals and organisations other than the owner(s). Liabilities must have arisen from past transactions or events such as supplying goods or lending money to the business. When a liability is settled it will normally be through an outflow of assets (usually cash).

Once a claim from the owners or outsiders has been incurred by a business, it will remain as an obligation until it is settled.

Now that the meaning of the terms *assets* and *claims* has been established, we can go on and discuss the relationship between the two. This relationship is quite straightforward. If a business wishes to acquire assets, it will have to raise the necessary funds from somewhere. It may raise the funds from the owner(s) or from other outside parties or from both. Example 2.2 illustrates this relationship.

Example 2.2

Jerry and Company start a business by depositing £20,000 in a bank account on 1 March. This amount was raised partly from the owner (£6,000) and partly from borrowing (£14,000). Raising funds in this way will give rise to a claim on the business by both the owner (equity) and the lender (liability). If a balance sheet of Jerry and Company is prepared following the above transactions, it will appear as follows:

Jerry and Company
Balance sheet as at 1 March

	£
Assets	
Cash at bank	20,000
Total assets	20,000
Claims	
Equity (owner's capital)	6,000
Liabilities – borrowing	14,000
Total equity and liabilities	20,000

We can see from the balance sheet that the total claims are the same as the total assets. Thus:

Assets = Equity + Liabilities.

This equation – which is often referred to as the *balance sheet equation* – will always hold true. Whatever changes may occur to the assets of the business or the claims against it, there will be compensating changes elsewhere that will ensure that the balance sheet always 'balances'. By way of illustration, consider the following transactions for Jerry and Company:

2 March	Bought a motor van for £5,000, paying by cheque.
3 March	Bought inventories (that is, goods to be sold) on one month's credit for £3,000. (This means that the inventories were bought on 3 March, but payment will not be made to the supplier until 3 April.)
4 March	Repaid £2,000 of the amount borrowed to the lender, by cheque.
6 March	Owner introduced another £4,000 into the business bank account.

A balance sheet may be drawn up after each day in which transactions have taken place. In this way, the effect can be seen of each transaction on the assets and claims of the business. The balance sheet as at 2 March will be:

Jerry and Company
Balance sheet as at 2 March

	£
Assets	
Cash at bank (20,000 – 5,000)	15,000
Motor van	5,000
Total assets	20,000
Claims	
Equity	6,000
Liabilities – borrowing	14,000
Total equity and liabilities	20,000

As can be seen, the effect of buying the motor van is to decrease the balance at the bank by £5,000 and to introduce a new asset – a motor van – to the balance sheet. The total assets remain unchanged. It is only the 'mix' of assets that has changed. The claims against the business remain the same because there has been no change in the way in which the business has been funded.

The balance sheet as at 3 March, following the purchase of inventories, will be:

Jerry and Company
Balance sheet as at 3 March

	£
Assets	
Cash at bank	15,000
Motor van	5,000
Inventories	3,000
Total assets	23,000
Claims	
Equity	6,000
Liabilities – borrowing	14,000
Liabilities – trade payable	3,000
Total equity and liabilities	23,000

The effect of buying inventories has been to introduce another new asset (inventories) to the balance sheet. In addition, the fact that the goods have not yet been paid for means that the claims against the business will be increased by the £3,000 owed to the supplier, who is referred to as a *trade payable* (or trade creditor) on the balance sheet.

Activity 2.4

Try drawing up a balance sheet for Jerry and Company as at 4 March.

The balance sheet as at 4 March, following the repayment of part of the loan, will be:

Jerry and Company
Balance sheet as at 4 March

	£
Assets	
Cash at bank (15,000 – 2,000)	13,000
Motor van	5,000
Inventories	3,000
Total assets	21,000
Claims	
Equity	6,000
Liabilities – borrowing (14,000 – 2,000)	12,000
Liabilities – trade payable	3,000
Total equity and liabilities	21,000

The repayment of £2,000 of the borrowing will result in a decrease in the balance at the bank of £2,000 and a decrease in the lender's claim against the business by the same amount.

Activity 2.5

Try drawing up a balance sheet as at 6 March for Jerry and Company.

The balance sheet as at 6 March, following the introduction of more funds, will be:

Jerry and Company
Balance sheet as at 6 March

	£
Assets	
Cash at bank (13,000 + 4,000)	17,000
Motor van	5,000
Inventories	3,000
Total assets	25,000
Claims	
Equity (6,000 + 4,000)	10,000
Liabilities – borrowing	12,000
Liabilities – trade payable	3,000
Total equity and liabilities	25,000

The introduction of more funds by the owner will result in an increase in the equity of £4,000 and an increase in the cash at bank by the same amount.

Example 2.2 illustrates the point that the balance sheet equation (assets equals equity plus liabilities) will always hold true, because it reflects the fact that, if a business wishes to acquire more assets, it must raise funds equal to the cost of those assets. The funds raised must be provided by the owners (equity), or by others (liabilities), or by a combination of the two. Hence the total cost of assets acquired should always equal the total equity plus liabilities.

It is worth pointing out that in real life, businesses do not normally draw up a balance sheet after each day, as shown in the example above. Such an approach is not likely to be useful, given the relatively small number of transactions each day. We have done this in our examples to see the effect on the balance sheet, transaction by transaction. In real life, a balance sheet for the business is usually prepared at the end of a defined reporting period.

Determining the length of the reporting interval will involve weighing up the costs of producing the information against the perceived benefits of the information for decision-making purposes. In practice, the reporting interval will vary between businesses; it could be monthly, quarterly, half-yearly or annually. For external reporting purposes, an annual reporting cycle is the norm (although certain businesses, typically larger ones, report more frequently than this). However, for internal reporting purposes to managers, many businesses produce monthly financial statements.

The effect of trading operations on the balance sheet

In the example we have just considered (Jerry and Company), we dealt with the effect on the balance sheet of a number of different types of transactions that a business might undertake. These transactions covered the purchase of assets for cash and on credit, the repayment of a loan, and the injection of equity. However, one form of transaction, trading, has not yet been considered. To deal with the effect of trading transactions on the balance sheet, let us return to our example.

Example 2.2 (continued)

The balance sheet that we drew up for Jerry and Company as at 6 March was as follows:

Jerry and Company
Balance sheet as at 6 March

	£
Assets	
Cash at bank (13,000 + 4,000)	17,000
Motor van	5,000
Inventories	3,000
Total assets	25,000

Claims	
Equity (6,000 + 4,000)	10,000
Liabilities – borrowing	12,000
Liabilities – trade payable	3,000
Total equity and liabilities	25,000

On 7 March, the business managed to sell all of the inventories for £5,000 and received a cheque immediately from the customer for this amount. The balance sheet on 7 March, after this transaction has taken place, will be:

Jerry and Company
Balance sheet as at 7 March

	£
Assets	
Cash at bank (17,000 + 5,000)	22,000
Motor van	5,000
Inventories (3,000 – 3,000)	–
Total assets	27,000
Claims	
Equity (10,000 + (5,000 – 3,000))	12,000
Liabilities – borrowing	12,000
Liabilities – trade payable	3,000
Total equity and liabilities	27,000

We can see that the inventories (£3,000) have now disappeared from the balance sheet, but the cash at bank has increased by the selling price of the inventories (£5,000). The net effect has therefore been to increase assets by £2,000 (that is, £5,000 less £3,000). This increase represents the net increase in wealth (the profit) that has arisen from trading. Also note that the equity of the business has increased by £2,000, in line with the increase in assets. This increase in equity reflects the fact that increases in wealth, as a result of trading or other operations, will be to the benefit of the owners and will increase their stake in the business.

Activity 2.6

What would have been the effect on the balance sheet if the inventories had been sold on 7 March for £1,000 rather than £5,000?

The balance sheet on 7 March would then have been:

Jerry and Company
Balance sheet as at 7 March

	£
Assets	
Cash at bank (17,000 + 1,000)	18,000
Motor van	5,000
Inventories (3,000 – 3,000)	–
Total assets	23,000
Claims	
Equity (10,000 + (1,000 – 3,000))	8,000
Liabilities – borrowing	12,000
Liabilities – trade payable	3,000
Total equity and liabilities	23,000

As we can see, the inventories (£3,000) will disappear from the balance sheet, but the cash at bank will rise by only £1,000. This will mean a net reduction in assets of £2,000. This reduction represents a loss arising from trading and will be reflected in a reduction in the equity of the owner.

We can see that any decrease in wealth (that is, a loss) arising from trading or other transactions will lead to a reduction in the owner's stake in the business. If the business wished to maintain the level of assets as at 6 March, it would be necessary to obtain further funds from the owner or from borrowing, or both.

What we have just seen means that the balance sheet equation can be extended as follows:

Assets (at the end = Equity (amount at the start of the period
  of the period)   + profit (or – loss) for the period)
                        + Liabilities (at the end of the period)

(This is assuming that the owner makes no injections or withdrawals of equity during the period.)

As we have seen, the profit (or loss) for the period is shown on the balance sheet as an addition to (or a reduction of) equity. Any funds introduced or withdrawn by the owner for living expenses or other reasons also affect equity, but are shown separately. When this is done, more comprehensive information is provided for users of the financial statements. If Jerry and Company sold the inventories for £5,000, as in Example 2.2, and the owner withdrew £1,500 for his or her own use, the equity of the owner would appear as follows on the balance sheet:

	£
Equity (owner's equity)	
Opening balance	10,000
Profit	2,000
Drawings	(1,500)
Closing balance	10,500

If the drawings were in cash, the balance of cash would decrease by £1,500 in the balance sheet.

Note that, like all balance sheet items, the amount of equity is cumulative. This means that any profit made that is not taken out as drawings by the owner(s) remains in the business. These retained (or 'ploughed-back') profits have the effect of expanding the business.

The classification of assets

If the items on the balance sheet are listed haphazardly, with assets listed on one side and claims on the other, though it may be mathematically correct, it can be confusing. To help users to understand more clearly the information that is presented, assets and claims are usually grouped into categories. Assets may be categorised as being either current or non-current.

Current assets

→ Current assets are basically assets that are held for the short term. To be more precise, they are assets that meet any of the following conditions:

- they are held for sale or consumption in the normal course of a business's operating cycle;
- they are expected to be sold within the next year;
- they are held primarily for trading;
- they are cash, or near equivalents to cash such as easily marketable, short-term investments.

The most common current assets are inventories, amounts owed by customers for goods or services supplied on credit (known as trade receivables), and cash.

Perhaps it is worth making the point here that most sales made by most businesses are made on credit. This is to say that the goods pass to, or the service is rendered to, the customer at one point but the customer pays later. Retail sales are the only significant exception to this general point.

For businesses that sell goods, rather than render a service, the current assets of inventories, trade receivables and cash are interrelated. They circulate within a business as shown in Figure 2.2. We can see that cash can be used to buy inventories, which are then sold on credit. When the credit customers (trade receivables) pay, the business receives an injection of cash, and so on.

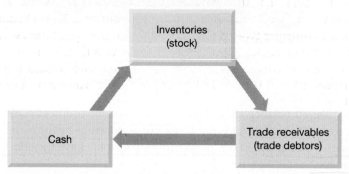

Figure 2.2 The circulating nature of current assets

Inventories may be sold on credit to customers. When the customers pay, the trade receivables will be converted into cash, which can then be used to purchase more inventories, and so the cycle begins again.

For purely service businesses, the situation is similar, except that inventories are not involved.

Non-current assets

 Non-current assets (also called fixed assets) are simply assets that do not meet the definition of current assets. Generally speaking, they are held for long-term operations.

This distinction between assets that are continuously circulating within the business and assets used for long-term operations may be helpful when trying to assess the appropriateness of the mix of assets held. Most businesses will need a certain amount of both types of asset to operate effectively.

Activity 2.7

Can you think of two examples of assets that may be classified as non-current assets for an insurance business?

Examples of assets that may be defined as being non-current are:

■ property
■ motor vehicles
■ computers
■ computer software
■ reference books
■ furniture.

This is not an exhaustive list. You may have thought of others.

Classification issues

It is important to appreciate that whether a particular asset is classified as current or non-current may vary according to the nature of the business. This is because the *purpose* for which a particular type of asset is held may differ from business to business. For example, a motor vehicle manufacturer will normally hold inventories of the finished motor vehicles produced for resale, and would therefore classify them as part of the current assets. On the other hand, a business that uses motor vehicles for delivering its goods to customers (that is, as part of its long-term operations) would classify them as non-current assets.

Activity 2.8

The assets of Kunalun and Co., a large advertising agency, are as follows:

- cash at bank — *cash*
- fixtures and fittings
- office equipment
- motor vehicles
- property
- computer equipment
- work in progress (that is, partly completed work for clients).

Which of these do you think should be classified as non-current assets, and which as current assets?

Your answer should be as follows:

Non-current assets	Current assets
Fixtures and fittings	Cash at bank
Office equipment	Work in progress
Motor vehicles	
Property	
Computer equipment	

The classification of claims

As we have already seen, claims are normally classified into equity or capital (owner's claim) and liabilities (claims of outsiders). Liabilities are further classified as either current or non-current.

Current liabilities

Current liabilities are basically amounts due for settlement in the short term. To be more precise, they are liabilities that meet any of the following conditions:

- they are expected to be settled within the normal course of the business's operating cycle;
- they are due to be settled within twelve months following the date of the balance sheet on which they appear;
- they are held primarily for trading purposes;
- there is no right to defer settlement beyond twelve months following the date of the balance sheet on which they appear.

Non-current liabilities

Non-current liabilities represent amounts due that do not meet the definition of current liabilities.

Classification issues

Note that it is quite common for non-current liabilities to become current liabilities. For example, borrowings that are due to be repaid within eighteen months following the date of a particular balance sheet will appear as a non-current liability, but, if the borrowings have not been paid off in the meantime, they will appear as a current liability in the balance sheet as at one year later.

This classification of liabilities can help the user to gain a clear impression of the ability of the business to meet its maturing obligations (that is, claims that must shortly be met). The value of the current liabilities (that is, the amounts that must be paid within the normal operating cycle) can be compared with the value of the current assets (that is, the assets that either are cash or will turn into cash within the same period).

The classification of liabilities should also help to highlight how the long-term finance of the business is raised. If long-term borrowings are relied on to finance the business, the financial risks associated with the business will increase. This is because these borrowings will bring a commitment to make interest payments and repayments of the amounts borrowed and the business may be forced to stop trading if this commitment is not fulfilled. Thus, when raising long-term finance, a business must strike the right balance between non-current liabilities and owner's equity. We shall consider this issue in more detail in Chapter 6.

Activity 2.9

Can you think of one example of a current liability and one of a non-current liability?

An example of a current liability would be amounts owing to suppliers for goods supplied on credit (known as trade payables or trade creditors) or a bank overdraft (a form of short-term bank borrowing that is repayable on demand). An example of a non-current liability would be a long-term loan.

Balance sheet layouts

Now that we have looked at the classification of assets and liabilities, we shall consider the layout of the balance sheet. Although there is an almost infinite number of ways in which the same balance sheet information could be presented, one particular layout has become clearly the most common, certainly among the larger, better-known businesses. This is the style that we adopted with Jerry and Company earlier (see pages 39–43). A more comprehensive example of this style is shown in Example 2.3.

Example 2.3

Brie Manufacturing
Balance sheet as at 31 December 2008

	£000
Non-current assets	
Property	45
Plant and equipment	30
Motor vans	19
	94
Current assets	
Inventories	23
Trade receivables	18
Cash at bank	12
	53
Total assets	147
Equity (owner's capital)	
Opening balance	50
Profit	14
Drawings	(4)
	60
Non-current liabilities	
Long-term borrowings	50
Current liabilities	
Trade payables	37
Total equity and liabilities	147

The non-current assets have a total of £94,000, which together with the current assets total of £53,000 gives a total of £147,000 for assets. Similarly, the equity totals £60,000, which together with the £50,000 for non-current liabilities and £37,000 for current liabilities gives a total for equity and liabilities of £147,000.

Within each category of asset (non-current and current) shown in Example 2.3, the items are listed in reverse order of liquidity (nearness to cash). This means that the assets that are furthest from cash appear first and the assets that are closest to cash come last. In the case of non-current assets, the property comes first as this asset is usually the most difficult to turn into cash. Motor vans are shown last as there is usually a ready market for them. In the case of current assets, we have already seen that inventories are converted to trade receivables and then trade receivables are converted to cash. This means that, under the heading of current assets, inventories appear first, followed by trade receivables and finally cash itself. This ordering of assets is a normal practice, which is followed irrespective of the layout used.

Note that, in addition to a grand total for assets held, subtotals for non-current assets and current assets are shown. Subtotals are also used for non-current liabilities and current liabilities when more than one item appears within these categories.

A slight variation from the standard layout illustrated in Example 2.3 is as shown in Example 2.4.

Example 2.4

Brie Manufacturing
Balance sheet as at 31 December 2008

	£000
Non-current assets	
Property	45
Plant and equipment	30
Motor vans	19
	94
Current assets	
Inventories	23
Trade receivables	18
Cash at bank	12
	53
Total assets	147
Non-current liabilities	
Long-term borrowings	(50)
Current liabilities	
Trade payables	(37)
Total liabilities	(87)
Net assets	60
Equity (owner's capital)	
Opening balance	50
Profit	14
Drawings	(4)
Total equity	60

We can see that the total liabilities are deducted from the total assets. This derives a figure for net assets – which is equal to total equity. Using this format, the basic accounting equation is rearranged so that

$$\textbf{Assets} - \textbf{Liabilities} = \textbf{Equity.}$$

? Self-assessment question 2.1

The following information relates to Simonson Engineering as at 30 September 2008:

	£
Plant and equipment	25,000
Trade payables	18,000
Short-term borrowing	26,000
Inventories	45,000
Property	72,000
Long-term borrowing	51,000
Trade receivables	48,000
Equity at 1 October 2007	117,500
Cash	1,500
Motor vehicles	15,000
Fixtures and fittings	9,000
Profit for the year to 30 September 2008	18,000
Drawings for the year to 30 September 2008	15,000

Required:
Prepare a balance sheet as at 30 September 2008 for the business, using the standard lay-out illustrated in Example 2.3.

The answer to this question can be found at the back of the book in Appendix B.

The balance sheet and time

As we have already seen, the balance sheet is a statement of the financial position of the business at *a specified point in time.* The balance sheet has been compared to a still photograph, in that the balance sheet 'freezes' a particular moment in time and will represent the situation only at that moment. Events may be quite different immediately before and immediately after the particular moment at which the 'snapshot' of the business was taken. When examining a balance sheet, therefore, it is important to establish the date at which it has been drawn up. This information should be prominently displayed in the balance sheet heading, as it is in Example 2.4. When we are using the balance sheet to assess the business's current financial position, the more recent the balance sheet date, the better.

A business will normally prepare a balance sheet as at the close of business on the last day of its accounting year. In the UK, businesses are free to choose their accounting year. When making a decision on which year-end date to choose, commercial convenience can often be a deciding factor. For example, a business operating in the retail trade may choose to have a year-end date early in the calendar year (for example, 31 January) because trade tends to be slack during that period and more staff time is available to help with the tasks involved in the preparation of the annual financial statements (such as checking the amount of inventories held). Since trade is slack, it is also a time when the amount of inventories held by the retail business is likely to be unusually low as compared with other times of the year. Thus the balance sheet, though showing a fair view of what it purports to show, may not show a picture of what is more typically the position of the business over the rest of the year.

Accounting conventions and the balance sheet

Accounting has a number of rules or conventions that have evolved over time. They have evolved as attempts to deal with practical problems experienced by preparers and users of financial statements, rather than to reflect some theoretical ideal. In preparing the balance sheets shown earlier, we have followed various accounting conventions, although they have not been explicitly mentioned. We shall now identify and discuss the major conventions that we have applied.

Business entity convention

For accounting purposes, the business and its owner(s) are treated as being quite separate and distinct. This is why owners are treated as being claimants against their own business in respect of their investment in the business. The business entity convention must be distinguished from the legal position that may exist between businesses and their owners. For sole proprietorships and partnerships, the law does not make any distinction between the business and its owner(s). For limited companies, on the other hand, there is a clear legal distinction between the business and its owners. (As we shall see in Chapter 4, the limited company is regarded as having a separate legal existence.) For accounting purposes these legal distinctions are irrelevant, and the business entity convention applies to all businesses.

Historic cost convention

The historic cost convention holds that the value of assets shown on the balance sheet should be based on their acquisition cost (that is, historic cost). This method of measuring asset value takes preference over other methods based on some form of current value. Many people, however, find the historic cost convention difficult to support, as outdated historic costs are unlikely to help in the assessment of current financial position. It is often argued that recording assets at their current value would provide a more realistic view of financial position and would be relevant for a wide range of decisions. However, a system of measurement based on current values can present a number of problems.

Activity 2.10

Plumber and Company has some motor vans that are used by staff when visiting customers' premises to carry out work. It is now the last day of the business's accounting year.

If it were decided to show the vans on the balance sheet at a current value (rather than a value based on their historic cost), how might the business arrive at a suitable value and how reliable would this figure be?

Two ways of deriving a current value are to find out:

■ how much would have to be paid to buy vans of a similar type and condition;
■ how much a motor van dealer would pay for the vans, were the company to sell them.

Both options will normally rely on opinion and so a range of possible values could be produced for each. Moreover, the range of values for each option could be significantly different. (The selling prices of the vans are likely to be lower than the amount required to replace them.) Thus, any value finally decided upon could arouse some debate.

Activity 2.10 illustrates that the term 'current value' can be defined in different ways. It can be defined broadly as either the current replacement cost or the current realisable value (selling price) of an asset. These two types of valuation may result in quite different figures being produced to represent the current value of an item. Furthermore, the broad terms 'replacement cost' and 'realisable value' can be defined in different ways. We must therefore be clear about what kind of current value accounting we wish to use.

Activity 2.10 also illustrates the practical problems associated with current value accounting. Current values, however defined, are often difficult to establish with any real degree of objectivity. The figures produced may be heavily dependent on the opinion of managers. Unless current value figures are capable of some form of independent verification, there is a danger that the financial statements will lose their credibility among users.

By reporting assets at their historic cost, it is argued that more reliable information is produced. Reporting in this way reduces the need for judgements, as the amount paid for a particular asset is usually a matter of demonstrable fact. Information based on past costs, however, may not always be relevant to the needs of users.

Later in the chapter, we shall consider the valuation of assets in the balance sheet in more detail. We shall see that the historic cost convention is not always rigidly adhered to. Departures from this convention are becoming more frequent.

Prudence convention

The prudence convention holds that caution should be exercised when making accounting judgements. Uncertainty about the future is dealt with by recording all losses at once and in full; this refers to both actual losses and expected losses. Profits, on the

other hand, are recognised only when they actually arise. Greater emphasis is, therefore, placed on expected losses than on expected profits. To illustrate the application
of this convention, let us assume that certain inventories held by a business prove
unpopular with customers and so a decision is made to sell them below their original
cost. The prudence convention requires that the expected loss from future sales be
recognised immediately rather than when the goods are eventually sold. If, however,
these inventories could have been sold above their original cost, profit would only be
recognised at the time of sale.

The prudence convention evolved to counteract the excessive optimism of some
managers and owners and is designed to prevent an overstatement of financial position. There is, however, a risk that it will introduce a bias towards understatement of
financial position.

Activity 2.11

What problems might arise if an excessively prudent view is taken of the financial position and performance of a business?

Excessive prudence will lead to an overstatement of losses and an understatement of
profits and financial position. This will obscure the underlying financial reality and may lead
users to make bad decisions. The owners, for example, may sell their stake in the business
at a lower price than they would have received if a fairer picture of the financial health of
the business had been presented.

In recent years, the prudence convention has weakened its grip on accounting and
has become a less dominant force. Nevertheless, it remains an important convention.

Going concern convention

The going concern convention holds that the financial statements should be prepared
on the assumption that the business will continue operations for the foreseeable future,
unless this is known not to be true. In other words, it is assumed that there is no intention, or need, to sell off the non-current assets of the business. Such a sale may arise
where the business is in financial difficulties and needs to pay amounts borrowed that
are due for repayment. This convention is important because the market (sale) value
of many non-current assets is often low in relation to the values at which they appear
in the balance sheet. This means that were a forced sale to occur, there is the likelihood that assets would be sold for less than their balance sheet value. Such anticipated
losses should be fully recorded as soon as the business's going concern status is called
into question. However, where there is no expectation of a need to sell off the assets,
the value of non-current assets can continue to be shown at their recorded values (that
is, based on historic cost). This convention therefore provides some support for the
historic cost convention under normal circumstances.

Dual aspect convention

→ The dual aspect convention asserts that each transaction has two aspects, both of which will affect the balance sheet. Thus the purchase of a motor car for cash results in an increase in one asset (motor car) and a decrease in another (cash). The repayment of borrowings results in the decrease in a liability (borrowings) and the decrease in an asset (cash).

Activity 2.12

What are the two aspects of each of the following transactions?

1 Purchase £1,000 inventories on credit.
2 Owner withdraws £2,000 in cash.
3 Repayment of borrowings of £3,000.

Your answer should be as follows:

1 Inventories increase by £1,000, trade payables increase by £1,000.
2 Equity reduces by £2,000, cash reduces by £2,000.
3 Borrowings reduce by £3,000, cash reduces by £3,000.

Recording the dual aspect of each transaction ensures that the balance sheet will continue to balance.

Money measurement

We saw earlier that a resource will only be regarded as an asset and included on the balance sheet if it can be measured in monetary terms, with a reasonable degree of reliability. Some resources of a business, however, do not meet this criterion and so are excluded from the balance sheet. As a result, the scope of the balance sheet is limited.

Activity 2.13

Can you think of resources of a business that cannot usually be measured reliably in monetary terms?

In answering this activity you may have thought of the following:

■ the quality of the human resources of the business
■ the reputation of the business's products
■ the location of the business
■ the relationship a business enjoys with its customers.

There have been occasional attempts to measure and report resources of a business that are normally excluded from the balance sheet so as to provide a more complete picture of its financial position. These attempts, however, invariably fail the reliability test. We saw in Chapter 1 that a lack of reliability affects the quality of financial statements. Unreliable measurement can lead to inconsistency in reporting and can create uncertainty among users, which in turn undermines the credibility of the financial statements.

Some key resources of a business that normally defy reliable measurement are discussed below.

Goodwill and brands

Some intangible non-current assets are similar to tangible non-current assets: they have a clear and separate identity and the cost of acquiring the asset can be reliably measured. Examples normally include patents, trademarks, copyrights and licences. Other intangible non-current assets, however, are quite different. They lack a clear and separate identity and reflect a hotchpotch of attributes, which are part of the essence of the business. Goodwill and product brands can provide examples of assets that lack a clear and separate identity.

The term 'goodwill' is often used to cover attributes such as the skill of the workforce and the relationship with customers. The term 'product brands' is also used to cover various attributes, such as the brand image, the quality of the product, the trademark and so on. Where goodwill and product brands have been generated internally by the business, it is often difficult to determine their cost or to measure their current market value or even to be clear that they really exist. They are, therefore, excluded from the balance sheet.

When they are acquired through an arm's-length transaction, however, the problems of uncertainty about their existence and measurement are resolved. (An 'arm's-length' transaction is one that is undertaken between two unconnected parties.) If goodwill is acquired when taking over another business, or if a business acquires a particular product brand from another business, these items will be separately identified and a price agreed for them. Under these circumstances, they can be regarded as assets by the business that acquired them and included on the balance sheet.

To agree a price for acquiring goodwill or product brands means that some form of valuation must take place and this raises the question as to how it is done. Usually, the valuation will be based on estimates of future earnings from holding the asset, a process that is fraught with difficulties. Nevertheless, a number of specialist businesses now exist that are prepared to take on this challenge. Real World 2.1 reveals how one specialist business ranked and valued the top ten brands in the world.

Real World 2.1

Valuing brands

Millward Brown Optimor, part of WPP marketing services group, recently produced a report which ranked and valued the top ten world brands for 2007 as follows:

Ranking	Brand	Value ($m)
1	Google	66,434
2	GE (General Electric)	61,880
3	Microsoft	54,951
4	Coca-Cola	44,134
5	China Mobile	41,214
6	Marlboro	39,166
7	Wal-Mart	36,880
8	Citi	33,706
9	IBM	33,572
10	Toyota	33,427

We can see that the valuations placed on the brands are remarkable; they show how much of a company's value can be tied up in brand equity.

Source: '2007 Brandz Top 100 Most Powerful Brands' by Millward Brown Optimor, p. 10.

Human resources

Attempts have been made to place a monetary measurement on the human resources of a business, but without any real success. There are, however, certain limited circumstances in which human resources are measured and reported in the balance sheet. These circumstances normally arise with professional football clubs. While football clubs cannot own players, they can own the rights to the players' services. Where these rights are acquired by compensating other clubs for releasing the players from their contracts, an arm's-length transaction arises and the amounts paid provide a reliable basis for measurement. This means that the rights to services can be regarded as an asset of the club for accounting purposes (assuming, of course, that the player will also bring benefits to the club).

Real World 2.2 describes how one leading club reports its investment in players on the balance sheet.

Real World 2.2

Dimitar is on the team sheet and on the balance sheet

Tottenham Hotspur Football Club (Spurs) has acquired several key players as a result of paying transfer fees to other clubs. In common with most UK football clubs, Spurs reports the cost of acquiring the rights to the players' services on its balance sheet. The club's balance sheet for 2007 shows the cost of registering its squad of players as about £109m. The item of players' registrations is shown as an intangible asset in the balance sheet as it is the rights to services, not the players, that are the assets. This figure of £74m includes the cost of bought-in players such as Dimitar Berbatov (for just under £11m from Bayer Leverkusen) and Jermaine Defoe (from West Ham United for £7m). The figure does not include 'home-grown' players such as Ledley King, because Spurs did not pay a transfer fee for them and so no clear-cut value can be placed on their services.

Source: Tottenham Hotspur plc Annual Report 2007.

Monetary stability

When using money as the unit of measurement, we normally fail to recognise the fact that it will change in value over time. In the UK and throughout much of the world, however, inflation has been a persistent problem. This has meant that the value of money has declined in relation to other assets. In past years, high rates of inflation have resulted in balance sheets, which were prepared on a historic cost basis, reflecting figures for assets that were much lower than they would have been if current values had been employed. Rates of inflation have been relatively low in recent years and so the disparity between historic cost values and current values has been less pronounced. Nevertheless, it can still be significant and has added fuel to the debate concerning how to measure asset values on the balance sheet. It is to this issue that we now turn.

Valuing assets on the balance sheet

It was mentioned earlier that, when preparing the balance sheet, the historic cost convention is normally applied for the reporting of assets. However, this point requires further elaboration as, in practice, it is not simply a matter of recording each asset on the balance sheet at its original cost. We shall see that things are a little more complex than this. Before discussing the valuation rules in some detail, however, we should point out that these rules are based on international financial reporting (or accounting) standards, which are rules that are generally accepted throughout much of the world. The nature and role of financial reporting standards will be discussed in Chapter 4.

Tangible non-current assets (property, plant and equipment)

→ Tangible non-current assets normally consist of property, plant and equipment, and we shall refer to them in this way from now on. This is a rather broad term that covers all items mentioned in its title plus other items such as motor vehicles and fixtures and fittings. All of these items are, in essence, the 'tools' used by the business to generate wealth, that is, they are used to produce or supply goods and services or for administration purposes. They tend to be held for the longer term, which typically means for more than one accounting period.

Initially these items are recorded at their historic cost, which will include any amounts spent on getting them ready for use. However, they will normally be used up over time as a result of wear and tear, obsolescence and so on. The amount used up, which is referred to as *depreciation*, must be measured for each accounting period for which the assets are held. Although we shall leave a detailed examination of depreciation until Chapter 3, we need to know that when an asset has been depreciated, this must be reflected in the balance sheet.

The total depreciation that has accumulated over the period since the asset was acquired must be deducted from its cost. This net figure (that is, the cost of the asset less the total depreciation to date) is referred to as the *carrying amount, net book value, or written-down value*. The procedure just described is not really a contravention of the historic cost convention. It is simply recognition of the fact that a proportion of the historic cost of the non-current asset has been consumed in the process of generating benefits for the business.

Although using historic cost (less any depreciation) is the 'benchmark treatment' for recording these assets, an alternative is allowed. Property, plant and equipment can be recorded using fair values provided that these values can be measured reliably. The fair values, in this case, are usually the current market values (that is, the exchange values in an arm's-length transaction). The use of fair values, rather than depreciated cost figures, can provide users with more up-to-date information, which may well be more relevant to their needs. It may also place the business in a better light, since the value of assets such as property may have increased significantly over time. Of course, merely increasing the balance sheet value of an asset does not make that asset more valuable. However, perceptions of the business may be altered by such a move.

One consequence of the upward revaluation of non-current assets is that the depreciation charge will be increased. This is because the depreciation charge is based on the new (increased) value of the asset.

Real World 2.3 shows that one well-known business revalued its land and buildings and, by doing so, greatly improved the look of its balance sheet.

Real World 2.3

Retailer marks up land and buildings

The balance sheet of Marks and Spencer plc, a major high street retailer, as at 1 April 2006 reveals land and buildings at a carrying amount (or net book value) of £2,310.0m. A firm of independent surveyors revalued these land and buildings two years earlier and this has been reflected in subsequent balance sheets. The effect of the revaluation was to give an uplift of £530.9m against the previous carrying amount.

Source: Marks and Spencer plc Annual Report 2006, p. 74, www.marksandspencer.com.

Activity 2.14

Refer to the format balance sheet of Brie Manufacturing, shown earlier in Example 2.3 (page 49). What would be the effect of revaluing the property to a figure of £110,000 on the balance sheet?

The effect on the balance sheet would be to increase the property to £110,000 and the gain on revaluation (that is, £110,000 – £45,000 = £65,000) would be added to the equity of the owner, as it is the owner who will benefit from the gain. The revised balance sheet would therefore be as follows:

Brie Manufacturing
Balance sheet as at 31 December 2008

	£000
Non-current assets (property, plant and equipment)	
Property	110
Plant and equipment	30
Motor vans	19
	159
Current assets	
Inventories	23
Trade receivables	18
Cash at bank	12
	53
Total assets	212
Equity (owner's capital)	
Opening balance	50
Revaluation gain	65
Profit	14
	129
Drawings	(4)
	125
Non-current liabilities	
Long-term borrowings	50
Current liabilities	
Trade payables	37
Total equity and liabilities	212

Once assets are revalued, the frequency of revaluation then becomes an important issue as assets recorded at out-of-date values can mislead users. Using out-of-date revaluations on the balance sheet is the worst of both worlds. It lacks the objectivity and verifiability of historic cost; it also lacks the realism of current values. Revaluations should therefore be frequent enough to ensure that the carrying amount of the revalued asset does not differ materially from its fair value at the balance sheet date.

When an item of property, plant or equipment is revalued on the basis of fair values, all assets within that particular group must be revalued. Thus, it is not acceptable to revalue some property but not others. Although this provides some degree of consistency within a particular group of assets, it does not, of course, prevent the balance sheet from containing a mixture of valuations.

Intangible non-current assets

For these assets, the 'benchmark treatment' is, once again, that they are measured initially at historic cost. What follows, however, will depend on whether the asset has a finite or an infinite useful life. (Purchased goodwill can provide an example of an asset with an infinitely useful life.) Where the asset has a finite life, any depreciation (or *amortisation* as it is usually termed for intangible non-current assets) following acquisition will be deducted from its cost. Where, however, the asset has an infinite life, it will not be amortised. Instead, it will be tested annually to see whether there has been any fall in value. This point is discussed in more detail in the following section.

Once again, the alternative of revaluing intangible assets using fair values is available. However, this can only be used where an active market exists, which allows fair values to be properly determined. In practice, this is a rare occurrence.

The impairment of non-current assets

There is always a risk that both types of non-current asset (tangible and intangible) may suffer a significant fall in value. This may be due to factors such as changes in market conditions, technological obsolescence and so on. In some cases, this fall in value may lead to the carrying amount (or net book value) of the asset being higher than the amount that could be recovered from the asset through its continued use or through its sale. When this occurs, the asset value is said to be impaired and the general rule is to reduce the value of the asset on the balance sheet to its recoverable amount. Unless this is done, the asset will be overstated on the balance sheet.

Activity 2.15

With which one of the accounting conventions that we discussed earlier is this accounting treatment consistent?

The answer is the prudence convention, which states that actual or anticipated losses should be recognised in full.

In many situations, a business may use either historic cost, less any depreciation, or a value-based measure when reporting its non-current assets. However, where the former is greater than the latter, the business has no choice; the use of depreciated historic cost is not an option. Real World 2.4 provides an example of where the application of the 'impairment rule', as it is called, resulted in huge write-downs (that is, reductions in the balance sheet value of the assets) for a well-known mobile phone operator.

Real World 2.4

Talking telephone numbers

Vodafone Group plc (Vodafone), the mobile phone operator, had to incur massive goodwill impairment charges during the year ended 31 March 2007. These totalled £11,600m which, to place it in context, compares with sales revenue for the year of £31,104m. This helped to lead to a loss for the business of £2,383m for the year. This followed similar impairment charges totalling £23,515m for the previous accounting year. These rate as some of the largest impairment charges ever incurred by any business anywhere.

The problem arose from Vodafone's purchase, in 2000, of the German business Mannesmann, which operated mobile phone networks in Germany and Italy. Vodafone paid £101,000m for Mannesmann's business.

Vodafone blamed the large impairment charges on an assessment of the longer-term prospects in the German and Italian markets, which are being hit by tough price competition.

Sources: 'Goodwill charges at record levels', FT.com, 30 May 2006; Vodafone Group plc Annual Report 2007.

We saw earlier that intangible, non-current assets with infinite lives must be tested annually to see whether there has been any impairment. Other non-current assets, however, must be also tested where events suggest that impairment has taken place.

Inventories

It is not only non-current assets that run the risk of a significant fall in value. The inventories of a business could also suffer this fate, which could be caused by factors such as reduced selling prices, obsolescence, deterioration, damage and so on. Where a fall in value means that the amount likely to be recovered from the sale of the inventories will be lower than their cost, this loss must be reflected in the balance sheet. Thus, if the net realisable value (that is, selling price less any selling costs) falls below the historic cost of inventories held, the former should be used as the basis of valuation. This reflects, once again, the influence of the prudence convention on the balance sheet.

Real World 2.5 shows how one well-known business wrote down the inventories of one of its products following a sharp reduction in selling prices.

Real World 2.5

You're fired!

'You're fired!' is what some investors might like to tell Amstrad, run by *Apprentice* star Sir Alan Sugar. . . . Shares in the company fell nearly 10 per cent as it revealed that sales of its much-vaunted videophone have failed to take off.

Amstrad launched the E3, a phone allowing users to hold video calls with each other, in a blaze of publicity last year. But, after cutting the price from £99 to £49, Amstrad sold just 61,000 E3s in the year to June and has taken a £5.7m stock [inventories] write down.

Source: 'Amstrad (AMT)', *Investors Chronicle*, 7 October 2005.

The published financial statements of large businesses will normally show the basis on which inventories are valued. Real World 2.6 shows how one well-known business reports this information.

Uses and usefulness of the balance sheet

The balance sheet is the oldest of the three main financial statements and many businesses have consistently prepared one on a regular basis, even where there was no regulation requiring it to be produced. It is clearly, therefore, seen as being capable of providing useful information. The balance sheet can be seen as having several uses, including the following:

- *It provides an insight into how the business is financed and how its funds are deployed.* We can see how much finance is contributed by the owners and how much is contributed by outside lenders. We can also see the different kinds of assets acquired and how much is invested in each kind.
- *It can provide a basis for assessing the value of the business.* Since the balance sheet lists, and places a value on, the various assets and the claims, it can provide a starting point for assessing the value of the business. It is, however, severely limited in the extent to which it can do this. We have seen earlier that accounting rules may result in assets being shown at their historic cost and that the restrictive definition of assets may exclude certain business resources from the balance sheet. Ultimately, the value of a business will be based on its ability to generate wealth in the future. Because of this, assets need to be valued on the basis of their wealth-generating potential. Also, other business resources that do not meet the restrictive definition of assets, such as brand values, need to be similarly valued and included. In Chapter 10 we shall see how assets and other business resources can be valued on the basis of their future wealth-generating ability.
- *Relationships between assets and claims can be assessed.* It can be useful to look at relationships between balance sheet items, for example the relationship between how much wealth is tied up in current assets and how much is owed in the short term (current liabilities). From this relationship, we can see whether the business has

sufficient short-term assets to cover its maturing obligations. We shall look at this and other relationships between balance sheet items in some detail in Chapter 6.

■ *Performance can be assessed.* The effectiveness of a business in generating wealth (making a profit) can usefully be assessed against the amount of investment that was involved. The relationship between profit earned over a particular period and the value of the net assets involved can be very helpful to many of those involved with the business concerned. This is particularly likely to be of interest to the owners and the managers. This and similar relationships will also be explored in detail in Chapter 6.

Summary

The main points of the chapter may be summarised as follows.

The major financial statements

■ There are three major financial statements: the cash flow statement, the income statement (profit and loss account) and the balance sheet (statement of financial position).

■ The cash flow statement shows the cash movements over a particular period.

■ The income statement shows the wealth (profit) generated over a particular period.

■ The balance sheet shows the accumulated wealth at a particular point in time.

The balance sheet

■ This sets out the assets of the business, on the one hand, and the claims against those assets, on the other.

■ Assets are resources of the business that have certain characteristics, such as the ability to provide future benefits.

■ Claims are obligations on the part of the business to provide cash, or some other benefit, to outside parties.

■ Claims are of two types: equity and liabilities.

■ Equity represents the claim(s) of the owner(s) and liabilities represent the claims of others, apart from the owner(s).

Classification of assets and liabilities

■ Assets are normally categorised as being current or non-current.

■ Current assets are cash or near cash or are held for sale or consumption in the normal course of business, or for trading, or for the short term.

■ Non-current assets are assets that are not current assets. They are normally held for the long-term operations of the business.

■ Liabilities are normally categorised as being current or non-current liabilities.

■ Current liabilities represent amounts due in the normal course of the business's operating cycle, or are held for trading, or are to be settled within twelve months of, or cannot be deferred for at least twelve months after, the end of the reporting period.

■ Non-current liabilities represent amounts due that are not current liabilities.

Balance sheet layouts

■ The standard layout begins with the assets at the top of the balance sheet and places equity and liabilities underneath.

■ A variation of the standard layout begins with the assets at the top of the balance sheet. From the total assets figure are deducted the non-current and current liabilities to arrive at a net assets figure. Equity is placed underneath.

Accounting conventions

■ Accounting conventions are the rules of accounting that have evolved to deal with practical problems experienced by those preparing financial statements.

■ The main conventions relating to the balance sheet include business entity, historic cost, prudence, going concern and dual aspect.

Money measurement

■ Using money as the unit of measurement limits the scope of the balance sheet.

■ Certain resources such as goodwill, product brands and human resources are difficult to measure. An 'arm's-length transaction' is normally required before such assets can be reliably measured and reported on the balance sheet.

■ Money is not a stable unit of measurement – it changes in value over time.

Asset valuation

■ The 'benchmark treatment' is to show property, plant and equipment at historic cost less any amounts written off for depreciation. However, fair values may be used rather than depreciated cost.

■ The 'benchmark treatment' for intangible non-current assets is to show the items at historic cost. Only assets with a finite life will be amortised (depreciated) and fair values will rarely be used.

■ Where the recoverable amount from tangible non-current assets is below their carrying amount, this lower amount is reflected in the balance sheet.

■ Inventories are shown at the lower of cost or net realisable value.

Balance sheet uses

■ The balance sheet shows how finance has been raised and how it has been been deployed.

■ It provides a basis for valuing the business, though the conventional balance sheet can only be a starting point.

■ Relationships between various balance sheet items can usefully be explored.

■ Relationships between wealth generated and wealth invested can be helpful indicators of business effectiveness.

→ **Key terms**

cash flow statement p. 30	non-current (fixed) assets p. 46
income statement p. 30	current liabilities p. 47
balance sheet p. 30	non-current liabilities p. 48
final accounts p. 34	accounting conventions p. 52
assets p. 35	business entity convention p. 52
claims p. 35	historic cost convention p. 52
tangible assets p. 37	prudence convention p. 53
intangible assets p. 37	going concern convention p. 54
equity p. 38	dual aspect convention p. 55
liabilities p. 38	property, plant and equipment p. 58
current assets p. 45	fair values p. 59

Further reading

If you would like to explore the topics covered in this chapter in more depth, we recommend the following books:

Elliott, B. and Elliott, J., *Financial Accounting and Reporting* (12th edn), Financial Times Prentice Hall, 2008, chapters 16 and 18.

International Accounting Standards Board, International Financial Reporting Standards IAS 16 (revised December 2003), IAS 36 (revised March 2004) and IAS 38 (revised March 2004).

Kirk, R.J., *International Financial Reporting Standards in Depth, Vol. 1. Theory and Practice*, CIMA Publishing, 2005, chapters 2 and 3.

Sutton, T., *Corporate Financial Accounting and Reporting* (2nd edn), Financial Times Prentice Hall, 2004, chapters 2 and 8.

? Review questions

Answers to these questions can be found at the back of the book in Appendix C.

2.1 An accountant prepared a balance sheet for a business. In the balance sheet, the equity of the owner was shown next to the liabilities. This confused the owner, who argued: 'My equity is my major asset and so should be shown as an asset on the balance sheet.' How would you explain this misunderstanding to the owner?

2.2 'The balance sheet shows how much a business is worth.' Do you agree with this statement? Discuss.

2.3 What is meant by the balance sheet equation? How does the form of this equation differ between the two balance sheet layouts mentioned in the chapter?

2.4 In recent years there have been attempts to place a value on the 'human assets' of a business in order to derive a figure that can be included on the balance sheet. Do you think humans should be treated as assets? Would 'human assets' meet the conventional definition of an asset for inclusion on the balance sheet?

✳ Exercises

Exercise 2.5 is more advanced than Exercises 2.1 to 2.4. Those exercises with coloured numbers have answers at the back of the book in Appendix D.

If you wish to try more exercises, visit MyAccountingLab/

2.1 On Thursday, the fourth day of his business venture, Paul, the street trader in wrapping paper (see pp. 31–33), bought more inventories for £53 cash. During the day he sold inventories that had cost £33 for a total of £47.

Required:
Draw up the three financial statements for Paul's business venture for Thursday.

2.2 While on holiday in Bridlington, Helen had her credit cards and purse stolen from the beach while she was swimming. She was left with only £40, which she had kept in her hotel room, but she had three days of her holiday remaining. She was determined to continue her holiday and decided to make some money to enable her to do so. She decided to sell orange juice to holidaymakers using the local beach. On day 1 she bought 80 cartons of orange juice at £0.50 each for cash and sold 70 of these at £0.80 each. On the following day she bought 60 cartons at £0.50 each for cash and sold 65 at £0.80 each. On the third and final day she bought another 60 cartons at £0.50 each for cash. However, it rained and, as a result, business was poor. She managed to sell 20 at £0.80 each but sold off the rest of her inventories at £0.40 each.

Required:
Prepare an income statement and cash flow statement for each day's trading and prepare a balance sheet at the end of each day's trading.

2.3 On 1 March, Joe Conday started a new business. During March he carried out the following transactions:

1 March	Deposited £20,000 in a bank account.
2 March	Bought fixtures and fittings for £6,000 cash, and inventories £8,000 on credit.
3 March	Borrowed £5,000 from a relative and deposited it in the bank.
4 March	Bought a motor car for £7,000 cash and withdrew £200 in cash for his own use.
5 March	A further motor car costing £9,000 was bought. The motor car bought on 4 March was given in part exchange at a value of £6,500. The balance of the purchase price for the new car was paid in cash.
6 March	Joe won £2,000 in a lottery and paid the amount into the business bank account. He also repaid £1,000 of the loan.

$\rightarrow$

Required:

Draw up a balance sheet for the business at the end of each day.

2.4 The following is a list of the assets and claims of Crafty Engineering Ltd at 30 June last year:

	£000
Trade payables	86
Motor vehicles	38
Long-term borrowings from Industrial Finance Co.	260
Equipment and tools	207
Short-term borrowings	116
Inventories	153
Property	320
Trade receivables	185

Required:

(a) Prepare the balance sheet of the business as at 30 June last year from the above information using the standard layout. (*Hint*: There is a missing item that needs to be deduced and inserted.)

(b) Discuss the significant features revealed by this financial statement.

2.5 The balance sheet of a business at the start of the week is as follows:

	£
Assets	
Property	145,000
Furniture and fittings	63,000
Inventories	28,000
Trade receivables	33,000
Total assets	269,000
Claims	
Equity	203,000
Short-term borrowing (bank overdraft)	43,000
Trade payables	23,000
Total equity and liabilities	269,000

During the week the following transactions take place:

(a) Inventories sold for £11,000 cash; these inventories had cost £8,000.
(b) Sold inventories for £23,000 on credit; these inventories had cost £17,000.
(c) Received cash from trade receivables totalling £18,000.
(d) The owners of the business introduced £100,000 of their own money, which was placed in the business bank account.
(e) The owners brought a motor van, valued at £10,000, into the business.
(f) Bought inventories on credit for £14,000.
(g) Paid trade payables £13,000.

Required:

Show the balance sheet after all of these transactions have been reflected.

Chapter 3

Measuring and reporting financial performance

Introduction

In this chapter we continue our examination of the major financial statements by looking at the income statement. This statement was briefly considered in Chapter 2 and we shall now examine it in some detail. We shall see how it is prepared and how it links with the balance sheet. We shall also consider some of the key measurement problems to be faced when preparing the income statement.

Learning outcomes

When you have completed this chapter, you should be able to:

- discuss the nature and purpose of the income statement;
- prepare an income statement from relevant financial information;
- discuss the main recognition and measurement issues that must be considered when preparing the income statement;
- explain the main accounting conventions underpinning the income statement.

What does it mean?

Tate and Lyle plc, whose business is sweeteners, starches and sugar refining, reported sales revenue of £3,814m and a profit of £217m for the year ending on 31 March 2007. To understand fully the significance of these figures, we must be clear about the nature of revenue and profit. This means that we must be able to answer questions such as:

- Does the sales revenue of £3,814m represent the cash generated from sales for the period?
- What is the relationship between the sales revenue and the profit for the period?
- Can the profit for the period of £217m be measured with complete accuracy and certainty?
- Does the profit figure of £217m mean that the business had £217m *more* in the bank at the end of the year than it had at the beginning?
- How can the sales revenue and profit figures help in assessing performance?

The answers to these and other questions are covered in the chapter.

The income statement

In Chapter 2 we examined the nature and purpose of the balance sheet. We saw that this statement is concerned with setting out the financial position of a business at a particular moment in time. However, it is not usually enough for users of the financial statements to have information relating only to the amount of wealth held by a business at one moment in time. Businesses exist for the primary purpose of generating wealth, or profit, and it is the profit generated *during a period* that is the main concern of many users of financial statements. Although the amount of profit generated is of particular interest to the owners of a business, other groups such as managers, employees and suppliers will also have an interest in the profit-generating ability of the business. The purpose of the income statement – or profit and loss account, as it is sometimes called – is to measure and report how much profit (wealth) the business has generated over a period. As with the balance sheet, which we examined in Chapter 2, the principles of preparation are the same irrespective of whether the income statement is for a sole proprietorship business or for a limited company.

The measurement of profit requires that the total revenue of the business, generated during a particular period, be identified. Revenue is simply a measure of the inflow of economic benefits arising from the ordinary activities of a business. These benefits, which accrue to the owners, will result in either an increase in assets (such as cash or amounts owed to the business by its customers) or a decrease in liabilities. Different forms of business enterprise will generate different forms of revenue. Some examples of the different forms that revenue can take are as follows:

- sales of goods (for example, by a manufacturer)
- fees for services (for example, of a solicitor)

- subscriptions (for example, of a club)
- interest received (for example, on an investment fund).

Real World 3.1 shows the various forms of revenue generated by a leading UK manufacturer.

Real World 3.1

Generating revenues!

Rolls-Royce plc, the well-known engine and power-generator manufacturer, had total sales turnover for the year ended 31 December 2006 of £7,156m. A breakdown of this amount is shown in Figure 3.1.

Figure 3.1 Revenues generated by Rolls-Royce plc during the year ended 31 December 2006

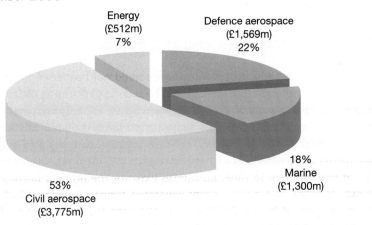

The two main sources of revenue are from aerospace (civil and defence). Together, these account for about 75 per cent of the total revenue generated.

Source: Based on information taken from Rolls-Royce plc Annual Report 2006.

The total expenses relating to each period must also be identified. Expense is really the opposite of revenue. It represents the outflow of economic benefits arising from the ordinary activities of a business. This loss of benefits will result in either a decrease in assets (such as cash) or an increase in liabilities (such as amounts owed to suppliers). Expenses are incurred in the process of generating revenue, or attempting to generate it. The nature of the business will again determine the type of expenses that will be incurred. Examples of some of the more common types of expenses are:

- the cost of buying the goods that are sold during the period concerned – known as *cost of sales* or *cost of goods sold*
- salaries and wages
- rent and rates

- motor vehicle running expenses
- insurances
- printing and stationery
- heat and light
- telephone and postage.

The income statement simply shows the total revenue generated during a particular period and deducts from this the total expenses incurred in generating that revenue. The difference between the total revenue and total expenses will represent either profit (if revenue exceeds expenses) or loss (if expenses exceed revenue). Thus, we have:

Profit (or loss) for the period = Total revenue for the period *less* Total expenses incurred in generating that revenue

The period over which profit or loss is normally measured is usually known as the accounting period, but sometimes known as the 'reporting period' or 'financial period'.

The income statement and the balance sheet

The income statement and the balance sheet should not be viewed in any way as substitutes for one another. Rather they should be seen as performing different functions. The balance sheet is, as stated earlier, a statement of the financial position of a business at a single moment in time – a 'snapshot' of the make-up of the wealth held by the business. The income statement, on the other hand, is concerned with the *flow* of wealth over a period of time. The two statements are, however, closely related.

The income statement links the balance sheets at the beginning and the end of an accounting period. Thus, at the start of a new accounting period, the balance sheet shows the opening financial position. After an appropriate period, an income statement is prepared to show the wealth generated over that period. A balance sheet is then also prepared to reveal the new financial position at the end of the period. This balance sheet will incorporate the changes in wealth that have occurred since the previous balance sheet was drawn up.

We saw in Chapter 2 (page 44) that the effect on the balance sheet of making a profit (or loss) means that the equation can be extended as follows:

Assets (at the end of the period) = Equity (amount at the start of the period
+ profit (or – loss) for the period)
+ Liabilities (at the end of the period).

The amount of profit or loss for the period affects the balance sheet as an adjustment to equity.

The above equation can be extended to:

Assets (at the end of the period) = Equity (amount at the start of the period)
+ (sales revenue – expenses)
+ Liabilities (at the end of the period).

In theory, it would be possible to calculate the profit (or loss) for the period by making all adjustments for revenue and expenses through the equity section of the balance sheet. However, this would be rather cumbersome. A better solution is to have an 'appendix' to the equity section, in the form of an income statement. By deducting expenses from revenue for the period, the income statement derives the profit (or loss) for adjustment to the equity figure in the balance sheet. This profit (or loss) figure represents the net effect of trading for the period. By providing this 'appendix', users are presented with a detailed and more informative view of performance.

Income statement layout

The layout of the income statement will vary according to the type of business to which it relates. To illustrate an income statement, let us consider the case of a retail business (that is, a business that buys goods in their completed state and resells them). This type of business usually has straightforward operations and, as a result, the income statement is relatively easy to understand.

Example 3.1 sets out a typical layout for the income statement of a retail business.

Example 3.1

Better-Price Stores
Income statement for the year ended 31 October 2008

	£
Sales revenue	232,000
Cost of sales	(154,000)
Gross profit	78,000
Salaries and wages	(24,500)
Rent and rates	(14,200)
Heat and light	(7,500)
Telephone and postage	(1,200)
Insurance	(1,000)
Motor vehicle running expenses	(3,400)
Depreciation – fixtures and fittings	(1,000)
Depreciation – motor van	(600)
Operating profit	24,600
Interest received from investments	2,000
Loan interest	(1,100)
Profit for the year	25,500

We can see that revenue, which arises from selling the goods, is the first item to appear. Deducted from this item is the cost of sales (also called the cost of the goods sold) during the period. We saw in Chapter 2 that brackets are used to denote when an item is to be deducted. This convention is used by accountants in preference to + or – signs and will be used throughout the text.

Gross profit

→ The first part of the income statement is concerned with calculating the gross profit for the period. This is simply the difference between the revenue and cost of sales figures and represents the profit from buying and selling goods, without taking into account any other revenues or expenses associated with the business.

Operating profit

From the gross profit, other expenses (overheads) that have been incurred in operating the business (salaries and wages, rent and rates, and so on) are deducted.

→ The resulting figure is known as the operating profit for the accounting period. This represents the wealth generated during the period from the normal activities of the business.

Operating profit does not take account of any income that the business may have from activities that are not included in its normal operations. Better-Price Stores in Example 3.1 is a retailer, so the interest on some spare cash that the business has lent is not part of its operating profit.

Costs of financing the business are also ignored in the calculation of the operating profit.

Profit for the year

Having established the operating profit, we add any non-operating income (such as interest receivable) and deduct any interest payable on borrowings made by the

→ business, to arrive at the profit for the year (or net profit). This is the income that is attributable to the owner(s) of the business and which will be added to the equity figure in the balance sheet. As can be seen, profit for the year is a residual: that is, the amount remaining after deducting all expenses incurred in generating the sales revenue for the period and taking account of non-operating income.

Some further issues

Having set out the main principles involved in preparing an income statement, we need to consider some further points.

Cost of sales

→ The cost of sales (or cost of goods sold) figure for a period can be identified in different ways. In some businesses, the cost of sales amount for each individual sale is identified at the time of the transaction. Each sales revenue is closely matched with the relevant cost of that sale and so identifying the cost of sales figure for inclusion in the income statement is not a problem. Many large retailers (for example, supermarkets) have point-of-sale (checkout) devices that not only record each sale but also simultaneously pick up the cost of the goods that are the subject of the particular sale. Other businesses that sell a relatively small number of high-value items (for example, an engineering business that produces custom-made equipment) also tend to match sales revenue with the cost of the goods sold, at the time of the sale. However, some businesses (for example, small retailers) do not usually find it practical to match each sale to a particular cost of sales figure as the accounting period progresses. They find it easier to identify the cost of sales figure at the end of the accounting period.

Deriving the cost of sales after the end of the accounting period

To understand how this is done, it is important to recognise that the cost of sales figure represents the cost of goods that were *sold* by the business during the period rather than the cost of goods that were *bought* by that business during the period. Part of the goods bought during a particular period may remain in the business, as inventories, and not be sold until a later period. To derive the cost of sales for a period, it is necessary to know the amount of opening and closing inventories for the period and the cost of goods bought during the period. Example 3.2 illustrates how the cost of sales is derived.

Example 3.2

Better-Price Stores, which we considered in Example 3.1 above, began the accounting year with unsold inventories of £40,000 and during that year bought inventories at a cost of £189,000. At the end of the year, unsold inventories of £75,000 were still held by the business.

The opening inventories at the beginning of the year *plus* the goods bought during the year will represent the total goods available for resale. Thus:

	£
Opening inventories	40,000
Goods bought	189,000
Goods available for resale	229,000

The closing inventories will represent that portion of the total goods available for resale that remains unsold at the end of the period. Thus, the cost of goods actually sold during the period must be the total goods available for resale *less* the inventories remaining at the end of the period. That is:

	£
Goods available for resale	229,000
Closing inventories	(75,000)
Cost of sales (or cost of goods sold)	154,000

These calculations are sometimes shown on the face of the income statement as in Example 3.3.

Example 3.3

	£	£
Sales revenue		232,000
Cost of sales:		
Opening inventories	40,000	
Goods bought	189,000	
Closing inventories	(75,000)	(154,000)
Gross profit		78,000

The above is just an expanded version of the first section of the income statement for Better-Price Stores, as set out in Example 3.1. We have simply included the additional information concerning inventories balances and purchases for the year provided in Example 3.2.

Classification of expenses

The classifications for the revenue and expense items, as with the classifications of various assets and claims in the balance sheet, are often a matter of judgement by those who design the accounting system. Thus, the income statement set out in Example 3.1 could have included the insurance expense with the telephone and postage expense under a single heading – say, 'general expenses'. Such decisions are normally based on how useful a particular classification will be to users. This will usually mean, however, that expense items of material size will be shown separately. For businesses that trade as limited companies, there are rules that dictate the classification of various items appearing in the financial statements for external reporting purposes. These rules will be discussed in Chapter 4.

Activity 3.1

The following information relates to the activities of H & S Retailers for the year ended 30 April 2008:

	£
Motor vehicle running expenses	1,200
Closing inventories	3,000
Rent and rates payable	5,000
Motor vans – cost less depreciation	6,300
Annual depreciation – motor vans	1,500
Heat and light	900
Telephone and postage	450
Sales revenue	97,400
Goods purchased	68,350
Insurance	750
Loan interest payable	620
Balance at bank	4,780
Salaries and wages	10,400
Opening inventories	4,000

Prepare an income statement for the year ended 30 April 2008. (*Hint*: Not all items shown above should appear on this statement.)

Your answer to this activity should be as follows:

H & S Retailers
Income statement for the year ended 30 April 2008

	£	£
Sales revenue		97,400
Cost of sales:		
Opening inventories	4,000	
Purchases	68,350	
Closing inventories	(3,000)	(69,350)
Gross profit		28,050
Salaries and wages		(10,400)
Rent and rates		(5,000)
Heat and light		(900)
Telephone and postage		(450)
Insurance		(750)
Motor vehicle running expenses		(1,200)
Depreciation – motor vans		(1,500)
Operating profit		7,850
Loan interest		(620)
Profit for the year		7,230

Note that neither the motor vans nor the bank balance are included in this statement, because they are both assets and so neither revenues nor expenses.

The accounting period

We have seen already that for reporting to those outside the business, a financial reporting cycle of one year is the norm, though some large businesses produce a half-yearly, or interim, financial statement to provide more frequent feedback on progress. For those who manage a business, however, it is probably essential to have much more frequent feedback on performance. Thus it is quite common for income statements to be prepared on a quarterly, monthly, weekly or even daily basis in order to show how things are progressing.

Recognising revenue

A key issue in the measurement of profit concerns the point at which revenue is recognised. Revenue arising from the sale of goods or provision of a service could be recognised at various points. Where, for example, a motor car dealer receives an order for a new car from one of its business clients, the associated revenue could be recognised by the dealer

- at the time that the order is placed by the customer;
- at the time that the car is collected by the customer; or
- at the time that the customer pays the dealer.

These three points could well be quite far apart, particularly where the order relates to a specialist car that is sold to the customer on credit.

The point chosen is not simply a matter of academic interest: it can have a profound impact on the total revenues reported for a particular accounting period. This, in turn, could have a profound effect on profit. If the car transaction straddled the end of an accounting period, the choice made between the three possible times for recognising the revenue could determine whether it is included as revenue of an earlier accounting period or a later one.

When dealing with the sale of goods or the provision of services, the main criteria for recognising revenue are that

- the amount of revenue can be measured reliably, and
- it is probable that the economic benefits will be received.

An additional criterion, however, must be applied where the revenue comes from the sale of goods, which is that

- ownership and control of the items should pass to the buyer.

Activity 3.2 provides an opportunity to apply these criteria to a practical problem.

Activity 3.2

A manufacturing business sells goods on credit (that is, the customer pays for the goods some time after they are received). Below are four points in the production/selling cycle at which revenue might be recognised by the business:

1 when the goods are produced;
2 when an order is received from the customer;
3 when the goods are delivered to, and accepted by, the customer;
4 when the cash is received from the customer.

A significant amount of time may elapse between these different points. At what point do you think the business should recognise revenue?

All of the three criteria mentioned above will usually be fulfilled at point 3: when the goods are passed to, and accepted by, the customer. This is because

- the selling price and the settlement terms will have been agreed and therefore the amount of revenue can be reliably measured;
- delivery and acceptance of the goods leads to ownership and control passing to the buyer;
- transferring ownership gives the seller legally enforceable rights that makes it probable that the buyer will pay.

We can see that the effect of applying these criteria is that a sale on credit is usually recognised *before* the cash is received. Thus, the total sales revenue figure shown in the income statement may include sales transactions for which the cash has yet to be received. The total sales revenue figure in the income statement for a period will often, therefore, be different from the total cash received from sales during that period.

Where goods are sold for cash rather than on credit, the revenue will normally be recognised at the point of sale. It is at this point that all the criteria will usually be met. For cash sales, there will be no difference in timing between reporting sales revenue and cash received.

Real World 3.2 sets out the revenue recognition criteria for one well-known travel business, First Choice Holidays plc. Note that even where clients have already paid for part of their trip (as a deposit), this is not recognised as revenue until the trip takes place.

Real World 3.2

Selling point

(i) Goods sold and services rendered
Revenue from sale of goods is recognised in the income statement when the significant risks and rewards or ownership have been transferred to the buyer.

Revenue in respect of in-house product is recognised on the date of departure. Travel agency commissions and other revenues received from the sale of third-party product are recognised when they are earned on receipt of final payment.

No revenue is recognised if there are significant uncertainties regarding recovery of the consideration due, associated costs or possible return of goods.

(ii) Client monies received in advance (deferred income)
Client monies received at the balance sheet date relating to holidays commencing and flights departing after the year end is deferred and included within trade and other payables.

Source: First Choice Holidays plc Annual Report 2006.

Long-term contracts

Some contracts, both for goods and for services, can last for more than one accounting period. If the business providing the goods or service were to wait until the contract is fulfilled before recognising revenue, the income statement could give a misleading impression of the wealth generated in the various accounting periods covered by the contract. This is a particular problem for businesses that undertake major long-term contracts, where a single contract could represent a large proportion of their total activities.

Construction contracts

Construction contracts often extend over a long period of time. Suppose that a customer enters into a contract with a builder to have a new factory built, that will take three years to complete. In such a situation, it is possible to recognise revenue *before* the factory is completed provided that the building work can be broken down into a number of stages and each stage can be measured reliably. Let us assume that building the factory could be broken down into the following stages:

Stage 1 – clearing and levelling the land and putting in the foundations.
Stage 2 – building the walls.
Stage 3 – putting on the roof.
Stage 4 – putting in the windows and completing all the interior work.

Each stage can be awarded a separate price with the total for all the stages being equal to the total contract price for the factory. This means that, as each stage is completed, the builder can recognise the price for that stage as revenue and bill the customer accordingly.

If the builder were to wait until the factory was completed before recognising revenue, the income statement covering the final year of the contract would recognise all of the revenue on the contract and the income statements for each preceding year would recognise no revenue. This would give a misleading impression, as it would not reflect the work done during each period.

Real World 3.3 sets out the revenue recognition criteria for one large construction business.

Real World 3.3

Tracking revenue

Jarvis plc is a business operating in the areas of road and rail infrastructure renewal, facilities management and plant hire. The point at which revenue on long-term contracts is recognised by the business is as follows:

> When the outcome of a long-term contract can be estimated reliably, contract revenue is recognised by reference to the degree of completion of each contract, based on the amounts certified and to be certified by the customer.

Source: Jarvis plc Annual Report and Accounts 2007, p. 45.

Services

Revenue from contracts for services may also be recognised in stages. Suppose a consultancy business has a contract to install a new computer system for the government, which will take several years to complete. Revenue can be recognised *before* the contract is completed as long as the contract can be broken down into stages and the particular stages of completion can be measured reliably. This is really the same approach as that used in the construction contract mentioned above.

Sometimes a continuous service is provided to a customer; for example, a telecommunications business may provide open access to the Internet to those who subscribe to the service. In this case, revenue is usually recognised as the service is rendered. Benefits from providing the service are usually assumed to flow evenly over time and so revenue is recognised evenly over the subscription period.

Where it is not possible to break down a service into particular stages of completion, or to assume that benefits from providing the service accrue evenly over time, revenue will not usually be recognised until the service is fully completed. A solicitor handling a house purchase for a client would be one such example.

Real World 3.4 provides an example of how one major business recognises revenue from providing services.

When a service is provided, there will normally be a timing difference between the recognition of revenue and the receipt of cash. Revenue for providing services is often recognised *before* the cash is received, as with the sale of goods on credit. However, there are occasions when it is the other way around, usually because the business demands payment before providing the service.

Activity 3.3

Can you think of any examples where cash may be demanded in advance of a service being provided? (*Hint*: Try to think of services that you may use.)

Examples of cash being received in advance of the service being provided may include:

- rent received from letting premises
- telephone line rental charges
- TV licence (BBC) or subscription (for example, Sky) fees
- subscriptions received for the use of health clubs or golf clubs.

You may have thought of others.

Recognising expenses

Having decided on the point at which revenue is recognised, we can now turn to the issue of the recognition of expenses. The matching convention in accounting is designed to provide guidance concerning the recognition of expenses. This convention states that expenses should be matched to the revenue that they helped to generate. In other words, the expenses that are associated with a particular revenue must be taken into account in the income statement for the same accounting period as that in which that revenue is included in the total sales revenue figure. Applying this convention may mean that a particular expense reported in the income statement for a period may not be the same figure as the cash paid for that item during the period. The expense reported might be either more or less than the cash paid during the period. Let us consider two examples that illustrate this point.

When the expense for the period is more than the cash paid during the period

Example 3.4

Domestic Ltd sells household electrical appliances. It pays its sales staff a commission of 2 per cent of sales revenue generated. Total sales revenue for last year amounted to £300,000. This will mean that the commission to be paid in respect of the sales for the year will be £6,000. However, by the end of the period, the amount of sales commission that had actually been paid to staff was £5,000. If the business reported only the amount paid, it would mean that the income statement would not reflect the full expense for the year. This would contravene the *matching convention* because not all of the expenses associated with the revenue of the year would have been matched in the income statement. This will be remedied as follows:

- Sales commission expense in the income statement will include the amount paid plus the amount outstanding (that is, £6,000 = £5,000 + £1,000).
- The amount outstanding (£1,000) represents an outstanding liability at the balance sheet date and will be included under the heading accrued expenses, or 'accruals', in the balance sheet. As this item will have to be paid within twelve months of the balance sheet date, it will be treated as a current liability.
- The cash will already have been reduced to reflect the commission paid (£5,000) during the period.

These points are illustrated in Figure 3.2.

In principle, all expenses should be matched to the period in which the sales revenue to which they relate is reported. However, it is sometimes difficult to match certain expenses to sales revenue in the same precise way that we have matched sales commission to sales revenue. It is unlikely, for example, that electricity charges incurred can be linked directly to particular sales in this way. As a result, the electricity charges incurred by, say, a retailer would be matched to the *period* to which they relate. Example 3.5 illustrates this.

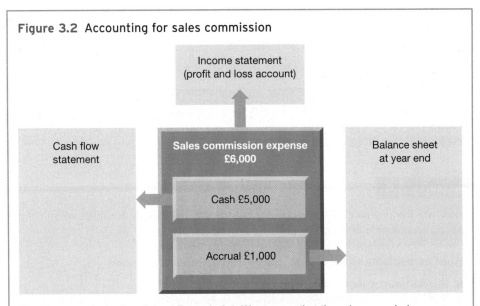

Figure 3.2 Accounting for sales commission

This illustrates the main points of Example 3.4. We can see that the sales commission expense of £6,000 (which appears in the income statement) is made up of a cash element of £5,000 and an accrued element of £1,000. The cash element appears in the cash flow statement and the accrued element will appear as a year-end liability in the balance sheet.

Example 3.5

Domestic Ltd has reached the end of its accounting year and has only paid for electricity for the first three-quarters of the year (amounting to £1,900). This is simply because the electricity company has yet to send out bills for the quarter that ends on the same date as Domestic Ltd's year end. The amount of Domestic Ltd's bill for the last quarter is £500. In this situation, the amount of the electricity expense outstanding is dealt with as follows:

■ Electricity expense in the income statement will include the amount paid, plus the amount of the bill for the last quarter (that is, £1,900 + £500 = £2,400) in order to cover the whole year.

■ The amount of the outstanding bill (£500) represents a liability at the balance sheet date and will be included under the heading 'accruals' or 'accrued expenses' in the balance sheet. This item would normally have to be paid within twelve months of the end of the accounting year and will, therefore, be treated as a current liability.

■ The cash will already have been reduced to reflect the electricity paid (£1,900) during the period.

This treatment will mean that the correct figure for the electricity expense for the year will be included in the income statement. It will also have the effect of showing that, at the end of the accounting year, Domestic Ltd owed the amount of the last quarter's electricity bill. Dealing with the outstanding amount in this way reflects the dual aspect of the item and will ensure that the balance sheet equation is maintained.

Domestic Ltd may wish to draw up its income statement before it is able to discover how much it owes for the last quarter's electricity. In this case it is quite normal to make a reasonable estimate of the amount of the bill and to use this estimated amount as described above.

Activity 3.4

How will the payment of the electricity bill for the last quarter be dealt with in the accounting records of Domestic Ltd?

When the electricity bill is eventually paid, it will be dealt with as follows:

- Reduce cash by the amount of the bill.
- Reduce the amount of the accrued expense as shown on the balance sheet by the same amount.

If an estimated figure is used and there is a slight error in the estimate, a small adjustment (either negative or positive depending on the direction of the error) can be made to the following year's expense. Dealing with the estimation error in this way is not strictly correct, but the amount is likely to be insignificant.

Activity 3.5

Can you think of other expenses for a retailer, apart from electricity charges, that cannot be linked directly to sales revenue and for which matching will therefore be done on a time basis?

You may have thought of the following examples:

- rent and rates
- insurance
- interest payments
- licence fees payable.

This is not an exhaustive list. You may have thought of others.

When the amount paid during the year is more than the full expense for the period

It is not unusual for a business to be in a situation where it has paid more during the year than the full expense for that year. Example 3.6 illustrates how we deal with this.

Example 3.6

Images Ltd, an advertising agency, normally pays rent for its premises quarterly in advance (on 1 January, 1 April, 1 July and 1 October). On the last day of the last accounting year (31 December), it paid the next quarter's rent (£4,000) to the following 31 March, which was a day earlier than required. This would mean that a total of five quarters' rent was paid during the year. If Images Ltd reports all of the cash paid as an expense in the income statement, this would be more than the full expense for the year. This would contravene the matching convention because a higher figure than the expenses associated with the revenue of the year would appear in the income statement.

The problem is overcome by dealing with the rental payment as follows:

- Show the rent for four quarters as the appropriate expense in the income statement (that is, 4 × £4,000 = £16,000).
- The cash (that is, 5 × £4,000 = £20,000) would already have been paid during the year.
- Show the quarter's rent paid in advance (£4,000) as a prepaid expense under assets in the balance sheet. (The rent paid in advance will appear as a current asset in the balance sheet, under the heading prepaid expenses or 'prepayments'.)

In the next accounting period, this prepayment will cease to be an asset and will become an expense in the income statement of that period. This is because the rent prepaid relates to the next period and will be 'used up' during it.

These points are illustrated in Figure 3.3.

In practice, the treatment of accruals and prepayments will be subject to the materiality convention of accounting. This convention states that, where the amounts involved are immaterial, we should consider only what is reasonable. This may mean that an item will be treated as an expense in the period in which it is paid, rather than being strictly matched to the revenue to which it relates. For example, a business may find that, at the end of an accounting period, a bill of £5 has been paid for stationery that has yet to be delivered. For a business of any size, the time and effort involved in recording this as a prepayment would not be justified by the little effect that this would have on the measurement of profit or financial position. The amount would, therefore, be treated as an expense when preparing the income statement for the current period and ignored in the following period.

Profit, cash and accruals accounting

As we have just seen, revenue does not usually represent cash received, and expenses are not the same as cash paid. As a result, the profit figure (that is, total revenue minus total expenses) will not normally represent the net cash generated during a period. It is therefore important to distinguish between profit and liquidity. Profit is a measure of achievement, or productive effort, rather than a measure of cash generated. Although

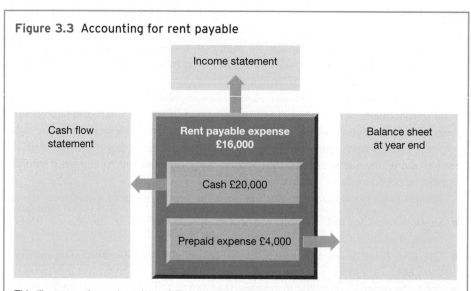

Figure 3.3 Accounting for rent payable

This illustrates the main points of Example 3.6. We can see that the rent expense of £16,000 (which appears in the income statement) is made up of four quarters' rent at £4,000 per quarter. This is the amount that relates to the period and is 'used up' during the period. The cash paid of £20,000 (which appears in the cash flow statement) is made up of the cash paid during the period, which is five quarters at £4,000 per quarter. Finally, the prepayment of £4,000 (which appears on the balance sheet) represents the payment made on 31 December and relates to the next financial year.

making a profit will increase wealth, as we have already seen in Chapter 2, cash is only one form in which that wealth may be held.

The above points are reflected in the accruals convention of accounting, which asserts that profit is the excess of revenue over expenses for a period, not the excess of cash receipts over cash payments. Leading on from this, the approach to accounting that is based on the accruals convention is frequently referred to as accruals accounting. Thus, the balance sheet and the income statement are both prepared on the basis of accruals accounting. The cash flow statement, on the other hand, is not, as it simply deals with cash receipts and payments.

Depreciation

The expense of depreciation, which appeared in the income statement in Activity 3.1, requires further explanation. Most non-current assets do not have a perpetual existence. They are eventually used up in the process of generating revenue for the business. In essence, depreciation is an attempt to measure that portion of the cost (or fair value) of a non-current asset that has been used up in generating the revenue recognised during a particular period. The depreciation charge is considered to be an expense of the period to which it relates. Depreciation tends to be relevant both to tangible non-current assets (property, plant and equipment) and to intangible non-current assets.

We should be clear that the principle is the same for both types of non-current asset. We shall deal with each of the two in turn.

Tangible non-current assets (property, plant and equipment)

To calculate a depreciation charge for a period, four factors have to be considered:

- the cost (or fair value) of the asset
- the useful life of the asset
- the residual value of the asset
- the depreciation method.

The cost (or fair value) of the asset

The cost of an asset will include all costs incurred by the business to bring the asset to its required location and to make it ready for use. Thus, in addition to the costs of acquiring the asset, any delivery costs, installation costs (for example, setting up a new machine) and legal costs incurred in the transfer of legal title (for example, in purchasing property) will be included as part of the total cost of the asset. Similarly, any costs incurred in improving or altering an asset in order to make it suitable for its intended use within the business will also be included as part of the total cost.

Activity 3.6

Andrew Wu (Engineering) Ltd bought a new motor car for its marketing director. The invoice received from the motor car supplier showed the following:

	£
New BMW 325i	26,350
Delivery charge	80
Alloy wheels	660
Sun roof	200
Petrol	30
Number plates	130
Road fund licence	165
	27,615
Part exchange – Reliant Robin	(1,000)
Amount outstanding	26,615

What is the total cost of the new car that will be treated as part of the business's property, plant and equipment?

The cost of the new car will be as follows:

	£
New BMW 325i	26,350
Delivery charge	80
Alloy wheels	660
Sun roof	200
Number plates	130
	27,420

→

This cost includes delivery charges, which are necessary to bring the asset into use, and it includes number plates, as they are a necessary and integral part of the asset. Improvements (alloy wheels and sun roof) are also regarded as part of the total cost of the motor car. The petrol and road fund licence, however, represent costs of operating the asset rather than a part of the total cost of acquiring it and making it ready for use: hence these amounts will be charged as an expense in the period incurred (although part of the cost of the licence may be regarded as a prepaid expense in the period incurred).

The part-exchange figure shown is part payment of the total amount outstanding and so is not relevant to a consideration of the total cost.

The fair value of an asset was defined in Chapter 2 as the exchange value that could be obtained in an arm's-length transaction. We have already seen that assets may be revalued to fair value only if this can be measured reliably. When a revaluation is carried out, all items within the same class must be revalued and revaluations must be kept up to date.

The useful life of the asset

A tangible non-current asset has both a *physical life* and an *economic life*. The physical life will be exhausted through the effects of wear and tear and/or the passage of time. It is possible, however, for the physical life to be extended considerably through careful maintenance, improvements and so on. The economic life is decided by the effects of technological progress and by changes in demand. After a while, the benefits of using the asset may be less than the costs involved. This may be because the asset is unable to compete with newer assets, or because it is no longer relevant to the needs of the business. The economic life of a non-current tangible asset may be much shorter than its physical life. For example, a computer may have a physical life of eight years and an economic life of three years.

It is the economic life that will determine the expected useful life for the purpose of calculating depreciation. Forecasting the economic life, however, may be extremely difficult in practice: both the rate at which technology progresses and shifts in consumer tastes can be swift and unpredictable.

Residual value (disposal value)

When a business disposes of a tangible non-current asset that may still be of value to others, some payment may be received. This payment will represent the residual value, or *disposal value*, of the asset. To calculate the total amount to be depreciated, the residual value must be deducted from the cost of the asset. The likely amount to be received on disposal can, once again, be difficult to predict. The best guide is often past experience of similar assets sold.

Depreciation method

Once the amount to be depreciated (that is, the cost, or fair value, of the asset less any residual value) has been estimated, the business must select a method of allocating this depreciable amount between the accounting periods covering the asset's useful life. Although there are various ways in which the total depreciation may be allocated and, from this, a depreciation charge for each period derived, there are really only two methods that are commonly used in practice.

The first of these is known as the straight-line method. This method simply allocates the amount to be depreciated evenly over the useful life of the asset. In other words, an equal amount of depreciation is charged for each year that the asset is held.

Example 3.7

To illustrate this method, consider the following information:

Cost of machine	£78,124
Estimated residual value at the end of its useful life	£2,000
Estimated useful life	4 years

To calculate the depreciation charge for each year, the total amount to be depreciated must be calculated. This will be the total cost less the estimated residual value: that is, £78,124 – £2,000 = £76,124. Having done this, the annual depreciation charge can be derived by dividing the amount to be depreciated by the estimated useful life of the asset of four years. The calculation is therefore:

$$\frac{£76,124}{4} = £19,031$$

Thus, the annual depreciation charge that appears in the income statement in relation to this asset will be £19,031 for each of the four years of the asset's life.

The amount of depreciation relating to the asset will be accumulated for as long as the asset continues to be owned by the business. This accumulated depreciation figure will increase each year as a result of the annual depreciation amount charged to the income statement. This accumulated amount will be deducted from the cost of the asset on the balance sheet. At the end of the second year, for example, the accumulated depreciation will be £19,031 × 2 = £38,062, and the asset details will appear on the balance sheet as follows:

	£
Machine at cost	78,124
Accumulated depreciation	(38,062)
	40,062

The balance of £40,062 shown above is referred to as the carrying amount (sometimes also known as the written-down value or net book value) of the asset. It represents that portion of the cost (or fair value) of the asset that has still to be charged as an expense (written off) in future years. It must be emphasised that this figure does not represent the current market value, which may be quite different.

The straight-line method derives its name from the fact that the carrying amount of the asset at the end of each year, when plotted against time, will result in a straight line, as shown in Figure 3.4.

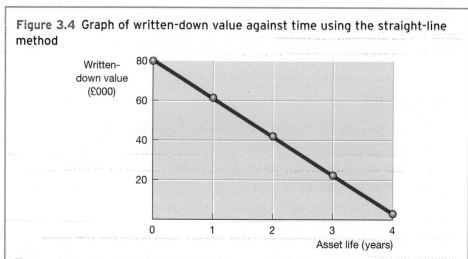

Figure 3.4 Graph of written-down value against time using the straight-line method

The carrying amount of the asset declines by a constant amount each year. This is because the straight-line method provides a constant depreciation charge each year. The result, when plotted on a graph, is a straight line.

The second approach to calculating depreciation for a period, which is found in practice, is referred to as the reducing-balance method. This method applies a fixed percentage rate of depreciation to the carrying amount of an asset each year. The effect of this will be high annual depreciation charges in the early years and lower charges in the later years. To illustrate this method, let us take the same information that was used in Example 3.7. By using a fixed percentage of 60 per cent of the carrying amount to determine the annual depreciation charge, the effect will be to reduce the carrying amount to £2,000 after four years.

The calculations will be as follows:

	£
Cost of machine	78,124
Year 1 Depreciation charge (60%* of cost)	(46,874)
Carrying amount	31,250
Year 2 Depreciation charge (60% of carrying amount)	(18,750)
Carrying amount	12,500
Year 3 Depreciation charge (60% of carrying amount)	(7,500)
Carrying amount	5,000
Year 4 Depreciation charge (60% of carrying amount)	(3,000)
Residual value	2,000

* See Box 3.1 for an explanation of how to derive the fixed percentage.

Box 3.1
Deriving the fixed percentage

Deriving the fixed percentage to be applied requires the use of the following formula:

$$P = (1 - \sqrt[n]{R/C}) \times 100\%$$

where: P = the depreciation percentage
 n = the useful life of the asset (in years)
 R = the residual value of the asset
 C = the cost, or fair value, of the asset.

The fixed percentage rate will, however, be given in all examples used in this text.

We can see that the pattern of depreciation is quite different for the two methods. If we plot the carrying amount of the asset, which has been derived using the reducing-balance method, against time, the result will be as shown in Figure 3.5.

Figure 3.5 Graph of written-down value against time using the reducing-balance method

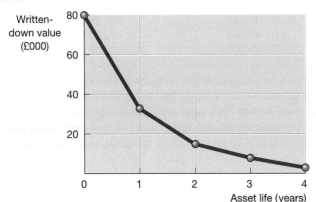

Under the reducing-balance method, the carrying amount of an asset falls by a larger amount in the earlier years than in the later years. This is because the depreciation charge is based on a fixed-rate percentage of the carrying amount.

Activity 3.7

Assume that the machine used in the example above was owned by a business that made a profit before depreciation of £40,000 for each of the four years in which the asset was held.

Calculate the profit for the business for each year under each depreciation method, and comment on your findings.

Your answer should be as follows:

Straight-line method

	(a) Profit before depreciation £	(b) Depreciation £	(a − b) Profit £
Year 1	40,000	19,031	20,969
Year 2	40,000	19,031	20,969
Year 3	40,000	19,031	20,969
Year 4	40,000	19,031	20,969

Reducing-balance method

	(a) Profit before depreciation £	(b) Depreciation £	(a − b) Profit/(loss) £
Year 1	40,000	46,874	(6,874)
Year 2	40,000	18,750	21,250
Year 3	40,000	7,500	32,500
Year 4	40,000	3,000	37,000

The straight-line method of depreciation results in a constant profit figure over the four-year period. This is because both the profit before depreciation and the depreciation charge are constant over the period. The reducing-balance method, however, results in a changing profit figure over time, despite the fact that in this example the pre-depreciation profit is the same each year. In the first year a loss is reported, and thereafter a rising profit is reported.

Although the *pattern* of profit over the four-year period will be quite different, depending on the depreciation method used, the *total* profit for the period (£83,876) will remain the same. This is because both methods of depreciating will allocate the same amount of total depreciation (£76,124) over the four-year period. It is only the amount allocated *between years* that will differ.

In practice, the use of different depreciation methods may not have such a dramatic effect on profits as suggested in Activity 3.7. Where a business replaces some of its assets each year, the total depreciation charge calculated under the reducing-balance method will reflect a range of charges (from high through to low), as assets will be at different points in the replacement cycle. This could mean that each year's total depreciation charge may not be significantly different from the total depreciation charge that would be derived under the straight-line method.

Selecting a depreciation method

How does a business choose which depreciation method to use for a particular asset? The answer is the one that best matches the depreciation expense to the pattern of economic benefits that the asset provides. Where these benefits are provided evenly over time (buildings, for example), the straight-line method is usually appropriate. Where assets lose their efficiency (as with certain types of machinery), the benefits provided will decline over time and so the reducing-balance method may be more appropriate. Where the pattern of economic benefits provided by the asset is uncertain, the straight-line method is normally chosen.

There is an international financial reporting standard (or international accounting standard) to deal with the depreciation of property, plant and equipment. As we shall see in Chapter 4, the purpose of accounting standards is to narrow areas of accounting difference and to try to ensure that information provided to users is transparent and comparable. The relevant standard endorses the view that the depreciation method chosen should reflect the pattern of economic benefits provided but does not specify particular methods to be used. It states that the useful life, depreciation method and residual values of non-current assets should be reviewed at least annually and adjustments made where appropriate.

Real World 3.5 sets out the depreciation policies of Thorntons plc.

Real World 3.5

Sweet talk on depreciation policies

Thorntons plc, the manufacturer and retailer of confectionery, uses the straight-line method to depreciate all its non-current assets. In practice, this appears to be the most widely used method of depreciation. The financial statements for the year ended 30 June 2007 show the period over which different classes of tangible non-current assets are depreciated as follows:

In equal annual instalments	
Freehold premises	50 years
Short leasehold land and buildings	Period of the lease
Retail fixtures and fittings	Up to 5 years
Retail equipment	4 to 5 years
Retail store improvements	Up to 10 years
Other equipment and vehicles	3 to 7 years
Manufacturing plant and machinery	10 to 15 years
Computer licenses and software	3 to 5 years

We can see that there are wide variations in the expected useful lives of the various non-current assets held.

Source: Thorntons plc Annual Report and Accounts 2007, p. 28.

It seems that Thorntons plc is typical of UK businesses in that most use the straight-line approach. The reducing-balance method is not very much used.

The approach taken to calculating depreciation is summarised in Figure 3.6.

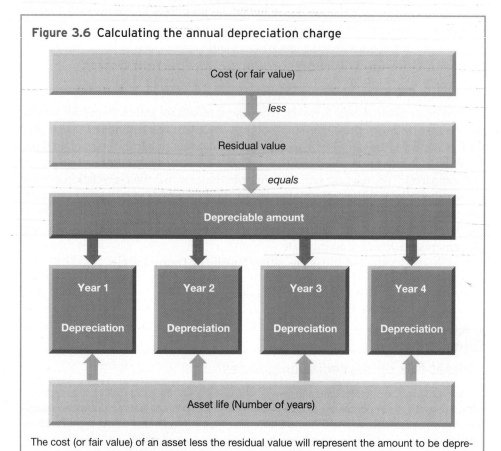

Figure 3.6 Calculating the annual depreciation charge

The cost (or fair value) of an asset less the residual value will represent the amount to be depreciated. This amount is depreciated over the useful life (four years in this particular case) of the asset using an appropriate depreciation method.

Depreciating intangible assets

Where an intangible asset has a finite life, the approach taken for the depreciation (or *amortisation* as it is usually called with intangibles) is broadly the same as that for property, plant and equipment (tangible non-current assets). The asset is amortised (depreciated) over its useful life and the amortisation method used should reflect the pattern of benefits provided. Some differences arise, however, because of the valuation problems surrounding these assets. Intangible assets are normally reported at cost rather than their fair value. They are rarely revalued because there is usually no active market from which to establish fair values. For similar reasons, the residual value of an intangible asset is normally assumed to be zero.

We saw in Chapter 2 that some intangible assets, which may include acquired goodwill, have an indefinite useful life. These assets are not amortised but instead are tested for impairment at least annually. While intangible assets with finite lives and property, plant and equipment are also subject to impairment testing, this will only occur when there is some indication that impairment has taken place.

Depreciation and the replacement of non-current assets

There seems to be a misunderstanding in the minds of some people that the purpose of depreciation is to provide the funds for the replacement of an asset when it reaches the end of its useful life. However, this is not the purpose of depreciation as conventionally defined. It was mentioned earlier that depreciation represents an attempt to allocate the cost, or fair value (less any residual value), of an asset over its expected useful life. The resulting depreciation charge in each accounting period represents an expense, which is then used in the calculation of profit for the period. Calculating the depreciation charge for a period is therefore necessary for the proper measurement of financial performance, and must be done whether or not the business intends to replace the asset in the future.

If there is an intention to replace the asset, the depreciation charge in the income statement will not ensure that liquid funds are set aside by the business specifically for this purpose. Although the effect of a depreciation charge is to reduce profit, and therefore to reduce the amount available for withdrawal by the owners, the amounts retained within the business as a result may be invested in ways that are unrelated to the replacement of the specific asset.

Depreciation and judgement

When reading the above sections on depreciation, it may have struck you that accounting is not as precise and objective as is sometimes suggested. There are areas where subjective judgement is required, and depreciation provides a good illustration of this.

Activity 3.8

What kinds of judgements must be made to calculate a depreciation charge for a period?

You may have thought of the following:

- the expected residual or disposal value of the asset
- the expected useful life of the asset
- the choice of depreciation method.

Making different judgements on these matters would result in a different pattern of depreciation charges over the life of the asset, and therefore in a different pattern of reported profits. However, underestimations or overestimations that are made in relation to the above will be adjusted for in the final year of an asset's life, and so the total depreciation charge (and total profit) over the asset's life will not be affected by estimation errors.

Real World 3.6 describes the effect of extending the useful life of property, plant and equipment on the short-term profits of one large business.

Real World 3.6

Sports massage

JJB Sports plc, a leading retailer, reported interim financial results for the six months ended 30 June 2005 that caused some disquiet among investors and analysts. The business changed the estimates for the useful life of its property, plant and equipment when calculating depreciation. It explained that this was due to new requirements to adopt International Financial Reporting Standards (IFRSs) when preparing financial statements. The article below, however, suggests that not everyone believed this.

JJB massages results to boost profits
High street retailer JJB Sports massaged last week's disappointing interim results by changing its depreciation calculations, in order to boost flagging profits by £4.3m.

Analysts admitted that they were caught on the hop, as the company reported a 35.8% drop in operating profits from £27.4m to £17.6m for six months ended June 2005 on revenues down 6% to £340.4m. Operating profits would have plummeted even further to £14.3m had the company not changed its accounting for depreciation. 'The company explained the change as coming out of its IFRS conversion review, but it was clearly there for other reasons,' said Teather & Greenwood retail analyst Sanjay Vidyarthi.

JJB said that an impairment review ahead of its IFRS transition had forced a rethink on the carrying value of property, plant and equipment.

It concluded that these items had useful economic lives that more closely matched the length of the short-term lease of the property, rather than the 10-year economic life, which had formed the basis of the depreciation charge in previous accounting periods.

Richard Ratner, head of equity research at Seymour Pierce, said: 'They said the way they had depreciated assets previously was not correct but I haven't seen any other companies make this kind of change.'

JJB's share price fell from 168.2p before the results to 164.7p at the end of last week.

Source: 'JJB massages results to boost profits', *Accountancy Age*, 20 October 2005, p. 3.

Costing inventories

The way in which we measure the cost of inventories is important because the cost of inventories sold during a period will affect the calculation of profit and the remaining inventories held at the end of the period will affect the portrayal of financial position in the balance sheet. In Chapter 2, we saw that historic cost is often the basis for reporting assets, and so it is tempting to think that determining the cost of inventories held is very straightforward. However, in a period of changing prices, the costing of inventories can be a problem.

A business must determine the cost of the inventories sold during the period and the cost of the inventories remaining at the end of the period. To do this, some assumption must be made about the way in which the inventories are physically handled. The assumption need have nothing to do with how the inventories are *actually* handled; it is concerned only with providing useful accounting information.

Two common assumptions used are:

- first in, first out (FIFO) – the earliest acquired inventories held are the first to be used;
- last in, first out (LIFO) – the latest acquired inventories held are the first to be used.

Another approach to deriving the cost of inventories is to assume that inventories acquired lose their separate identity and go into a 'pool'. Any issues of inventories then reflect the average cost of the inventories held. This is the weighted average cost (AVCO) method, where the weights used in deriving the average cost figures are the quantities of each batch of inventories acquired.

Example 3.8 provides a simple illustration of the way in which each method is applied.

Example 3.8

A business commenced on 1 May to supply oil to factories. During this month, the following transactions took place:

	Tonnes	Cost per tonne
May 2 Purchased	10,000	£10
10 Purchased	20,000	£13
18 Sold	9,000	

First in, first out (FIFO)

Using the first in, first out approach, 9,000 tonnes of the 10,000 tonnes bought on 2 May are treated as if these are the ones to be sold. The remaining inventories bought on 2 May (1,000 tonnes) and the inventories bought on 3 May (20,000 tonnes) will become the closing inventories. Thus we have:

Cost of sales	(9,000 @ £10 per tonne)	£90,000
Closing inventories		
		£
	(1,000 @ £10 per tonne)	10,000
	(20,000 @ £13 per tonne)	260,000
		270,000

Last in, first out (LIFO)

Using the last in, first out approach, 9,000 tonnes of the inventories bought on 10 May will be treated as if these are the first to be sold. The earlier inventories bought on 2 May (10,000 tonnes) and the remainder of the inventories bought on 10 May (11,000 tonnes) will become the closing inventories. Thus we have:

Cost of sales	(9,000 @ £13 per tonne)	£117,000

Closing inventories

		£
(11,000 @ £13 per tonne)		143,000
(10,000 @ £10 per tonne)		100,000
		243,000

Weighted average cost (AVCO)

Since newly acquired inventories are treated, for accounting purposes, as if they lose their separate identity, any issues should reflect the weighted average cost of the inventories that are held. The weights used in deriving the average cost figures are the quantities of each batch of inventories bought.

Using this approach, a weighted average cost will be determined that will be used to derive both the cost of goods sold and the cost of the remaining inventories held. This simply means that the cost of the inventories bought on 2 May and 10 May are added together and then divided by the total number of tonnes to obtain the weighted average cost per tonne. That is:

Average cost = ((10,000 × £10) + (20,000 × £13))/(10,000 + 20,000) = £12 per tonne.

Both the cost of sales and the value of the closing inventories are then based on this average cost per tonne. Thus we have:

Cost of sales	(9,000 @ £12 per tonne)	£108,000
Closing inventories	(21,000 × £12 per tonne)	£252,000

Activity 3.9

Suppose that the 9,000 tonnes of inventories in Example 3.8 were sold for £15 a tonne.

(a) Calculate the gross profit for the period under each of the three costing methods.
(b) What do you note about the different profit and closing inventories valuations when using each method, when prices are rising?

Your answer should be along the following lines:

(a) Gross profit calculation:

	FIFO	LIFO	AVCO
	£000	£000	£000
Sales revenue (9,000 @ £15)	135	135	135
Cost of sales	(90)	(117)	(108)
Gross profit	45	18	27
Closing inventories figure	270	243	252

(b) These figures show that FIFO will give the highest gross profit during a period of rising prices. This is because sales revenue is matched with the earlier (and cheaper) purchases. LIFO will give the lowest gross profit because sales revenue is matched against the more recent (and dearer) purchases. The AVCO method will normally give a figure that is between these two extremes.

The closing inventories figure in the balance sheet will be highest with the FIFO method. This is because the cost of oil still held will be based on the more recent (and dearer) purchases. LIFO will give the lowest closing inventories figure as the oil held will be based on the earlier (and cheaper) purchases. Once again, the AVCO method will normally give a figure that is between these two extremes. During a period of falling prices, the position of FIFO and LIFO is reversed.

The different costing methods will only have an effect on the reported profit from one year to the next. The figure derived for closing inventories will be carried forward and matched with sales revenue in a later period. Thus, if the cheaper purchases of inventories are matched to sales revenue in the current period, it will mean that the dearer purchases will be matched to sales revenue in a later period. Over the life of the business, therefore, the total profit will be the same whichever costing method has been used.

Inventories – some further issues

We saw in Chapter 2 that the convention of prudence requires that inventories be valued at the lower of cost and net realisable value. (The net realisable value of inventories is the estimated selling price less any further costs that may be necessary to complete the goods and any costs involved in selling and distributing the goods.) This rule may mean that the valuation method applied to inventories (cost or net realisable value) will switch from one year to the next, depending on which of cost and net realisable value is the lower. In practice, however, the cost of the inventories held is usually below the current net realisable value – particularly during a period of rising prices. It is, therefore, the cost figure that will normally appear in the balance sheet.

Activity 3.10

Can you think of any circumstances where the net realisable value will be lower than the cost of inventories held, even during a period of generally rising prices?

The net realisable value may be lower where:

■ goods have deteriorated or become obsolete;
■ there has been a fall in the market price of the goods;
■ the goods are being used as a 'loss leader';
■ bad buying decisions have been made.

There is an international financial reporting standard that deals with inventories. It states that the cost of inventories should normally be determined using either FIFO or AVCO. The LIFO approach is not an acceptable method to use. The standard also requires the 'lower of cost or net realisable value' rule to be used.

Real World 3.7 sets out the costing methods of two large businesses.

Real World 3.7

Costing inventories in practice

Tate and Lyle plc, the sugar and other starch-based food processor, reports inventories on either a 'first in, first out' basis or weighted average costs basis.

Kingfisher plc, the home improvement business (that owns B and Q and other outlets worldwide), uses weighted average cost only.

Sources: Tate and Lyle plc Annual Report 2007, p. 92; Kingfisher plc Annual Report and Accounts 2007, p. 59.

Costing inventories and depreciation provide two examples where the consistency convention must be applied. This convention holds that once a particular method of accounting is selected, it should be applied consistently over time. Thus, it would not be acceptable to switch from, say, FIFO to AVCO between periods (unless exceptional circumstances make it appropriate). The purpose of this convention is to help users make valid comparisons of performance and position from one period to the next.

Activity 3.11

Reporting inventories in the financial statements provides a further example of the need to apply subjective judgement. For the inventories of a retail business, what are the main areas where judgement is required?

The main areas are:

■ the choice of cost method (FIFO, LIFO, AVCO);
■ deducing the net realisable value figure for inventories held.

Dealing with trade receivables' problems

We have seen that, when businesses sell goods or services on credit, revenue will often be recognised before the customer pays the amounts owing. Recording the dual aspect of a credit sale will involve increasing sales revenue, and increasing trade receivables, by the amount of the revenue from the credit sale.

With this type of sale there is always the risk that the customer will not pay the amount due, however reliable they might have appeared to be at the time of the sale. When it becomes reasonably certain that the customer will never pay, the amount owed is considered to be a bad debt and this must be taken into account when preparing the financial statements.

Activity 3.12

When preparing the financial statements, what would be the effect on the income statement, and on the balance sheet, of not taking into account the fact that a particular debt is bad?

The effect would be to overstate the assets (trade receivables) on the balance sheet, and to overstate profit in the income statement, as the revenue which has been recognised will not result in any future benefit.

To provide a more realistic picture of financial performance and position, the bad debt must be 'written off'. This will involve reducing the trade receivables, and increasing expenses (by creating an expense known as 'bad debts written off'), by the amount of the bad debt.

The matching convention requires that the bad debt is written off in the same period in which the sale that gave rise to the debt is recognised.

Note that, when a debt is bad, the accounting response is not simply to cancel the original sale. If this were done, the income statement would not be so informative. Reporting the bad debts as an expense can be extremely useful in assessing management performance.

Activity 3.13

The treatment of bad debts represents another area where judgement is needed to derive an appropriate expense figure.

What will be the effect of different judgements concerning the appropriate amount of bad debts expense on the profit for a particular period and on the total profit reported over the life of the business?

Judgement is often required in deriving a figure for bad debts incurred during a period. There may be situations where views will differ concerning whether or not a debt is irrecoverable. The decision concerning whether or not to write off a bad debt will have an effect on the expenses for the period and, hence, the reported profit. However, over the life of the business the total reported profit would not be affected, as incorrect judgements in one period will be adjusted for in a later period.

Suppose that a debt of £100 was written off in a period and that, in a later period, the amount owing was actually received. The increase in expenses of £100 in the period in which the bad debt was written off would be compensated for by an increase in revenue of £100 when the amount outstanding was finally received (bad debt recoverable). If, on the other hand, the amount owing of £100 was never written off in the first place, the profit for the two periods would not be affected by the bad debt adjustment and would, therefore, be different – but the total profit for the two periods would be the same.

Real World 3.8 discusses the approach taken by banks trying to avoid bad debts.

Real World 3.8

Banking on bad debts

Nervousness in the world's financial markets, sparked by sub-prime lending in the US, is causing banks and other financial institutions to take a closer look at their customers.

Banks are tightening their lending policies to shield themselves from the possibility of debtors defaulting. Already, reports are emerging of banks shunning some categories of new borrower and limiting the credit available to existing ones.

But how do they make these decisions?

According to the British Bankers' Association, banks now collect four kinds of data to assess client risk: negative data, such as county-court fines and convictions; 'positive' information on people's financial commitments and loans etc; income data; and reports on spending behaviour.

Apacs, a UK association for the banking industry, says lenders tend to grab these from three sources – the electoral roll, their own systems, which are tied up with other payments organisations such as Visa, and credit-checking agencies.

'People are creatures of habit,' says Eric Leenders, executive director of the BBA. 'You put a salary in your account once a month and may go to the supermarket weekly. From that analysis, you see the ability of someone to repay.

'The software has to achieve the same end and banks all look at the same data.'

While turning some customers away, banks are arguing that lending criteria are unchanged. Mr Leenders says this is true: 'Banks have not recently changed the lending criteria. All they do is raise or lower the threshold score. When you raise the bar, fewer people are accepted for credit. The name of the game is to minimise the risk of whom you lend to.'

Methods used to assess customers, on the other hand, have changed. Lenders now either use their own analytics software, or systems from vendors, such as Fair Isaac. These can calculate a customer's risk based on the available data. HBOS bank, for example, uses Callcredit's software to monitor missed payments in a bid to intervene on bad debts before they mount up.

'The data is held entirely within the bank's own systems,' says Ian Turvill, a senior director at Fair Isaac. 'What may be common across banks is the expertise in developing the analytics that review the data to work out whether delinquency or bankruptcy is likely to take place.

'Most banks have automated links with the credit agencies – now typically using web services – that deliver data automatically into the customer databases. The banks rely on the internal quality processes that the agencies apply to ensure that the data is of an appropriate integrity.'

Martha Bennett, director of research for financial services at analyst Datamonitor, adds: 'There is always an issue around a neural network and predicting the propensity of someone who will fail on a loan. The technology is reasonably sophisticated with that, but the problem is what do you do with the result?'

Today, the same type of CRM systems that allow retailers to monitor spending of customers who carry loyalty cards also run in banks, and these enable them to build more accurate profiles. Combined with predictive software, this can be a powerful alarm system.

'If a business with a fleet of cars has a cash crunch, they will commonly send out the vehicles to fuel up,' says Carl Clump, chief executive of Retail Decisions. 'They'll break through their credit limits all at once.'

'You can see similar acts with consumers – if you start to see lots of expenses on payment cards for food shopping, way more than usual, it would seem they are having a cash crunch.'

Mr Turvill adds: 'There is a whole class of applications called credit account management systems, including Fair Isaac's Triad and Probe from Experian, the credit-checking agency. They are sometimes classified as CRM systems, but they are distinct. They are linked to what is called the master data file, a centralised database maintained by the credit card companies.'

Zopa, by contrast, is an online service that allows individuals to lend and borrow money from each other. For its business to operate and to gain the trust of lenders, it bought software from SAS, the data-mining company, to help with credit scoring. It now boasts a 'bad-debt rate' of some 0.05 per cent. This is because the company's IT system performs real-time authentication and credit checks with the Equifax credit rating body. The software then scores the customer into one of four bands: A*, A, B or C.

'But over the industry in general there is still some difficulty in getting a single view of a client,' says Bart Patrick, head of risk strategy for SAS. 'You basically have various systems linking up the client records.'

'We do customer experience analytics – looking at what a customer buys and what they could buy. We are getting demand for joining up lending and marketing systems.'

Sources close to the banks, which are reluctant to talk about decision-making processes, say lenders also demand more real-time information.

With increasing sales of financial products over the internet, banks require faster answers on applications for instant mortgage quotes, for example.

But again, this means greater sharing of data, which raises serious security questions over how safe that information is.

Data protection laws are set in many countries to prevent data being shared without consent of the subject. Banks argue this is optional, but in many cases an individual cannot apply for a loan without providing that consent.

'Lenders are sharing more information and that means a more informed decision,' says Peter Brooker, director of public affairs for Experian. 'The information we hold is by consent. A lender cannot search your credit report without your consent. It must be fully transparent.'

Source: 'How the banks assess their customers', Dan Ilett, *Financial Times*, 23 October 2007.

Let us now try to bring together some of the points that we have raised in this chapter through a self-assessment question.

? Self-assessment question 3.1

TT and Co. is a new business that started trading on 1 January 2008. The following is a summary of transactions that occurred during the first year of trading:

1 The owners introduced £50,000 of equity, which was paid into a bank account opened in the name of the business.
2 Premises were rented from 1 January 2008 at an annual rental of £20,000. During the year, rent of £25,000 was paid to the owner of the premises.
3 Rates (a tax on business premises) were paid during the year as follows:

For the period 1 January 2008 to 31 March 2008	£500
For the period 1 April 2008 to 31 March 2009	£1,200

4 A delivery van was bought on 1 January 2008 for £12,000. This is expected to be used in the business for four years and then to be sold for £2,000.

5 Wages totalling £33,500 were paid during the year. At the end of the year, the business owed £630 of wages for the last week of the year.

6 Electricity bills for the first three quarters of the year were paid totalling £1,650. After 31 December 2008, but before the financial statements had been finalised for the year, the bill for the last quarter arrived showing a charge of £620.

7 Inventories totalling £143,000 were bought on credit.

8 Inventories totalling £12,000 were bought for cash.

9 Sales revenue on credit totalled £152,000 (cost of sales £74,000).

10 Cash sales revenue totalled £35,000 (cost of sales £16,000).

11 Receipts from trade receivables totalled £132,000.

12 Payments to trade payables totalled £121,000.

13 Van running expenses paid totalled £9,400.

At the end of the year it was clear that a trade receivable who owed £400 would not be able to pay any part of the debt. The business uses the straight-line method for depreciating non-current assets.

Required:
Prepare a balance sheet as at 31 December 2008 and an income statement for the year to that date.

The answer to this question can be found at the back of the book in Appendix B.

Uses and usefulness of the income statement

The income statement, like the balance sheet, has been around for a long time. Most major businesses seem to prepare an income statement on a frequent basis (monthly or even more frequently). This is despite there being no rule requiring an income statement to be produced more frequently than once, or in some cases twice, a year. Income statements are, therefore, seen as being capable of providing useful information. The income statement can be seen as being useful in several ways, including the following:

■ *It provides information on how effective the business has been in generating wealth.* Since wealth generation appears to be a primary reason for most businesses to exist, assessing how much wealth has been created is an important issue. A problem with the profit figure for a particular period, however, is that, had different judgements been made in key areas like depreciation, inventories valuation and bad debts, a different profit figure could have emerged. Whilst these different judgements may be made in good faith, it highlights the fact that there is no single 'correct' profit figure. This can call into question the integrity of the reported profit figure and cause scepticism among users. The problem, however, should not be overstated. For most businesses in most years, making different judgements would probably not affect the profit figure to a significant extent.

■ *It provides information on how the profit was made.* For some users, the only item of concern may be the final profit figure, or *bottom line* as it is sometimes called. Whilst this is a primary measure of performance, and its importance is difficult to overstate, the income statement contains other information that should also be of interest. To evaluate business performance effectively, it is important to find out how the final profit figure was derived. Thus the level of sales revenue, the nature and amount of expenses incurred, and the profit in relation to sales revenue are important factors in understanding the performance of the business over a period. The analysis and interpretation of financial statements is considered in detail in Chapter 6.

Summary

The main points of this chapter may be summarised as follows.

The income statement (profit and loss account)

■ The income statement measures and reports how much profit (or loss) has been generated over a period.

■ Profit (or loss) for the period is the difference between the total revenue and total expenses for the period.

■ The income statement links the balance sheets at the beginning and end of an accounting period.

■ The income statement of a retail business will first calculate gross profit and then deduct any overheads for the period. The final figure derived is the profit (or loss) for the period.

■ Gross profit represents the difference between the sales revenue for the period and the cost of sales.

Expenses and revenue

■ Cost of sales may be identified either by matching the cost of each sale to the particular sale or by adjusting the goods bought during the period to take account of opening and closing inventories.

■ The classification of expenses is often a matter of judgement, although there are rules for businesses that trade as limited companies.

■ Revenue is recognised when the amount of revenue can be measured reliably and it is probable that the economic benefits will be received.

■ Where there is a sale of goods, there is an additional criterion that ownership and control must pass to the buyer before revenue can be recognised.

■ Revenue can be recognised after partial completion provided that a particular stage of completion can be measured reliably.

- The matching convention states that expenses should be matched to the revenue that they help generate.
- A particular expense reported in the income statement may not be the same as the cash paid. This will result in some adjustment for accruals or prepayments.
- The materiality convention states that where the amounts are immaterial, we should consider only what is expedient.
- 'Accruals accounting' is preparing the income statement and balance sheet following the accruals convention, which says that profit = revenue less expenses (not cash receipts less cash payments).

Depreciation of non-current assets

- Depreciation requires a consideration of the cost (or fair value), useful life and residual value of an asset. It also requires a consideration of the method of depreciation.
- The straight-line method of depreciation allocates the amount to be depreciated evenly over the useful life of the asset.
- The reducing-balance method applies a fixed percentage rate of depreciation to the carrying amount of an asset each year.
- The depreciation method chosen should reflect the pattern of benefits associated with the asset.
- Depreciation is an attempt to allocate the cost (or fair value), less the residual value, of an asset over its useful life. It does not provide funds for replacement of the asset.

Costing inventories

- The way in which we derive the cost of inventories is important in the calculation of profit and the presentation of financial position.
- The first in, first out (FIFO) method approaches matters as if the earliest inventories held are the first to be used.
- The last in, first out (LIFO) method approaches matters as if the latest inventories are the first to be used.
- The weighted average cost (AVCO) method applies an average cost to all inventories used.
- When prices are rising, FIFO gives the lowest cost of sales figure and highest closing inventories figure and LIFO gives the highest cost of sales figure and the lowest closing inventories figure. AVCO gives figures for cost of sales and closing inventories that lie between FIFO and LIFO.
- When prices are falling, the positions of FIFO and LIFO are reversed.
- Inventories are shown at the lower of cost and net realisable value.
- When a particular method of accounting, such as an inventories costing method, is selected, it should be applied consistently over time.

Bad debts

- Where it is reasonably certain that a credit customer will not pay, the debt is regarded as 'bad' and written off.

Uses of the income statement

- Provides a profit figure.
- Provides information on how the profit was derived.

→ **Key terms**

profit p. 70
revenue p. 70
expense p. 71
income statement p. 72
accounting period p. 72
gross profit p. 74
operating profit p. 74
profit for the year p. 74
cost of sales p. 74
matching convention p. 81
accrued expenses p. 82
prepaid expenses p. 85
materiality convention p. 85
accruals convention p. 86

accruals accounting p. 86
depreciation p. 86
residual value p. 88
straight-line method p. 89
carrying amount p. 89
written-down value p. 89
net book value p. 89
reducing-balance method p. 90
first in, first out (FIFO) p. 97
last in, first out (LIFO) p. 97
weighted average cost (AVCO) p. 97
consistency convention p. 100
bad debt p. 101

Further reading

If you would like to explore the topics covered in this chapter in more depth, we recommend the following books:

Elliott, B. and Elliott, J., *Financial Accounting and Reporting* (12th edn), Financial Times Prentice Hall, 2008, chapters 2, 16, 18 and 19.

Kirk, R.J., *International Financial Reporting Standards in Depth*, CIMA Publishing, 2005, chapters 2 and 3.

KPMG, *KPMG's Practical Guide to International Financial Reporting Standards* (3rd edn), Thomson, 2006, sections 3.2, 3.3 and 3.8.

Sutton, T., *Corporate Financial Accounting and Reporting* (2nd edn), Financial Times Prentice Hall, 2004, chapters 2, 8, 9 and 10.

? Review questions

Answers to these questions can be found at the back of the book in Appendix C.

3.1 'Although the income statement is a record of past achievement, the calculations required for certain expenses involve estimates of the future.' What does this statement mean? Can you think of examples where estimates of the future are used?

3.2 'Depreciation is a process of allocation and not valuation.' What do you think is meant by this statement?

3.3 What is the convention of consistency? Does this convention help users in making a more valid comparison between businesses?

3.4 'An asset is similar to an expense.' Do you agree?

✳ Exercises

Exercises 3.4 and 3.5 are more advanced than Exercises 3.1 to 3.3. Those with coloured numbers have answers at the back of the book in Appendix D.

> If you wish to try more exercises, visit MyAccountingLab/

3.1 You have heard the following statements made. Comment critically on them.

(a) 'Equity only increases or decreases as a result of the owners putting more cash into the business or taking some out.'
(b) 'An accrued expense is one that relates to next year.'
(c) 'Unless we depreciate this asset we shall be unable to provide for its replacement.'
(d) 'There is no point in depreciating the factory building. It is appreciating in value each year.'

3.2 Singh Enterprises has an accounting year to 31 December and uses the straight-line method of depreciation. On 1 January 2006 the business bought a machine for £10,000. The machine had an expected useful life of four years and an estimated residual value of £2,000. On 1 January 2007 the business bought another machine for £15,000. This machine had an expected useful life of five years and an estimated residual value of £2,500. On 31 December 2008 the business sold the first machine bought for £3,000.

Required:
Show the relevant income statement extracts and balance sheet extracts for the years 2006, 2007 and 2008.

3.3 The owner of a business is confused, and comes to you for help. The financial statements for the business, prepared by an accountant, for the last accounting period revealed a profit of £50,000. However, during the accounting period the bank balance declined by £30,000. What reasons might explain this apparent discrepancy?

3.4 The following is the balance sheet of TT and Co. at the end of its first year of trading (from Self-assessment question 3.1):

TT and Co. Balance sheet as at 31 December 2008

	£
Non-current assets	
Property, plant and equipment	
Delivery van at cost	12,000
Depreciation	(2,500)
	9,500
Current assets	
Inventories	65,000
Trade receivables	19,600
Prepaid expenses*	5,300
Cash	750
	90,650
Total assets	100,150
Equity	
Original	50,000
Retained profit	26,900
	76,900
Current liabilities	
Trade payables	22,000
Accrued expenses†	1,250
	23,250
Total equity and liabilities	100,150

* The prepaid expenses consisted of rates (£300) and rent (£5,000).
† The accrued expenses consisted of wages (£630) and electricity (£620).

During 2009, the following transactions took place:

1 The owners withdrew equity in the form of cash of £20,000.
2 Premises continued to be rented at an annual rental of £20,000. During the year, rent of £15,000 was paid to the owner of the premises.
3 Rates on the premises were paid during the year as follows: for the period 1 April 2009 to 31 March 2010 £1,300.
4 A second delivery van was bought on 1 January 2009 for £13,000. This is expected to be used in the business for four years and then to be sold for £3,000.
5 Wages totalling £36,700 were paid during the year. At the end of the year, the business owed £860 of wages for the last week of the year.
6 Electricity bills for the first three quarters of the year and £620 for the last quarter of the previous year were paid totalling £1,820. After 31 December 2009, but before the financial statements had been finalised for the year, the bill for the last quarter arrived showing a charge of £690.
7 Inventories totalling £67,000 were bought on credit.
8 Inventories totalling £8,000 were bought for cash.
9 Sales revenue on credit totalled £179,000 (cost £89,000).
10 Cash sales revenue totalled £54,000 (cost £25,000).

→

11 Receipts from trade receivables totalled £178,000.
12 Payments to trade payables totalled £71,000.
13 Van running expenses paid totalled £16,200.

The business uses the straight-line method for depreciating non-current assets.

Required:
Prepare a balance sheet as at 31 December 2009 and an income statement for the year
to that date.

3.5 The following is the balance sheet of WW Associates as at 31 December 2007:

Balance sheet as at 31 December 2007

	£
Non-current assets	
Machinery	25,300
Current assets	
Inventories	12,200
Trade receivables	21,300
Prepaid expenses (rates)	400
Cash	8,300
Total assets	67,500
Equity	
Original	25,000
Retained profit	23,900
	48,900
Current liabilities	
Trade payables	16,900
Accrued expenses (wages)	1,700
	18,600
Total equity and liabilities	67,500

During 2008, the following transactions took place:

1 The owners withdrew equity in the form of cash of £23,000.
2 Premises were rented at an annual rental of £20,000. During the year, rent of £25,000
was paid to the owner of the premises.
3 Rates on the premises were paid during the year for the period 1 April 2008 to 31
March 2009 and amounted to £2,000.
4 Some machinery (a non-current asset), which was bought on 1 January 2007 for
£13,000, has proved to be unsatisfactory. It was part-exchanged for some new
machinery on 1 January 2008, and WW Associates paid a cash amount of £6,000. The
new machinery would have cost £15,000 had the business bought it without the
trade-in.
5 Wages totalling £23,800 were paid during the year. At the end of the year, the business owed £860 of wages.
6 Electricity bills for the four quarters of the year were paid totalling £2,700.
7 Inventories totalling £143,000 were bought on credit.
8 Inventories totalling £12,000 were bought for cash.

9 Sales revenue on credit totalled £211,000 (cost £127,000).

10 Cash sales revenue totalled £42,000 (cost £25,000).

11 Receipts from trade receivables totalled £198,000.

12 Payments to trade payables totalled £156,000.

13 Van running expenses paid totalled £17,500.

The business uses the reducing-balance method of depreciation for non-current assets at the rate of 30 per cent each year.

Required:

Prepare a balance sheet as at 31 December 2008 and an income statement (profit and loss account) for the year to that date.

Chapter 4

Accounting for limited companies

Introduction

Most businesses in the UK, except the very smallest, operate in the form of limited companies. More than 2 million limited companies now exist and they account for the majority of UK business activity and employment. The economic significance of this type of business is not confined to the UK; it can be seen in many of the world's developed countries.

In this chapter we consider the nature of limited companies and how they differ from sole proprietorship businesses and partnerships. We examine the ways in which the owners provide finance as well as the rules governing the way in which limited companies must account to their owners and to other interested parties. We shall also see how the financial statements, which were discussed in the previous two chapters, are prepared for this type of business.

Learning outcomes

When you have completed this chapter, you should be able to:

- discuss the nature of the limited company;
- describe the main features of the owners' claim in a limited company;
- discuss the framework of rules that surround accounting for limited companies;
- explain how the income statement and balance sheet of a limited company differ in detail from those of sole proprietorships and partnerships.

Why limited companies?

Although there are very many businesses in the UK that trade as sole proprietorships, partnerships and other forms, overwhelmingly the most important business form is the limited company. In terms of sales revenue generated, wealth created, number of people employed, exports achieved and virtually any other measure, the limited companies dominate the business scene. We shall be seeing in this chapter that limited companies are subject to a great deal of regulation, particularly in the areas of finance and accounting. This is particularly true of those limited companies whose shares are traded on the London Stock Exchange. All of this regulation can be very tiresome for the companies and, importantly, very expensive.

In this chapter we shall be looking at a number of issues, including:

- What is a limited company?
- Why are limited companies so popular?
- What regulation must limited companies accept?
- Why do some limited companies have their shares traded on the London Stock Exchange, when this leads to even more regulation, at great expense?

We shall be answering these and other questions during this chapter.

The main features of limited companies

Legal nature

Let us begin our examination of limited companies by discussing their legal nature. A limited company has been described as an artificial person that has been created by law. This means that a company has many of the rights and obligations that 'real' people have. It can, for example, sue or be sued by others and can enter into contracts in its own name. This contrasts sharply with other types of businesses, such as sole proprietorships and partnerships (that is, unincorporated businesses), where it is the owner(s) rather than the business that must sue, enter into contracts and so on, because the business has no separate legal identity.

With the rare exceptions of those that are created by Act of Parliament or by Royal Charter, all UK companies are created (or *incorporated*) by registration. To create a company the person or persons wishing to create it (usually known as *promoters*) fill in a few simple forms and pay a modest registration fee. After having ensured that the necessary formalities have been met, the Registrar of Companies, a UK government official, enters the name of the new company on the Registry of Companies. Thus, in the UK, companies can be formed very easily and cheaply (for about £100).

A limited company may be owned by just one person, but most have more than one owner and some have many owners. The owners are usually known as *members* or *shareholders*. The ownership of a company is normally divided into a number, frequently a large number, of shares, each of equal size. Each owner, or shareholder, owns one or more shares in the company. Large companies typically have a very large number of shareholders. For example, at 31 March 2007, BT Group plc, the telecommunications business, had nearly 1.3 million different shareholders.

As a limited company has its own legal identity, it is regarded as being quite separate from those that own and manage it.

It is worth emphasising that this legal separateness of owners and the company has no connection whatsoever with the business entity convention of accounting, which we discussed in Chapter 2. This accounting convention applies equally well to all business types, including sole proprietorships and partnerships where there is certainly no legal distinction between the owner(s) and the business.

The legal separateness of the limited company and its shareholders leads to two important features of the limited company: perpetual life and limited liability. These are now explained.

Perpetual life

A company is normally granted a perpetual existence and so will continue even where an owner of some, or even all, of the shares in the company dies. The shares of the deceased person will simply pass to the beneficiary of his or her estate. The granting of perpetual existence means that the life of a company is quite separate from the lives of those individuals who own or manage it. It is not, therefore, affected by changes in ownership that arise when individuals buy and sell shares in the company.

Though a company may be granted a perpetual existence when it is first formed, it is possible for either the shareholders or the courts to bring this existence to an end. When this is done, the assets of the company are sold off to meet outstanding liabilities. Any surplus arising from the sale will then be used to pay the shareholders. Shareholders may agree to end the life of a company where it has achieved the purpose for which it was formed or where they feel that the company has no real future. The courts may bring the life of a company to an end where creditors have applied to the courts for this to be done because they have not been paid amounts owing.

Where shareholders agree to end the life of a company, it is referred to as a 'voluntary liquidation'. Real World 4.1 describes the demise of one company by this method.

Monotub Industries in a spin as founder gets Titan for £1

Monotub Industries, maker of the Titan washing machine, yesterday passed into corporate history with very little ceremony and with only a whimper of protest from minority shareholders.

At an extraordinary meeting held in a basement room of the group's West End headquarters, shareholders voted to put the company into voluntary liquidation and sell its assets and intellectual property to founder Martin Myerscough for £1. [The shares in the company were at one time worth 650p each.]

The only significant opposition came from Giuliano Gnagnatti who, along with other shareholders, has seen his investment shrink faster than a wool twin-set on a boil wash.

The not-so-proud owner of 100,000 Monotub shares, Mr Gnagnatti, the managing director of an online retailer . . . described the sale of Monotub as a 'free gift' to Mr Myerscough. This assessment was denied by Ian Green, the chairman of Monotub, who said the closest the beleaguered company had come to a sale was an offer for £60,000 that gave no guarantees against liabilities, which are thought to amount to £750,000.

The quiet passing of the washing machine, eventually dubbed the Titanic, was in strong contrast to its performance in many kitchens.

Originally touted as the 'great white goods hope' of the washing machine industry with its larger capacity and removable drum, the Titan ran into problems when it kept stopping during the spin cycle, causing it to emit a loud bang and leap into the air.

Summing up the demise of the Titan, Mr Green said: 'Clearly the machine had some revolutionary aspects, but you can't get away from the fact that the machine was faulty and should not have been launched with those defects.'

The usually-vocal Mr Myerscough, who has promised to pump £250,000 into the company and give Monotub shareholders £4 for every machine sold, refused to comment on his plans for the Titan or reveal who his backers were. But . . . he did say that he intended to 'take the Titan forward'.

Source: 'Monotub Industries in a spin as founder gets Titan for £1', Lisa Urquhart, *Financial Times*, 23 January 2003, FT.com.

Limited liability

Since the company is a legal person in its own right, it must take responsibility for its own debts and losses. This means that once the shareholders have paid what they have agreed to pay for the shares, their obligation to the company, and to the company's creditors, is satisfied. Thus shareholders can limit their losses to the amount that they have paid, or agreed to pay, for their shares. This is of great practical importance to potential shareholders since they know that what they can lose, as part owners of the business, is limited.

Contrast this with the position of sole proprietors or partners. They cannot 'ring-fence' assets that they do not want to put into the business. If a sole proprietary or partnership business finds itself in a position where liabilities exceed the business assets, the law gives unsatisfied creditors the right to demand payment out of what the sole proprietor or partner may have regarded as 'non-business' assets. Thus the sole proprietor or partner could lose everything – house, car, the lot. This is because the law sees Jill, the sole proprietor, as being the same as Jill the private individual. The shareholder, by contrast, can lose only the amount committed to that company. Legally, the business operating as a limited company, in which Jack owns shares, is not the same as Jack himself. This is true even if Jack were to own all of the shares in the company.

Real World 4.2 gives an example of a well-known case where the shareholders of a particular company were able to avoid any liability to those that had lost money as a result of dealing with the company.

Real World 4.2

Carlton and Granada 1 - Nationwide Football League 0

Two television broadcasting companies, Carlton and Granada, each owned 50 per cent of a separate company, ITV Digital (formerly ON Digital). ITV Digital signed a contract to pay the Nationwide Football League (in effect the three divisions of English football below the Premiership) more than £89m on both 1 August 2002 and 1 August 2003 for the rights to broadcast football matches over three seasons. ITV Digital was unable to sell enough sub-scriptions for the broadcasts and collapsed because it was unable to meet its liabilities. The Nationwide Football League tried to force Carlton and Granada (ITV Digital's only share-holders) to meet the ITV Digital's contractual obligations. It was unable to do so because the shareholders could not be held legally liable for the amounts owing.

Carlton and Granada merged into one business in 2003, but at the time of ITV Digital were two independent companies.

Activity 4.1

The fact that shareholders can limit their losses to that which they have paid, or have agreed to pay, for their shares is of great practical importance to potential shareholders.

Can you think of any practical benefit to a private-sector economy, in general, of this ability of shareholders to limit losses?

Business is a risky venture – in some cases very risky. People with money to invest will usually be happier to do so when they know the limit of their liability. If investors are given limited liability, new businesses are more likely to be formed and existing ones are likely to find it easier to raise more finance. This is good for the private-sector economy and may ultimately lead to the generation of greater wealth for society as a whole.

→   Although limited liability has this advantage to the providers of equity finance (the shareholders), it is not necessarily to the advantage of all others who have a stake in the business, like the Nationwide Football League clubs (see Real World 4.2). Limited liability is attractive to shareholders because they can, in effect, walk away from the unpaid debts of the company if their contribution has not been sufficient to meet those debts. This is likely to make any individual, or another business, that is con-sidering entering into a contract, wary of dealing with the limited company. This can be a real problem for smaller, less established companies. Suppliers may insist on cash payment before delivery of goods or the rendering of a service. Alternatively, they may require a personal guarantee from a major shareholder that the debt will be paid before allowing trade credit. In the latter case, the supplier circumvents the company's limited liability status by demanding the personal liability of an individual. Larger, more established companies, on the other hand, tend to have built up the confidence of suppliers.

Legal safeguards

Various safeguards exist to protect individuals and businesses contemplating dealing with a limited company. These include the requirement to indicate limited liability status in the name of the company. By doing this, an alert is issued to prospective suppliers and lenders.

A further safeguard is the restrictions placed on the ability of shareholders to withdraw their equity from the company. These restrictions are designed to prevent shareholders from protecting their own investment and, as a result, leaving lenders and suppliers in an exposed position. We shall consider this point in more detail later in the chapter.

Finally, limited companies are required to produce annual financial statements (income statement, balance sheet and cash flow statement), and make them publicly available. This means that anyone interested can gain an impression of the financial performance and position of the company. The form and content of these statements are considered in some detail later in the chapter.

Public and private companies

When a company is registered with the Registrar of Companies, it must be registered either as a public or as a private company. The main practical difference between these is that a public company can offer its shares for sale to the general public, but a private company is restricted from doing so. A public limited company must signal its status to all interested parties by having the words 'public limited company', or its abbreviation 'plc', in its name. For a private limited company, the word 'limited' or 'Ltd' must appear as part of its name.

Private limited companies tend to be smaller businesses where the ownership is divided among relatively few shareholders who are usually fairly close to one another – for example, a family company. Numerically, there are vastly more private limited companies in the UK than there are public ones. Of the 2.1 million UK limited companies now in existence, only 11,500 (representing 0.5 per cent of the total) are public limited companies.

Since individual public companies tend to be larger, they are often economically more important. In some industry sectors, such as banking, insurance, oil refining and grocery retailing, they are completely dominant. Although some large private limited companies exist, many private limited companies are little more than the vehicle through which one-person businesses operate.

Real World 4.3 shows the extent of market dominance of public limited companies in one particular business sector.

A big slice of the market

The grocery sector is dominated by four large players: Tesco, Sainsbury, Morrison and Asda. The first three are public limited companies and the fourth, Asda, is owned by a large US public company, Wal-Mart. Figure 4.1 shows the share of the grocery market enjoyed by each.

Figure 4.1 Market share of the four largest grocers: 12 weeks to 15 July 2007

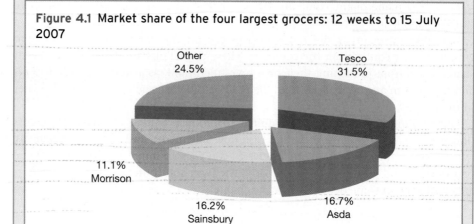

This diagram shows that Tesco had by far the largest market share and that the four largest grocers, when taken together, had more than 75 per cent of the total market during the period.

Source: Compiled from information in 'Tesco share of the UK grocery market is 31.5 per cent', www.investing.reuters. co.uk, 26 July 2007.

Taxation

Another consequence of the legal separation of the limited company from its owners is that companies must be accountable to the tax authorities for tax on their profits and gains. This leads to the reporting of tax in the financial statements of limited companies. The charge for tax is shown in the income statement (profit and loss account). The tax charge for a particular year is based on that year's profit. Since only 50 per cent of a company's tax liability is due for payment during the year concerned, the other 50 per cent will appear on the end-of-year balance sheet as a short-term liability. This will be illustrated a little later in the chapter. The tax position of companies contrasts with that of sole proprietorships and partnerships, where tax is levied not on the business but on the owner(s). Thus tax does not impact on the financial statements of unincorporated businesses, but is an individual matter between the owner(s) and the tax authorities.

→ Companies are charged corporation tax on their profits and gains. The percentage rates of tax tend to vary from year to year, but have recently been 30 per cent for larger companies and 20 per cent for smaller companies. These rates of tax are levied on the company's taxable profit, which is not necessarily the same as the profit shown on the income statement. This is because tax law does not, in every respect, follow the normal accounting rules. Generally, however, the taxable profit and the company's accounting profit are pretty close to one another.

Transferring share ownership: the role of the Stock Exchange

We have already seen that shares in a company may be transferred from one owner to another. The desire of some shareholders to sell their shares, coupled with the desire of others to buy those shares, has led to the existence of a formal market in which shares can be bought and sold. The London Stock Exchange and similar organisations around the world provide a marketplace in which shares in public companies may be bought and sold. Share prices are determined by the laws of supply and demand, which are, in turn, determined by investors' perceptions of the future economic prospects of the companies concerned. Only the shares of certain companies (listed companies) may be traded on the London Stock Exchange. About 1,300 UK companies are listed. This represents only 1 in about 1,600 of all UK companies (public and private) and about 1 in 9 public limited companies. However, many of these 1,300 listed companies are massive. Nearly all of the 'household-name' UK businesses (for example, Tesco, Next, BT, Cadbury Schweppes, Vodafone, BP and so on) are listed companies.

Activity 4.2

If, as has been pointed out earlier, the change in ownership of shares does not directly affect the particular company, why do many public companies actively seek to have their shares traded in a recognised market?

The main reason is that investors are generally very reluctant to pledge their money unless they can see some way in which they can turn their investment back into cash. In theory, the shares of a particular company may be very valuable because the company has bright prospects. However, unless this value is capable of being turned into cash, the benefit to the shareholders is dubious. After all, we cannot spend shares; we generally need cash.

This means that potential shareholders are much more likely to be prepared to buy new shares from the company (thereby providing the company with new finance) where they can see a way of liquidating their investment (turning it into cash) as and when they wish. Stock Exchanges provide the means of liquidation.

Although the buying and selling of 'second-hand' shares does not provide the company with cash, the fact that the buying and selling facility exists will make it easier for the company to raise new share capital when it needs to do so.

Managing a company

A limited company may have legal personality, but it is not a human being capable of making decisions and plans about the business and exercising control over it. People must undertake these management tasks. The most senior level of management of a company is the board of directors.

→ The shareholders elect directors (by law there must be at least one director for a private limited company and two for a public limited company) to manage the company on a day-to-day basis on behalf of those shareholders. In a small company, the board may be the only level of management and consist of all of the shareholders. In larger companies, the board may consist of ten or so directors out of many thousands of shareholders. Indeed, directors are not even required to be shareholders. Below the board of directors of the typical large company could be several layers of management comprising thousands of people.

→ In recent years, the issue of corporate governance has generated much debate. The term is used to describe the ways in which companies are directed and controlled. The issue of corporate governance is important because, with larger companies, those who own the company (that is, the shareholders) are usually divorced from the day-to-day control of the business. The shareholders employ the directors to manage the company for them. Given this position, it may seem reasonable to assume that the best interests of shareholders will guide the directors' decisions. However, in practice this does not always occur. The directors may be more concerned with pursuing their own interests, such as increasing their pay and 'perks' (such as expensive motor cars, overseas visits and so on) and improving their job security and status. As a result, a conflict can occur between the interests of shareholders and the interests of directors.

Where directors pursue their own interests at the expense of the shareholders, there is clearly a problem for the shareholders. However, it may also be a problem for society as a whole. If shareholders feel that their funds are likely to be mismanaged, they will be reluctant to invest. A shortage of funds will mean that fewer investments can be made and the costs of funds will increase as businesses compete for what funds are available. Thus, a lack of concern for shareholders can have a profound effect on the performance of individual companies and, with this, the health of the economy. To avoid these problems, most competitive market economies have a framework of rules to help monitor and control the behaviour of directors.

These rules are usually based around three guiding principles:

■ *Disclosure*. This lies at the heart of good corporate governance. An OECD report (*Corporate Governance: Improving Competitiveness and Access to Capital in Global Markets*, report by Business Sector Advisory Group on Corporate Governance, OECD, 1998) summed up the benefits of disclosure as follows:

> Adequate and timely information about corporate performance enables investors to make informed buy-and-sell decisions and thereby helps the market reflect the value of a corporation under present management. If the market determines that present management is not performing, a decrease in stock [share] price will sanction management's failure and open the way to management change. (p. 14)

- *Accountability*. This involves defining the roles and duties of the directors and establishing an adequate monitoring process. In the UK, company law requires that the directors of a business act in the best interests of the shareholders. This means, among other things, that they must not try to use their position and knowledge to make gains at the expense of the shareholders. The law also requires larger companies to have their annual financial statements independently audited. The purpose of an independent audit is to lend credibility to the financial statements prepared by the directors. We shall take a brief look at audit later in this chapter.
- *Fairness*. Directors should not be able to benefit from access to 'inside' information that is not available to shareholders. As a result, both the law and the Stock Exchange place restrictions on the ability of directors to buy and sell the shares of the business. One example of these restrictions is that the directors cannot buy or sell shares immediately before the announcement of the annual trading results of the business or before the announcement of a significant event such as a planned merger or the loss of the chief executive.

Strengthening the framework of rules

The number of rules designed to safeguard shareholders has increased considerably over the years. This has been in response to weaknesses in corporate governance procedures, which have been exposed through well-publicised business failures and frauds, excessive pay increases to directors and evidence that some financial reports were being 'massaged' so as to mislead shareholders. (This last point will be discussed later in the chapter.) Some believe, however, that the shareholders must shoulder some of the blame for any weaknesses. Not all shareholders in large companies are private individuals owning just a few shares each. In fact, ownership, by market value, of the shares listed on the London Stock Exchange is dominated by investing institutions such as insurance businesses, banks and pension funds. These are often massive operations, owning large quantities of the shares of the companies in which they invest. These institutional investors employ specialist staff to manage their portfolios of shares in various companies. It has been argued that the large institutional shareholders, despite their size and relative expertise, have not been very active in corporate governance matters. Thus there has been little monitoring of directors. However, things seem to be changing. There is increasing evidence that institutional investors are becoming more proactive in relation to the companies in which they hold shares.

The Combined Code

During the 1990s there was a real effort by the accountancy profession and the London Stock Exchange to address the problems mentioned above. A Code of Best Practice on Corporate Governance emerged in 1992. This was concerned with accountability and financial reporting. In 1995, a separate code of practice emerged. This dealt with directors' pay and conditions. These two codes were revised, 'fine-tuned' and amalgamated to produce the Combined Code, which was issued in 1998.

The Combined Code was revised in 2003, following the recommendations of the Higgs Report, and modified slightly in 2006. These recommendations were mainly concerned with the roles of the company chairman (the senior director) and the other directors. The report was particularly concerned with the role of 'non-executive' directors. Non-executive directors do not work full-time in the company, but act solely in the role of director. This contrasts with 'executive' directors who are salaried employees. For example, the finance director of most large companies is a full-time employee. This person is a member of the board of directors and, as such, takes part in the key decision-making at board level. At the same time, he or she is also responsible for managing the departments of the company that act on those board decisions as far as finance is concerned.

The view reflected in the 2003 Combined Code is that executive directors can become too embroiled in the day-to-day management of the company to be able to take a broad view. It also reflects the view that, for executive directors, conflicts can arise between their own interests and those of the shareholders. The advantage of non-executive directors can be that they are much more independent of the company than are their executive colleagues. Non-executive directors are remunerated by the company for their work, but this would normally form only a small proportion of their total income. This gives them an independence that the executive directors may lack. Non-executive directors are often senior managers in other businesses or people who have had good experience of such roles.

The Combined Code has the backing of the London Stock Exchange. This means that companies listed on the London Stock Exchange are expected to comply with the requirements of the Code or must give their shareholders good reason why they do not. Failure to do one or other of these can lead to the company's shares being suspended from listing. This is an important sanction against non-compliant directors.

The Combined Code sets out a number of principles relating to such matters as the role of the directors, their relations with shareholders, and their accountability. Real World 4.4 outlines some of the more important of these.

Real World 4.4

The Combined Code

Some of the key elements of the Combined Code are as follows:

■ Every listed company should have a board of directors to lead and control the company.
■ There should be a clear division of responsibilities between the chairman and the chief executive officer of the company to ensure that a single person does not have unbridled power.
■ There should be a balance between executive and non-executive (who are often part-time and independent) members of the board, to ensure that small groups of individuals cannot dominate proceedings.

- The board should receive timely information that is of sufficient quality to enable them to carry out their duties.
- Appointments to the board should be the subject of rigorous, formal and transparent procedures.
- All directors should submit themselves for re-election at regular intervals, subject to satisfactory performance.
- There should be formal and transparent procedures for developing policy on directors' remuneration.
- The board has a responsibility for ensuring that a satisfactory dialogue with shareholders occurs.
- Boards should use the annual general meeting to communicate with private investors and encourage their participation.
- Institutional shareholders have a responsibility to use their votes.
- The board should publish a balanced and understandable assessment of the company's position and performance.
- Internal controls should be in place to protect the shareholders' wealth.
- Formal and transparent arrangements for applying financial reporting and internal control principles and for maintaining an appropriate relationship with auditors should be in place.

Strengthening the framework of rules has improved the quality of information available to shareholders, resulted in better checks on the powers of directors, and provided greater transparency in corporate affairs. However, rules can only be a partial answer. A balance must be struck between the need to protect shareholders and the need to encourage the entrepreneurial spirit of directors, which could be stifled under a welter of rules. This implies that rules should not be too tight and so unscrupulous directors may still find ways around them.

Financing limited companies

The owners' claim

The owner's claim of a sole proprietorship is normally encompassed in one figure on the balance sheet, usually labelled 'equity' (or 'capital'). With companies, this is usually a little more complicated, although in essence the same broad principles apply. With a company, the owners' claim is divided between shares (for example, the original investment), on the one hand, and reserves (that is, profits and gains subsequently made), on the other. There is also the possibility that there will be more than one type of shares and of reserves. Thus, within the basic divisions of share capital and reserves, there might well be further subdivisions. This might seem quite complicated, but we shall shortly consider the reasons for these subdivisions and all should become clearer. The sum of share capital and reserves is commonly known as equity.

The basic division

When a company is first formed, those who take steps to form it (the promoters) will decide how much needs to be raised by the potential shareholders to set the company up with the necessary assets to operate. Example 4.1 acts as a basis for illustration.

Example 4.1

A group of friends get together and decide to form a company to operate an office cleaning business. They estimate that the company will need £50,000 to obtain the necessary assets to operate. Between them, they raise the cash, which they use to buy shares in the company, on 31 March 2008, with a nominal value (or par value) of £1 each.

At this point the balance sheet of the company would be:

Balance sheet as at 31 March 2008

	£
Net assets (all in cash)	50,000
Equity	
Share capital	
50,000 shares of £1 each	50,000

The company now buys the necessary non-current assets (vacuum cleaners and so on) and inventories (cleaning materials) and starts to trade. During the first year, the company makes a profit of £10,000. This, by definition, means that the equity expands by £10,000. During the year, the shareholders (owners) make no drawings of their claim, so at the end of the year the summarised balance sheet looks like this:

Balance sheet as at 31 March 2009

	£
Net assets (various assets less liabilities*)	60,000
Equity	
Share capital	
50,000 shares of £1 each	50,000
Reserves (revenue reserve)	10,000
Total equity	60,000

* We know from Chapter 2 that Assets = Equity + Liabilities. This can be rearranged so that Assets − Liabilities = Equity.

The profit is shown in a reserve, known as a revenue reserve, because it arises from generating revenue (making sales). Note that we do not simply merge the profit with the share capital: we must keep the two amounts separate (to satisfy company law). The reason for this is that there is a legal restriction on the maximum drawings of

→ the shareholders' claim (or payment of a dividend) that the owners can make. This is defined by the amount of revenue reserves, and so it is helpful to show these separately. We shall look at why there is this restriction, and how it works, a little later in the chapter.

Share capital

Ordinary shares

→ Shares represent the basic units of ownership of a business. All companies issue ordinary shares. Ordinary shares are often known as *equities*. The nominal value of such shares is at the discretion of the people that start up the company. For example, if the initial share capital is to be £50,000, this could be two shares of £25,000 each, 5 million shares of one penny each or any other combination that gives a total of £50,000. All shares must have equal value.

Activity 4.3

The initial financial requirement for a new company is £50,000. There are to be two equal shareholders. Would you advise them to issue two shares of £25,000 each? Why?

Such large-denomination shares tend to be unwieldy. Suppose that one of the shareholders wanted to sell her shareholding. She would have to find one buyer. If there were shares of smaller denomination, it would be possible to sell part of the shareholding to various potential buyers. Furthermore, it would be possible to sell just part of the holding and retain a part.

In practice, £1 is the normal maximum nominal value for shares. Shares of 25 pence each and 50 pence each are probably the most common.

Altering the nominal value of shares

We have already seen that the promoters of a new company may make their own choice of the nominal or par value of the shares. This value need not be permanent. At a later date the shareholders can decide to change it.

Suppose that a company has 1 million ordinary shares of £1 each and a decision is made to change the nominal value of the shares from £1 to £0.50, in other words to halve the value. This would lead the company to issue each shareholder with a new share certificate (the shareholders' evidence of ownership of their shareholding) for exactly twice as many shares, each with half the nominal value. The result would be that each shareholder retains a holding of the same total nominal value. This process → is known, not surprisingly, as splitting the shares. The opposite, reducing the number of shares and increasing their nominal value per share to compensate, is known as → consolidating.

Since each shareholder would be left, after a split or consolidation, with exactly the same proportion of ownership of the company's assets as before, the process should not increase the value of the total shares held.

Splitting is fairly common. The objective is probably to avoid individual shares becoming too valuable and making them a bit unwieldy, in the way discussed in the answer to Activity 4.3. If a company trades successfully, the value of each share is likely to rise, and in time could increase to a level that makes them less marketable. Splitting would solve this problem. Consolidating is relatively rare.

Preference shares

Some companies also issue other classes of shares, preference shares being the most common. Preference shares guarantee that *if a dividend is paid*, the preference share-holders will be entitled to the first part of it up to a maximum value. This maximum is normally defined as a fixed percentage of the nominal value of the preference shares. If, for example, a company issues 10,000 preference shares of £1 each with a dividend rate of 6 per cent, this means that the preference shareholders are entitled to receive the first £600 (that is, 6 per cent of £10,000) of any dividend that is paid by the company for a year. The excess over £600 goes to the ordinary shareholders. Normally, any undistributed profits and gains also accrue to the ordinary shareholders.

The ordinary shareholders are the primary risk-takers as they are entitled to share in the profits of the company only after other claims have been satisfied. There are no upper limits, however, on the amount by which they may benefit. The potential rewards available to ordinary shareholders reflect the risks that they are prepared to take. Since ordinary shareholders take most of the risks, power normally resides in their hands. Usually, only the ordinary shareholders are able to vote on issues that affect the company, such as who the directors should be.

It is open to the company to issue shares of various classes – perhaps with some having unusual and exotic conditions – but in practice it is rare to find other than straight-forward ordinary and preference shares. Although a company may have different classes of shares whose holders have different rights, within each class all shares must be treated equally. The rights of the various classes of shareholders, as well as other matters relating to a particular company, are contained in that company's set of rules, known as the 'articles and memorandum of association'. A copy of these rules must be lodged with the Registrar of Companies, who makes it available for inspection by the general public.

Reserves

Reserves are profits and gains that have been made by a company, which still form part of the shareholders' (owners') claim or equity. One reason that past profits and gains may not remain part of equity is that they have been paid out to shareholders (as dividends and so on). Another reason is that reserves will be reduced by the amount of any losses that the company might suffer. In the same way that profits increase equity, losses reduce it.

The shareholders' claim consists of share capital and reserves.

Activity 4.4

Are reserves amounts of cash? Can you think of a reason why this is an odd question?

To deal with the second point first, it is an odd question because reserves are a claim, or part of one, on the assets of the company, whereas cash is an asset. So reserves cannot be cash.

Reserves are classified as either revenue reserves or capital reserves. In Example 4.1 we came across one type of reserve, the revenue reserve. We should recall that this reserve represents the company's retained trading profits and gains on the disposal of non-current assets. It is worth mentioning that retained profits, or earnings, as they are often called, represent overwhelmingly the largest source of new finance for UK companies. For most companies they amount to more than share issues and borrowings combined.

Capital reserves arise for two main reasons:

- issuing shares at above their nominal value (for example, issuing £1 shares at £1.50);
- revaluing (upwards) non-current assets.

Where a company issues shares at above their nominal value, UK law requires that the excess of the issue price over the nominal value be shown separately.

Activity 4.5

Can you think why shares might be issued at above their nominal value? (*Hint*: This would not usually happen when a company is first formed and the initial shares are being issued.)

Once a company has traded and has been successful, the shares would normally be worth more than the nominal value at which they were issued. If additional shares are to be issued to new shareholders to raise finance for further expansion, unless they are issued at a value higher than the nominal value, the new shareholders will be gaining at the expense of the original ones.

Example 4.2 shows how this works.

Example 4.2

Based on future prospects, the net assets of a company are worth £1.5m. There are currently 1 million ordinary shares in the company, each with a face (nominal) value of £1. The company wishes to raise an additional £0.6m of cash for expansion and has decided to raise it by issuing new shares. If the shares are issued for £1 each (that is 600,000 shares), the total number of shares will be

$$1.0m + 0.6m = 1.6m$$

and their total value will be the value of the existing net assets plus the new injection of cash:

$$£1.5m + £0.6m = £2.1m.$$

This means that the value of each share after the new issue will be

$$£2.1m/1.6m = £1.3125.$$

The current value of each share is

$$£1.5m/1.0m = £1.50$$

so the original shareholders will lose

$$£1.50 - £1.3125 = £0.1875 \text{ a share}$$

and the new shareholders will gain

$$£1.3125 - £1.0 = £0.3125 \text{ a share.}$$

The new shareholders will, no doubt, be delighted with this outcome; the original ones will not.

Things could be made fair between the two sets of shareholders described in Example 4.2 by issuing the new shares at £1.50 each. In this case it would be necessary to issue 400,000 shares to raise the necessary £0.6 million. £1 a share of the £1.50 is the nominal value and will be included with share capital in the balance sheet (£400,000 in total). The remaining £0.50 is a share premium, which will be shown as a capital reserve known as the share premium account (£200,000 in total).

It is not clear why UK company law insists on the distinction between nominal share values and the premium. In some other countries (for example, the United States) with similar laws governing the corporate sector, there is not the necessity of distinguishing between share capital and share premium. Instead, the total value at which shares are issued is shown as one comprehensive figure on the company balance sheet. Real World 4.5 shows the shareholders' claim of one well-known business.

Real World 4.5

easyFunding

The budget airline easyJet plc had the following share capital and reserves as at 31 March 2007:

	£m
Share capital (25p ordinary shares)	104.7
Share premium account	632.9
Other reserves (capital)	(9.4)
Retained earnings	262.3
Total equity	990.5

> Note how the nominal share capital figure is only about one-sixth of the share premium account figure. This implies that easyJet has issued shares at higher prices than the 25p a share nominal value. This reflects its trading success since the company was first formed. Note also how, at balance sheet values, retained earnings (profits) make up only 26 per cent of the total for share capital and reserves. This is probably on the low side of the average for UK companies and reflects the fact that easyJet is a fairly young company.
>
> *Source:* easyJet plc Interim Report 2007.

Bonus shares

It is always open to a company to take reserves of any kind (irrespective of whether they are capital or revenue) and turn them into share capital. This will involve transferring the desired amount from the reserve concerned to share capital and then distributing the appropriate number of new shares to the existing shareholders. New shares arising from such a conversion are known as bonus shares. Issues of bonus shares are quite frequently encountered in practice. Example 4.3 illustrates this aspect of share issues.

Example 4.3

The summary balance sheet of a company is as follows:

Balance sheet as at 31 March 2008

	£
Net assets (various assets less liabilities)	128,000
Equity	
Share capital	
50,000 shares of £1 each	50,000
Reserves	78,000
Total equity	128,000

The company decides that it will issue existing shareholders with one new share for every share currently owned by each shareholder. The balance sheet immediately following this will appear as follows:

Balance sheet as at 31 March 2008

	£
Net assets (various assets less liabilities)	128,000
Equity	
Share capital	
100,000 shares of £1 each (50,000 + 50,000)	100,000
Reserves (78,000 − 50,000)	28,000
Total equity	128,000

We can see that the reserves have decreased by £50,000 and share capital has increased by the same amount. Share certificates for the 50,000 ordinary shares of £1 each that have been created from reserves will be issued to the existing shareholders to complete the transaction.

Activity 4.6

A shareholder of the company in Example 4.3 owned 100 shares before the bonus issue. How will things change for this shareholder as regards the number of shares owned and the value of the shareholding?

The answer should be that the number of shares will double, from 100 to 200. Now the shareholder owns one five-hundredth of the company (that is, 200/100,000). Before the bonus issue, the shareholder also owned one five-hundredth of the company (that is, 100/50,000). The company's assets and liabilities have not changed as a result of the bonus issue and so, logically, one five-hundredth of the value of the company should be identical to what it was before. Thus, each share is worth half as much.

→ A bonus issue simply takes one part of the owners' claim (a reserve) and puts it into another part (share capital). The transaction has no effect on the company's assets or liabilities, so there is no effect on shareholders' wealth.

Note that a bonus issue is not the same as a share split. A split does not affect the reserves.

Activity 4.7

Can you think of any reasons why a company might want to make a bonus issue if it has no economic consequence?

We think that there are three possible reasons:

- *Share price.* To lower the value of each share without reducing the shareholders' collective or individual wealth. This has a similar effect to share splitting.
- *Shareholder confidence.* To provide the shareholders with a 'feel-good factor'. It is believed that shareholders like bonus issues because they seem to make them better off, although in practice they should not affect their wealth.
- *Lender confidence.* Where reserves arising from operating profits and/or realised gains on the sale of non-current assets are used to make the bonus issue, it has the effect of taking part of that portion of the shareholders' equity that could be drawn by the shareholders, as drawings (or dividends), and locking it up. The amount transferred becomes part of the permanent equity base of the company. (We shall see a little later in this chapter that there are severe restrictions on the extent to which shareholders may make drawings from their claim.) An individual or business contemplating lending money to the company may insist that the dividend payment possibilities are restricted as a condition of making the loan. This point will be explained shortly.

Real World 4.6 provides an example of a bonus share issue.

Real World 4.6

Banking on a bonus

Royal Bank of Scotland Group plc (RBS), the UK banking business, made a 2-for-1 bonus issue of shares on 4 May 2007. The nominal value of a share in the company is 25p and a total of 6,435 million new shares was issued. Following the issue, each RBS shareholder would have had three times as many shares as before the issue. Though RBS was not specific as to why it had made the bonus issue, it seems that the objective was to reduce the market price per share.

Source: Based on information contained in an announcement published by RBS on www.investors.rbs.com.

Share capital jargon

Before leaving our detailed discussion of share capital, it might be helpful to clarify some of the jargon relating to shares that is used in company financial statements.

Share capital that has been issued to shareholders is known as the issued share capital (or allotted share capital). Sometimes, but not very often, a company may not require shareholders to pay the whole amount that is due to be paid for the shares at the time of issue. This may happen where the company does not need the money all at once. Some money would normally be paid at the time of issue and the company would 'call' for further instalments until the shares were fully paid. That part of the total issue price that has been 'called' is known as the called-up share capital. That part that has been called and paid is known as the paid-up share capital.

Raising share capital

Once the company has made its initial share issue to start business (usually soon after the company is first formed) it may decide to make further issues of new shares. These may be

- *rights issues*, that is, issues made to existing shareholders, in proportion to their existing shareholding
- *public issues*, that is, issues made to the general investing public
- *private placings*, that is, issues made to selected individuals who are usually approached and asked if they would be interested in taking up new shares.

During its lifetime a company may use all three of these approaches to raising funds through issuing new shares (although only public companies can make appeals to the general public). These approaches will be discussed in detail in Chapter 11.

Borrowings

Most companies borrow money to supplement that raised from share issues and ploughed-back profits. Company borrowing is often on a long-term basis, perhaps on a ten-year contract. Lenders may be banks and other professional providers of loan finance. Many companies raise loan finance in such a way that small investors, including private individuals, are able to lend small amounts. This is particularly the case with the larger, Stock Exchange listed, companies and involves their making a loan notes issue, which, though large in total, can be taken up in small slices by individual investors, both private individuals and investing institutions, such as pension funds and insurance companies. In some cases, these slices of loans can be bought and sold through the Stock Exchange. This means that investors do not have to wait the full term of the loan to obtain repayment, but can sell their slice of the loan to another would-be lender at intermediate points in the term of the loan. Loan notes are often known as *loan stock* or *debentures*.

Some of the features of loan notes financing, particularly the possibility that the loan notes may be traded on the Stock Exchange, can lead to a confusion that loan notes are shares by another name. We should be clear that this is not the case. It is the shareholders who own the company and, therefore, who share in its losses and profits. Holders of loan notes lend money to the company under a legally binding contract that normally specifies the rate of interest, the interest payment dates and the date of repayment of the loan itself. Usually, long-term loans are secured on assets of the company. This would give the lender the right to seize the assets concerned, sell them and satisfy the repayment obligation, should the company fail to pay either its interest payments or the repayment of the loan itself, on the dates specified in the contract between the company and the lender. A mortgage granted to a private individual buying a house or a flat is a very common example of a secured loan.

Long-term financing of companies can be depicted as in Figure 4.2.

Figure 4.2 Sources of long-term finance for a typical limited company

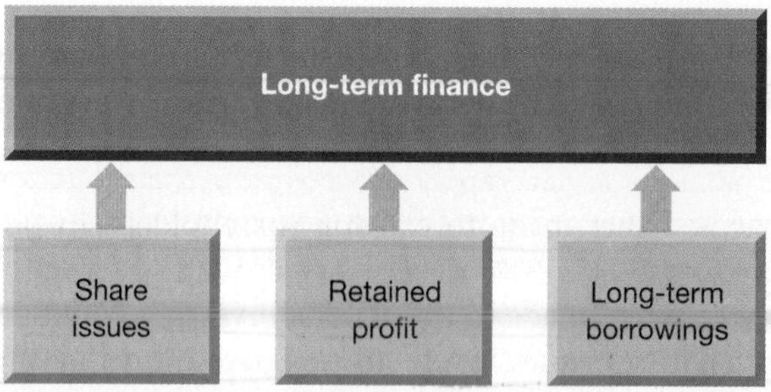

Companies derive their long-term financing needs from three sources: new share issues, retained profit and long-term borrowings. For a typical company, the sum of the first two (jointly known as 'equity finance') exceeds the third. Retained profit usually exceeds either of the other two in terms of the amount of finance raised in most years.

It is important to the prosperity and stability of a company that it strikes a suitable balance between finance provided by the shareholders (equity) and from borrowing. This topic will be explored in Chapter 6. Equity and loan notes are, of course, not the only forms of finance available to a company. In Chapter 11, we consider other sources of finance available to businesses, including companies.

Withdrawing equity

Companies are legally obliged to distinguish, on the balance sheet, between that part of the shareholders' equity that may be withdrawn and that part which may not.

The withdrawable part consists of profits arising from trading and from the disposal of non-current assets. It is represented in the balance sheet by *revenue reserves.*

It is important to appreciate that the total of revenue reserves appearing in the balance sheet is rarely the total of all trading profits and profits on disposals of non-current assets generated by the company. This total will normally have been reduced by at least one of the following three factors:

- corporation tax paid on those profits
- any dividends paid
- any losses from trading and the disposal of non-current assets.

The non-withdrawable part consists of profits arising from shareholders buying shares in the company and from upward revaluations of assets still held. It is represented in the balance sheet by *share capital* and *capital reserves.*

The law does not specify how large the non-withdrawable part of a particular company's shareholders' equity should be. However, when seeking to impress prospective lenders and credit suppliers, the larger this part, the better. Those considering doing business with the company must be able to see from the company's balance sheet how large it is.

Activity 4.8

Why are limited companies required to distinguish different parts of their shareholders' claim whereas sole proprietorship and partnership businesses are not?

The reason stems from the limited liability that company shareholders enjoy but which owners of unincorporated businesses do not. If a sole proprietor or partner withdraws all of the owners' claim, or even an amount in excess of this, the position of the lenders and credit suppliers of the business is not weakened since they can legally enforce their claims against the sole proprietor or partner as an individual. With a limited company, the business and the owners are legally separated and such right to enforce claims against individuals does not exist. To protect the company's lenders and credit suppliers, however, the law insists that the shareholders cannot normally withdraw a specific part of their claim.

Let us now look at another example.

Example 4.4

The summary balance sheet of a company at a particular date is as follows:

Balance sheet

	£
Total assets	43,000
Equity	
Share capital	
20,000 shares of £1 each	20,000
Reserves (revenue)	23,000
Total equity	43,000

A bank has been asked to make a £25,000 long-term loan to the company. If the loan were to be made, the balance sheet immediately following would appear as follows:

Balance sheet (after the loan)

	£
Total assets (£43,000 + £25,000)	68,000
Equity	
Share capital	
20,000 shares of £1 each	20,000
Reserves (revenue)	23,000
	43,000
Non-current liability	
Borrowings – loan	25,000
Total equity and liabilities	68,000

As things stand, there are assets to a total balance sheet value of £68,000 to meet the bank's claim of £25,000. It would be possible and perfectly legal, however, for the company to pay a dividend (withdraw part of their claim) of £23,000. The balance sheet would then appear as follows:

Balance sheet

	£
Total assets (£68,000 – £23,000)	45,000
Equity	
Share capital	
20,000 shares of £1 each	20,000
Reserves [revenue (£23,000 – £23,000)]	–
	20,000
Non-current liabilities	
Borrowings – loan	25,000
Total equity and liabilities	45,000

This leaves the bank in a very much weaker position, in that there are now total assets with a balance sheet value of £45,000 to meet a claim of £25,000. Note that the difference between the amount of the borrowings (bank loan) and the total assets equals the equity (share capital and reserves) total. Thus, the equity represents a margin of safety for lenders and suppliers. The larger the amount of the owners' claim withdrawable by the shareholders, the smaller is the potential margin of safety for lenders and suppliers.

As we have already seen, the law says nothing about how large the margin of safety must be. It is up to each company to decide what is appropriate.

As a practical footnote to Example 4.4, it is worth pointing out that long-term lenders would normally seek to secure a loan against an asset of the company, such as land.

Activity 4.9

Would you expect a company to pay all of its revenue reserves as a dividend? What factors might be involved with a dividend decision?

It would be rare for a company to pay all of its revenue reserves as a dividend: the fact that it is legally possible does not necessarily make it a good idea. Most companies see ploughed-back profits as a major – usually *the* major – source of new finance. The factors that influence the dividend decision are likely to include

■ the availability of cash to pay a dividend; it would not be illegal to borrow to pay a dividend, but it would be unusual and, possibly, imprudent;
■ the needs of the business for finance for new investment;
■ the expectations of shareholders concerning the amount of dividends to be paid.

You may have thought of others.

If we look back at Real World 4.5 (pages 128–9), we can see that at 31 March 2007, easyJet could legally have paid a dividend totalling £262.3m. Of course, the company did not do this, presumably because the funds concerned were tied up in aircraft and other assets, not lying around in the form of cash

The law states, however, that shareholders cannot, under normal circumstances, withdraw that part of their claim that is represented by shares and capital reserves. This means that potential lenders and credit suppliers know the maximum amount of the shareholders' equity that can be withdrawn. Figure 4.3 shows the important division between that part of the shareholders' equity that can be withdrawn as a dividend and that part which cannot.

The main financial statements

As we might expect, the financial statements of a limited company are, in essence, the same as those of a sole proprietor or partnership. There are, however, some differences of detail, and we shall now consider these. Example 4.5 sets out the income statement (profit and loss account) and balance sheet of a limited company.

Figure 4.3 Availability for dividends of various parts of the shareholders' claim

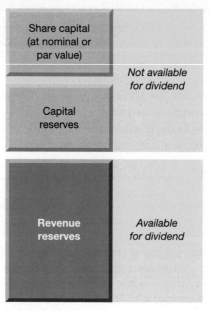

Total equity finance of limited companies consists of share capital, capital reserves and revenue reserves. Only the revenue reserves (which arise from realised profits and gains) can be used to fund a dividend. In other words, the maximum legal dividend is the amount of the revenue reserves.

Example 4.5

Da Silva plc
Income statement for the year ended 31 December 2008

	£m
Revenue	840
Cost of sales	(520)
Gross profit	320
Wages and salaries	(98)
Heat and light	(18)
Rent and rates	(24)
Motor vehicle expenses	(20)
Insurance	(4)
Printing and stationery	(12)
Depreciation	(45)
Audit fee	(4)
Operating profit	95
Interest payable	(10)
Profit before taxation	85
Taxation	(24)
Profit for the year	61

Balance sheet as at 31 December 2008

	£m
Non-current assets	
Property, plant and equipment	203
Intangible assets	100
	303
Current assets	
Inventories	65
Trade receivables	112
Cash	36
	213
Total assets	516
Equity	
Ordinary shares of £0.50 each	200
Share premium account	30
Other reserves	50
Retained earnings	25
	305
Non-current liabilities	
Borrowings	100
Current liabilities	
Trade payables	99
Taxation	12
	111
Total equity and liabilities	516

Let us now go through these statements and pick up those aspects that are unique to limited companies.

The income statement

There are a few features in the income statement that need consideration.

Profit

We can see that, following the calculation of operating profit, two further measures of profit are shown.

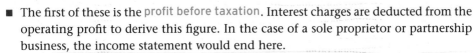

- The first of these is the profit before taxation. Interest charges are deducted from the operating profit to derive this figure. In the case of a sole proprietor or partnership business, the income statement would end here.

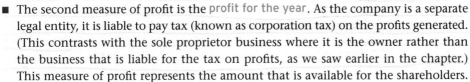

- The second measure of profit is the profit for the year. As the company is a separate legal entity, it is liable to pay tax (known as corporation tax) on the profits generated. (This contrasts with the sole proprietor business where it is the owner rather than the business that is liable for the tax on profits, as we saw earlier in the chapter.) This measure of profit represents the amount that is available for the shareholders.

Audit fee

Companies beyond a certain size are required to have their financial statements audited by an independent firm of accountants, for which a fee is charged. As we shall see later in this chapter, the purpose of the audit is to lend credibility to the financial statements. Although it is also open to sole proprietors and partnerships to have their financial statements audited, relatively few do, so this is an expense that is most often seen in the income statement of a company.

The balance sheet

The main points for consideration in the balance sheet are as follows.

Taxation

The amount that appears as part of the current liabilities represents 50 per cent of the tax on the profit for the year 2008. It is, therefore, 50 per cent (£12m) of the charge that appears in the income statement (£24m); the other 50 per cent (£12m) will already have been paid. The unpaid 50 per cent will be paid shortly after the balance sheet date. These payment dates are set down by law.

Other reserves

This will include any reserves that are not separately identified on the face of the balance sheet. It may include a *general reserve*, which normally consists of trading profits that have been transferred to this separate reserve for reinvestment ('ploughing back') into the operations of the company. It is not at all necessary to set up a separate reserve for this purpose. The trading profits could remain unallocated and still swell the retained earnings of the company. It is not entirely clear why directors decide to make transfers to general reserves, since the profits concerned remain part of the revenue reserves, and are, therefore, still available for dividend. The most plausible explanation seems to be that directors feel that placing profits in a separate reserve indicates an intention to invest the funds, represented by the reserve, permanently in the company and, therefore, not to use them to pay a dividend. Of course, the retained earnings appearing on the balance sheet are also a reserve, but that fact is not indicated in its title.

Dividends

We have already seen that dividends represent drawings by the shareholders of the company. Dividends are paid out of the revenue reserves and should be deducted from these reserves (usually retained earnings) when preparing the balance sheet. Shareholders are often paid an annual dividend, perhaps in two parts. An 'interim' dividend may be paid part way through the year and a 'final' dividend shortly after the year end.

Dividends declared by the directors during the year but still unpaid at the year end *may* appear as a liability in the balance sheet. To be recognised as a liability, however, they must be properly authorised before the balance sheet date. This normally means that the shareholders must approve the dividend.

The directors' duty to account

With most large companies, it is not possible for all shareholders to take part in the management of the company, nor do most of them wish to be involved. Instead, they appoint directors to act on their behalf. This separation of ownership from day-to-day control creates the need for directors to be accountable for their stewardship (management) of the company's assets. Thus, the law requires that directors

- maintain appropriate accounting records
- prepare annual financial statements and a directors' report, and make these available to all shareholders and to the public at large.

The financial statements are made available to the public by submitting a copy to the Companies Registry (Department of Trade and Industry), which allows anyone who wishes to do so to inspect them. In addition, listed companies are required to publish their financial statements on their website.

Activity 4.10

Why does the law require directors to account in this way and who benefits from these requirements?

We thought of the following benefits and beneficiaries:

- *To inform and protect shareholders.* If shareholders do not receive information about the performance and position of their investment, they will have problems in appraising their investment. Under these circumstances, they would probably be reluctant to invest and this, in turn, would affect the functioning of the private sector. Any society with a significant private sector needs to encourage equity investment.
- *To inform and protect suppliers of labour, goods, services and finance, particularly those supplying credit (loans) or goods and services on credit.* Individuals and organisations would be reluctant to engage in commercial relationships, such as supplying goods or lending money, where a company does not provide information about its financial health. The fact that a company has limited liability increases the risks involved in dealing with the company. An unwillingness to engage in commercial relationships with limited companies will, once again, affect the functioning of the private sector.
- *To inform and protect society more generally.* Some companies exercise enormous power and influence in society generally, particularly on a geographically local basis. For example, a particular company may be the dominant employer and purchaser of commercial goods and services in a particular town or city. Legislators have tended to take the view that society has the right to information about the company and its activities.

The need for accounting rules

If we accept the need for directors to prepare and publish financial statements, we must also accept the need for a framework of rules concerning how these statements are prepared and presented. Without rules, there is a much greater risk that unscrupulous directors will adopt policies and practices that portray an unrealistic view of financial health. There is also a much greater risk that the financial statements will not be comparable over time or with those of other companies. These risks are likely to undermine the integrity of financial statements in the eyes of users.

Users must, however, be realistic about what can be achieved through regulation. Problems of manipulation and of concealment can still occur even within a highly regulated environment and some examples of both will be considered later in the chapter. The scale of these problems, however, should be reduced. Problems of comparability can also still occur, as accounting is not a precise science. Judgements and estimates must be made when preparing financial statements (for example, relating to depreciation), and these may hinder comparisons. Furthermore, no two companies are identical and the accounting policies adopted may vary between companies for valid reasons.

Sources of accounting rules

In recent years there has been a trend towards the internationalisation of business, which seems set to continue. This trend has led to calls for the international harmonisation of accounting rules to help both users and companies. Harmonisation should help investors and other users of financial statements by making it easier to compare the performance and position of different companies operating in different countries. It should help companies with international operations by reducing the time and cost of producing financial statements: different sets of financial statements would no longer have to be prepared to comply with the rules of different countries.

The International Accounting Standards Board (IASB) is an independent body, which is at the forefront of the move towards harmonisation. The Board, which is based in the UK, is dedicated to developing a single set of high quality, global accounting rules that provide transparent and comparable information in financial statements. These rules, which are known as International Financial Reporting Standards (IFRSs) or International Accounting Standards, deal with key issues such as:

- what information should be disclosed;
- how information should be presented;
- how assets should be valued;
- how profit should be measured.

In fact we have already met some of the IFRSs when we considered areas including depreciation and inventories valuation in Chapters 2 and 3.

The overriding requirement for financial statements prepared according to IASB standards is to provide a fair representation of the company's financial position, financial performance and cash flows. There is a presumption that this fair representation will be achieved where the financial statements are drawn up in accordance with the various IASB standards that have been issued.

The authority of the IASB was given a huge boost when the European Commission adopted a regulation requiring nearly all Stock Exchange listed companies of EU member states to prepare their financial statements according to IASB standards for accounting periods commencing on or after 1 January 2005. Although non-listed UK companies are not currently required to adopt IASB standards, they have the option to do so. Many informed observers believe, however, that IASB standards will soon become a requirement for all UK companies.

The EU regulation overrides any laws in force in member states that could either hinder or restrict compliance with IASB standards. The ultimate aim is to achieve a single framework of accounting rules for companies from all member states. The EU recognises that this will be achieved only if individual governments do not add to the requirements imposed by the various IASB standards. Thus, it seems that accounting rules developed within individual EU member countries will eventually disappear. For the time being, however, the EU accepts that the governments of member states may need to impose additional disclosures for some corporate governance matters and regulatory requirements. In the UK, company law requires disclosure relating to various corporate governance issues. There is, for example, a requirement to disclose details of directors' remuneration in the published financial statements, which goes beyond anything required by IASB standards. Furthermore, the Financial Services Authority (FSA), in its role as the UK (Stock Exchange) listing authority, imposes rules on Stock Exchange listed companies. These include the requirement to publish a condensed set of interim (half-year) financial statements in addition to the annual financial statements. (These statements are not required by the IASB, although there is a standard providing guidance on their content and structure.)

Figure 4.4 sets out the main sources of accounting rules for Stock Exchange listed companies discussed above. While company law and the FSA still play an important role, in the longer term IASB standards seem set to become the sole source of company accounting rules.

Directors' report

In addition to preparing the financial statements, the law requires the directors to prepare an annual report to shareholders and other interested parties. This report contains information of both a financial and a non-financial nature and goes beyond that which is contained in the financial statements. The information disclosed covers a variety of topics, including details of share ownership, details of directors and their

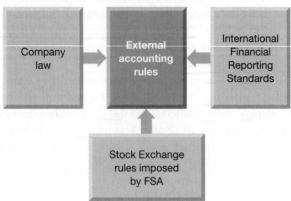

Figure 4.4 Sources of external accounting rules for a UK public limited company listed on the London Stock Exchange

International Financial Reporting Standards provide the basic framework of accounting rules for nearly all Stock Exchange listed companies. These rules are augmented by company law and by the Financial Services Authority (FSA) in its role as the UK listing authority.

financial interests in the company, employment policies, and charitable and political donations. The auditors do not carry out an audit of the directors' report. However, they will check to see that the information in the report is consistent with that contained in the audited financial statements.

The auditors' role

Shareholders are required to elect a qualified and independent person or, more usually, a firm to act as auditors. The auditors' main duty is to report whether, in their opinion, the financial statements do what they are supposed to do, namely to show a true and fair view of the financial performance, position and cash flows of the company by complying with the relevant accounting rules. To be able to form such an opinion, auditors must scrutinise both the annual financial statements and the evidence upon which they are based. The auditors' opinion must be included with the financial statements sent to the shareholders and to the Registrar of Companies.

The relationship between the shareholders, the directors and the auditors is illustrated in Figure 4.5.

The shareholders elect the directors to act on their behalf, in the day-to-day running of the company. The directors are then required to 'account' to the shareholders on the performance, position and cash flows of the company, on an annual basis. The shareholders also elect auditors, whose role it is to give the shareholders an independent view of the truth and fairness of the financial statements prepared by the directors.

> **Figure 4.5** The relationship between the shareholders, the directors and the auditors
>
>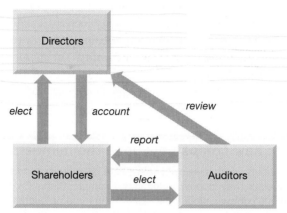
>
> The directors are appointed by the shareholders to manage the company on the shareholders' behalf. The directors are required to report each year to the shareholders, principally by means of financial statements, on the company's performance, position and cash flows. To give greater confidence in the statements, the shareholders also appoint auditors to investigate the reports and to express an opinion on their reliability.

Creative accounting

Despite the proliferation of accounting rules and the independent checks that are imposed, concerns over the quality of published financial statements surface from time to time. Some directors apply particular accounting policies or structure particular transactions in such a way as to portray a picture of financial health that is in line with what they would like users to see rather than what is a true and fair view of financial position and performance. This practice is referred to as creative accounting and it poses a major problem for accounting rule makers and for society generally.

Activity 4.11

Why might the directors of a company engage in creative accounting?

There are many reasons, and these include:

- to get around restrictions (for example, to report sufficient profit to pay a dividend);
- to avoid government action (for example, the taxation of excessive profits);
- to hide poor management decisions;
- to achieve sales revenue or profit targets, thereby ensuring that performance bonuses are paid to the directors;
- to attract new share capital or loan finance by showing a healthy financial position;
- to satisfy the demands of major investors concerning levels of return.

Creative accounting methods

The ways in which unscrupulous directors can manipulate the financial statements are many and varied. However, they usually involve adopting unorthodox practices for reporting key elements of the financial statements such as revenue, expenses, assets and liabilities. They may also involve the use of complicated or obscure transactions in an attempt to hide the underlying economic reality. The manipulation carried out may be designed to bend the rules or may be designed to break the rules.

Real World 4.7 identifies some of the more popular approaches to creative accounting.

Real World 4.7

Dirty laundry: how companies fudge the numbers

Hollow swaps: telecoms companies sell useless fibre optic capacity to each other in order to generate revenues on their income statements. Example: Global Crossing.

Channel stuffing: a company floods the market with more products than its distributors can sell, artificially boosting its sales. SSL, the condom maker, shifted £60 million in excess inventories on to trade customers. Also known as 'trade loading'.

Round tripping: also known as 'in-and-out trading'. Used to notorious effect by Enron. Two or more traders buy and sell energy among themselves for the same price and at the same time. Inflates trading volumes and makes participants appear to be doing more business than they really are.

Pre-dispatching: goods such as carpets are marked as 'sold' as soon as an order is placed. This inflates sales and profits.

Off-balance sheet activities: companies use special purpose entities and other devices such as leasing to push assets and liabilities off their balance sheets.

Source: 'Dirty laundry: how companies fudge the numbers', *The Times*, Business Section, 22 September 2002.

A few years ago there was a wave of creative accounting scandals, particularly in the US but also in Europe; however, it seems that this wave has now subsided. The quality of financial statements is improving and, it is to be hoped, trust among investors and others is being restored. As a result of the actions taken by various regulatory bodies and by accounting rule makers, creative accounting has become a more risky and difficult process for those who attempt it. However, it will never disappear completely and a further wave of creative accounting scandals may occur in the future.

As Real World 4.8 shows, creative accounting is not a thing of the past. The US computer business Dell was engaged in creative accounting as recently as 2007.

Real World 4.8

Recomputing the numbers

In August 2007, Dell admitted that some unnamed 'senior executives' had been involved in a scheme to overstate sales revenue figures during the period 2003 to 2007. This was done in an attempt to make it appear that quarterly sales targets had been met, when in fact this was not the case. The overstatement of sales revenue was estimated to amount to $92m, about 1 per cent of total profit over the period concerned.

Source: 'Dell reduces profit by $92m', Kevin Allison, *Financial Times*, 30 October 2007.

The recent wave coincided with a period of strong economic growth, and during good economic times, investors and auditors become less vigilant. Thus, the opportunity to manipulate the figures becomes easier. We must not, therefore, become too complacent. Things may change again when we next experience a period of strong growth.

? Self-assessment question 4.1

This question requires you to correct some figures on a set of company financial statements. It should prove useful practice for the material that you covered in Chapters 2 and 3, as well as helping you to become familiar with the financial statements of a company.

Presented below is a draft set of simplified financial statements for Pear Limited for the year ended 30 September 2008.

Income statement for the year ended 30 September 2008

	£000
Revenue	1,456
Cost of sales	(768)
Gross profit	688
Salaries	(220)
Depreciation	(249)
Other operating costs	(131)
Operating profit	88
Interest payable	(15)
Profit before taxation	73
Taxation at 30%	(22)
Profit for the year	51

Balance sheet as at 30 September 2008

	£000
Non-current assets	
Property, plant and equipment	
Cost	1,570
Depreciation	(690)
	880
Current assets	
Inventories	207
Trade receivables	182
Cash at bank	21
	410
Total assets	1,290
Equity	
Share capital	300
Share premium account	300
Retained earnings at beginning of year	104
Profit for year	51
	755

→

Non-current liabilities	
Borrowings (10% loan notes repayable 2012)	300
Current liabilities	
Trade payables	88
Other payables	20
Taxation	22
Borrowings (bank overdraft)	105
	235
Total equity and liabilities	1,290

The following information is available:

1 Depreciation has not been charged on office equipment with a carrying amount of £100,000. This class of assets is depreciated at 12 per cent a year using the reducing-balance method.

2 A new machine was purchased, on credit, for £30,000 and delivered on 29 September 2008 but has not been included in the financial statements. (Ignore depreciation.)

3 A sales invoice to the value of £18,000 for September 2008 has been omitted from the financial statements. (The cost of sales figure is stated correctly.)

4 A dividend of £25,000 had been approved by the shareholders before 30 September 2006, but was unpaid at that date. This is not reflected in the financial statements.

5 The interest payable on the loan notes for the second half-year was not paid until 1 October 2008 and has not been included in the financial statements.

6 An allowance for receivables is to be made at the level of 2 per cent of receivables.

7 An invoice for electricity to the value of £2,000 for the quarter ended 30 September 2008 arrived on 4 October and has not been included in the financial statements.

8 The charge for taxation will have to be amended to take account of the above information. Make the simplifying assumption that tax is payable shortly after the end of the year, at the rate of 30 per cent of the profit before tax.

Required:
Prepare a revised set of financial statements for the year ended 30 September 2008 incorporating the additional information in 1 to 8 above. (Work to the nearest £1,000.)

The answer to this question can be found at the back of the book in Appendix B.

Summary

The main points of this chapter may be summarised as follows.

Main features of a limited company

■ It is an artificial person that has been created by law.

■ It has a separate life to its owners and is granted a perpetual existence.

■ It must take responsibility for its own debts and losses but its owners are granted limited liability.

- A public company can offer its shares for sale to the public; a private company cannot.
- It is governed by a board of directors, which is elected by the shareholders.
- Corporate governance is a major issue; various scandals have led to the emergence of the Combined Code.

Financing the limited company

- The share capital of a company can be of two main types: ordinary shares and preference shares.
- Holders of ordinary shares (equities) are the main risk-takers and are given voting rights; they form the backbone of the company.
- Holders of preference shares are given a right to a fixed dividend before ordinary shareholders receive a dividend.
- Reserves are profits and gains made by the company and form part of the ordinary shareholders' claim.
- Borrowings provide another major source of finance.

Share issues

- Bonus shares are issued to existing shareholders when part of the reserves of the company is converted into share capital. No funds are raised.
- Rights issues give existing shareholders the right to buy new shares in proportion to their existing holding.
- Public issues are made direct to the general investing public.
- Private placings are share issues to particular investors.
- The shares of public companies may be bought and sold on a recognised Stock Exchange.

Reserves

- Reserves are of two types: revenue reserves and capital reserves.
- Revenue reserves arise from trading profits and from realised profits on the sale of non-current assets.
- Capital reserves arise from the issue of shares above their nominal value or from the upward revaluation of non-current assets.
- Revenue reserves can be withdrawn as dividends by the shareholders whereas capital reserves normally cannot.

Financial statements of limited companies

- The financial statements of limited companies are based on the same principles as those of sole proprietorship and partnership businesses. However, there are some differences in detail.
- The income statement has three measures of profit displayed after the gross profit figure: operating profit, profit before taxation and profit for the year.

- The income statement also shows audit fees and tax on profits for the year.
- Any unpaid tax and unpaid, but authorised, dividends will appear in the balance sheet as current liabilities.
- The share capital plus the reserves make up 'equity'.

Directors' duty

- The directors have a duty to
  - maintain appropriate accounting records;
  - prepare and publish financial statements and a directors' report.

The need for accounting rules

- Accounting rules are necessary to
  - avoid unacceptable accounting practices;
  - improve the comparability of financial statements.

Accounting rules

- The International Accounting Standards Board (IASB) has become an important source of rules.
- Company law and the London Stock Exchange are also sources of rules for UK companies.

Other statutory reports

- The auditors' report provides an opinion by an independent auditor concerning whether the financial statements provide a true and fair view of the financial health of a business.
- The directors' report contains information of a financial and a non-financial nature, which goes beyond that contained in the financial statements.

Creative accounting

- Despite the accounting rules in place there have been examples of creative accounting by directors.
- This involves using accounting practices to show what the directors would like users to see rather than what is a fair representation of reality.

→ Key terms

equity p. 123
nominal value p. 124
par value p. 124
revenue reserve p. 124
dividend p. 125
ordinary shares p. 125
splitting p. 125
consolidating p. 125
preference shares p. 126
capital reserves p. 127
share premium account p. 128
bonus shares p. 129
bonus issue p. 130
issued share capital p. 131

allotted share capital p. 131
fully paid shares p. 131
called-up share capital p. 131
paid-up share capital p. 131
loan notes p. 132
profit before taxation p. 137
profit for the year p. 137
International Financial Reporting
    Standards p. 140
International Accounting Standards
    p. 140
directors' report p. 142
auditors p. 142
creative accounting p. 143

Further reading

If you would like to explore the topics covered in this chapter in more depth, we recommend the following books:

Elliott, B. and Elliott, J., *Financial Accounting and Reporting* (12th edn), Financial Times Prentice Hall, 2008, chapters 5, 6, 8 and 21–23.
KPMG, *KPMG's Practical Guide to International Financial Reporting Standards* (3rd edn), Thomson, 2006, section 2.5.
Sutton, T., *Corporate Financial Accounting and Reporting* (2nd edn), Financial Times Prentice Hall, 2004, chapters 6 and 12.

? Review questions

Answers to these questions can be found at the back of the book in Appendix C.

4.1 How does the liability of a limited company differ from the liability of a real person, in respect of amounts owed to others?

4.2 Some people are about to form a company, as a vehicle through which to run a new business. What are the advantages to them of forming a private limited company rather than a public one?

4.3 What is a reserve? Distinguish between a revenue reserve and a capital reserve.

4.4 What is a preference share? Compare the main features of a preference share with those of
(a) an ordinary share, and
(b) loan notes.

✳ Exercises

Exercises 4.4 and 4.5 are more advanced than Exercises 4.1 to 4.3. Those with coloured numbers have answers at the back of the book in Appendix D.

If you wish to try more exercises, visit MyAccountingLab/

4.1 Comment on the following quote:

> Limited companies can set a limit on the amount of debts that they will meet. They tend to have reserves of cash, as well as share capital and they can use these reserves to pay dividends to the shareholders. Many companies have preference as well as ordinary shares. The preference shares give a guaranteed dividend. The shares of many companies can be bought and sold on the Stock Exchange, and shareholders selling their shares can represent a useful source of new finance to the company.

4.2 Comment on the following quotes:

(a) 'Bonus shares increase the shareholders' wealth because, after the issue, they have more shares, but each one of the same nominal value as they had before.'
(b) 'By law, once shares have been issued at a particular nominal value, they must always be issued at that value in any future share issues.'
(c) 'By law, companies can pay as much as they like by way of dividends on their shares, provided that they have sufficient cash to do so.'
(d) 'Companies do not have to pay tax on their profits because the shareholders have to pay tax on their dividends.'

4.3 Briefly explain each of the following expressions that you have seen in the financial statements of a limited company:

(a) dividend
(b) audit fee
(c) share premium account.

4.4 Presented below is a draft set of financial statements for Chips Limited.

Chips Limited
Income statement for the year ended 30 June 2008

	£000
Revenue	1,850
Cost of sales	(1,040)
Gross profit	810
Depreciation	(220)
Other operating costs	(375)
Operating profit	215
Interest payable	(35)
Profit before taxation	180
Taxation	(60)
Profit for the year	120

Balance sheet as at 30 June 2008

	Cost £000	Depreciation £000	£000
Non-current assets			
Property, plant and equipment			
Buildings	800	(112)	688
Plant and equipment	650	(367)	283
Motor vehicles	102	(53)	49
	1,552	(532)	1,020
Current assets			
Inventories			950
Trade receivables			420
Cash at bank			16
			1,386
Total assets			2,406
Equity			
Ordinary shares of £1, fully paid			800
Reserves at 1 July 2007			248
Profit for the year			120
			1,168
Non-current liabilities			
Borrowings (secured 10% loan notes)			700
Current liabilities			
Trade payables			361
Other payables			117
Taxation			60
			538
Total equity and liabilities			2,406

The following additional information is available:

1 Purchase invoices for goods received on 29 June 2008 amounting to £23,000 have not been included. This means that the cost of sales figure in the income statement has been understated.

2 A motor vehicle costing £8,000 with depreciation amounting to £5,000 was sold on 30 June 2008 for £2,000, paid by cheque. This transaction has not been included in the company's records.

3 No depreciation on motor vehicles has been charged. The annual rate is 20 per cent of cost at the year end.

4 A sale on credit for £16,000 made on 1 July 2008 has been included in the financial statements in error. The cost of sales figure is correct in respect of this item.

5 A half-yearly payment of interest on the secured loan due on 30 June 2008 has not been paid.

6 The tax charge should be 30 per cent of the reported profit before taxation. Assume that it is payable, in full, shortly after the year end.

Required:
Prepare a revised set of financial statements incorporating the additional information in 1 to 6 above. (Work to the nearest £1,000.)

4.5 Rose Limited operates a small chain of retail shops that sell high quality teas and coffees. Approximately half of sales are on credit. Abbreviated and unaudited financial statements are given below.

Rose Limited
Income statement for the year ended 31 March 2008

	£000
Revenue	12,080
Cost of sales	(6,282)
Gross profit	5,798
Labour costs	(2,658)
Depreciation	(625)
Other operating costs	(1,003)
Operating profit	1,512
Interest payable	(66)
Profit before taxation	1,446
Taxation	(434)
Profit for the year	1,012

Balance sheet as at 31 March 2008

	£000
Non-current assets	2,728
Current assets	
Inventories	1,583
Trade receivables	996
Cash	26
	2,605
Total assets	5,333
Equity	
Share capital (50p shares, fully paid)	750
Share premium	250
Retained earnings	1,468
	2,468
Non-current liabilities	
Borrowings – Secured loan notes (2011)	300
Current liabilities	
Trade payables	1,118
Other payables	417
Tax	434
Borrowings – Overdraft	596
	2,565
Total equity and liabilities	5,333

Since the unaudited financial statements for Rose Limited were prepared, the following information has become available:

1 An additional £74,000 of depreciation should have been charged on fixtures and fittings.
2 Invoices for credit sales on 31 March 2008 amounting to £34,000 have not been included; cost of sales is not affected.

3 Trade receivables totalling £20 are recognised as having gone bad, but they have not yet been written off.
4 Inventories which had been purchased for £2,000 have been damaged and are unsaleable. This is not reflected in the financial statements.
5 Fixtures and fittings to the value of £16,000 were delivered just before 31 March 2008, but these assets were not included in the financial statements and the purchase invoice had not been processed.
6 Wages for Saturday-only staff, amounting to £1,000, have not been paid for the final Saturday of the year. This is not reflected in the financial statements.
7 Tax is payable at 30 per cent of profit after taxation. Assume that it is payable shortly after the year end.

Required:
Prepare revised financial statements for Rose Limited for the year ended 31 March 2008, incorporating the information in 1 to 7 above. (Work to the nearest £1,000.)

Chapter 5

Measuring and reporting cash flows

Introduction

This chapter is devoted to the third major financial statement identified in Chapter 2: the cash flow statement. This statement reports the movements of cash over a period and the effect of these movements on the cash position of the business. It is an important financial statement because cash is vital to the survival of a business. Without cash, no business can operate.

In this chapter we shall see how the cash flow statement is prepared and how the information that it contains may be interpreted. We shall also see why the deficiencies of the income statement in revealing cash flows over time make a separate cash flow statement necessary.

The cash flow statement is being considered after the chapter on limited companies because the format of the statement requires an understanding of this type of business. Limited companies are required to provide a cash flow statement for shareholders and other interested parties, as well as the more traditional income statement and balance sheet.

Learning outcomes

When you have completed this chapter, you should be able to:

■ discuss the crucial importance of cash to a business;

■ explain the nature of the cash flow statement and discuss how it can be helpful in identifying cash flow problems;

■ prepare a cash flow statement;

■ interpret a cash flow statement.

The cash flow statement (or statement of cash flows)

The cash flow statement is a fairly recent addition to the set of financial statements provided to shareholders and to others. There used to be no regulation requiring companies to produce more than an income statement and a balance sheet. The prevailing view seems to have been that any financial information required would be contained within these two statements. This view may have been based partly on the assumption that if a business were profitable, it would also have plenty of cash. Although in the very long run this is likely to be true, it is not necessarily true in the short to medium term.

We have already seen in Chapter 3 that the income statement sets out the revenue and expenses, rather than the cash receipts and cash payments, for the period. This means that profit (or loss), which represents the difference between the revenue and expenses for the period, may have little or no relation to the cash generated for the period. To illustrate this point, let us take the example of a business making a sale (generating a revenue). This may well lead to an increase in wealth and that will be reflected in the income statement. However, if the sale is made on credit, no cash changes hands – at least not at the time of sale. Instead, the increase in wealth is reflected in another asset: an increase in trade receivables. Furthermore, if an item of inventories is the subject of the sale, wealth is lost to the business through the reduction in inventories. This means an expense is incurred in making the sale, which will be shown in the income statement. Once again, however, no cash has changed hands at the time of sale. For such reasons, the profit and the cash generated for a period will rarely go hand in hand.

The following activity should help to underline how profit and cash for a period may be affected differently by particular transactions or events.

Activity 5.1

The following is a list of business/accounting events. In each case, state the effect (increase, decrease or no effect) on both profit and cash:

		Effect	
		on profit	*on cash*
1	Repayment of borrowings	___	___
2	Making a sale on credit	___	___
3	Buying a current asset on credit	___	___
4	Receiving cash from a credit customer (trade receivable)	___	___
5	Depreciating a non-current asset	___	___
6	Buying some inventories for cash	___	___
7	Making a share issue for cash	___	___

You should have come up with the following:

		Effect	
		on profit	on cash
1	Repayment of borrowings	none	decrease
2	Making a sale on credit	increase	none
3	Buying a current asset on credit	none	none
4	Receiving cash from a credit customer (trade receivable)	none	increase
5	Depreciating a non-current asset	decrease	none
6	Buying some inventories for cash	none	decrease
7	Making a share issue for cash	none	increase

The reasons for these answers are as follows:

1 Repaying borrowings requires that cash be paid to the lender. This means that two figures in the balance sheet will be affected, but none in the income statement.
2 Making a sale on credit will increase the sales revenue figure (and a profit or a loss, unless the sale was made for a price that precisely equalled the expenses involved). No cash will change hands at this point, however.
3 Buying a current asset on credit affects neither the cash balance nor the profit figure.
4 Receiving cash from a credit customer increases the cash balance and reduces the credit customer's balance. Both of these figures are on the balance sheet. The income statement is unaffected.
5 Depreciating a non-current asset means that an expense is recognised. This causes the carrying amount of the asset, as it is recorded on the balance sheet, to fall by an amount equal to the amount of the expense. No cash is paid or received.
6 Buying some inventories for cash means that the value of the inventories will increase and the cash balance will decrease by a similar amount. Profit is not affected.
7 Making a share issue for cash increases the owners' claim and increases the cash balance; profit is unaffected.

It is clear from the above that if we are to gain an insight into cash movements over time, the income statement is not the place to look. Instead we need a separate financial statement. This fact has become widely recognised in recent years, and in 1991 a UK financial reporting standard, FRS 1, emerged that required all but the smallest companies to produce and publish a cash flow statement. This standard has been superseded for many companies from 2005 by the International Financial Reporting (Accounting) Standard IAS 7. The two standards have broadly similar requirements. This chapter follows the provisions of IAS 7.

Why is cash so important?

It is worth asking why cash is so important. After all, cash is just an asset that the business needs to help it to function. In that sense, it is no different from inventories or non-current assets.

The reason for the importance of cash is that people and organisations will not normally accept other than cash in settlement of their claims against the business. If a business wants to employ people, it must pay them in cash. If it wants to buy a new non-current asset to exploit a business opportunity, the seller of the asset will normally insist on being paid in cash, probably after a short period of credit. When businesses fail, it is their inability to find the cash to pay the amounts owed that really pushes them under.

These factors lead to cash being the pre-eminent business asset. Cash is the thing that analysts tend to watch most carefully when trying to assess the ability of businesses to survive and/or to take advantage of commercial opportunities as they arise. The fact that cash and profits do not always go hand in hand is illustrated in Real World 5.1. This explains how Eurotunnel, the cross-channel business between England and France, continues to struggle to achieve profit, yet generates positive cash flows.

Cash flows under the channel

Despite making a loss for the year of £143m for 2006, Eurotunnel managed to increase its bank balance by £71m. This occurred partly because depreciation (of non-current assets) of £115m is an expense in the income statement, but it did not give rise to a cash outflow during 2006.

At the same time the interest expense charged in the income statement amounted to £333m, but the cash outflow was only £237m. This was because the business was authorised by the French Commercial Court to delay these interest payments.

Eurotunnel in 2006 shows a striking example of differences between reported profit and reported cash flow.

Source: Based on information contained in Eurotunnel's 2006 Annual Accounts.

The main features of the cash flow statement

The cash flow statement is a summary of the cash receipts and payments over the period concerned. All payments of a particular type, for example cash payments to acquire additional non-current assets or other investments, are added together to give just one figure that appears in the statement. The net total of the statement is the net increase or decrease of the cash (and cash equivalents) of the business over the period. The statement is basically an analysis of the business's cash (and cash equivalents) movements for the period.

A definition of cash and cash equivalents

IAS 7 defines cash as notes and coins in hand and deposits in banks and similar institutions that are accessible to the business on demand. Cash equivalents are short-term, highly liquid investments that are readily convertible to known amounts of cash and which are subject to an insignificant risk of changes of value. Cash equivalents are held for the purpose of meeting short-term cash commitments rather than for investment or other purposes.

Activity 5.2 should clarify the types of items that fall within the definition of 'cash equivalents'.

Activity 5.2

At the end of its accounting period, Zeneb plc's balance sheet included the following items:

1 *A bank deposit account where one month's notice of withdrawal is required.* This deposit was made because the business has a temporary cash surplus that it will need to use in the short term for operating purposes;
2 *Ordinary shares in Jones plc (a Stock Exchange listed business).* These were acquired because Zeneb plc has a temporary cash surplus and its directors believed that the shares represent a good short-term investment. The funds invested will need to be used in the short term for operating purposes.
3 *A bank deposit account that is withdrawable instantly.* This represents an investment of surplus funds that are not seen as being needed in the short term.
4 *An overdraft on the business's bank current account.*

Which (if any) of these four items would be included in the figure for cash and cash equivalents?

Your response should have been as follows:

1 A cash equivalent because the deposit is part of the business's normal cash management activities and there is little doubt about how much cash will be obtained when the deposit is withdrawn.
2 Not a cash equivalent. Although the investment was made as part of normal cash management, there is a significant risk that the amount expected (hoped for!) when the shares are sold may not actually be forthcoming.
3 Not a cash equivalent because this represents an investment rather than a short-term surplus amount of cash.
4 This is cash itself, though a negative amount of it. The only exception to this classification would be where the business is financed in the longer term by an overdraft, when it would be part of the financing of the business, rather than negative cash.

As can be seen from the responses to Activity 5.2, whether a particular item falls within the definition of cash and cash equivalent depends on two factors:

- the nature of the item; and
- why it has arisen.

In practice, it is not usually difficult to decide whether an item is a cash equivalent.

The relationship between the primary financial statements

The cash flow statement is now accepted, along with the income statement and the balance sheet, as a primary financial statement. The relationship between the three statements is shown in Figure 5.1. The balance sheet reflects the combination of assets (including cash) and claims (including the shareholders' equity) of the business *at a particular point in time*. The cash flow statement and the income statement explain the *changes over a period* to two of the items in the balance sheet. The cash flow statement explains the changes to cash. The income statement explains changes to equity, arising from trading.

Figure 5.1 The relationship between the balance sheet, the income statement and the cash flow statement

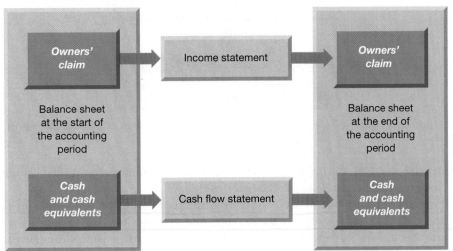

The balance sheet shows the position, at a particular point in time, of the business's assets and claims. The income statement explains how, over a period between two balance sheets, the owners' claim figure in the first balance sheet has altered as a result of trading operations. The cash flow statement also looks at changes over the accounting period, but this statement explains the alteration in the cash (and cash equivalent) balances from the first to the second of the two consecutive balance sheets.

The form of the cash flow statement

The standard layout of the cash flow statement is summarised in Figure 5.2. Explanations of the terms used in the cash flow statement are given below.

Cash flows from operating activities

This is the net inflow or outflow from trading operations, after tax and financing costs. It is equal to the sum of cash receipts from trade receivables, and cash receipts from cash sales where relevant, less the sums paid to buy inventories, to pay rent, to pay

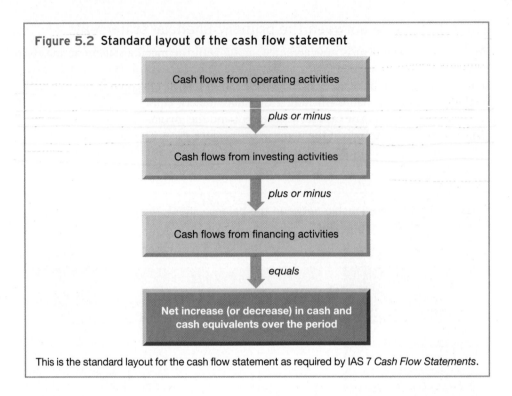

Figure 5.2 Standard layout of the cash flow statement

Cash flows from operating activities

plus or minus

Cash flows from investing activities

plus or minus

Cash flows from financing activities

equals

Net increase (or decrease) in cash and cash equivalents over the period

This is the standard layout for the cash flow statement as required by IAS 7 *Cash Flow Statements*.

wages and so on. From this are also deducted payments for interest on the business's borrowings, corporation tax and dividends paid.

Note that it is the amounts of cash received and paid during the period that feature in the cash flow statement, not the revenue and expenses for that period. It is, of course, the income statement that deals with the revenue and expenses. Similarly the tax and dividend payments that appear in the cash flow statement are those made in the period of the statement. Companies normally pay tax on their profits in four equal instalments. Two of these are during the year concerned, and the other two are during the following year. As a result, by the end of each accounting year, half of the tax will have been paid and the remainder will be a current liability at the end of the year, to be paid off during the following year. During any particular year, therefore, the tax payment would normally equal 50 per cent of the previous year's tax charge and 50 per cent of that of the current year.

The net figure for this section is intended to indicate the net cash flows for the period that arose from normal day-to-day trading activities after taking account of the tax that has to be paid on them and the cost of servicing the finance (equity and borrowings) needed to support them.

Cash flows from investing activities

This section of the statement is concerned with cash payments made to acquire additional non-current assets and with cash receipts from the disposal of non-current assets. These non-current assets will tend to be the usual items such as buildings and machinery. They might also include loans made by the business or shares in another company bought by the business.

The net cash flows from making new investments and/or disposing of existing ones also appear here.

This section also includes cash receipts arising from financial investments (loans and equities) made outside the business. These receipts are interest on loans made by the business and dividends from shares in other companies that are owned by the business.

Cash flows from financing activities

This part of the statement is concerned with the long-term financing of the business. So here we are considering borrowings (other than very short-term) and finance from share issues. This category is concerned with repayment/redemption of finance as well as with the raising of it. It is permissible under IAS 7 to include dividend payments made by the business here, as an alternative to including them in 'Cash flows from operating activities' (above).

This section shows the net cash flows from raising and/or paying back long-term finance.

Net increase or decrease in cash and cash equivalents

The total of the statement must, of course, be the net increase or decrease in cash and cash equivalents over the period concerned.

The effect on a business's cash and cash equivalents of its various activities is shown in Figure 5.3. As explained in the diagram, the arrows show the *normal* direction of cash flow for the typical healthy, profitable business in a typical year.

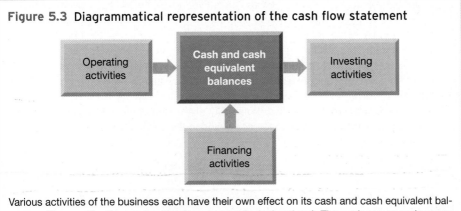

Figure 5.3 Diagrammatical representation of the cash flow statement

Various activities of the business each have their own effect on its cash and cash equivalent balances, either positive (increasing them) or negative (reducing them). The net increase or decrease in the cash and cash equivalent balances over a period will be the sum of these individual effects, taking account of the direction (cash in or cash out) of each activity.

Note that the direction of the arrow shows the *normal* direction of the cash flow in respect of each activity. In certain circumstances, each of these arrows could be reversed in direction.

The normal direction of cash flows

Normally 'operating activities' provide positive cash flows, that is, they help to increase the business's cash resources. In fact, for most UK businesses, in most time periods, cash generated from day-to-day trading, even after deducting tax, interest and dividends, is overwhelmingly the most important source of new finance.

Activity 5.3

Last year's cash flow statement for Angus plc showed a negative cash flow from operating activities. What could be the reason for this, and should the business's management be alarmed by it? (*Hint*: We think that there are two broad possible reasons for a negative cash flow.)

The two reasons are:

■ The business is unprofitable. This leads to more cash being paid out to employees, suppliers of goods and services, interest and so on, than is received from trade receivables in respect of sales. This would be particularly alarming, because a major expense for most businesses is depreciation of non-current assets. Since depreciation does not lead to a cash flow, it is not considered in 'net cash inflows from operating activities'. This means that a negative operating cash flow might well indicate a very much larger trading loss – in other words, a significant loss of the business's wealth; something to concern management.

■ The other reason might be less alarming. A business that is expanding its activities (level of sales revenue) would tend to spend quite a lot of cash relative to the amount of cash coming in from sales. This is because it will probably be expanding its assets (non-current and current) to accommodate the increased demand. For example, a business may well have to have inventories in place before additional sales can be made. Similarly, staff have to be employed and paid. Even when the additional sales are made, those sales would normally be made on credit, with the cash inflow lagging behind the sale. All of this means that, in the first instance, in cash flow terms, the business would not necessarily benefit from the additional sales revenue. This would be particularly likely to be true of a new business, which would be expanding inventories and other assets from zero. It would also need to employ and pay staff. Expansion typically causes cash flow strains for the reasons just explained. This can be a particular problem because the business's increased profitability might encourage a feeling of optimism, which could lead to lack of attention being paid to the cash flow problem.

Investing activities typically cause net negative cash flows. This is because many types of non-current asset wear out, and many that do not wear out become obsolete. Also, businesses tend to seek to expand their asset base. When a business sells some non-current assets, the sale will give rise to positive cash flows, but in net terms the cash flows are normally negative with cash spent on new assets outweighing that received from disposal of old ones.

Financing can go in either direction, depending on the financing strategy at the time. Since businesses seek to expand, there is a general tendency for this area to lead to cash coming into the business rather than leaving it.

Real World 5.2 shows the summarised cash flow statement of Tesco plc, the UK-based supermarket.

Cashing in

An abridged version of the published summarised cash flow statement for Tesco plc for the year ended 24 February 2007 shows the cash flows of the business under each of the headings described above.

Summarised cash flow statement for the year ended 24 February 2007

	£m
Net cash from operating activities	2,611
Net cash used in investing activities	(2,343)
Net cash used in financing activities	(533)
Net (decrease)/increase in cash and cash equivalents	(265)
Cash and cash equivalents at beginning of year	1,325
Effects of foreign exchange rate changes [*]	(18)
Cash and cash equivalents at end of period	1,042

* This adjustment is required because transactions are undertaken by the business in different currencies and movements in exchange rates can lead to gains or losses.

Source: Adapted from Tesco Annual Report 2007.

As we shall see shortly, more detailed information under each of the main headings is provided in the cash flow statement presented to the business's shareholders (and others).

Preparing the cash flow statement

Deducing net cash flows from operating activities

The first section of the cash flow statement is the 'cash flows from operating activities'. There are two approaches that can be taken to deriving this figure: the direct method and the indirect method.

The direct method

The direct method involves an analysis of the cash records of the business for the period, picking out all payments and receipts relating to operating activities. These are summarised to give the total figures for inclusion in the cash flow statement. Done on the computer, this would be a simple matter, but not many businesses adopt this approach.

The indirect method

The indirect method is the more popular method. It relies on the fact that, broadly, sales revenue gives rise to cash inflows, and expenses give rise to outflows. This means that the profit for the year figure will be closely linked to the net cash inflows from operating activities. Since businesses have to produce an income statement in any case, information from it can be used as a starting point to deduce the cash flows from operating activities.

Of course, within a particular accounting period, profit for the year will not normally equal the net cash inflows from operating activities. We saw in Chapter 3 that, when sales are made on credit, the cash receipt occurs some time after the sale. This means that sales revenue made towards the end of an accounting year will be included in that year's income statement, but most of the cash from those sales will flow into the business, and should be included in the cash flow statement, in the following year. Fortunately it is easy to deduce the cash received from sales if we have the relevant income statement and balance sheets, as we shall see in Activity 5.4.

Activity 5.4

How can we deduce the cash inflows from sales using the income statement and balance sheet for the business?

The balance sheet will tell us how much was owed in respect of credit sales at the beginning and end of the year (trade receivables). The income statement tells us the sales revenue figure. If we adjust the sales revenue figure by the increase or decrease in trade receivables over the year, we deduce the cash from sales for the year.

Example 5.1

The sales revenue figure for a business for the year was £34m. The trade receivables totalled £4m at the beginning of the year, but had increased to £5m by the end of the year.

Basically, the trade receivables figure is affected by sales revenue and cash receipts. It is increased when a sale is made and decreased when cash is received from a credit customer. If, over the year, the sales revenue and the cash receipts had been equal, the beginning-of-year and end-of-year trade receivables figures would have been equal. Since the trade receivables figure increased, it must mean that less cash was received than sales revenues were made. This means that the cash receipts from sales must be £33m (that is, 34 − (5 − 4)).

Put slightly differently, we can say that as a result of sales, assets of £34m flowed into the business during the year. If £1m of this went to increasing the asset of trade receivables, this leaves only £33m that went to increase cash.

The same general point is true in respect of nearly all of the other items that are taken into account in deducing the operating profit figure. The exception is depreciation. This is not necessarily associated with any movement in cash during the accounting period.

All of this means that we can take the profit before taxation (that is, the profit after interest but before taxation) for the year, add back the depreciation and interest expense charged in arriving at that profit, and adjust this total by movements in inventories, trade (and other) receivables and payables. If we then go on to deduct payments made during the accounting period for taxation, interest on borrowings and dividends, we have the net cash from operating activities.

Example 5.2

The relevant information from the financial statements of Dido plc for last year is as follows:

	£m
Profit before taxation (after interest)	122
Depreciation charged in arriving at profit before taxation	34
Interest expense	6
At the beginning of the year:	
Inventories	15
Trade receivables	24
Trade payables	18
At the end of the year:	
Inventories	17
Trade receivables	21
Trade payables	19

The following further information is available about payments during last year:

	£m
Taxation paid	32
Interest paid	5
Dividends paid	9

The cash flow from operating activities is derived as follows:

	£m
Profit before taxation (after interest)	122
Depreciation	34
Interest expense	6
Increase in inventories (17 – 15)	(2)
Decrease in trade receivables (21 – 24)	3
Increase in trade payables (19 – 18)	1
Cash generated from operating activities	164
Less Interest paid	(5)
Taxation paid	(32)
Dividends paid	(9)
Net cash from operating activities	118

As we can see, the net increase in working capital* (that is, current assets less current liabilities), as a result of trading, was £162m. Of this, £2m went into increased inventories. More cash was received from trade receivables than sales revenue was made, and less cash was paid to trade payables than purchases of goods and services on credit. Both of these had a favourable effect on cash, which increased by £164m. When account was taken of the payments for interest, tax and dividends, the net cash flow from operating activities was £118m (inflow).

Note that we needed to adjust the profit before taxation (after interest) by the depreciation and interest expenses to derive the profit before depreciation, interest and taxation.

* Working capital is a term widely used in accounting and finance, not just in the context of cash flow statements. We shall encounter it several times in later chapters.

The indirect method of deducing the net cash flow from operating activities is summarised in Figure 5.4.

Activity 5.5

The relevant information from the financial statements of Pluto plc for last year is as follows:

	£m
Profit before taxation (after interest)	165
Depreciation charged in arriving at operating profit	41
Interest expense	21
At the beginning of the year:	
Inventories	22
Trade receivables	18
Trade payables	15
At the end of the year:	
Inventories	23
Trade receivables	21
Trade payables	17

The following further information is available about payments during last year:

	£m
Taxation paid	49
Interest paid	25
Dividends paid	28

What figure should appear in the cash flow statement for 'Cash flows from operating activities'?

Net cash inflows from operating activities:

	£m
Profit before taxation (after interest)	165
Depreciation	41
Interest expense	21
Increase in inventories (23 – 22)	(1)
Increase in trade receivables (21 – 18)	(3)
Increase in trade payables (17 – 15)	2
Cash generated from operating activities	225
Interest paid	(25)
Taxation paid	(49)
Dividends paid	(28)
Net cash from operating activities	123

Figure 5.4 The indirect method of deducing the net cash flows from operating activities

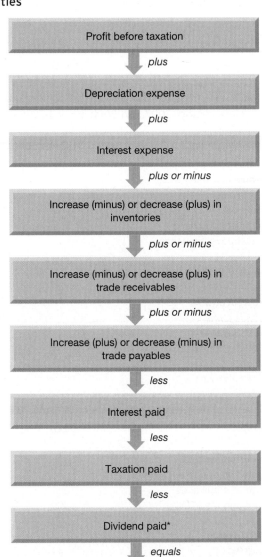

Determining the net cash from operating activities firstly involves adding back the depreciation and the interest expense to the profit before taxation. Next, adjustment is made for increases or decreases in inventories, trade receivables and trade payables. Lastly, cash paid for interest, taxation and dividends is deducted.

* Note that dividends could alternatively be included under the heading 'Cash flows from financing activities'.

Deducing the other areas of the cash flow statement

We can now go on to take a look at the preparation of a complete cash flow statement through Example 5.3.

Example 5.3

Torbryan plc's income statement for the year ended 31 December 2008 and the balance sheets as at 31 December 2007 and 2008 are as follows:

Income statement for the year ended 31 December 2008

	£m
Revenue	576
Cost of sales	(307)
Gross profit	269
Distribution expenses	(65)
Administrative expenses	(26)
	178
Other operating income	21
Operating profit	199
Interest receivable	17
	216
Interest payable	(23)
Profit before taxation	193
Taxation	(46)
Profit for the year	147

Balance sheets as at 31 December 2007 and 2008

	2007 £m	2008 £m
Non-current assets		
Property, plant and equipment		
Land and buildings	241	241
Plant and machinery	309	325
	550	566
Current assets		
Inventories	44	41
Trade receivables	121	139
	165	180
Total assets	715	746
Equity		
Called-up ordinary share capital	150	200
Share premium account	–	40
Retained earnings	26	123
	176	363

Non-current liabilities		
Borrowings – loan notes	400	250
Current liabilities		
Borrowings (all bank overdraft)	68	56
Trade payables	55	54
Taxation	16	23
	139	133
Total equity and liabilities	715	746

During 2008, the business spent £95m on additional plant and machinery. There were no other non-current-asset acquisitions or disposals. A dividend of £50m was paid on ordinary shares during the year. The interest receivable revenue and the interest payable expenses for the year were equal to the cash inflow and outflow respectively.

The cash flow statement would be as follows:

Torbryan plc
Cash flow statement for the year ended 31 December 2008

	£m
Cash flows from operating activities	
Profit before taxation (after interest) (see Note 1 below)	193
Adjustments for:	
Depreciation (Note 2)	79
Interest receivable (Note 3)	(17)
Interest payable (Note 4)	23
Increase in trade receivables (139 – 121)	(18)
Decrease in trade payables (55 – 54)	(1)
Decrease in inventories (44 – 41)	3
Cash generated from operations	262
Interest paid	(23)
Taxation paid (Note 5)	(39)
Dividend paid	(50)
Net cash from operating activities	150
Cash flows from investing activities	
Payments to acquire tangible non-current assets	(95)
Interest received (Note 3)	17
Net cash used in investing activities	(78)
Cash flows from financing activities	
Repayments of loan notes (Note 6)	(150)
Issue of ordinary shares (Note 7)	90
Net cash used in financing activities	(60)
Net increase in cash and cash equivalents	12
Cash and cash equivalents at 1 January 2008 (Note 8)	(68)
Cash and cash equivalents at 31 December 2008	(56)

To see how this relates to the cash of the business at the beginning and end of the year it can be useful to provide a reconciliation as follows:

**Analysis of cash and cash equivalents during the year
ended 31 December 2008**

	£m
Overdraft balance at 1 January 2008	(68)
Net cash inflow	12
Overdraft balance at 31 December 2008	(56)

Notes:

1 This is simply taken from the income statement for the year.
2 Since there were no disposals, the depreciation charges must be the difference between the start and end of the year's plant and machinery (non-current assets) values, adjusted by the cost of any additions.

	£m
Carrying amount at 1 January 2008	309
Additions	95
	404
Depreciation (balancing figure)	(79)
Carrying amount at 31 December 2008	325

3 Interest receivable must be taken away to work towards the profit before crediting it, because it is not part of operations but of investing activities. The cash inflow from this source appears under the 'Cash flows from investing activities' heading.
4 Interest payable expense must be taken out, by adding it back to the profit figure. We subsequently deduct the cash paid for interest payable during the year. In this case the two figures are identical.
5 Taxation is paid by companies 50 per cent during their accounting year and 50 per cent in the following year. As a result the 2008 payment would have been half the tax on the 2007 profit (that is, the figure that would have appeared in the current liabilities at the end of 2007), plus half of the 2008 taxation charge (that is, $16 + (\frac{1}{2} \times 46) = 39$). Probably the easiest way to deduce the amount paid during the year to 31 December 2008 is by following this approach:

	£m
Taxation owed at start of the year (from the balance sheet as at 31 December 2007)	16
Taxation charge for the year (from the income statement)	46
	62
Less Taxation owed at the end of the year (from the balance sheet as at 31 December 2008)	(23)
Taxation paid during the year	39

This follows the logic that if we start with what the business owed at the beginning of the year, add the increase in what was owed as a result of the current year's taxation charge and then deduct what was owed at the end, the resulting figure must be what was paid during the year.

6 It has been assumed that the loan notes were redeemed for their balance sheet value. This is not, however, always the case.
7 The share issue raised £90m, of which £50m went into the share capital total on the balance sheet and £40m into share premium.
8 There were no 'cash equivalents', just cash (though negative).

What does the cash flow statement tell us?

The cash flow statement tells us how the business has generated cash during the period and where that cash has gone. Since cash is properly regarded as the lifeblood of just about any business, this is potentially very useful information.

Tracking the sources and uses of cash over several years could show financing trends that a reader of the statements could use to help to make judgements about the likely future behaviour of the business.

Looking specifically at the cash flow statement for Torbryan plc, in Example 5.3, we can see the following:

- Net cash flow from operations was strong, much larger than the profit for the year figure, after taking account of the dividend paid. This would be expected because depreciation is deducted in arriving at profit. There was a general tendency for working capital to absorb some cash. This would not be surprising had there been an expansion of activity (sales revenue) over the year. From the information supplied, we do not know whether there was an expansion or not. (We have only one year's income statement.)
- There were net outflows of cash for investing activities, but this would not be unusual. Many items of property, plant and equipment have limited lives and need to be replaced with new ones. The expenditure during the year was not out of line with the depreciation expense for the year, which is what we might expect.
- There was a fairly major outflow of cash to redeem some borrowings, partly offset by the proceeds of a share issue. This presumably represents a change of financing strategy. Together with the ploughed-back profit from trading, there has been a significant shift in the equity/borrowings balance.

Real World 5.3 looks at the cash flow statement of an emerging business, LiDCO Group plc, that is experiencing negative cash flows as it seeks to establish a profitable market for its products.

Real World 5.3

Not losing heart

LiDCO Group plc is a smaller business whose shares are listed on the Alternative Investment Market (AIM). AIM is a section of the London Stock Exchange that specialises in providing a market for the shares of smaller up-and-coming businesses. We shall discuss AIM in Chapter 11.

LiDCO makes highly sophisticated equipment for monitoring the hearts of cardiac patients, typically in hospitals and clinics. The business was started by four doctors and scientists. It has spent £6.8m over ten years developing its products, obtaining registration for their use from both the UK and US authorities and creating manufacturing facilities.

LiDCO's cash flow statement for the year to 31 January 2007 was as follows:

	£000
Net cash outflow from operating activities	(1,366)
Returns on invetment and servicing of financing	
Interest received	69
Interest paid	(35)
Net cash inflow from returns on investment	34
Taxation	283
Capital expenditure and financial investment	
Purchase of tangible fixed assets	(137)
Purchase of intangible fixed assets	(410)
Net cash outflow from capital expenditure and financial investment	(547)
Financing activities	
Issue of ordinary share capital	3,245
Convertible loan drawdowns	(1,126)
Net cash inflow from financing	2,119
Increase/(decrease) in cash	523

[Note that this was the statement that appeared in the business's annual report. Some more detail was supplied in the way of notes to the accounts.]

To put these figures into context, the sales revenue for the year was £3,443,000. This means that the net cash outflow from operating activities was equal to nearly 40 per cent of the revenue figure. (This was an improvement, since it was over 50 per cent in 2006.) Such cash flow profiles are fairly typical of 'high-tech' businesses that have enormous start-up costs to bring their products to the market in sufficient quantities to yield a profit. Of course, not all such businesses achieve this, but LiDCO seems confident of success.

Source: Information taken from LiDCO Group plc Annual Report 2007 and AIM company profile, www.londonstockexchange.com.

? Self-assessment question 5.1

Touchstone plc's income statements for the years ended 31 December 2007 and 2008 and the balance sheets as at 31 December 2007 and 2008 are as follows:

Income statements for the years ended 2007 and 2008

	2007	2008
	£m	£m
Revenue	173	207
Cost of sales	(96)	(101)
Gross profit	77	106
Distribution expenses	(18)	(20)
Administrative expenses	(24)	(26)
Other operating income	3	4
Operating profit	38	64
Interest payable	(2)	(4)
Profit before taxation	36	60
Taxation	(8)	(16)
Profit for the year	28	44

Balance sheets as at 31 December 2007 and 2008

	2007 £m	2008 £m
Non-current assets		
Property, plant and equipment		
Land and buildings	94	110
Plant and machinery	53	62
	147	172
Current assets		
Inventories	25	24
Treasury bills (short-term investments)	–	15
Trade receivables	16	26
Cash at bank and in hand	4	4
	45	69
Total assets	192	241
Equity		
Called-up ordinary share capital	100	100
Retained earnings	30	56
	130	156
Non-current liabilities		
Borrowings – loan notes (10%)	20	40
Current liabilities		
Trade payables	38	37
Taxation	4	8
	42	45
Total equity and liabilities	192	241

Included in 'cost of sales', 'distribution costs' and 'administration expenses', depreciation was as follows:

	2007 £m	2008 £m
Land and buildings	5	6
Plant and machinery	6	10

There were no non-current asset disposals in either year.

The interest payable expense equalled the cash payment made during the year, in both cases.

The business paid dividends on ordinary shares of £14m during 2007 and £18m during 2008.

The Treasury bills represent a short-term investment of funds that will be used shortly in operations. There is insignificant risk that this investment will lose value.

Required:
Prepare a cash flow statement for the business for 2008.

The answer to this question can be found at the back of the book in Appendix B.

Summary

The main points of this chapter may be summarised as follows.

The need for a cash flow statement

- Cash is important because no business can operate without it.
- The cash flow statement is specifically designed to reveal movements in cash over a period.
- Cash movements cannot be readily detected from the income statement, which focuses on revenue and expenses rather than on cash receipts and cash payments.
- Profit (or loss) and cash generated for the period are rarely equal.
- The cash flow statement is a primary financial statement, along with the income statement and the balance sheet.

Preparing the cash flow statement

- The layout of the statement contains three categories of cash movement:
  - cash flows from operating activities;
  - cash flows from investing activities;
  - cash flows from financing activities.
- The total of the cash movements under these three categories will provide the net increase or decrease in cash and cash equivalents for the period.
- A reconciliation can be undertaken to check that the opening balance of cash and cash equivalents plus the net increase (or decrease) for the period equals the closing balance.

Calculating the cash generated from operations

- The net cash flows from operating activities can be derived by either the direct method or the indirect method.
- The direct method is based on an analysis of the cash records for the period, whereas the indirect method uses information contained within the income statement and balance sheets of the business.
- The indirect method takes the net operating profit for the period, adds back any depreciation charge and then adjusts for changes in inventories, receivables and payables during the period.

Interpreting the cash flow statement

- The cash flow statement shows the main sources and uses of cash.
- Tracking the cash movements over several periods may reveal financing and investing patterns and may help predict future management action.

Key terms

direct method p. 163
indirect method p. 163
working capital p. 165

Further reading

If you would like to explore the topics covered in this chapter in more depth, we recommend the following books:

Elliott, B. and Elliott, J., *Financial Accounting and Reporting* (12th edn), Financial Times Prentice Hall, 2008, chapter 27.
KPMG, *KPMG's Practical Guide to International Financial Reporting Standards* (3rd edn), Thomson, 2006, section 2.4.
Sutton, T., *Corporate Financial Accounting and Reporting* (2nd edn), Financial Times Prentice Hall, 2004, chapters 6 and 18.

? Review questions

Answers to these questions can be found at the back of the book in Appendix C.

5.1 The typical business outside the service sector has about 50 per cent more of its resources tied up in inventories than in cash, yet there is no call for a 'inventories flow statement' to be prepared. Why is cash regarded as more important than inventories?

5.2 What is the difference between the direct and indirect methods of deducing cash generated from operations?

5.3 Taking each of the categories of the cash flow statement in turn, in which direction would you normally expect the cash flow to be? Explain your answer.
(a) Cash flows from operating activities.
(b) Cash flows from investing activities.
(c) Cash flows from financing activities.

5.4 What causes the profit for the year not to equal the net cash inflow?

✳ Exercises

Exercises 5.3 to 5.5 are more advanced than Exercises 5.1 and 5.2. Those with coloured numbers have answers at the back of the book in Appendix D.

> If you wish to try more exercises, visit MyAccountingLab/

5.1 How will each of the following events ultimately affect the amount of cash?
(a) An increase in the level of inventories.
(b) A rights issue of ordinary shares.
(c) A bonus issue of ordinary shares.
(d) Writing off part of the value of some inventories.
(e) The disposal of a large number of the business's shares by a major shareholder.
(f) Depreciating a non-current asset.

5.2 The following information has been taken from the financial statements of Juno plc for last year and the year before last:

	Year before last £m	Last year £m
Operating profit	156	187
Depreciation charged in arriving at operating profit	47	55
Inventories held at the end of:	27	31
Trade receivables at the end of:	24	23
Trade payables at the end of:	15	17

Required:
What is the figure for cash generated from operations for Juno plc for last year?

5.3 Torrent plc's income statement for the year ended 31 December 2008 and the balance sheets as at 31 December 2007 and 2008 are as follows:

Income statement

	£m
Revenue	623
Cost of sales	(353)
Gross profit	270
Distribution expenses	(71)
Administrative expenses	(30)
Rental income	27
Operating profit	196
Interest payable	(26)
Profit before taxation	170
Taxation	(36)
Profit for the year	134

Balance sheets as at 31 December 2007 and 2008

	2007 £m	2008 £m
Non-current assets		
Property, plant and equipment		
Land and buildings	310	310
Plant and machinery	325	314
	635	624
Current assets		
Inventories	41	35
Trade receivables	139	145
	180	180
Total assets	815	804
Equity		
Called-up ordinary share capital	200	300
Share premium account	40	–
Revaluation reserve	69	9
Retained earnings	123	197
	432	506
Non-current liabilities		
Borrowings – loan notes	250	150
Current liabilities		
Borrowings (all bank overdraft)	56	89
Trade payables	54	41
Taxation	23	18
	133	148
Total equity and liabilities	815	804

During 2008, the business spent £67m on additional plant and machinery. There were no other non-current asset acquisitions or disposals.

There was no share issue for cash during the year. The interest payable expense was equal in amount to the cash outflow. A dividend of £60m was paid.

Required:
Prepare the cash flow statement for Torrent plc for the year ended 31 December 2008.

5.4 Chen plc's income statements for the years ended 31 December 2007 and 2008 and the balance sheets as at 31 December 2007 and 2008 are as follows:

Income statement

	2007 £m	2008 £m
Revenue	207	153
Cost of sales	(101)	(76)
Gross profit	106	77
Distribution expenses	(22)	(20)
Administrative expenses	(20)	(28)
Operating profit	64	29
Interest payable	(4)	(4)
Profit before taxation	60	25
Taxation	(16)	(6)
Profit for the year	44	19

Balance sheets as at 31 December 2007 and 2008

	2007 £m	2008 £m
Non-current assets		
Property, plant and equipment		
Land and buildings	110	130
Plant and machinery	62	56
	172	186
Current assets		
Inventories	24	25
Trade receivables	26	25
Cash at bank and in hand	19	–
	69	50
Total assets	241	236
Equity		
Called-up ordinary share capital	100	100
Retained earnings	56	57
	156	157
Non-current liabilities		
Borrowings – loan notes (10%)	40	40
Current liabilities		
Borrowings (all bank overdraft)	–	2
Trade payables	37	34
Taxation	8	3
	45	39
Total equity and liabilities	241	236

Included in 'cost of sales', 'distribution costs' and 'administrative expenses', depreciation was as follows:

	2007 £m	2008 £m
Land and buildings	6	10
Plant and machinery	10	12

There were no non-current asset disposals in either year. The amount of cash paid for interest equalled the expense in both years. Dividends were paid totalling £18m in each year.

Required:
Prepare a cash flow statement for the business for 2008.

5.5 The following financial statements for Blackstone plc are a slightly simplified set of published accounts. Blackstone plc is an engineering business that developed a new range of products in 2006. These products now account for 60 per cent of its turnover.

Income statement for the years ended 31 March

	Notes	2007 £m	2008 £m
Revenue		7,003	11,205
Cost of sales		(3,748)	(5,809)
Gross profit		3,255	5,396
Operating expenses		(2,205)	(3,087)
Operating profit		1,050	2,309
Interest payable	1	(216)	(456)
Profit before taxation		834	1,853
Taxation		(210)	(390)
Profit for the year		624	1,463

Balance sheets as at 31 March

	Notes	2007 £m	2008 £m
Non-current assets			
Property, plant and equipment	2	4,300	7,535
Intangible assets	3	–	700
		4,300	8,235
Current assets			
Inventories		1,209	2,410
Trade receivables		641	1,173
Cash at bank		123	–
		1,973	3,583
Total assets		6,273	11,818
Equity			
Share capital		1,800	1,800
Share premium		600	600
Capital reserves		352	352
Retained profits		685	1,748
		3,437	4,500
Non-current liabilities			
Borrowings – bank loan (repayable 2012)		1,800	3,800
Current liabilities			
Trade payables		931	1,507
Taxation		105	195
Borrowings (all bank overdraft)		–	1,816
		1,036	3,518
Total equity and liabilities		6,273	11,818

Notes:

1 The expense and the cash outflow for interest payable are equal.

2 The movements in property, plant and equipment during the year are set out below.

	Land and buildings £m	Plant and machinery £m	Fixtures and fittings £m	Total £m
Cost				
At 1 April 2007	4,500	3,850	2,120	10,470
Additions	–	2,970	1,608	4,578
Disposals	–	(365)	(216)	(581)
At 31 March 2008	4,500	6,455	3,512	14,467
Depreciation				
At 1 April 2007	1,275	3,080	1,815	6,170
Charge for year	225	745	281	1,251
Disposals	–	(305)	(184)	(489)
At 31 March 2008	1,500	3,520	1,912	6,932
Carrying amount				
At 31 March 2008	3,000	2,935	1,600	7,535

3 Intangible assets represent the amounts paid for the goodwill of another engineering business acquired during the year.

4 Proceeds from the sale of non-current assets in the year ended 31 March 2008 amounted to £54m.

5 Dividends were paid on ordinary shares of £300m in 2007 and £400m in 2008.

Required:

Prepare a cash flow statement for Blackstone plc for the year ended 31 March 2008. (*Hint*: A loss (deficit) on disposal of non-current assets is simply an additional amount of depreciation and should be dealt with as such in preparing the cash flow statement.)

Chapter 6

Analysing and interpreting financial statements

Introduction

In this chapter we shall consider the analysis and interpretation of the financial statements discussed in Chapters 2 and 3. We shall see how financial (or accounting) ratios can help in assessing the financial health of a business. We shall also consider the problems that are encountered when applying this technique.

Financial ratios can be used to examine various aspects of financial position and performance and are widely used for planning and control purposes. As we shall see in later chapters, they can be very helpful to managers in a wide variety of decision areas, such as profit planning, pricing, working capital management, financial structure and dividend policy.

Learning outcomes

When you have completed this chapter, you should be able to:

■ identify the major categories of ratios that can be used for analysis purposes;

■ calculate important ratios for assessing the financial performance and position of a business;

■ explain the significance of the ratios calculated;

■ discuss the limitations of ratios as a tool of financial analysis.

Financial ratios

Financial ratios provide a quick and relatively simple means of assessing the financial health of a business. A ratio simply relates one figure appearing in the financial statements to some other figure appearing there (for example, operating profit in relation to capital employed) or, perhaps, to some resource of the business (for example, operating profit per employee, sales revenue per square metre of selling space, and so on).

Ratios can be very helpful when comparing the financial health of different businesses. Differences may exist between businesses in the scale of operations, and so a direct comparison of, say, the operating profit generated by each business may be misleading. By expressing operating profit in relation to some other measure (for example, capital (or funds) employed), the problem of scale is eliminated. A business with an operating profit of, say, £10,000 and capital employed of £100,000 can be compared with a much larger business with an operating profit of, say, £80,000 and sales revenue of £1,000,000 by the use of a simple ratio. The operating profit to capital employed ratio for the smaller business is 10 per cent (that is, (10,000/100,000) × 100%) and the same ratio for the larger business is 8 per cent (that is, (80,000/1,000,000) × 100%). These values (10% and 8%) can be directly compared whereas comparison of the absolute operating profit figures would be less meaningful. The need to eliminate differences in scale through the use of ratios can also apply when comparing the performance of the same business over time.

By calculating a small number of ratios it is often possible to build up a good picture of the position and performance of a business. It is not surprising, therefore, that ratios are widely used by those who have an interest in businesses and business performance. Although ratios are not difficult to calculate, they can be difficult to interpret, and so it is important to appreciate that they are really only the starting point for further analysis.

Ratios help to highlight the financial strengths and weaknesses of a business, but they cannot, by themselves, explain why those strengths or weaknesses exist or why certain changes have occurred. Only a detailed investigation will reveal these underlying reasons. Ratios tend to enable us to know which questions to ask, rather than provide the answers.

Ratios can be expressed in various forms, for example as a percentage or as a proportion. The way that a particular ratio is presented will depend on the needs of those who will use the information. Although it is possible to calculate a large number of ratios, only a few, based on key relationships, tend to be helpful to a particular user. Many ratios that could be calculated from the financial statements (for example, rent payable in relation to current assets) may not be considered because there is no clear or meaningful relationship between the two items.

There is no generally accepted list of ratios that can be applied to the financial statements, nor is there a standard method of calculating many ratios. Variations in both the choice of ratios and their calculation will be found in practice. However, if ratios are to be helpful in drawing comparisons, it is important to be consistent in the way in which ratios are calculated. The ratios that we shall discuss here are those that are widely used. They are popular because many consider them to be among the more important for decision-making purposes.

Financial ratio classifications

Ratios can be grouped into categories, each of which relates to a particular aspect of financial performance or position. The following five broad categories provide a useful basis for explaining the nature of the financial ratios to be dealt with.

- *Profitability*. Businesses generally exist with the primary purpose of creating wealth for their owners. Profitability ratios provide an insight to the degree of success in achieving this purpose. They express the profit made (or figures bearing on profit, such as sales revenue or particular expenses, like labour cost) in relation to other key figures in the financial statements or to some business resource.
- *Efficiency*. The efficiency with which particular resources have been used by the business is a key issue and ratios may be used to assess this. Efficiency ratios are also referred to as *activity* ratios.
- *Liquidity*. It is vital to the survival of a business that there are sufficient liquid resources available to meet maturing obligations (that is, amounts owing that must be paid in the near future). Some liquidity ratios examine the relationship between liquid resources held and amounts due for payment in the near future.
- *Financial gearing*. This is the relationship between the contribution to financing the business made by the owners of the business (typically the shareholders) and the amount contributed by lenders, for example a bank loan. The level of gearing has an important effect on the degree of risk associated with a business, as we shall see. Gearing is, therefore, something that managers must consider when making financing decisions. Gearing ratios tend to highlight the extent to which the business uses borrowings.
- *Investment*. Certain ratios are concerned with assessing the returns and performance of shares in a particular business from the perspective of shareholders who are not involved with the management of the business.

The analyst who is carrying out an assessment of a business's performance must be clear *who* needs the information and *why* they need it. Different users of financial information are likely to have different information needs, which will in turn determine the ratios that they find useful. For example, shareholders are likely to be interested in their returns in relation to the level of risk associated with their investment. Profitability, investment and gearing ratios will, therefore, be of particular interest. Long-term lenders are concerned with the long-term viability of the business and, to help them to assess this, the profitability and gearing ratios of the business are also likely to be of particular interest. Short-term lenders, such as suppliers of goods and services on credit (trade payables), will be interested in the ability of the business to repay the amounts owing in the short term. As a result, the liquidity ratios should be of interest.

We shall consider ratios falling into each of the five categories (profitability, efficiency, liquidity, gearing and investment) a little later in the chapter.

The need for comparison

Merely calculating a ratio will not tell us very much about the position or performance of a business. For example, if a ratio revealed that the business was generating £100 in sales revenue per square metre of counter space, it would not be possible to deduce from this information alone whether this particular level of performance was good, bad or indifferent. It is only when we compare this ratio with some 'benchmark' that the information can be interpreted and evaluated.

Activity 6.1

Can you think of any bases that could be used to compare a ratio you have calculated from the financial statements of a particular period?
We feel that there are three sensible possibilities.

You may have thought of the following bases:

■ past periods for the same business
■ similar businesses for the same or past periods
■ planned performance for the business.

We shall now take a closer look at these three in turn.

Past periods

By comparing the ratio we have calculated with the same ratio, but for a previous period, it is possible to detect whether there has been an improvement or deterioration in performance. Indeed, it is often useful to track particular ratios over time (say, five or ten years) to see whether it is possible to detect trends. The comparison of ratios from different periods brings certain problems, however. In particular, there is always the possibility that trading conditions were quite different in the periods being compared. There is the further problem that, when comparing the performance of a single business over time, operating inefficiencies may not be clearly exposed. For example, the fact that sales revenue per employee has risen by 10 per cent over the previous period may at first sight appear to be satisfactory. This may not be the case, however, if similar businesses have shown an improvement of 50 per cent for the same period.

Finally, there is the problem that inflation may have distorted the figures on which the ratios are based. Inflation can lead to an overstatement of profit and an understatement of asset values, as will be discussed later in the chapter.

Similar businesses

In a competitive environment, a business must consider its performance in relation to that of other businesses operating in the same industry. Survival may depend on the ability to achieve comparable levels of performance. A useful basis for comparing a particular ratio, therefore, is the ratio achieved by similar businesses during the same period. This basis is not, however, without its problems. Competitors may have different year ends and, therefore, trading conditions may not be identical. They may also have different accounting policies, for example, different approaches to calculating depreciation or valuing inventories, which can have a significant effect on reported profits and asset values. Finally, it may be difficult to obtain the financial statements of competitor businesses. Sole proprietorships and partnerships, for example, are not obliged to make their financial statements available to the public. In the case of limited companies, there is a legal obligation to do so. However, a diversified business may not provide a breakdown of activities that is sufficiently detailed to enable analysts to compare the activities with those of other businesses.

Planned performance

Ratios may be compared with the targets that management developed before the start of the period under review. The comparison of planned performance with actual performance may therefore be a useful way of revealing the level of achievement attained. However, the planned levels of performance must be based on realistic assumptions if they are to be useful for comparison purposes.

Planned performance is likely to be the most valuable benchmark for the managers to assess their own business. Businesses tend to develop planned ratios for each aspect of their activities. When formulating its plans, a business may usefully take account of its own past performance and that of other businesses. There is no reason, however, why a particular business should seek to achieve either its own previous performance or that of other businesses. Neither of these may be seen as an appropriate target.

Analysts outside the business do not normally have access to the business's plans. For these people, past performance and the performances of other, similar, businesses may be the only practical benchmarks.

Calculating the ratios

Probably the best way to explain financial ratios is through an example. Example 6.1 provides an income statement and a balance sheet from which we can calculate important ratios.

Example 6.1

The following financial statements relate to Alexis plc, which operates a wholesale carpet business:

Balance sheets as at 31 March

	2007	2008
	£m	£m
Non-current assets		
Property, plant and equipment (at cost less depreciation)		
Land and buildings	381	427
Fixtures and fittings	129	160
	510	587
Current assets		
Inventories at cost	300	406
Trade receivables	240	273
Cash at bank	4	–
	544	679
Total assets	1,054	1,266
Equity		
£0.50 ordinary shares (Note 1)	300	300
Retained earnings	263	234
	563	534
Non-current liabilities		
Borrowings – 9% loan notes (secured)	200	300
Current liabilities		
Trade payables	261	354
Taxation	30	2
Short-term borrowings (all bank overdraft)	–	76
	291	432
Total equity and liabilities	1,054	1,266

Income statements for the year ended 31 March

	2007	2008
	£m	£m
Revenue (Note 2)	2,240	2,681
Cost of sales (Note 3)	(1,745)	(2,272)
Gross profit	495	409
Operating expenses	(252)	(362)
Operating profit	243	47
Interest payable	(18)	(32)
Profit before taxation	225	15
Taxation	(60)	(4)
Profit for the year	165	11

Notes:

1 The market value of the shares of the business at the end of the year was £2.50 for 2007 and £1.50 for 2008.
2 All sales and purchases are made on credit.
3 The cost of sales figure can be analysed as follows:

	2007 £m	2008 £m
Opening inventories	241	300
Purchases (Note 2)	1,804	2,378
	2,045	2,678
Closing inventories	(300)	(406)
Cost of sales	1,745	2,272

4 At 31 March 2006, the trade receivables stood at £223m and the trade payables at £203m.
5 A dividend of £40m had been paid to the shareholders in respect of each of the years.
6 The business employed 13,995 staff at 31 March 2007 and 18,623 at 31 March 2008.
7 The business expanded its capacity during 2008 by setting up a new warehouse and distribution centre in the north of England.
8 At 1 April 2006, the total of equity stood at £438m and the total of equity and non-current liabilities stood at £638m.

A brief overview

Before we start our detailed look at the ratios for Alexis plc (in Example 6.1), it is helpful to take a quick look at what information is obvious from the financial statements. This will usually pick up some issues that the ratios may not be able to identify. It may also highlight some points that could help us in our interpretation of the ratios. Starting at the top of the balance sheet, the following points can be noted:

■ *Expansion of non-current assets.* These have increased by about 15 per cent (from £510m to £587m). Note 7 mentions a new warehouse and distribution centre, which may account for much of the additional investment in non-current assets. We are not told when this new facility was established, but it is quite possible that it was well into the year. This could mean that not much benefit was reflected in terms of additional sales revenue or cost saving during 2008. Sales revenue, in fact, expanded by about 20 per cent (from £2,240m to £2,681m), a greater expansion than that in non-current assets.
■ *Major expansion in the elements of working capital.* Inventories increased by about 35 per cent, trade receivables by about 14 per cent and trade payables by about 36 per cent between 2007 and 2008. These are major increases, particularly in inventories and payables (which are linked because the inventories are all bought on credit – see Note 2).
■ *Reduction in the cash balance.* The cash balance fell from £4m (in funds) to a £76m overdraft between 2007 and 2008. The bank may be putting the business under pressure to reverse this, which could raise difficulties.

- *Apparent debt capacity*. Comparing the non-current assets with the long-term borrowings implies that the business may well be able to offer security on further borrowing. This is because potential lenders usually look at the value of assets that can be offered as security when assessing loan requests. Lenders are particularly attracted to land and, to a lesser extent, buildings as security. This is because they tend to hold their market value. For example, at 31 March 2008, non-current assets had a balance sheet value of £587m, but long-term borrowing was only £300m (though there was also an overdraft of £76m). Balance sheet values are not normally, of course, market values. On the other hand, land and buildings tend to have a market value higher than their balance sheet value due to inflation in property values.
- *Lower operating profit*. Though sales revenue expanded by 20 per cent between 2007 and 2008, both cost of sales and operating expenses rose by a greater percentage, leaving both gross profit and, particularly, operating profit massively reduced. The level of staffing, which increased by about 33 per cent (from 13,995 to 18,623 employees), may have greatly affected the operating expenses. (Without knowing when the additional employees were recruited during 2008, we cannot be sure of the effect on operating expenses.) Increasing staffing by 33 per cent must put an enormous strain on management, at least in the short term. It is not surprising, therefore, that 2008 was not successful for the business.

Having had a quick look at what is fairly obvious without calculating the normal ratios, we shall now go on to calculate and interpret them.

Profitability

The following ratios may be used to evaluate the profitability of the business:

- return on ordinary shareholders' funds
- return on capital employed
- operating profit margin
- gross profit margin.

We shall now look at each of these in turn.

Return on ordinary shareholders' funds (ROSF)

The return on ordinary shareholders' funds ratio compares the amount of profit for the period available to the owners with the owners' average stake in the business during that same period. The ratio (which is normally expressed in percentage terms) is as follows:

$$\text{ROSF} = \frac{\text{Profit for the year (net profit) less any preference dividend}}{\text{Ordinary share capital + Reserves}} \times 100$$

The profit for the year (less preference dividend, if any) is used in calculating the ratio because this figure represents the amount of profit that is left for the owners.

In the case of Alexis plc, the ratio for the year ended 31 March 2007 is

$$\text{ROSF} = \frac{165}{(438 + 563)/2} \times 100 = 33.0\%$$

Note that, when calculating the ROSF, the average of the figures for ordinary share-holders' funds as at the beginning and at the end of the year has been used. It is prefer-able to use an average figure as this is likely to be more representative. This is because the shareholders' funds did not have the same total throughout the year, yet we want to compare it with the profit earned during the whole period. We know, from Note 8, that the total of the shareholders' funds at 1 April 2006 was £438m. By a year later, however, it had risen to £563m, according to the balance sheet as at 31 March 2007.

The easiest approach to calculating the average amount of shareholders' funds is to take a simple average based on the opening and closing figures for the year. This is often the only information available, as is the case with Example 6.1. Averaging in this way is generally valid for all ratios that combine a figure for a period (such as profit for the year) with one taken at a point in time (such as shareholders' funds).

Where we do not even have the beginning-of-year figure, we are forced to rely on just the year-end figure. This is not ideal, but provided that this approach is con-sistently adopted it should provide ratios that are useful.

Activity 6.2

Calculate the ROSF for Alexis plc for the year to 31 March 2008.

The ratio for 2008 is

$$\text{ROSF} = \frac{11}{(563 + 534)/2} \times 100 = 2.0\%$$

Broadly, businesses seek to generate as high a value as possible for this ratio, pro-vided that it is not achieved at the expense of potential future returns by, for example, taking on more risky activities. In view of this, the 2008 ratio is very poor by any standards; a very safe bank deposit account will yield a better return than this. We need to try to find out why things went so badly wrong in 2008. As we look at other ratios, we should find some clues.

Return on capital employed (ROCE)

The return on capital employed ratio is a fundamental measure of business performance. This ratio expresses the relationship between the operating profit generated during a period and the average long-term capital invested in the business during that period. The ratio is expressed in percentage terms and is as follows:

$$\text{ROCE} = \frac{\text{Operating profit}}{\text{Share capital} + \text{Reserves} + \text{Non-current liabilities}} \times 100$$

Note, in this case, that the profit figure used is the operating profit (that is, the net profit *before* interest and taxation), because the ratio attempts to measure the returns to all suppliers of long-term finance before any deductions for interest payable on borrowings, or payments of dividends to shareholders, are made.

For the year to 31 March 2007, the ratio for Alexis plc is

$$ROCE = \frac{243}{(638 + 763)/2} \times 100 = 34.7\%$$

ROCE is considered by many to be a primary measure of profitability. It compares inputs (capital invested) with outputs (operating profit). This comparison is vital in assessing the effectiveness with which funds have been deployed. Once again, an average figure for capital employed may be used where the information is available.

Activity 6.3

Calculate the ROCE for Alexis plc for the year to 31 March 2008.

For 2008, the ratio is

$$ROCE = \frac{47}{(763 + 834)/2} \times 100 = 5.9\%$$

This ratio tells much the same story as ROSF, namely, a poor performance, with the return on the assets being less than the rate that the business has to pay for most of its borrowed funds (that is, 9 per cent for the loan notes).

Real World 6.1 shows how financial ratios are used by businesses as a basis for setting profitability targets.

Real World 6.1

Targeting profitability

The ROCE ratio is widely used by businesses when establishing targets for profitability. These targets are sometimes made public and here are some examples:

Tesco plc, the supermarket business, in 2004 set a target to achieve a growth in ROCE of 2 per cent from its 2004 figure of 10.4 per cent. It achieved this with 12.5 per cent in 2006 and increased it further in 2007. Tesco has set a further 2 per cent target growth for ROCE for 2008 and beyond. Tesco uses performance against a target ROCE as a basis of rewarding its senior managers, indicating the importance that the business attaches to this measure of performance.

The satellite broadcaster BSkyB plc has a target ROCE of 15 per cent by 2011 for its broadband operation.

Air France-KLM, the world's largest airline (on the basis of sales revenue), has set itself the target of increasing ROCE from 6.5 per cent in 2006 to 8.5 per cent by 2010.

Sources: Information taken from Tesco plc Annual Report 2007, 'BSkyB/triple play', *Financial Times*, 12 July 2006, and 'Air France-KLM raises targets', K. Done, *Financial Times*, 24 May 2007.

Real World 6.2 provides some insight to the levels of ROCE achieved by UK businesses.

Real World 6.2

Achieving profitability

UK businesses reported an average ROCE of 15.1 per cent for the first quarter of 2007, improving on the 2006 rate of 14.5 per cent. This was the highest level of ROCE since the Office of National Statistics first kept records.

Service sector businesses were much the more successful with an average ROCE of 21.1 per cent, compared with 5.3 per cent among manufacturers. In fact, manufacturers' average ROCE had fallen from 7.7 per cent in 2006.

Source: Information taken from 'Corporate profitability', Office of National Statistics, www.statistics.gov.uk/cci, 3 July 2007.

Operating profit margin

The operating profit margin ratio relates the operating profit for the period to the sales revenue during that period. The ratio is expressed as follows:

$$\text{Operating profit margin} = \frac{\text{Operating profit}}{\text{Sales revenue}} \times 100$$

The operating profit (that is, net profit before interest and taxation) is used in this ratio as it represents the profit from trading operations before the interest payable expense is taken into account. This is often regarded as the most appropriate measure of operational performance, when used as a basis of comparison, because differences arising from the way in which the business is financed will not influence the measure.

For the year ended 31 March 2007, Alexis plc's operating profit margin ratio is

$$\text{Operating profit margin} = \frac{243}{2,240} \times 100 = 10.8\%$$

This ratio compares one output of the business (operating profit) with another output (sales revenue). The ratio can vary considerably between types of business. For example, supermarkets tend to operate on low prices and, therefore, low operating profit margins. This is done in an attempt to stimulate sales and thereby increase the total amount of operating profit generated. Jewellers, on the other hand, tend to have high operating profit margins but have much lower levels of sales volume. Factors such as the degree of competition, the type of customer, the economic climate and industry characteristics (such as the level of risk) will influence the operating profit margin of a business. This point is picked up again later in the chapter.

Activity 6.4

Calculate the operating profit margin for Alexis plc for the year to 31 March 2008.

The ratio for 2008 is

$$\text{Operating profit margin} = \frac{47}{2,681} \times 100 = 1.8\%$$

Once again, this shows a very weak performance compared with that of 2007. Whereas in 2007 for every £1 of sales revenue an average of 10.8p (that is, 10.8 per cent) was left as operating profit, after paying the cost of the carpets sold and other expenses of operating the business, for 2008 this had fallen to only 1.8p for every £1. It seems that the reason for the poor ROSF and ROCE ratios was partially, perhaps wholly, a high level of expenses relative to sales revenue. The next ratio should provide us with a clue as to how the sharp decline in this ratio occurred.

Real World 6.3 describes how one well-known business intends to increase its operating profit margin over time.

Real World 6.3

Operating profit margin taking off at BA

British Airways plc, the airline business, more than achieved its 10 per cent operating profit margin target during the three months up to 30 June 2007. The figure was 12 per cent, up from 9.2 per cent for the previous period.

Source: Information taken from 'BA ahead despite Heathrow woes', K. Done, *Financial Times*, 3 August 2007.

Gross profit margin

→ The gross profit margin ratio relates the gross profit of the business to the sales revenue generated for the same period. Gross profit represents the difference between sales revenue and the cost of sales. The ratio is therefore a measure of profitability in buying (or producing) and selling goods or services before any other expenses are taken into account. As cost of sales represents a major expense for many businesses, a change in this ratio can have a significant effect on the 'bottom line' (that is, the profit for the year). The gross profit margin ratio is calculated as follows:

$$\textbf{Gross profit margin} = \frac{\textbf{Gross profit}}{\textbf{Sales revenue}} \times \textbf{100}$$

For the year to 31 March 2007, the ratio for Alexis plc is

$$\text{Gross profit margin} = \frac{495}{2,240} \times 100 = 22.1\%$$

Calculate the gross profit margin for Alexis plc for the year to 31 March 2008.

The ratio for 2008 is

$$\text{Gross profit margin} = \frac{409}{2{,}681} \times 100 = 15.3\%$$

The decline in this ratio means that gross profit was lower *relative* to sales revenue in 2008 than it had been in 2007. Bearing in mind that

Gross profit = Sales revenue – Cost of sales (or cost of goods sold)

this means that cost of sales was higher *relative* to sales revenue in 2008 than in 2007. This could mean that sales prices were lower and/or that the purchase cost of goods sold had increased. It is possible that both sales prices and prices of goods sold had reduced, but the former at a greater rate than the latter. Similarly they may both have increased, but with sales prices having increased at a lesser rate than the cost of the goods sold.

Clearly, part of the decline in the operating profit margin ratio is linked to the dramatic decline in the gross profit margin ratio. Whereas, after paying for the carpets sold, for each £1 of sales revenue 22.1p was left to cover other operating expenses and leave an operating profit in 2007, this was only 15.3p in 2008.

The profitability ratios for the business over the two years can be set out as follows:

	2007	2008
	%	%
ROSF	33.0	2.0
ROCE	34.7	5.9
Operating profit margin	10.8	1.8
Gross profit margin	22.1	15.3

What do you deduce from a comparison of the declines in the operating profit and gross profit margin ratios?

It occurs to us that the decline in the operating profit margin was 9 per cent (that is, 10.8 per cent to 1.8 per cent), whereas that of the gross profit margin was only 6.8 per cent (that is, from 22.1 per cent to 15.3 per cent). This can only mean that operating expenses were greater compared with sales revenue in 2008 than they had been in 2007. The declines in both ROSF and ROCE were caused partly, therefore, by the business incurring higher inventories costs relative to sales revenue and partly through higher operating expenses relative to sales revenue. We should need to compare these ratios with the planned levels for them before we could usefully assess the business's success.

The analyst must now carry out some investigation to discover what caused the increases in both cost of sales and operating expenses, relative to sales revenue, from 2007 to 2008. This will involve checking on what has happened with sales and inventories prices over the two years. Similarly, it will involve looking at each of the individual areas that make up operating expenses to discover which ones were responsible for the increase, relative to sales revenue. Here, further ratios, for example, staff expenses (wages and salaries) to sales revenue, could be calculated in an attempt to isolate the cause of the change from 2007 to 2008. In fact, as we discussed when we took an overview of the financial statements, the increase in staffing may well account for most of the increase in operating expenses.

Real World 6.4 is a *Financial Times* article that discusses the reasons for improving profitability at 'Bollywood'.

Real World 6.4

Investing in Bollywood

Alas for investors, the economics of Bollywood have long been about as predictable as, but rather less uplifting than, the plotline of the average Hindi movie. The world's biggest movie market in terms of number of tickets sold – a massive 3.7bn – has traditionally offered miserable returns to its backers. Instead, revenues were swallowed up by a blend of piracy, taxes and inefficiencies.

Now the script appears to be changing. Big backers – in the shape of international entertainment giants such as Walt Disney and Viacom, and venture capitalists – are starting to enter Bollywood. With a brace of Indian film production companies listed on London's Alternative Investment Market and a third due to follow shortly, smaller investors are also getting in on the act. That is testament to improving industry dynamics. Digital technology and tougher regulation is helping reduce piracy while tax strains are being mitigated either by new rules at home – such as scrapping entertainment tax for multiplexes – or shifting production abroad.

Entertainment companies are also sharpening up their acts and evolving from one-stop shops to specialists in, say, production or distribution. Cleaner corporate structures enable them to access a broader range of financing. The economics of movie-making are improving too. Perhaps 40 per cent of Indian movies are now shot overseas, benefiting from tax breaks, 'captive' actors and producers and – in Europe – longer working days. As a result, a movie may be in the can in perhaps a quarter of the time it would normally take in India.

Evolution in other parts of the media world also plays into the hands of Bollywood moguls; for example, the growth in satellite TV means more channels to bid on movie licensing rights. Industry analysts reckon Bollywood now offers a return on capital employed of about 30–35 per cent, not too dissimilar from Hollywood. Years of tears followed by a happy ending? How Bollywood.

Source: 'Investing in Bollywood', Lex column, *Financial Times*, 26 June 2007.

Efficiency

Efficiency ratios examine the ways in which various resources of the business are managed. The following ratios consider some of the more important aspects of resource management:

- average inventories turnover period
- average settlement period for trade receivables
- average settlement period for trade payables
- sales revenue to capital employed
- sales revenue per employee.

We shall now look at each of these in turn.

Average inventories turnover period

Inventories often represent a significant investment for a business. For some types of business (for example, manufacturers), inventories may account for a substantial proportion of the total assets held (see Real World 12.1, page 443). The average inventories turnover period ratio measures the average period for which inventories are being held. The ratio is calculated as follows:

$$\text{Average inventories turnover period} = \frac{\text{Average inventories held}}{\text{Cost of sales}} \times 365$$

The average inventories for the period can be calculated as a simple average of the opening and closing inventories levels for the year. However, in the case of a highly seasonal business, where inventories levels may vary considerably over the year, a monthly average may be more appropriate.

In the case of Alexis plc, the inventories turnover period for the year ended 31 March 2007 is

$$\text{Average inventories turnover period} = \frac{(241 + 300)/2}{1,745} \times 365 = 56.6 \text{ days}$$

(The opening inventories figure was taken from Note 3 to the financial statements.)

This means that, on average, the inventories held are being 'turned over' every 56.6 days. So, a carpet bought by the business on a particular day would, on average, have been sold about eight weeks later. A business will normally prefer a short inventories turnover period to a long one, because holding inventories has a cost, for example the opportunity cost of the funds tied up. When judging the amount of inventories to carry, the business must consider such things as the likely demand for the inventories, the possibility of supply shortages, the likelihood of price rises, the amount of storage space available, and the perishability/susceptibility to obsolescence of the inventories. The management of inventories will be considered in more detail in Chapter 12.

This ratio is sometimes expressed in terms of months rather than days. Multiplying by 12 rather than 365 will achieve this.

Activity 6.7

Calculate the average inventories turnover period for Alexis plc for the year ended 31 March 2008.

The ratio for 2008 is:

$$\text{Average inventories turnover period} = \frac{(300 + 406)/2}{2{,}272} \times 365 = 56.7 \text{ days}$$

The inventories turnover period is virtually the same in both years.

Average settlement period for trade receivables

A business will usually be concerned with amount of funds tied up in trade receivables and try to keep this to a minimum. The speed of payment can have a significant effect on the business's cash flow. The average settlement period for trade receivables ratio calculates how long, on average, credit customers take to pay the amounts that they owe to the business. The ratio is as follows:

$$\text{Average settlement period for trade receivables} = \frac{\text{Average trade receivables}}{\text{Credit sales revenue}} \times 365$$

A business will normally prefer a shorter average settlement period to a longer one as, once again, funds are being tied up that may be used for more profitable purposes. Although this ratio can be useful, it is important to remember that it produces an *average* figure for the number of days for which debts are outstanding. This average may be badly distorted by, for example, a few large customers who are very slow or very fast payers.

Since all sales made by Alexis plc are on credit, the average settlement period for trade receivables for the year ended 31 March 2007 is:

$$\text{Average settlement period for trade receivables} = \frac{(223 + 240)/2}{2{,}240} \times 365 = 37.7 \text{ days}$$

(The opening trade receivables figure was taken from Note 4 to the financial statements.)

Activity 6.8

Calculate the average settlement period for Alexis plc's trade receivables for the year ended 31 March 2008.

The ratio for 2008 is:

$$\text{Average settlement period for trade receivables} = \frac{(240 + 273)/2}{2{,}681} \times 365 = 34.9 \text{ days}$$

On the face of it, this reduction in the settlement period is welcome. It means that less cash was tied up in trade receivables for each £1 of sales revenue in 2008 than in 2007. Only if the reduction were achieved at the expense of customer goodwill or a high direct financial cost might the desirability of the reduction be questioned. For example, the reduction may have been due to chasing customers too vigorously or as a result of incurring higher expenses, such as discounts allowed to customers who pay quickly.

Average settlement period for trade payables

The average settlement period for trade payables ratio measures how long, on average, the business takes to pay those who have supplied goods and services on credit. The ratio is calculated as follows:

$$\text{Average settlement period for trade payables} = \frac{\text{Average trade payables}}{\text{Credit purchases}} \times 365$$

This ratio provides an average figure, which, like the average settlement period for trade receivables ratio, can be distorted by the payment period for one or two large suppliers.

As trade payables provide a free source of finance for the business, it is perhaps not surprising that some businesses attempt to increase their average settlement period for trade payables. However, such a policy can be taken too far and result in a loss of suppliers, goodwill. We shall return to the issues concerning the management of trade receivables and trade payables in Chapter 12.

For the year ended 31 March 2007, Alexis plc's average settlement period for trade payables is:

$$\text{Average settlement period for trade payables} = \frac{(203 + 261)/2}{1,804} \times 365 = 46.9 \text{ days}$$

(The opening trade payables figure was taken from Note 4 to the financial statements.)

Activity 6.9

Calculate the average settlement period for trade payables for Alexis plc for the year ended 31 March 2008. (For the sake of consistency, use a year-end figure for trade payables.)

The ratio for 2008 is:

$$\text{Average settlement period for trade payables} = \frac{(261 + 354)/2}{2,378} \times 365 = 47.2 \text{ days}$$

There was a very slight increase, between 2007 and 2008, in the average length of time that elapsed between buying inventories and services and paying for them. Had this increase been significant, it would, on the face of it, been beneficial because the business is using free finance provided by suppliers. If, however, this would lead to a loss of supplier goodwill that could have adverse consequences for Alexis plc, it would not necessarily be advantageous.

Sales revenue to capital employed

The sales revenue to capital employed ratio (or asset turnover ratio) examines how effectively the assets of the business are being used to generate sales revenue. It is calculated as follows:

$$\frac{\text{Sales revenue to}}{\text{capital employed ratio}} = \frac{\text{Sales revenue}}{\text{Share capital + Reserves + Non-current liabilities}}$$

Generally speaking, a higher asset turnover ratio is preferred to a lower one. A higher ratio will normally suggest that assets are being used more productively in the generation of revenue. However, a very high ratio may suggest that the business is 'overtrading on its assets', that is, it has insufficient assets to sustain the level of sales revenue achieved. When comparing this ratio for different businesses, factors such as the age and condition of assets held, the valuation bases for assets and whether assets are leased or owned outright can complicate interpretation.

A variation of this formula is to use the total assets less current liabilities (which is equivalent to long-term capital employed) in the denominator (lower part of the fraction). The identical result is obtained.

For the year ended 31 March 2007 this ratio for Alexis plc is:

$$\text{Sales revenue to capital employed} = \frac{2,240}{(638 + 763)/2} = 3.20 \text{ times}$$

(The opening capital employed figure comes from Note 8 to the financial statements)

Activity 6.10

Calculate the sales revenue to capital employed ratio for Alexis plc for the year ended 31 March 2008.

The sales revenue to capital employed ratio for the 2008 is:

$$\text{Sales revenue to capital employed} = \frac{2,681}{(763 + 834)/2} = 3.36 \text{ times}$$

This seems to be an improvement, since in 2008 more sales revenue was being generated for each £1 of capital employed (£3.36) than was the case in 2007 (£3.20). Provided that overtrading is not an issue and that the additional sales are generating an acceptable profit, this is to be welcomed.

Sales revenue per employee

The sales revenue per employee ratio relates sales revenue generated to a particular business resource, that is, labour. It provides a measure of the productivity of the workforce. The ratio is:

$$\text{Sales revenue per employee} = \frac{\text{Sales revenue}}{\text{Number of employees}}$$

Generally, businesses would prefer to have a high value for this ratio, implying that they are using their staff efficiently.

For the year ended 31 March 2007, the ratio for Alexis plc is:

$$\text{Sales revenue per employee} = \frac{£2,240m}{13,995} = £160,057$$

Activity 6.11

Calculate the sales revenue per employee for Alexis plc for the year ended 31 March 2008.

The ratio for 2008 is:

$$\text{Sales revenue per employee} = \frac{£2,681m}{18,623} = £143,962$$

This represents a fairly significant decline and probably one that merits further investigation. Labour is a particularly important resource and how well it is managed is a crucial issue for nearly all businesses. As we discussed previously, the number of employees had increased quite notably (by about 33 per cent) during 2008 and the analyst will probably try to discover why this had not generated sufficient additional sales revenue to maintain the ratio at its 2007 level. It could be that the additional employees were not appointed until late in the year ended 31 March 2008.

The efficiency, or activity, ratios may be summarised as follows:

	2007	2008
Average inventories turnover period	56.6 days	56.7 days
Average settlement period for trade receivables	37.7 days	34.9 days
Average settlement period for trade payables	46.9 days	47.2 days
Sales revenue to capital employed (asset turnover)	3.20 times	3.36 times
Sales revenue per employee	£160,057	£143,962

Activity 6.12

What do you deduce from a comparison of the efficiency ratios over the two years?

We feel that maintaining the inventories turnover period at the 2007 level might be reasonable, though whether this represents a satisfactory period can probably only be assessed by looking at the business's planned inventories period. The inventories holding period for other businesses operating in carpet retailing, particularly those regarded as the market leaders, may have been helpful in formulating the plans. On the face of things, a shorter receivables collection period and a marginally longer payables payment period are both desirable. On the other hand, these may have been achieved at the cost of a loss of the goodwill of customers and suppliers, respectively. The increased asset turnover ratio seems beneficial, provided that the business can manage this increase. The decline in the sales revenue per employee ratio is undesirable but, as we have already seen, is probably related to the dramatic increase in the level of staffing. As with the inventories turnover period, these other ratios need to be compared with the planned standard of efficiency.

Relationship between profitability and efficiency

In our earlier discussions concerning profitability ratios, we saw that return on capital employed (ROCE) is regarded as a key ratio by many businesses. The ratio is:

$$\text{ROCE} = \frac{\text{Operating profit}}{\text{Long-term capital employed}} \times 100$$

where long-term capital comprises share capital plus reserves plus long-term borrowings. This ratio can be broken down into two elements, as shown in Figure 6.1. The first ratio is the operating profit margin ratio, and the second is the sales revenue to capital employed (asset turnover) ratio, both of which we discussed earlier.

Figure 6.1 The main elements of the ROCE ratio

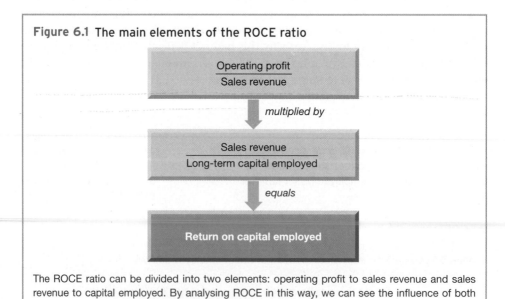

The ROCE ratio can be divided into two elements: operating profit to sales revenue and sales revenue to capital employed. By analysing ROCE in this way, we can see the influence of both profitability and efficiency on this important ratio.

By breaking down the ROCE ratio in this manner, we highlight the fact that the overall return on funds employed within the business will be determined both by the profitability of sales and by efficiency in the use of capital.

Example 6.2

Consider the following information, for last year, concerning two different businesses operating in the same industry:

	Antler plc	Baker plc
Operating profit	£20m	£15m
Average long-term capital employed	£100m	£75m
Sales revenue	£200m	£300m

The ROCE for each business is identical (20 per cent). However, the manner in which that return was achieved by each business was quite different. In the case of Antler plc, the operating profit margin is 10 per cent and the sales revenue to capital employed ratio is 2 times (so ROCE = 10% × 2 = 20%). In the case of Baker plc, the operating profit margin is 5 per cent and the sales revenue to capital employed ratio is 4 times (and so ROCE = 5% × 4 = 20%).

Example 6.2 demonstrates that a relatively high sales revenue to capital employed ratio can compensate for a relatively low operating profit margin. Similarly, a relatively low sales revenue to capital employed ratio can be overcome by a relatively high operating profit margin. In many areas of retail and distribution (for example, supermarkets and delivery services), the operating profit margins are quite low but the ROCE can be high, provided that the assets are used productively (that is, low margin, high turnover).

Activity 6.13

Show how the ROCE ratio for Alexis plc can be analysed into the two elements for each of the years 2007 and 2008. What conclusions can you draw from your figures?

	ROCE	=	Operating profit margin	×	Sales revenue to capital employed
2007	34.7%		10.8%		3.20
2008	5.9%		1.8%		3.36

As we can see, the relationship between the three ratios holds for Alexis plc for both years. The small apparent differences arise because the three ratios are stated here only to one or two decimal places.

Although the business was more effective at generating sales revenue (sales revenue to capital employed ratio increased) in 2008 than in 2007, in 2008 it fell well below the level necessary to compensate for the sharp decline in the effectiveness of each sale (operating profit margin). As a result, the 2008 ROCE was well below the 2007 value.

N

Liquidity

Liquidity ratios are concerned with the ability of the business to meet its short-term financial obligations. The following ratios are widely used:

- current ratio
- acid test ratio.

These two will now be considered.

Current ratio

The current ratio compares the 'liquid' assets (that is, cash and those assets held that will soon be turned into cash) of the business with the current liabilities. The ratio is calculated as follows:

$$\text{Current ratio} = \frac{\text{Current assets}}{\text{Current liabilities}}$$

Some people seem to believe that there is an 'ideal' current ratio (usually 2 times or 2:1) for all businesses. However, this fails to take into account the fact that different types of business require different current ratios. For example, a manufacturing business will often have a relatively high current ratio because it is necessary to hold inventories of finished goods, raw materials and work in progress. It will also normally sell goods on credit, thereby giving rise to trade receivables. A supermarket chain, on the other hand, will have a relatively low ratio, as it will hold only fast-moving inventories of finished goods and all of its sales will be made for cash (no credit sales). (See Real World 12.1 on page 443.)

The higher the ratio, the more liquid the business is considered to be. As liquidity is vital to the survival of a business, a higher current ratio might be thought to be preferable to a lower one. If a business has a very high ratio, however, it may be that funds are tied up in cash or other liquid assets and are not, therefore, being used as productively as they might otherwise be.

As at 31 March 2007, the current ratio of Alexis plc is:

$$\text{Current ratio} = \frac{544}{291} = 1.9 \text{ times (or 1.9:1)}$$

Activity 6.14

Calculate the current ratio for Alexis plc as at 31 March 2008.

The ratio as at 31 March 2008 is:

$$\text{Current ratio} = \frac{679}{432} = 1.6 \text{ times (or 1.6:1)}$$

Although this is a decline from 2007 to 2008, it is not necessarily a matter of concern. The next ratio may provide a clue as to whether there seems to be a problem.

Acid test ratio

→ The acid test ratio is very similar to the current ratio, but it represents a more stringent test of liquidity. It can be argued that, for many businesses, inventories cannot be converted into cash quickly. (Note that, in the case of Alexis plc, the inventories turnover period was about 57 days in both years (see pages 195–196).) As a result, it may be better to exclude this particular asset from any measure of liquidity. The acid test ratio is a variation of the current ratio, but normally excludes inventories.

The minimum level for this ratio is often stated as 1.0 times (or 1:1; that is, current assets (excluding inventories) equals current liabilities). In many highly successful businesses that are regarded as having adequate liquidity, however, it is not unusual for the acid test ratio to be below 1.0 without causing particular liquidity problems. (See Real World 12.1 on page 143.)

The acid test ratio is calculated as follows:

$$\text{Acid test ratio} = \frac{\text{Current assets (excluding inventories)}}{\text{Current liabilities}}$$

The acid test ratio for Alexis plc as at 31 March 2007 is:

$$\text{Acid test ratio} = \frac{544 - 300}{291} = 0.8 \text{ times (or 0.8:1)}$$

We can see that the 'liquid' current assets do not quite cover the current liabilities, so the business may be experiencing some liquidity problems.

Activity 6.15

Calculate the acid test ratio for Alexis plc as at 31 March 2008.

The ratio as at 31 March 2008 is:

$$\text{Acid test ratio} = \frac{679 - 406}{432} = 0.6 \text{ times}$$

The 2008 ratio is significantly below that for 2007. The 2008 level may well be a cause for concern. The rapid decline in this ratio should lead to steps being taken, at least, to stop further decline.

The liquidity ratios for the two-year period may be summarised as follows:

	2007	2008
Current ratio	1.9	1.6
Acid test ratio	0.8	0.6

Activity 6.16

What do you deduce from the liquidity ratios set out above?

Although it is probably not really possible to make a totally valid judgement without knowing the planned ratios, there appears to have been a worrying decline in liquidity. This is indicated by both of these ratios. The apparent liquidity problem may, however, be planned, short-term and linked to the expansion in non-current assets and staffing. It may be that when the benefits of the expansion come on stream, liquidity will improve. On the other hand, short-term claimants may become anxious when they see signs of weak liquidity. This anxiety could lead to steps being taken to press for payment, and this could cause problems for Alexis plc.

Financial gearing

→ Financial gearing occurs when a business is financed, at least in part, by borrowing instead of by finance provided by the owners (the shareholders) as equity. A business's level of gearing (that is, the extent to which it is financed from sources that require a fixed return) is an important factor in assessing risk. Where a business borrows, it takes on a commitment to pay interest charges and make capital repayments. Where the borrowing is heavy, this can be a significant financial burden; it can increase the risk of the business becoming insolvent. Nevertheless, most businesses are geared to some extent. (Costain Group plc, the building and construction business, is a rare example of a UK business with no borrowings.)

Given the risks involved, we may wonder why a business would want to take on gearing (that is, to borrow). One reason may be that the owners have insufficient funds, so the only way to finance the business adequately is to borrow from others. Another reason is that gearing can be used to increase the returns to owners. This is possible provided the returns generated from borrowed funds exceed the cost of paying interest. Example 6.3 illustrates this point.

Example 6.3

The long-term capital structures of two new businesses, Lee Ltd and Nova Ltd, are as follows:

	Lee Ltd £	Nova Ltd £
£1 ordinary shares	100,000	200,000
10% loan notes	200,000	100,000
	300,000	300,000

In their first year of operations, they each make an operating profit (that is, profit before interest and taxation) of £50,000. The tax rate is 30 per cent of the profit before taxation after interest.

Lee Ltd would probably be considered relatively highly geared, as it has a high proportion of borrowed funds in its long-term capital structure. Nova Ltd is much lower-geared. The profit available to the shareholders of each business in the first year of operations will be:

	Lee Ltd £	Nova Ltd £
Operating profit	50,000	50,000
Interest payable	(20,000)	(10,000)
Profit before taxation	30,000	40,000
Taxation (30%)	(9,000)	(12,000)
Profit for the year (available to ordinary shareholders)	21,000	28,000

The return on ordinary shareholders' funds (ROSF) for each business will be:

Lee Ltd

$$\frac{21,000}{100,000} \times 100 = 21\%$$

Nova Ltd

$$\frac{28,000}{200,000} \times 100 = 14\%$$

We can see that Lee Ltd, the more highly geared business, has generated a better ROSF than Nova Ltd. This is despite the fact that the ROCE (return on capital employed) is identical for both businesses (that is, (£50,000/£300,000) × 100 = 16.7%).

Note that at the £50,000 level of operating profit, the shareholders of both Lee Ltd and Nova Ltd benefit from gearing. Were the two businesses totally reliant on equity financing, the profit for the year (after taxation) would be £35,000 (that is, £50,000 less 30 per cent taxation), giving an ROSF of 11.7 per cent (that is, £35,000/£300,000). Both businesses generate higher ROSFs than this as a result of financial gearing.

An effect of gearing is that returns to shareholders become more sensitive to changes in operating profit. For a highly geared business, a change in operating profit will lead to a proportionately greater change in the ROSF ratio.

Activity 6.17

Assume that the operating profit was 20 per cent higher for each business than stated above (that is, each had an operating profit of £60,000). What would be the effect of this on ROSF?

The revised profit available to the shareholders of each business in the first year of operations will be:

	Lee Ltd £	Nova Ltd £
Operating profit	60,000	60,000
Interest payable	(20,000)	(10,000)
Profit before taxation	40,000	50,000
Taxation (30%)	(12,000)	(15,000)
Profit for the year (available to ordinary shareholders)	28,000	35,000

→

The ROSF for each business will now be:

Lee Ltd	Nova Ltd

$$\frac{28,000}{100,000} \times 100 = 28\% \qquad \frac{35,000}{200,000} \times 100 = 17.5\%$$

We can see that for Lee Ltd, the higher-geared business, the returns to shareholders have increased by one-third (from 21 per cent to 28 per cent), whereas for the lower-geared business, Nova Ltd, the benefits of gearing are less pronounced, increasing ROSF by only one-quarter (from 14 per cent to 17.5 per cent). The effect of gearing can, of course, work in both directions. So, for a highly geared business, a small decline in operating profit will bring about a much greater decline in the returns to shareholders. This makes gearing risky to shareholders.

The reason that gearing tends to be beneficial to shareholders is that interest rates for borrowings are low by comparison with the returns that the typical business can earn. On top of this, interest expenses are tax-deductible, in the way shown in Example 6.3 and Activity 6.17, making the effective cost of borrowing quite cheap. It is debatable whether the apparent low interest rates really are beneficial to the shareholders. Some argue that since borrowing increases the risk to shareholders, there is a hidden cost of borrowing. What are not illusory, however, are the benefits to the shareholders of the tax-deductibility of loan interest.

The effect of gearing is like that of two intermeshing cogwheels of unequal size (see Figure 6.2). The movement in the larger cog (operating profit) causes a more than proportionate movement in the smaller cog (returns to ordinary shareholders). The subject of gearing is discussed further in Chapter 11.

Two ratios are widely used to assess gearing:

- gearing ratio
- interest cover ratio.

Gearing ratio

The gearing ratio measures the contribution of long-term lenders to the long-term capital structure of a business:

$$\text{Gearing ratio} = \frac{\text{Long-term (non-current) liabilities}}{\text{Share capital + Reserves + Long-term (non-current) liabilities}} \times 100$$

The gearing ratio for Alexis plc, as at 31 March 2007, is:

$$\text{Gearing ratio} = \frac{200}{(563 + 200)} \times 100 = 26.2\%$$

A gearing ratio of 26.2% would not normally be considered to be very high.

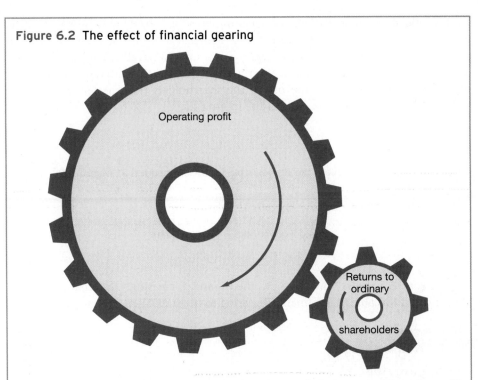

Figure 6.2 The effect of financial gearing

Operating profit

Returns to ordinary

shareholders

The cogs link the two wheels, so that a small circular movement in the large wheel (operating profit) leads to a relatively large circular movement in the small wheel (returns to ordinary shareholders).

Activity 6.18

Calculate the gearing ratio of Alexis plc as at 31 March 2008.

The ratio as at 31 March 2008 is:

$$\text{Gearing ratio} = \frac{300}{(534 + 300)} \times 100 = 36.0\%$$

This is a substantial increase in the level of gearing over the year.

Interest cover ratio

The interest cover ratio measures the amount of operating profit available to cover interest payable. The ratio may be calculated as follows:

$$\text{Interest cover ratio} = \frac{\textbf{Operating profit}}{\textbf{Interest payable}}$$

The ratio for Alexis plc for the year ended 31 March 2007 is:

$$\text{Interest cover ratio} = \frac{243}{18} = 13.5 \text{ times}$$

This ratio shows that the level of operating profit is considerably higher than the level of interest payable. This means that a significant fall in operating profit could occur before operating profit levels failed to cover interest payable. The lower the level of operating profit coverage, the greater the risk to lenders that interest payments will not be met, and the greater the risk to the shareholders that the lenders will take action against the business to recover the interest due.

Activity 6.19

Calculate the interest cover ratio of Alexis plc for the year ended 31 March 2008.

The ratio for the year ended 31 March 2008 is:

$$\text{Interest cover ratio} = \frac{47}{32} = 1.5 \text{ times}$$

Real World 6.5 shows how Tesco plc, the UK and, increasingly, international super-market chain was able to use financial gearing to boost ROSF in the early 2000s.

Real World 6.5

Changing gear at Tesco

Figure 6.3 plots the ROSF, ROCE and interest cover ratios for Tesco plc over the period 2000 to 2007.

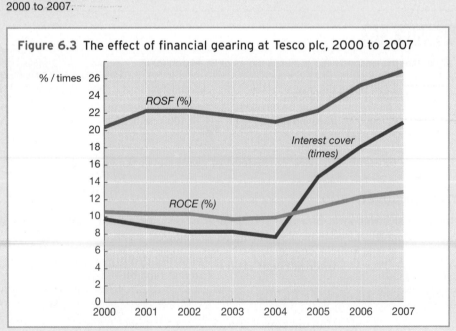

Figure 6.3 The effect of financial gearing at Tesco plc, 2000 to 2007

Tesco was able to boost returns to shareholders (ROSF), despite the business not producing a better ROCE (which reduced slightly between 1999 and 2003). This was achieved as a result of increasing financial gearing (as measured by interest cover) over that period. Since 2004, Tesco has gradually reduced gearing. Now ROSF continued to increase, but as a result of increasing ROCE.

Source: Based on information contained in Tesco plc Annual Reports from 2003 to 2007.

Alexis plc's gearing ratios are:

	2007	2008
Gearing ratio	26.2%	36.0%
Interest cover ratio	13.5 times	1.5 times

Activity 6.20

What do you deduce from a comparison of Alexis plc's gearing ratios over the two years?

The gearing ratio altered significantly. This is mainly due to the substantial increase in long-term lenders to the financing of the business.

The interest cover ratio has declined dramatically from a position where operating profit covered interest 13.5 times in 2007, to one where operating profit covered interest only 1.5 times in 2008. This was partly caused by the increase in borrowings in 2008, but mainly caused by the dramatic decline in profitability in that year. The later situation looks hazardous; only a small decline in future profitability in 2008 would leave the business with insufficient operating profit to cover the interest payments. The gearing ratio at 31 March 2008 would not necessarily be considered to be very high for a business that was trading successfully. It is the low profitability that is the problem.

Without knowing what the business planned these ratios to be, it is not possible to reach a valid conclusion on Alexis plc's gearing.

Real World 6.6 provides some evidence concerning the gearing of listed businesses.

Real World 6.6

The gearing of listed businesses

Larger listed businesses tend to have higher levels of gearing than smaller ones. A Bank of England report on the financing of small businesses found that the average level of gearing among smaller listed businesses was 27 per cent compared with 37 per cent for the top 350 listed businesses. Over recent years the level of borrowing by larger listed businesses has risen steadily (Tesco plc – see Real World 6.5 – provides an example of an exception to this general trend) whereas the level of borrowing for smaller listed businesses has remained fairly stable. This difference in gearing levels between larger and smaller businesses flies in the face of conventional wisdom.

Recent government investigations have found that smaller listed businesses often find it hard to attract investors. Many large institutional investors, who dominate the stock market, are not interested in the shares of smaller listed businesses because the amount of investment required is too small. As a result, shares in smaller businesses are less marketable. In such circumstances, it may be imagined that smaller businesses would become more reliant on borrowing and so would have higher levels of gearing than larger businesses. However, this is clearly not the case.

Although smaller businesses increase the level of shareholder funds by paying relatively low dividends and retaining more profits, they tend to be less profitable than larger businesses. So, higher retained profits do not seem to explain this phenomenon satisfactorily.

The only obvious factors that could explain this difference between smaller and larger businesses are the level of tax relief on interest on borrowings, and borrowing capacity. Broadly, larger businesses pay tax at a higher rate than their smaller counterparts. This means that the tax benefits of borrowing tend to be greater per £ of interest paid for larger businesses than for smaller ones. It may well be that larger businesses can borrow at lower interest rates than smaller ones, if only because they tend to borrow larger sums and so economies of scale may apply. Also, larger businesses tend to be less likely to get into financial difficulties than smaller ones, so they may be able to borrow at lower interest rates.

Source: Adapted from 'Small companies surprise on lending', *Financial Times*, 25 April 2003.

Investment ratios

There are various ratios available that are designed to help investors assess the returns on their investment. The following are widely used:

■ dividend payout ratio
■ dividend yield ratio
■ earnings per share
■ price/earnings ratio.

Dividend payout ratio

The dividend payout ratio measures the proportion of earnings (profit for the year) that a business pays out to shareholders in the form of dividends. The ratio is calculated as follows:

$$\text{Dividend payout ratio} = \frac{\text{Dividends announced for the year}}{\text{Profit for the year}} \times 100$$

This ratio is normally expressed as a percentage.

The dividend payout ratio for Alexis plc for the year ended 31 March 2007 is:

$$\text{Dividend payout ratio} = \frac{40}{165} \times 100 = 24.2\%$$

The information provided by this ratio is often expressed slightly differently as the dividend cover ratio. Here the calculation is:

$$\text{Dividend cover ratio} = \frac{\text{Profit for the year}}{\text{Dividend announced for the year}}$$

In the case of Alexis plc (for 2007) it would be 165/40 = 4.1 times. That is to say, the earnings available for dividend cover the actual dividend by just over four times.

Calculate the dividend payout ratio of Alexis plc for the year ended 31 March 2008.

The ratio for 2008 is:

$$\text{Dividend payout ratio} = \frac{40}{11} \times 100 = 363.6\%$$

This would normally be considered to be a very alarming increase in the ratio over the two years. Paying a dividend of £40m in 2008 would probably be regarded as very imprudent.

Dividend yield ratio

The dividend yield ratio relates the cash return from a share to its current market value. This can help investors to assess the cash return on their investment in the business. The ratio, expressed as a percentage, is:

$$\text{Dividend yield} = \frac{\text{Dividend per share}/(1 - t)}{\text{Market value per share}} \times 100$$

where t is the 'dividend tax credit' rate of income tax. This requires some explanation. In the UK, investors who receive a dividend from a business also receive a tax credit. As this tax credit can be offset against any tax liability arising from the dividends received, the dividends are effectively issued net of income tax, at the dividend tax credit rate.

Investors may wish to compare the returns from shares with the returns from other forms of investment. As these other forms of investment are typically quoted on a 'gross' (that is, pre-tax) basis it is useful to 'gross up' the dividend to make comparison easier. We can achieve this by dividing the dividend per share by $(1 - t)$, where t is the 'dividend tax credit' rate of income tax.

Using the 2007/8 dividend tax credit rate of 10 per cent, the dividend yield for Alexis plc for the year ended 31 March 2007 is:

$$\text{Dividend yield} = \frac{0.067^*/(1 - 0.10)}{2.50} \times 100 = 3.0\%$$

* Dividend proposed/number of shares = 40/(300 × 2) = £0.067 dividend per share (the 300 is multiplied by 2 because they are £0.50 shares).

Calculate the dividend yield for Alexis plc for the year ended 31 March 2008.

The ratio for 2008 is:

$$\text{Dividend yield} = \frac{0.067^*/(1 - 0.10)}{1.50} \times 100 = 4.9\%$$

* 40/(300 × 2) = £0.067.

Earnings per share

→ The earnings per share (EPS) ratio relates the profit for the year to the number of shares in issue. The ratio is calculated as follows:

$$\text{Earnings per share} = \frac{\textbf{Profit for the year}}{\textbf{Number of ordinary shares in issue}}$$

In the case of Alexis plc, the earnings per share for the year ended 31 March 2007 is as follows:

$$\text{EPS} = \frac{£165m}{600m} = 27.5p$$

Many investment analysts regard the EPS ratio as a fundamental measure of share performance. The trend in earnings per share over time is used to help assess the investment potential of a business's shares. Although it is possible to make total profit rise through ordinary shareholders investing more in the business, this will not necessarily mean that the profitability *per share* will rise as a result.

It is not usually very helpful to compare the EPS of one business with that of another. Differences in the constituents of equity (for example, in the nominal value of shares issued or the relative levels of shares and reserves) can render any such comparison meaningless. However, it can be very useful to monitor the changes that occur in this ratio for a particular business over time.

Activity 6.23

Calculate the earnings per share of Alexis plc for the year ended 31 March 2008.

The ratio for 2008 is:

$$\text{EPS} = \frac{£11m}{600m} = 1.8p$$

Price/earnings (P/E) ratio

→ The price/earnings ratio relates the market value of a share to the earnings per share. This ratio can be calculated as follows:

$$\text{P/E ratio} = \frac{\textbf{Market value per share}}{\textbf{Earnings per share}}$$

The P/E ratio for Alexis plc as at 31 March 2007 is:

$$\text{P/E ratio} = \frac{£2.50}{27.5p^*} = 9.1 \text{ times}$$

* The EPS figure (27.5p) was calculated above.

This means that the capital value of the share is 9.1 times higher than the current level of earnings attributable to it. The ratio is a measure of market confidence in the future of the business concerned. The higher the P/E ratio, the greater the confidence in the future earning power of the business and, consequently, the more investors are prepared to pay in relation to the earnings stream of the business.

P/E ratios provide a useful guide to market confidence concerning the future and they can, therefore, be helpful when comparing different businesses. However, differences in accounting policies between businesses can lead to different profit and earnings per share figures, and this can distort comparisons.

Activity 6.24

Calculate the P/E ratio of Alexis plc as at 31 March 2008.

The ratio for 2008 is:

$$\text{P/E ratio} = \frac{£1.50}{1.8p} = 83.3 \text{ times}$$

The investment ratios for Alexis plc over the two-year period are as follows:

	2007	2008
Dividend payout ratio	24.2%	363.6%
Dividend yield ratio	3.0%	4.9%
Earnings per share	27.5p	1.8p
P/E ratio	9.1 times	83.3 times

Activity 6.25

What do you deduce from the investment ratios set out above?

Can you offer an explanation why the share price has not fallen as much as it might have done, bearing in mind the very poor (relative to 2007) trading performance in 2008?

We thought that, although the EPS has fallen dramatically and the dividend payment for 2008 seems very imprudent, the share price seems to have held up remarkably well (fallen from £2.50 to £1.50 – see page 187). This means that dividend yield and P/E value for 2008 look better than those for 2007. This is an anomaly of these two ratios, which stems from using a forward-looking value (the share price) in conjunction with historic data (dividends and earnings). Share prices are based on investors' assessments of the business's future. It seems with Alexis plc that, at the end of 2008, the 'market' was not happy with the business, relative to 2007. This is evidenced by the fact that the share price had fallen by £1 a share. On the other hand, the share price has not fallen as much as the profit for the year. It appears that investors believe that the business will perform better in the future than it did in 2008. This may well be because they believe that the large expansion in assets and employee numbers that occurred in 2008 will yield benefits in the future; benefits that the business was not able to generate during 2008.

Real World 6.7 gives some information about the shares of several large, well-known UK businesses. This type of information is provided on a daily basis by several newspapers, notably the *Financial Times*.

Real World 6.7

Market statistics for some well-known businesses

The following data were extracted from the *Financial Times* on 6 October 2007, relating to the previous day's trading of the shares of some well-known businesses on the London Stock Exchange.

Share	Price	Chng	2007 High	Low	Y'ld	P/E	Volume 000s
BP	572.5	+10.5	617	504.5	3.6	12.4	100,518
J D Wetherspoon	571.5	+11	772.5	505	2.1	17.6	289
BSkyB	696	+3	721	521	2.2	24.5	7,463
Marks and Spencer	640	–	759	561	2.9	15.8	11,769
Rolls-Royce	545	+7.5	579	436.65	1.8	14.2	8,642
Vodafone	169.9	+0.80	179.8	133.7	3.6	14.0	207,567

The column headings are as follows:

Price   Mid-market price in pence (that is, the price midway between buying and selling price) of the shares at the end of 5 October 2007.

Chng   Gain or loss in the mid-market price during 5 October 2007.

High/Low   Highest and lowest prices reached by the share during the year 2007 until 5 October 2007.

Y'ld   Gross dividend yield, based on the most recent year's dividend and the current share price.

P/E   Price/earnings ratio, based on the most recent year's (after-tax) profit for the year and the current share price.

Volume   The number of shares (in thousands) that were bought/sold on 5 October 2007.

So, for example, for BP, the oil business,

■ the shares had a mid-market price of £5.725 each at the close of Stock Exchange trading on 5 October 2007;

■ the shares had increased in price by 10.5 pence during trading on 5 October;

■ the shares had highest and lowest prices during 2007 until 5 October of £6.17 and £5.045, respectively;

■ the shares had a dividend yield, based on the 5 October price (and the dividend for the most recent year) of 3.6 per cent;

■ the shares had a P/E ratio, based on the 5 October price (and the after-taxation earnings per share for the most recent year) of 12.4;

■ during trading in the shares on 5 October 2007, 100,518,000 (that is, about 100.5m) of the business's shares had changed hands from one investor to another. To put this into perspective, according to BP's Annual Report for 2006, the total number of shares in the hands of investors was 21,457.3m. This means that the number of BP shares transacted on the London Stock Exchange on that day represented only 0.47 per cent (that is, about 1 in 214) of the total.

Real World 6.8 shows how investment ratios can vary between different industry sectors.

Real World 6.8

How investment ratios vary between industries

Investment ratios can vary significantly between businesses and between industries. To give some indication of the range of variations that occur, the average dividend yield ratios and average P/E ratios for listed businesses in twelve different industries are shown in Figures 6.4 and 6.5, respectively.

The dividend yield ratios are calculated from the current market value of the shares and the most recent year's dividend paid.

Some industries tend to pay out lower dividends than others, leading to lower dividend yield ratios. The average for all Stock Exchange listed businesses was (as is shown in Figure 6.4) 2.83, but there is a wide variation with Chemicals at 1.68 and Banks at 4.43.

Figure 6.4 Average dividend yield ratios for businesses in a range of industries

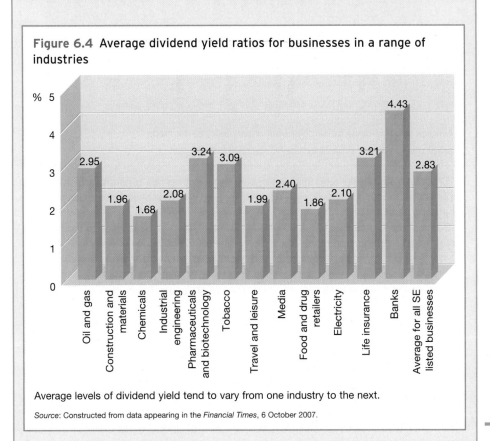

Average levels of dividend yield tend to vary from one industry to the next.

Source: Constructed from data appearing in the *Financial Times*, 6 October 2007.

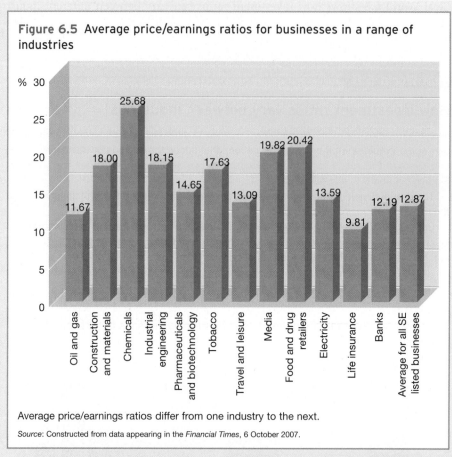

Figure 6.5 Average price/earnings ratios for businesses in a range of industries

Average price/earnings ratios differ from one industry to the next.

Source: Constructed from data appearing in the *Financial Times*, 6 October 2007.

Chemicals businesses tend to invest heavily in developing new products, which possibly explains their tendency to pay low dividends compared with their share prices. Banks, on the other hand, tend not to devote such a large percentage of their profits in new developments.

Some of the differences in the dividend yield ratios from one business to the next can be explained by the nature of the calculation of the ratio. The prices of shares at any given moment are based on expectations of their economic futures; dividends are actual past events. A business that had a good trading year recently may have paid a dividend that, in the light of investors' assessment on the business's economic future, may be high (a high dividend yield).

The P/E ratios are calculated from the current market value of the shares and the most recent year's earnings per share (EPS).

Businesses that have a high share price relative to their recent historic earnings have high P/E ratios. This may be because their future is regarded as economically bright, which may be the result of investing heavily in the future at the expense of recent profits (earnings). On the other hand, high P/Es also arise where businesses have recent low earnings but investors believe that their future is brighter. The average for all Stock Exchange listed businesses was 12.87, but Life Insurance was as low as 9.81 and Chemicals as high as 25.68.

Both Ali plc and Bhaskar plc operate electrical stores throughout the UK. The financial statements of each business for the year ended 30 June 2008 are as follows:

Balance sheets as at 30 June 2008

	Ali plc £000	Bhaskar plc £000
Non-current assets		
Property, plant and equipment		
(cost less depreciation)		
Land and buildings	360.0	510.0
Fixtures and fittings	87.0	91.2
	447.0	601.2
Current assets		
Inventories	592.0	403.0
Trade receivables	176.4	321.9
Cash at bank	84.6	91.6
	853.0	816.5
Total assets	1,300.0	1,417.7
Equity		
£1 ordinary shares	320.0	250.0
Retained profit	367.6	624.6
	687.6	874.6
Non-current liabilities		
Borrowings – loan notes	190.0	250.0
Current liabilities		
Trade payables	406.4	275.7
Taxation	16.0	17.4
	422.4	293.1
Total equity and liabilities	1,300.0	1,417.7

Income statements for the year ended 30 June 2008

	Ali plc £000	Bhaskar plc £000
Revenue	1,478.1	1,790.4
Cost of sales	(1,018.3)	(1,214.9)
Gross profit	459.8	575.5
Operating expenses	(308.5)	(408.6)
Operating profit	151.3	166.9
Interest payable	(19.4)	(27.5)
Profit before taxation	131.9	139.4
Taxation	(32.0)	(34.8)
Profit for the year	99.9	104.6

All purchases and sales were on credit. Ali plc had announced its intention to pay a dividend of £135,000 and Bhaskar plc £95,000 in respect of the year. The market values of a share in Ali plc and Bhaskar plc at the end of the year were £6.50 and £8.20 respectively.

Required:
For each business, calculate two ratios that are concerned with liquidity, gearing and investment (six ratios in total). What can you conclude from the ratios that you have calculated?

The answer to this question can be found at the back of the book in Appendix B.

Trend analysis

It is often helpful to see whether ratios are indicating trends. Key ratios can be plotted on a graph to provide a simple visual display of changes occurring over time. The trends occurring within a business may, for example, be plotted against trends for rival businesses or for the industry as a whole for comparison purposes. An example of trend analysis is shown in Real World 6.9.

Real World 6.9

Trend setting

In Figure 6.6 the current ratio of three of the UK's leading supermarkets is plotted over time. We can see that the current ratio of Tesco plc has risen slightly over the period but it was, nevertheless, consistently lower than that of Sainsbury and Morrison until 2005, when it overtook Morrison.

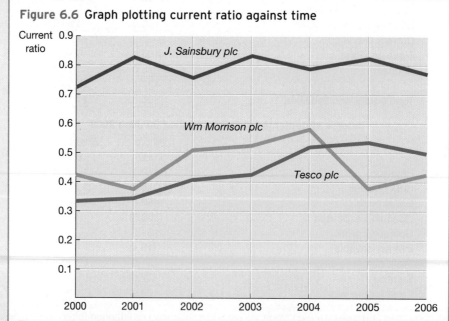

Figure 6.6 Graph plotting current ratio against time

The current ratio for three leading UK supermarkets is plotted for the financial years ending 2000 to 2006. This enables comparisons to be made regarding the ratio, both over time and between the businesses.

Many larger businesses publish certain key financial ratios as part of their annual reports to help users identify significant trends. These ratios typically cover several years' activities. Real World 6.10 shows part of the table of 'key performance measures' of Marks and Spencer plc (M&S), the well-known UK high street store.

Real World 6.10

Key performance measures of Marks and Spencer plc

	2007 52 weeks	2006 52 weeks	2005 52 weeks	2004 53 weeks	2003 52 weeks
Gross margin $\dfrac{\text{Gross profit}}{\text{Revenue}}$	38.9%	38.3%	34.7%	35.4%	34.8%
Net margin $\dfrac{\text{Operating profit}}{\text{Revenue}}$	12.2%	10.9%	8.0%	9.9%	8.6%
Net margin excluding property disposals and exceptional items	12.2%	11.0%	8.7%	10.2%	9.2%
Profitability $\dfrac{\text{Profit before tax}}{\text{Revenue}}$	10.9%	9.6%	6.7%	9.4%	8.4%
Profitability excluding property disposals and exceptional items	11.2%	9.6%	7.4%	9.7%	9.0%
Basic earnings per share $\dfrac{\text{Basic earnings}}{\substack{\text{Weighted average} \\ \text{ordinary shares in issue}}}$	39.1p	31.3p	17.6p	24.2p	21.8p
Earnings per share adjusted for property disposals and exceptional items	40.4p	31.4p	19.2p	24.7p	23.3p
Dividend cover $\dfrac{\substack{\text{Profit attributable} \\ \text{to shareholders}}}{\text{Dividend payable}}$	2.1x	2.2×	2.9×	2.1×	2.1×
Return on equity $\dfrac{\substack{\text{Profit attributable} \\ \text{to shareholders}}}{\substack{\text{Average equity} \\ \text{shareholders' funds}}}$	46.3%	50.0%	35.1%	25.2%	22.4%

Source: Marks and Spencer plc Annual Report 2007. Reproduced by kind permission of Marks and Spencer plc. The 2003 and 2004 results have not been restated following the adoption of the International Financial Reporting Standards in 2005. This means that the results over the five years are not strictly comparable.

After many years of profitable growth, M&S suffered a decline in its fortunes during the late 1990s. This was seen by the directors, and by many independent commentators, as arising from the business allowing itself to be drawn away from its traditional areas of strength. M&S reached its low point in the year ended March 2001 when it incurred a significant overall loss, with an operating profit well below that achieved in 1998. Steps were taken to deal with the problem and the improvements since 2003 are very clear from the table above. The return on equity (return on ordinary shareholders' funds) in 2007 is significantly better than for any other of the five years, except 2006. Although in 2005 both the gross profit and net (operating profit) margins are lower than in 2004, they both recovered strongly in 2006 and continued in 2007.

Using ratios to predict future outcomes

Financial ratios, based on current or past performance, are often used to help predict the future, though both the choice of ratios and the interpretation of results are normally dependent on the judgement of the analyst. Attempts have been made, however, to develop a more rigorous and systematic approach to the use of ratios for prediction purposes. In particular, researchers have shown an interest in the use of ratios to predict financial distress in a business. By financial distress we mean a business getting into financial difficulties or even being made 'bankrupt' and forced out of existence. Several methods and models using ratios have been developed that are claimed to predict future financial distress. Researchers have also developed ratio-based models with which to assess the supposed vulnerability of a business to takeover by another business. These areas, of course, are of interest to all those connected with the business. In the future, it is likely that further ratio-based models will be developed that predict other aspects of future performance.

Limitations of ratio analysis

Although ratios offer a quick and useful method of analysing the position and performance of a business, they are not without their problems and limitations. Some of the more important limitations are described below.

Quality of financial statements

It must always be remembered that ratios are based on financial statements, and the results of ratio analysis are dependent on the quality of these underlying statements. Ratios will inherit the limitations of the financial statements on which they are based. A significant example of this arises from the application of the prudence convention to internally generated intangible non-current assets (as compared with purchased ones). This convention tends to lead to assets of considerable value, such as goodwill and brand names, being excluded from the balance sheet. This can mean that ratios such as ROSF, ROCE and the gearing ratio fail to take account of these assets.

There is also the problem of deliberate attempts to make the financial statements misleading. We discussed this problem of *creative accounting* in Chapter 4.

Inflation

A persistent, though recently less severe, problem, in most western countries is that the financial statements of businesses can be distorted as a result of inflation. One effect of inflation is that the balance sheet values of assets held for any length of time may bear little relation to current values. Generally speaking, the balance sheet value of assets will be understated in current terms during a period of inflation as they are usually recorded at their original cost (less any amounts written off for depreciation).

This means that comparisons, either between businesses or between periods, will be hindered. A difference in, say, ROCE may simply be owing to the fact that assets in one of the balance sheets being compared were acquired more recently (ignoring the effect of depreciation on the asset values). Another effect of inflation is to distort the measurement of profit. Sales revenue for a period is often matched against costs from an earlier period because there is often a time lag between acquiring a particular resource and using it to help generate sales revenue. For example, inventories may be acquired at one point in time and sold perhaps a month or so later. During a period of inflation, this will mean that the expense may not reflect current prices. The cost of sales figure is usually based on the historic cost of the inventories concerned. As a result, expenses will be understated in the income statement and this, in turn, means that profit will be overstated. One effect of this will be to distort the profitability ratios discussed earlier.

The restricted vision of ratios

It is important not to rely exclusively on ratios, thereby losing sight of information contained in the underlying financial statements. As we saw earlier in the chapter, some items reported in these statements can be vital in assessing position and performance. For example, the total sales revenue, capital employed and profit figures may be useful in assessing changes in absolute size that occur over time, or differences in scale between businesses. Ratios do not provide such information. Ratios measure *relative* performance and position, and therefore provide only part of the picture. When comparing two businesses, therefore, it will often be useful to assess the absolute size of profits, as well as the relative profitability of each business. For example, Business A may generate £1m operating profit and have a ROCE of 15 per cent, and Business B may generate £100,000 operating profit and have a ROCE of 20 per cent. Although Business B has a higher level of *profitability*, as measured by ROCE, it generates lower total operating profits.

The basis for comparison

We saw earlier that if ratios are to be useful they require a basis for comparison. Moreover, it is important that the analyst compares like with like. However, no two businesses are identical, and the greater the differences between the businesses being compared, the greater the limitations of ratio analysis. Furthermore, any differences in accounting policies, financing methods (gearing levels) and financial year ends between businesses will add to the problems of comparison.

Balance sheet ratios

Because the balance sheet is only a 'snapshot' of the business at a particular moment in time, any ratios based on balance sheet figures, such as the liquidity ratios, may not be representative of the financial position of the business for the year as a whole. For example, it is common for a seasonal business to have a financial year end that coincides with a low point in business activity. As a result, inventories and trade receivables may be low at the balance sheet date, and so the liquidity ratios may also be low. A more representative picture of liquidity can only really be gained by taking additional measurements at other points in the year.

Real World 6.11 points out another way in which ratios are limited.

Real World 6.11

Remember, it's people that really count . . .

Lord Weinstock (1924–2002) was an influential industrialist whose management style and philosophy helped to shape management practice in many UK businesses. During his long and successful reign at GEC plc, a major engineering business, Lord Weinstock relied heavily on financial ratios to assess performance and to exercise control. In particular, he relied on ratios relating to sales revenue, expenses, trade receivables, profit margins and inventories turnover. However, he was keenly aware of the limitations of ratios and recognised that, ultimately, people produce profits.

In a memo written to GEC managers he pointed out that ratios are an aid to good management rather than a substitute for it. He wrote:

> The operating ratios are of great value as measures of efficiency but they are only the measures and not efficiency itself. Statistics will not design a product better, make it for a lower cost or increase sales. If ill-used, they may so guide action as to diminish resources for the sake of apparent but false signs of improvement.
>
> Management remains a matter of judgement, of knowledge of products and processes and of understanding and skill in dealing with people. The ratios will indicate how well all these things are being done and will show comparison with how they are done elsewhere. But they will tell us nothing about how to do them. That is what you are meant to do.

Source: Extract from *Arnold Weinstock and the Making of GEC*, S. Aris (Aurum Press, 1998), published in *The Sunday Times*, 22 February 1998, p. 3.

Summary

The main points of this chapter may be summarised as follows.

Ratio analysis

- Compares two related figures, usually both from the same set of financial statements.

- Is an aid to understanding what the financial statements really mean.

- Is an inexact science so results must be interpreted cautiously.

- Past periods, the performance of similar businesses and planned performance are often used to provide benchmark ratios.

- A brief overview of the financial statements can often provide insights that may not be revealed by ratios and/or may help in the interpretation of them.

Profitability ratios - concerned with effectiveness at generating profit

- Return on ordinary shareholders' funds (ROSF).
- Return on capital employed (ROCE).
- Operating profit margin.
- Gross profit margin.

Efficiency ratios - concerned with efficiency of using assets/resources

- Average inventories turnover period.
- Average settlement period for trade receivables.
- Average settlement period for trade payables.
- Sales revenue to capital employed.
- Sales revenue per employee.

Liquidity ratios - concerned with the ability to meet short-term obligations

- Current ratio.
- Acid test ratio.

Gearing ratios - concerned with the relationship between equity and debt financing

- Gearing ratio.
- Interest cover ratio.

Investment ratios - concerned with returns to shareholders

- Dividend payout ratio.
- Dividend yield ratio.
- Earnings per share.
- Price/earnings ratio.

Trend analysis

- Individual ratios can be tracked (for example, plotted on a graph) to detect trends.

Ratios as predictors of future outcomes

- Ratios can be used to help predict the future, particularly financial distress.

Limitations of ratio analysis

- Ratios are only as reliable as the financial statements from which they derive.
- Inflation can distort the information.
- Ratios have restricted vision.
- It can be difficult to find a suitable benchmark (for example, another business) as comparator.
- Some ratios could mislead due to the 'snapshot' nature of the balance sheet.

→ **Key terms**

return on ordinary shareholders' funds ratio (ROSF) p. 188
return on capital employed ratio (ROCE) p. 189
operating profit margin ratio p. 190
gross profit margin ratio p. 192
average inventories turnover period ratio p. 195
average settlement period for trade receivables ratio p. 196
average settlement period for trade payables ratio p. 197
sales revenue to capital employed ratio p. 198

sales revenue per employee ratio p. 199
current ratio p. 202
acid test ratio p. 203
financial gearing p. 204
gearing ratio p. 206
interest cover ratio p. 207
dividend payout ratio p. 210
dividend cover ratio p. 210
dividend yield ratio p. 211
dividend per share p. 211
earnings per share (EPS) p. 212
price/earnings ratio p. 212

Further reading

If you would like to explore the topics covered in this chapter in more depth, we recommend the following books:

Elliott, B. and Elliott, J., *Financial Accounting and Reporting* (12th edn), Financial Times Prentice Hall, 2008, chapters 28 and 29.

Revsine, L., Collins, D. and Johnson, W.B., *Financial Reporting and Analysis* (3rd edn), Prentice Hall, 2005, chapter 5.

Sutton, T., *Corporate Financial Accounting and Reporting* (2nd edn), Financial Times Prentice Hall, 2004, chapter 19.

Wild, J., Subramanyam, K. and Halsey, R., *Financial Statement Analysis* (9th edn), McGraw-Hill, 2006, chapters 8, 9 and 11.

? Review questions

Answers to these questions can be found at the back of the book in Appendix C.

6.1 Some businesses operate on a low operating profit margin (for example, a supermarket chain). Does this mean that the return on capital employed from the business will also be low?

6.2 What potential problems arise for the external analyst from the use of balance sheet figures in the calculation of financial ratios?

6.3 Two businesses operate in the same industry. One has an inventories turnover period that is longer than the industry average. The other has an inventories turnover period that is shorter than the industry average. Give three possible explanations for each business's inventories turnover period ratio.

6.4 Identify and discuss three reasons why the P/E ratio of two businesses operating within the same industry may differ.

 Exercises

Exercises 6.4 and 6.5 are more advanced than Exercises 6.1 to 6.3. Those with coloured numbers have answers at the back of the book in Appendix D.

> If you wish to try more exercises, visit MyAccountingLab/

6.1 I. Jiang (Western) Ltd has recently produced its financial statements for the current year. The directors are concerned that the return on capital employed (ROCE) had decreased from 14 per cent last year to 12 per cent for the current year.

The following reasons were suggested as to why this reduction in ROCE had occurred:

1 an increase in the gross profit margin;
2 a reduction in sales revenue;
3 an increase in overhead expenses;
4 an increase in amount of inventories held;
5 the repayment of some borrowings at the year end; and
6 an increase in the time taken for credit customers (trade receivables) to pay.

Required:
Taking each of these six suggested reasons in turn, state, with reasons, whether each of them could lead to a reduction in ROCE.

6.2 Amsterdam Ltd and Berlin Ltd are both engaged in retailing, but they seem to take a different approach to it according to the following information:

Ratio	Amsterdam Ltd	Berlin Ltd
Return on capital employed (ROCE)	20%	17%
Return on ordinary shareholders' funds (ROSF)	30%	18%
Average settlement period for trade receivables	63 days	21 days
Average settlement period for trade payables	50 days	45 days
Gross profit margin	40%	15%
Operating profit margin	10%	10%
Average inventories turnover period	52 days	25 days

Required:
Describe what this information indicates about the differences in approach between the two businesses. If one of them prides itself on personal service and one of them on competitive prices, which do you think is which and why?

6.3 Conday and Co. Ltd has been in operation for three years and produces antique repro-
duction furniture for the export market. The most recent set of financial statements for the
business is set out as follows:

Balance sheet as at 30 November

	£000
Non-current assets	
Property, plant and equipment (cost less depreciation)	
Land and buildings	228
Plant and machinery	762
	990
Current assets	
Inventories	600
Trade receivables	820
	1,420
Total assets	2,410
Equity	
Ordinary shares of £1 each	700
Retained earnings	365
	1,065
Non-current liabilities	
Borrowings – 9% loan notes (Note 1)	200
Current liabilities	
Trade payables	665
Taxation	48
Short-term borrowings (all bank overdraft)	432
	1,145
Total equity and liabilities	2,410

Income statement for the year ended 30 November

	£000
Revenue	2,600
Cost of sales	(1,620)
Gross profit	980
Selling and distribution expenses (Note 2)	(408)
Administration expenses	(194)
Operating profit	378
Finance expenses	(58)
Profit before taxation	320
Taxation	(95)
Profit for the year	225

Notes:
1 The loan notes are secured on the freehold land and buildings.
2 Selling and distribution expenses include £170,000 in respect of bad debts.
3 A dividend of £160,000 was paid on the ordinary shares during the year.
4 The directors have invited an investor to take up a new issue of ordinary shares in the
   business at £6.40 each making a total investment of £200,000. The directors wish to
   use the funds to finance a programme of further expansion.

Required:

(a) Analyse the financial position and performance of the business and comment on any features that you consider to be significant.

(b) State, with reasons, whether or not the investor should invest in the business on the terms outlined.

6.4 Threads Limited manufactures nuts and bolts, which are sold to industrial users. The abbreviated financial statements for 2007 and 2008 are as follows:

Income statements for the year ended 30 June

	2007 £000	2008 £000
Revenue	1,180	1,200
Cost of sales	(680)	(750)
Gross profit	500	450
Operating expenses	(200)	(208)
Depreciation	(66)	(75)
Operating profit	234	167
Interest	(–)	(8)
Profit before taxation	234	159
Taxation	(80)	(48)
Profit for the year	154	111

Balance sheets as at 30 June

	2007 £000	2008 £000
Non-current assets		
Property, plant and equipment	702	687
Current assets		
Inventories	148	236
Trade receivables	102	156
Cash	3	4
	253	396
Total assets	955	1,083
Equity		
Ordinary share capital of £1 (fully paid)	500	500
Retained earnings	256	295
	756	795
Non-current liabilities		
Borrowings – bank loan	–	50
Current liabilities		
Trade payables	60	76
Other payables and accruals	18	16
Taxation	40	24
Short-term borrowings (all bank overdraft)	81	122
	199	238
Total equity and liabilities	955	1,083

Dividends were paid on ordinary shares of £70,000 and £72,000 in respect of 2007 and 2008, respectively.

Required:

(a) Calculate the following financial ratios for *both* 2007 and 2008 (using year-end figures for balance sheet items):

1 return on capital employed
2 operating profit margin
3 gross profit margin
4 current ratio
5 acid test ratio
6 settlement period for trade receivables
7 settlement period for trade payables
8 inventories turnover period.

(b) Comment on the performance of Threads Limited from the viewpoint of a business considering supplying a substantial amount of goods to Threads Limited on usual trade credit terms.

6.5 Bradbury Ltd is a family-owned clothes manufacturer based in the southwest of England. For a number of years the chairman and managing director was David Bradbury. During his period of office, sales revenue had grown steadily at a rate of 2 to 3 per cent each year. David Bradbury retired on 30 November 2007 and was succeeded by his son Simon. Soon after taking office, Simon decided to expand the business. Within weeks he had successfully negotiated a five-year contract with a large clothes retailer to make a range of sports and leisurewear items. The contract will result in an additional £2m in sales revenue during each year of the contract. To fulfil the contract, Bradbury Ltd acquired new equipment and premises.

Financial information concerning the business is given below.

Income statements for the year ended 30 November

	2007	2008
	£000	£000
Revenue	9,482	11,365
Operating profit	914	1,042
Interest charges	(22)	(81)
Profit before taxation	892	961
Taxation	(358)	(386)
Profit for the year	534	575

Balance sheets as at 30 November

	2007 £000	2008 £000
Non-current assets		
Property, plant and equipment		
(cost less depreciation)		
Premises	5,240	7,360
Plant and equipment	2,375	4,057
	7,615	11,417
Current assets		
Inventories	2,386	3,420
Trade receivables	2,540	4,280
	4,926	7,700
Total assets	12,541	19,117
Equity		
Share capital	2,000	2,000
Reserves	7,813	8,268
	9,813	10,268
Non-current liabilities		
Borrowing – loans	1,220	3,675
Current liabilities		
Trade payables	1,157	2,245
Taxation	179	193
Short-term borrowings (all bank overdraft)	172	2,736
	1,508	5,174
Total equity and liabilities	12,541	19,117

Dividends of £120,000 were paid on ordinary shares in respect of each of the two years.

Required:
(a) Calculate, for each year (using year-end figures for balance sheet items), the following ratios:
   1 operating profit margin
   2 return on capital employed
   3 current ratio
   4 gearing ratio
   5 days trade receivables (settlement period)
   6 sales revenue to capital employed.
(b) Using the above ratios, and any other ratios or information you consider relevant, comment on the results of the expansion programme.

Part 2

MANAGEMENT ACCOUNTING

Chapter 7

Cost-volume-profit analysis

Introduction

This chapter is concerned with the relationship between volume of activity, costs and profit. Broadly, costs can be analysed as those that are fixed, relative to the volume of activity, and those that vary with the volume of activity. We shall consider how we can use knowledge of this relationship to make decisions and to assess risk, particularly in the context of short-term decisions. Though the distinction between financial accounting and management accounting is rather blurred, and much relating to the financial statements that we have discussed so far in the book relates to providing information to managers, this chapter is the first one that is clearly in the area of management accounting.

Learning outcomes

When you have completed this chapter, you should be able to:

- distinguish between fixed costs and variable costs and use this distinction to explain the relationship between costs, volume and profit;

- prepare a break-even chart and deduce the break-even point for some activity;

- discuss the weaknesses of break-even analysis;

- demonstrate the way in which marginal analysis can be used when making short-term decisions.

The behaviour of costs

Costs represent the resources that have to be sacrificed to achieve a business objective. The objective may be, for example, to make a particular product, to provide a particular service, or to operate a particular hospital for a month. The costs incurred by a business may be classified in various ways and one important way is according to how they behave in relation to changes in the volume of activity. There are costs that are fixed (stay the same) when changes occur to the volume of activity, and costs that vary according to the volume of activity. These are known as fixed costs and variable costs respectively.

A restaurant manager's salary would normally provide an example of a fixed cost of operating the restaurant. The cost to the restaurant of buying the raw food would be a typical variable cost.

We shall see in this chapter that it can be of great value to the decision-maker to know how much of each type of cost is associated with some particular activity.

Fixed costs

The way in which fixed costs behave can be shown by preparing a graph that plots the fixed costs of a business against the level of activity, as in Figure 7.1. The distance 0F represents the amount of fixed costs, and this stays the same irrespective of the volume of activity.

Activity 7.1

Can you give some examples of costs that are likely to be fixed for a hairdressing salon? (Assume here that the business does not own its premises and that all those working in the salon are employees.)

We came up with the following:

- rent
- insurance
- cleaning costs
- staff salaries.

These costs seem likely to be the same irrespective of the number of customers having their hair cut or styled.

Staff salaries and wages tend to be fixed costs. People are generally not paid according to the volume of output, and it is not normal to dismiss staff when there is a short-term downturn in activity. If there is a long-term downturn, or at least if it looks

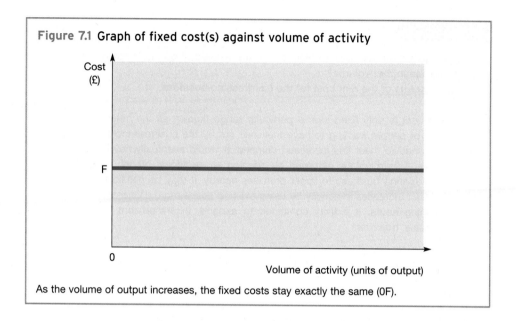

Figure 7.1 Graph of fixed cost(s) against volume of activity

Cost (£)

F

0

Volume of activity (units of output)

As the volume of output increases, the fixed costs stay exactly the same (0F).

that way to management, redundancies may occur, with fixed-cost savings. This, however, is true of all costs. If there is seen to be a likely reduction in demand, the business may decide to close some branches and make rental cost savings. Thus 'fixed' does not mean set in stone for all time; it usually means fixed over the short to medium term.

There are circumstances in which labour costs are variable (for example, where employees are paid according to how much output they produce), but this is relatively unusual. Whether labour costs are fixed or variable depends on the circumstances in the particular case concerned.

It is important to be clear that 'fixed', in this context, means only that the cost is not altered by changes in the volume of activity. Fixed costs are likely to be affected by inflation. If rent (a typical fixed cost) goes up because of inflation, a fixed cost will have increased, but not because of a change in the volume of activity.

Similarly, the level of fixed costs does not stay the same, irrespective of the time period involved. Fixed costs are almost always *time-based*: that is, they vary with the length of time concerned. The rental charge for two months is normally twice that for one month. Thus fixed costs normally vary with time, but (of course) not with the volume of output. We should note that when we talk of fixed costs being, say, £1,000, we must add the period concerned, say, £1,000 a month.

Activity 7.2

Do fixed costs stay the same irrespective of the volume of output, even where there is a massive rise in that volume?

Think in terms of the rent cost for the hairdressing business.

In fact, the rent is only fixed over a particular range (known as the 'relevant' range). If the number of people wanting to have their hair cut by the business increased, and the business wished to meet this increased demand, it would eventually have to expand its physical size. This might be achieved by opening an additional branch, or perhaps by moving the existing business to larger premises nearby. It may be possible to cope with relatively minor increases in activity by using existing space more efficiently, or by having longer opening hours. If activity continued to expand, increased rent charges would seem inevitable, however.

In practice, the situation described in Activity 7.2 would look something like Figure 7.2.

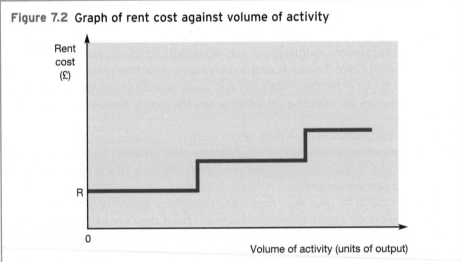

Figure 7.2 Graph of rent cost against volume of activity

As the volume of activity increases from zero, the rent (a fixed cost) is unaffected. At a particular point, the volume of activity cannot increase further without additional space being rented. The cost of renting the additional space will cause a 'step' in the rent cost. The higher rent cost will continue unaffected if volume rises further until eventually another step point is reached.

At lower volumes of activity, the rent cost shown in Figure 7.2 would be OR. As the volume of activity expands, the accommodation becomes inadequate and further expansion requires an increase in premises and, therefore, cost. This higher level of accommodation provision will enable further expansion to take place. Eventually, additional costs will need to be incurred if further expansion is to occur. Fixed costs that behave like this are often referred to as stepped fixed costs.

Variable costs

We saw earlier that variable costs are costs that vary with the volume of activity. In a manufacturing business, for example, this would include raw materials used.

Variable costs can be represented graphically as in Figure 7.3. At zero volume of activity the variable cost is zero. The cost increases in a straight line as activity increases.

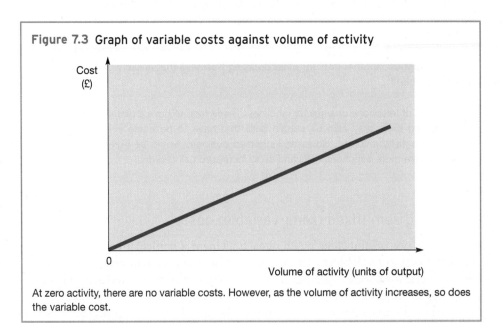

Figure 7.3 Graph of variable costs against volume of activity

At zero activity, there are no variable costs. However, as the volume of activity increases, so does the variable cost.

Activity 7.3

Can you think of some examples of variable costs in the hairdressing business?

We can think of a couple:

- lotions and other materials used;
- laundry costs for washing towels.

As with many types of business activity, variable costs of hairdressers tend to be relatively light in comparison with fixed costs, that is, fixed costs tend to make up the bulk of total costs.

The straight line for variable cost on the graph implies that the variable cost will normally be the same per unit of activity, irrespective of the volume of activity concerned. We shall consider the practicality of this assumption a little later in this chapter.

Semi-fixed (semi-variable) costs

In some cases, costs have an element of both fixed and variable cost. These can be described as semi-fixed (semi-variable) costs. An example might be the electricity cost for the hairdressing business. Some of this will be for heating and lighting, and this part is probably fixed, at least until the volume of activity expands to a point where longer opening hours or larger premises are necessary. The other part of the cost will vary with the volume of activity. Here we are talking about such things as power for hairdryers.

Activity 7.4

Can you suggest another cost for a hairdressing business that is likely to be semi-fixed (semi-variable)?

We thought of telephone charges for landlines. These tend to have a rental element, which is fixed, and there may also be certain calls that have to be made irrespective of the volume of activity involved. However, increased business would be likely to lead to the need to make more telephone calls and so to increased call charges.

Estimating semi-fixed (semi-variable) costs

Usually, it is not obvious how much of each element a particular cost contains. It is normally necessary to look at past experience. If we have data on what the electricity cost has been for various volumes of activity, say the relevant electricity bills over several recent three-month periods (electricity is usually billed by the quarter), we can estimate the fixed and variable portions. This may be done graphically, as shown in Figure 7.4. We tend to use past data here purely because they provide us with an estimate of future costs.

Each of the dots in Figure 7.4 is the electricity charge for a particular quarter plotted against the volume of activity (probably measured in terms of sales revenue) for the same quarter. The diagonal line on the graph is the *line of best fit*. This means that this was the line that best seemed (to us, at least) to represent the data. A better estimate can usually be made using a statistical technique (*least squares regression*), which does not involve drawing graphs and making estimates. In practice, though, it probably makes little difference which approach is taken.

From the graph we can say that the fixed element of the electricity cost is the amount represented by the vertical distance from the origin at zero (bottom left-hand corner) to the point where the line of best fit crosses the vertical axis of the graph. The variable cost per unit is the amount that the graph rises for each increase in the volume of activity.

By breaking down semi-fixed costs in this way into their fixed and variable elements we are left with just two types of cost: fixed costs and variable costs. Armed with this knowledge it is possible to make predictions regarding total and per-unit costs at

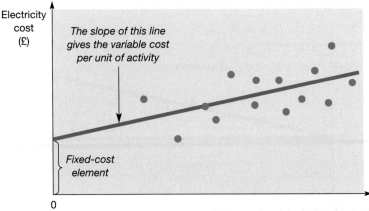

Figure 7.4 Graph of electricity cost against volume of activity

The slope of this line gives the variable cost per unit of activity

Electricity cost (£)

Fixed-cost element

0

Volume of activity (units of output)

Here the electricity bill for a time period (for example, three months) is plotted against the volume of activity for that same period. This is done for a series of periods. A line is then drawn that best 'fits' the various points on the graph. From this line we can then deduce both the cost at zero activity (the fixed element) and the slope of the line (the variable element).

various projected levels of output. Such predictive information can be very useful to decision-makers and much of the rest of this chapter will be devoted to seeing how, starting with break-even analysis.

Finding the break-even point

If, in respect of a particular activity, we know the total fixed costs for a period and the total variable cost per unit, we can produce a graph like the one shown in Figure 7.5.

The bottom part of Figure 7.5 shows the fixed-cost area. Added to this is the variable cost, the wedge-shaped portion at the top of the graph. The uppermost line represents the total cost at any particular volume of activity. This total is the vertical distance between the graph's horizontal axis and the uppermost line for the particular volume of activity concerned. Logically, the total cost at zero activity is the amount of the fixed costs. This is because, even where there is nothing going on, the business will still be paying rent, salaries and so on, at least in the short term. The fixed cost is augmented by the amount of the relevant variable costs, to give the total cost, as the volume of activity increases.

If we take this total cost graph in Figure 7.5, and superimpose on it a line representing total revenue for each volume of activity, we obtain the break-even chart. This is shown in Figure 7.6.

Note in Figure 7.6 that, at zero volume of activity (zero sales), there is zero sales revenue. The profit (or loss), which is the difference between total sales revenue and

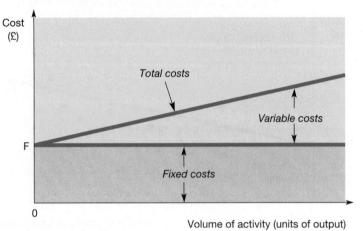

Figure 7.5 Graph of total cost against volume of activity

The bottom part of the graph represents the fixed-cost element. To this is added the wedge-shaped top portion, which represents the variable costs. The two parts together represent total cost. At zero activity, the variable costs are zero, so total costs equal fixed costs. As activity increases so does total cost, but only because variable costs increase. We are assuming that there are no steps in the fixed costs.

Figure 7.6 Break-even chart

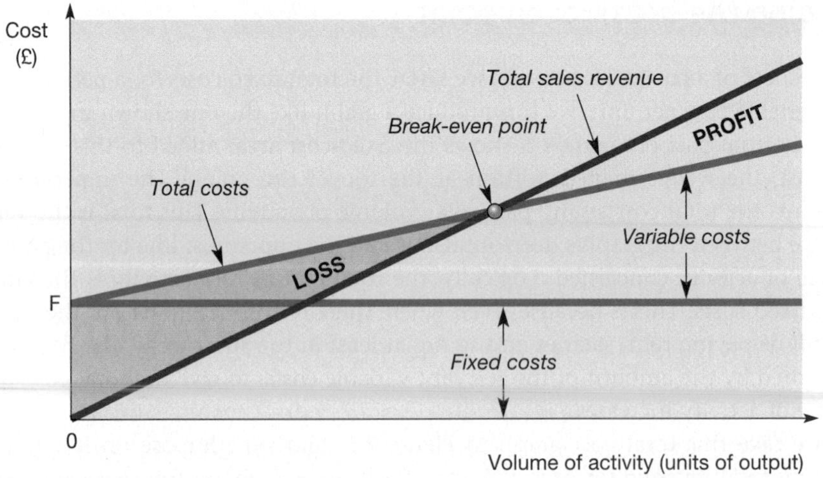

The sloping line starting at zero represents the sales revenue at various volumes of activity. The point at which this finally catches up with the sloping total cost line, which starts at F, is the break-even point (BEP). Below this point a loss is made, above it a profit.

total cost, for some particular volume of activity is the vertical distance between the total sales revenue line and the total cost line at that volume of activity. Where the volume of activity is at break-even point (BEP), there is no vertical distance between these two lines (total sales revenue equals total costs) and so there is no profit or loss; that is, the activity *breaks even*. Where the volume of activity is below the BEP, a loss will be incurred because total costs exceed total sales revenue. Where the business operates at a volume of activity above the BEP, there will be a profit because total sales revenue will exceed total costs. The further below the BEP, the higher the loss: the further above the BEP, the higher the profit.

As may be imagined, deducing BEPs by graphical means is a laborious business. However, since the relationships in the graph are all linear (that is, the lines are all straight), it is easy to calculate the BEP.

We know that at the BEP (but not at any other point):

Total sales revenue = Total costs

(At all other points except the BEP, either total sales revenue will exceed total cost or the other way round. Only at the BEP are they equal.) That is,

Total sales revenue = Fixed costs + Total variable costs

If we call the number of units of output at BEP *b*, then

$$b \times \text{Sales revenue per unit} = \text{Fixed costs} + (b \times \text{Variable costs per unit})$$

so:

$$(b \times \text{Sales revenue per unit}) - (b \times \text{Variable costs per unit}) = \text{Fixed costs}$$

or

$$b \times (\text{Sales revenue per unit} - \text{Variable costs per unit}) = \text{Fixed costs}$$

giving

$$b = \frac{\text{Fixed costs}}{\text{Sales revenue per unit} - \text{Variable costs per unit}}$$

If we look at the break-even chart in Figure 7.6, this seems logical. The total cost line starts off at point F, higher than the starting point for the total sales revenue line (zero) by amount F (the amount of the fixed costs). Because the sales revenue per unit is greater than the variable cost per unit, the sales revenue line will gradually catch up with the total cost line. The rate at which it will catch up is dependent on the relative steepness of the two lines and the amount that it has to catch up (the fixed costs). Bearing in mind that the slopes of the two lines are the variable cost per unit and the selling price per unit, the above equation for calculating *b* looks perfectly logical.

Although the BEP can be calculated quickly and simply, as shown, it does not mean that the graphical approach of the break-even chart is without value. The chart shows the relationship between cost, volume and profit over a range of output and in a form that can easily be understood by non-financial managers. The break-even chart can therefore be a useful device for explaining this relationship.

Example 7.1

Cottage Industries Ltd makes baskets. The fixed costs of operating the workshop for a month total £500. Each basket requires materials that cost £2. Each basket takes one hour to make, and the business pays the basket-makers £10 an hour. The basket-makers are all on contracts such that if they do not work for any reason, they are not paid. The baskets are sold to a wholesaler for £14 each.

What is the BEP for basket-making for the business?

The BEP (in number of baskets) is:

$$\text{BEP} = \frac{\text{Fixed costs}}{(\text{Sales revenue per unit} - \text{Variable costs per unit})}$$

$$= \frac{£500}{£14 - (£2 + £10)} = 250 \text{ baskets per month}$$

Note that the BEP must be expressed with respect to a period of time.

Real World 7.1 shows information on the BEPs of three well-known businesses.

Real World 7.1

BE at BA, Ryanair and easyJet

Commercial airlines seem to pay a lot of attention to their BEPs and their 'load factors', that is, their actual level of activity. Figure 7.7 shows the BEPs and load factors for three

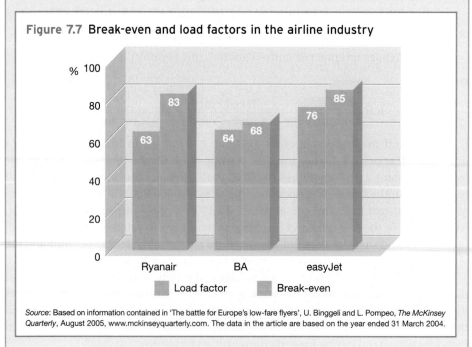

Figure 7.7 Break-even and load factors in the airline industry

Source: Based on information contained in 'The battle for Europe's low-fare flyers', U. Binggeli and L. Pompeo, *The McKinsey Quarterly*, August 2005, www.mckinseyquarterly.com. The data in the article are based on the year ended 31 March 2004.

well-known airlines operating from the UK. British Airways (BA) is a traditional airline. Ryanair and easyJet are both 'no-frills' carriers, which means that passengers receive lower levels of service in return for lower fares. All three operate flights within the UK and from the UK to other European countries. Only BA operates flights beyond Europe. We can see that all three airlines are making operating profits as each has a load factor greater than its BEP.

Activity 7.5

Can you think of reasons why the managers of a business might find it useful to know the BEP of some activity that they are planning to undertake?

The usefulness of being able to deduce the BEP is that it makes it possible to compare the planned or expected volume of activity with the BEP and so make a judgement about risk. Planning to operate only just above the break-even volume of activity may indicate that it is a risky venture, since only a small fall from the planned level could lead to a loss.

Activity 7.6

Cottage Industries Ltd (see Example 7.1) expects to sell 500 baskets a month. The business has the opportunity to rent a basket-making machine. Doing so would increase the total fixed costs of operating the workshop for a month to £3,000. Using the machine would reduce the labour time to half an hour per basket. The basket-makers would still be paid £10 an hour.

(a) How much profit would the business make each month from selling baskets
  ■ assuming that the basket-making machine is not rented and
  ■ assuming that it is rented?
(b) What is the BEP if the machine is rented?
(c) What do you notice about the figures that you calculate?

(a) Estimated monthly profit from basket-making:

		Without the machine £	With the machine £
Sales revenue	(500 × £14)	7,000	7,000
Materials	(500 × £2)	(1,000)	(1,000)
Labour	(500 × 1 × £10)	(5,000)	
	(500 × ½ × £10)		(2,500)
Fixed costs		(500)	(3,000)
Profit		500	500

(b) The BEP (in number of baskets) with the machine:

$$BEP = \frac{Fixed\ costs}{Sales\ revenue\ per\ unit - Variable\ costs\ per\ unit}$$

$$= \frac{£3,000}{£14 - (£2 + £5)} = 429\ baskets\ a\ month$$

The BEP without the machine is 250 baskets per month (see Example 7.1).

(c) There seems to be nothing to choose between the two manufacturing strategies regarding profit, at the projected sales volume. There is, however, a distinct difference between the two strategies regarding the BEP. Without the machine, the actual volume of sales could fall by a half of that which is projected (from 500 to 250) before the business would fail to make a profit. With the machine, however, just a 14 per cent fall (from 500 to 429) would be enough to cause the business to fail to make a profit. On the other hand, for each additional basket sold above the estimated 500, an additional profit of only £2 (that is, £14 – (£2 + £10)) would be made without the machine, whereas £7 (that is, £14 – (£2 + £5)) would be made with the machine. (Note that knowledge of the BEP and the projected volume of activity gives some basis for assessing the riskiness of the activity.)

We shall take a closer look at the relationship between fixed costs, variable costs and break-even, together with any advice that we might give the management of Cottage Industries Ltd, after we have briefly considered the notion of contribution.

Contribution

The bottom part of the break-even formula (sales revenue per unit less variable costs per unit) is known as the contribution per unit. Thus, for the basket-making activity, without the machine the contribution per unit is £2, and with the machine it is £7. This can be quite a useful figure to know in a decision-making context. It is called 'contribution' because it contributes to meeting the fixed costs and, if there is any excess, it also contributes to profit.

We shall see, a little later in this chapter, how knowing the amount of the contribution generated by a particular activity can be valuable in making short-term decisions of various types, as well as being useful in the BEP calculation.

Margin of safety

The margin of safety is the extent to which the planned volume of output or sales lies above the BEP. Going back to Activity 7.6, we saw that the following situation exists:

	Number of baskets	
	Without the machine	With the machine
Expected volume of sales	500	500
BEP	250	429
Difference (margin of safety):		
Number of baskets	250	71
Percentage of estimated volume of sales	50%	14%

Activity 7.7

What advice would you give Cottage Industries Ltd about renting the machine, on the basis of the values for margin of safety?

It is a matter of personal judgement, which in turn is related to individual attitudes to risk, as to which strategy to adopt. Most people, however, would prefer the strategy of not renting the machine, since the margin of safety between the expected volume of activity and the BEP is much greater. Thus, for the same level of return the risk will be lower without renting the machine.

The relative margins of safety are directly linked to the relationship between the selling price per basket, the variable costs per basket and the fixed costs per month. Without the machine the contribution (selling price less variable costs) per basket is £2; with the machine it is £7. On the other hand, without the machine the fixed costs are £500 a month; with the machine they are £3,000. This means that, with the machine, the contributions have more fixed costs to 'overcome' before the activity becomes profitable. However, the rate at which the contributions can overcome fixed costs is higher with the machine, because variable costs are lower. This means that one more, or one less, basket sold has a greater impact on profit than it does if the machine is not rented. The contrast between the two scenarios is shown graphically in Figures 7.8(a) and (b).

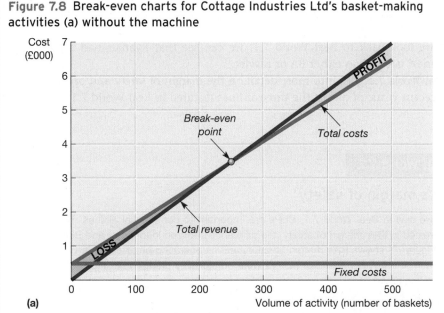

Figure 7.8 Break-even charts for Cottage Industries Ltd's basket-making activities (a) without the machine

Without the machine the contribution is low. Thus, each additional basket sold does not make a dramatic difference to the profit or loss. With the machine, however, the opposite is true, and small increases or decreases in the sales volume will have a marked effect on the profit or loss.

Figure 7.8 (b) with the machine

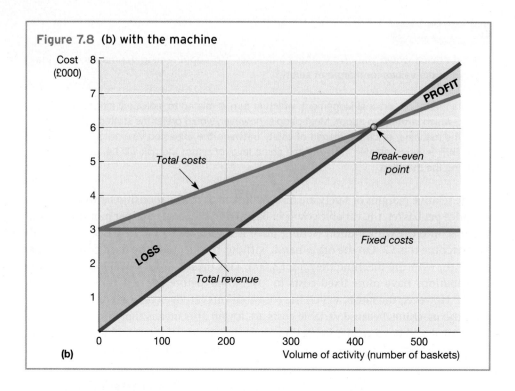

(b)

If we look back to Real World 7.1, we can see that Ryanair had a much larger margin of safety than either BA or easyJet.

Real World 7.2 goes into more detail on the margin of safety and operating profit, over recent years, of one of the three airlines featured in Real World 7.1.

BA's margin of safety

As we saw in Real World 7.1, BEPs are important to commercial airlines. They are also interested in their margin of safety (the difference between load factor and BEP).

Figure 7.9 shows BA's margin of safety and its operating profit over a five-year period. In each of the years, the load factors were comfortably greater than the BEP. This led to operating profits.

Source: British Airways plc Annual Reports 2003 to 2007.

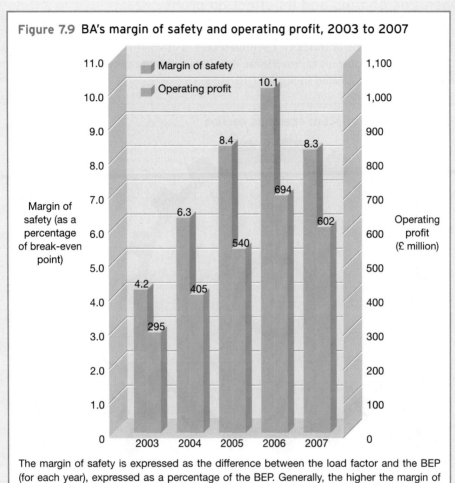

Figure 7.9 BA's margin of safety and operating profit, 2003 to 2007

The margin of safety is expressed as the difference between the load factor and the BEP (for each year), expressed as a percentage of the BEP. Generally, the higher the margin of safety, the higher the operating profit.

Source: Derived from information contained in British Airways plc Annual Reports 2003 to 2007.

Operating gearing

The relationship between contribution and fixed costs is known as operating gearing (or operational gearing). An activity with relatively high fixed costs compared with its variable costs is said to have high operating gearing. Thus, Cottage Industries Ltd has higher operating gearing using the machine than not using it. Renting the machine increases the level of operating gearing quite dramatically because it causes an increase in fixed costs, but at the same time it leads to a reduction in variable costs per basket.

Operating gearing and its effect on profit

The reason for the word 'gearing' to be used in this context is that, as with inter-meshing gear wheels of different circumferences, a circular movement in one of the factors (volume of output) causes a more than proportionate circular movement in the other (profit), as illustrated in Figure 7.10.

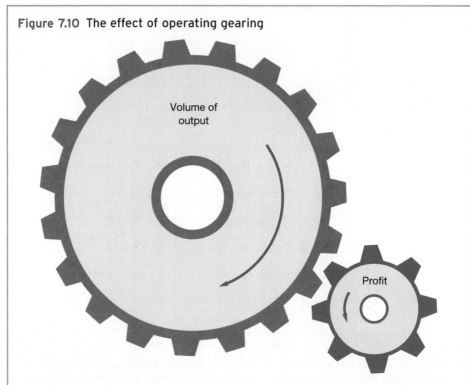

Figure 7.10 The effect of operating gearing

Where operating gearing is relatively high, as in the diagram, a small amount of circular motion in the volume wheel causes a relatively large amount of circular motion in the profit wheel. An increase in volume would cause a disproportionately greater increase in profit. The equivalent would also be true of a decrease in activity, however.

Increasing the level of operating gearing makes profits more sensitive to changes in the volume of activity. We can demonstrate operating gearing with Cottage Industries Ltd's basket-making activities as follows:

	Without the machine			With the machine		
Volume (number of baskets)	500	1,000	1,500	500	1,000	1,500
	£	£	£	£	£	£
Contributions*	1,000	2,000	3,000	3,500	7,000	10,500
Less fixed costs	(500)	(500)	(500)	(3,000)	(3,000)	(3,000)
Profit	500	1,500	2,500	500	4,000	7,500

* £2 per basket without the machine and £7 per basket with it.

Note that, without the machine (low operating gearing), a doubling of the output from 500 to 1,000 units brings a trebling of the profit. With the machine (high operating gearing), doubling output causes profit to rise by eight times. At the same time, reductions in the volume of output tend to have a more damaging effect on profit where the operating gearing is higher.

Operating gearing is quite similar in nature and effect to financial gearing, which we met in Chapter 6.

Activity 7.8

In general terms, what types of business activity tend to have the highest operating gearing? (*Hint*: Cottage Industries Ltd might give you some idea.)

In general, activities that are capital-intensive tend to have higher operating gearing. This is because renting or owning capital equipment gives rise to additional fixed costs, but it can also give rise to lower variable costs.

Real World 7.3 shows how a very well-known business has benefited from high operating gearing.

Real World 7.3

Sky-high operating gearing

British Sky Broadcasting Group plc (Sky), the satellite television broadcaster, is an obvious example of a business with high operating gearing. Nearly all of its costs are fixed in that they do not vary with the number of subscribers that it has or the value of its advertising revenues. This means that any increase in total revenues is likely to have a stron favourable effect on profit. The business acknowledged this in its 2006 annual report where it said:

> We currently expect our operating margin to grow in the long-term, as a result of the operational gearing of our business as we expect total revenues to increase at a faster rate than operating costs.

Source: British Sky Broadcasting Group plc Annual Report 2006, p. 45.

Profit-volume charts

A slight variant of the break-even chart is the profit-volume (PV) chart. A typical PV chart is shown in Figure 7.11.

The PV chart is obtained by plotting loss or profit against volume of activity. The slope of the graph is equal to the contribution per unit, since each additional unit sold

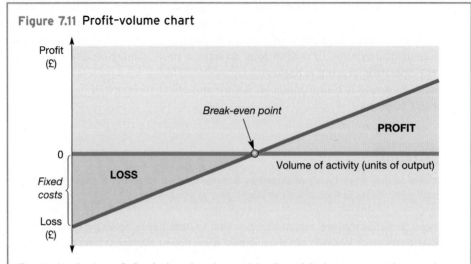

Figure 7.11 Profit-volume chart

The sloping line is profit (loss) plotted against activity. As activity increases, so does total contribution (sales revenue less variable costs). At zero activity there are no contributions, so there will be a loss equal in amount to the total fixed costs.

decreases the loss, or increases the profit, by the sales revenue per unit less the variable cost per unit. At zero volume of activity there are no contributions, so there is a loss equal to the amount of the fixed costs. As the volume of activity increases, the amount of the loss gradually decreases until the BEP is reached. Beyond the BEP, profits increase as activity increases.

As we can see, the PV chart does not tell us anything not shown by the break-even chart. On the other hand, information is perhaps more easily absorbed from the PV chart. This is particularly true of the profit (or loss) at any volume of activity. The break-even chart shows this as the vertical distance between the total cost and total sales revenue lines. The PV chart, in effect, combines the total sales revenue and total variable cost lines, which means that profit (or loss) is directly readable.

Failing to break even

Where a business fails to reach its BEP, or only just achieves it, steps must be taken to remedy the problem: there must be an increase in sales revenue or a reduction in costs, or both of these. Real World 7.4 discusses the results for the year ended 3 March 2007 of Blacks Leisure Group plc (the retailer of outdoor wear and camping equipment, which trades through Blacks, Millets, O'Neill, Freespirit and Mambo). It points out that, because the business has high operating (operational) gearing, a fall in sales revenue from the previous year had a disproportionate effect on profit.

Real World 7.4

Blacks nearly in the red

Results for the year to March 3 showed the outdoor wear group just managed to break even, with underlying profit of £100,000 on sales little changed at £298m, in line with expectations after its most recent profit warning.

Russell Hardy, chief executive of Blacks, said there had been 'some pleasing signs of good growth from the camping business' but that the company had endured a 'tough April'.

Blacks has traditionally performed well in wet summers and cold winters and claims that 'global warming' has brought about much of its weaker performance.

'In terms of weather proofing the business, we've done a lot of work for this season but my sense is it's going to take another couple of seasons to put the business in a position where it can cope with consistently drier weather,' said Mr Hardy.

During the year, like-for-like sales fell 2.7 per cent and high operational gearing meant margins fell sharply.

Source: Extracts from 'Blacks Leisure falls into the red', Tom Braithwaiteand Maggie Urry, *Financial Times*, 4 May 2007.

Weaknesses of break-even analysis

As we have seen, break-even analysis can provide some useful insights concerning the important relationship between fixed costs, variable costs and the volume of activity. It does, however, have its weaknesses. There are three general problems:

- *Non-linear relationships*. The normal approach to break-even analysis assumes that the relationships between sales revenues, variable costs and volume are strictly straight-line (linear) ones. In real life this is unlikely to be the cases; we shall look at the reasons for this in Activity 7.9 (below). Non-linear relationships are probably not a major problem, since
  - break-even analysis is normally conducted in advance of the activity actually taking place. Our ability to predict future costs, revenues and so on is somewhat limited, so what are probably minor variations from strict linearity are likely to be insignificant, compared with other forecasting errors; and
  - most businesses operate within a narrow range of volume of activity; over short ranges, curved lines tend to be relatively straight;
- *Stepped fixed costs*. Most fixed costs are not fixed over all volumes of activity. They tend to be 'stepped' in the way depicted in Figure 7.2. This means that, in practice, great care must be taken in making assumptions about fixed costs. The problem is particularly heightened because most activities will involve fixed costs of various types (rent, supervisory salaries, administration costs and so on), all of which are likely to have steps at different points.
- *Multi-product businesses*. Most businesses do not offer just one product or service. This is a problem for break-even analysis since it raises the question of the effect of additional sales of one product or service on sales of another of the business's products

or services. There is also the problem of identifying the fixed costs of one particular activity. Fixed costs tend to relate to more than one activity – for example, two activities may be carried out in the same rented premises. There are ways of dividing fixed costs between activities, but these tend to be arbitrary, and this calls into question the value of the break-even analysis and any conclusions reached.

Activity 7.9

We saw above that, in practice, relationships between costs, revenues and volumes of activity are not necessarily straight-line ones.
  Can you think of any reasons for this and examples of it?

We thought of the following:

- *Economies of scale with labour.* A business may do things more economically where there is a high volume of activity than is possible at lower levels of activity. It may, for example, be possible for employees to specialise.
- *Economies of scale with buying goods or services.* A business may find it cheaper to buy in goods and services where it is buying in bulk.
- *Diseconomies of scale.* This may mean that the per-unit cost of output is higher at higher levels of activity. For example, it may be necessary to pay higher rates of pay to workers to recruit the additional staff needed at higher volumes of activity.
- *Lower sales prices at high levels of activity.* It may not be possible to achieve high levels of sales activity without lowering the selling price.

Despite some problems, the notions of break-even analysis and BEP seem to be widely used. The media frequently refer to the BEP for businesses and activities. For example, there is seemingly constant discussion about Eurotunnel's BEP and whether it will ever be reached. Similarly, the number of people regularly needed to pay to watch a football team so that the club breaks even often seems to be referred to.

Real World 7.5 shows specific references to break-even point for three organisations.

Real World 7.5

Breaking even is breaking out all over

Waterford breaking even

Waterford Wedgwood plc, the ceramics and crystal business, expects to break even in the year ending 31 March 2008, following several years of heavy losses.

Source: 'Waterford chipping away at losses', John Murray Brown, *Financial Times*, 28 June 2007.

Superjumbo break-even point grows

German industrial group EADS is developing the Airbus A380 aircraft. The aircraft can carry up to 555 passengers on each flight. When EADS approved development of the plane in 2000, it was estimated that the business would need to sell 250 of them to break even. By

2005, the break-even number had increased to 270, but by late 2006 the costs of development had increased to the point where it was estimated that it would require sales of 420 of the aircraft for it to break even. Total sales of the aircraft are expected to be 750 over its commercial lifetime, but by August 2007 the business had only 173 firm orders.

Source: Taken from 'Airbus raises A380 break even target', Kevin Done and Gerrit Wiesmann, *Financial Times*, 20 October 2006, and 'Airbus sets departure date for A380 after 19-month delay', Kevin Done, *Financial Times*, 17 August 2007.

Harry Potter only breaks even
Waterstone's sales benefited from the release of the book *Harry Potter and the Deathly Hallows* during the summer of 2007, but this did not help profits as the book was sold at half price and so only broke even. Waterstone is a part of the HMV Group plc.

Source: Taken from 'HMV in cautious summer recovery', Tom Braithwaite and Lucy Killgren, *Financial Times*, 7 September 2007.

A 2003 survey of management accounting practice in the United States (Ernst and Young, *Survey of Management Accounting*, 2003) found that 62 per cent of businesses use break-even analysis extensively, with a further 22 per cent considering using the technique in the future. The situation is probably much the same in other developed countries.

Using contribution to make decisions: marginal analysis

When we are trying to decide between two or more possible courses of action, *only costs that vary with the decision should be included in the decision analysis.*

Activity 7.10

A householder wants a house decorated. Two decorators have been asked to price the job. One of them will do the work for £250, the other one wants £300, in both cases on the basis that the householder will supply the materials. It is believed that the two decorators will do an equally good job. The materials will cost £200 irrespective of which decorator does the work. Assuming that the householder wants the house decorated at the lower cost, which decorator should be asked to do the work? Is the cost of the materials relevant to the decision?

Clearly the first of the two decorators should be selected. The cost of the materials is irrelevant because it will be the same in each case. It is only possible to distinguish rationally between courses of action on the basis of differences between them.

In Activity 7.10 a distinction is made between relevant and irrelevant costs. For many decisions that involve

- relatively small variations from existing practice, and/or
- relatively limited periods of time

all fixed costs are irrelevant to the decision, because they will be the same irrespective of the decision made, because either

- fixed costs tend to be impossible to alter in the short term, or
- managers are reluctant to alter them in the short term.

Activity 7.11

Ali plc owns premises from which it provides a PC repair and maintenance service. There has been a fall in demand for the service and it would be possible for the business to continue operations from smaller, cheaper premises.

Can you think of any reasons why the business might not immediately move to smaller, cheaper premises?

We thought of broadly three reasons:

- It is not usually possible to find a buyer for the existing premises and to buy, or rent, new premises at very short notice.
- It may be difficult to move premises quickly where there is, say, delicate equipment to be moved.
- Management may feel that the downturn might not be permanent, and so would be reluctant to take such a dramatic step and deny itself the opportunity to benefit from a possible revival of trade.

The business's premises in Activity 7.11 may provide an example of one of the more inflexible types of cost, but most fixed costs tend to be broadly similar in this context.

We shall now consider some types of decisions where fixed costs can be regarded as irrelevant. In making these decisions, we should have as our key strategic objective the enhancement of owners' (shareholders') wealth. Since these decisions are short-term in nature, this means that wealth will normally be increased by trying to generate as much net cash inflow as possible.

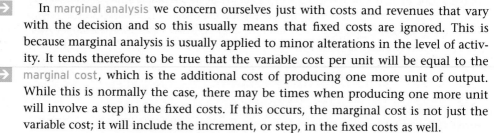

In marginal analysis we concern ourselves just with costs and revenues that vary with the decision and so this usually means that fixed costs are ignored. This is because marginal analysis is usually applied to minor alterations in the level of activity. It tends therefore to be true that the variable cost per unit will be equal to the marginal cost, which is the additional cost of producing one more unit of output. While this is normally the case, there may be times when producing one more unit will involve a step in the fixed costs. If this occurs, the marginal cost is not just the variable cost; it will include the increment, or step, in the fixed costs as well.

Marginal analysis may be used in four key areas of decision-making:

- accepting/rejecting special contracts;
- determining the most efficient use of scarce resources;
- make-or-buy decisions;
- closing or continuation decisions.

We shall now consider each of these areas in turn.

Accepting/rejecting special contracts

To understand how marginal analysis may be used in decisions as to whether to accept or reject special contracts, let us consider the following activity.

Activity 7.12

Cottage Industries Ltd (see Example 7.1 on page 242) has spare capacity in that its basket-makers have some spare time. An overseas retail chain has offered the business an order for 300 baskets at a price of £13 each.

Without considering any wider issues, should the business accept the order? (Assume that the business does not rent the machine.)

Since the fixed costs will be incurred in any case, they are not relevant to this decision. All we need to do is see whether the price offered will yield a contribution. If it will, the business will be better off by accepting the contract than by refusing it.

	£
Additional revenue per unit	13
Additional cost per unit	(12)
Additional contribution per unit	1

For 300 units, the additional contribution will be £300 (that is, 300 × £1). Since no fixed cost increase is involved, irrespective of what else is happening to the business, it will be £300 better off by taking this contract than by refusing it.

As ever with decision-making, there are other factors that are either difficult or impossible to quantify. These should be taken into account before reaching a final decision. In the case of Cottage Industries Ltd's decision on the overseas customer, these could include the following:

■ It is possible that the spare capacity will have been 'sold off' cheaply when there might be another potential customer who will offer a higher price after the capacity has been fully committed. It is a matter of commercial judgement how likely this will be.
■ Selling the same product, but at different prices, could lead to a loss of customer goodwill. The fact that a different price will be set for customers in different countries (that is, in different markets) may be sufficient to avoid this potential problem.
■ If the business is going to suffer continually from being unable to sell its full production potential at the 'usual' price, it might be better, in the long run, to reduce capacity and make fixed-cost savings. Using the spare capacity to produce marginal benefits may lead to the business failing to address this issue.
■ On a more positive note, the business may see this as a way of breaking into the overseas market. This is something that might be impossible to achieve if the business charges its usual price.

The most efficient use of scarce resources

It is often the level of market demand that restricts output. That is to say, it is the ability of a business to sell that will limit production, rather than sales being limited by the business's ability to produce. In some cases, however, it is a limit on what can be produced that limits sales. Limited production might stem from a shortage of any factor of production – for example, labour, raw materials, space, machinery. Such scarce factors are often known as *key factors* or *limiting factors*.

The most profitable combination of products will occur where the *contribution per unit of the scarce factor* is maximised. Example 7.2 should illustrate this point.

Example 7.2

A business provides three different services, the details of which are as follows:

Service (code name)	AX107	AX109	AX220
Selling price per unit (£)	50	40	65
Variable cost per unit (£)	(25)	(20)	(35)
Contribution per unit (£)	25	20	30
Labour time per unit (hours)	5	3	6

The market will take as many units of each service as can be provided, but the ability to provide the service is limited by the availability of labour, all of which needs to be skilled. Fixed costs are not affected by the choice of service provided because all three services use the same facilities.

The most profitable service is AX109 because it generates a contribution of £6.67 (£20/3) an hour. The other two generate only £5.00 each an hour (£25/5 and £30/6). So, to maximise profit, priority should be given to the production that maximises the contribution per unit of limiting factor.

Our first reaction may have been that the business should provide only service AX220, because this is the one that yields the highest contribution per unit sold. If so, we should have been making the mistake of thinking that it is the ability to sell that is the limiting factor. If the above analysis is not convincing, we can take an imaginary number of available labour hours and ask ourselves what is the maximum contribution (and, therefore, profit) that could be made by providing each service exclusively. Bear in mind that there is no shortage of anything else, including market demand, just a shortage of labour.

Activity 7.13

A business makes three different products, the details of which are as follows:

Product (code name)	B14	B17	B22
Selling price per unit (£)	25	20	23
Variable cost per unit (£)	10	8	12
Weekly demand (units)	25	20	30
Machine time per unit (hours)	4	3	4

Fixed costs are not affected by the choice of product because all three products use the same machine. Machine time is limited to 148 hours a week.

Which combination of products should be manufactured if the business is to produce the highest profit?

	B14	B17	B22
Selling price per unit (£)	25	20	23
Variable cost per unit (£)	(10)	(8)	(12)
Contribution per unit (£)	15	12	11
Machine time per unit	4 hours	3 hours	4 hours
Contribution per machine hour	£3.75	£4.00	£2.75
Order of priority	2nd	1st	3rd

Therefore produce:

20 units of product B17 using	60 hours
22 units of product B14 using	88 hours
	148 hours

This leaves unsatisfied the market demand for a further 3 units of product B14 and 30 units of product B22.

Activity 7.14

What steps could be contemplated that could lead to a higher level of contribution for the business in Activity 7.13?

The possibilities for improving matters that occurred to us are as follows:

- Consider obtaining additional machine time. This could mean buying or renting a new machine, subcontracting the machining to another business, or perhaps squeezing a few more hours a week out of the business's existing machine. Perhaps a combination of two or more of these is a possibility.
- Redesign the products in a way that requires less time per unit on the machine.
- Increase the price per unit of the three products. This might well have the effect of dampening demand, but the existing demand cannot be met at present, and it may be more profitable in the long run to make a greater contribution on each unit sold than to take one of the other courses of action to overcome the problem.

Activity 7.15

Going back to Activity 7.13, what is the maximum price that the business concerned would logically be prepared to pay to have the remaining B14s machined by a subcontractor, assuming that no fixed or variable costs would be saved as a result of not doing the machining in-house?

Would there be a different maximum if we were considering the B22s?

If the business could find a subcontractor who would machine the remaining three B14s for no cost, the business would be able to earn a contribution of £15 a unit, which it would not otherwise be able to gain. Therefore, any price up to £15 a unit would be worth paying to a subcontractor to undertake the machining. Naturally, the business would prefer to pay as little as possible, but anything up to £15 would still make it worthwhile subcontracting the machining.

The maximum for the B22s would be £11, because that is their contribution per unit.

Real World 7.6 is an extract from a *Financial Times* article about a UK government announcement relating to the financing of Britain's train network.

Real World 7.6

On track

Freight operators will also face higher fees. Currently they pay only the marginal cost of running each train: electricity, signalling and wear to the track that would not have been incurred had the train not run.

Source: 'The tricky question of who pays', Robert Wright, *Financial Times*, 25 July 2007.

Make-or-buy decisions

Businesses are frequently confronted by the need to decide whether to produce the product or service that they sell themselves, or to buy it in from some other business. For example, a producer of electrical appliances might decide to subcontract the manufacture of one of its products to another business, perhaps because there is a shortage of production capacity in the producer's own factory, or because it believes it to be cheaper to subcontract than to make the appliance itself.

It might just be part of a product or service that is subcontracted. For example, the producer may have a component for the appliance made by another manufacturer. In principle, there is hardly any limit to the scope of make-or-buy decisions. Virtually any part, component or service that is required in production of the main product or service, or the main product or service itself, could be the subject of a make-or-buy decision. So, for example, the personnel (human resources) function of a business, which is normally performed in-house, could be subcontracted. At the same time, electrical power, which is typically provided by an outside electrical utility business, could be generated in-house. Obtaining services or products from a subcontractor is often called outsourcing.

Real World 7.7 provides an example of outsourcing by a well-known international retailer.

Real World 7.7

IBM minds the Gap IT requirements

During 2006, Gap Inc., the US-based clothing retailer, decided to subcontract or 'out-source' its IT activities to IBM. Now, instead of employing its own IT staff, Gap has a 10-year contract for IBM to run its IT facility. Gap said that it expects to improve cap-abilities while reducing costs.

Outsourcing this type of activity is becoming very common in the UK and elsewhere.

Source: www.ibm.com.

Activity 7.16

Shah Ltd needs a component for one of its products. It can subcontract production of the component to a subcontractor who will provide the components for £20 each. The business can produce the components internally for total variable costs of £15 per component. Shah Ltd has spare capacity.

Should the component be subcontracted or produced internally?

The answer is that Shah Ltd should produce the component internally, since the variable cost of subcontracting is greater by £5 than the variable cost of internal manufacture.

Activity 7.17

Now assume that Shah Ltd (Activity 7.16) has no spare capacity, so it can only produce the component internally by reducing its output of another of its products. While it is making each component, it will lose contributions of £12 from the other product.

Should the component be subcontracted or produced internally?

The answer is to subcontract.

The relevant cost of internal production of each component is:

	£
Variable cost of production of the component	15
Opportunity cost of lost production of the other product	12
	27

This is obviously more costly than the £20 per component that will have to be paid to the subcontractor.

Activity 7.18

What factors, other than the immediately financially quantifiable, would you consider when making a make-or-buy decision?

We feel that there are two major factors:

1 The general problems of subcontracting:
   (a) loss of control of quality;
   (b) potential unreliability of supply.
2 Expertise and specialisation. It is possible for most businesses, with sufficient determination, to do virtually everything in-house. This may, however, require a level of skill and
   facilities that most businesses neither have nor feel inclined to acquire. For example,
   although it is true that most businesses could generate their own electricity, their man-
   agements tend to take the view that this is better done by a specialist generator business. Specialists can often do things more cheaply, with less risk of things going wrong.

Closing or continuation decisions

It is quite common for businesses to produce separate financial statements for each
department or section, to try to assess the relative effectiveness of each one.

Example 7.3

Goodsports Ltd is a retail shop that operates through three departments, all in the
same premises. The three departments occupy roughly equal-sized areas of the
premises. The trading results for the year just finished showed the following:

	Total £000	Sports equipment £000	Sports clothes £000	General clothes £000
Sales revenue	534	254	183	97
Costs	(482)	(213)	(163)	(106)
Profit/(loss)	52	41	20	(9)

It would appear that if the general clothes department were to close, the business
would be more profitable, by £9,000 a year, assuming last year's performance to be
a reasonable indication of future performance.

When the costs are analysed between those that are variable and those that
are fixed, however, the contribution of each department can be deduced and the
following results obtained:

	Total £000	Sports equipment £000	Sports clothes £000	General clothes £000
Sales revenue	534	254	183	97
Variable costs	(344)	(167)	(117)	(60)
Contribution	190	87	66	37
Fixed costs				
(rent and so on)	(138)	(46)	(46)	(46)
Profit/(loss)	52	41	20	(9)

Now it is obvious that closing the general clothes department, without any other
developments, would make the business worse off by £37,000 (the department's
contribution). The department should not be closed, because it makes a positive
contribution. The fixed costs would continue whether the department were closed
or not. As can be seen from the above analysis, distinguishing between variable and
fixed costs, and deducing the contribution, can make the picture a great deal clearer.

Activity 7.19

In considering Goodsports Ltd (Example 7.3), we saw that the general clothes department should not be closed 'without any other developments'. What 'other developments' could affect this decision, making continuation either more attractive or less attractive?

The things that we could think of are as follows:

■ Expansion of the other departments or replacing the general clothes department with a completely new activity. This would make sense only if the space currently occupied by the general clothes department could generate contributions totalling at least £37,000 a year.
■ Subletting the space occupied by the general clothes department. Once again, this would need to generate a net rent greater than £37,000 a year to make it more financially beneficial than keeping the department open.
■ Keeping the department open, even if it generated no contribution whatsoever (assuming that there is no other use for the space), may still be beneficial. If customers are attracted into the shop because it has general clothing, they may then buy something from one of the other departments. In the same way, the activity of a sub-tenant might attract customers into the shop. (On the other hand, it might drive them away.)

? Self-assessment question 7.1

Khan Ltd can render three different types of service (Alpha, Beta and Gamma) using the same staff. Various estimates for next year have been made as follows:

	Alpha	Beta	Gamma
Selling price (£/unit)	30	39	20
Variable material costs (£/unit)	15	18	10
Other variable costs (£/unit)	6	10	5
Share of fixed costs (£/unit)	8	12	4
Staff time required (hours/unit)	2	3	1

Fixed costs for next year are expected to total £40,000.

Required:
(a) If the business were to render only service Alpha next year, how many units of the service would it need to provide in order to break even? (Assume for this part of the question that there is no effective limit to market size and staffing level.)
(b) If the business has a maximum of 10,000 staff hours next year, in which order of preference would the three services come?
(c) If the maximum market for next year for the three services is as follows:

Alpha	3,000 units
Beta	2,000 units
Gamma	5,000 units

what quantities of which service should the business provide next year and how much profit would this be expected to yield?

The answer to this question can be found at the back of the book in Appendix B.

Summary

The main points in this chapter may be summarised as follows.

Behaviour of costs

- Fixed costs are those that are independent of the level of activity (for example, rent).

- Variable costs are those that vary with the level of activity (for example, raw materials).

- Semi-fixed (semi-variable) costs are a mixture of the two (for example, electricity).

Break-even analysis

- The break-even point (BEP) is the level of activity (in units of output or sales revenue) at which total costs (fixed + variable) = total sales revenue.

- Calculation of BEP is as follows:

$$\text{BEP (in units of output)} = \frac{\text{Fixed costs for the period}}{\text{Contribution per unit}}$$

- Use of knowledge of BEP for a particular activity: risk assessment.

- Contribution per unit = sales revenue per unit less variable cost per unit.

- Margin of safety = excess of planned volume of activity over BEP.

- Operating gearing = the extent to which the total costs of some activity are fixed rather than variable.

- Profit–volume (PV) chart is an alternative approach to break-even chart.

Weaknesses of break-even analysis

- Non-linear relationships.

- Stepped fixed costs.

- Multi-product businesses.

Marginal analysis (ignores fixed costs where these are not affected by the decision)

- Accepting/rejecting special contracts – consider only the effect on contributions.

- Using scarce resources – the limiting factor is most effectively used by maximising its contribution per unit.

- Make-or-buy decisions – take the action that leads to the highest total contributions.

- Closing/continuing an activity – should be assessed by net effect on total contributions.

fixed costs p. 234
variable costs p. 234
stepped fixed costs p. 236
semi-fixed (semi-variable) costs p. 238
break-even analysis p. 239
break-even chart p. 239
break-even point (BEP) p. 241
contribution per unit p. 244

margin of safety p. 244
operating gearing p. 247
operational gearing p. 247
profit–volume (PV) chart p. 249
marginal analysis p. 254
marginal cost p. 254
outsourcing p. 258

Further reading

If you would like to explore the topics covered in this chapter in more depth, we recommend the following books:

Drury, C., *Management and Cost Accounting* (7th edn), Thomson Learning, 2007, Chapter 8.
Hilton, R., *Managerial Accounting* (7th edn). McGraw-Hill/Irwin, 2007, Chapter 8.
Horngren, C., Datar, S. and Foster, G., *Cost Accounting: A Managerial Emphasis* (12th edn), Prentice Hall, 2006, Chapter 3.

? Review questions

Answers to these questions can be found at the back of the book in Appendix C.

7.1 Define the terms *fixed cost* and *variable cost*. Explain how an understanding of the distinction between fixed costs and variable costs can be useful to managers.

7.2 What is meant by the *break-even point* for an activity? How is the BEP calculated? Why is it useful to know the BEP?

7.3 When we say that some business activity has *high operating gearing*, what do we mean? What are the implications for the business of high operating gearing?

7.4 If there is a scarce resource that is restricting sales, how will the business maximise its profit? Explain the logic of the approach that you have identified for maximising profit.

✳ Exercises

Exercises 7.3 to 7.5 are more advanced than Exercises 7.1 and 7.2. Those with coloured numbers have answers at the back of the book in Appendix D.

If you wish to try more exercises, visit MyAccountingLab/

7.1   The management of a business is concerned about its inability to obtain enough fully trained labour to enable it to meet its present budget projection for its three services, Alpha, Beta and Gamma.

	Alpha £000	Beta £000	Gamma £000	Total £000
Variable costs				
Materials	6	4	5	15
Labour	9	6	12	27
Expenses	3	2	2	7
Allocated fixed costs	6	15	12	33
Total cost	24	27	31	82
Profit	15	2	2	19
Sales revenue	39	29	33	101

The amount of labour likely to be available will cost £20,000. All of the variable labour is paid at the same hourly rate. You have been asked to prepare a statement of plans ensuring that at least 50 per cent of the budgeted sales revenues are achieved for each service, and that the balance of labour is used to produce the greatest profit.

Required:
(a) Prepare a statement, with explanations, showing the greatest profit available from the limited amount of skilled labour available, within the constraint stated. *Hint:* Remember that all labour is paid at the same rate.
(b) What steps could the business take in an attempt to improve profitability, in the light of the labour shortage?

7.2   A hotel group prepares financial statements on a quarterly basis. The senior management is reviewing the performance of one hotel and making plans for next year.

The managers have in front of them the results for this year (based on some actual results and some forecasts to the end of this year):

Quarter	Sales revenue £000	Profit/(loss) £000
1	400	(280)
2	1,200	360
3	1,600	680
4	800	40
Total	4,000	800

The total estimated number of visitors (guest nights) for this year is 50,000. The results follow a regular pattern; there are no unexpected cost fluctuations beyond the seasonal trading pattern shown above. The management intends to incorporate into its plans for next year an anticipated increase in unit variable costs of 10 per cent and a profit target for the hotel of £1m.

Required:
(a) Calculate the total variable and total fixed costs of the hotel for this year. Show the provisional annual results for this year in total, showing variable and fixed costs separately. Show also the revenue and costs per visitor.
(b) (1) If there is no increase in visitors for next year, what will be the required revenue rate per hotel visitor to meet the profit target?
    (2) If the required revenue rate per visitor is not raised above this year's level, how many visitors will be required to meet the profit target?
(c) Outline and briefly discuss the assumptions that are made in typical PV or break-even analysis, and assess whether they limit the usefulness of such analysis.

7.3 A business makes three products, A, B and C. All three products require the use of two types of machine: cutting machines and assembling machines. Estimates for next year include the following:

	A	B	C
Selling price (£/unit)	25	30	18
Sales demand (units)	2,500	3,400	5,100
Material cost (£/unit)	12	13	10
Variable production cost (£/unit)	7	4	3
Time required per unit on cutting machines (hours)	1.0	1.0	0.5
Time required per unit on assembling machines (hours)	0.5	1.0	0.5

Fixed costs for next year are expected to total £42,000. It is the business's policy for each unit of production to absorb these in proportion to its total variable costs.

The business has cutting machine capacity of 5,000 hours a year and assembling machine capacity of 8,000 hours a year.

Required:
(a) State, with supporting workings, which products in which quantities the business should plan to make next year on the basis of the above information. (*Hint:* First determine which machines will be a limiting factor (scarce resource).)
(b) State the maximum price per product that it would be worth the business paying to a subcontractor to carry out that part of the work that could not be done internally.

7.4 Darmor Ltd has three products, X, Y and Z, which require the same production facilities. Information about the production costs for one unit of its products is as follows:

	X	Y	Z
	£	£	£
Labour: Skilled	6	9	3
Unskilled	2	4	10
Materials	12	25	14
Other variable costs	3	7	7
Fixed costs	5	10	10

All labour and materials are variable costs. Skilled labour is paid £12 an hour, and unskilled labour is paid £8 an hour. All references to labour costs, above, are based on basic rates of pay. Skilled labour is scarce, which means that the business could sell more than the maximum that it is able to make of any of the three products.

Product X is sold in a regulated market, and the regulators have set a price of £30 per unit for it.

Required:
(a) State, with supporting workings, the price that must be charged for products Y and Z such that the business would find it equally profitable to make and sell any of the three products.
(b) State, with supporting workings, the maximum rate of overtime premium that the business would logically be prepared to pay its skilled workers to work beyond the basic time.

7.5 Gandhi Ltd renders a promotional service to small retailing businesses. There are three levels of service: the 'basic', the 'standard' and the 'comprehensive'. On the basis of past experience, the business plans next year to work at absolute full capacity as follows:

	Number of units of the service	Selling price £	Variable cost per unit £
Basic	11,000	50	25
Standard	6,000	80	65
Comprehensive	16,000	120	90

The business's fixed costs total £660,000 a year. Each service takes about the same length of time, irrespective of the level.

One of the accounts staff has just produced a report that seems to show that the standard service is unprofitable. The relevant extract from the report is as follows:

Standard service cost analysis

	£	
Selling price per unit	80	
Variable cost per unit	(65)	
Fixed cost per unit	(20)	[£660,000/(11,000 + 6,000 + 16,000)]
Loss	(5)	

The producer of the report suggests that the business should not offer the standard service next year.

Required:
(a) Should the standard service be offered next year, assuming that the quantity of the other services could not be expanded to use the spare capacity?
(b) Should the standard service be offered next year, assuming that the released capacity could be used to render a new service, the 'nova', for which customers would be charged £75, and which would have variable costs of £50 and take twice as long as the other three services?
(c) What is the minimum price that could be accepted for the basic service, assuming that the necessary capacity to expand it will come only from not offering the standard service?

Chapter 8

Full costing

Introduction

In this chapter, we examine methods of deducing the cost of a unit of output that take account of all of the costs. These methods contrast with the approach that we looked at in Chapter 7, where we concentrated on just the variable costs. These full costing methods, as they are called, are widely used in practice. We shall first look at the traditional full costing method and consider its usefulness for management purposes. We shall then go on to consider activity-based costing, which represents an alternative to the traditional approach.

Learning outcomes

When you have completed this chapter, you should be able to:

- discuss the usefulness of deducing the full cost of a unit of output for decision-making purposes;
- deduce the full cost of a unit of output both in a single-product environment and in a multi-product environment using the traditional full cost method.
- discuss the problems of charging full costs to jobs in a multi-product environment;
- explain the role and nature of activity-based costing.

Why do managers want to know the full cost?

We saw in Chapter 1 that the only point in producing accounting information is to help users make more informed decisions. For managers, information concerning the full cost of a unit of output can be useful in four main areas of decision-making. These are:

- *Pricing and output decisions.* Having full cost information can help managers make decisions on the price to be charged to customers for the business's products or services and how many to provide.
- *Exercising control.* Managers need information to check that the performance of the business conforms to earlier plans. Budgets (that is, short-term financial plans) are typically expressed in full-cost terms. This means that periodic reports that compare actual performance with budgets need to be expressed in the same full-cost terms.
- *Assessing relative efficiency.* Full cost information can help managers to compare the cost of doing something in one way, or location, with its cost if done in a different manner or place. For example, a car manufacturer may find it useful to compare the cost of building a particular model of car in one of its plants rather than in another. This may help the manufacturer to make a decision on where to locate future production.
- *Assessing performance.* The level of profit, or income, generated over a period is an important measure of business performance. To measure profit, or income, we need to compare sales revenue with the associated expenses. With a business that produces a product or service, a major expense will be the cost of making the product or rendering the service. Logically this is the full cost of what was sold. Measuring income provides managers (and other users) with information that can help them to make a wide range of decisions.

Figure 8.1 shows the four uses of full costing information.

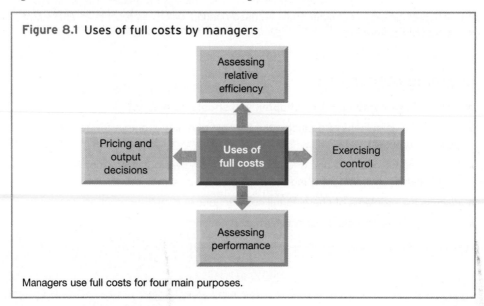

Figure 8.1 Uses of full costs by managers

Managers use full costs for four main purposes.

Now let us consider Real World 8.1.

Real World 8.1

Operating costs

An interesting example of the use of full costs for pricing decisions occurs in the National Health Service (NHS). In recent years, the funding of hospitals has radically changed. A new system of Payment by Results (PBR) requires the Department of Health to produce a list of prices for an in-patient spell in hospital that covers different types of surgical operations. This list, which is revised annually, reflects the prices that hospitals will be paid by the government for carrying out the different operations.

For 2005/6, the price list included the following figures:

£7,211 for carrying out a knee replacement operation
£6,362 for carrying out a hip replacement operation.

These figures are based on the full cost of undertaking each type of operation in 2003/4 (but adjusted for inflation). Full cost figures were submitted by all NHS hospitals for that year as part of their annual accounting process and an average for each type of operation was then calculated. Figures for other surgical operations on the price list were derived in the same way.

Source: Payment by results: The New Funding System for the NHS in England: Practical Support for Allied Health Professionals, a Workbook, Chartered Society of Physiotherapy, 2005, p. 6.

When looking at the information in Real World 8.1, an important question that arises is 'what does the full cost of each type of operation actually include?' Does it simply include the cost of the salaries earned by doctors and nurses during the time spent with the patient or does it also include other costs? If other costs are included, what are they and how are they identified? Would they include, for example, a charge for

- the artificial knee/hip provided for the patient
- equipment used in the operating theatre
- administrative and support staff within the hospital
- maintaining the hospital buildings
- laundry and cleaning?

If such costs are included, how can an appropriate charge be determined? If, on the other hand, they are not included, are the figures of £7,211 and £6,362 potentially misleading?

These questions are the subject of this chapter.

What is full costing?

Full cost is the total amount sacrificed to achieve a particular objective. It includes all amounts sacrificed and so, if the objective were to supply a customer with a product or service, all costs relating to the production of the product or provision of the service would be included as part of the full cost. To derive the full cost figure, we must accumulate the costs incurred and then assign them to the particular product or service.

The logic of full costing is that all of the costs of running a particular facility, say an office, are part of the cost of the output of that office. The rent, for example, may be a cost that will not alter merely because we provide one more unit of the service. If the office were not rented, there would be nowhere for the staff, who provide the service, to work. So rent is an important element of the cost of each unit of output.

In the two sections that follow, we shall first see how traditional full costing is applied to a single-product business and then see how it is done for a multi-product one.

Single-product businesses

The simplest case for which to deduce the full cost per unit is where the business has only one product or service, that is, each unit of its production is identical. Here it is simply a question of adding up all the costs of production incurred in the period (materials, labour, rent, fuel, power and so on) and dividing this total by the total number of units of output for the period.

Activity 8.1

Fruitjuice Ltd has just one product, a sparkling orange drink that is marketed as Orange Fizz. During last month, the business produced 7,300 litres of the drink. The costs incurred were as follows:

	£
Ingredients (oranges and so on)	390
Fuel	85
Rent of premises	350
Depreciation of equipment	75
Labour	880

What is the full cost per litre of producing Orange Fizz?

The full cost figure is found by simply adding together all of the costs incurred and then dividing by the number of litres produced:

$$£(390 + 85 + 350 + 75 + 880)/7,300 = £0.24 \text{ per litre}$$

In practice, there can be problems in deciding exactly how much cost was incurred. In the case of Fruitjuice Ltd, for example, how is the cost of depreciation deduced? It is certainly an estimate, and so its reliability is open to question. The cost of raw materials may also be a problem. Should we use the 'relevant' cost of the raw materials (in this case, almost certainly the replacement cost), or the actual price paid for it (historic cost)? If the cost per litre is to be used for some decision-making purpose, the replacement cost is probably more logical. In practice, however, it seems that historic costs are more often used to deduce full costs.

There can also be problems in deciding precisely how many units of output there were. If making Orange Fizz is not a very fast process, some of the drink will probably be in the process of being made at any given moment. This, in turn, means that some of the costs incurred last month were for some Orange Fizz that was work in progress at the end of the month, so is not included in last month's output quantity of 7,300 litres. Similarly, part of the 7,300 litres might well have been started and incurred costs in the previous month, yet all of those litres were included in the 7,300 litres that we used in our calculation of the cost per litre. Work in progress is not a serious problem, but some adjustment for the value of opening and closing work in progress for a period needs to be made if reliable full cost information is to be obtained.

The approach to full costing which is usually taken with identical, or near identical, units of output (of goods or services) is often referred to as process costing.

Multi-product businesses

Most businesses produce more than one type of product or service. In this situation, the units of output of the product, or service, will not be identical and so the approach that we used with litres of Orange Fizz in Activity 8.1 probably cannot be used. Although it is reasonable to assign an identical cost to units of output that are identical, it is not reasonable to do this where the units of output are obviously different. It would not be reasonable, for example, to assign the same costs to each car repair carried out by a garage, irrespective of the complexity and size of the repair.

Direct and indirect costs

To provide full cost information, we need to have a systematic approach to accumulating costs and then assigning these costs to particular units of product or service on some reasonable basis. Where units of output are not identical, the starting point is to separate costs into two categories: direct costs and indirect costs.

- Direct costs. These are costs that can be identified with specific cost units. That is to say, the effect of the cost can be measured in respect of each particular unit of output. (A cost unit is simply a unit of whatever is having its cost determined – usually one unit of a service or a manufactured item.) The main examples of direct costs are direct materials and direct labour. This means that, in costing a motor car repair by a garage, both the cost of spare parts used in the repair and the cost of the mechanic's time would be direct costs. Collecting direct costs is a simple matter of having a cost-recording system that is capable of capturing the cost of direct materials used on each job and the cost, based on the hours worked and the rate of pay, of direct workers.
- Indirect costs (or overheads). These are all other costs, that is, those that cannot be directly measured in respect of each particular unit of output. Thus the rent of the garage premises would be an indirect cost of a motor car repair.

We shall use the terms 'indirect costs' and 'overheads' interchangeably for the remainder of this book. Overheads are also sometimes known as common costs because they are common to all outputs of the production unit (for example, factory or department) for the period.

Real World 8.2 provides some insight into the direct/indirect cost balance in practice.

Real World 8.2

Direct and indirect costs in practice

A survey of 176 fairly large UK businesses, conducted during 1999, revealed that, on average, total costs of businesses are in the following proportions:

- direct costs: 70 per cent
- indirect costs: 30 per cent.

Perhaps surprisingly, these proportions did not vary greatly between manufacturers, retailers and service businesses. The only significant variation from the 70/30 proportions was with financial and commercial businesses (for example, banks), which had an average 52/48 split.

Source: Based on information in *Cost Systems Design and Profitability Analysis in UK Manufacturing Companies*, C. Drury and M. Tayles, CIMA Publishing, 2000.

An extensive (nearly 2,000 responses) and more recent (2003) survey of management accounting practice in the US showed similar results. Like the 1999 UK survey, the US survey tended to relate to larger businesses. About 40 per cent were manufacturers and about 16 per cent financial services; the remainder were from a range of other industries. This survey revealed that, of total costs, indirect costs accounted for between

- 34 per cent for retailers (lowest) and
- 42 per cent for manufacturers (highest),

with other industries' proportions of indirect costs falling within the 34 to 42 per cent range. Financial and commercial businesses showed an indirect cost percentage of 38 per cent.

Source: *2003 Survey of Management Accounting*, Ernst and Young.

The differences between the UK and the US could be accounted for by a higher level of capital intensity in US industry, which would tend to increase indirect costs relative to direct ones. The fact that the US survey is more recent may also affect the results.

Job costing

The term job costing is used to describe the way in which we identify the full cost per unit of output (job) where the units of output differ. To cost (that is, deduce the full cost of) a particular unit of output (job), we first identify the direct costs of the job, which, by the definition of direct costs, is fairly straightforward. We then seek to 'charge' each unit of output with a fair share of indirect costs. Put another way, cost units (products) absorb overheads. This leads to full costing also being called absorption costing. This is shown graphically in Figure 8.2.

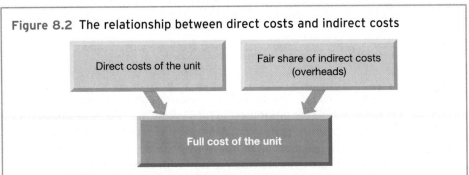

Figure 8.2 The relationship between direct costs and indirect costs

The full cost of any particular job is the sum of those costs that can be measured specifically in respect of the job (direct costs) and a share of those costs that create the environment in which production (of an object or service) can take place, but which do not relate specifically to any particular job (overheads).

Sparky Ltd is a business that employs a number of electricians. The business undertakes a range of work for its customers, from replacing fuses to installing complete wiring systems in new houses.

In respect of a particular job done by Sparky Ltd, into which category (direct or indirect) would each of the following costs fall?

1 The wages of the electrician who did the job.
2 Depreciation of the tools used by the electrician.
3 The salary of Sparky Ltd's accountant.
4 The cost of cable and other materials used on the job.
5 Rent of the premises where Sparky Ltd stores its inventories of cable and other materials.

Only the electrician's wages earned while working on the particular job and the cost of the materials used on the job are direct costs. This is because it is possible to measure how much time was spent on the particular job (and therefore the direct labour cost) and the amount of materials used (and therefore the direct material cost).

All the other costs are general costs of running the business and, as such, must form part of the full cost of doing the job, but they cannot be directly measured in respect of the particular job.

It is important to note that whether a cost is direct or indirect depends on the item being costed – the cost objective. People sometimes refer to overheads without stating what the cost objective is; this is incorrect.

Into which category, direct or indirect, would each of the costs listed in Activity 8.2 fall if we were seeking to find the cost of operating the entire business of Sparky Ltd for a month?

The answer is that all of them will be direct costs, since they can all be related to, and measured in respect of, running the business for a month.

Naturally, broader-reaching cost objectives, such as operating Sparky Ltd for a month, tend to include a higher proportion of direct costs than do more limited ones, such as a particular job done by Sparky Ltd. As we shall see shortly, this makes costing broader cost objectives rather more straightforward than costing narrower ones. It is generally the case that direct costs are easier to deal with than indirect ones.

Full (absorption) costing and the behaviour of costs

We saw in Chapter 7 that the full cost of doing something (or total cost, as it is usually known in the context of marginal analysis) can be analysed between the fixed and the variable elements. This is illustrated in Figure 8.3.

Figure 8.3 The relationship between fixed costs, variable costs and total costs

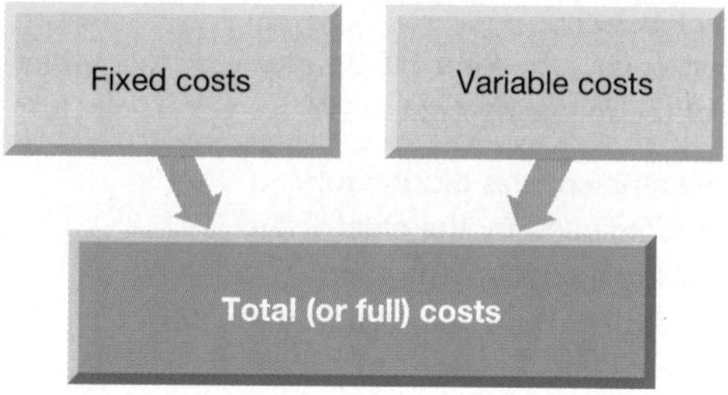

The total cost of a job is the sum of those costs that remain the same irrespective of the level of activity (fixed costs) and those that vary according to the level of activity (variable costs).

The similarity of what is shown in Figure 8.3 to that depicted in Figure 8.2 seems to lead some people to believe, mistakenly, that variable costs and direct costs are the same and that fixed costs and overheads are the same. This is incorrect.

The notions of fixed and variable are concerned entirely with cost behaviour in the face of changes in the volume of activity. Directness of costs, on the other hand, is concerned with collecting together the elements that make up full cost, that is, with the extent to which costs can be measured directly in respect of particular units of output or jobs. These are two entirely different concepts. Although it may be true that there is a tendency for fixed costs to be indirect costs (overheads) and for variable costs to be direct costs, there is no link, and there are many exceptions to this tendency. For example, most activities have variable overheads. Labour is a major element of direct cost in most types of business activity but is usually a fixed cost, at least over the short term.

The relationship between the reaction of costs to volume changes (cost behaviour), on the one hand, and how costs need to be gathered to deduce the full cost (cost collection), on the other, in respect of a particular job is shown in Figure 8.4.

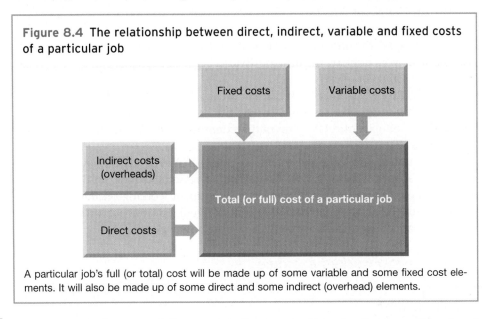

Figure 8.4 The relationship between direct, indirect, variable and fixed costs of a particular job

A particular job's full (or total) cost will be made up of some variable and some fixed cost elements. It will also be made up of some direct and some indirect (overhead) elements.

Total cost is the sum of direct and indirect costs. It is also the sum of fixed and variable costs. These two facts are independent of one another. A particular cost may be fixed, relative to the level of output, but that fact tells us nothing about whether it is a direct or an indirect cost.

The problem of indirect costs

Distinguishing between direct and indirect costs is related only to deducing full cost in a job-costing environment, that is, where units of output differ. When we were considering costing a litre of Orange Fizz drink in Activity 8.1, whether particular elements of cost were direct or indirect was of absolutely no consequence, because all costs were shared equally between the litres of Orange Fizz. Where we have units of output that are not identical, however, we have to look more closely at the make-up of the costs to achieve a fair measure of the full cost of a particular job.

Indirect costs of any activity must form part of the cost of each unit of output. By definition, however, they cannot be directly related to individual cost units. This raises a major practical issue: how are indirect costs to be apportioned to individual cost units or products?

Overheads as service renderers

It is reasonable to view the overheads as rendering a service to the cost units. A legal case undertaken by a firm of solicitors for a particular client can be seen as being rendered a service by the office in which the work is done. In this sense, it is reasonable to charge each case (cost unit) with a share of the costs of running the office (rent, lighting, heating, cleaning, building maintenance and so on). It also seems reasonable to relate the charge for the 'use' of the office to the level of service that the particular case has received from the office.

The next step is the difficult one. How might the cost of running the office, which is a cost of all work done by the firm, be divided between individual cases that are not similar in size and complexity?

One possibility is sharing this overhead cost equally between each case handled by the firm within the period. Most of us would not propose this method unless the cases were close to being identical in terms of the extent to which they had 'benefited' from the overheads.

If we are not to propose equal shares, we must identify something observable and measurable about the cases that we feel provides a reasonable basis for distinguishing between one case and the next. In practice, time spent working on the cost unit or product by direct labour is the basis that is most popular. It must be stressed that this is not the 'correct' way, and it certainly is not the only way.

Job costing: a worked example

To see how job costing (as it is usually called) works, let us consider Example 8.1.

Example 8.1

Johnson Ltd, a business that provides a personal computer service to its customers, has overheads of £10,000 each month. Each month 1,000 direct labour hours are worked and charged to units of output (repairs carried out by the business). A particular repair undertaken by the business used direct materials costing £15. Direct labour worked on the repair was 3 hours and the wage rate is £16 an hour. Overheads are charged to jobs on a direct labour hour basis. What is the full (absorption) cost of the repair?

First, let us establish the overhead absorption (recovery) rate, that is, the rate at which individual repairs will be charged with overheads. This is £10 (that is, £10,000/1,000) per direct labour hour.

So, the full cost of the repair is:

	£
Direct materials	15
Direct labour (3 × £16)	48
Total direct cost (or prime cost)	63
Overheads (3 × £10)	30
Full cost of the job	93

Note, in Example 8.1, that the number of labour hours (3 hours) appears twice in deducing the full cost: once to deduce the direct labour cost and a second time to deduce the overheads to be charged to the repair. These are really two separate issues, though they are both based on the same number of labour hours.

Note also that if all of the repair jobs that are undertaken during the month are assigned overheads in a similar manner, all £10,000 of overheads will be charged to the jobs between them. Jobs that involve a lot of direct labour will be assigned a large share of overheads, and those that involve little direct labour will be assigned a small share of overheads.

Activity 8.4

Can you think of reasons why the direct labour hours basis is regarded as the most logical basis for sharing overheads between cost units?

The reasons that occurred to us are as follows:

■ Large jobs should logically attract large amounts of overheads because they are likely to have been rendered more 'service' by the overheads than small ones. The length of time that they are worked on by direct labour may be seen as a rough and ready way of measuring relative size, although other means of doing this may be found – for example, relative physical size, where the cost unit is a physical object such as a manufactured product.

■ Most overheads are related to time. Rent, heating, lighting, non-current asset depreciation, supervisors' and managers' salaries and loan interest, which are all typical overheads, are all more or less time-based: the overhead cost for one week tends to be about half of that for a similar two-week period. Thus, a basis of allotting overheads to jobs that takes account of the length of time that the units of output benefited from the 'service' rendered by the overheads seems logical.

■ Direct labour hours are capable of being measured for each job. They will normally be measured to deduce the direct labour element of cost in any case. Thus, a direct labour hour basis of dealing with overheads is practical to apply in the real world.

It cannot be emphasised enough that there is no 'correct' way to allot overheads to jobs. Overheads (indirect costs), by definition, do not naturally relate to individual jobs. If, nevertheless, we wish to take account of the fact that overheads are part of the cost of all jobs, we must find some acceptable way of including a share of the total overheads in each job. If a particular means of doing this is accepted by those who use the full cost deduced, then the method is as good as any other method. Accounting is concerned only with providing useful information to decision-makers. In practice, the method that seems to be regarded as being the most useful is the direct labour hour method.

Activity 8.5

Marine Suppliers Ltd undertakes a range of work, including making sails for small sailing boats on a made-to-measure basis.

The business expects to incur the following costs during the next month:

Direct labour costs	£60,000
Direct labour time	6,000 hours
Indirect labour cost	£9,000
Depreciation of machinery	£3,000
Rent and rates	£5,000
Heating, lighting and power	£2,000
Machine time	2,000 hours
Indirect materials	£500
Other miscellaneous indirect costs	£200
Direct materials cost	£3,000

The business has received an enquiry about a sail. It is estimated that the particular sail will take twelve direct labour hours to make and will require 20 square metres of sailcloth, which costs £2 per square metre.

The business normally uses a direct-labour-hour basis of charging overheads to individual jobs.

What is the full (absorption) cost of making the sail?

The direct costs of making the sail can be identified as follows:

	£
Direct materials (20 × £2)	40.00
Direct labour (12 × (£60,000/6,000))	120.00
	160.00

To deduce the indirect cost element that must be added to derive the full cost of the sail, we first need to total these costs as follows:

	£
Indirect labour	9,000
Depreciation	3,000
Rent and rates	5,000
Heating, lighting and power	2,000
Indirect materials	500
Other miscellaneous indirect costs	200
Total indirect costs	19,700

Since the business uses a direct-labour-hour basis of charging overheads to jobs, we need to deduce the indirect cost (or overhead) recovery rate per direct labour hour. This is simply £19,700/6,000 = £3.28 per direct labour hour.

Thus, the full cost of the sail would be expected to be:

	£
Direct materials (20 × £2)	40.00
Direct labour (12 × (£60,000/6,000))	120.00
Indirect costs (12 × £3.28)	39.36
Full cost	199.36

Figure 8.5 shows the process for applying overheads and direct costs to the sail that was the subject of Activity 8.5.

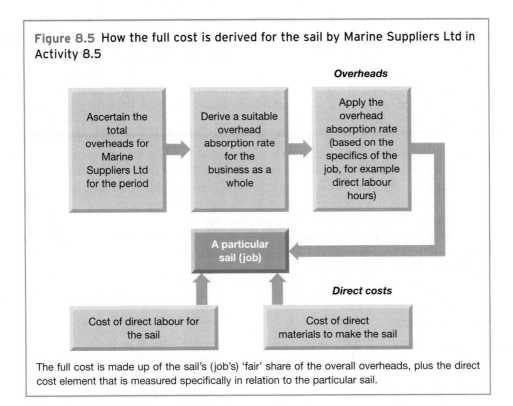

Figure 8.5 How the full cost is derived for the sail by Marine Suppliers Ltd in Activity 8.5

The full cost is made up of the sail's (job's) 'fair' share of the overall overheads, plus the direct cost element that is measured specifically in relation to the particular sail.

Activity 8.6

Suppose that Marine Suppliers Ltd (see Activity 8.5) used a machine hour basis of charging overheads to jobs. What would be the cost of the job detailed if it was expected to take 5 machine hours (as well as 12 direct labour hours)?

The total overheads of the business will of course be the same irrespective of the method of charging them to jobs. Thus, the overhead recovery rate, on a machine-hour basis, will be £19,700/2,000 = £9.85 per machine hour.

The full cost of the sail would, therefore, be:

	£
Direct materials (20 × £2)	40.00
Direct labour (12 × (£60,000/6,000))	120.00
Indirect costs (5 × £9.85)	49.25
Full cost	209.25

Selecting a basis for charging overheads

A question now presents itself as to which of the two costs for this sail is the correct one, or simply the better one. The answer is that neither is correct, as was pointed out earlier. Which is the better one is a matter of judgement. This judgement is concerned entirely with the usefulness of information, which is difficult to assess.

It is probably reasonable to take the view that the nature of the overheads should influence the choice of the basis of charging the overheads to jobs. Where production is capital-intensive and overheads are primarily machine-based (depreciation, machine maintenance, power and so on), machine hours might be favoured. Otherwise direct labour hours might be preferred.

It could appear that one of these bases might be preferred to the other simply because it apportions either a higher or a lower amount of overheads to a particular job. This would probably be irrational, however. Since the total overheads are the same irrespective of the method of dividing that total between individual jobs, a method that gives a higher share of overheads to one particular job must give a lower share to the remaining jobs. There is one cake of fixed size. If one person is to be given a relatively large slice, others must on average receive relatively small slices. To illustrate further this issue of apportioning overheads, consider Example 8.2.

Example 8.2

A business that provides a service expects to incur overheads totalling £20,000 next month. The total direct labour time worked is expected to be 1,600 hours and machines are expected to operate for a total of 1,000 hours.

During the month, the business expects to do just two large jobs. Information concerning each job is as follows:

	Job 1	Job 2
Direct labour hours	800	800
Machine hours	700	300

How much of the total overheads will be charged to each job if overheads are to be charged on

(a) a direct-labour-hour basis; and
(b) a machine-hour basis?

What do you notice about the two sets of figures that you calculate?

(a) *Direct-labour-hour basis*

Overhead recovery rate = £20,000/1,600 = £12.50 per direct labour hour.

$$\text{Job 1:} \quad £12.50 \times 800 = £10,000$$
$$\text{Job 2:} \quad £12.50 \times 800 = £10,000$$

(b) *Machine-hour basis*

Overhead recovery rate = £20,000/1,000 = £20.00 per machine hour.

$$\text{Job 1:} \quad £20.00 \times 700 = £14,000$$
$$\text{Job 2:} \quad £20.00 \times 300 = £6,000$$

It is clear from these calculations that the total of the overheads charged to jobs is the same (that is, £20,000) whichever method is used. So, whereas the machine-hour basis gives Job 1 a higher share than the direct-labour-hour basis, the opposite is true for Job 2.

It is not practical to charge overheads on one basis to one job and on the other basis to the other job. This is because either total overheads will not be fully charged to the jobs, or the jobs will be overcharged with overheads. For example, using the direct-labour-hour method for Job 1 (£10,000) and the machine-hour basis for Job 2 (£6,000) will mean that only £16,000 of a total £20,000 of overheads will be charged to jobs. As a result, the objective of full (absorption) costing, which is to charge all overheads to jobs done, will not be achieved. In this particular case, if selling prices are based on full costs, the business may not charge high enough prices to cover all of its costs.

Figure 8.6 shows the effect of the two different bases of charging overheads to Jobs 1 and 2.

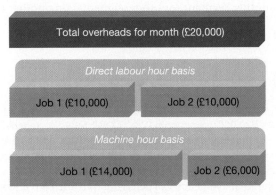

Figure 8.6 The effect of different bases of charging overheads to jobs in Example 8.2

Total overheads for month (£20,000)

Direct labour hour basis

Job 1 (£10,000)　　Job 2 (£10,000)

Machine hour basis

Job 1 (£14,000)　　Job 2 (£6,000)

The share of the total overheads for the month charged to jobs can differ significantly depending on the basis used.

Activity 8.7

The point was made above that it would normally be irrational to prefer one basis of charging overheads to jobs simply because it apportions either a higher or a lower amount of overheads to a particular job. This is because the total overheads are the same irrespective of the method of charging the total to individual jobs. Can you think of any circumstances where it would not necessarily be so irrational?

This might apply where, for a particular job, a customer has agreed to pay a price based on full cost plus an agreed fixed percentage for profit. Here it would be beneficial to the producer for the total cost of the job to be as high as possible. This would be relatively unusual, but in the past public-sector organisations, particularly central and local government departments, have entered into contracts to have work done with the price to be deduced on a cost-plus basis after the work has been completed. Such contracts are rare these days, probably because they are open to abuse in the way described. Usually, contract prices are agreed in advance, typically in conjunction with competitive tendering.

Survey evidence in the early 1990s (Drury, Braund, Osborne and Tayles: *A Survey of Management Accounting Practices in UK Manufacturing Companies*, 1993) showed that the direct labour hour basis of charging overheads to cost units was overwhelmingly the most popular, even where activities were automated. There is no reason to believe that current practice is very different from this and, in the absence of more recent information, it provides some impression of what happens in practice.

Segmenting the overheads

As we have just seen, charging the same overheads to different jobs on different bases is not possible. It is possible, however, to charge one segment of the total overheads on one basis and another segment (or other segments) on another basis (or bases).

Activity 8.8

Taking the same business as in Example 8.2, on closer analysis we find that of the overheads totalling £20,000 next month, £8,000 will relate to machines (depreciation, maintenance, rent of the space occupied by the machines, and so on) and the remaining £12,000 to more general overheads. The other information about the business is exactly as it was before.

How much of the total overheads will be charged to each job if the machine-related overheads are to be charged on a machine-hour basis and the remaining overheads on a direct-labour-hour basis?

Direct-labour-hour basis

> Overhead recovery rate = £12,000/1,600 = £7.50 per direct labour hour

Machine-hour basis

> Overhead recovery rate = £8,000/1,000 = £8.00 per machine hour

Overheads charged to jobs

	Job 1 £	Job 2 £
Direct-labour-hour basis:		
£7.50 × 800	6,000	
£7.50 × 800		6,000
Machine-hour basis:		
£8.00 × 700	5,600	
£8.00 × 300		2,400
Total	11,600	8,400

We can see from this that the expected overheads of £20,000 are charged in total.

Segmenting the overheads in this way may well be seen as providing a better basis of charging overheads to jobs. This is quite often found in practice, and is usually done by dividing a business into separate 'areas' for costing purposes and charging overheads differently from one area to the next, according to the nature of the work done there.

Although it has been made clear that there is no single correct basis of charging overheads, the direct-labour-hour and machine-hour bases do have something to commend them and are popular in practice. We have seen that a sensible method does need to identify something about each job that can be measured and which distinguishes it from other jobs. There is also a lot to be said for methods that are concerned with time, because most overheads are time-related.

Dealing with overheads on a departmental basis

In general, all but the smallest businesses are divided into departments. Normally, each department deals with a separate activity. The reasons for dividing a business into departments include the following:

- Many businesses are too large and complex to be managed as a single unit. It is usually more practical to operate each business as a series of relatively independent units (departments) with each one having its own manager.
- Each department normally has its own area of specialism and is managed by a specialist.
- Each department can have its own accounting records that enable its performance to be assessed. This can lead to greater management control and motivation among the staff.

Many businesses charge overheads to cost units on a department-by-department basis. They do this in the expectation that it will give rise to a more useful way of charging overheads. It is probably often the case that it does not lead to any great improvement in the usefulness of the resulting full costs. Although it may not be of enormous benefit in many cases, it is probably not an expensive exercise to apply overheads on a departmental basis. Since each department collects costs for other purposes (particularly control), to apply overheads on a department-by-department basis is a relatively simple matter.

Example 8.3 looks at how the departmental approach to deriving full costs works in a service-industry context.

Example 8.3

Autosparkle Ltd offers a motor vehicle paint-respray service. The jobs that it undertakes range from painting a small part of a saloon car, usually following a minor accident, to a complete respray of a double-decker bus.

Each job starts life in the preparation department, where it is prepared for the paintshop department. In the preparation department the job is worked on by direct workers, in most cases taking some direct materials from the stores with which to treat the old paintwork to render the vehicle ready for respraying. Thus the job will be charged with direct materials, direct labour and a share of the preparation department's overheads. The job then passes into the paintshop department, already valued at the costs that it picked up in the preparation department.

In the paintshop, the staff draw direct materials (mainly paint) from the stores and direct workers spend time respraying, using sophisticated spraying apparatus as well as working by hand. So, in the paintshop, the job is charged with direct materials, direct labour and a share of that department's overheads. The job now passes into the finishing department, valued at the cost of the materials, labour and overheads that it accumulated in the first two departments.

In the finishing department, jobs are cleaned and polished ready to go back to the customers. Further direct labour and, in some cases, materials are added. All jobs also pick up a share of that department's overheads. The job, now complete, passes back to the customer.

Figure 8.7 shows graphically how this works for a particular job.

The basis of charging overheads to jobs (for example, direct labour hours) might be the same for all three departments, or it might be different from one department to another. It is possible that spraying apparatus costs dominate the paintshop costs, so that department's overheads might well be charged to jobs on a machine-hour basis. The other two departments are probably labour-intensive, so that a direct-labour-hour basis may be seen as being appropriate there.

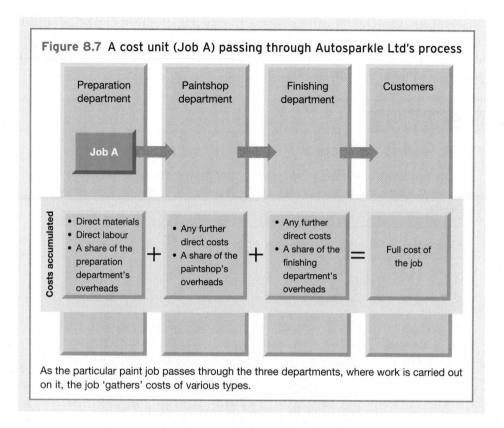

Figure 8.7 A cost unit (Job A) passing through Autosparkle Ltd's process

As the particular paint job passes through the three departments, where work is carried out on it, the job 'gathers' costs of various types.

The passage of the job through the departments, picking up costs as it goes, can be compared to a snowball being rolled across snow: as it rolls, it picks up more and more snow.

Where costs are dealt with departmentally, each department is known as a cost centre. This can be defined as some physical area or some activity or function for which costs are separately identified. The process of charging direct costs to jobs, in a departmental system, is exactly the same as where the whole business is one single cost centre. It is simply a matter of keeping a record of

- the number of hours of direct labour worked on the particular job and the grade of labour, assuming that there are different grades with different rates of pay;
- the cost of the direct materials taken from stores and applied to the job; and
- any other direct costs, for example some subcontracted work, associated with the job.

This record-keeping will normally be done departmentally in a departmental system.

It is obviously necessary to break down the production overheads of the entire business on a departmental basis. This means that the total overheads of the business must be divided between the departments such that the sum of the departmental overheads equals the overheads for the entire business. By charging all of their overheads to jobs, the departments will, between them, charge all of the overheads of the business to jobs. Real World 8.3 provides an indication of the number of different cost centres that businesses tend to use in practice.

Real World 8.3

Cost centres in practice

It is not unusual for businesses to have several cost centres. Figure 8.8 shows the results of a recent survey by Drury and Tayles of 186 larger UK businesses involved in various activities.

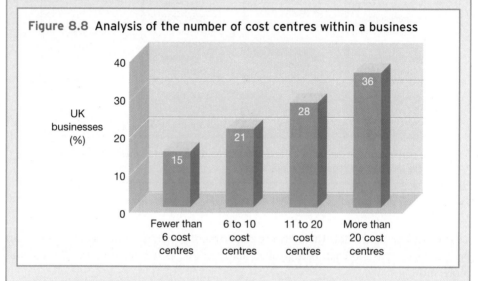

Figure 8.8 Analysis of the number of cost centres within a business

We can see from the figure that 85 per cent of businesses surveyed had six or more cost centres and that 36 per cent of businesses had more than twenty cost centres. Though this is not shown on the diagram, 3 per cent of businesses surveyed had a single cost centre (that is, there was a business-wide or overall overhead rate used). Clearly, businesses that deal with overheads on a business-wide basis are rare.

Source: Based on 'Profitability analysis in UK organisations', C. Drury and M. Tayles, *British Accounting Review*, December 2006.

Batch costing

The production of many types of goods and services (particularly goods) involves producing in a batch of identical, or nearly identical, units of output, but where each batch is distinctly different from other batches. For example, a theatre may put on a production whose nature (and therefore costs) is very different from that of other productions. On the other hand, ignoring differences in the desirability of the various types of seating, all of the individual units of output (tickets to see the production) are identical.

In these circumstances, we should normally deduce the cost per ticket by using a job-costing approach (taking account of direct and indirect costs and so on) to find the cost of mounting the production and then we should simply divide this by the expected number of tickets to be sold to find the cost per ticket. This is known as batch costing.

Figure 8.9 shows the process for deriving the cost of one cost unit (product) in a batch.

Figure 8.9 Deriving the cost of one cost unit where production is in batches

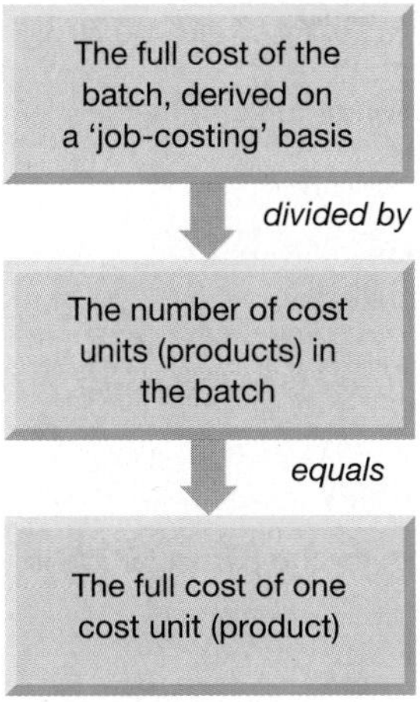

The full cost of the batch, derived on a 'job-costing' basis

divided by

The number of cost units (products) in the batch

equals

The full cost of one cost unit (product)

The cost for the batch is derived using a job-costing basis and this is divided by the number of units in the batch to determine the cost for each cost unit.

Full (absorption) cost as the break-even price

It should be clear that, if all goes according to plan (so that direct costs, overheads and the basis of charging overheads, for example direct labour hours, prove to be as expected), then selling the output for its full cost should cause the business to break even exactly. This means that whatever profit (in total) is loaded on to full cost to set selling prices will, if plans are achieved, result in that level of profit being earned for the period.

Predicting full costs in advance

Although deducing full costs can be done after the work has been completed, it is often done in advance. In other words, costs are frequently predicted. Where, for example, full costs are needed as a basis on which to set selling prices, it will usually be necessary to set the price before the customer will accept the job being done. Even where no particular customer has been identified, some idea of the ultimate price will need to be known before the business will be able to make a judgement as to whether potential customers will buy the product, and in what quantities. There is a risk, of course, that the actual outcome will differ from that which was predicted. If this occurs, corrections are subsequently made to the full costs originally calculated.

? Self-assessment question 8.1

Promptprint Ltd, a printing business, has received an enquiry from a potential customer for the quotation of a price for a job. The pricing policy of the business is based on the plans for the next financial year shown below.

	£
Sales revenue (billings to customers)	196,000
Materials (direct)	(38,000)
Labour (direct)	(32,000)
Variable overheads	(2,400)
Advertising (for business)	(3,000)
Depreciation	(27,600)
Administration	(36,000)
Interest	(8,000)
Profit (before taxation)	49,000

A first estimate of the direct costs for the particular job is:

Direct materials: £4,000
Direct labour: £3,600

Required:
(a) Prepare a recommended price for the job based on the plans, commenting on your method.
(b) Comment on the validity of using financial plans in pricing, and recommend any improvements you would consider desirable for the pricing policy used in (a).

The answer to this question can be found at the back of the book in Appendix B.

Activity-based costing

What we have considered so far in this chapter is the traditional approach to job/batch costing (deriving the full cost of output where one unit/batch of output differs from another). This approach is to collect, for each job/batch, those costs that can be unequivocally linked to, and measured in respect of, the particular job/batch (direct costs). All other costs (overheads) are thrown into a pool of costs and charged to individual jobs/batches according to some formula, often the number of direct labour hours worked on each particular job/batch.

Costing in the traditional way

This traditional and still widely used approach to product costing was developed around the time of the Industrial Revolution, when industry was characterised by:

- *Direct-labour-intensive and direct-labour-paced production.* Labour was at the heart of production. Where machinery was used, it was to support the efforts of direct labour, and the speed of production was dictated by direct labour.
- *A low level of overheads relative to direct costs.* Little was spent on power, personnel services, machinery (leading to low depreciation charges) or other areas typical of the overheads of modern businesses.
- *A relatively uncompetitive market.* Transport difficulties, limited industrial production worldwide and a lack of knowledge by customers of competitors' prices meant that businesses could prosper without being too scientific in costing and pricing their output. Customers tended to accept what the supplier offered, rather than demanding precisely what they wanted.

Since overheads at that time represented a relatively small element of total costs, it was acceptable and practical to deal with them in a fairly arbitrary manner. Little effort was devoted to controlling the cost of overheads because the benefits of better control were relatively small, particularly compared with the benefits from firmer control of direct labour and material costs. It was also reasonable to charge overheads to individual jobs on a direct-labour-hour basis. Most of the overheads were incurred directly in support of direct labour: providing a place to work, heating and lighting that workplace, employing people to supervise the direct workers, and so on. Direct workers, perhaps aided by machinery, carried out all production.

At that time, service industries were a relatively unimportant part of the economy and would have largely consisted of self-employed individuals. These individuals would probably have been uninterested in trying to do more than work out a rough hourly/daily rate for their time and to try to base prices on this.

Costing in the new environment

In recent years, the world of industrial production has fundamentally altered. Most of it is now characterised by:

- *Capital-intensive and machine-paced production.* Machines are at the heart of much production, including service provision. Most labour supports the efforts of machines, for example technically maintaining them. Also, machines often dictate the pace of production.
- *A high level of overheads relative to direct costs.* Modern businesses tend to have very high depreciation, servicing and power costs. There are also high costs of a nature scarcely envisaged in the early days of industrial production, such as personnel and staff training costs. At the same time, there are very low (sometimes no) direct labour costs. Although direct material cost often remains an important element of total cost, more efficient production methods lead to less waste and, therefore, less total material cost, again tending to make overheads more dominant.

■ *A highly competitive, international market.* Production, much of it highly sophistic-ated, is carried out worldwide. Transport, including fast airfreight, is relatively cheap. Fax, telephone and, particularly, the Internet ensure that potential customers can quickly and cheaply find the prices of a range of suppliers. Markets now tend to be highly price-competitive. Customers increasingly demand products custom made to their own requirements. This means that businesses need to know their product costs with a greater degree of accuracy than in the past. Businesses also need to take a considered and informed approach to pricing their output.

In the UK, as in many developed countries, service industries now dominate the economy, employing the great majority of the workforce and producing most of the value of productive output. Although there are many self-employed individuals supplying services, many service providers are vast businesses such as banks, insur-ance companies and cinema operators. For most of these larger service providers, the activities closely resemble modern manufacturing activity. They too are character-ised by high capital intensity, overheads dominating direct costs and a competitive international market.

In the past, overhead recovery rates (that is, rates at which overheads are absorbed by jobs/batches) were typically of a much lower value for each direct labour hour than the rate paid to direct workers as wages or salaries. It is now, however, becoming increas-ingly common for overhead recovery rates to be between five and ten times the hourly rate of pay, because overheads are now much more significant and the direct labour input much less so. When production is dominated by direct labour paid, say, £8 an hour, it might be reasonable to have an overhead recovery rate of, say, £1 an hour. When, however, direct labour plays a relatively small part in production, to have overhead recovery rates of, say, £50 for each direct labour hour is likely to lead to very arbitrary costing. Even a small change in the amount of direct labour worked on a job/batch could massively affect the total cost deduced. This is not because the direct worker is very highly paid, but because of the effect of the direct labour change on the overhead loading. Also, overheads are still typically charged on a direct-labour-hour basis even though those overheads may not be particularly closely related to direct labour.

Real World 8.4 provides a rather disturbing view of costing and cost control in large banks.

Real World 8.4

Bank accounts

In a study of the cost structures of 52 international banks, the German consultancy firm, Droege, found that indirect costs could represent as much as 85 per cent of total costs. However, whilst direct costs were generally under tight management control, indirect costs were not. The indirect costs, which include such items as IT development, risk control, auditing, marketing and public relations, were often not allocated between operating divisions or were allocated in a rather arbitrary manner.

Source: Based on information in 'Banks have not tackled indirect costs,' A. Skorecki, ft.com, 7 January 2004.

An alternative approach to full costing

As a result of changes in the business environment, the whole question of overheads, what causes them and how they are charged to jobs/batches, has been receiving much closer attention. Historically, businesses have been content to accept that overheads exist and, therefore, for product costing purposes they must be dealt with in as practical a way as possible. In recent years, however, there has been an increasing acceptance of the fact that overheads do not just happen; they must be caused by something. To illustrate this point, let us consider Example 8.4.

Example 8.4

Modern Producers Ltd has, like virtually all manufacturers, a storage area that is set aside for its inventories of finished goods. The costs of running the stores include a share of the factory rent and other establishment costs, such as heating and lighting. They also include the salaries of staff employed to look after the inventories and the cost of financing the inventories held in the stores.

The business has two product lines: A and B. Product A tends to be made in small batches, and low levels of finished inventories are held. The business prides itself on its ability to supply Product B in relatively large quantities instantly. As a consequence, most of the space in the finished goods store is filled with finished Product Bs ready to be dispatched immediately an order is received.

Traditionally, the whole cost of operating the stores would have been treated as a general overhead and included in the total of overheads charged to batches, probably on a direct-labour-hour basis. This means that when assessing the cost of Products A and B, the cost of operating the stores has fallen on them according to the number of direct labour hours worked on each one, a factor that has nothing to do with storage.

In fact, most of the stores cost should be charged to Product B, since this product causes (and benefits from) the stores cost much more than does Product A. Failure to account more precisely for the cost of running the stores is masking the fact that Product B is not as profitable as it seems to be. It may even be leading to losses as a result of the relatively high stores-operating cost that it causes. So far, much of this cost has been charged to Product A without regard to the fact that Product A causes little of it.

What drives the costs?

Realisation that overheads do not just occur, but are caused by activities – such as holding products in stores – that 'drive' the costs, is at the heart of activity-based costing (ABC). The traditional approach is that direct labour hours are the cost driver, which probably used to be true. ABC recognises that this is often not the case.

There is a basic philosophical difference between the traditional and the ABC approaches. Traditionally we tend to think of overheads as *rendering a service to cost units*, the cost of which must be charged to those units. ABC sees overheads as being *caused by activities*, and so it is the cost units that cause the activities that must be charged with the costs that they cause.

Activity 8.9

Can you think of any other purpose that identification of the cost drivers serves, apart from deriving more accurate costs?

Identification of the activities that cause costs puts management in a position where it may well be able to control them more effectively.

It is not always easy to see how and why some overhead costs have arisen. This has traditionally made them more difficult to control than direct labour and material costs. If, however, an analysis of overheads can identify the cost drivers, questions can be asked about whether the activity driving certain costs is necessary at all, and whether the cost justifies the benefit. In Example 8.4, it may well be a good marketing policy that Product B can be supplied immediately from inventories held, but this causes a cost that should be recognised and assessed against the benefit.

Adopting ABC requires that most overheads can be analysed and the cost drivers identified. This means that it might be possible to gain much clearer insights about the overhead costs that are caused, activity by activity, so that fairer and more accurate product costs can be identified, and costs can be controlled more effectively.

Cost pools

Under ABC, an overhead cost pool is established for each cost driver in which all of the costs caused by that driver are placed. So, the business in Example 8.4 would create a cost pool for operating the stores. All costs associated with this activity would be allocated to that cost pool. The total costs in that pool would then be allocated to output (Products A and B, in this case), using the cost driver identified, according to the extent to which each unit of output 'drove' those costs.

Example 8.5

The management accountant at Modern Producers Ltd (see Example 8.4) has estimated that the costs of running the finished goods stores for next year will be £90,000. This will be the amount allocated to the 'finished goods stores cost pool'.

It is estimated that each Product A will spend an average of one week in the stores before being sold. With Product B, the equivalent period is four weeks. Both products are of roughly similar size and have similar storage needs. It is felt, therefore, that the quantity of each product and the period spent in the stores ('product weeks') are the cost drivers.

It is estimated that, next year, 50,000 Product As and 25,000 Product Bs will pass through the stores. So the total number of 'product weeks' in store will be:

Product A (50,000 × 1 week)	50,000
B (25,000 × 4 weeks)	100,000
	150,000

The stores cost for each 'product week' is given by

$$£90,000/150,000 = £0.60$$

Therefore each Product A will be charged with £0.60 for finished stores costs, and each Product B with £2.40 (that is, £0.60 × 4).

Allocating overhead costs to cost pools, as is necessary with ABC, contrasts with the traditional approach, where the overheads are normally allocated to production departments (cost centres). In both cases, however, the overheads are then charged to cost units (goods or services). The two different approaches are illustrated in Figure 8.10.

With the traditional approach, overheads are apportioned to product departments (cost centres). Each department would then derive an overhead recovery rate, typically overheads per direct labour hour. Overheads would then be applied to units of output according to how many direct labour hours were worked on them.

With ABC, the overheads are analysed into cost pools, with one cost pool for each cost driver. The overheads are then charged to units of output, through activity cost driver rates (for example, £0.60 per 'product week' for the stores cost in Example 8.5). These rates are an attempt to represent the extent to which each cost unit is believed to cause the particular part of the overheads.

Cost pools are much the same as cost centres, except that each cost pool is linked to a particular *activity* (operating the stores in Examples 8.4 and 8.5), rather than being more general, as is the case with cost centres in traditional product costing.

ABC and service industries

Much of our discussion of ABC has concentrated on manufacturing industry, perhaps because early users of ABC were manufacturing businesses. In fact, ABC is possibly even more relevant to service industries because, in the absence of a direct material element, a service business's total costs are likely to be largely made up of overheads. There is certainly evidence that ABC has been adopted more readily by businesses that sell services rather than goods, as we shall see later.

Activity 8.10

What is the difference in the way in which direct costs are accounted for when using ABC, relative to their treatment taking a traditional approach to full costing?

The answer is that there is no difference at all. ABC is concerned only with the way in which overheads are charged to jobs to derive the full cost.

Figure 8.10 Traditional versus activity-based costing

Traditional approach

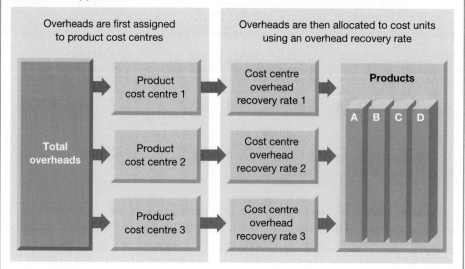

Overheads are first assigned to product cost centres

Overheads are then allocated to cost units using an overhead recovery rate

Total overheads

Product cost centre 1 → Cost centre overhead recovery rate 1

Product cost centre 2 → Cost centre overhead recovery rate 2

Product cost centre 3 → Cost centre overhead recovery rate 3

Products A B C D

ABC approach

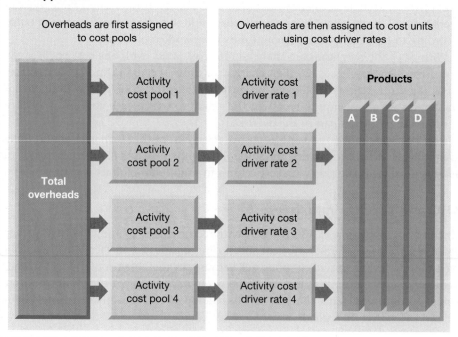

Overheads are first assigned to cost pools

Overheads are then assigned to cost units using cost driver rates

Total overheads

Activity cost pool 1 → Activity cost driver rate 1

Activity cost pool 2 → Activity cost driver rate 2

Activity cost pool 3 → Activity cost driver rate 3

Activity cost pool 4 → Activity cost driver rate 4

Products A B C D

With the traditional approach, overheads are first assigned to product cost centres and then overheads are absorbed by cost units based on an overhead recovery rate (using direct labour hours worked on the cost units, or some other approach) for each department. With activity-based costing, overheads are assigned to cost pools and then cost units are charged with overheads to the extent that they drive the costs in the various pools.

Source: Adapted from *Activity Based Costing: A Review with Case Studies*, J. Innes and F. Mitchell, CIMA Publishing, 1990.

Criticisms of ABC

Critics of ABC argue that analysing overheads in order to identify cost drivers is time-consuming and costly, and that the benefit of doing so, in terms of more accurate product costing and the potential for cost control, does not justify the cost of carrying out the analysis.

ABC is also criticised for the same reason that full costing is generally criticised, which is that it does not provide relevant information for decision-making. This point will be addressed in the following section.

Even if ABC-derived product costs were not really helpful (and many would argue that they *are* helpful), identifying the activities that cause the costs may still be well worth doing. As was pointed out above, knowing what drives the costs may make cost control more effective.

Real World 8.5 shows how ABC came to be used at the Royal Mail.

Real World 8.5

Delivering ABC

Early in the 2000s the publicly owned Royal Mail adopted ABC and used it to find the cost of making postal deliveries. Royal Mail identified 340 activities that gave rise to costs and created a cost pool and identified a cost driver for each of these.

Roger Tabour, Royal Mail's Enterprise Systems Programme Director, explained 'A new regulatory and competitive environment, plus a down-turned economy, led management to seek out more reliable sources of information on performance and profitability', and this led to the introduction of ABC.

The Royal Mail is a public-sector organisation that is subject to supervision by Postcomm, the UK-government-appointed regulatory body. The government requires the Royal Mail to operate on a commercial basis and to make profits.

Source: www.sas.com.

Real World 8.6 provides some indication of the extent to which ABC is used in practice.

Real World 8.6

ABC in practice

A survey was carried out of 528 businesses that are all members of BetterManagement, a division of SAS Institute, the world's largest private software business. It covered various industries with a wide international spread and showed that 34 per cent were actively using ABC, 20 per cent were piloting ABC within the business and 32 per cent were considering using ABC. However, these figures varied significantly according to size and industry. Figure 8.11 shows the breakdown according to the size of the business.

The survey shows that the greater the size of the business, the more likely it is to use ABC.

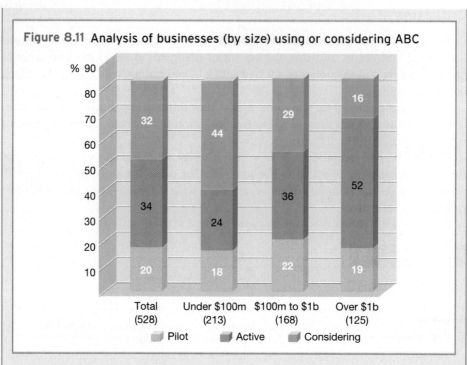

Figure 8.11 Analysis of businesses (by size) using or considering ABC

Figure 8.12 shows the breakdown according to industry type.

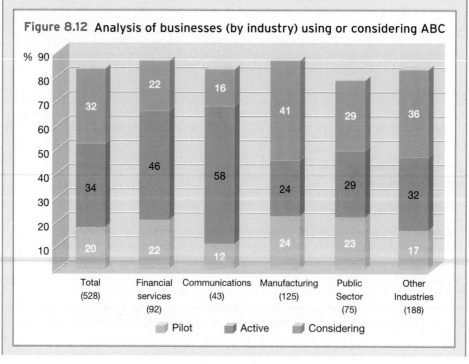

Figure 8.12 Analysis of businesses (by industry) using or considering ABC

We can see that communications and financial services appear to have embraced ABC much more enthusiastically than other industries identified. Interestingly, manufacturing businesses have shown a relatively low level of interest in ABC, when compared with other industries in the survey.

Source: 'Activity Based Costing: How ABC is used in the organisation', Bettermanagement, www.sas.com, September 2005, pp. 2 and 3.

A separate survey of businesses within the UK food and drinks industry – which is the largest manufacturing industry in the UK – revealed only a lukewarm response to ABC. The findings are, therefore, broadly consistent with those mentioned above. When asked to indicate the degree of importance assigned to ABC, the following answers (based on 112 respondents) were given:

	Percentage of respondents
Important	12
Moderately important	34
Not important	54
	100

This means that fewer than 50 per cent of respondents to the survey regarded ABC as important to them.

Source: 'Management accounting practices in the food and drinks industry', M. Abdel-Kader and R. Luther, CIMA Research, 2006, p. 15.

Criticisms of full (absorption) costing methods

Both the traditional and the ABC methods have been criticised because, in practice, they tend to use past (historic) costs. It can be argued that past costs are irrelevant, irrespective of the purpose for which the information is to be used. This is basically because it is not possible to make decisions about the past, only about the future. Advocates of full costing methods would argue, however, that they provide a useful guide to long-run average cost.

Despite the criticisms made of full costing methods, research evidence suggests that their use is widespread. An International Accounting Standard (IAS 2 *Inventories*) requires that all inventories, including work in progress, be valued at full cost in the published financial reports. This fact demands the use of full costing. As a result, businesses that have work in progress and/or inventories of finished goods at the end of their financial periods apply full costing for income measurement purposes. (This will include the many service providers that tend to have work in progress.)

Summary

The main points in this chapter may be summarised as follows.

Full (absorption) cost

■ Full (absorption) cost is the total amount of resources sacrificed to achieve a particular objective.

Uses of full (absorption) cost information

■ Pricing and output decisions.

■ Exercising control.

■ Assessing relative efficiency.

■ Income measurement.

Single-product businesses

■ Where all units of output are identical, the full cost can be calculated as follows:

$$\text{Cost per unit} = \frac{\text{Total cost of output}}{\text{Number of units produced}}$$

Multi-product businesses – job costing

■ Where units of output are not identical, it is necessary to divide the costs into two categories: direct costs and indirect costs.

■ Direct costs are costs that can be identified with specific cost units (for example, labour of a garage mechanic, in relation to a particular job).

■ Indirect costs (overheads) are costs that cannot be directly measured in respect of a particular job (for example, the rent of a garage).

■ Full (absorption) cost = direct cost + indirect cost.

■ The direct/indirect distinction is not linked to the variable/fixed distinction.

■ Indirect costs are difficult to relate to individual cost units. Arbitrary bases are used and there is no single correct method.

■ Traditionally, indirect costs are seen as the costs of providing a 'service' to cost units.

■ The direct-labour-hour basis of applying indirect costs to cost units is the most popular in practice.

Dealing with overheads on a departmental basis

■ Indirect costs can be segmented, usually on a departmental basis. Each department has its own overhead recovery rate.

■ Each department is a separate cost centre, that is, an area, activity or function for which costs are separately collected.

Batch costing

■ Batch costing is a variation of job costing where each job consists of a number of identical (or near identical) cost units.

■ The cost per unit can be calculated as follows:

$$\text{Cost per unit} = \frac{\text{Cost of the batch (direct + indirect)}}{\text{Number of units in the batch}}$$

Break-even price and full (absorption) costing

■ If the full (absorption) cost is charged as the sales price and things go according to plan, the business will break even.

Criticisms of full (absorption) costing

■ Full cost information is seen by some as not very useful because it can be backward-looking: it includes information irrelevant to decision-making, but excludes some relevant information.

Activity-based costing

■ Activity-based costing is an approach to dealing with overheads (in full costing) that treats all costs as being caused or 'driven' by activities.

■ Advocates argue that it is more relevant to the modern commercial environment than is the traditional approach.

■ Identification of the cost drivers can lead to more relevant indirect cost treatment in full costing.

■ Identification of the cost drivers can also lead to better control of overheads.

■ Critics argue that ABC is time-consuming and expensive to apply – not justified by the possible improvement in the quality of information.

→ Key terms

Further reading

If you would like to explore the topics covered in this chapter in more depth, we recommend the following books:

Atkinson, A., Kaplan, R., Young, S. M. and Matsumura, E. *Management Accounting*, (5th edn), Prentice Hall, 2007, chapter 3.

Atrill, P. and McLaney, E. *Management Accounting for Decision Makers*, (5th edn), FT/Prentice Hall 2007, chapters 4 and 5.

Drury, C. *Management and Cost Accounting*, (8th edn), Thomson Learning, 2008, chapters 3, 4, 5 and 10.

Horngren, C., Foster, G. and Datar, S. *Cost Accounting: A Managerial Emphasis*, (12th edn), Prentice Hall, 2006, chapter 4.

? Review questions

Answers to these questions can be found at the back of the book in Appendix C.

8.1 What problem does the existence of work in progress cause in process costing?

8.2 What is the point of distinguishing direct costs from indirect ones? Why is this not necessary in process-costing environments?

8.3 Are direct costs and variable costs the same thing? Explain your answer.

8.4 It is sometimes claimed that the full cost of pursuing some objective represents the long-run break-even selling price. Why is this said, and what does it mean?

✳ Exercises

Exercises 8.4 and 8.5 are more advanced than Exercises 8.1 to 8.3. Those with coloured numbers have answers at the back of the book in Appendix D.

If you wish to try more exercises, visit MyAccountingLab/

8.1 Distinguish between

- job costing,
- process costing, and
- batch costing.

What tend to be the problems specifically associated with each of these?

8.2 Pieman Products Ltd makes road trailers to the precise specifications of individual customers. The following are predicted to occur during the forthcoming year, which is about to start.

Direct materials cost	£50,000
Direct labour costs	£160,000
Direct labour time	16,000 hours
Indirect labour cost	£25,000
Depreciation of machine	£8,000
Rent and rates	£10,000
Heating, lighting and power	£5,000
Indirect materials	£2,000
Other indirect costs	£1,000
Machine time	3,000 hours

All direct labour is paid at the same hourly rate.

A customer has asked the business to build a trailer for transporting a racing motor-cycle to races. It is estimated that this will require materials and components that will cost £1,150. It will take 250 direct labour hours to do the job, of which 50 will involve the use of machinery.

Required:

Deduce a logical cost for the job, and explain the basis of dealing with overheads that you propose.

8.3 Athena Ltd is an engineering business doing work for its customers to their particular requirements and specifications. It determines the full cost of each job taking a 'job-costing' approach, accounting for overheads on a departmental basis. It bases its prices to customers on this full cost figure. The business has two departments: a machining department, where each job starts, and a fitting department, which completes all of the jobs. Machining department overheads are charged to jobs on a machine-hour basis and those of the fitting department on a direct-labour-hour basis. The budgeted information for next year is as follows:

Heating and lighting	£25,000	(allocated equally between the two departments)
Machine power	£10,000	(all allocated to the machining department)
Direct labour	£200,000	(£150,000 allocated to the fitting department and £50,000 to the machining department. All direct workers are paid £10 an hour)
Indirect labour	£50,000	(apportioned to the departments in proportion to the direct labour cost)
Direct materials	£120,000	(all applied to jobs in the machining department)
Depreciation	£30,000	(all relates to the machining department)
Machine time	20,000 hours	(all worked in the machining department)

Required:

(a) Prepare a statement showing the budgeted overheads for next year, analysed between the two departments. This should be in the form of three columns: one for the total figure for each type of overhead and one column each for the two departments, where each type of overhead is analysed between the two departments. Each column should also show the total of overheads for the year.

(b) Derive the appropriate rate for charging the overheads of each department to jobs (that is, a separate rate for each department).

(c) Athena Ltd has been asked by a customer to specify the price that it will charge for a particular job that will, if the job goes ahead, be undertaken early next year. The job is expected to use direct materials costing Athena Ltd £1,200, to need 50 hours of machining time, 5 hours of machining department direct labour and 20 hours of fitting department direct labour. Athena Ltd charges a profit loading of 20% to the full cost of jobs to determine the selling price.

Show workings to derive the proposed selling price for this job.

8.4 Kaplan plc makes a range of suitcases of various sizes and shapes. There are ten different models of suitcase produced by the business. In order to keep inventories of finished suitcases to a minimum, each model is made in a small batch. Each batch is costed as a separate job and the cost for each suitcase deduced by dividing the batch cost by the number of suitcases in the batch.

At present, the business derives the cost of each batch using a traditional job-costing approach. Recently, however, a new management accountant was appointed, who is advocating the use of activity-based costing (ABC) to deduce the cost of the batches. The management accountant claims that ABC leads to much more reliable and relevant costs and that it has other benefits.

Required:

(a) Explain how the business deduces the cost of each suitcase at present.

(b) Discuss the purposes to which the knowledge of the cost for each suitcase, deduced on a traditional basis, can be put and how valid the cost is for the purpose concerned.

(c) Explain how ABC could be applied to costing the suitcases, highlighting the differences between ABC and the traditional approach.

(d) Explain what advantages the new management accountant probably believes ABC to have over the traditional approach.

8.5 Consider this statement:

'In a job costing system, it is necessary to divide up the business into departments. Fixed costs (or overheads) will be collected for each department. Where a particular fixed cost relates to the business as a whole, it must be divided between the departments. Usually this is done on the basis of area of floor space occupied by each department relative to the entire business. When the total fixed costs for each department have been identified, this will be divided by the number of hours that were worked in each department to deduce an overhead recovery rate. Each job that was worked on in a department will have a share of fixed costs allotted to it according to how long it was worked on. The total cost for each job will therefore be the sum of the variable costs of the job and its share of the fixed costs. It is essential that this approach is taken in order to deduce a selling price for the business's output.'

Required:

Prepare a table of two columns. In the first column you should show any phrases or sentences in the above statement with which you do not agree, and in the second column you should show your reason for disagreeing with each one.

Chapter 9

Budgeting

Introduction

Budgets are an important tool for management planning and control. In this chapter, we examine the role and nature of budgets and see how budgets are prepared. Preparing budgets relies on an understanding of the financial statements (balance sheet and income statement), which we considered in Chapters 2 and 3. It also requires an understanding of issues relating to the behaviour of costs and full costing, which we considered in Chapters 7 and 8.

Budgets do not exist in a vacuum; they are an important part of a planning framework that is adopted by well-run businesses. Thus, to understand fully the nature of budgets, we must also understand the framework within which they are set. The chapter begins with a discussion of this planning framework before going on to consider detailed aspects of the budgeting process.

Learning outcomes

When you have completed this chapter, you should be able to:

- define a budget and show how budgets, strategic objectives and strategic plans are related;
- explain the budgeting process and the interlinking of the various budgets within the business;
- indicate the uses of budgeting and construct various budgets, including the cash budget, from relevant data;
- explain how flexing the budget can be used to exercise control over a business.

How budgets link with strategic plans and objectives

It is vital that businesses develop plans for the future. Whatever a business is trying to achieve, it is unlikely to come about unless its managers are clear what the future direction of the business is going to be. The development of plans involves five key steps:

→ 1 *Establish mission and objectives.* The mission statement is a statement of broad intent. A food manufacturer, for example, may have a mission to be *'the supplier of choice for UK retailers in convenience foods'*. Strategic (long-term) objectives are then developed to translate this broad intent into more specific and, often, quantifiable goals.

2 *Undertake a position analysis.* This is to assess where the business is currently placed relative to where it wants to be, as defined by its objectives.

3 *Identify and assess the strategic options.* Here the business considers the various ways in which it might move from where it is now (identified in step 2) to where it wants to be (identified in step 1).

4 *Select strategic options.* This involves selecting what seems to be the best of the courses of action or strategies (identified in step 3) and formulating a strategic plan. The plan is normally broken down into a series of plans, one for each element of

→ the business. These plans are the budgets. A budget is a business plan for the short term – typically one year. It is likely to be expressed mainly in financial terms and its role is to convert the strategic plans into actionable blueprints for the immediate future. Budgets will define precise targets concerning such things as
   - cash receipts and payments
   - sales volumes and revenues, broken down into amounts and prices for each of the products or services provided by the business
   - detailed inventories requirements
   - detailed labour requirements
   - specific production requirements.

5 *Perform, review and control.* Here the business pursues the budgets derived in step 4. By comparing the actual outcome with the budgets, managers can see if things are going according to plan. Action would be taken to exercise control where actual performance appears not to be matching the budgets.

The relationship between the mission, strategic objectives, strategic plans and budgets is that:

- the mission sets the overall direction and, once set, is likely to last for quite a long time – perhaps throughout the life of the business;
- the strategic objectives, which are also long-term, will articulate how the mission can be achieved;
- the strategic plans identify how each objective will be pursued; and
- the budgets set out, in detail, the short-term plans and targets necessary to fulfil the strategic objectives.

An analogy might be found in terms of a student enrolling on a course of study. His or her mission might be to have a happy and fulfilling life. A key strategic objective flowing from this mission might be to embark on a career that will be rewarding in various ways. He or she might have identified the particular study course as the most effective way to work towards this objective. Successfully completing the course would then be the strategic plan. In working towards this strategic plan, passing a particular stage of the course might be identified as the target for the forthcoming year. This short-term target is analogous to the budget. Having achieved the 'budget' for the first year, the budget for the second year becomes passing the second stage.

Collecting information on performance and exercising control

However well planned the activities of a business might be, they will come to nothing unless steps are taken to try to achieve them in practice. The process of making planned events actually occur is known as control. This is part of step 5 (above).

Control can be defined as compelling events to conform to plan. This definition is valid in any context. For example, when we talk about controlling a motor car, we mean making the car do what we plan that it should do. In a business context, management accounting is very useful in the control process. This is because it is possible to state plans in accounting terms (as budgets). Since it is also possible to state *actual* outcomes in the same terms, making comparison between actual and planned outcomes is a relatively simple matter. Where actual outcomes are at variance with budgets, this variance should be highlighted by accounting information. Managers can then take steps to get the business back on track towards the achievement of the budgets. We shall be looking more closely at the control aspect of budgeting later in the chapter.

It should be emphasised that planning (including budgeting) is the responsibility of managers rather than accountants. Although management accountants play a major role in the planning process, by supplying relevant information to managers and by contributing to decision-making as part of the management team, they should not dominate the process. In practice, it seems that the budgeting aspect of planning is in danger of being dominated by accountants, perhaps because most budgets are expressed in financial terms. However, managers are failing in their responsibilities if they allow this to happen.

Figure 9.1 shows the planning and control process in diagrammatic form.

Time horizon of plans and budgets

Setting strategic plans is typically a major exercise, performed about every five years. Budgets are usually set annually for the forthcoming year. It does not have to be the case that strategic plans are set for five years and that budgets are set for one year: it is up to the management concerned. Businesses involved in certain industries – say, information technology – may feel that five years is too long a planning period since new developments can, and do, occur virtually overnight. Such businesses may feel that a planning horizon of two or three years is more feasible. Similarly, a budget need not be set for one year, although this appears to be a widely used time horizon.

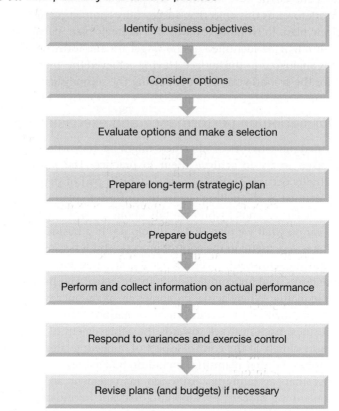

Figure 9.1 The planning and control process

Identify business objectives

Consider options

Evaluate options and make a selection

Prepare long-term (strategic) plan

Prepare budgets

Perform and collect information on actual performance

Respond to variances and exercise control

Revise plans (and budgets) if necessary

Once the objectives of the business have been determined, the various options that can fulfil them must be considered and evaluated and a strategic plan derived. The budget is a short-term financial plan for the business that is prepared within the framework of the strategic plan. Control can be exercised through the comparison of budgeted and actual performance. Where a significant divergence emerges, some form of corrective action should be taken. If the budget figures prove to be based on incorrect assumptions about the future, it might be necessary to revise the budget.

Activity 9.1

Can you think of any reason why most businesses prepare detailed budgets for the forthcoming year, rather than for a shorter or longer period?

The reason is probably that a year represents a long enough time for the budget preparation exercise to be worthwhile, yet short enough into the future for detailed plans to be capable of being made. The process of formulating budgets can be a time-consuming exercise, but there are economies of scale – for example, preparing the budget for the next year would not normally take twice as much time and effort as preparing the budget for the next six months.

An annual budget sets targets for the forthcoming year for all aspects of the business. It is usually broken down into monthly budgets, which define monthly targets. Indeed, in many instances, the annual budget will be built up from monthly figures. For example, the sales staff will be required to set sales targets for each month of the budget period. Other budgets will be set, for each month of the budget period, as we shall explain below.

Limiting factors

There will always be some aspect of the business that will stop it achieving its objectives to the maximum extent. This is often a limited ability of the business to sell its products. Sometimes, it is some production shortage (such as labour, materials or plant capacity) that is the limiting factor, or, linked to these, a shortage of funds. Often, production shortages can be overcome by an increase in funds – for example, more plant can be bought or leased. This is not always a practical solution because no amount of money will buy certain labour skills or increase the world supply of some raw material.

It is sometimes possible to ease an initial limiting factor: for example, subcontracting can eliminate a plant capacity problem. This means that some other factor, perhaps sales, will replace the production problem, though at a higher level of output. Ultimately, however, the business will hit a ceiling; some limiting factor will prove impossible to ease.

It is important that the limiting factor is identified. Ultimately, most, if not all, budgets will be affected by the limiting factor, and so if it can be identified at the outset, all managers can be informed of the restriction early in the process. This will enable them to take account of the limiting factor when preparing the budgets.

Budgets and forecasts

As we have seen, a budget may be defined as a business plan for the short term. Budgets are, to a great extent, expressed in financial terms. Note, particularly, that a budget is a *plan*, not a forecast. To talk of a plan suggests an intention or determination to achieve the targets; forecasts tend to be predictions of the future state of the environment.

Clearly, forecasts are helpful to the planner/budget-setter. If, for example, a reputable forecaster has forecast the number of new cars to be purchased in the UK during next year, it will be valuable for managers in a car manufacturing business to take account of this forecast figure when setting next year's sales budgets. However, a forecast and a budget are distinctly different.

Periodic and continual budgets

Budgeting can be undertaken on a periodic or a continual basis. A periodic budget is prepared for a particular period (usually one year). Managers will agree the budget for the year and then allow the budget to run its course. Although it may be necessary to revise the budget on occasions, the budget is prepared just once during each financial year. A continual budget, as the name suggests, is continually updated. We have seen that an annual budget will normally be broken down into smaller time intervals (usually monthly periods) to help control the activities of a business. A continual budget will add a new month to replace the month that has just passed, thereby ensuring that, at all times, there will be a budget for a full planning period. Continual budgets are also referred to as rolling budgets.

Activity 9.2

Which method of budgeting do you think is likely to be more costly and which method is likely to be of more benefit for forward planning?

Periodic budgeting will usually take less time and effort to prepare and will therefore be less costly. However, as time passes, the budget period shortens, and towards the end of the financial year managers will be working to a very short planning period. Continual budgeting, on the other hand, will ensure that managers always have a full year's budget to help them make decisions. It is claimed that continual budgeting ensures that managers plan throughout the year rather than just once each year. In this way it encourages a forward-looking attitude.

Although continual budgeting encourages a forward-looking attitude, there is a danger that it will become a mechanical exercise. Managers may not have time to step back from their other tasks each month and consider the future carefully. It may be unreasonable to expect managers continually to take this future-oriented perspective.

How budgets link to one another

A business will prepare more than one budget for a particular period. Each budget prepared will relate to a specific aspect of the business. The ideal situation is, perhaps, where there is a separate budget for each person who is in a managerial position, no matter how junior. The contents of all of the individual budgets will be summarised in master budgets, usually consisting of a budgeted income statement and balance sheet. The cash flow statement (in summarised form) is considered by some to be a third master budget.

Figure 9.2 illustrates the interrelationship and interlinking of individual budgets, using a manufacturing business as an example.

The sales budget is usually the first budget to be prepared (at the left of Figure 9.2), as the level of sales often determines the overall level of activity for the forthcoming period. This is because it is probably the most common limiting factor (see above). The level of sales tends to dictate the finished inventories requirement, though this would

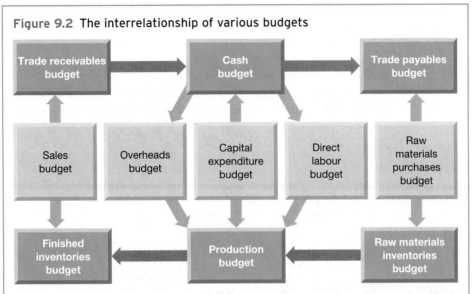

Figure 9.2 The interrelationship of various budgets

This is the interrelationship between budgets in a manufacturing business. The starting point is usually the sales budget. The expected level of sales frequently defines the overall level of activity for the business; the other budgets will be drawn up in accordance with this. Thus the sales budget will largely define the finished inventories requirements and from this we can define the production requirements and so on.

also be dictated by the policy of the business on the amount of finished products to be held in inventories. The requirement for finished inventories will define the required production levels, which will, in turn, dictate the requirements of the individual production departments or sections. The demands of manufacturing, in conjunction with the business's policy on how long it holds raw materials before they enter production, define the raw materials inventories budget. The purchases budget will be dictated by the materials inventories budget, which will, in conjunction with the policy of the business on taking credit from suppliers, dictate the trade payables budget. One of the determinants of the cash budget will be the trade payables budget; another will be the trade receivables budget, which itself derives, through the business's policy on credit periods granted to credit customers, from the sales budget. Cash will also be affected by overheads and direct labour costs (themselves linked to production) and by capital expenditure. The factors that affect policies on matters such as inventories holding and trade receivables collection and trade payables payment periods will be discussed in some detail in Chapter 12.

A manufacturing business has been used as the example in Figure 9.2 simply because it has all of the types of budgets found in practice. Service businesses have similar arrangements of budgets, but obviously do not have inventories budgets. All of the issues relating to budgets apply equally well to all types of business.

It may prove to be the case that it is not sales demand that is the limiting factor. Assuming that the budgeting process takes the order just described, it might be found in practice that there is some constraint other than sales demand. For example, the production capacity of the business may be incapable of meeting the necessary levels of output to match the sales budget for one or more months. In this case, it might be reasonable to look at ways of overcoming the problem. As a last resort, it might be necessary to revise the sales budget to a lower level to enable production to meet the target.

Activity 9.3

Can you think of any ways in which a manufacturer's short-term shortage of production facilities might be overcome?

We thought of the following:

- higher production in previous months and stockpiling to meet periods of higher demand
- increasing production capacity, perhaps by working overtime and/or acquiring (buying or leasing) additional plant
- subcontracting some production
- encouraging potential customers to change the timing of their buying by offering discounts or other special terms during quiet months.

You might well have thought of other approaches.

There will be the horizontal relationships between budgets, which we have just looked at, but there will usually be vertical ones as well. For example, the sales budget may be broken down into a number of subsidiary budgets, perhaps one for each regional sales manager. The overall sales budget will be a summary of the subsidiary ones. The same may be true of virtually all of the other budgets, most particularly the production budget.

Figure 9.3 shows the vertical relationship for the sales budgets for a business. The business has four geographical sales regions, each one the responsibility of a separate manager who is probably located in the region concerned. Each regional manager is responsible to the overall sales manager for the business. The overall sales budget is the sum of the budgets for the four sales regions.

Although sales are often managed on a geographical basis and so their budgets reflect this, sales may be managed on some other basis. For example, a business that sells a range of products may manage sales on a product-type basis, with a specialist manager responsible for each type of product. For example, an insurance business may have separate sales managers, and so separate sales budgets, for life insurance, household insurance, motor insurance and so on. Very large businesses may even have separate product-type managers for each geographical region. Each of these managers would have a separate budget, and these would combine to form the overall sales budget for the business as a whole.

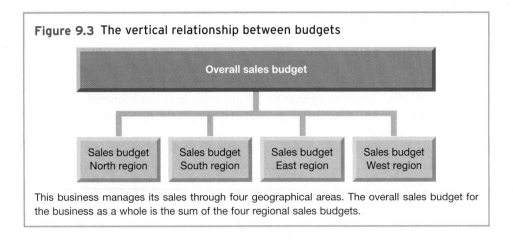

Figure 9.3 The vertical relationship between budgets

This business manages its sales through four geographical areas. The overall sales budget for the business as a whole is the sum of the four regional sales budgets.

All of the operating budgets that we have just reviewed have to be consistent with the overall short-term plans laid out in the master budget, that is, the budgeted income statement and balance sheet.

How budgets help managers

Budgets are generally regarded as having five areas of usefulness. These are:

■ *Budgets tend to promote forward thinking and the possible identification of short-term problems.* We saw above that a shortage of production capacity might be identified during the budgeting process. Making this discovery in good time could leave a number of means of overcoming the problem open to exploration. If the potential production problem is picked up early enough, all of the suggestions in the answer to Activity 9.3 and, possibly, other ways of overcoming the problem can be explored. Early identification of the potential problem gives managers time for calm and rational consideration of the best way of overcoming it. The best solution to the potential problem may be feasible only if action can be taken well in advance. This would be true of all of the suggestions made in the answer to Activity 9.3.

■ *Budgets can help co-ordinate various sections of the business.* It is crucially important that the activities of the various departments and sections of the business are linked so that the activities of one are complementary to those of another. For example, the activities of the purchasing/procurement department of a manufacturing business should dovetail with the raw materials needs of the production departments. If this is not the case, production could run out of raw materials, leading to expensive production stoppages. Possibly just as undesirable, excessive amounts of raw materials could be bought, leading to large and unnecessary inventories-holding costs. We shall see how this co-ordination tends to work in practice later in this chapter.

■ *Budgets can motivate managers to better performance.* Having a stated task can motivate managers and staff in their performance. It is generally accepted that to tell managers to do their best is not very motivating, but to define a required level of achievement for each manager is more likely to encourage good performance. It is felt that managers will be better motivated by being able to relate their particular role in the business to the overall business objectives. Since budgets are directly derived from these objectives, budgeting makes this possible. It is clearly not possible to allow managers to operate in an unconstrained environment. Having to operate in a way that matches the goals of the business is a price of working in an effective organisation.

■ *Budgets can provide a basis for control.* As mentioned earlier in the chapter, control is concerned with ensuring that events conform to plans. If senior management wishes to control and monitor the performance of more junior staff, it needs some yardstick against which the performance can be measured and assessed. It is possible to compare current performance with past performance or perhaps with what happens in another business. However, the most logical yardstick is usually planned performance. If there is information available concerning the actual performance for a period, and this can be compared with the planned performance, then a basis for control will have been established. Such a basis will enable the use of management by exception, a technique where senior managers can spend most of their time dealing with those staff or activities that have failed to achieve the budget (the exceptions). This means that senior managers do not have to spend too much time on those that are performing well. It also allows junior managers to exercise self-control. By knowing what is expected of them and what they have actually achieved, they can assess how well they are performing and take steps to correct matters where they are failing to achieve.

■ *Budgets can provide a system of authorisation for managers to spend up to a particular limit.* Some activities (for example, staff development and research expenditure) are allocated a fixed amount of funds at the discretion of senior management. This provides the authority to spend.

Figure 9.4 shows the benefits of budgets in diagrammatic form.

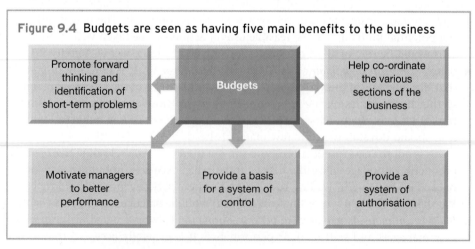

Figure 9.4 Budgets are seen as having five main benefits to the business

Promote forward thinking and identification of short-term problems	Budgets	Help co-ordinate the various sections of the business
Motivate managers to better performance	Provide a basis for a system of control	Provide a system of authorisation

The following two activities pick up issues that relate to some of the uses of budgets.

Activity 9.4

The third point on the above list of the uses of budgets (motivation) implies that managers are set stated tasks. Do you think there is a danger that requiring managers to work towards such predetermined targets will stifle their skill, flair and enthusiasm?

If the budgets are set in such a way as to offer challenging yet achievable targets, the manager is still required to show skill, flair and enthusiasm. There is the danger, however, that if targets are badly set (either unreasonably demanding or too easy to achieve), they will become a demotivating force and will fail to exploit the talents of managers.

Activity 9.5

The fourth point on the above list of the uses of budgets (control) implies that current management performance is compared with some yardstick. What is wrong with comparing actual performance with past performance, or the performance of others, in an effort to exercise control?

There is no automatic reason to believe that what happened in the past, or is happening elsewhere, represents a sensible target for the current year of a particular business. Considering what happened last year, and in other businesses, may help in the formulation of plans, but past events and the performance of others should not automatically be seen as the target.

The five identified uses of budgets can conflict with one another on occasions. Where, for example, a budget is being used as a system of authorisation, managers may be motivated to spend to the limit of their budget, even though this may be wasteful. This may occur where the managers are not allowed to carry over unused funds to the next budget period or where they believe that the budget for the next period will be reduced because not all the funds for the current period were spent. The wasting of resources in this way conflicts with the role of budgets as a means of exercising control.

Conflict between the different uses will mean that managers must decide which particular uses for budgets should be given priority; managers must be prepared, if necessary, to trade off the benefits resulting from one particular use for the benefits of another.

Using budgets in practice

There is quite a lot of recent survey evidence that reveals the extent to which budgeting is used by businesses in practice. Real World 9.1 reviews some of this evidence and shows that most businesses prepare and use budgets.

Real World 9.1

Budgeting in practice

A recent survey of 41 UK manufacturing businesses found that 40 of the 41 prepare budgets.

Source: 'Contemporary management accounting practices in UK manufacturing', D. Dugdale, C. Jones and S. Green, CIMA Research, 2005.

Another recent survey of UK businesses, but this time businesses involved in the food and drink sector, found that virtually all of them use budgets.

Source: 'Management accounting practices in the food and drinks industry', M. Abdel-Kader and R. Luther, CIMA Research, 2006.

A survey of management accounting practice in the US was conducted in 2003. Nearly 2,000 businesses replied to the survey. These tended to be larger businesses, of which about 40 per cent were manufacturers and about 16 per cent financial services; the remainder were across a range of other industries.

The survey revealed that 75 per cent use operational budgeting extensively, with a further 16 per cent considering using the technique in the future.

Source: 2003 Survey of Management Accounting, Ernst and Young.

Although these three surveys relate to UK and US businesses, they provide some insights about what is likely also to be practice elsewhere in the developed world.

Real World 9.2 gives the results of a survey of budgeting practice in small and medium-sized enterprises (SMEs). It shows that not all such businesses fully use budgeting. It seems that some smaller businesses prepare budgets only for what they see as key areas. The budget that is most frequently prepared by such businesses is the sales budget, followed by the budgeted income statement and the overheads budget. Perhaps surprisingly, the cash budget is prepared by less than two-thirds of the small businesses surveyed.

Real World 9.2

Preparation of budgets in SMEs

A study of budgeting practice in SMEs revealed that the most frequently prepared budget is the sales budget, followed by the budgeted income statement and the overheads budget (see Figure 9.5).

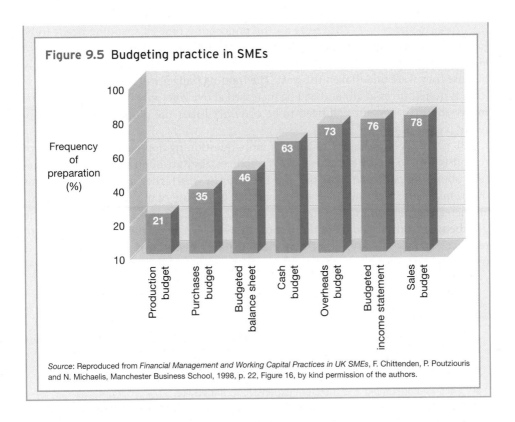

Figure 9.5 Budgeting practice in SMEs

Source: Reproduced from *Financial Management and Working Capital Practices in UK SMEs*, F. Chittenden, P. Poutziouris and N. Michaelis, Manchester Business School, 1998, p. 22, Figure 16, by kind permission of the authors.

Incremental and zero-base budgeting

Traditionally, much budget-setting has been on the basis of what happened in the previous year, with some adjustment for any changes in factors that are expected to affect the forthcoming budget period (for example, inflation). This approach is sometimes known as incremental budgeting; it is often used for 'discretionary' budgets, such as research and development and staff training, where the budget holder (the manager responsible for the budget) is allocated a sum of money to be spent in the area of activity concerned. They are referred to as discretionary budgets because the sum allocated is normally at the discretion of senior management. These budgets are very common in local and central government (and in other public bodies), but are also used in commercial businesses to cover certain types of activity.

Discretionary budgets are often used for activities where there is no clear relationship between inputs (resources applied) and outputs (benefits). Compare this with, say, a raw materials usage budget in a manufacturing business, where the amount of material used and, therefore, the amount of funds involved, is clearly related to the level of production and, ultimately, to sales volumes. It is easy for discretionary budgets to eat up funds with no clear benefit being derived. Often only proposed increases in these budgets are closely scrutinised.

315

➡ Zero-base budgeting (ZBB) rests on the philosophy that all spending needs to be justified. For example, when establishing, say, the training budget each year, it is not automatically accepted that training courses should be financed in the future simply because they were undertaken this year. The training budget will start from a zero base (that is no resources at all) and will be increased above zero only if a good case can be made. Top management will need to be convinced that the proposed activities represent 'value for money'.

ZBB encourages managers to adopt a more questioning approach to their areas of responsibility. To justify the allocation of resources, they are often forced to think carefully about the particular activities and the ways in which they are undertaken. This questioning approach should result in a more efficient use of business resources. With an increasing portion of the total costs of most businesses being in areas where the link between outputs and inputs is not always clear, and where commitment of resources is discretionary rather than demonstrably essential to production, ZBB is increasingly relevant.

Activity 9.6

Can you think of any disadvantages of using ZBB?

The principal problems with ZBB are:

- It is time-consuming and therefore expensive to undertake.
- Managers whose sphere of responsibility is subjected to ZBB can feel threatened by it.

The benefits of a ZBB approach can be gained to some extent – perhaps at not too great a cost – by using the approach on a selective basis. For example, a particular budget area could be subjected to ZBB-type scrutiny only every third or fourth year. In any case, if ZBB is used more frequently, there is the danger that managers will use the same arguments each year to justify their activities. The process will simply become a mechanical exercise and the benefits will be lost. For a typical business, some areas are likely to benefit from ZBB more than others. ZBB could, in these circumstances, be applied only to those areas that will benefit from it, and not to the others. The areas that are most likely to benefit from ZBB are discretionary spending ones, such as training, advertising, and research and development.

If senior management is aware of the potentially threatening nature of this form of budgeting, care can be taken to apply ZBB with sensitivity. However, in the quest for cost control and value for money, the application of ZBB can result in some tough decisions being made.

Real World 9.3 provides some insight to the extent that ZBB is used in practice.

ZBB is not food and drink to many businesses

The 2001 survey of businesses in the UK food and drink sector found that ZBB is not much used by them. Only 48 per cent ever use it and only 16 per cent use it 'often' or 'very often'.

ZBB is, however most appropriate with 'spending' budgets, such as training, advertising and so on, which probably represent a minority for the types of business in this survey.

Source: 'Management accounting practices in the food and drinks industry', M. Abdel-Kader and R. Luther, CIMA Research, 2006.

Preparing the cash budget

We shall now look in some detail at how the various budgets used by the typical business are prepared, starting with the cash budget and then looking at the others. It is helpful for us to start with the cash budget because

■ it is a key budget (some observers see it as a 'master budget' – along with the budgeted income statement and balance sheet); most economic aspects of a business are reflected in cash sooner or later, so that for a typical business, the cash budget reflects the whole business more than any other single budget;

■ very small, unsophisticated businesses (for example, a corner shop) may feel that full-scale budgeting is not appropriate to their needs, but almost certainly they should prepare a cash budget as a minimum (despite the survey evidence mentioned in Real World 9.2).

Since budgets are documents that are to be used only internally by a business, their style is a question of management choice and will vary from one business to the next. However, as managers, irrespective of the business, are likely to be using budgets for similar purposes, some consistency of approach tends to be found. In most businesses, the cash budget will probably possess the following features:

1 The budget period would be broken down into sub-periods, typically months.
2 The budget would be in columnar form, with one column for each month.
3 Receipts of cash would be analysed under various headings and a total for each month's receipts shown.
4 Payments of cash would be analysed under various headings and a total for each month's payments shown.
5 The surplus of total cash receipts over payments, or of payments over receipts, for each month would be identified.
6 The running cash balance would be identified. This would be achieved by taking the balance at the end of the previous month and adjusting it for the surplus or deficit of receipts over payments for the current month.

Typically, all of the pieces of information in points 3 to 6 above would be useful to management for one reason or another.

Probably the best way to deal with this topic is through an example.

Example 9.1

Vierra Popova Ltd is a wholesale business. The budgeted income statements for each of the next six months are as follows:

	Jan £000	Feb £000	Mar £000	Apr £000	May £000	June £000
Sales revenue	52	55	55	60	55	53
Cost of goods sold	(30)	(31)	(31)	(35)	(31)	(32)
Salaries and wages	(10)	(10)	(10)	(10)	(10)	(10)
Electricity	(5)	(5)	(4)	(3)	(3)	(3)
Depreciation	(3)	(3)	(3)	(3)	(3)	(3)
Other overheads	(2)	(2)	(2)	(2)	(2)	(2)
Total expenses	(50)	(51)	(50)	(53)	(49)	(50)
Profit for the month	2	4	5	7	6	3

The business allows all of its customers one month's credit (this means, for example, that cash from January sales will be received in February). Sales revenue during December totalled £60,000.

The business plans to maintain inventories at their existing level until some time in March, when they are to be reduced by £5,000. Inventories will remain at this lower level indefinitely. Inventories purchases are made on one month's credit. December purchases totalled £30,000. Salaries, wages and 'other overheads' are paid in the month concerned. Electricity is paid quarterly in arrears in March and June. The business plans to buy and pay for a new delivery van in March. This will cost a total of £15,000, but an existing van will be traded in for £4,000 as part of the deal.

The business expects to have £12,000 in cash at the beginning of January.

The cash budget for the six months ending in June will be as follows:

	Jan £000	Feb £000	Mar £000	Apr £000	May £000	June £000
Receipts						
Trade receivables (Note 1)	60	52	55	55	60	55
Payments						
Trade payables (Note 2)	(30)	(30)	(31)	(26)	(35)	(31)
Salaries and wages	(10)	(10)	(10)	(10)	(10)	(10)
Electricity			(14)			(9)
Other overheads	(2)	(2)	(2)	(2)	(2)	(2)
Van purchase	–	–	(11)	–	–	–
Total payments	(42)	(42)	(68)	(38)	(47)	(52)
Cash surplus for the month	18	10	(13)	17	13	3
Opening balance (Note 3)	12	30	40	27	44	57
Closing balance	30	40	27	44	57	60

Notes:

1 The cash receipts from trade receivables lag a month behind sales because customers are given a month in which to pay for their purchases. So, December sales will be paid for in January, and so on.

2 In most months, the purchases of inventories will equal the cost of goods sold. This is because the business maintains a constant level of inventories. For inventories to remain constant at the end of each month, the business must replace exactly the amount that has been used. During March, however, the business plans to reduce its inventories by £5,000. This means that inventories purchases will be lower than inventories usage in that month. The payments for inventories purchases lag a month behind purchases because the business expects to be allowed a month to pay for what it buys.

3 Each month's cash balance is the previous month's figure plus the cash surplus (or minus the cash deficit) for the current month. The balance at the start of January is £12,000 according to the information provided earlier.

4 Depreciation does not give rise to a cash payment. In the context of profit measurement (in the income statement), depreciation is a very important aspect. Here, however, we are interested only in cash.

Activity 9.7

Looking at the cash budget of Vierra Popova Ltd, what conclusions do you draw and what possible course of action do you recommend regarding the cash balance over the period concerned?

There appears to be a fairly large cash balance, given the size of the business, and it seems to be increasing. Management might consider putting some of the cash into an income-yielding deposit. Alternatively, it could be used to expand the trading activities of the business by, for example, increasing the investment in non-current assets.

Activity 9.8

Vierra Popova Ltd (Example 9.1) now wishes to prepare its cash budget for the second six months of the year. The budgeted income statements for each month of the second half of the year are as follows:

	July £000	Aug £000	Sept £000	Oct £000	Nov £000	Dec £000
Sales revenue	57	59	62	57	53	51
Cost of goods sold	(32)	(33)	(35)	(32)	(30)	(29)
Salaries and wages	(10)	(10)	(10)	(10)	(10)	(10)
Electricity	(3)	(3)	(4)	(5)	(6)	(6)
Depreciation	(3)	(3)	(3)	(3)	(3)	(3)
Other overheads	(2)	(2)	(2)	(2)	(2)	(2)
Total expenses	(50)	(51)	(54)	(52)	(51)	(50)
Profit for the month	7	8	8	5	2	1

The business will continue to allow all of its customers one month's credit.

It plans to increase inventories from the 30 June level by £1,000 each month until, and including, September. During the following three months, inventories levels will be decreased by £1,000 each month.

Inventories purchases, which had been made on one month's credit until the June payment, will, starting with the purchases made in June, be made on two months' credit.

Salaries, wages and 'other overheads' will continue to be paid in the month concerned. Electricity is paid quarterly in arrears in September and December.

At the end of December, the business intends to pay off part of some borrowings. This payment is to be such that it will leave the business with a cash balance of £5,000 with which to start next year.

Prepare the cash budget for the six months ending in December. (Remember that any information you need that relates to the first six months of the year, including the cash balance that is expected to be brought forward on 1 July, is given in Example 9.1.)

The cash budget for the six months ended 31 December is:

	July £000	Aug £000	Sept £000	Oct £000	Nov £000	Dec £000
Receipts						
Trade receivables	53	57	59	62	57	53
Payments						
Trade payables (Note 1)	–	(32)	(33)	(34)	(36)	(31)
Salaries and wages	(10)	(10)	(10)	(10)	(10)	(10)
Electricity	–	–	(10)	–	–	(17)
Other overheads	(2)	(2)	(2)	(2)	(2)	(2)
Borrowings repayment (Note 2)	–	–	–	–	–	(131)
Total payments	(12)	(44)	(55)	(46)	(48)	(191)
Cash surplus for the month	41	13	4	16	9	(138)
Opening balance	60	101	114	118	134	143
Closing balance	101	114	118	134	143	5

Notes:

1 There will be no payment to trade payables in July because the June purchases will be made on two months' credit and will therefore be paid in August. The July purchases, which will equal the July cost of sales figure plus the increase in inventories made in July, will be paid for in September, and so on.

2 The amount of the borrowings repayment is simply the amount that will cause the balance at 31 December to be £5,000.

Preparing other budgets

Though each one will have its own particular features, other budgets will tend to follow the same sort of pattern as the cash budget, that is, they will show inflows and outflows during each month and the opening and closing balances in each month.

Example 9.2

To illustrate some of the other budgets, we shall continue to use the example of Vierra Popova Ltd that we considered in Example 9.1. To the information given there, we need to add the fact that the inventories balance at 1 January was £30,000.

Trade receivables budget

This would normally show the planned amount owing from credit sales to the business at the beginning and at the end of each month, the planned total sales revenue for each month and the planned total cash receipts from receivables. The layout would be something like the following:

	Jan £000	Feb £000	Mar £000	Apr £000	May £000	June £000
Opening balance	60	52	55	55	60	55
Sales revenue	52	55	55	60	55	53
Cash receipts	(60)	(52)	(55)	(55)	(60)	(55)
Closing balance	52	55	55	60	55	53

The opening and closing balances represent the amount that the business plans to be owed (in total) by credit customers (trade receivables) at the beginning and end of each month, respectively.

Trade payables budget

Typically this shows the planned amount owed to suppliers by the business at the beginning and at the end of each month, the planned purchases for each month and the planned total cash payments to trade payables. The layout would be something like the following:

	Jan £000	Feb £000	Mar £000	Apr £000	May £000	June £000
Opening balance	30	30	31	26	35	31
Purchases	30	31	26	35	31	32
Cash payment	(30)	(30)	(31)	(26)	(35)	(31)
Closing balance	30	31	26	35	31	32

The opening and closing balances represent the amount planned to be owed (in total) by the business to suppliers (trade payables), at the beginning and end of each month respectively.

Inventories budget

This would normally show the planned amount of inventories to be held by the business at the beginning and at the end of each month, the planned total inventories purchases for each month and the planned total monthly inventories usage. The layout would be something like the following:

	Jan £000	Feb £000	Mar £000	Apr £000	May £000	June £000
Opening balance	30	30	30	25	25	25
Purchases	30	31	26	35	31	32
Inventories used	(30)	(31)	(31)	(35)	(31)	(32)
Closing balance	30	30	25	25	25	25

The opening and closing balances represent the amount of inventories, at cost, planned to be held by the business at the beginning and end of each month respectively.

A *raw materials inventories budget*, for a manufacturing business, would follow a similar pattern, with the 'inventories usage' being the cost of the inventories put into production. A *finished inventories budget* for a manufacturer would also be similar to the above, except that 'inventories manufactured' would replace 'purchases'. A manufacturing business would normally prepare both a raw materials inventories budget and a finished inventories budget. Both of these would typically be based on the full cost of the inventories (that is, including overheads). There is no reason why the inventories should not be valued on the basis of either variable cost or direct costs, should managers feel that this would provide more useful information.

The inventories budget will normally be expressed in financial terms, but may also be expressed in physical terms (for example, kg or metres) for individual inventories items.

Note how the trade receivables, trade payables and inventories budgets in Example 9.2 link to one another, and to the cash budget for the same business in Example 9.1. Note particularly that

- purchases in the trade payables budget and in the inventories budget are identical;
- cash payments in the trade payables budget and in the cash budget are identical;
- cash receipts in the trade receivables budget and in the cash budget are identical.

Other values would link different budgets in a similar way. For example, the row of sales revenue figures in the trade receivables budget would be identical to the sales revenue figures that will be found in the sales budget. This is how the linking (co-ordination), which was discussed earlier in this chapter, is achieved.

Activity 9.9

Have a go at preparing the trade receivables budget for Vierra Popova Ltd for the six months from July to December (see Activity 9.8 and Example 9.2).

The trade receivables budget for the six months ended 31 December is:

	July £000	Aug £000	Sept £000	Oct £000	Nov £000	Dec £000
Opening balance (Note 1)	53	57	59	62	57	53
Sales revenue (Note 2)	57	59	62	57	53	51
Cash receipts (Note 3)	(53)	(57)	(59)	(62)	(57)	(53)
Closing balance (Note 4)	57	59	62	57	53	51

Notes:
1 The opening trade receivables figure is the previous month's sales revenue figure (sales are on one month's credit).
2 The sales revenue is the current month's figure.
3 The cash received each month is equal to the previous month's sales revenue figure.
4 The closing balance is equal to the current month's sales revenue figure.

Note that if we knew any three of the four figures each month, we could deduce the fourth.

This budget could be set out in any manner that would have given the sort of information that management would require in respect of planned levels of trade receivables and associated transactions.

Activity 9.10

Have a go at preparing the trade payables budget for Vierra Popova Ltd for the six months from July to December (see Activity 9.8 and Example 9.2). (*Hint*: Remember that the payment period for trade payables alters from the June purchases onwards.)

The trade payables budget for the six months ended 31 December is:

	July £000	Aug £000	Sept £000	Oct £000	Nov £000	Dec £000
Opening balance	32	65	67	70	67	60
Purchases	33	34	36	31	29	28
Cash payments	–	(32)	(33)	(34)	(36)	(31)
Closing balance	65	67	70	67	60	57

This, again, could be set out in any manner that would have given the sort of information that management would require in respect of planned levels of trade payables and associated transactions.

Non-financial measures in budgeting

The efficiency of internal operations and customer satisfaction levels are critically important to businesses operating in an increasingly competitive environment. Non-financial performance indicators have a vital role to play in assessing performance in such key areas as customer/supplier delivery times, set-up times, defect levels and customer satisfaction levels.

There is no reason why budgeting need be confined to financial targets and measures. Non-financial measures can also be used as the basis for targets. They can also be incorporated into the budgeting process and reported alongside the financial targets for the business.

Self-assessment question 9.1 should pull together what we have seen about preparing budgets.

? Self-assessment question 9.1

Antonio Ltd has planned production and sales for the next nine months as follows:

	Production units	Sales units
May	350	350
June	400	400
July	500	400
August	600	500
September	600	600
October	700	650
November	750	700
December	750	800
January	750	750

During the period, the business plans to advertise in order to generate these increases in sales. Payments for advertising of £1,000 and £1,500 will be made in July and October, respectively.

The selling price per unit will be £20 throughout the period. Forty per cent of sales are normally made on two months' credit. The other 60 per cent are settled within the month of the sale.

Raw materials will be held for one month before they are taken into production. Purchases of raw materials will be on one month's credit (buy one month, pay the next). The cost of raw materials is £8 per unit of production.

Other direct production expenses, including labour, are £6 per unit of production. These will be paid in the month concerned.

Various production overheads, which during the period to 30 June had run at £1,800 a month, are expected to rise to £2,000 each month from 1 July to 31 October. These are expected to rise again from 1 November to £2,400 a month and to remain at that level for the foreseeable future. These overheads include a steady £400 each month for depreciation. Overheads are planned to be paid 80 per cent in the month of production and 20 per cent in the following month.

To help to meet the planned increased production, a new item of plant will be bought and delivered in August. The cost of this item is £6,600; the contract with the supplier will specify that this will be paid in three equal amounts in September, October and November.

Raw materials inventories are planned to be 500 units on 1 July. The balance at the bank on the same day is planned to be £7,500.

Required:
(a) Draw up the following for the six months ending 31 December:
    (i)   A raw materials inventories budget, showing both physical quantities and financial values.
    (ii) A trade payables budget.
    (iii) A cash budget.
(b) The cash budget reveals a potential cash deficiency during October and November. Can you suggest any ways in which a modification of plans could overcome this problem?

The answer to this question can be found at the back of the book in Appendix B.

Budgeting for control

We have seen that budgets provide a useful basis for exercising control over a business as they provide a yardstick against which performance can be assessed. We must, however, measure actual performance in the same terms as those in which the budget is stated. If they are not in the same terms, valid comparison will not be possible.

Exercising control involves finding out where and why things did not go according to plan and then seeking ways to put them right for the future. One reason why things may not have gone according to plan is that the budget targets were unachievable. In this case, it may be necessary to revise the budgets for future periods so that targets become achievable.

This last point should not be taken to mean that budget targets can simply be ignored if the going gets tough; rather that they should be adaptable. Unrealistic budgets cannot form a basis for exercising control and little can be gained by sticking with them. Budgets may become unrealistic for a variety of reasons, including unexpected changes in the commercial environment (for example, an unexpected collapse in demand for services of the type that the business provides).

Real World 9.4 reveals how one important budget had to be dramatically revised because it had become so unrealistic.

Real World 9.4

No medals for budgeting

The government's dramatic increase this spring in the budget for the 2012 Olympic games, almost tripling the £3.3bn cost to the taxpayer estimated at the time of winning the 2005 bid, has put the event on a 'firmer financial footing', says a report by the National Audit Office (NAO).

Nevertheless, the revised £9.3bn London Olympics budget contains 'significant areas of uncertainty' that could drive costs up, unless effective controls are exercised. Sir John Bourn, head of the NAO, warned the government it still had to 'work to contain funding and achieve value for money'. He highlighted areas of uncertainty affecting costs, including the design specifications and future use of the Olympic venues, the level of price inflation in the construction sector and the contracts negotiated by suppliers.

The NAO, in effect, gives the revised budget its seal of approval, saying it 'should be sufficient' to cover the estimated costs of the games, provided – a 'most important proviso' – the assumptions on which the budget is based hold good. But its report calls for action by the government to ensure proper controls over the huge project.

Source: Adapted from 'Watchdog warns on Olympic costs', Jean Eaglesham, ft.com, 20 July 2007.

We saw earlier that budgets enable a management-by-exception environment to be created where senior management can focus on areas where things are not going according to plan (the exceptions – it is to be hoped). To create this environment, a comparison of the budget and the actual results must be undertaken to see whether any variances between the two exist. We are now going to discuss the way in which this may be done.

Measuring variances from budget

We saw in Chapter 1 that the key financial objective of a business is to increase the wealth of its owners (shareholders). Since profit is the net increase in wealth from business operations, the most important budget target to meet is the profit target. We shall therefore take this as our starting point when comparing the budget with the actual results. Example 9.3 shows the budgeted and actual income statement for Baxter Ltd for the month of May.

Example 9.3

The following are the budgeted and actual income statements for Baxter Ltd, a manufacturing business, for the month of May:

	Budget	Actual
Output (production and sales)	1,000 units	900 units
	£	£
Sales revenue	100,000	92,000
Raw materials	(40,000) (40,000 metres)	(36,900) (37,000 metres)
Labour	(20,000) (2,500 hours)	(17,500) (2,150 hours)
Fixed overheads	(20,000)	(20,700)
Operating profit	20,000	16,900

From these figures it is clear that the budgeted profit was not achieved. As far as May is concerned, this is a matter of history. However, the business (or at least one aspect of it) is out of control. Senior management must discover where things went wrong during May and try to ensure that these mistakes are not repeated in later months. It is not enough to know that things went wrong overall. We need to know where and why. The approach taken is to compare the budgeted and actual figures for the various items (sales revenue, raw materials and so on) in the above statement.

Activity 9.11

Can you see any problems in comparing the various items (sales, raw materials and so on) for the budget and the actual performance of Baxter Ltd in order to draw conclusions as to which aspects were out of control?

The problem is that the actual level of output was not as budgeted. The actual level of output was 10 per cent less than budget. This means that we cannot, for example, say that there was a labour cost saving of £2,500 (that is, £20,000 – £17,500) and conclude that all is well in that area.

Flexing the budget

One practical way to overcome our difficulty is to 'flex' the budget to what it would have been had the planned level of output been 900 units rather than 1,000 units. Flexing the budget simply means revising it, assuming a different volume of output.

To exercise control, the budget is usually flexed to reflect the volume that actually occurred, where this is higher or lower than that originally planned. This means that we need to know which revenues and costs are fixed and which are variable relative to the volume of output. Once we know this, flexing is a simple operation. We shall assume that sales revenue, material cost and labour cost vary strictly with volume. Fixed overheads, by definition, will not. Whether, in real life, labour cost does vary with the volume of output is not so certain, but it will serve well enough as an assumption for our purposes. Were labour costs actually fixed, we should simply take this into account in the flexing process.

On the basis of our assumptions regarding the behaviour of revenues and costs, the flexed budget would be as follows:

	Flexed budget
Output (production and sales)	900 units
	£
Sales revenue	90,000
Raw materials	(36,000) (36,000 metres)
Labour	(18,000) (2,250 hours)
Fixed overheads	(20,000)
Operating profit	16,000

This is simply the original budget, with the sales revenue, raw materials and labour cost figures scaled down by 10 per cent (the same factor as the actual output fell short of the budgeted one).

Putting the original budget, the flexed budget and the actual for May together, we obtain the following:

	Original budget	Flexed budget	Actual
Output (production and sales)	1,000 units	900 units	900 units
	£	£	£
Sales revenue	100,000	90,000	92,000
Raw materials	(40,000)	(36,000) (36,000m)	(36,900) (37,000m)
Labour	(20,000)	(18,000) (2,250 hr)	(17,500) (2,150 hr)
Fixed overheads	(20,000)	(20,000)	(20,700)
Operating profit	20,000	16,000	16,900

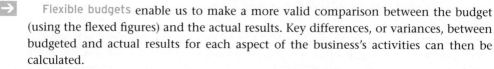 Flexible budgets enable us to make a more valid comparison between the budget (using the flexed figures) and the actual results. Key differences, or variances, between budgeted and actual results for each aspect of the business's activities can then be calculated.

It may seem as if we are saying that it does not matter if there are volume shortfalls because we just revise the budget and carry on as if all is well. However, this is not the case, because losing sales means losing profit. The first point that we must pick up therefore is the loss of profit arising from the loss of sales of 100 units.

Activity 9.12

What will be the loss of profit arising from the sales volume shortfall, assuming that everything except sales volume was as planned?

The answer is simply the difference between the original and flexed budget profit figures. The only difference between these two profit figures is the volume of sales; everything else was the same. (That is to say that the flexing was carried out assuming that the per-unit sales revenue, raw material cost and labour cost were all as originally budgeted.) This means that the figure for the loss of profit due to the volume shortfall, taken alone, is £4,000 (that is, £20,000 – £16,000).

Where a variance between the flexed budget and the actual results has the effect of making the actual profit lower than the budgeted profit, it is known as an adverse variance. The variance arising from the sales volume shortfall is, therefore an adverse variance. Where a variance has the opposite effect, it is known as a favourable variance. We can therefore say that a variance is the effect of that factor (taken alone) on the budgeted profit. When looking at some particular aspect, such as sales volume, we assume that all other factors went according to plan. This is shown in Figure 9.6.

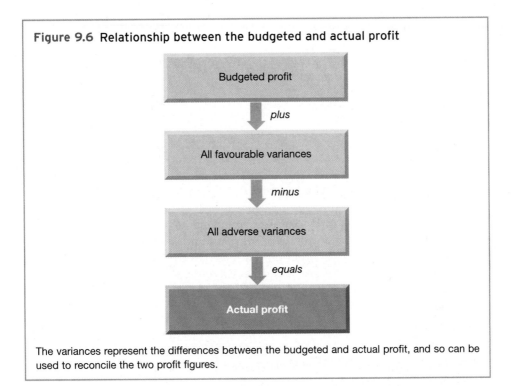

Figure 9.6 Relationship between the budgeted and actual profit

Budgeted profit

plus

All favourable variances

minus

All adverse variances

equals

Actual profit

The variances represent the differences between the budgeted and actual profit, and so can be used to reconcile the two profit figures.

For the month of May, we have already identified one of the reasons that the budgeted profit of £20,000 was not achieved and that the actual profit was only £16,900. This was the £4,000 loss of profit (adverse variance) that arose from the sales volume shortfall. Now that the budget is flexed, we can compare like with like and reach further conclusions about May's trading.

The fact that the sales revenue, raw materials and labour figures differ between the flexed budget and the actual results (see page 328) suggests that the adverse sales volume variance was not the only problem area. To identify the value of the differences that arose from these other three areas (sales revenue, raw materials and labour), we need to compare the flexed budget and actual values for each of them.

Activity 9.13

Compare the sales revenue, raw materials and labour values between the flexed budget and the actual results and reconcile the original budget and the actual profit for Baxter Ltd. Remember that the sales volume variance is also part of the difference.

This is calculated as follows:

	£
Budgeted profit	20,000
Favourable variances	
Sales price (92,000 – 90,000)	2,000
Labour (18,000 – 17,500)	500
Total favourable variances	2,500
Adverse variances	
Sales volume (as above)	(4,000)
Raw materials (36,000 – 36,900)	(900)
Fixed overheads (20,000 – 20,700)	(700)
	(5,600)
Actual profit	16,900

The variance between flexed budget sales revenue and actual sales revenue (£2,000) can only arise from higher prices being charged than were envisaged in the original budget. This is because any variance arising from volume difference has already been 'stripped out' in the flexing process. Less was spent on labour than was allowed for a volume of 900 units. More was spent on raw materials than should have been for an output of 900 units. There was also an overspend on fixed overheads.

Activity 9.14

If you were managing director of Baxter Ltd, what attitude would you take to the overall variance between the budgeted profit and the actual one?

How would you react to the five individual variances that are the outcome of the analysis shown in the solution to Activity 9.13?

You would probably be concerned about how large the variances are and their direction (favourable or adverse). In particular you may have thought of the following:

■ The overall adverse profit variance is £3,100 (that is £20,000 – £16,900). This represents 15.5 per cent of the budgeted profit (that is £3,100/£20,000 × 100%) and you (as managing director) would pretty certainly see it as significant and worrying.
■ The £4,000 adverse sales volume variance represents 20 per cent of budgeted profit and it too would be a major cause of concern.
■ The £2,000 favourable sales price variance represents 10 per cent of budgeted profit. Since this is favourable it might be seen as a cause for celebration rather than concern.

On the other hand it means that Baxter's output was, on average, sold at prices 10 per cent above the planned price. This could have been the cause of the worrying adverse sales volume variance. Baxter may have sold fewer units because it charged higher prices.

- The £900 adverse raw materials variance represents 4.5 per cent of budgeted profit. It would be unrealistic to expect the actuals to hit the precise budget figure each month. The question is whether 4.5 per cent for this variance represents a significant amount and a cause for concern.
- The £500 favourable labour variance represents 2.5 per cent of budgeted profit. Since this is favourable and relatively small it may not be seen as a major cause for concern.
- The £700 fixed overhead adverse variance represents 3.5 per cent of budgeted profit. The managing director may be concerned about this.

The managing director will now need to ask some questions as to why things went so badly wrong in several areas and what can be done to improve things for the future.

The variance between the actual and flexed figures that has been calculated for both raw materials and labour overheads can be broken down further. The total materials overheads variance (£900) can be analysed to see the extent to which it is caused by a difference (between budget and actual) in the amount of raw material used and by a difference in the prices at which the materials were bought. A similar analysis can be carried out for the total labour variance (£500). These further analyses may provide much more helpful information than the broad variances for each of these two areas. A detailed discussion of the ways in which these overhead variances can be broken down is beyond the scope of this book. If you would like to pursue this topic, the further reading at the end of the chapter provides some appropriate references.

Real World 9.5 shows how two UK-based businesses, Next plc, the retailer, and British Airways plc, the airline operator, use variance analysis to exercise control over their operations. Many businesses explain in their annual reports how they operate systems of budgetary control.

Real World 9.5

Exercising control

What Next?

According to its annual report, Next plc has the following arrangements:

The Board is responsible for approving semi-annual Group budgets. Performance against budget is reported to the Board monthly and any substantial variances are explained.

BA at the controls

BA plc makes it clear that it too uses budgets and variance analysis to help keep control over its activities. The annual report says:

A comprehensive management accounting system is in place providing financial and operational performance measurement indicators to management. Detailed management accounts are prepared monthly to cover each major area of the business. Variances from plan are analysed, explained and acted on in a timely manner.

The boards of directors of these businesses will not seek explanations of variances arising at each branch/flight/department, but they will be looking at figures for the businesses as a whole or the results for major divisions of them.

Equally certainly, branch/department managers will receive a monthly (or perhaps more frequent) report of variances arising within their area of responsibility alone.

Sources: Next plc Annual Report 2007, p. 20; British Airways plc Annual Report 2007, p. 48.

Real World 9.6 gives some indication of the importance of flexible budgeting in practice.

Real World 9.6

Flexing the budgets

A study of the UK food and drink industry by Abdel-Kader and Luther provides some insight as to the importance attached by management accountants to flexible budgeting. The study asked those in charge of the management accounting function to rate the importance of flexible budgeting by selecting one of three possible categories: 'not important', 'moderately important' or 'important'. Figure 9.7 sets out the results, from the sample of 117 respondents.

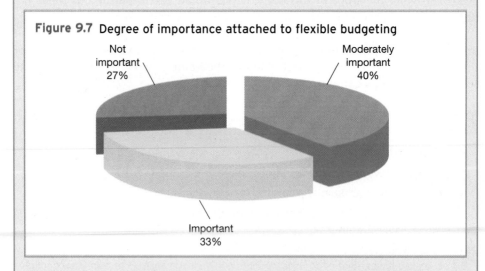

Figure 9.7 Degree of importance attached to flexible budgeting

Not important 27%

Moderately important 40%

Important 33%

Respondents were also asked to state the frequency with which flexible budgeting was used within the business, using a five-point scale ranging from 1 (never) through to 5 (very often). Figure 9.8 sets out the results.

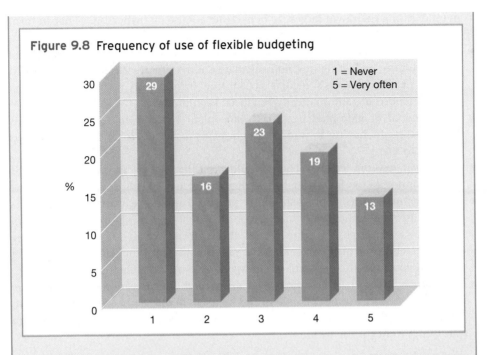

Figure 9.8 Frequency of use of flexible budgeting

1 = Never
5 = Very often

We can see that although flexible budgeting is regarded as important by a significant proportion of management accountants and is being used in practice, not all businesses use it.

Source: Based on information in 'Management accounting practices in the food and drinks industry', M. Abdel-Kader and R. Luther, CIMA Research, 2006.

Making budgetary control effective

It should be clear from what we have seen of budgetary control that a system, or a set of routines, must be put in place to enable the potential benefits to be gained. Most businesses that operate successful budgetary control systems tend to share some common features. These include the following:

- *A serious attitude taken to the system.* This approach should apply to all levels of management, right from the very top. For example, senior managers need to make clear to junior managers that they take notice of the monthly variance reports and base some of their actions and decisions upon them.
- *Clear demarcation between areas of managerial responsibility.* It needs to be clear which manager is responsible for each business area, so that accountability can more easily be ascribed for any area that seems to be going out of control.
- *Budget targets that are challenging yet achievable.* Setting unachievable targets is likely to have a demotivating effect. There may be a case for getting managers to participate

in establishing their own targets to help create a sense of 'ownership'. This, in turn, can increase the managers' commitment and motivation.

- *Established data collection, analysis and reporting routines.* These should take the actual results and the budget figures, and calculate and report the variances. This should be part of the business's regular accounting information system, so that the required reports are automatically produced each month.
- *Reports aimed at individual managers, rather than general-purpose documents.* This avoids managers having to wade through reams of reports to find the part that is relevant to them.
- *Fairly short reporting periods.* These would typically be one month long, so that things cannot go too far wrong before they are picked up.
- *Timely variance reports.* Reports should be produced and made available to managers shortly after the end of the relevant reporting period. If it is not until the end of June that a manager is informed that the performance in May was below the budgeted level, it is quite likely that the performance for June will be below target as well. Reports on the performance in May ideally need to emerge in early June.
- *Action being taken to get operations back under control if they are shown to be out of control.* The report will not change things by itself. Managers need to take action to try to ensure that the reporting of significant adverse variances leads to action to put things right for the future.

Behavioural issues

Budgets are prepared with the objective of affecting the attitudes and behaviour of managers. We saw earlier that budgets are intended to motivate managers, and research evidence generally shows that budgets can be effective in achieving this. More specifically, the research shows that

- the existence of budgets generally tends to improve performance;
- demanding, yet achievable, budget targets tend to motivate better than less demanding targets – it seems that setting the most demanding targets that will be accepted by managers is a very effective way to motivate them;
- unrealistically demanding targets tend to have an adverse effect on managers' performance;
- the participation of managers in setting their targets tends to improve motivation and performance. This is probably because those managers feel a sense of commitment to the targets and a moral obligation to achieve them.

It has been suggested that allowing managers to set their own targets will lead to slack (that is, easily achievable targets) being introduced. This would make achievement of the target that much easier. On the other hand, in an effort to impress, a manager may select a target that is not really achievable. These points imply that care must be taken in the extent to which managers have unfettered choice of their own targets.

Summary

The main points of this chapter may be summarised as follows.

Budgets

- A budget is a short-term business plan, mainly expressed in financial terms.
- Budgets are the short-term means of working towards the business's objectives.
- They are usually prepared for a one-year period with sub-periods of a month.
- There is usually a separate budget for each key area.
- The budgets for each area are summarised in master budgets (budgeted income statement and balance sheet).
- Budgets are plans rather than forecasts.
- Periodic budgets are usually agreed for a year and then allowed to run their course.
- Continual budgets are updated each month to replace the month just passed.

Uses of budgets

- Promote forward thinking.
- Help co-ordinate the various aspects of the business.
- Motivate performance.
- Provide the basis of a system of control.
- Provide a system of authorisation.

Zero-base budgeting

- Zero-base budgeting seeks to ensure that all spending is justified.
- It encourages a questioning approach but can be time-consuming.
- Probably best used selectively.

Preparing budgets

- There is no standard style – practicality and usefulness are the key issues.
- They are usually prepared in columnar form, with a column for each month (or similarly short period).
- Each budget must link (co-ordinate) with others.
- Non-financial measures (such as units of output) can be used when budgeting.

Controlling through budgets

- To exercise control, budgets can be flexed to match actual volume of output.
- A variance is an increase (favourable) or decrease (adverse) in profit, relative to the budgeted profit, as a result of some aspect of the business's activities when taken alone.

→

- Budgeted profit plus all favourable variances less all adverse variances equals actual profit.

Effective budgetary control

- Good budgetary control requires establishing systems and routines to ensure such things as a clear distinction between individual managers' areas of responsibility; prompt, frequent and relevant variance reporting; and senior management commitment.

- There are behavioural aspects of control relating to management style, participation in budget-setting and the failure to meet budget targets that should be taken into account by senior managers.

→ Key terms

mission statement p. 304
budget p. 304
control p. 305
limiting factor p. 307
forecast p. 307
periodic budget p. 307
continual budget p. 308
rolling budget p. 308
master budget p. 308
management by exception p. 312
incremental budgeting p. 315

budget holder p. 315
discretionary budget p. 315
zero-base budgeting (ZBB) p. 316
flexing the budget p. 327
flexible budgets p. 328
adverse variance p. 329
favourable variance p. 329
variance p. 329
variance analysis p. 331
budgetary control p. 332

Further reading

If you would like to explore the topics covered in this chapter in more depth, we recommend the following books:

Atkinson, A., Kaplan, R., Young, S. M. and Matsumura, E., *Management Accounting* (5th edn), Prentice Hall, 2007, chapter 10.

Atrill, P. and McLaney, E., *Management Accounting for Decision Makers* (5th edn), Prentice Hall, 2007, chapters 6 and 7.

Drury, C., *Management and Cost Accounting* (8th edn), Thomson Learning, 2008, chapters 15 and 16.

Horngren, C., Datar, S. and Foster, G., *Cost Accounting: A Managerial Emphasis* (12th edn), Prentice Hall, 2006, chapter 6.

 **? Review questions**

Answers to these questions can be found at the back of the book in Appendix C.

9.1 Define a budget. How is a budget different from a forecast?

9.2 What were the five uses of budgets that were identified in the chapter?

9.3 What is meant by a *variance*? What is the point in analysing variances?

9.4 What is the point in flexing the budget in the context of variance analysis? Does flexing imply that differences between budget and actual in the volume of output are ignored in variance analysis?

✳ Exercises

Exercises 9.3 to 9.5 are more advanced than Exercises 9.1 and 9.2. Those with coloured numbers have answers at the back of the book in Appendix D.

> If you wish to try more exercises, visit MyAccountingLab/

9.1 You have overheard the following statements:

  (a) 'A budget is a forecast of what is expected to happen in a business during the next year.'
  (b) 'Monthly budgets must be prepared with a column for each month so that you can see the whole year at a glance, month by month.'
  (c) 'Budgets are OK but they stifle all initiative. No manager worth employing would work for a business that seeks to control through budgets.'
  (d) 'Any sensible person would start with the sales budget and build up the other budgets from there.'

Required:
Critically discuss these statements, explaining any technical terms.

9.2 Daniel Chu Ltd, a new business, will start production on 1 April, but sales will not start until 1 May. Planned sales for the next nine months are as follows:

	Sales Units
May	500
June	600
July	700
August	800
September	900
October	900
November	900
December	800
January	700

The selling price of a unit will be a consistent £100 and all sales will be made on one month's credit. It is planned that sufficient finished goods inventories for each month's sales should be available at the end of the previous month.

Raw materials purchases will be such that there will be sufficient raw materials inventories available at the end of each month precisely to meet the following month's planned production. This planned policy will operate from the end of April. Purchases of raw materials will be on one month's credit. The cost of raw material is £40 a unit of finished product.

The direct labour cost, which is variable with the level of production, is planned to be £20 a unit of finished production. Production overheads are planned to be £20,000 each month, including £3,000 for depreciation. Non-production overheads are planned to be £11,000 a month, of which £1,000 will be depreciation.

Various non-current assets costing £250,000 will be bought and paid for during April.

Except where specified, assume that all payments take place in the month in which the cost is incurred.

The business will raise £300,000 in cash from a share issue in April.

Required:
Draw up the following for the six months ending 30 September:
(a) A finished inventories budget, showing just physical quantities.
(b) A raw materials inventories budget showing both physical quantities and financial values.
(c) A trade payables budget.
(d) A trade receivables budget.
(e) A cash budget.

9.3 A nursing home, which is linked to a large hospital, has been examining its budgetary control procedures, with particular reference to overhead costs.

The level of activity in the facility is measured by the number of patients treated in the budget period. For the current year, the budget stands at 6,000 patients and this is expected to be met.

For months 1 to 6 of this year (assume 12 months of equal length), 2,700 patients were treated. The actual variable overhead costs incurred during this six-month period are as follows:

Expense	£
Staffing	59,400
Power	27,000
Supplies	54,000
Other	8,100
Total	148,500

The hospital accountant believes that the variable overhead costs will be incurred at the same rate during months 7 to 12 of the year.

Fixed overhead costs are budgeted for the whole year as follows:

Expense	£
Supervision	120,000
Depreciation/financing	187,200
Other	64,800
Total	372,000

Required:

(a) Present an overheads budget for months 7 to 12 of the year. You should show each expense, but should not separate individual months. What is the total overhead cost for each patient that would be incorporated into any statistics?

(b) The home actually treated 3,800 patients during months 7 to 12, the actual variable overheads were £203,300, and the fixed overheads were £190,000. In summary form, examine how well the home exercised control over its overheads.

(c) Interpret your analysis and point out any limitations or assumptions.

9.4 Linpet Ltd is to be incorporated on 1 June. The opening balance sheet of the business will then be as follows:

	£
Cash at bank	60,000
Share capital (£1 ordinary shares)	60,000

During June, the business intends to make payments of £40,000 for a leasehold property, £10,000 for equipment and £6,000 for a motor vehicle. The business will also purchase initial trading inventories costing £22,000 on credit.

The business has produced the following estimates:

1 Sales revenue for June will be £8,000 and will increase at the rate of £3,000 a month until September. In October, sales revenue will rise to £22,000 and in subsequent months will be maintained at this figure.

2 The gross profit percentage on goods sold will be 25 per cent.

3 There is a risk that supplies of trading inventories will be interrupted towards the end of the accounting year. The business therefore intends to build up its initial level of inventories (£22,000) by purchasing £1,000 of inventories each month in addition to the monthly purchases necessary to satisfy monthly sales requirements. All purchases of inventories (including the initial inventories) will be on one month's credit.

4 Sales revenue will be divided equally between cash and credit sales. Credit customers are expected to pay two months after the sale is agreed.

5 Wages and salaries will be £900 a month. Other overheads will be £500 a month for the first four months and £650 thereafter. Both types of expense will be payable when incurred.

6 Eighty per cent of sales revenue will be generated by sales people who will receive 5 per cent commission on sales revenue. The commission is payable one month after the sale is agreed.

7 The business intends to purchase further equipment in November for £7,000 cash.

8 Depreciation is to be provided at the rate of 5 per cent a year on freehold property and 20 per cent a year on equipment. (Depreciation has not been included in the overheads mentioned in point 5 above.)

Required:
(a) State why a cash budget is required for a business.
(b) Prepare a cash budget for Linpet Ltd for the six-month period to 30 November.

9.5 Newtake Records Ltd owns a chain of 14 shops selling DVDs and CDs. At the beginning of June the business had an overdraft of £35,000 and the bank had asked for this to be eliminated by the end of November. As a result, the directors have recently decided to review their plans for the next six months.

The following plans were prepared for the business some months earlier:

	May £000	June £000	July £000	Aug £000	Sept £000	Oct £000	Nov £000
Sales revenue	180	230	320	250	140	120	110
Purchases	135	180	142	94	75	66	57
Administration expenses	52	55	56	53	48	46	45
Selling expenses	22	24	28	26	21	19	18
Taxation payment	–	–	–	22	–	–	–
Finance payments	5	5	5	5	5	5	5
Shop refurbishment	–	–	14	18	6	–	–

Notes:
1 The inventories level at 1 June was £112,000. The business believes it is preferable to maintain a minimum inventories level of £40,000 over the period to 30 November.
2 Suppliers allow one month's credit.
3 The gross profit margin is 40 per cent.
4 All sales proceeds are received in the month of sale. However, 50 per cent of customers pay with a credit card. The charge made by the credit card business to Newtake Records Ltd is 3 per cent of the sales revenue value. These charges are in addition to the selling expenses identified above. The credit card business pays Newtake Records Ltd in the month of sale.
5 The business has a bank loan, which it is paying off in monthly instalments of £5,000. The interest element represents 20 per cent of each instalment.
6 Administration expenses are paid when incurred. This item includes a charge of £15,000 each month in respect of depreciation.
7 Selling expenses are payable in the following month.

Required (working to the nearest £1,000):

(a) Prepare an inventory budget for the six months to 30 November also based on the table of plans above.

(b) Prepare a cash budget for the six months ending 30 November which shows the cash balance at the end of each month also based on the plans set out in the table above.

(c) Prepare a budgeted income statement for the whole of the six-month period ending 30 November. (A monthly breakdown of profit is *not* required.)

(d) What problems is Newtake Records Ltd likely to face in the next six months? Can you suggest how the business might deal with these problems?

Part 3

FINANCIAL MANAGEMENT

Chapter 10

Making capital investment decisions

Introduction

This chapter is the first of three dealing with the area generally known as *financial management*. In this chapter we shall look at how businesses can make decisions involving investments in new plant, machinery, buildings and similar long-term assets. In making these decisions, businesses should be trying to pursue their key financial objective, which is to enhance the wealth of the owners (shareholders).

Investment appraisal is a very important area for businesses; expensive and far-reaching consequences can flow from bad investment decisions.

Learning outcomes

When you have completed this chapter, you should be able to

- explain the nature and importance of investment decision-making;
- identify the four main investment appraisal methods found in practice;
- use each method to reach a decision on a particular investment opportunity;
- discuss the attributes of each of the methods.

The nature of investment decisions

The essential feature of investment decisions is *time*. Investment involves making an outlay of something of economic value, usually cash, at one point in time, which is expected to yield economic benefits to the investor at some other point in time. Usually, the outlay precedes the benefits. Also, the outlay is typically one large amount and the benefits arrive as a series of smaller amounts over a fairly protracted period.

Investment decisions tend to be of profound importance to the business because:

- *Large amounts of resources are often involved.* Many investments made by businesses involve laying out a significant proportion of their total resources (see Real World 10.2). If mistakes are made with the decision, the effects on the businesses could be significant, if not catastrophic.
- *It is often difficult and/or expensive to bail out of an investment once it has been undertaken.* It is often the case that investments made by a business are specific to its needs. For example, a hotel business may invest in a new, custom-designed hotel complex. The specialist nature of this complex will probably lead to its having a rather limited second-hand value to another potential user with different needs. If the business found, after having made the investment, that room occupancy rates were not as buoyant as was planned, the only possible course of action might be to close down and sell the complex. This would probably mean that much less could be recouped from the investment than it had originally cost, particularly if the costs of design are included as part of the cost, as they logically should be.

Real World 10.1 gives an illustration of a major investment by a well-known business operating in the UK.

Real World 10.1

Brittany Ferries launches an investment

Brittany Ferries, the cross-channel ferry operator, recently ordered a new ship to be named *Amorique*. The ship will cost the business about €81m and will be used on the Plymouth to Roscoff route as from autumn 2008. Although Brittany Ferries is a substantial business, this level of expenditure is significant. Clearly, the business believes that acquisition of the new ship will be profitable for it, but how would it have reached this conclusion? Presumably the anticipated future cash flows from passengers and freight operators will have been major inputs to the decision. The ship was specifically designed for Brittany Ferries, so it would be difficult for the business to recoup a large proportion of its €81m should these projected cash flows not materialise.

Source: 'New €81m passenger cruise-ferry to be named Amorique', www.brittany-ferries.co.uk.

The issues raised by Brittany Ferries' investment will be the main subject of this chapter.

Real World 10.2 indicates the level of annual net investment for a number of randomly selected, well-known UK businesses. It can be seen that the scale of investment varies from one business to another. (It also tends to vary from one year to the next for a particular business.) In nearly all of these businesses the scale of investment is very significant.

The scale of investment by UK businesses

	Expenditure on additional non-current assets as a percentage of:	
	Annual sales revenue	End-of-year non-current assets
BT plc (telecommunications)	15.9	17.5
Babcock International Group plc (support services)	6.8	20.6
Tesco plc (supermarkets)	5.5	11.6
J D Wetherspoon plc (pub operator)	12.5	9.0
Marks and Spencer plc (stores)	7.6	14.4
National Grid plc (utilities)	48.0	19.8
J. Sainsbury plc (supermarkets)	4.0	8.9
First Group plc (passenger transport)	5.7	13.1

Source: Annual reports of the businesses concerned for the financial year ending in 2007.

Real World 10.2 is limited to considering the non-current asset investment, but most non-current asset investment also requires a level of current asset investment to support it (additional inventories, for example), meaning that the real scale of investment is even greater, typically considerably so, than indicated above.

Activity 10.1

When managers are making decisions involving capital investments, what should the decision seek to achieve?

Investment decisions must be consistent with the objectives of the particular business. For a private-sector business, increasing the wealth of the owners (shareholders) is usually assumed to be the key financial objective.

Investment appraisal methods

Given the importance of investment decisions, it is essential that there is proper screening of investment proposals. An important part of this screening process is to ensure that the business uses appropriate methods of evaluation.

Research shows that there are basically four methods used in practice by businesses throughout the world to evaluate investment opportunities. They are:

- accounting rate of return (ARR)
- payback period (PP)
- net present value (NPV)
- internal rate of return (IRR).

It is possible to find businesses that use variants of these four methods. It is also possible to find businesses, particularly smaller ones, which do not use any formal appraisal method but rely instead on the 'gut feeling' of their managers. Most businesses, however, seem to use one (or more) of these four methods.

We are going to assess the effectiveness of each of these methods and we shall see that only one of them (NPV) is a wholly logical approach. The other three all have flaws. We shall also see how popular these four methods seem to be in practice.

To help us to examine each of the methods, it might be useful to consider how each of them would cope with a particular investment opportunity. Let us consider the following example.

Example 10.1

Billingsgate Battery Company has carried out some research that shows that the business could provide a standard service that it has recently developed.

Provision of the service would require investment in a machine that would cost £100,000, payable immediately. Sales of the service would take place throughout the next five years. At the end of that time, it is estimated that the machine could be sold for £20,000.

Inflows and outflows from sales of the service would be expected to be as follows:

Time		£000
Immediately	Cost of machine	(100)
1 year's time	Operating profit before depreciation	20
2 years' time	Operating profit before depreciation	40
3 years' time	Operating profit before depreciation	60
4 years' time	Operating profit before depreciation	60
5 years' time	Operating profit before depreciation	20
5 years' time	Disposal proceeds from the machine	20

Note that, broadly speaking, the operating profit before deducting depreciation (that is, before non-cash items) equals the net amount of cash flowing into the business. Apart from depreciation, all of this business's expenses cause cash to flow out of the business. Sales revenues lead to cash flowing in. If, for the time being, we assume that inventories, trade receivables and trade payables remain constant, operating profit before depreciation will equal the cash inflow.

To simplify matters, we shall assume that the cash from sales and for the expenses of providing the service are received and paid, respectively, at the end of each year. This is clearly unlikely to be true in real life. Money will have to be paid to employees (for salaries and wages) on a weekly or a monthly basis. Customers will pay within a month or two of buying the service. On the other hand, making the assumption probably does not lead to a serious distortion. It is a simplifying assumption that is often made in real life, and it will make things more straightforward for us now. We should be clear, however, that there is nothing about any of the four methods that *demands* that this assumption is made.

Having set up the example, we shall now go on to consider how each of the appraisal methods works.

Accounting rate of return (ARR)

The accounting rate of return (ARR) method takes the average accounting operating profit that the investment will generate and expresses it as a percentage of the average investment made over the life of the project. Thus:

$$ARR = \frac{\text{Average annual operating profit}}{\text{Average investment to earn that profit}} \times 100\%$$

We can see from the equation that, to calculate the ARR, we need to deduce two pieces of information about the particular project:

■ the average annual operating profit; and
■ the average investment.

In our example, the average annual operating profit *before depreciation* over the five years is £40,000 (that is, £(20 + 40 + 60 + 60 + 20)/5). Assuming 'straight-line' depreciation (that is, equal annual amounts), the annual depreciation charge will be £16,000 (that is, £(100,000 − 20,000)/5). Thus the average annual operating profit *after depreciation* is £24,000 (that is, £40,000 − £16,000).

The average investment over the five years can be calculated as follows:

$$\text{Average investment} = \frac{\text{Cost of machine} + \text{Disposal value}}{2}$$
$$= \frac{£100,000 + £20,000}{2}$$
$$= £60,000$$

Thus, the ARR of the investment is:

$$ARR = \frac{£24,000}{£60,000} \times 100\% = 40\%$$

Users of ARR should apply the following decision rules:

- For any project to be acceptable it must achieve a target ARR as a minimum.
- Where there are competing projects that all seem capable of exceeding this minimum rate (that is, where the business must choose between more than one project), the one with the higher or highest ARR would normally be selected.

To decide whether the 40 per cent return is acceptable, we need to compare this percentage return with the minimum rate required by the business.

Activity 10.2

Chaotic Industries is considering an investment in a fleet of ten delivery vans to take its products to customers. The vans will cost £15,000 each to buy, payable immediately. The annual running costs are expected to total £20,000 for each van (including the driver's salary). The vans are expected to operate successfully for six years, at the end of which period they will all have to be sold, with disposal proceeds expected to be about £3,000 a van. At present, the business uses a commercial carrier for all of its deliveries. It is expected that this carrier will charge a total of £230,000 each year for the next six years to undertake the deliveries.

What is the ARR of buying the vans? (Note that cost savings are as relevant a benefit from an investment as are net cash inflows.)

The vans will save the business £30,000 a year (that is, £230,000 − (£20,000 × 10)), before depreciation, in total. Thus, the inflows and outflows will be:

Time		£000
Immediately	Cost of vans (10 × £15,000)	(150)
1 year's time	Net saving before depreciation	30
2 years' time	Net saving before depreciation	30
3 years' time	Net saving before depreciation	30
4 years' time	Net saving before depreciation	30
5 years' time	Net saving before depreciation	30
6 years' time	Net saving before depreciation	30
6 years' time	Disposal proceeds from the vans (10 × £3,000)	30

The total annual depreciation expense (assuming a straight-line method) will be £20,000 (that is, (£150,000 − £30,000)/6). Thus, the average annual saving, after depreciation, is £10,000 (that is, £30,000 − £20,000).

The average investment will be

$$\text{Average investment} = \frac{£150,000 + £30,000}{2} = £90,000$$

and the ARR of the investment is

$$\text{ARR} = \frac{£10,000}{£90,000} \times 100\% = 11.1\%$$

ARR and ROCE

We should note that ARR and the return on capital employed (ROCE) ratio (which we met in Chapter 6) take the same approach to performance measurement, in that they both relate accounting profit to the cost of the assets invested to generate that profit. ROCE is a popular means of assessing the performance of a business, as a whole, *after* it has performed. ARR is an approach that assesses the potential performance of a particular investment, taking the same approach as ROCE, but *before* it has performed.

As we have just seen, managers using ARR will require that any investment undertaken should achieve a target ARR as a minimum. Perhaps this minimum target would be based on the rate that previous investments had actually achieved (as measured by ROCE). Perhaps it would be the industry-average ROCE.

Since private-sector businesses are normally seeking to increase the wealth of their owners, ARR may seem to be a sound method of appraising investment opportunities. Operating profit can be seen as a net increase in wealth over a period, and relating it to the size of investment made to achieve it seems a logical approach.

ARR is said to have a number of advantages as a method of investment appraisal. It was mentioned earlier that ROCE seems to be a widely used measure of business performance. Shareholders seem to use this ratio to evaluate management performance, and sometimes the financial objective of a business will be expressed in terms of a target ROCE. It therefore seems sensible to use a method of investment appraisal that is consistent with this overall approach to measuring business performance. It also gives the result expressed as a percentage. It seems that some managers feel comfortable using measures expressed in percentage terms.

Problems with ARR

Activity 10.3

ARR suffers from a very major defect as a means of assessing investment opportunities. Can you reason out what this is? Consider the three competing projects whose profits are shown below. All three involve investment in a machine that is expected to have no residual value at the end of the five years. Note that all of the projects have the same total operating profits over the five years.

Time		Project A £000	Project B £000	Project C £000
Immediately	Cost of machine	(160)	(160)	(160)
1 year's time	Operating profit after depreciation	20	10	160
2 years' time	Operating profit after depreciation	40	10	10
3 years' time	Operating profit after depreciation	60	10	10
4 years' time	Operating profit after depreciation	60	10	10
5 years' time	Operating profit after depreciation	20	160	10

The problem with ARR is that it almost completely ignores the time factor. In this example, exactly the same ARR would have been computed for each of the three projects.

Since the same total operating profit over the five years (£200,000) arises in all three of these projects, and the average investment in each project is £80,000 (that is, £160,000/2), this means that each will give rise to the same ARR of 50 per cent (that is, £40,000/£80,000).

Given a financial objective of increasing the wealth of the owners of the business, any rational decision-maker faced with a choice between the three projects set out in Activity 10.3 would strongly prefer Project C. This is because most of the benefits from the investment arise within twelve months of investing the £160,000 to establish the project. Project A would rank second and Project B would come a poor third. Any appraisal technique that is not capable of distinguishing between these three situations is seriously flawed. We shall look at why timing is so important later in the chapter.

There are further problems associated with the use of ARR. One of these problems concerns the approach taken to derive the average investment in a project.

Example 10.2 illustrates the daft result that ARR can produce.

Example 10.2

George put forward an investment proposal to his boss. The business uses ARR to assess investment proposals using a minimum 'hurdle' rate of 27 per cent. Details of the proposal were as follows:

Cost of equipment	£200,000
Estimated residual value of equipment	£40,000
Average annual operating profit before depreciation	£48,000
Estimated life of project	10 years
Annual straight-line depreciation charge	£16,000 (that is, (200,000 − £40,000)/10)

The ARR of the project will be:

$$\text{ARR} = \frac{48,000 - 16,000}{(200,000 + 40,000)/2} \times 100\% = 26.7\%$$

The boss rejected George's proposal because it failed to achieve an ARR of at least 27 per cent. Although George was disappointed, he realised that there was still hope. In fact, all that the business had to do was to give away the piece of equipment at the end of its useful life rather than to sell it. The residual value of the equipment then became zero and the annual depreciation charge became ([£200,000 − £0]/10) = £20,000 a year. The revised ARR calculation was then as follows:

$$\text{ARR} = \frac{48,000 - 20,000}{(200,000 + 0)/2} \times 100\% = 28\%$$

ARR is based on the use of accounting profit. When measuring performance over the whole life of a project, however, it is cash flows rather than accounting profits that are important. Cash is the ultimate measure of the economic wealth generated by an investment. This is because it is cash that is used to acquire resources and for distribution to owners. Accounting profit, on the other hand is more appropriate for reporting achievement on a periodic basis. It is a useful measure of productive effort for a relatively short period, such as a year or half-year. It is really a question of 'horses for courses'. Accounting profit is fine for measuring performance over a short period but cash is the appropriate measure when considering the performance over the life of a project.

The ARR method can also create problems when considering competing investments of different size.

Activity 10.4

Sinclair Wholesalers plc is currently considering opening a new sales outlet in Coventry. Two possible sites have been identified for the new outlet. Site A has an area of 30,000 sq m. It will require an average investment of £6m, and will produce an average operating profit of £600,000 a year. Site B has an area of 20,000 sq m. It will require an average investment of £4m, and will produce an average operating profit of £500,000 a year.

What is the ARR of each investment opportunity? Which site would you select, and why?

The ARR of Site A is £600,000/£6m = 10 per cent. The ARR of Site B is £500,000/£4m = 12.5 per cent. Thus, Site B has the higher ARR. However, in terms of the absolute operating profit generated, Site A is the more attractive. If the ultimate objective is to increase the wealth of the shareholders of Sinclair Wholesalers plc, it might be better to choose Site A even though the percentage return is lower. It is the absolute size of the return rather than the relative (percentage) size that is important. This is a general problem of using comparative measures, such as percentages, when the objective is measured in absolute ones, like an amount of money. If businesses were seeking through their investments to generate a percentage rate of return on investment, ARR would be more helpful. The problem is that most businesses seek to achieve increases in their absolute wealth (measured in pounds, euros, dollars and so on), through their investment decisions.

Real World 10.3 illustrates how using percentage measures can lead to confusion.

Real World 10.3

Increasing road capacity by sleight of hand

During the 1970s, the Mexican government wanted to increase the capacity of a major four-lane road. It came up with the idea of repainting the lane markings so that there were six narrower lanes occupying the same space as four wider ones had previously done. This increased the capacity of the road by 50 per cent (that is, $2/4 \times 100$). A tragic outcome of the narrower lanes was an increase in deaths from road accidents. A year later the Mexican government had the six narrower lanes changed back to the original four wider ones. This reduced the capacity of the road by 33 per cent (that is, $^2/_6 \times 100$). The Mexican government reported that, overall, it had increased the capacity of the road by 17 per cent (that is, 50% − 33%), despite the fact that its real capacity was identical to that which it had been originally. The confusion arose because each of the two percentages (50 per cent and 33 per cent) is based on different bases (four and six).

Source: Reckoning with Risk, G. Gigerenzer, Penguin, 2002.

Payback period (PP)

The payback period (PP) is the length of time it takes for an initial investment to be repaid out of the net cash inflows from a project. Since it takes time into account, the PP method seems to go some way to overcoming the timing problem of ARR – or at first glance it does.

It might be useful to consider PP in the context of the Billingsgate Battery example. We should recall that the project's cash flows are:

Time		£000
Immediately	Cost of machine	(100)
1 year's time	Operating profit before depreciation	20
2 years' time	Operating profit before depreciation	40
3 years' time	Operating profit before depreciation	60
4 years' time	Operating profit before depreciation	60
5 years' time	Operating profit before depreciation	20
5 years' time	Disposal proceeds	20

Note that all of these figures are amounts of cash to be paid or received (we saw earlier that operating profit before depreciation is a rough measure of the cash flows from the project).

As the payback period is the length of time it takes for the initial investment to be repaid out of the net cash inflows, it will be three years before the £100,000 outlay is covered by the inflows. This is still assuming that the cash flows occur at year ends. The payback period can be derived by calculating the cumulative cash flows as follows:

Time		Net cash flows £000	Cumulative cash flows £000	
Immediately	Cost of machine	(100)	(100)	
1 year's time	Operating profit before depreciation	20	(80)	(−100 + 20)
2 years' time	Operating profit before depreciation	40	(40)	(−80 + 40)
3 years' time	Operating profit before depreciation	60	20	(−40 + 60)
4 years' time	Operating profit before depreciation	60	80	(20 + 60)
5 years' time	Operating profit before depreciation	20	100	(80 + 20)
5 years' time	Disposal proceeds	20	120	(100 + 20)

We can see that the cumulative cash flows become positive at the end of the third year. (Had we assumed that the cash flows arise evenly over the year, the precise payback period would be:

$$2 \text{ years} + (^{40}\!/_{60}) \text{ years} = 2^2\!/_3 \text{ years}$$

where 40 represents the cash flow still required at the beginning of the third year to repay the initial outlay, and 60 is the projected cash flow during the third year.)

We must now ask how to decide whether three years is an acceptable payback period. The decision rule for using PP is:

■ For a project to be acceptable it would need to have a payback period shorter than a maximum payback period set by the business.
■ If there were two (or more) competing projects whose payback periods were all shorter than the maximum payback period requirement, the decision-maker should select the project with the shorter (shortest) payback period.

If, for example, Billingsgate Battery had a maximum acceptable payback period of four years, the project would be undertaken. A project with a longer payback period than four years would not be acceptable.

Activity 10.5

What is the payback period of the Chaotic Industries project from Activity 10.2?

The inflows and outflows are expected to be:

Time		Net cash flows £000	Cumulative net cash flows £000
Immediately	Cost of vans	(150)	(150)
1 year's time	Net saving before depreciation	30	(120) (−150 + 30)
2 years' time	Net saving before depreciation	30	(90) (−120 + 30)
3 years' time	Net saving before depreciation	30	(60) (−90 + 30)
4 years' time	Net saving before depreciation	30	(30) (−60 + 30)
5 years' time	Net saving before depreciation	30	0 (−30 + 30)
6 years' time	Net saving before depreciation	30	30 (0 + 30)
6 years' time	Disposal proceeds from the machine	30	60 (30 + 30)

The payback period here is five years; that is, it is not until the end of the fifth year that the vans will pay for themselves out of the savings that they are expected to generate.

The PP method has certain advantages. It is quick and easy to calculate, and can be easily understood by managers. The logic of using PP is that projects that can recoup their cost quickly are economically more attractive than those with longer payback periods, that is, it emphasises liquidity. PP is probably an improvement on ARR in respect of the timing of the cash flows. PP is not, however, the whole answer to the problem.

Problems with PP

Activity 10.6

In what respect is PP not the whole answer as a means of assessing investment opportunities? Consider the cash flows arising from three competing projects:

Time		Project 1 £000	Project 2 £000	Project 3 £000
Immediately	Cost of machine	(200)	(200)	(200)
1 year's time	Operating profit before depreciation	40	10	80
2 years' time	Operating profit before depreciation	80	20	100
3 years' time	Operating profit before depreciation	80	170	20
4 years' time	Operating profit before depreciation	60	20	200
5 years' time	Operating profit before depreciation	40	10	500
5 years' time	Disposal proceeds	40	10	20

(*Hint*: Again, the defect is not concerned with the ability of the manager to forecast future events. This is a problem, but it is a problem whatever approach we take.)

The PP for each project is three years and so the PP method would regard the projects as being equally acceptable. It cannot distinguish between those projects that pay back a significant amount early in the three-year payback period and those that do not.

In addition, this method ignores cash flows after the payback period. A decision-maker concerned with increasing owners' wealth would prefer Project 3 because the cash flows come in earlier (most of the initial cost of making the investment has been repaid by the end of the second year) and they are greater in total.

The cumulative cash flows of each project in Activity 10.6 are set out in Figure 10.1. We can see that the PP method is not concerned with the profitability of projects; it is concerned simply with their payback period. Thus cash flows arising beyond the payback period are ignored. While this neatly avoids the practical problems of forecasting cash flows over a long period, it means that relevant information may be ignored.

We may feel that, by favouring projects with a short payback period, the PP method does at least provide a means of dealing with the problems of risk and uncertainty. However, this is a fairly crude approach to the problem. It looks only at the risk that the project will end earlier than expected. However, this is only one of many risk areas. What, for example, about the risk that the demand for the product may be less than expected? There are more systematic approaches to dealing with risk that can be used.

PP takes some note of the timing of the costs and benefits from the project. Its key deficiency, however, is that it is not linked to promoting increases in the wealth of the business and its owners. PP will tend to recommend undertaking projects that pay for themselves quickly.

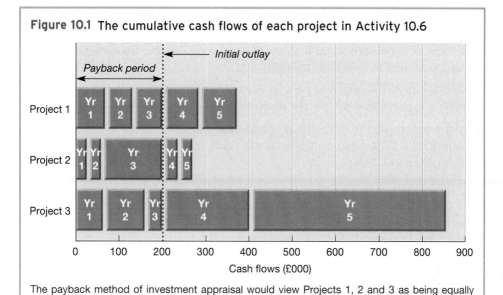

Figure 10.1 The cumulative cash flows of each project in Activity 10.6

The payback method of investment appraisal would view Projects 1, 2 and 3 as being equally attractive. In doing so, the method completely ignores the fact that Project 3 provides the payback cash earlier in the three-year period and goes on to generate large benefits in later years.

The PP method requires the managers of a business to select a maximum acceptable payback period. This maximum period, in practice, will vary from one business to the next. Real World 10.4 provides some evidence of the length of payback period required by small and medium-sized businesses when investing in new forms of energy generation.

Real World 10.4

Payback time

When it comes to self-generation of renewable energy, UK SMEs (small and medium-sized enterprises) want an unrealistically quick return on investment according to research carried out by energy consultancy energyTEAM. Nearly three-quarters would need payback within three years in order to justify introducing such measures. Only 4 per cent are prepared for this process to take over five years despite growing concern over commercial energy usage. EnergyTEAM's study revealed that 40 per cent of enterprises with 50 to 500 employees would have to be convinced of a return on investment in just one year before they would proceed down the route of self-generation.

When asked which method of self-generation they would be most inclined to choose, over half of respondents highlighted solar power as the preferred method. This is despite the fact that solar has one of the largest payback times, at around ten years.

Brian Rickerby, joint Managing Director of energyTEAM, said: 'I can understand that seeking a quick return is a pragmatic, business-like approach, but unfortunately this is not realistic when it comes to energy issues. Self-generation technologies must be viewed as a long-term strategy that will have a significant positive impact for many years to come.'

Source: 'SMEs' unrealistic demands on renewables', *Sustain*, vol. 8, issue 5, 2007, p. 74.

Net present value (NPV)

From what we have seen so far it seems that, to make sensible investment decisions, we need a method of appraisal that both

- considers *all* of the costs and benefits of each investment opportunity; and
- makes a logical allowance for the *timing* of those costs and benefits.

 The net present value (NPV) method provides us with this.

Consider the Billingsgate Battery example's cash flows, which we should recall can be summarised as follows:

Time		£000
Immediately	Cost of machine	(100)
1 year's time	Operating profit before depreciation	20
2 years' time	Operating profit before depreciation	40
3 years' time	Operating profit before depreciation	60
4 years' time	Operating profit before depreciation	60
5 years' time	Operating profit before depreciation	20
5 years' time	Disposal proceeds	20

Given that the principal financial objective of the business is to increase owners' wealth, it would be very easy to assess this investment if all of the cash inflows and outflows were to occur now (all at the same time). All that we should need to do would be to add up the cash inflows (total £220,000) and compare them with the cash outflows (£100,000). This would lead us to the conclusion that the project should go ahead because the business, and its owners, would be better off by £120,000. Of course, it is not as easy as this because time is involved. The cash outflow (payment) will occur immediately if the project is undertaken. The inflows (receipts) will arise at a range of later times.

The time factor is an important issue because people do not normally see £100 paid out now as equivalent in value to £100 receivable in a year's time. If we were to be offered £100 in 12 months' time in exchange for paying out £100 now, we should not be prepared to do so unless we wished to do someone a favour.

Activity 10.7

Why would you see £100 to be received in a year's time as not equal in value to £100 to be paid immediately? (There are basically three reasons.)

The reasons are:

- interest lost
- risk
- effects of inflation.

We shall now take a closer look at these three reasons in turn.

Interest lost

If we are to be deprived of the opportunity to spend our money for a year, we could equally well be deprived of its use by placing it on deposit in a bank or building society. In this case, at the end of the year we could have our money back and have interest as well. Thus, by investing the funds in some other way, we shall be incurring an *opportunity cost*. An opportunity cost occurs where one course of action, for example making an investment, deprives us of the opportunity to derive some benefit from an alternative action, for example putting the money in the bank and earning interest.

From this we can see that any investment opportunity must, if it is to make us wealthier, do better than the returns that are available from the next best opportunity. Thus, if Billingsgate Battery Company sees putting the money in the bank on deposit as the alternative to investment in the machine, the return from investing in the machine must be better than that from investing in the bank. If the bank offered a better return, the business, and its owners, would become wealthier by putting the money on deposit.

Risk

Buying a machine to manufacture a product, or to provide a service, to be sold in the market, on the strength of various estimates made in advance of buying the machine, exposes the business to risk. Things may not turn out as expected.

Activity 10.8

Can you suggest some areas where things could go other than according to plan in the Billingsgate Battery Company example?

We have come up with the following:

- The machine might not work as well as expected; it might break down, leading to loss of the business's ability to provide the service.
- Sales of the service may not be as buoyant as expected.
- Labour costs may prove to be higher than expected.
- The sale proceeds of the machine could prove to be less than were estimated.

It is important to remember that the decision whether to invest in the machine must be taken *before* any of these things are known. It is only after the machine has been purchased that we could discover that the level of sales, which had been estimated before the event, is not going to be achieved. It is not possible to wait until we know for certain whether the market will behave as we expected before we buy the machine. We can study reports and analyses of the market. We can commission sophisticated market surveys, and these may give us more confidence in the likely outcome. We can advertise widely and try to promote sales. Ultimately, however, we have to decide whether to jump off into the dark and accept the risk if we want the opportunity to make profitable investments.

Real World 10.5 gives some impression of the extent to which businesses believe that investment outcomes turn out as expected.

Real World 10.5

Size matters

A sample of 99 Cambridgeshire manufacturing businesses were surveyed and asked the extent to which past investments performed in line with earlier expectations. The results, broken down according to business size, are set out below.

	Large	Medium	Small	All
		Size of business		
	Large	*Medium*	*Small*	*All*
Under-performed	8%	14%	32%	14%
Performed as expected	82%	72%	68%	77%
Over-performed	10%	14%	0%	9%

It seems that smaller businesses are much more likely to get it wrong than medium-sized or larger businesses. This may be because small businesses are often younger and, therefore, less experienced in the techniques of both forecasting and managing investment projects. They are also likely to have less financial expertise. It also seems that small businesses have a distinct bias towards over-optimism and do not take full account of the possibility that things will turn out worse than expected.

Source: 'Unpacking the black box: An econometric analysis of investment strategies in real world firms', M. Baddeley, CEPP Working Paper No. 08/05, University of Cambridge, p. 14.

Normally, people expect to receive greater returns where they perceive risk to be a factor. Examples of this in real life are not difficult to find. One such example is that banks tend to charge higher rates of interest to borrowers whom the bank perceives as more risky. Those who can offer good security for a loan, and who can point to a regular source of income, tend to be charged lower rates of interest.

Going back to Billingsgate Battery Company's investment opportunity, it is not enough to say that we should not advise making the investment unless the returns from it are as high as those from investing in a bank deposit. Clearly we should want returns above the level of bank deposit interest rates, because the logical equivalent of investing in the machine is not putting the money on deposit but making an alternative investment that is risky.

In practice, we tend to expect a higher rate of return from investment projects where the risk is perceived as being higher. How risky a particular project is, and therefore how large this risk premium should be, are matters that are difficult to handle. It is usually necessary to make some judgement on these questions.

Inflation

If we are to be deprived of £100 for a year, when we come to spend that money it will not buy as many goods and services as it would have done a year earlier. Generally, we shall not be able to buy as many tins of baked beans or loaves of bread or bus tickets as we could have done a year earlier. This is because of the loss in the purchasing power of money, or inflation, which occurs over time. Clearly, the investor needs compensating for this loss of purchasing power if the investment is to be made. This compensation is on top of a return that takes account of what could have been gained from an alternative investment of similar risk.

In practice, interest rates observable in the market tend to take inflation into account. Rates that are offered to potential building society and bank depositors include an allowance for the rate of inflation that is expected in the future.

What will a logical investor do?

A logical investor who is seeking to increase his or her wealth will only be prepared to make investments that will compensate for the loss of interest and purchasing power of the money invested and for the fact that the returns expected may not materialise (risk). This is usually assessed by seeing whether the proposed investment will yield a return that is greater than the basic rate of interest (which would include an allowance for inflation) plus a risk premium.

These three factors (interest lost, risk and inflation) are set out in Figure 10.2.

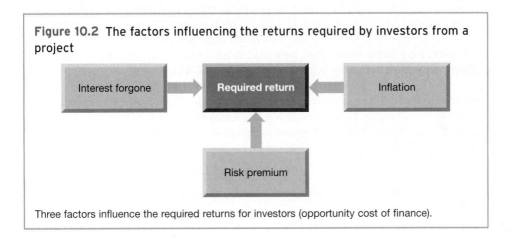

Figure 10.2 The factors influencing the returns required by investors from a project

Three factors influence the required returns for investors (opportunity cost of finance).

Naturally, investors need at least the minimum returns before they are prepared to invest. However, it is in terms of the effect on their wealth that they should logically assess an investment project. Usually it is the investment with the highest percentage return that will make the investor most wealthy, but we shall see later in this chapter that this is not always the case. For the time being, therefore, we shall concentrate on wealth.

Let us now return to the Billingsgate Battery Company example. We should recall that the cash flows expected from this investment are:

Time		£000
Immediately	Cost of machine	(100)
1 year's time	Operating profit before depreciation	20
2 years' time	Operating profit before depreciation	40
3 years' time	Operating profit before depreciation	60
4 years' time	Operating profit before depreciation	60
5 years' time	Operating profit before depreciation	20
5 years' time	Disposal proceeds	20

We have already seen that it is not sufficient just to compare the basic cash inflows and outflows for the investment. It would be useful if we could express each of these cash flows in similar terms, so that we could make a direct comparison between the sum of the inflows over time and the immediate £100,000 investment. Fortunately, we can.

Let us assume that, instead of making this investment, the business could make an alternative investment with similar risk and obtain a return of 20 per cent a year.

Activity 10.9

We know that Billingsgate Battery Company could alternatively invest its money at a rate of 20 per cent a year. How much do you judge the present (immediate) value of the expected first year receipt of £20,000 to be? In other words, if instead of having to wait a year for the £20,000, and being deprived of the opportunity to invest it at 20 per cent, you could have some money now, what sum to be received now would you regard as exactly equivalent to getting £20,000 but having to wait a year for it?

We should obviously be happy to accept a lower amount if we could get it immediately than if we had to wait a year. This is because we could invest it at 20 per cent (in the alternative project). Logically, we should be prepared to accept the amount that, with a year's income, will grow to £20,000. If we call this amount PV (for present value) we can say:

$$PV + (PV \times 20\%) = £20,000$$

– that is, the amount plus income from investing the amount for the year equals the £20,000.

If we rearrange this equation we find:

$$PV \times (1 + 0.2) = £20,000$$

(Note that 0.2 is the same as 20 per cent, but expressed as a decimal.) Further rearranging gives:

$$PV = £20,000/(1 + 0.2) = £16,667$$

Thus, rational investors who have the opportunity to invest at 20 per cent a year would not mind whether they have £16,667 now or £20,000 in a year's time. In this sense we can say that, given a 20 per cent alternative investment opportunity, the present value of £20,000 to be received in one year's time is £16,667.

If we could derive the present value (PV) of each of the cash flows associated with Billingsgate's machine investment, we could easily make the direct comparison between the cost of making the investment (£100,000) and the various benefits that will derive from it in years 1 to 5. In fact, we can do this.

We can make a more general statement about the PV of a particular cash flow. It is:

PV of the cash flow of year n = actual cash flow of year n divided by $(1 + r)^n$

where n is the year of the cash flow (that is, how many years into the future) and r is the opportunity investing rate expressed as a decimal (instead of as a percentage).

We have already seen how this works for the £20,000 inflow for year 1 for the Billingsgate project. For year 2 the calculation would be:

PV of year 2 cash flow (that is, £40,000) $= £40,000/(1 + 0.2)^2 = £40,000/(1.2)^2$
$$= £40,000/1.44 = £27,778$$

Thus the present value of the £40,000 to be received in two years' time is £27,778.

Activity 10.10

See if you can show that an investor would find £27,778, receivable now, as equally acceptable to receiving £40,000 in two years' time, assuming that there is a 20 per cent investment opportunity.

The reasoning goes like this:

	£
Amount available for immediate investment	27,778
Add Interest for year 1 (20% × 27,778)	5,556
	33,334
Add Interest for year 2 (20% × 33,334)	6,667
	40,001

(The extra £1 is only a rounding error.)

This is to say that since the investor can turn £27,778 into £40,000 in two years, these amounts are equivalent. We can say that £27,778 is the present value of £40,000 receivable after two years (given a 20 per cent rate of return).

Now let us calculate the present values of all of the cash flows associated with the Billingsgate machine project and from them the *net present value (NPV)* of the project as a whole.

The relevant cash flows and calculations are as follows:

Time	Cash flow £000	Calculation of PV	PV £000
Immediately (time 0)	(100)	$(100)/(1 + 0.2)^0$	(100.00)
1 year's time	20	$20/(1 + 0.2)^1$	16.67
2 years' time	40	$40/(1 + 0.2)^2$	27.78
3 years' time	60	$60/(1 + 0.2)^3$	34.72
4 years' time	60	$60/(1 + 0.2)^4$	28.94
5 years' time	20	$20/(1 + 0.2)^5$	8.04
5 years' time	20	$20/(1 + 0.2)^5$	8.04
Net present value (NPV)			24.19

Note: $(1 + 0.2)^0 = 1$.

Once again, we must ask how we can decide whether the machine project is acceptable to the business. In fact, the decision rule for NPV is simple:

- If the NPV is positive the project should be accepted; if it is negative the project should be rejected.
- If there are two (or more) competing projects that have positive NPVs, the decision-maker should select the project with the higher (or highest) NPV.

In this case, the NPV is positive, so we should accept the project and buy the machine. The reasoning behind this decision rule is quite straightforward. Investing in the machine will make the business, and its owners, £24,190 better off than they would be by taking up the next best opportunity available. The gross benefits from investing in this machine are worth a total of £124,190 today, and since the business can 'buy' these benefits for just £100,000 today, the investment should be made. If, however, the present value of the gross benefits were below £100,000, it would be less than the cost of 'buying' those benefits.

Activity 10.11

What is the *maximum* the Billingsgate Battery Company should be prepared to pay for the machine, given the potential benefits of owning it?

The business should logically be prepared to pay up to £124,190, since the wealth of the owners of the business would be increased up to this price – although the business would prefer to pay as little as possible.

Using discount tables

Deducing the present values of the various cash flows is a little laborious using the approach that we have just taken. To deduce each PV we took the relevant cash flow and multiplied it by $1/(1 + r)^n$. There is a slightly different way to do this. Tables exist that show values of this discount factor for a range of values of r and n. Such a table appears in Appendix E. Take a look at it.

Look at the column for 20 per cent and the row for one year. We find that the factor is 0.833. This means that the PV of a cash flow of £1 receivable in one year is £0.833. So the present value of a cash flow of £20,000 receivable in one year's time is £16,660 (that is, 0.833 × £20,000), the same result as we found doing it in longhand.

Activity 10.12

What is the NPV of the Chaotic Industries project from Activity 10.2, assuming a 15 per cent opportunity cost of finance (discount rate)? You should use the discount table in Appendix E.

Remember that the inflows and outflow are expected to be:

Time		£000
Immediately	Cost of vans	(150)
1 year's time	Net saving before depreciation	30
2 years' time	Net saving before depreciation	30
3 years' time	Net saving before depreciation	30
4 years' time	Net saving before depreciation	30
5 years' time	Net saving before depreciation	30
6 years' time	Net saving before depreciation	30
6 years' time	Disposal proceeds from the machine	30

The calculation of the NPV of the project is as follows:

Time	Cash flows £000	Discount factor (15% – from the table)	Present value £000
Immediately	(150)	1.000	(150.00)
1 year's time	30	0.870	26.10
2 years' time	30	0.756	22.68
3 years' time	30	0.658	19.74
4 years' time	30	0.572	17.16
5 years' time	30	0.497	14.91
6 years' time	30	0.432	12.96
6 years' time	30	0.432	12.96
		NPV	(23.49)

How would you interpret this result?

The fact that the project has a negative NPV means that the present values of the benefits from the investment are worth less than the cost of entering into it. Any cost up to £126,510 (the present value of the benefits) would be worth paying, but not £150,000.

The discount table shows how the value of £1 diminishes as its receipt goes further into the future. Assuming an opportunity cost of finance of 20 per cent a year, £1 to be received immediately, obviously, has a present value of £1. However, as the time before it is to be received increases, the present value diminishes significantly, as is shown in Figure 10.3.

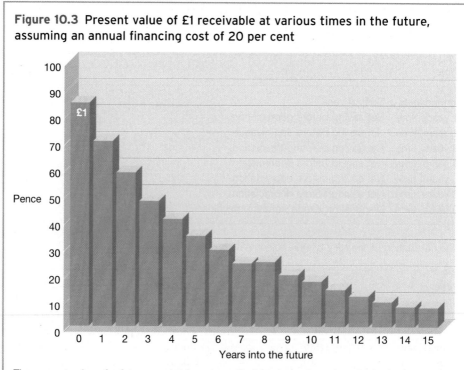

Figure 10.3 Present value of £1 receivable at various times in the future, assuming an annual financing cost of 20 per cent

The present value of a future receipt (or payment) of £1 depends on how far in the future it will occur. Those that will occur in the near future will have a larger present value than those whose occurrence is more distant in time.

The discount rate and the cost of capital

We have seen that the appropriate discount rate to use in NPV assessments is the opportunity cost of finance. This is often known as the cost of capital.

Why NPV is better

From what we have seen, NPV seems to be a better method of appraising investment opportunities than either ARR or PP. This is because it fully takes account of each of the following:

- *The timing of the cash flows.* By discounting the various cash flows associated with each project according to when each one is expected to arise, NPV takes account of the time value of money. Associated with this is the fact that by discounting, using the opportunity cost of finance (that is, the return that the next best alternative opportunity would generate), the net benefit *after* financing costs have been met is identified (as the NPV of the project).
- *The whole of the relevant cash flows.* NPV includes *all* of the relevant cash flows irrespective of when they are expected to occur. It treats them differently according to their date of occurrence, but they are all taken into account in the NPV, and they all have an influence on the decision.
- *The objectives of the business.* NPV is the only method of appraisal in which the output of the analysis has a direct bearing on the wealth of the owners of the business (with a limited company, the shareholders). Positive NPVs enhance wealth; negative ones reduce it. Since we assume that private-sector businesses seek to increase owners' wealth, NPV is superior to the other two methods (ARR and PP) that we have already discussed.

We saw earlier that a business should take on all projects with positive NPVs, when their cash flows are discounted at the opportunity cost of finance. Where a choice has to be made between projects, the business should normally select the one with the higher or highest NPV.

NPV's wider application

NPV is considered the most logical approach to making business decisions about investments in productive assets. The same logic makes NPV equally valid as the best approach to take when trying to place a value on any economic asset, that is, an asset that seems capable of yielding financial benefits. This would include a share in a limited company and a loan. In fact, when we talk of *economic value*, we mean a value that has been derived by adding together the discounted (present) values of all future cash flows from the asset concerned.

Real World 10.6 provides an estimate of the NPV that is expected from one interesting project.

Real World 10.6

A real diamond geezer

Alan Bond, the disgraced Australian businessman and America's Cup winner, is looking at ways to raise money in London for an African diamond mining project. Lesotho Diamond Corporation (LDC) is a private company in which Mr Bond has a large interest. LDC's main asset is a 93 per cent stake in the Kao diamond project in the southern African kingdom of Lesotho.

Mr Bond says, on his personal website, that the Kao project is forecast to yield 5m carats of diamonds over the next ten years and could become Lesotho's biggest foreign currency earner.

SRK, the mining consultants, has estimated the net present value of the project at £129m.

It is understood that Mr Bond and his family own about 40 per cent of LDC. Mr Bond has described himself as 'spearheading' the Kao project.

Source: Adapted from 'Bond seeks funds in London to mine African diamonds', Rebecca Bream, ft.com, 23 April 2007.

Internal rate of return (IRR)

This is the last of the four major methods of investment appraisal that are found in practice. It is quite closely related to the NPV method in that, like NPV, it also involves discounting future cash flows. The internal rate of return (IRR) of a particular investment is the discount rate that, when applied to its future cash flows, will produce an NPV of precisely zero. In essence, it represents the yield from an investment opportunity.

Activity 10.14

We should recall that, when we discounted the cash flows of the Billingsgate Battery Company machine investment opportunity at 20 per cent, we found that the NPV was a positive figure of £24,190 (see page 364). What does the NPV of the machine project tell us about the rate of return that the investment will yield for the business?

The fact that the NPV is positive when discounting at 20 per cent implies that the rate of return that the project generates is more than 20 per cent. The fact that the NPV is a pretty large figure implies that the actual rate of return is quite a lot above 20 per cent. We should expect increasing the size of the discount rate to reduce NPV, because a higher discount rate gives a lower discounted figure.

It is somewhat laborious to deduce the IRR by hand, since it cannot usually be calculated directly. Iteration (trial and error) is the approach that must usually be adopted. Fortunately, computer spreadsheet packages can deduce the IRR with ease. The package will also use a trial and error approach, but at high speed.

Despite it being laborious, we shall now go on and derive the IRR for the Billingsgate project by hand.

Let us try a higher rate, say 30 per cent, and see what happens.

Time	Cash flow £000	Discount factor (30%)	PV £000
Immediately (time 0)	(100)	1.000	(100.00)
1 year's time	20	0.769	15.38
2 years' time	40	0.592	23.68
3 years' time	60	0.455	27.30
4 years' time	60	0.350	21.00
5 years' time	20	0.269	5.38
5 years' time	20	0.269	5.38
			NPV (1.88)

In increasing the discount rate from 20 per cent to 30 per cent, we have reduced the NPV from £24,190 (positive) to £1,880 (negative). Since the IRR is the discount rate that will give us an NPV of exactly zero, we can conclude that the IRR of Billingsgate Battery Company's machine project is very slightly below 30 per cent. Further trials could lead us to the exact rate, but there is probably not much point, given the likely inaccuracy of the cash flow estimates. It is probably good enough, for practical purposes, to say that the IRR is about 30 per cent.

The relationship between the NPV method discussed earlier and the IRR is shown graphically in Figure 10.4 using the information relating to the Billingsgate Battery Company.

Figure 10.4 The relationship between the NPV and IRR methods

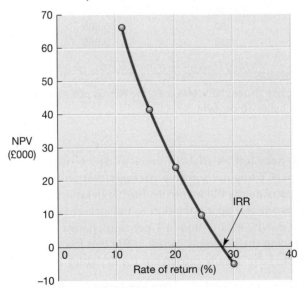

If the discount rate were zero, the NPV would be the sum of the net cash flows. In other words, no account would be taken of the time value of money. However, if we assume increasing discount rates, there is a corresponding decrease in the NPV of the project. When the NPV line crosses the horizontal axis there will be a zero NPV, and the point where it crosses is the IRR.

We can see that, where the discount rate is zero, the NPV will be the sum of the net cash flows. In other words, no account is taken of the time value of money. However, as the discount rate increases there is a corresponding decrease in the NPV of the project. When the NPV line crosses the horizontal axis there will be a zero NPV, and that represents the IRR.

Activity 10.15

What is the internal rate of return of the Chaotic Industries project from Activity 10.2? You should use the discount table in Appendix E. (*Hint*: Remember that you already know the NPV of this project at 15 per cent (from Activity 10.12).)

Since we know that, at a 15 per cent discount rate, the NPV is a relatively large negative figure, our next trial is using a lower discount rate, say 10 per cent:

Time	Cash flows £000	Discount factor (10%)	Present value £000
Immediately	(150)	1.000	(150.00)
1 year's time	30	0.909	27.27
2 years' time	30	0.826	24.78
3 years' time	30	0.751	22.53
4 years' time	30	0.683	20.49
5 years' time	30	0.621	18.63
6 years' time	30	0.565	16.95
6 years' time	30	0.565	16.95
			NPV (2.40)

This figure is close to zero NPV. However, the NPV is still negative and so the precise IRR will be a little below 10 per cent.

We could undertake further trials in order to derive the precise IRR. In practice, most businesses have computer software packages that will do this quickly. If, however, we have to calculate the IRR manually, further iterations can be time-consuming. We can get an acceptable approximation to the answer fairly quickly by first calculating the change in NPV arising from a 1 per cent change in the discount rate. This can be done by taking the difference between the two trials (that is, 15 per cent and 10 per cent) that we have already carried out (in Activities 10.12 and 10.15):

Trial	Discount factor %	Present value £000
1	15	(23.49)
2	10	(2.40)
Difference	5	21.09

The change in NPV for every 1 per cent change in the discount rate will be:

$$(21.09/5) = 4.22$$

The reduction in the 10% discount rate required to achieve a zero NPV would therefore be:

$$(2.40)/4.22 = 0.57\%$$

The IRR is therefore:

$$(10.00 - 0.57) = 9.43\%$$

However, to say that the IRR is about 9 per cent is near enough for most purposes.

Note that this approach assumes a straight-line relationship between the discount rate and NPV. We can see from Figure 10.4, however, that this assumption is not strictly correct. Over a relatively short range, however, this simplifying assumption is not usually a problem and so we can still arrive at a reasonable approximation using the approach that we took in deriving the 9.43 per cent IRR.

Users of the IRR method should apply the following decision rules:

■ For any project to be acceptable, it must meet a minimum IRR requirement. This is often referred to as the *hurdle rate* and, logically, this should be the opportunity cost of finance.

■ Where there are competing projects (that is, the business can choose only one of two or more viable projects), the one with the higher (or highest) IRR would be selected.

IRR has certain attributes in common with NPV. All cash flows are taken into account, and their timing is logically handled.

Real World 10.7 provides some idea of the IRR for one form of renewable energy.

Real World 10.7

The answer is blowin' in the wind

'Wind farms are practically guaranteed to make returns once you have a licence to operate,' says Bernard Lambilliotte, chief investment officer at Ecofin, a financial group that runs Ecofin Water and Power Opportunities, an investment trust.

'The risk is when you have bought the land and are seeking a licence,' says Lambilliotte. 'But once it is built and you are plugged into the grid it is risk-free. It will give an internal rate of return in the low to mid teens.' Ecofin's largest investment is in Sechilienne, a French company that operates wind farms in northern France and generates capacity in the French overseas territories powered by sugar cane waste.

Source: 'A hot topic, but poor returns', Charles Batchelor, ft.com, 27 August 2005.

Real World 10.8 gives some examples of IRRs sought in practice.

Real World 10.8

Rates of return

IRR rates for investment projects can vary considerably. Here are a few examples of the expected returns from investment projects of large businesses.

■ Associated British Ports, the UK's largest port operator, concentrates on projects that generate an IRR of at least 15 per cent.
■ Brascan, a Canadian property and energy business, made a bid to acquire Canary Wharf, a property estate in London, and expected to generate an IRR of at least 20 per cent if the bid price was accepted.
■ Hutchison Whampoa, a large telecommunications business, requires an IRR of at least 25 per cent from its telecom projects.
■ Airbus expects an IRR of 13 per cent from the sale of its A380 superjumbo aircraft.

Sources: 'Brascan raises offer for Canary Wharf', ft.com, 13 February 2004; 'Spread of risks gives ABP confident outlook', FT.com, 13 February 2003; Lex column, Hutchison Whampoa, ft.com, 31 March 2004; 'Airbus hikes A380 break-even target', FT.com, 20 October 2006.

Problems with IRR

The main disadvantage of IRR, relative to NPV, is the fact that it does not correctly address the question of wealth generation. It could therefore lead to the wrong decision being made. This is because IRR would, for example, always see an IRR of 25 per cent as being preferable to a 20 per cent IRR, assuming an opportunity cost of finance of, say, 15 per cent. Although accepting the project with the higher percentage return will often generate more wealth, this may not always be the case. This is because IRR completely ignores the *scale of investment*.

With a 15 per cent cost of finance, £15 million invested at 20 per cent for one year will make us wealthier by £0.75 million (that is, $15 \times (20 - 15)\% = 0.75$). With the same cost of finance, £5 million invested at 25 per cent for one year will make us only £0.5 million (that is, $5 \times (25 - 15)\% = 0.50$). IRR does not recognise this. It should be acknowledged that it is not usual for projects to be competing where there is such a large difference in scale. Even though the problem may be rare and so, typically, IRR will give the same signal as NPV, a method that is always reliable (NPV) must be better to use than IRR. This problem with percentages is another example of that illustrated by the Mexcian road discussed in Real World 10.3 (pp. 353–4).

A further problem with the IRR method is that it has difficulty handling projects with unconventional cash flows. In the examples studied so far, each project has a negative cash flow arising at the start of its life and then positive cash flows thereafter. However, in some cases, a project may have both positive and negative cash flows at future points in its life. Such a pattern of cash flows can result in there being more than one IRR, or even no IRR at all. This would make the IRR method impossible to use, although it should be said that this is quite rare in practice.

Some practical points

When undertaking an investment appraisal, there are several practical points that we should bear in mind:

■ *Past costs.* As with all decisions, we should take account only of relevant costs in our analysis. This means that only costs that vary with the decision should be considered. Thus, all past costs should be ignored as they cannot vary with the decision. In some cases, a business may incur costs (such as development costs and market research costs) *before* the evaluation of an opportunity to launch a new product. As those costs have already been incurred, they should be disregarded, even though the amounts may be substantial. Costs that have already been committed but not yet paid should also be disregarded. Where a business has entered into a binding contract to incur a particular cost, it becomes in effect a past cost even though payment may not be due until some point in the future.

■ *Common future costs.* It is not only past costs that do not vary with the decision; some future costs may also be the same. For example, the cost of raw materials may not vary with the decision whether to invest in a new piece of manufacturing plant or to continue to use existing plant.

■ *Opportunity costs.* Opportunity costs arising from benefits forgone must be taken into account. Thus, for example, when considering a decision concerning whether or not to continue to use a machine already owned by the business, the realisable value of the machine might be an important opportunity cost.

These points concerning costs are brought together in Activity 10.16 below.

Activity 10.16

A garage has an old car that it bought several months ago for £3,000. The car needs a replacement engine before it can be sold. It is possible to buy a reconditioned engine for £300. This would take seven hours to fit by a mechanic who is paid £12 an hour. At present, the garage is short of work, but the owners are reluctant to lay off any mechanics or even cut down their basic working week because skilled labour is difficult to find and an upturn in repair work is expected soon.

Without the engine, the car could be sold for an estimated £3,500. What is the minimum price at which the garage should sell the car, with a reconditioned engine fitted, to avoid making a loss? (Ignore any timing differences in receipts and payments.)

The minimum price is the amount required to cover the relevant costs of the job. At this price, the business will make neither a profit nor a loss. Any price below this amount will result in a reduction in the wealth of the business. Thus, the minimum price is:

	£
Opportunity cost of the car	3,500
Cost of the reconditioned engine	300
Total	3,800

The original cost of the car is a past cost and is, therefore, irrelevant. However, we are told that, without the engine, the car could be sold for £3,500. This is the opportunity cost of the car, which represents the real benefits forgone, and should be taken into account.

The cost of the new engine is relevant because, if the work is done, the garage will have to pay £300 for the engine; it will pay nothing if the job is not done. The £300 is a future cost that varies with the decision and should be taken into account.

The labour cost is irrelevant because the same cost will be incurred whether the mechanic undertakes the work or not. This is because the mechanic is being paid to do nothing if this job is not undertaken; thus the additional labour cost arising from this job is zero.

■ *Taxation.* Owners will be interested in the after-tax returns generated from the business, and so taxation will usually be an important consideration when making an investment decision. The profits from the project will be taxed, the capital investment may attract tax relief, and so on. Tax is levied at significant rates. This means that, in real life, unless tax is formally taken into account, the wrong decision could easily be made. The timing of the tax outflow should also be taken into account when preparing the cash flows for the project.

■ *Cash flows not profit flows.* We have seen that for the NPV, IRR and PP methods, it is cash flows rather than profit flows that are relevant to the assessment of investment projects. In an investment appraisal requiring the application of any of these methods we may be given details of the profits for the investment period. These need to be adjusted in order to derive the cash flows. We should remember that the operating profit *before* non-cash items (such as depreciation) is an approximation to the cash flows for the period, and so we should work back to this figure.

When the data are expressed in profit rather than cash flow terms, an adjustment in respect of working capital may also be necessary. Some adjustment should be made to take account of changes in working capital. For example, launching a new product may give rise to an increase in the net investment made in trade receivables, inventories and trade payables, requiring an immediate outlay of cash. This outlay for additional working capital should be shown in the NPV calculations as part of the initial cost. However, at the end of the life of the project, the additional working capital will be released. This divestment, resulting in an inflow of cash at the end of the project, should also be taken into account at the point at which it is received.

■ *Year-end assumption.* In the examples and activities that we have considered so far in this chapter, we have assumed that cash flows arise at the end of the relevant year. This is a simplifying assumption that is used to make the calculations easier. (However, it is perfectly possible to deal more precisely with the cash flows.) The assumption is clearly unrealistic, as money will have to be paid to employees on a weekly or monthly basis and credit customers will pay within a month or two of buying the product or service. Nevertheless, it is probably not a serious distortion. We should be clear, however, that there is nothing about any of the four appraisal methods that demands that this assumption be made.

■ *Interest payments.* When using discounted cash flow techniques (NPV and IRR), interest payments should not be taken into account in deriving the cash flows for the period. The discount factor already takes account of the costs of financing, and so to take account of interest charges in deriving cash flows for the period would be double counting.

■ *Other factors.* Investment decision-making must not be viewed as simply a mechanical exercise. The results derived from a particular investment appraisal method will be only one input to the decision-making process. There may be broader issues connected to the decision that have to be taken into account but which may be difficult or impossible to quantify.

The reliability of the forecasts and the validity of the assumptions used in the evaluation will also have a bearing on the final decision.

Activity 10.17

The directors of Manuff (Steel) Ltd are considering closing one of the business's factories. There has been a reduction in the demand for the products made at the factory in recent years, and the directors are not optimistic about the long-term prospects for these products. The factory is situated in the north of England, in an area where unemployment is high.

The factory is leased, and there are still four years of the lease remaining. The directors are uncertain whether the factory should be closed immediately or at the end of the period of the lease. Another business has offered to sublease the premises from Manuff at a rental of £40,000 a year for the remainder of the lease period.

The machinery and equipment at the factory cost £1,500,000, and have a balance sheet value of £400,000. In the event of immediate closure, the machinery and equipment could be sold for £220,000. The working capital at the factory is £420,000, and could be liquidated for that amount immediately, if required. Alternatively, the working capital can be liquidated in full at the end of the lease period. Immediate closure would result in redundancy payments to employees of £180,000.

If the factory continues in operation until the end of the lease period, the following operating profits (losses) are expected:

	Year 1 £000	Year 2 £000	Year 3 £000	Year 4 £000
Operating profit (loss)	160	(40)	30	20

The above figures include a charge of £90,000 a year for depreciation of machinery and equipment. The residual value of the machinery and equipment at the end of the lease period is estimated at £40,000.

Redundancy payments are expected to be £150,000 at the end of the lease period if the factory continues in operation. The business has an annual cost of capital of 12 per cent. Ignore taxation.

Required:
(a) Determine the relevant cash flows arising from a decision to continue operations until the end of the lease period rather than to close immediately.
(b) Calculate the net present value of continuing operations until the end of the lease period, rather than closing immediately.

→

(c) **What other factors might the directors take into account before making a final decision on the timing of the factory closure?**

(d) **State, with reasons, whether or not the business should continue to operate the factory until the end of the lease period.**

Your answer should be as follows:

(a) *Relevant cash flows*

	Years				
	0	1	2	3	4
	£000	£000	£000	£000	£000
Operating cash flows (Note 1)		250	50	120	110
Sale of machinery (Note 2)	(220)				40
Redundancy costs (Note 3)	180				(150)
Sublease rentals (Note 4)		(40)	(40)	(40)	(40)
Working capital invested (Note 5)	(420)				420
	(460)	210	10	80	380

Notes:

1 Each year's operating cash flows are calculated by adding back the depreciation charge for the year to the operating profit for the year. In the case of the operating loss, the depreciation charge is deducted.

2 In the event of closure, machinery could be sold immediately. Thus an opportunity cost of £220,000 is incurred if operations continue.

3 By continuing operations, there will be a saving in immediate redundancy costs of £180,000. However, redundancy costs of £150,000 will be paid in four years' time.

4 By continuing operations, the opportunity to sublease the factory will be forgone.

5 Immediate closure would mean that working capital could be liquidated. By continuing operations this opportunity is forgone. However, working capital can be liquidated in four years' time.

(b)

	Years				
	0	1	2	3	4
Discount rate 12 per cent	1.000	0.893	0.797	0.712	0.636
Present value (£000s)	(460)	187.5	8.0	57.0	241.7
Net present value (£000s)	34.2				

(c) Other factors that may influence the decision include:

■ *The overall strategy of the business.* The business may need to set the decision within a broader context. It may be necessary to manufacture the products at the factory because they are an integral part of the business's product range. The business may wish to avoid redundancies in an area of high unemployment for as long as possible.

■ *Flexibility*. A decision to close the factory is probably irreversible. If the factory continues, however, there may be a chance that the prospects for the factory will brighten in the future.

■ *Creditworthiness of sub-lessee*. The business should investigate the creditworthiness of the sub-lessee. Failure to receive the expected sublease payments would make the closure option far less attractive.

■ *Accuracy of forecasts*. The forecasts made by the business should be examined carefully. Inaccuracies in the forecasts or any underlying assumptions may change the expected outcomes.

(d) The NPV of the decision to continue operations rather than close immediately is positive. Hence, shareholders would be better off if the directors took this course of action. The factory should therefore continue in operation rather than close down. This decision is likely to be welcomed by employees and would allow the business to maintain its flexibility.

Investment appraisal in practice

Many surveys have been conducted in the UK into the methods of investment appraisal used by businesses. They have shown the following features:

■ Businesses tend to use more than one method to assess each investment decision, increasingly so over time.

■ The discounting methods (NPV and IRR) have become increasingly popular over time, with these two becoming the most popular in recent years.

■ ARR and PP continue to be popular despite their theoretical shortcomings and the rise in popularity of the discounting methods.

■ Larger businesses tend to use the discounting methods and to use more than one method in respect of each decision.

Real World 10.9 shows the results of one of the most recent (1997) surveys of UK businesses regarding their use of investment appraisal methods.

Real World 10.9

A survey of UK business practice

Method	Percentage of businesses using the method
Net present value	80
Internal rate of return	81
Payback period	70
Accounting rate of return	56
	287

Source: 'The theory–practice gap in capital budgeting: evidence from the United Kingdom', G. C. Arnold and P. D. Hatzopoulos, *Journal of Business Finance and Accounting*, June/July 2000. Reproduced by kind permission of Blackwell Publishing Ltd.

A more recent survey of US businesses also shows considerable support for the NPV and IRR methods. There is less support, however, for the payback method and ARR. Real World 10.10 sets out some of the main findings.

Real World 10.10

A survey of US practice

A survey of the chief financial officers (CFOs) of 392 US businesses examined the popularity of various methods of investment appraisal. Figure 10.5 shows the percentage of businesses surveyed that always, or almost always, used the four methods discussed in this chapter.

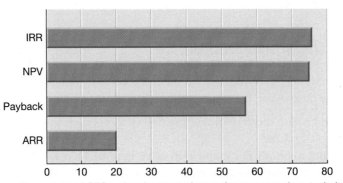

Figure 10.5 The use of investment appraisal methods among US businesses

Percentage of CFOs who always or almost always use a given technique

Both the IRR and NPV methods are widely used and are much more popular than PP and ARR. Nevertheless, PP is still used always, or almost always, by a majority of US businesses.

Source: Based on information in 'How do CFOs make capital budgeting and capital structure decisions?', R. Graham and C. Harvey, *Journal of Applied Corporate Finance*, vol. 15, no. 1, 2002.

Activity 10.18

Earlier in the chapter we discussed the theoretical limitations of the PP method. How do you explain the fact that it still seems to be a popular method of investment appraisal among businesses?

A number of possible reasons may explain this finding:

- PP is easy to understand and use.
- It can avoid the problems of forecasting far into the future.
- It gives emphasis to the early cash flows when there is greater certainty concerning the accuracy of their predicted value.
- It emphasises the importance of liquidity. Where a business has liquidity problems, a short payback period for a project is likely to appear attractive.

PP can provide a convenient, though rough and ready, assessment of the profitability of a project, in the way that it is used in Real World 10.11.

Real World 10.11

An investment lifts off

SES Global is the world's largest commercial satellite operator. This means that it rents satellite capacity to broadcasters, governments, telecommunications groups and Internet service providers. This is a risky venture that few are prepared to undertake. As a result, a handful of businesses dominates the market.

Launching a satellite requires a huge initial outlay of capital, but relatively small cash outflows following the launch. Revenues only start to flow once the satellite is in orbit. A satellite launch costs around €250m. The main elements of this cost are the satellite (€120m), the launch vehicle (€80m), insurance (€40m) and ground equipment (€10m).

According to Romain Bausch, president and chief executive of SES Global, it takes three years to build and launch a satellite. However, the average lifetime of a satellite is fifteen years, during which time it is generating revenues. The revenues generated are such that the payback period is around four to five years.

Source: 'Satellites need space to earn', Tim Burt, FT.com, 14 July 2003.

The popularity of PP may suggest a lack of sophistication by managers concerning investment appraisal. This criticism is most often made against managers of smaller businesses. This point is borne out by both of the surveys discussed above which have found that smaller businesses are much less likely to use discounted cash flow methods (NPV and IRR) than are larger ones. Other surveys have tended to reach a similar conclusion.

The survey evidence suggests that many businesses use more than one method to appraise investments. The sum of percentage usage for each appraisal method in the UK survey, for example, is 287 per cent (see Real World 10.9). This survey also suggests that most businesses use one, or both, of the two discounted cash flow methods. Generally survey evidence has shown a strong increase in the rate of usage of both NPV and IRR, in the UK, over the years. Similar trends seem to prevail in most of the world.

IRR may be as popular as NPV, despite its shortcomings, because it expresses outcomes in percentage terms rather than in absolute terms. This form of expression appears to be more acceptable to managers, despite the problems of percentage measures that we discussed earler. This may be because managers are used to using percentage figures as targets (for example, return on capital employed).

Real World 10.12 shows extracts from the 2006 annual report of a well-known business: Rolls-Royce plc, the builder of engines for aircraft and other purposes.

Real World 10.12

The use of NPV at Rolls-Royce

In its 2006 annual report and accounts, Rolls-Royce plc stated that:

> The Group continues to subject all investments to rigorous examination of risks and future cash flows to ensure that they create shareholder value. All major investments require Board approval.
>
> The Group has a portfolio of projects at different stages of their life cycles. Discounted cash flow analysis of the remaining life of projects is performed on a regular basis.

Source: Rolls-Royce plc Annual Report and Accounts 2006.

Rolls-Royce makes clear that it uses NPV (the report refers to creating shareholder value and to discounted cash flow, which strongly imply NPV). It is interesting to note that Rolls-Royce not only assesses new projects but also reassesses existing ones. This must be a sensible commercial approach. Businesses should not continue with existing projects unless those projects have a positive NPV based on future cash flows. Just because a project seemed to have a positive NPV before it started does not mean that this will persist under changing circumstances. Activity 10.17 considered a decision whether to close down a project.

? Self-assessment question 10.1

Beacon Chemicals plc is considering buying some equipment to produce a chemical named X14. The new equipment's capital cost is estimated at £100,000. If its purchase is approved now, the equipment can be bought and production can commence by the end of this year. £50,000 has already been spent on research and development work. Estimates of revenues and costs arising from the operation of the new equipment appear below:

	Year 1	Year 2	Year 3	Year 4	Year 5
Sales price (£/litre)	100	120	120	100	80
Sales volume (litres)	800	1,000	1,200	1,000	800
Variable costs (£/litre)	50	50	40	30	40
Fixed costs (£000)	30	30	30	30	30

If the equipment is bought, sales of some existing products will be lost, and this will result in a loss of contribution of £15,000 a year over its life.

The accountant has informed you that the fixed costs include depreciation of £20,000 a year on the new equipment. They also include an allocation of £10,000 for fixed overheads. A separate study has indicated that if the new equipment were bought, additional overheads, excluding depreciation, arising from producing the chemical would be £8,000 a year. Production would require additional working capital of £30,000.

For the purposes of your initial calculations ignore taxation.

Required:

(a) Deduce the relevant annual cash flows associated with buying the equipment.

(b) Deduce the payback period.

(c) Calculate the net present value using a discount rate of 8 per cent.

(*Hint*: You should deal with the investment in working capital by treating it as a cash outflow at the start of the project and an inflow at the end.)

The answer to this question can be found at the back of the book in Appendix B.

As a footnote to our discussion of business investment decision-making, Real World 10.13 looks at one of the world's biggest investment projects which has proved to be a commercial disaster, despite being a technological success.

Real World 10.13

Wealth lost in the chunnel

The tunnel, which runs for 31 miles between Folkestone in the UK and Sangatte in northern France, was started in 1986 and opened for public use in 1994. From a technological and social perspective it has been a success, but from a financial point of view it has been a disaster. The tunnel was purely a private-sector venture for which a new business, Eurotunnel plc, was created. Relatively little public money was involved. To be a commercial success the tunnel needed to cover all of its costs, including interest charges, and leave sufficient to enhance the shareholders' wealth. In fact, the providers of long-term finance (lenders and shareholders) have lost virtually all of their investment. Although the main losers were banks and institutional investors, many individuals, particularly in France, bought shares in Eurotunnel.

Key inputs to the pre-1986 assessment of the project were the cost of construction and creating the infrastructure, the length of time required to complete construction and the level of revenue that the tunnel would generate when it became operational.

In the event,

- construction cost was £10bn – it was originally planned to cost £5.6bn;
- construction time was seven years – it was planned to be six years;
- revenues from passengers and freight have been well below what was projected – for example, 21 million annual passenger journeys on Eurostar trains were projected; the numbers have consistently remained at around 7 million.

The failure to generate revenues at the projected levels has probably been the biggest contributor to the problem. When preparing the pre-1986 projection, planners failed to take adequate account of two crucial factors:

- fierce competition from the ferry operators – at the time, many thought that the ferries would roll over and die; and
- the rise of no-frills, cheap air travel between the UK and the continent.

The commercial failure of the tunnel means that it will be very difficult in future for projects of this nature to be funded by private funds.

Sources: Annual reports of Eurotunnel plc; 'How Eurotunnel went wrong', J. Randall, BBC news, www.newsvote.bbc.co.uk.

Summary

The main points of this chapter may be summarised as follows.

Accounting rate of return

- **Accounting rate of return (ARR) is the average accounting profit from the project expressed as a percentage of the average investment.**

- Decision rule: projects with an ARR above a defined minimum are acceptable; the greater the ARR, the more attractive the project becomes.

- Conclusions on ARR:
    - it does not relate directly to shareholders' wealth – can lead to illogical conclusions;
    - takes almost no account of the timing of cash flows;
    - ignores some relevant information and may take account of some that is irrelevant;
    - relatively simple to use;
    - much inferior to NPV.

Payback period

- **Payback period (PP) is the length of time that it takes for the cash outflow for the initial investment to be repaid out of resulting cash inflows.**

- Decision rule: projects with a PP up to a defined maximum period are acceptable; the shorter the PP, the more desirable.

- Conclusions on PP:
    - does not relate to shareholders' wealth;
    - ignores inflows after the payback date;
    - takes little account of the timing of cash flows;
    - ignores much relevant information;
    - does not always provide clear signals and can be impractical to use;
    - much inferior to NPV, but it is easy to understand and can offer a liquidity insight, which might be the reason for its widespread use.

Net present value

- **Net present value (NPV) is the sum of the discounted values of the net cash flows from the investment.**

- Money has a time value.

- Decision rule: all positive NPV investments enhance shareholders' wealth; the greater the NPV, the greater the enhancement and the more desirable.

- PV of a cashflow = cashflow $\times 1/(1 + r)^n$, assuming a constant discount rate.

- The act of discounting brings cash flows at different points in time to a common valuation basis (their present value), which enables them to be directly compared.

- Conclusions on NPV:

- relates directly to shareholders' wealth objective;
- takes account of the timing of cash flows;
- takes all relevant information into account;
- provides clear signals and practical to use.

Internal rate of return

■ **Internal rate of return (IRR) is the discount rate that, when applied to the cash flows of a project, causes it to have a zero NPV.**

■ Represents the average percentage return on the investment, taking account of the fact that cash may be flowing in and out of the project at various points in its life.

■ Decision rule: projects that have an IRR greater than the cost of capital are acceptable; the greater the IRR, the more attractive the project.

■ Cannot normally be calculated directly; a trial and error approach is often necessary.

■ Conclusions on IRR:
- does not relate directly to shareholders' wealth;
- usually gives the same signals as NPV but can mislead where there are competing projects of different size;
- takes account of the timing of cash flows;
- takes all relevant information into account;
- problems of multiple IRRs when there are unconventional cash flows;
- inferior to NPV.

Use of appraisal methods in practice

■ All four methods identified are widely used.

■ The discounting methods (NPV and IRR) show a steady increase in usage over time.

■ Many businesses use more than one method.

■ Larger businesses seem to be more sophisticated in their choice and use of appraisal methods than smaller ones.

→ **Key terms**

accounting rate of return (ARR) p. 349
payback period (PP) p. 354
net present value (NPV) p. 358
risk p. 359
risk premium p. 360
inflation p. 361
discount factor p. 365
internal rate of return (IRR) p. 368
relevant cost p. 373
opportunity cost p. 373

Further reading

If you would like to explore the topics covered in this chapter in more depth, we recommend the following books:

Arnold, G., *Corporate Financial Management* (3rd edn), Financial Times Prentice Hall, 2005, chapters 2, 3 and 4.

Drury, C., *Management and Cost Accounting* (8th edn), Thomson Learning, 2008, chapters 13 and 14.

McLaney, E., *Business Finance: Theory and Practice* (8th edn), Financial Times Prentice Hall, 2009, chapters 4, 5 and 6.

Pike, R. and Neale, B., *Corporate Finance and Investment* (5th edn), Prentice Hall, 2005, chapters 5, 6 and 7.

? Review questions

Answers to these questions can be found at the back of the book in Appendix C.

10.1 Why is the net present value method of investment appraisal considered to be theoretically superior to other methods that are found in practice?

10.2 The payback method has been criticised for not taking the time value of money into account. Could this limitation be overcome? If so, would this method then be preferable to the NPV method?

10.3 Research indicates that the IRR method is a more popular method of investment appraisal than the NPV method. Why might this be?

10.4 Why are cash flows rather than profit flows used in the IRR, NPV and PP methods of investment appraisal?

* Exercises

Exercises 10.3 to 10.5 are more advanced than Exercises 10.1 and 10.2. Those with coloured numbers have answers at the back of the book in Appendix D.

If you wish to try more exercises, visit MyAccountingLab/

10.1 The directors of Mylo Ltd are currently considering two mutually exclusive investment projects. Both projects are concerned with the purchase of new plant. The following data are available for each project:

	Project 1 £000	Project 2 £000
Cost (immediate outlay)	(100)	(60)
Expected annual operating profit (loss):		
Year 1	29	18
2	(1)	(2)
3	2	4
Estimated residual value of the plant	7	6

The business has an estimated cost of capital of 10 per cent, and uses the straight-line method of depreciation for all non-current (fixed) assets when calculating operating profit. Neither project would increase the working capital of the business. The business has sufficient funds to meet all capital expenditure requirements.

Required:
(a) Calculate for each project:
  (i) The net present value.
  (ii) The approximate internal rate of return.
  (iii) The payback period.
(b) State which, if any, of the two investment projects the directors of Mylo Ltd should accept, and why.
(c) State, in general terms, which method of investment appraisal you consider to be most appropriate for evaluating investment projects, and why.

10.2 C. George (Controls) Ltd manufactures a thermostat that can be used in a range of kitchen appliances. The manufacturing process is, at present, semi-automated. The equipment used costs £540,000, and has a written-down (balance sheet) value of £300,000. Demand for the product has been fairly stable, and output has been maintained at 50,000 units a year in recent years.

The following data, based on the current level of output, have been prepared in respect of the product:

	Per unit	
	£	£
Selling price		12.40
Less		
Labour	3.30	
Materials	3.65	
Overheads: Variable	1.58	
Fixed	1.60	
	10.13	
Operating profit		2.27

Although the existing equipment is expected to last for a further four years before it is sold for an estimated £40,000, the business has recently been considering purchasing new equipment that would completely automate much of the production process. The new equipment would cost £670,000 and would have an expected life of four years, at the end of which it would be sold for an estimated £70,000. If the new equipment is purchased, the old equipment could be sold for £150,000 immediately.

The assistant to the business's accountant has prepared a report to help assess the viability of the proposed change, which includes the following data:

	Per unit	
	£	£
Selling price		12.40
Less		
Labour	1.20	
Materials	3.20	
Overheads: Variable	1.40	
Fixed	3.30	
		9.10
Operating profit		3.30

Depreciation charges will increase by £85,000 a year as a result of purchasing the new machinery; however, other fixed costs are not expected to change.

In the report the assistant wrote:

> The figures shown above that relate to the proposed change are based on the current level of output and take account of a depreciation charge of £150,000 a year in respect of the new equipment. The effect of purchasing the new equipment will be to increase the operating profit to sales revenue ratio from 18.3% to 26.6%. In addition, the purchase of the new equipment will enable us to reduce our inventories level immediately by £130,000.
>
> In view of these facts, I recommend purchase of the new equipment.

The business has a cost of capital of 12 per cent. Ignore taxation.

Required:
(a) Prepare a statement of the incremental cash flows arising from the purchase of the new equipment.
(b) Calculate the net present value of the proposed purchase of new equipment.
(c) State, with reasons, whether the business should purchase the new equipment.
(d) Explain why cash flow forecasts are used rather than profit forecasts to assess the viability of proposed capital expenditure projects.

10.3 The accountant of your business has recently been taken ill through overwork. In his absence his assistant has prepared some calculations of the profitability of a project, which are to be discussed soon at the board meeting of your business. His workings, which are set out below, include some errors of principle. You can assume that the statement below includes no arithmetical errors.

	Year 1 £000	Year 2 £000	Year 3 £000	Year 4 £000	Year 5 £000	Year 6 £000
Sales revenue	–	450	470	470	470	470
Less Costs:						
Materials	–	126	132	132	132	132
Labour	–	90	94	94	94	94
Overheads	–	45	47	47	47	47
Depreciation	–	120	120	120	120	120
Working capital	180	–	–	–	–	–
Interest on working capital	–	27	27	27	27	27
Write-off of development costs	–	30	30	30	–	–
Total costs	180	438	450	450	420	420
Operating profit/(loss)	(180)	12	20	20	50	50

$$\frac{\text{Total profit (loss)}}{\text{Cost of equipment}} = \frac{(£28,000)}{£600,000} = \text{Return on investment (4.7\%)}$$

You ascertain the following additional information:

- The cost of equipment contains £100,000, being the carrying (balance sheet) value of an old machine. If it were not used for this project it would be scrapped with a zero net realisable value. New equipment costing £500,000 will be purchased on 31 December Year 0. You should assume that all other cash flows occur at the end of the year to which they relate.
- The development costs of £90,000 have already been spent.
- Overheads have been costed at 50 per cent of direct labour, which is the business's normal practice. An independent assessment has suggested that incremental overheads are likely to amount to £30,000 a year.
- The business's cost of capital is 12 per cent.

Ignore taxation in your answer.

Required:
(a) Prepare a corrected statement of the incremental cash flows arising from the project. Where you have altered the assistant's figures you should attach a brief note explaining your alterations.
(b) Calculate:
  (i) The project's payback period.
  (ii) The project's net present value as at 31 December Year 0.
(c) Write a memo to the board advising on the acceptance or rejection of the project.

10.4 Newton Electronics Ltd has incurred expenditure of £5m over the past three years researching and developing a miniature hearing aid. The hearing aid is now fully developed, and the directors are considering which of three mutually exclusive options should be taken to exploit the potential of the new product. The options are as follows:

1 The business could manufacture the hearing aid itself. This would be a new departure, since the business has so far concentrated on research and development projects.

However, the business has manufacturing space available that it currently rents to another business for £100,000 a year. The business would have to purchase plant and equipment costing £9m and invest £3m in working capital immediately for production to begin.

A market research report, for which the business paid £50,000, indicates that the new product has an expected life of five years. Sales of the product during this period are predicted as follows:

	Predicted sales for the year ended 30 November				
	Year 1	Year 2	Year 3	Year 4	Year 5
Number of units (000s)	800	1,400	1,800	1,200	500

The selling price per unit will be £30 in the first year but will fall to £22 in the following three years. In the final year of the product's life, the selling price will fall to £20. Variable production costs are predicted to be £14 a unit, and fixed production costs (including depreciation) will be £2.4m a year. Marketing costs will be £2m a year.

The business intends to depreciate the plant and equipment using the straight-line method and based on an estimated residual value at the end of the five years of £1m. The business has a cost of capital of 10 per cent a year.

2 Newton Electronics Ltd could agree to another business manufacturing and marketing the product under licence. A multinational business, Faraday Electricals plc, has offered to undertake the manufacture and marketing of the product, and in return will make a royalty payment to Newton Electronics Ltd of £5 per unit. It has been estimated that the annual number of sales of the hearing aid will be 10 per cent higher if the multinational business, rather than Newton Electronics Ltd, manufactures and markets the product.

3 Newton Electronics Ltd could sell the patent rights to Faraday Electricals plc for £24m, payable in two equal instalments. The first instalment would be payable immediately and the second at the end of two years. This option would give Faraday Electricals the exclusive right to manufacture and market the new product.

Ignore taxation.

Required:

(a) Calculate the net present value of each of the options available to Newton Electronics Ltd.

(b) Identify and discuss any other factors that Newton Electronics Ltd should consider before arriving at a decision.

(c) State what you consider to be the most suitable option, and why.

10.5 Chesterfield Wanderers is a professional football club that has enjoyed considerable success in both national and European competitions in recent years. As a result, the club has accumulated £10m to spend on its further development. The board of directors is currently considering two mutually exclusive options for spending the funds available.

The first option is to acquire another player. The team manager has expressed a keen interest in acquiring Basil ('Bazza') Ramsey, a central defender, who currently plays for a rival club. The rival club has agreed to release the player immediately for £10m if required. A decision to acquire 'Bazza' Ramsey would mean that the existing central defender, Vinnie Smith, could be sold to another club. Chesterfield Wanderers has recently received an offer of £2.2m for this player. This offer is still open but will only be accepted if 'Bazza' Ramsey joins Chesterfield Wanderers. If this does not happen, Vinnie Smith will be expected to stay on with the club until the end of his playing career in five years' time. During this period, Vinnie will receive an annual salary of £400,000 and a loyalty bonus of £200,000 at the end of his five-year period with the club.

Assuming 'Bazza' Ramsey is acquired, the team manager estimates that gate receipts will increase by £2.5m in the first year and £1.3m in each of the four following years. There will also be an increase in advertising and sponsorship revenues of £1.2m for each of the next five years if the player is acquired. At the end of five years, the player can be sold to a club in a lower division and Chesterfield Wanderers will expect to receive £1m as a transfer fee. During his period at the club, 'Bazza' will receive an annual salary of £800,000 and a loyalty bonus of £400,000 after five years.

The second option is for the club to improve its ground facilities. The west stand could be extended and executive boxes could be built for businesses wishing to offer corporate hospitality to clients. These improvements would also cost £10m and would take one year to complete. During this period, the west stand would be closed, resulting in a reduction of gate receipts of £1.8m. However, gate receipts for each of the following four years would be £4.4m higher than current receipts. In five years' time, the club has plans to sell the existing grounds and to move to a new stadium nearby. Improving the ground facilities is not expected to affect the ground's value when it comes to be sold. Payment for the improvements will be made when the work has been completed at the end of the first year. Whichever option is chosen, the board of directors has decided to take on additional ground staff. The additional wages bill is expected to be £350,000 a year over the next five years.

The club has a cost of capital of 10 per cent. Ignore taxation.

Required:
(a) Calculate the incremental cash flows arising from each of the options available to the club.
(b) Calculate the net present value of each of the options.
(c) On the basis of the calculations made in (b) above, which of the two options would you choose and why?
(d) Discuss the validity of using the net present value method in making investment decisions for a professional football club.

Chapter 11

Financing the business

Introduction

In this chapter we shall examine various aspects of financing the business. We begin by considering the main sources of finance available. Some of these sources have already been touched upon when we discussed the financing of limited companies in Chapter 4. In this chapter we shall look at these in more detail as well as discuss other sources of finance that have not yet been mentioned. The factors to be taken into account when choosing an appropriate source of finance are also considered.

Following our consideration of the main sources of finance, we shall go on to examine various aspects of the capital markets, including the role of the Stock Exchange, the financing of smaller businesses and the ways in which share capital may be issued.

Learning outcomes

When you have completed this chapter, you should be able to:

■ identify the main sources of finance available to a business and explain the advantages and disadvantages of each;

■ outline the ways in which share capital may be issued;

■ explain the role and nature of the Stock Exchange;

■ discuss the ways in which smaller businesses may seek to raise finance.

Sources of finance

When considering the various sources of finance available to a business, it is useful to distinguish between *internal* and *external* sources of finance. By internal sources we mean sources that do not require the agreement of anyone beyond the directors and managers of the business. Thus, retained profit is considered an internal source because the directors of the business have power to retain profits without the agreement of the shareholders, whose profits they are. Finance from an issue of new shares, on the other hand, is an external source because it requires the compliance of potential shareholders.

Within each of the two categories just described, we can further distinguish between *long-term* and *short-term* sources of finance. There is no agreed definition concerning each of these terms but, for the purpose of this chapter, long-term sources of finance are defined as those that are expected to provide finance for at least one year. Short-term sources typically provide finance for a shorter period. As we shall see, sources that are seen as short-term when first used by the business often end up being used for quite long periods.

We shall begin the chapter by considering the various sources of internal finance available. We shall then go on to consider the various sources of external finance. This is probably an appropriate order since, in practice, businesses tend to look first to internal sources before going outside for new funds.

Sources of internal finance

Internal sources of finance usually have the advantage that they are flexible. They may also be obtained quickly – particularly from working capital sources – and need not require the compliance of other parties. The main sources of internal funds are described below and are summarised in Figure 11.1.

Long-term sources of internal finance

Retained profits

Retained profit is the major source of finance for most businesses. If profits are retained within the business rather than being distributed to shareholders in the form of dividends, the funds of the business are increased.

Figure 11.1 **The major sources of internal finance**

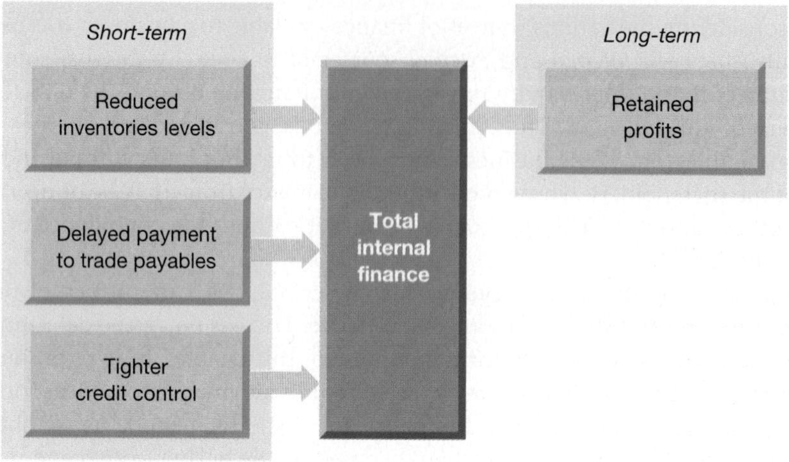

The major long-term source of internal finance is the profit that is retained rather than distributed to shareholders. The major short-term sources of internal finance involve reducing the level of trade receivables and inventories and increasing the level of trade payables.

Activity 11.1

Are retained profits a free source of finance to the business?

It is tempting to think that retained profits are a cost-free source of funds for a business. However, this is not the case. If profits are reinvested rather than distributed to shareholders in cash, those shareholders cannot invest this cash in other forms of investment. They will therefore expect a rate of return from the profits reinvested that is equivalent to what they would have received had the funds been invested in another opportunity with the same level of risk.

The reinvestment of profits can be a useful way of raising capital from ordinary share investors.

An obvious alternative way to increase equity investment is to issue new shares. When issuing new shares, however, the issue costs may be substantial and there may be uncertainty over the success of the issue. We shall look at these two problem areas later in the chapter. There are no issue costs associated with retaining profits, and the amount raised is certain, once the profit has been made.

Retaining profits will have no effect on the extent to which existing shareholders control the business, whereas when new shares are issued to outside investors there will be some dilution of control.

The decision to retain profits rather than pay them out as dividends to the share-holders is made by the directors. They may find it easier simply to retain profits rather than ask investors to subscribe to a new share issue. Retained profits are already held by the business, and so it does not have to wait to receive the funds. Moreover, there is often less scrutiny when profits are being retained for reinvestment purposes than when new shares are being issued. Investors and their advisers will closely examine the reasons for any new share issue. A problem with the use of profits as a source of finance, however, is that the timing and level of future profits cannot always be reliably estimated.

Some shareholders may prefer profits to be retained by the business, rather than be distributed in the form of dividends. By ploughing back profits, it may be expected that the business will expand, and that share values will increase as a result. An important reason for preferring profits to be retained is the effect of taxation on the share-holder. In the UK, dividends are treated as income for tax purposes and therefore attract income tax. Gains on the sale of shares attract capital gains tax. Generally capital gains tax bites less hard than income tax. A further advantage of capital gains over dividends is that the shareholder has a choice as to when to sell the shares and realise the gain. In the UK, it is only when the gain is realised that capital gains tax comes into play. Research indicates that investors may be attracted to particular businesses according to the dividend/retention policies that they adopt.

It would be wrong to get the impression that all businesses either retain all of their profit or pay it all out as a dividend. Where businesses pay dividends, and most of the larger ones do pay dividends, they typically pay no more than 50 per cent of the profit, retaining the remainder to fund expansion.

Retained profit is much the most important source of new finance for UK businesses, on average, in terms of value of funds raised.

Short-term sources of internal finance

Tighter credit control

By exerting tighter control over amounts owed by credit customers, it may be possible for a business to reduce the proportion of assets held in this form and so release funds for other purposes. Having funds tied up in trade receivables represents an opportunity cost in that those funds could be used for profit-generating activities. It is important, however, to weigh the benefits of tighter credit control against the likely costs in the form of lost customer goodwill and lost sales. To remain competitive, a business must take account of the needs of its customers and the credit policies adopted by rival businesses within the industry. We shall consider this further in Chapter 12.

Activity 11.2

Rusli Ltd provides a car valet service for car-hire businesses when their cars are returned from hire. Details of the service costs are as follows:

	Per car £
Car valet charge	20
Variable costs	(14)
Fixed costs	(4)
Profit	2

Sales revenue is £10m a year and is all on credit. The average credit period taken by Rusli Ltd's customers is 45 days, although the terms of credit state that payment should be made within 30 days. Allowances for receivables (bad debts) are currently £100,000 a year. Trade receivables are financed by a bank overdraft costing 10 per cent a year.

Rusli Ltd's credit control department believes it can eliminate allowances for receivables (bad debts) and can reduce the average credit period to 30 days if new credit control procedures are implemented. These will cost £50,000 a year and are likely to result in a loss of business leading to a reduction in sales revenue of 5 per cent a year.

Should Rusli Ltd implement the new credit control procedures? (*Hint*: To answer this activity it is useful to compare the current cost of trade credit with the costs under the proposed approach.)

The current annual cost of trade credit is:

	£
Allowances for receivables (bad debts)	100,000
Overdraft interest ((£10m × 45/365) × 10%)	123,288
	223,288

The annual cost of trade credit under the new policy would be:

	£
Overdraft interest ((95% × (£10m) × (30/365)) × 10%)	78,082
Cost of control procedures	50,000
Net cost of lost sales ((£(10m/20) × 5%) × (20 − 14*))	150,000
	278,082

* The loss will be the contribution per unit (that is, the difference between the selling price and the variable costs).

These calculations show that the business will be worse off if the new policies are adopted.

Reducing inventories levels

Reducing the level of inventories is an internal source of funds that may prove attractive to a business. If the business has a proportion of its assets in the form of inventories there is an opportunity cost, as the funds tied up cannot be used for other purposes. By reducing inventories, funds become available for those opportunities. However, a business must try to ensure that there are sufficient inventories available to meet likely future sales demand. Failure to do so will result in lost customer goodwill and lost sales revenue.

The nature and condition of the inventories held will determine whether it is possible to exploit this form of finance. A business may have excess inventories as a result of poor buying decisions. This may mean that a significant proportion of the inventories held are slow-moving or obsolete and cannot, therefore, be reduced easily. These issues will be picked up again in Chapter 12.

Delaying payment to trade payables

By providing a period of credit, suppliers are in effect offering a business an interest-free loan. If the business delays payment, the period of the 'loan' is extended and funds can be retained within the business. This can be a cheap form of finance for a business, though this is not always the case. If a business fails to pay within the agreed credit period, there may be significant costs. For example, the business may find it difficult to buy on credit when it has a reputation as a slow payer.

These so-called short-term sources are short-term to the extent that they can be reversed at short notice. For example, a reduction in the level of trade receivables can be reversed within a couple of weeks. Typically, however, once a business has established a reduced receivable collection period, a reduced inventories-holding period and/or an expanded payables payment period, it will tend to maintain these new levels.

As we shall see in Chapter 12, for the typical business, the level of funds involved with the working capital items is vast. This means that substantial amounts of funds can be raised through exercising tighter control of trade receivables and inventories and by exploiting opportunities to delay payment to trade payables.

Sources of external finance

Figure 11.2 summarises the main sources of long-term and short-term external finance.

Long-term sources of external finance

As Figure 11.2 reveals, the major forms of long-term external finance are

- ordinary shares
- preference shares
- borrowings
- finance leases, including sale-and-leaseback arrangements
- hire purchase agreements.

We shall now discuss each of the sources identified.

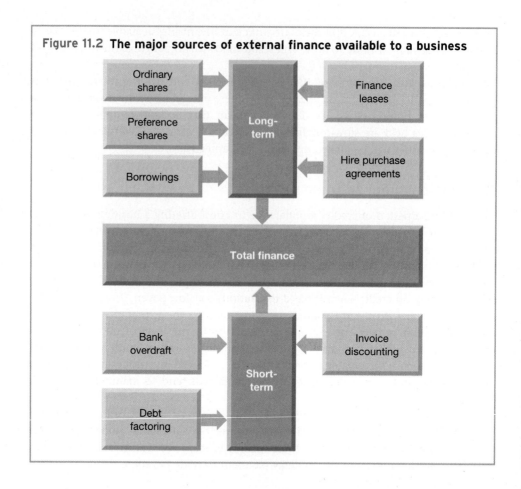

Figure 11.2 **The major sources of external finance available to a business**

Ordinary shares

As we saw in Chapter 4, ordinary shares form the backbone of the financial structure of a business. Ordinary share capital represents the business's risk capital. There is no fixed rate of dividend and ordinary shareholders can receive a dividend only if profits available for distribution still remain after other investors (preference shareholders and lenders, if any) have received their dividend or interest payments. If the business is wound up, the ordinary shareholders will receive any proceeds from asset disposals only after any lenders (including trade payables) and preference shareholders have received their entitlements. Because of the high risks associated with this form of investment, ordinary shareholders will normally require a comparatively high rate of return.

Although ordinary shareholders have a potential loss liability that is limited to the amount that they have invested or agreed to invest, the potential returns from their investment are unlimited. In other words, their downside risk is limited whereas their upside potential is not. Ordinary shareholders have control over the business, through their voting rights. This gives them the power both to elect the directors and to remove them from office.

From the business's (directors') perspective, ordinary shares can be an attractive form of financing, relative to borrowing. At times, it can be useful to be able to avoid paying a dividend. It is not usually possible to avoid paying interest on borrowings.

Activity 11.3

Under what circumstances might a business find it useful to avoid paying a dividend?

We feel that there are two main situations where this would apply:

■ An expanding business may prefer to retain funds to help fuel future growth.
■ A business in difficulties may need the funds to meet its operating costs and so may find making a dividend payment a real burden.

Real World 11.1 looks at the attitude of one well-known businessman to paying dividends.

Real World 11.1

No frills, no dividends and no brains

Michael O'Leary, the colourfully-spoken chief executive of the 'no-frills' airline Ryanair Holdings plc, was very clear on his attitude to dividends. He said, 'We are never paying a dividend as long as I live and breathe and as long as I'm the largest shareholder. If you are stupid enough to invest in an airline for its dividend flow you should be put back in the loony bin where you came from.' Presumably Ryanair is expanding at a rate that eats up all available finances.

Source: 'Ryanair blunted by Buzz takeover', A. Osborne, *Daily Telegraph*, 6 August 2004.

Although a business financed by ordinary shares can avoid making cash payments to shareholders when it is not prudent to do so, the market value of the shares may go down. The cost to the business of financing through ordinary shares may become higher if shareholders feel uncertain about future dividends. On the other hand, for a business like Ryanair, which is clearly expanding its operations in a profitable way, share prices are likely to reflect this despite the lack of dividends.

It is also worth pointing out that the business does not obtain any tax relief on dividends paid to shareholders, whereas interest on borrowings is tax-deductible. This makes it more expensive to the business to pay £1 of dividend than £1 of interest on borrowings.

Preference shares

Preference shares offer investors a lower level of risk than ordinary shares. Provided there are sufficient profits available, preference shares will normally be given a fixed rate of dividend each year, and preference shareholders will be paid the first slice of any dividend paid. Should the business be wound up, preference shareholders may be given priority over the claims of ordinary shareholders. (The business's own particular documents of incorporation will state the precise rights of preference shareholders in this respect.)

Activity 11.4

Would you expect the returns on preference shares to be higher or lower than those of ordinary shares?

We expect returns on preference shares to be lower than those on ordinary shares. This is because of the lower level of risk associated with this form of investment (preference shareholders have priority over ordinary shareholders regarding dividends).

Preference shares are no longer an important source of new finance. A major reason for this is that dividends paid to preference shareholders, like those paid to ordinary shareholders, are not allowable against taxable profits, whereas interest on loan capital is an allowable expense. From the business's point of view, preference shares and loans are quite similar, so the tax-deductibility of loan interest is an important issue.

Activity 11.5

Would you expect the market price of ordinary shares or of preference shares to be the more volatile? Why?

The share price, which reflects the expected future returns from the share, will normally be less volatile for preference shares than for ordinary shares. The dividends of preference shares tend to be fairly stable over time, and there is usually an upper limit on the returns that can be received.

Both preference shares and ordinary shares are, in effect, *redeemable*. The business is allowed to buy back the shares from shareholders at any time.

Borrowings

Most businesses rely on borrowings as well as equity to finance operations. Lenders enter into a contract with the business in which the rate of interest, dates of interest payments, capital repayments and security for the borrowings are clearly stated. In the event that the interest payments or capital repayments are not made on the due dates, the lender will usually have the right, under the terms of the contract, to seize the assets on which the loan is secured and sell them in order to repay the amount outstanding. Security for a loan may take the form of a fixed charge on particular assets of the business (land and buildings are often favoured by lenders) or a floating charge on the whole of its assets. A floating charge will 'float' over the assets and will only fix on particular assets in the event that the business defaults on its borrowing obligations.

Activity 11.6

What do you think is the advantage for the business of having a floating charge rather than a fixed charge on its assets?

A floating charge on assets allows the managers greater flexibility in their day-to-day operations than a fixed charge. Individual assets can be sold without reference to the lenders.

Term loans

One form of long-term loan is the term loan. This type of loan is offered by banks and other financial institutions, and is usually tailored to the needs of the client business. The amount of the loan, the time period, the repayment terms and the interest payable are all open to negotiation and agreement, which can be very useful. For example, where all of the funds to be borrowed are not required immediately, a business may agree with the lender that funds are drawn only as and when required. This means that interest will be paid only on amounts drawn and so the business will not have to pay interest on amounts borrowed that are temporarily surplus to requirements. Term loans tend to be cheap to set up (from the borrower business's perspective) and can be quite flexible as to conditions.

Loan notes (or loan stock)

Another form of long-term loan finance is the loan note (or loan stock). Loan notes are frequently divided into units (rather like share capital), and investors are invited to purchase the number of units they require. The loan notes may be redeemable or irredeemable. Loan notes of public limited companies are often traded on the Stock Exchange, and their listed value will fluctuate according to the fortunes of the business, movements in interest rates and so on.

Loan notes are usually referred to as *bonds* in the US and, increasingly, in the UK.

Real World 11.2 describes how a world-famous football club has made secured borrowings.

Real World 11.2

Gunning for success

The Arsenal Football Club plc (Arsenal) has recently moved from its traditional home to a new 'state-of-the-art' stadium at Ashburton Grove (the Emirates Stadium). It financed the stadium mainly with a £200m bond issue. The bonds are secured, not on the stadium itself, but on future cash receipts from ticket sales. This means that it is essential that Arsenal continues to be successful and generates a good level of attendances at matches. This type of security is quite common for UK and other European football clubs.

Source: Information taken from 'Gunners need on pitch success to pay off bond', *Accountancy Age*, 8 September 2005.

Eurobonds

 Eurobonds are unsecured loan notes denominated in a currency other than the home currency of the business that issued them. Eurobonds are issued by businesses (and other large organisations) in various countries, and the finance is raised on an international basis. They are often denominated in US dollars, but many are issued in other major currencies. Interest is normally paid annually. Eurobonds are part of an ever-expanding international capital market, and they are not subject to regulations imposed by authorities in particular countries. Numerous financial institutions throughout the world have created a market for eurobonds, where holders of eurobonds are able to sell them to would-be holders. The business issuing the eurobonds usually makes them available to large banks and other financial institutions, which may either retain them as an investment or sell them to their clients.

The extent of borrowing, by UK businesses, in currencies other than sterling has expanded massively in recent years. Businesses are often attracted to issuing eurobonds because of the size of the international capital market. Access to a large number of international investors is likely to increase the chances of a successful issue. In addition, the lack of regulation in the eurobond market means that national restrictions regarding loan issues may be overcome.

Real World 11.3 provides an example of a eurobond issue by a well-known UK business.

Real World 11.3

Taking off with Eurobonds

A growing number of companies are entering the euro bond market for the first time, encouraged by the opportunity to reach new investors with low financing costs. . . . This week BAA, the operator of Heathrow and six other airports in the UK, raised €750m ($913m) from its first euro-denominated bond. . . .

'This deal gave the company access to capital at a similar cost to what it could have done in sterling,' said Jean-Marc Mercier at HSBC's corporate syndicate desk, which managed the deal with BNP Paribas and Deutsche Bank.

'In addition, two-thirds of the investors in the deal were new to the company,' he added.

Diversifying the investor base is important for companies, as it increases their flexibility to raise capital when they need to.

Source: 'New appetite develops for euro bonds', Charles Batchelor, *Financial Times*, 17 September 2004, ft.com.

Activity 11.7

Would you expect the returns to loan capital to be higher or lower than those of preference shares?

Lenders are usually prepared to accept a lower rate of return. This is because they will normally view loans as being less risky than preference shares. Lenders have priority over any claims from preference shareholders, and will usually have security for their loans.

The risk/return characteristics of loan, preference share and ordinary share finance are shown graphically in Figure 11.3.

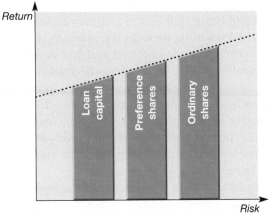

Figure 11.3 The risk/return characteristics of long-term capital

The higher the level of risk associated with a particular form of long-term finance, the higher will be the returns expected by investors. Ordinary shares are the most risky and have the highest expected return, and, as a general rule, loan capital is the least risky and has the lowest expected return.

Interest rates and deep discount bonds

Interest rates on loan finance may be either floating or fixed. A floating rate means that the rate of return required by lenders will rise and fall with market rates of interest. However, the market value of the lender's investment in the business is likely to remain fairly stable over time. The converse will normally be true for fixed-interest loans. The interest payments will remain unchanged with rises and falls in market rates of interest, but the value of the loan investment will fall when interest rates rise and will rise when interest rates fall.

A business may issue redeemable loan capital that offers a rate of interest below the market rate. In some cases, the loan capital may even have a zero rate of interest. Such loans are issued at a discount to their redeemable value and are referred to as deep discount bonds. Thus loan capital may be issued at, say, £80 for every £100 of nominal value. Although lenders will receive little or no interest during the period of the loan, they will receive a £20 gain when the loan is finally redeemed at the full £100. The redemption yield (that is, the effective rate of return to lenders over the life of the loan), as it is referred to, is often quite high and, when calculated on an annual basis, may compare favourably with returns from other forms of loan capital with the same level of risk. Deep discount bonds may have particular appeal to businesses with short-term cash flow problems. Such businesses receive an immediate injection of cash and there are no significant cash outflows associated with the loan until the maturity date. Deep discount bonds are likely to appeal to investors who do not have short-term cash flow needs, since they must wait for the loan to mature before receiving a cash return.

Convertible loan notes

 Convertible loan notes (or convertible bonds) give investors the right, but not the obligation, to exchange the loan notes for ordinary shares in the business at a specified price (the 'exercise' price) on a given future specified date or within a range of specified dates. The exercise price is usually higher than the market price of those ordinary shares at the time of issue of the convertible loan notes. In effect, the investor swaps the loan notes for a particular number of shares. The investor remains a lender to the business, and will receive interest on the amount of the loan, until such time as the conversion takes place. The investor is not obliged to convert to ordinary shares. This will be done only if the market price of the shares at the conversion date exceeds the specified conversion price.

An investor may find this form of investment a useful hedge against risk. This may be particularly useful when investment in a new business is being considered. Initially the investment is in the form of a loan, and regular interest payments will be made. If the business is successful, the investor can then decide to benefit from the success by converting the investment into ordinary shares.

The business may also find this form of financing useful. If the business is successful, the loan becomes self-liquidating (no cash payment is required), as investors will exercise their option to convert. The business may also be able to offer a lower rate of interest to investors because they expect future benefits to arise from conversion. There will be, however, some dilution of both control and earnings for existing shareholders if holders of convertible loans exercise their option to convert.

Real World 11.4 details one particular convertible loan issue.

Real World 11.4

Power conversion

In July 2006, International Power plc issued convertible bonds for a total of £140m. The business is a major generator of electricity throughout the world, including through six power stations in the UK. The business is listed on the London Stock Exchange.

It needed the cash to help finance a coal-fired electricity generation plant in Texas. The share price at which, in 2013, the bonds may be converted is £3.91 and, at the time of the issue, the market price of International Power's shares was £2.89. The offer was over-subscribed despite the annual interest rate attaching to the bonds being only 3.25 per cent (fixed). This implies a strong belief among investors that International Power's share price is set to rise.

Source: Information taken from 'Volatility prompts European issuance', Joanna Chung, *Financial Times*, 12 July 2006.

Warrants

Holders of warrants have the right, but not the obligation, to buy newly issued ordinary shares in a particular business, from that business, at a given price (the exercise price). As with convertible loan notes, the price at which shares may be bought is usually higher than the market price of those shares at the time of the issue of the warrants. The warrant will usually state the number of shares that the holder may buy and the time limit within which the option to buy them can be exercised. Occasionally, perpetual warrants are issued that have no set time limits. Warrants do not confer voting rights or entitle the holders to make any claims on the assets of the business. Warrants are themselves neither shares nor loan notes.

Share warrants are often sold to investors by the business concerned. In some cases, they are given away 'free' as a 'sweetener' to accompany an issue of loan notes, that is, as an incentive to potential lenders. The issue of warrants in this way may enable the business to offer lower rates of interest on the loan or to negotiate less restrictive loan conditions. Sometimes, businesses sell share warrants without there being a link to a loan notes issue. Warrants enable investors to benefit from any future increases in the business's ordinary share price without having to buy the shares themselves. On the other hand, if the share price remains below the exercise price, the warrant will not be used and the investor will lose out as a result.

Activity 11.8

Under what circumstances will the holders of share warrants exercise their option to purchase?

Holders will exercise this option only if the market price of the shares exceeds the exercise price within the time limit specified. If the exercise price were higher than the market price, it would be cheaper for the investor to buy the shares in the market.

To the business issuing the warrants, warrants represent a source of funds (the proceeds of selling them). Alternatively, they represent an encouragement for the issue of another source of funds (a loan notes issue) to be successful.

Share warrants issued with a loan may be *detachable*, which means that they can be sold separately from the loan capital. The warrants of businesses whose shares are listed on the Stock Exchange are often themselves listed, providing a ready market for buying and selling the warrants.

It is probably worth mentioning the difference in status within a business between holders of convertible loan notes and holders of loan notes with share warrants attached, if both groups decide to exercise their right to convert. Convertible loan note holders become ordinary shareholders and are no longer lenders to the business. They will have used the value of the loan notes to 'buy' the shares. Warrant holders become ordinary shareholders by paying cash for the shares. If the warrant holders hold loan notes, their position as lenders will be unaffected by them exercising their right to buy the shares bestowed by the warrant.

→ Both convertibles and warrants are examples of financial derivatives. These are any form of financial instrument, based on share or loan capital, that can be used by investors to increase their returns or reduce risk.

Mortgages

→ A mortgage is a form of loan that is secured on an asset, typically land. Financial institutions such as banks, insurance businesses and pension funds are often prepared to lend to businesses on this basis. The mortgage may be over a long period (twenty years or more).

Loan covenants

→ Lenders often impose certain obligations and restrictions on borrowers in an attempt to protect their loan. Loan covenants (as they are called) often form part of a loan agreement, and may deal with such matters as:

■ *Financial statements*. The lender may require access to the financial statements of the borrowing business on a regular basis.
■ *Other loans*. The lender may require the business to ask the lender's permission before taking on further loans from other sources.
■ *Dividend payments*. The lender may require dividend payments to be limited during the period of the loan.
■ *Liquidity*. The lender may require the business to maintain a certain level of liquidity during the period of the loan. This would typically be a requirement that the borrower business's current ratio is maintained at, or above, a specified level.

Any breach of these restrictive covenants can have serious consequences for the business. The lender may require immediate repayment of the loan in the event of a material breach.

Real World 11.5 shows how one well-known UK business was accused of breaching the covenants imposed by its lenders.

Real World 11.5

Capital problems

The stockbrokers Merrill Lynch (ML) claimed that GCap Media plc (Capital), the business that owns the London-based Capital Radio commercial station, breached its loan covenants. Capital's bankers required the business to maintain a net debt to annual earnings ratio of at most 3.0 and an interest cover ratio of at least 4.0. ML claims that both ratios were actually 3.3, meaning that Capital had broken the covenant on both counts. ML claimed that this had arisen as a result of falling advertising revenues for the radio station, particularly for its breakfast programme.

Capital denied breaching the covenants and referred to forecasts that it would do so as 'speculation'.

Source: Information taken from 'GCap attacks note on breaching covenants', *Financial Times*, 9 September 2006, ft.com.

Activity 11.9

Both preference shares and loan notes are forms of finance whose holders expect the business to provide a particular rate of return. What are the factors that may be taken into account by a business when deciding between these two sources of finance?

The main factors are as follows:

- Preference shares tend to have a higher rate of return than loan notes. From the investor's point of view, preference shares are more risky. The amount invested cannot be secured, and the return is paid after the returns paid to lenders.
- A business has a legal obligation to pay interest and, typically, make capital repayments on loan stocks at the agreed dates. It will usually make every effort to meet its obligations because failure to do so can have serious consequences. (These consequences have been mentioned earlier.) Failure to pay a preference dividend, on the other hand, is less important. There is no legal obligation to pay if profits are not available for distribution. Failure to pay a preference dividend may prove an embarrassment for the business, however, because it may make it difficult to persuade investors to take up future preference share issues.
- It was mentioned above that the taxation system in the UK permits interest on loans to be allowable against profits for taxation, whereas preference dividends are not. As a result, the cost of servicing loan capital is, £ for £, usually much less for a business than the cost of servicing preference shares.
- The issue of loan notes may result in the management of a business having to accept some restrictions on its freedom of action. We saw earlier that loan agreements often contain covenants that can be onerous. Preference shareholders can impose no such restrictions.

A further point is that preference shares issued form part of the permanent capital base of the business. If they are redeemed, the law requires that they be replaced, either by a new issue of shares or by a transfer from revenue reserves, so that the business's capital base stays intact. Loan capital, however, is not viewed in law as part of the business's permanent capital base, and therefore there is no legal requirement to replace any loan capital that has been redeemed.

Finance leases and sale-and-leaseback arrangements

When a business needs a particular asset (for example, an item of plant), instead of buying it direct from a supplier, the business may decide to arrange for another business (typically a bank) to buy it and then lease it to the first business. The business that owns the asset and leases it out is known as a 'lessor'. The one that uses it is known as the 'lessee'.

A finance lease, as such an arrangement is known, is, in essence, a form of lending. This is because, had the lessee borrowed the funds and then used them to buy the asset itself, the effect would be much the same. The lessee would have use of the asset, but have a financial obligation to the lender – much the same position as the leasing arrangement would lead to.

Although, with finance leasing, legal ownership of the asset rests with the financial institution (the lessor), a finance lease agreement transfers to the user (the lessee) virtually all the rewards and risks that are associated with the item being leased. The finance lease agreement covers a significant part of the life of the item being leased, and often cannot be cancelled.

Finance leasing is a very important source of finance for UK businesses. The Finance and Leasing Association estimates that 30 per cent of finance for non-current assets (excluding land and buildings) comes from finance leasing.

Finance leasing is by no means limited to smaller businesses. It is popular with many larger ones. Real World 11.6 gives an example of the use of finance leasing in a leading airline business.

Real World 11.6

BA's leased assets are taking off

Many airline businesses use finance leasing as a means of acquiring new aeroplanes. The financial statements for British Airways plc (BA) for the year ended 31 March 2007 show that almost 29 per cent (totalling £1,698m) of the net book value of its fleet of aircraft had been acquired through this method.

Source: British Airways plc Annual Report and Accounts 2007, p. 72.

A finance lease can be contrasted with an operating lease, where the rewards and risks of ownership stay with the owner and where the lease is short-term. An example of an operating lease is where a builder hires some earthmoving equipment for a week to carry out a particular job.

In recent years, some important benefits associated with finance leasing have disappeared. Changes in UK tax law no longer make it such a tax-efficient form of financing, and changes in accounting disclosure requirements no longer make it possible to conceal this form of 'borrowing' from investors. Nevertheless, the popularity of finance leases has continued. Other reasons must therefore exist for businesses to adopt this form of financing. These reasons are said to include the following:

■ *Ease of borrowing.* Leasing may be obtained more easily than other forms of long-term finance. Lenders normally require some form of security and a profitable track record before making advances to a business. However, a lessor may be prepared to lease assets to a new business without a track record, and to use the leased assets as security for the amounts owing.

■ *Cost.* Leasing agreements may be offered at reasonable cost. As the asset leased is used as security, standard lease arrangements can be applied and detailed credit checking of lessees may be unnecessary. This can reduce administrative costs for the lessor and, thereby, help in providing competitive lease rentals.

- *Flexibility*. Leasing can help provide flexibility where there are rapid changes in technology. If an option to cancel can be incorporated into the lease, the business may be able to exercise this option and invest in new technology as it becomes available. This will help the business to avoid the risk of obsolescence.
- *Cash flows*. Leasing, rather than purchasing an asset outright, means that large cash outflows can be avoided. The leasing option allows cash outflows to be smoothed out over the asset's life. In some cases, it is possible to arrange for low lease payments to be made in the early years of the asset's life, when cash inflows may be low, and for these to increase over time as the asset generates positive cash flows.

Real World 11.7 provides some impression of the importance of finance leasing over recent years.

Real World 11.7

Finance leasing 2002 to 2006

The amount of asset finance provided through finance leasing by FLA members over the five-year period has remained fairly stable (see Figure 11.4).

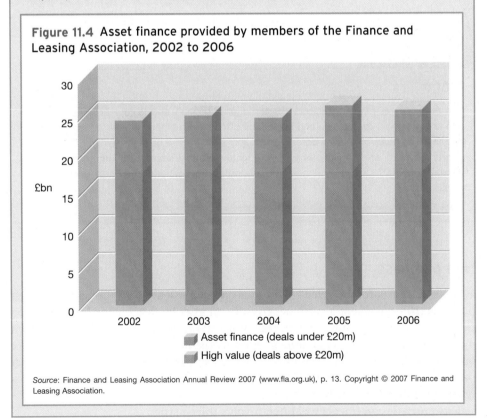

Figure 11.4 Asset finance provided by members of the Finance and Leasing Association, 2002 to 2006

- Asset finance (deals under £20m)
- High value (deals above £20m)

Source: Finance and Leasing Association Annual Review 2007 (www.fla.org.uk), p. 13. Copyright © 2007 Finance and Leasing Association.

→ A sale-and-leaseback arrangement involves a business raising finance by selling an asset to a financial institution. The sale is accompanied by an agreement to lease the asset back to the business to allow it to continue to use the asset. The lease payment is allowable against profits for taxation purposes. There are usually reviews at regular intervals throughout the period of the lease, and the amounts payable in future years may be difficult to predict. At the end of the lease agreement, the business must try either to renew the lease or to find an alternative asset. Although the sale of the asset will result in an immediate injection of cash for the business, the business will lose benefits from any future capital appreciation on the asset. Where a capital gain arises on the sale of the asset to the financial institution, a liability for taxation may also arise. Freehold property is often the asset that is the subject of such an arrangement. Many of the well-known UK high street retailers (for example, Boots, Debenhams, Marks and Spencer and Sainsbury) have recently sold off their store sites under sale-and-leaseback arrangements.

A sale-and-leaseback agreement can be used to help a business focus on its core areas of competence. In recent years, many hotel businesses have entered into sale-and-leaseback agreements to enable them to become purely hotel operators rather than a combination of hotel operators and owners.

Real World 11.8 provides an example of a sale-and-leaseback agreement undertaken by a well-known UK business.

Real World 11.8

Bingo

The Rank Group plc, the UK-based international gaming and leisure business, entered into an agreement for the sale and leaseback of 40 Mecca bingo clubs and four Grosvenor casinos. The deal, which was agreed on 14 July 2006, raised cash for Rank of £211m. The properties were sold to Solarus Estates Ltd and Earth Estates Ltd. Rank will now pay annual rents of £11.2m to lease back the properties, from Solarus and Earth, under 15-year leases.

Source: Information taken from 'Rank Group agrees sale and leaseback', 14 July 2006, ft.com.

Hire purchase

→ Hire purchase is a form of credit used to acquire an asset. Under the terms of a hire purchase (HP) agreement a customer pays for an asset by instalments over an agreed period. Normally, the customer will pay an initial deposit (down payment) and then make instalment payments at regular intervals (perhaps monthly) until the balance outstanding has been paid. The customer will usually take possession of the asset after payment of the initial deposit, although legal ownership of the asset will not be transferred until the final instalment has been paid.

Hire purchase agreements will often involve three parties:

- the supplier
- the customer
- a financial institution.

Although the supplier will deliver the asset to the customer, the financial institution will buy the asset from the supplier and then enter into a hire purchase agreement with the customer. This intermediary role played by the financial institution enables the supplier to receive immediate payment for the asset but allows the customer a period of extended credit.

Real World 11.9 describes how one well-known holiday operator uses hire purchase to help finance its assets.

Paying by instalments

Holidaybreak plc has a camping division that includes well-known brands such as Eurocamp and Keycamp. The division provides mobile homes for holidaymakers, and the company's 2006 annual report revealed that the cost of mobile homes purchased during the year was £3.0m. The company states:

> We have hire purchase agreements with various UK financial institutions to finance the purchase of mobile homes. Just over half of expenditure on mobile homes is financed from this source.

Source: Holidaybreak plc Annual Report 2006, p. 9.

HP agreements are similar to finance leases in so far that they allow a customer to obtain immediate possession of the asset without paying its full cost. Under the terms of an HP agreement, however, the customer will eventually become the legal owner of the asset, whereas under the terms of a finance lease, ownership will stay with the lessor.

Gearing and the long-term financing decision

In Chapter 6 we saw that financial gearing occurs when a business is financed, at least in part, by contributions from fixed-charge capital (preference shares and loans). We also saw that the level of gearing associated with a business is often an important factor in assessing the risk and returns to ordinary shareholders. In Example 11.1, we consider the implications of making a choice between a geared and an ungeared approach to raising long-term finance.

Chapter 11 Financing the business

Example 11.1

The following are the summarised financial statements of Woodhall Engineers plc.

Woodhall Engineers plc
Income statement for the year ended 31 December

	Year 1	Year 2
	£m	£m
Revenue	47	50
Operating costs	(42)	(48)
Operating profit	5	2
Interest payable	(1)	(1)
Profit before tax	4	1
Taxation	–	–
Profit for the year	4	1

Balance sheet at 31 December

	Year 1	Year 2
	£m	£m
Non-current assets (less depreciation)	21	20
Current assets		
Inventories	10	18
Receivables	16	17
Cash at bank	3	1
	29	36
Total assets	50	56
Equity		
Called-up share capital (25p ordinary shares)	16	16
Retained earnings	4	4
	20	20
Non-current liabilities		
Borrowings – long-term loans (secured)	15	15
Current liabilities		
Trade payables	10	10
Short-term borrowings	5	11
	15	21
Total equity and liabilities	50	56

The business is making plans to expand its premises. New plant will cost £8m, and an expansion in output will increase working capital by £4m. Over the 15 years' life of the project, incremental operating profit arising from the expansion will be £2m a year. In addition, Year 3's operating profit from its existing activities are expected to return to Year 1 levels.

Two possible methods of financing the expansion have been discussed by Woodhall's directors. The first is the issue of £12m of 10 per cent loan notes repayable in Year 18. The second is a rights issue of 40 million 25p ordinary shares, which will give the business 30p per share after expenses.

The business has substantial tax losses, which can be offset against future profits, so taxation can be ignored in the calculations. The Year 3 total dividend is expected to be £1.0m if the expansion is financed by loan notes and £1.6m if the rights issue is made.

Prepare Woodhall's projected income statement (excluding revenue and operating costs) for the year ended 31 December Year 3, and of its capital and reserves, long-term borrowings and number of shares outstanding at that date, assuming that the business issues

(a) loan notes
(b) ordinary shares.

The projected income statements under each financing option will be as follows:

Projected income statements for the year ended 31 December Year 3

	Loan issue	Share issue
	£m	£m
Operating profit (5.0 + 2.0)	7.0	7.0
Loan notes interest	(2.2)	(1.0)
Profit before tax	4.8	6.0
Taxation	–	–
Profit for the year	4.8	6.0

The capital structure of the business under each option as at the end of Year 3 will be as follows:

	Loan issue	Share issue
	£m	£m
Equity		
Share capital (25p ordinary shares)	16.0	26.0
Share premium account*	–	2.0
Retained earnings[†]	7.8	8.4
	23.8	36.4
Number of shares in issue (25p shares)	64 million	104 million

* This represents the amount received from the issue of shares that is above the nominal value of the shares. The amount is calculated as follows:

$$40m \text{ shares} \times (30p - 25p) = £2m$$

[†] This is the retained profit figure after deducting the dividend paid.

Activity 11.10

Compute Woodhall's interest cover and earnings per share for the year ended 31 December Year 3 and its gearing on that date, assuming that the business issues:

(a) loan notes;
(b) ordinary shares.

Your answer should be as follows:

	(a) Loan notes issue	(b) Share issue

Interest cover ratio

$\dfrac{\text{Operating profit}}{\text{Interest payable}}$

(a) $= \dfrac{7.0}{2.2}$ = 3.2 times

(b) $= \dfrac{7.0}{1.0}$ = 7.0 times

Earnings per share

$\dfrac{\text{Earnings available to ordinary shareholders}}{\text{Number of ordinary shares}}$

(a) $= \dfrac{£4.8m}{64m}$ = 7.5p

(b) $= \dfrac{£6.0m}{104m}$ = 5.8p

Gearing ratio

$\dfrac{\text{Non-current liabilities}}{\text{Share capital + Reserves + Non-current liabilities}}$

(a) $= \dfrac{£27m}{£23.8m + £27m}$ = 53.1%

(b) $= \dfrac{£15m}{£36.4m + £15m}$ = 29.2%

Activity 11.11

What would your views of the proposed schemes be in each of the following circumstances?

(a) If you were an investor who had been asked to take up some of the loan notes.
(b) If you were an ordinary shareholder in Woodhall and you were asked to subscribe to a rights issue.

(a) Investors may be unenthusiastic about lending money to the business. The gearing ratio of 53.1 per cent is rather high, and would leave the loan note holders in an exposed position. The existing loan is already secured on the business's assets, and it is not clear whether the business is in a position to offer an attractive form of security for the new loan. The interest cover ratio of 3.2 times is also rather low. If the business is unable to achieve the expected returns from the new project, or if it is unable to restore profits from the remainder of its operations to Year 1 levels, this ratio would be even lower.

(b) Ordinary share investors may need some convincing that it would be worthwhile to make further investments in the business. The return on ordinary shareholders' funds in Year 1 was 20 per cent (£4m/£20m). The incremental profit from the new project is £2m and the investment required is £12m, which represents a return of 16.7 per cent. Thus, the returns from the project are expected to be lower than for existing operations. In making their decision, investors should discover whether the new investment is of a similar level of risk to their existing investment and how the returns from the investment compare with those available from other opportunities with similar levels of risk.

Share issues

A business may issue shares in a number of ways. These may involve direct appeals to investors or the use of financial intermediaries. The most common methods of share issues for cash are:

- rights issues;
- offers for sale and public issues;
- private placings.

We shall now discuss these methods.

Rights issues

 As we saw in Chapter 4, rights issues are made when businesses that have been established for some time seek to raise additional share capital for expansion, or even to solve a liquidity problem (cash shortage) by issuing additional shares for cash. Company law gives existing shareholders the first right of refusal on these new shares, so the new shares would be offered to shareholders in proportion to their existing holding. Thus existing shareholders are each given the right to buy some new shares. Only where the existing shareholders agree to waive their right would the shares be offered to the investing public generally. Rights issues are now the most common form of share issue. The business (in effect, the existing shareholders) would typically prefer that existing shareholders buy the shares through a rights issue, irrespective of the legal position. This is for two reasons:

- The ownership (and, therefore, control) of the business remains in the same hands.
- The costs of making the issue (advertising, complying with various company law requirements) tend to be less if the shares are to be offered to existing shareholders.

To encourage existing shareholders to take up their 'rights' to buy some new shares, those shares are always offered at a price below the current market price of the existing ones.

Activity 11.12

In Chapter 4 (Example 4.2, pages 127–8) the point was made that issuing new shares at below their current worth was to the advantage of the new shareholders at the expense of the old ones. In view of this, does it matter that rights issues are always made at below the current value of the shares?

The answer is that it does not matter *in these particular circumstances*, because, in a rights issue, the existing shareholders and the new shareholders are exactly the same people. Moreover, the shareholders will hold the new shares in the same proportion as they currently hold the existing shares. Thus, shareholders will gain on the new shares exactly as much as they lose on the existing ones: in the end, no one is better or worse off as a result of the rights issue being made at a discount.

Calculating the value of the rights offer received by shareholders is quite straight-forward, as shown in Example 11.2.

Example 11.2

Shaw Holdings plc has 20 million ordinary shares of 50p in issue. These shares are currently valued on the Stock Exchange at £1.60 per share. The directors have decided to make a 1-for-4 issue (that is, one new share for every four shares held) at £1.30 per share.

The first step in the valuation process is to calculate the price of a share following the rights issue. This is known as the *ex-rights price*, and is simply a weighted average of the price of shares before the issue of rights and the price of the rights shares. In this example, we have a 1-for-4 rights issue. The theoretical ex-rights price is therefore calculated as follows:

	£
Price of four shares before the rights issue (4 × £1.60)	6.40
Price of taking up one rights share	1.30
	7.70
Theoretical ex-rights price = $£\dfrac{7.70}{5}$	= £1.54

As the price of each share, in theory, should be £1.54 following the rights issue and the price of a rights share is £1.30, the value of the rights offer will be the difference between the two:

$$£1.54 - £1.30 = £0.24 \text{ per share}$$

Market forces will usually ensure that the actual and theoretical price of rights will be fairly close.

Activity 11.13

An investor with 2,000 shares in Shaw Holdings plc (see Example 11.2) has contacted you for investment advice. She is undecided whether to take up the rights issue, sell the rights or allow the rights offer to lapse.

Calculate the effect on the net wealth of the investor of each of the options being considered.

Before the rights issue the position of the investor was:

	£
Value of shares (2,000 × £1.60)	3,200

If she takes up the rights issue, she will be in the following position:

	£
Value of holding after rights issue ((2,000 + 500) × £1.54)	3,850
Less cost of buying the rights shares (500 × £1.30)	650
	3,200

If the investor sells the rights, she will be in the following position:

	£
Value of holding after rights issue (2,000 × £1.54)	3,080
Sale of rights (500 × £0.24)	120
	3,200

If the investor lets the rights offer lapse, she will be in the following position:

	£
Value of holding after rights issue (2,000 × £1.54)	3,080

As we can see, the first two options should leave her in the same position concerning net wealth as before the rights issue. Before the rights issue she had 2,000 shares worth £1.60 each, or £3,200 in total. However, she will be worse off if she allows the rights offer to lapse than under the other two options. In practice, however, the business may sell the rights on behalf of the investor, and pass on the proceeds in order to ensure that she is not worse off as a result of the issue.

When considering a rights issue, the directors must first consider the amount of funds needing to be raised. This will depend on the future plans and commitments of the business (rights issues are frequently made to raise cash for expansion). The directors must then decide on the issue price of the rights shares. Normally, this decision is not critical. In Example 11.2, the business made a 1-for-4 issue with the price of the rights shares set at £1.30. However, it could have raised the same amount by making a 1-for-2 issue and setting the rights price at £0.65, a 1-for-1 issue and setting the price at £0.325, and so on. The issue price that is finally decided upon will not affect the value of the underlying assets of the business or the proportion of the underlying assets and earnings to which each shareholder is entitled. The directors must ensure that the issue price is not above the current market price of the shares, however, or the issue will be unsuccessful.

Real World 11.10 describes how Premier Foods plc, the well-known UK food business, made a rights issue to fund the acquisition of another business.

Real World 11.10

The rights stuff puts Campbell in the Premiership

In August 2006, Premier Foods plc made a 1-for-1 rights issue that raised £450m. Shareholders took up 98 per cent of the issue. The remaining 2 per cent of the shares were placed with other investors.

Premier Foods makes a number of household-name products, including Branston Pickle, Hartley's Jam, Ambrosia Rice, and Crosse and Blackwell's soups. The new finance was raised to fund the acquisition of the UK and Irish division of the US Campbell Soup Company.

Source: www.premierfoods.co.uk.

Offers for sale and public issues

→ An offer for sale involves a business that trades as a public limited company selling a new issue of shares to a financial institution known as an *issuing house*. However, shares that are already in issue may also be sold to an issuing house. In this case, existing shareholders agree to sell all or some of their shares to the issuing house. The issuing house will, in turn, sell the shares, purchased from either the business or its shareholders, to the public. The issuing house will publish a prospectus that sets out details of the business and the type of shares to be sold, and investors will be invited to apply for shares. The advantage of this type of issue, from the business's viewpoint, is that the sale proceeds of the shares are certain.

→ A public issue involves the business making a direct invitation to the public to purchase its shares. Typically, this is done through a newspaper advertisement. The shares may, once again, be either a new issue or those already in issue. An offer for sale and a public issue will both result in a widening of share ownership in the business.

In practical terms, the net effect on the business is much the same whether there is an offer for sale or a public issue.

Issue by tender

When making an issue of shares, the business or the issuing house will usually set a price for the shares. Establishing this may not be an easy task, however, particularly where the market is volatile or where the business has unique characteristics. One
→ way of dealing with this issue-price problem is to make a tender issue of shares. This involves the investors determining the price at which the shares are issued. Although the business (or issuing house) may publish a reserve price to help guide investors, it will be up to the individual investor to determine the number of shares to be purchased and the price the investor is prepared to pay. Once the offers from investors have all been received and recorded, a price at which all the shares can be sold will be established (known as the *striking price*). Investors who have made offers at, or above, the striking price will be issued shares at the striking price; offers received below the striking price will be rejected. Note that all of the shares will be issued at the same price irrespective of the prices actually offered by individual investors.

Although this form of issue is adopted occasionally, it is not popular with investors, and is therefore not in widespread use.

Private placings

→ A private placing does not involve an invitation to the public to subscribe for shares. Instead the shares are 'placed' with selected investors, such as large financial institutions. This can be a quick and relatively cheap form of raising funds, because savings can be made in advertising and legal costs. However, it can result in the ownership of the business being concentrated in a few hands. Sometimes, unlisted businesses seeking relatively small amounts of cash will make this form of issue.

Real World 11.11 describes how Aviva plc, the insurance business, used a placing to raise finance.

Insuring a successful placing

Aviva plc is the world's fifth largest insurance business and it strengthened its position still further by raising about £900m, in July 2006, through a placing of new ordinary shares. The shares were offered to clients of three leading merchant banks and were taken up by a variety of institutional and other investors. The funds raised led to an increase of about 5 per cent in Aviva plc's equity.

The cash raised by the placing provided most of the £1.6bn that Aviva plc is paying, in cash, to acquire AmerUs Group Company, a major US life insurance and annuity business.

Source: www.aviva.com.

Bonus issues

We should recall from Chapter 4 that a bonus issue is not a means of raising finance. It is simply converting one part of the equity (reserves) into another (ordinary shares). No cash changes hands; this benefits neither the business nor the shareholders.

The role of the Stock Exchange

Earlier we considered the various forms of long-term capital that are available to a business. In this section we examine the role that the Stock Exchange plays in providing finance for businesses. The Stock Exchange acts as both an important *primary* and *secondary* market in capital for businesses. As a primary market, its function is to enable businesses to raise new capital. As a secondary market, its function is to enable investors to sell their securities (including shares and loan notes) with ease. Thus, it provides a 'second-hand' market where shares and loan notes already in issue may be bought and sold.

To enable it to issue shares or loan notes through the Stock Exchange, a business must be 'listed'. Similarly, it must also be Stock Exchange listed before its existing shares and loan notes can be bought and sold there. Listing means that the business must meet fairly stringent requirements concerning size, profit history, information disclosure and so on.

Some share issues by Stock Exchange listed businesses arise from the initial listing of the business, often known as an *initial public offering (IPO)*. Other share issues are undertaken by businesses that are already listed and that are seeking additional finance from investors.

Real World 11.12 describes how Aer Lingus Group plc, the London Stock Exchange listed Irish airline, made a major IPO.

Real World 11.12

Aer Lingus off to a flying start

Aer Lingus Group plc was floated in September 2006 through an IPO that raised £335m. The shares offered were oversubscribed 3.8 times (for every share available 3.8 shares were sought by investors).

The group planned to use much of the funds raised to expand operations mainly by investing in additional planes.

Source: Information taken from 'Aer Lingus IPO has a smooth takeoff', Alistair Osborne and Stephen Seawright, *Daily Telegraph*, 28 September 2006.

Real World 11.13 explains how new issues are not always good investments for those who take up the shares concerned.

Real World 11.13

New issues but old problems

It seems that we should be cautious when invited to subscribe to a new issue of shares arising from an initial listing on the Stock Exchange. The following extract from the *Financial Times* tells us why investing in new business flotations may be bad for our wealth.

> Back in 1940 Benjamin Graham and David Dodd, the fathers of security analysis, wrote: 'the odds are so strongly against the man who buys into these new flotations that he might as well throw three-quarters of the money out the window and keep the rest in the bank.'
>
> Now confirmation of the poor record of recent new issues comes from an Ernst and Young survey. The accountancy group looked at the records of 200 companies that floated on the UK market between 1998 and 2002. It found that only 39% of the sample had increased profits since flotation (although 82% had seen their sales grow).
>
> This should not come as too much of a surprise. Companies are most likely to float on the market when their recent trading record is impressive. But periods of rapid growth can be very dangerous for a company – costs and management ambitions can get out of hand. Furthermore, no business can grow rapidly forever, and there is a risk that the flotation occurs just at the moment when the decline is beginning.
>
> And, as Ernst and Young points out, the very act of flotation incurs significant costs and can divert management focus from the business. The money raised can also burn a hole in the management's pockets, leading to a flurry of spending that would disgrace a football manager.
>
> All this is slightly discouraging, given that the primary role of the stock market is to allow growing businesses to raise capital. But perhaps a certain amount of investor greed (and gullibility) is necessary if industry is to gain access to finance. New issue investors have been fooled before; they will be fooled again.

Source: Financial Times, 8 August 2003, p. 22.

Despite the problems with IPOs they have been quite popular in terms of the value of funds raised over recent years, as is shown in Real World 11.14.

Real World 11.14

IPOs still popular

Figure 11.5 shows the number of IPOs, together with their average value, that have been made by businesses with a full London Stock Exchange listing during the ten years 1996 to 2005.

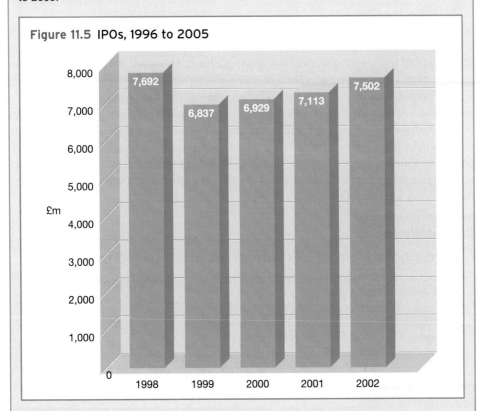

Figure 11.5 IPOs, 1996 to 2005

Although the number of issues has fluctuated quite widely, the average funds raised per IPO has tended to show an increase over time.

Source: Based on information contained on the KPMG Corporate Finance website, www.kpmg.co.uk.

Advantages of a listing

The secondary market role of the Stock Exchange means that shares and other financial claims are easily transferable. Furthermore, their prices are constantly under scrutiny by investors and skilled analysts. This helps to promote the tendency for the price quoted for a particular business's share to reflect its true worth at that particular time. These factors can bring real benefits to a business.

Activity 11.14

What kinds of benefits might a business gain from its shares being listed?

If it is generally accepted that shares can easily be sold for prices that tend to reflect their true worth, investors will have more confidence to invest. The business may benefit from this greater investor confidence by finding it easier to raise long-term finance and by obtaining this finance at a lower cost, as investors will view their investment as being less risky.

It is worth pointing out that investors are not obliged to use the Stock Exchange as the means of transferring shares in a listed business. However, it is usually the most convenient way of buying or selling shares.

The Stock Exchange can be a useful vehicle for a successful entrepreneur wishing to realise the value of the business that has been built up. By floating (listing) the shares on the Stock Exchange, and thereby making the shares available to the public, the entrepreneur will usually benefit from a gain in the value of the shares held and will be able to realise that gain easily, if required, by selling some shares. Real Worlds 15.15 and 15.16 give examples of businesses floating on the Stock Exchange and making their owners a lot of money.

Real World 11.15

Granny goes from Leicester market to Stock Market

Duelm Group plc floated on the London Stock Exchange and Jean Adderly realised £120m for her investment. The business was started, in 1979, by Jean (now a grandmother) and her husband Bill trading in curtains on a market stall in Leicester. The business has grown and expanded its range to include most types of household furnishings. It has also moved into more solid premises, with 82 retail outlets.

Source: Based on 'From the market to the market', Harry Wallop, *Daily Telegraph*, 22 September 2006.

Real World 11.16

Cashing in

Paul Doughty, the CFO (chief financial officer) of moneysupermarket.com, is nearly £3m richer after his company's IPO despite a below-par fundraising.

The internet broker, which helps consumers to find the cheapest financial products, completed its float last week but ended up with an offer price of £1.70 a share, at the foot of the £1.70 to £2.10 range.

A company spokesperson confirmed that Doughty had cashed in 1.6m shares, but even with the disappointing showing, the CFO of the UK's leading price-comparison website made himself close to £3m.

If the IPO offer price had been set at the top end of the range, Doughty would have earned close to £3.5m. But his windfall was dwarfed by that of chief executive Simon Nixon, who cashed in £60.3m shares, netting £100m. He still holds more than 57% of the company, which is worth more than £800m.

Source: 'Internet FD is in the money after floatation', David Jeyuah, *Accountancy Age*, 2 August 2007, p. 3.

Disadvantages of a listing

A Stock Exchange listing can have certain disadvantages for a business. These include:

- Strict rules are imposed on listed businesses, including requirements for levels of financial disclosure additional to those already imposed by International Financial Reporting Standards (for example, the listing rules require that half-yearly financial reports are published).
- Financial analysts, financial journalists and others tend to monitor closely the activities of listed businesses, particularly larger ones. Such scrutiny may not be welcome, particularly if the business is dealing with sensitive issues or is experiencing operational problems.
- It is often suggested that listed businesses are under pressure to perform well over the short term. This pressure may detract from undertaking projects that will yield benefits only in the longer term. If the market becomes disenchanted with the business, and the price of its shares falls, this may make it vulnerable to a takeover bid from another business.
- The costs of obtaining a listing are huge and this may be a real deterrent for some businesses.

To make an initial public offering, a business will rely on the help of various specialists such as lawyers, accountants and bankers. However, their services do not come cheap. Real World 11.17 provides some information.

Real World 11.17

Floating on heavy fees

According to the London Stock Exchange,

> While the total costs vary widely depending on individual circumstances, as a rule of thumb they tend to come to between four and eight percent of the total proceeds of the sale, although this proportion may be higher for relatively small share offers as some of the fees, for example for accountants and solicitors, are a fixed cost.

Source: *Practical Guide to Listing*, London Stock Exchange, p. 24.

Though there are over 1,000 UK businesses listed on the London Stock Exchange, in terms of equity market value, the market is dominated by just a few large ones, as is shown in Real World 11.18.

Real World 11.18

Listing to one side

At 31 August 2007 there were 1,138 businesses that had a London Stock Exchange listing. Just 134 of them (12 per cent) accounted for 85 per cent of their total equity market value.

A total of 320 businesses (28 per cent of listed businesses) accounted for nearly 95 per cent of total equity market value.

Source: *Main Market Fact Sheet*, London Stock Exchange, August 2007, Table 8.

Real World 11.19 provides an analysis of the ownership of shares in UK listed businesses at the end of 2006.

Real World 11.19

Ownership of UK listed shares

At the end of 2006, the proportion of shares of UK listed businesses held by various groups was as shown in Figure 11.6.

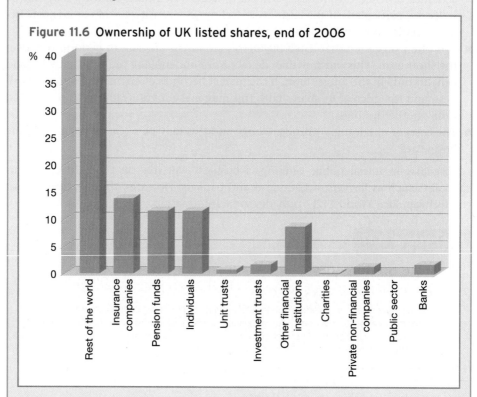

Figure 11.6 Ownership of UK listed shares, end of 2006

Ownership of UK listed shares is now dominated by large financial institutions. These figures do not fully portray the shareholdings of individuals, however, as individuals will also hold shares in unit trusts.

Source: Financial Statistics, Share Ownership 2006, Office for National Statistics, p. 1. Copyright © 2007 Crown Copyright. Crown copyright material is reproduced with the permission of the Controller of HMSO.

Going private

Such are the disadvantages of a stock market listing that many businesses have 'delisted'. This has obviously denied them the advantages of a listing, but it has avoided the disadvantages.

The Alternative Investment Market

The Alternative Investment Market (AIM) was established in June 1995 by the London Stock Exchange for smaller, young and growing businesses. AIM is similar in style to the main London Stock Exchange but it is cheaper for the business to enter. Obtaining an AIM listing and raising funds costs the typical business about £500,000. Many AIM listed businesses are family-based ones. AIM has proved to be a very successful market where new equity finance can be raised and shares can be traded. Businesses listed on AIM tend to have market values in the range £1m to £250m, though half of them fall within the £5m to £50m range, as is shown by Real World 11.20.

Real World 11.20

Take AIM

At 31 August 2007, there were 1,653 businesses that had an AIM listing. Their distribution according to market value is shown in Figure 11.7.

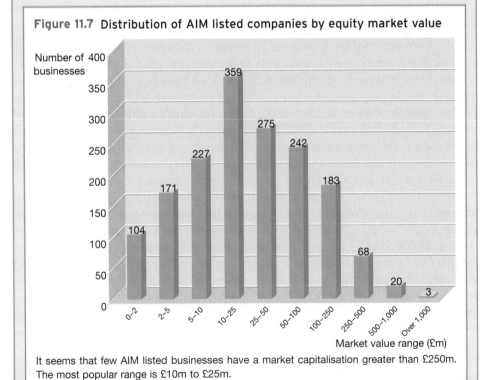

Figure 11.7 Distribution of AIM listed companies by equity market value

It seems that few AIM listed businesses have a market capitalisation greater than £250m. The most popular range is £10m to £25m.

Source: AIM Market Statistics, London Stock Exchange, August 2007.

The listing requirements of AIM are less stringent than those of a full listing. However AIM listed businesses tend to be more risky than fully listed ones, which can make AIM listed shares less attractive.

AIM listed companies include Monsoon plc, the high street fashion retailer, Heavitree Brewery plc, the Devon brewer and pub owner, and the football clubs Charlton Athletic and Preston North End. Also AIM listed is LiDCO Group plc, the heart monitoring equipment developer that we met in Real World 5.3 in the context of the cash flow statement.

Short-term sources of external finance

Short-term, in this context, is usually taken to mean up to one year. Figure 11.2 indicated that the major sources of short-term external finance are

- bank overdrafts
- debt factoring
- invoice discounting.

These are discussed below.

Bank overdrafts

A bank overdraft enables a business to maintain a negative balance on its bank account. It represents a very flexible form of borrowing as the size of the overdraft can (subject to bank approval) be increased or decreased more or less instantaneously. An overdraft is relatively inexpensive to arrange, and interest rates are often very competitive, though often higher than those for a term loan. As with all loans, the rate of interest charged on an overdraft will vary according to how creditworthy the customer is perceived to be by the bank. An overdraft is fairly easy to arrange – sometimes by a telephone call to the bank. In view of these advantages, it is not surprising that an overdraft is an extremely popular form of short-term finance.

Banks prefer to grant overdrafts that are self-liquidating, that is, the funds applied will result in cash inflows that will extinguish the overdraft balance. The banks may ask for a cash budget (projected cash flow statement) from the business to see when the overdraft will be repaid and how much finance is required. The bank may also require some form of security on amounts advanced. One potential drawback with this form of finance is that the overdraft is repayable on demand. This may pose problems for a business that is short of funds. However, many businesses operate for many years using an overdraft, simply because the bank remains confident of their ability to repay and the arrangement suits the business. Thus the bank overdraft, though in theory regarded as short-term, often becomes a long-term source of finance.

Debt factoring

Debt factoring is a service offered by a financial institution (known as a *factor*). Many of the large factors are subsidiaries of commercial banks. Debt factoring involves the factor taking over the business's debt collection. In addition to operating normal credit control procedures, a factor may offer to undertake credit investigations and to provide protection for approved credit sales. The factor is usually prepared to make an advance to the business of a maximum of 80 per cent of approved trade receivables. The charge made for the factoring service is based on total sales revenue, and is often 2 to 3 per cent of sales revenue. Any advances made to the business by the factor will attract a rate of interest similar to the rate charged on bank overdrafts.

Debt factoring is, in effect, outsourcing the trade receivables control to a specialist subcontractor. Many businesses find a factoring arrangement very convenient. It can result in savings in credit management and create more certainty with the cash flows. It can also release the time of key personnel for more profitable activities. This may be extremely important for smaller businesses that rely on the talent and skills of a few key individuals. However, there is a possibility that a factoring arrangement will be seen as an indication that the business is experiencing financial difficulties. This may have an adverse effect on the confidence of customers, suppliers and staff. For this reason, some businesses try to conceal the factoring arrangement by collecting debts on behalf of the factor. When considering a factoring agreement, the costs and likely benefits arising must be identified and carefully weighed.

Figure 11.8 shows the factoring process diagrammatically.

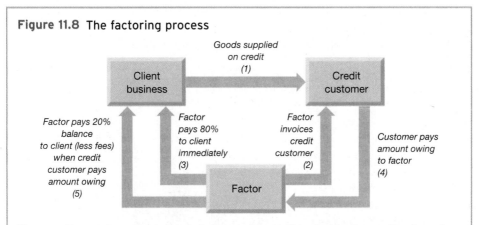

Figure 11.8 The factoring process

There are three main parties to the factoring agreement. The client business will sell goods or services on credit and the factor will take responsibility for invoicing the customer and collecting the amount owing. The factor will then pay the client business the invoice amount, less fees and interest, in two stages. The first stage typically represents 80 per cent of the invoice value and will be paid immediately after the goods or service have been delivered to the customer. The second stage will represent the balance outstanding and will usually be paid when the customer has paid the factor the amount owing.

Invoice discounting

Invoice discounting involves a factor or other financial institution providing a loan based on a proportion of the face value of a business's credit sales outstanding (that is, the trade receivables). The amount advanced is usually 75 to 80 per cent of the value of the approved sales invoices outstanding. The business must agree to repay the advance within a relatively short period, perhaps 60 or 90 days. The responsibility for collecting the trade receivables outstanding remains with the business, and repayment of the advance is not dependent on the trade receivables being collected. Invoice discounting will not result in such a close relationship developing between the business and the financial institution as results with factoring. It may be a short-term arrangement, whereas debt factoring usually involves a longer-term relationship.

There are three main reasons for the relative popularity of invoice discounting:

- It is a confidential form of financing that the business's customers will know nothing about.
- The service charge for invoice discounting is generally only 0.2 to 0.3 per cent of sales revenue, compared with 2.0 to 3.0 per cent for factoring.
- Many businesses are unwilling to relinquish control of their customers' records. Customers are an important resource of the business, and many wish to retain control over all aspects of their relationship with their customers.

Real World 11.21 shows the relative importance of invoice discounting and factoring.

Real World 11.21

The popularity of invoice discounting and factoring

Figure 11.9 Client sales: domestic invoice discounting and factoring, 2001 to 2006

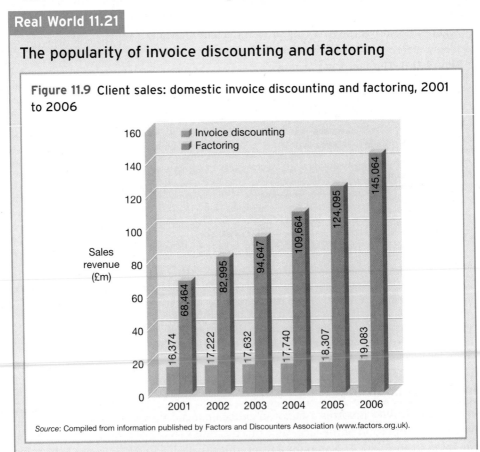

Source: Compiled from information published by Factors and Discounters Association (www.factors.org.uk).

> In recent years, client use of invoice discounting has risen much more sharply than client use of factoring. During 2006, for example, client use of factoring grew by 4 per cent whereas invoice discounting grew by 17 per cent. Client sales using invoice discounting in 2006 were more than seven times the client sales using factoring.

Factoring and invoice discounting are forms of asset-based financing, as the asset of trade receivables is in effect used as security for the cash advances received by the business.

Long-term versus short-term borrowing

Having decided that some form of borrowing is required to finance the business, managers must then decide whether it should be long-term or short-term in form. There are many issues that should be taken into account when making this decision. These include the following:

- *Matching*. The business may attempt to match the type of borrowing with the nature of the assets held. Thus, long-term borrowing might finance assets that form part of the permanent operating base of the business, including non-current assets and a certain level of current assets. This leaves assets held for a short period, such as current assets held to meet seasonal increases in demand (for example, inventories), to be financed by short-term borrowing, because short-term borrowing tends to be more flexible in that funds can be raised and repaid at short notice. Figure 11.10 (p. 428) shows this funding division graphically.

  A business may wish to match the asset life exactly with the period of the related loan; however, this may not be possible because of the difficulty of predicting the life of many assets.
- *Flexibility*. Short-term borrowing may be a useful means of postponing a commitment to taking on a long-term loan. This may be seen as desirable if interest rates are high and it is forecast that they will fall in the future. Short-term borrowing does not usually incur penalties if there is early repayment of the amount outstanding, whereas some form of financial penalty may arise if long-term borrowing is repaid early.
- *Refunding risk*. Short-term borrowing has to be renewed more frequently than long-term borrowing. This may create problems for the business if it is already in financial difficulties or if there is a shortage of funds available for lending.
- *Interest rates*. Interest payable on long-term borrowing is often higher than for short-term borrowing, as lenders require a higher return where their funds are locked up for a long period. This fact may make short-term borrowing a more attractive source of finance for a business. However, there may be other costs associated with borrowing (arrangement fees, for example) to be taken into account. The more frequently borrowings must be renewed, the higher these costs will be.

Figure 11.10 Short-term and long-term financing requirements

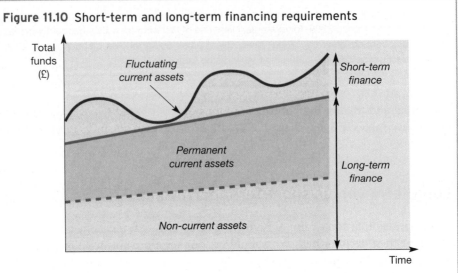

The broad consensus on financing seems to be that all of the permanent financial needs of the business should come from long-term sources. Only that part of current assets that fluctuates on a short-term, probably a seasonal, basis should be financed from short-term sources.

Activity 11.15

Some businesses may take up a less cautious financing position than that shown in Figure 11.10, and others may take up a more cautious one. How would the diagram differ under each of these options?

A less cautious position would mean relying on short-term finance to help fund part of the permanent capital base. A more cautious position would mean relying on long-term finance to help finance the fluctuating assets of the business.

Providing long-term finance for the small business

Although the Stock Exchange provides an important source of long-term finance for large businesses, it is not really suitable for small businesses. The aggregate market value of shares that are to be listed on the Stock Exchange must be at least £700,000 and, in practice, the amounts are much higher because of the high costs of listing. Thus, small businesses must look elsewhere for help in raising long-term finance. The more important sources of finance that are available to small businesses are venture capital, business angels and government assistance. We shall now consider these.

Venture capital

Venture capital is long-term capital provided to small and medium-sized businesses that wish to grow but do not have ready access to stock markets because of the prohibitively large costs of obtaining a listing. The businesses of interest to the venture capitalist will have higher levels of risk than would normally be acceptable to traditional providers of finance, such as the major clearing banks. The attraction for the venture capitalist of investing in higher-risk businesses is the prospect of higher returns.

Many small businesses are designed to provide the owners with a particular lifestyle and with job satisfaction. These kinds of businesses are not of interest to venture capitalists, as they are unlikely to provide the desired financial returns. Instead, venture capitalists look for businesses where the owners are seeking significant sales revenue and profit growth and need some outside help in order to achieve this.

The risks associated with the business can vary in practice. They are often due to the nature of the products or the fact that it is a new business that either lacks a trading record or has new management or both of these.

Venture capitalists provide long-term capital in the form of share and loan finance for different situations, including:

- *Start-up capital*. This is available to businesses that are not fully developed. They may need finance to help refine the business concept or to engage in product development or initial marketing. They have not yet reached the stage where they are trading.
- *Early-stage capital*. This is available for businesses that are ready to start trading.
- *Expansion capital*. This is aimed at providing additional funding for existing, growing businesses.
- *Buy-out or buy-in capital*. This is used to fund the acquisition of a business either by the existing management team ('buy-out') or by a new management team ('buy-in'). Management buy-outs (MBOs) and buy-ins (MBIs) often occur where a large business wishes to divest itself of one of its operating units or where a family business wishes to sell out because of succession problems.
- *Rescue capital* To help turn around businesses that are in difficulties.

The venture capitalist will often make a substantial investment in the business (usually more than £100,000), and this will often take the form of ordinary shares. However, some of the funding may be in the form of preference shares or loan capital. To keep an eye on the sum invested, the venture capitalist will usually require a representative on the board of directors as a condition of the investment. The venture capitalist may not be looking for a very quick return, and may well be prepared to invest in a business for five years or more. The return may take the form of a capital gain on the realisation of the investment (typically selling the shares).

Though venture capital is extremely important for some small businesses, the vast majority of small businesses obtain their finance from other sources. Real World 11.22 shows the main sources of finance for small businesses in the UK.

Real World 11.22

Small business funding

Bank finance, such as overdrafts and loans, is the main source of external finance for small businesses, as the pie chart in Figure 11.11 shows.

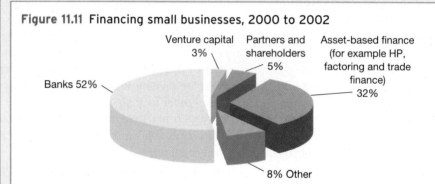

Figure 11.11 Financing small businesses, 2000 to 2002

Venture capital 3%
Partners and shareholders 5%
Asset-based finance (for example HP, factoring and trade finance) 32%
Banks 52%
8% Other

Venture capital, though very important to some small businesses, represents a very small part of the total finance raised. Bank finance remains the most important source of external finance, followed by asset-based finance, such as hire purchase, factoring and trade finance.

Source: Finance for Small Firms – An eleventh report, Bank of England, April 2004.

Business angels

 Business angels are often wealthy individuals who have been successful in business. They are usually willing to invest, through a shareholding, between £10,000 and £750,000 in a start-up business or in a business that is wishing to expand. If larger amounts are required, a syndicate of business angels may be formed to raise the money. Business angels typically make one or two investments over a three-year period and will usually be prepared to invest for a period of between three and five years. They normally have a minority stake in the business, and although they do not usually become involved in its day-to-day management, they tend to take an interest, more generally, in the way that the business is managed.

Business angels fill an important gap in the market as the size and nature of investments they find appealing are often not so appealing to venture capitalists. They can be attractive to small businesses because they may

- make investment decisions quickly, particularly if they are familiar with the industry in which the new business operates;
- offer useful skills, experience and business contacts;

- accept lower financial returns than those required from venture capitalists in order to have the opportunity to become involved in a new and interesting project.

Business angels offer an informal source of share finance and it is not always easy for owners of small businesses to identify a suitable angel. However, numerous business angel networks have now developed to help owners of small businesses find their 'perfect partner'.

Government assistance

One of the most effective ways in which the UK government assists small businesses is through the Small Firms Loan Guarantee scheme. This scheme aims to help small businesses that have viable business plans but lack the security to obtain a loan. The scheme guarantees:

- 75 per cent of the amount borrowed, for which the borrower pays a premium of 2 per cent on the outstanding loan
- loans of up to £250,000 for a maximum period of 10 years.

The scheme is available for businesses that are no more than five years old and have annual sales revenue of up to £5.6m.

In addition to other forms of financial assistance, such as government grants and tax incentives for investors to buy shares in small businesses, the government also helps by providing information concerning the sources of finance available.

? Self-assessment question 11.1

Helsim Ltd is a wholesaler and distributor of electrical components. The most recent draft financial statements of the business revealed the following:

Income statement for the year

	£m	£m
Sales revenue		14.2
Opening inventories	3.2	
Purchases	8.4	
	11.6	
Closing inventories	(3.8)	(7.8)
Gross profit		6.4
Administration expenses		(3.0)
Distribution expenses		(2.1)
Operating profit		1.3
Finance costs		(0.8)
Profit before taxation		0.5
Taxation		(0.2)
Profit for the period		0.3

Balance sheet as at the end of the year

	£m
Non-current assets	
Property, plant and equipment	
Land and buildings	3.8
Equipment	0.9
Motor vehicles	0.5
	5.2
Current assets	
Inventories	3.8
Trade receivables	3.6
Cash at bank	0.1
	7.5
Total assets	12.7
Equity	
Share capital	2.0
Retained earnings	1.8
	3.8
Non-current liabilities	
Loan notes (secured on freehold land)	3.5
Current liabilities	
Trade payables	1.8
Short-term borrowings	3.6
	5.4
Total equity and liabilities	12.7

Notes:

1 Land and buildings are shown at their current market value. Equipment and motor vehicles are shown at their written-down values (that is, cost less accumulated depreciation).

2 No dividends have been paid to ordinary shareholders for the past three years.

In recent months, trade payables have been pressing for payment. The managing director has therefore decided to reduce the level of trade payables to an average of 40 days outstanding. To achieve this, he has decided to approach the bank with a view to increasing the overdraft (the short-term borrowings comprise only a bank overdraft). The business is currently paying 10 per cent a year interest on the overdraft.

Required:

(a) Comment on the liquidity position of the business.

(b) Calculate the amount of finance required to reduce trade payables, from the level shown on the balance sheet, to an average of 40 days outstanding.

(c) State, with reasons, how you consider the bank would react to the proposal to grant an additional overdraft facility.

(d) Identify four sources of finance (internal or external, but excluding a bank overdraft) that may be suitable to finance the reduction in trade payables, and state, with reasons, which of these you consider the most appropriate.

The answer to this question can be found at the back of the book in Appendix B.

Summary

The main points in this chapter may be summarised as follows.

Sources of finance

■ Internal sources of finance do not require the agreement of anyone beyond the directors and managers of the business, whereas external sources of finance do require the compliance of 'outsiders'.

■ Long-term sources of finance are not due for repayment within one year whereas short-term sources are due for repayment within one year.

■ The higher the level of risk associated with investing in a particular form of finance, the higher the level of return that will be expected by investors.

Internal sources of finance

■ The major internal source of long-term finance is retained profits.

■ The main short-term sources of internal finance are tighter credit control of receivables, reducing inventories levels and delaying payments to trade payables.

External sources of finance

■ The main external, *long-term* sources of finance are ordinary shares, preference shares, loans, leases and hire purchase agreements.

■ Ordinary shares are normally considered to be the most risky form of investment and, therefore, provide the highest expected returns. Loan capital is normally the least risky and provides the lowest expected returns to investors.

■ Leases and hire purchase agreements allow a business to obtain immediate possession of an asset without having to pay the cost of acquiring the asset.

■ The level of gearing associated with a business is often an important factor in assessing the level of risk and returns to ordinary shareholders.

■ The main sources of external *short-term* finance are bank overdrafts, debt factoring and invoice discounting.

■ When considering the choice between long-term and short-term sources of borrowing, factors such as matching the type of borrowing with the nature of the assets held, the need for flexibility, refunding risk and interest rates should be taken into account.

Share issues

■ Share issues that involve the payment of cash by investors can take the form of a rights issue, public issue, offer for sale or a private placing.

■ A rights issue is made to existing shareholders. Most share issues are of this type as the law requires that shares that are to be issued for cash must first be offered to existing shareholders.

- A public issue involves a direct issue to the public and an offer for sale involves an indirect issue to the public.

- A private placing is an issue of shares to selected investors.

The Stock Exchange

- The Stock Exchange is an important primary and secondary market in capital for large businesses. However, obtaining a Stock Exchange listing can have certain drawbacks for a business.

The Alternative Investment Market (AIM)

- AIM is another important primary and secondary market managed by the London Stock Exchange for smaller, growing businesses. It tends to be a cheaper way for a business to become listed.

Small businesses

- Venture capital is long-term capital for small or medium-sized businesses that are not listed on the Stock Exchange. These businesses often have higher levels of risk but provide the venture capitalist with the prospect of higher levels of return.

- Business angels are wealthy individuals who are willing to invest in businesses at either an early stage or expansion stage of development.

- The government assists small businesses through guaranteeing loans and by providing grants and tax incentives.

→ **Key terms**

Further reading

If you would like to explore the topics covered in this chapter in more depth, we recommend the following books:

Arnold, G., *Corporate Financial Management* (3rd edn), Financial Times Prentice Hall, 2005, chapters 9 to 12.

Brealey, R., Myers, S. and Allen, F., *Corporate Finance* (8th edn), McGraw-Hill, 2005, chapters 14, 25 and 26.

McLaney, E., *Business Finance: Theory and Practice* (8th edn), Financial Times Prentice Hall, 2009, chapter 8.

Pike, R. and Neale, B., *Corporate Finance and Investment* (5th edn), Prentice Hall International, 2005, chapters 15 and 16.

? Review questions

Answers to these questions can be found at the back of the book in Appendix C.

11.1 What are the benefits to a business of issuing share warrants?

11.2 Why might a business that has a Stock Exchange listing revert to being unlisted?

11.3 Distinguish between an offer for sale and a public issue of shares.

11.4 Distinguish between invoice discounting and factoring.

* Exercises

Exercises 11.3 to 11.5 are more advanced than Exercises 11.1 to 11.2. Those with coloured numbers have answers at the back of the book in Appendix D.

> **If you wish to try more exercises, visit MyAccountingLab/**

11.1 H. Brown (Portsmouth) Ltd produces a range of central heating systems for sale to builders' merchants. As a result of increasing demand for the business's products, the directors have decided to expand production. The cost of acquiring new plant and machinery and the increase in working capital requirements are planned to be financed by a mixture of long-term and short-term borrowing.

Required:

(a) Discuss the major factors that should be taken into account when deciding on the appropriate mix of long-term and short-term borrowing necessary to finance the expansion programme.

(b) Discuss the major factors that a lender should take into account when deciding whether to grant a long-term loan to the business.

(c) Identify three conditions that might be included in a long-term loan agreement, and state the purpose of each.

11.2 Carpets Direct plc wishes to increase the number of its retail outlets in the south of England. The board of directors has decided to finance this expansion programme by raising the funds from existing shareholders through a 1-for-4 rights issue. The most recent income statement of the business is as follows:

Income statement for the year ended 30 April

	£m
Sales revenue	164.5
Operating profit	12.6
Interest	(6.2)
Profit before taxation	6.4
Taxation	(1.9)
Profit for the year	4.5

A £2m ordinary dividend had been paid in respect of the year.

The share capital consists of 120 million ordinary shares with a par value of £0.50 a share. These are currently being traded on the Stock Exchange at a price/earnings ratio of 22 times and the board of directors has decided to issue the new shares at a discount of 20 per cent on the current market value.

Required:

(a) Calculate the theoretical ex-rights price of an ordinary share in Carpets Direct plc.

(b) Calculate the price at which the rights in Carpets Direct plc are likely to be traded.

(c) Identify and evaluate, at the time of the rights issue, each of the options arising from the rights issue to an investor who holds 4,000 ordinary shares before the rights announcement.

(*Hint*: To answer part (a), first calculate the earnings per share and then use this and the P/E ratio to calculate the marker value per share.)

11.3 Raphael Ltd is a small engineering business that has annual sales revenue of £2.4m, all of which is on credit. In recent years, the business has experienced credit control problems. The average collection period for trade receivables has risen to 50 days even though the stated policy of the business is for payment to be made within 30 days. In addition, 1.5 per cent of sales are written off as bad debts each year.

The business has recently been in talks with a factor, which is prepared to make an advance to the business equivalent to 80 per cent of trade receivables, based on the assumption that customers will, in future, adhere to a 30-day payment period. The interest rate for the advance will be 11 per cent a year. The trade receivables are currently financed through a bank overdraft, which has an interest rate of 12 per cent a year. The factor will take over the credit control procedures of the business and this will result in a saving to the business of £18,000 a year. However, the factor will make a charge of 2 per cent of sales revenue for this service. The use of the factoring service is expected to eliminate the bad debts incurred by the business.

Required:
Calculate the net cost of the factor agreement to the business and state whether the business should take advantage of the opportunity to factor its trade receivables.

Hint: To answer this question, compare the cost of existing trade credit policies (cost of investment in trade receivables and cost of bad debts) with the cost of using a factor (interest and other charges less the credit control savings.)

11.4 Gainsborough Fashions Ltd operates a small chain of fashion shops in North Wales. In recent months the business has been under pressure from its suppliers to reduce the average credit period taken from three months to one month. As a result, the directors have approached the bank to ask for an increase in the existing overdraft for one year to be able to comply with the suppliers' demands. The most recent financial statements of the business are as follows:

Balance sheet as at 31 May

	£	£
Non-current assets		
Property, plant and equipment		
Fixtures and fittings at cost	90,000	
Less accumulated depreciation	23,000	67,000
Motor vehicles at cost	34,000	
Less accumulated depreciation	27,000	7,000
		74,000
Current assets		
Inventories at cost		198,000
Trade receivables		3,000
		201,000
Total assets		275,000
Equity		
£1 ordinary shares		20,000
General reserve		4,000
Retained profit		17,000
		41,000
Non-current liabilities		
Borrowings – loan notes repayable in just over one year's time		40,000
Current liabilities		
Trade payables		162,000
Accrued expenses		10,000
Borrowings – bank overdraft		17,000
Taxation		5,000
		194,000
Total equity and liabilities		275,000

→

Abbreviated income statement for the year ended 31 May

	£
Sales revenue	740,000
Operating profit	38,000
Interest charges	(5,000)
Profit before taxation	33,000
Taxation	(10,000)
Profit for the year	23,000

A dividend of £23,000 was paid for the year.

Notes:
1 The loan notes are secured by personal guarantees from the directors.
2 The current overdraft bears an interest rate of 12 per cent a year.

Required:
(a) Identify and discuss the major factors that a bank would take into account before deciding whether to grant an increase in the overdraft of a business.
(b) State whether, in your opinion, the bank should grant the required increase in the overdraft for Gainsborough Fashions Ltd. You should provide reasoned arguments and supporting calculations where necessary.

11.5 Telford Engineers plc, a medium-sized Midlands manufacturer of automobile components, has decided to modernise its factory by introducing a number of robots. These will cost £20m and will reduce operating costs by £6m a year for their estimated useful life of ten years starting next year (Year 10). To finance this scheme, the business can raise £20m by issuing either

1 20 million ordinary shares at 100p; or
2 loan notes at 7 per cent interest a year with capital repayments of £3m a year commencing at the end of Year 11.

Extracts from Telford Engineers' financial statements appear below.

Summary of balance sheet at 31 December

	Year 6 £m	Year 7 £m	Year 8 £m	Year 9 £m
Non-current assets	48	51	65	64
Current assets	55	67	57	55
	103	118	122	119
Equity	48	61	61	63
Non-current liabilities	30	30	30	30
Current liabilities				
Trade payables	20	27	25	18
Short-term borrowings	5	–	6	8
	25	27	31	26
	103	118	122	119
Number of issued 25p shares	80m	80m	80m	80m
Share price	150p	200p	100p	145p

Note that the short-term borrowings consisted entirely of bank overdrafts.

Summary of income statements for years ended 31 December

	Year 6 £m	Year 7 £m	Year 8 £m	Year 9 £m
Sales revenue	152	170	110	145
Operating profit	28	40	7	15
Interest payable	(4)	(3)	(4)	(5)
Profit before taxation	24	37	3	10
Taxation	(12)	(16)	(0)	(4)
Profit for the period	12	21	3	6
Dividends paid during each year	6	8	3	4

For your answer you should assume that the tax rate for Year 10 is 30 per cent, that sales revenue and operating profit will be unchanged from Year 9 except for the £6m cost saving arising from the introduction of the robots, and that Telford Engineers will pay the same dividend per share in Year 10 as in Year 9.

Required:
(a) Prepare, for each financing arrangement, Telford Engineers' projected income statement for the year ending 31 December Year 10 and a statement of its share capital, reserves and loans on that date.
(b) Calculate Telford's projected earnings per share for Year 10 for both schemes.
(c) Which scheme would you advise the business to adopt? You should give your reasons and state what additional information you would require.

Chapter 12

Managing working capital

Introduction

In this chapter we shall consider the factors that must be taken into account when managing the working capital of a business. Each element of working capital will be identified and the major issues surrounding them will be discussed. Working capital represents a significant investment for many businesses and so its proper management and control can be vital. We saw in Chapter 10 that an investment in working capital is typically an important aspect of new investment proposals. Some useful tools in the management of working capital are financial ratios, which were considered in Chapter 6, and budgets, which we examined in Chapter 9.

Learning outcomes

When you have completed this chapter, you should be able to:

■ identify the main elements of working capital;

■ discuss the purpose of working capital and the nature of the working capital cycle;

■ explain the importance of establishing policies for the control of working capital;

■ explain the factors that have to be taken into account when managing each element of working capital.

The nature and purpose of working capital

→ Working capital is usually defined as current assets less current liabilities. The major elements of current assets are:

- inventories
- trade receivables
- cash (in hand and at bank).

The major elements of current liabilities are:

- trade payables
- bank overdrafts.

The size and composition of working capital can vary between industries. For some types of business, the investment in working capital can be substantial. For example, a manufacturing business will typically invest heavily in raw material, work in progress and finished goods, and will normally sell its goods on credit, giving rise to trade receivables. A retailer, on the other hand, will hold only one form of inventories (finished goods), and will usually sell goods for cash. Many service businesses hold no inventories. Most businesses buy goods and/or services on credit, giving rise to trade payables. Few, if any, businesses operate without a cash balance, though in some cases it is a negative one (a bank overdraft).

Working capital represents a net investment in short-term assets. These assets are continually flowing into and out of the business, and are essential for day-to-day operations. The various elements of working capital are interrelated, and can be seen as part of a short-term cycle. For a manufacturing business, the working capital cycle can be depicted as shown in Figure 12.1.

For a retailer the situation would be as in Figure 12.1 except that there would be no work in progress and the raw materials and the finished goods inventories would be the same. For a purely service business, the working capital cycle would also be similar to that depicted in Figure 12.1 except that there would be no inventories of raw materials and finished goods. There may well be work in progress, however, since many services, for example cases handled by a firm of solicitors, will take some time to complete and costs will build up before the client is billed for them.

Managing working capital

The management of working capital is an essential part of the business's short-term planning process. It is necessary for management to decide how much of each element should be held. As we shall see later in this chapter, there are costs associated with holding either too much or too little of each element. Management must be aware of these costs, which include opportunity costs, in order to manage effectively. Hence, the potential benefits must be weighed against the likely costs in an attempt to achieve the optimum investment.

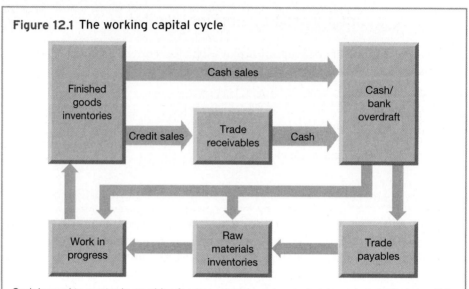

Figure 12.1 The working capital cycle

Cash is used to pay trade payables for raw materials, or raw materials are bought for immediate cash settlement. Cash is also spent on labour and other items that turn raw materials into work in progress and, finally, into finished goods. The finished goods are sold to customers either for cash or on credit. In the case of credit customers, there will be a delay before the cash is received from the sales. Receipt of cash completes the cycle.

The working capital needs of a particular business are likely to change over time as a result of changes in the business environment. This means that working capital decisions are constantly being made. Managers must try to identify changes in an attempt to ensure that the level of investment in working capital is appropriate.

Activity 12.1

What kinds of changes in the commercial environment might lead to a decision to change the level of investment in working capital? Try to identify four possible changes that could affect the working capital needs of a business.

These may include the following:

■ changes in interest rates
■ changes in market demand
■ changes in the seasons
■ changes in the state of the economy.

You may have thought of others.

In addition to changes in the external environment, changes arising within the business could alter the required level of investment in working capital. Examples of such internal changes include using different production methods (resulting, perhaps, in a need to hold less inventories) and changes in the level of risk that managers are prepared to take.

The scale of working capital

We might imagine that, compared with the scale of investment in non-current assets by the typical business, the amounts involved with working capital are pretty trivial. This would be unrealistic – the scale of the working capital elements for most businesses is vast.

Real World 12.1 gives some impression of the working capital involvement for five UK businesses that either are very well known by name or whose products are

A summary of the balance sheets of five UK businesses

Business:	Next plc	British Airways plc	Rolls-Royce plc	Tesco plc	Severn Trent plc
Balance sheet date:	28.1.07	31.3.07	31.12.06	24.2.07	31.3.07
	%	%	%	%	%
Non-current (fixed) assets	71	103	57	122	112
Current assets					
Inventories	34	1	23	12	–
Trade receivables	69	8	39	6	8
Other receivables	–	4	10	–	–
Cash and near cash	15	30	35	9	3
	118	43	107	27	11
Total assets	189	146	164	149	123
Equity and non-current liabilities	100	100	100	100	100
Current liabilities					
Trade payables	75	35	52	36	8
Taxation	10	1	3	3	1
Other short-term liabilities	–	5	3	–	–
Overdrafts and short-term loans	4	5	6	10	14
	89	46	64	49	23
Total equity and liabilities	189	146	164	149	123

The non-current assets, current assets and current liabilities are expressed as a percentage of the total net long-term investment (equity plus non-current liabilities) of the business concerned. Next is a major retail and home shopping business. British Airways (BA) is a major airline. Rolls-Royce makes aero and other engines. Tesco is one of the major UK supermarkets. Severn Trent is a major supplier of water, sewerage services and waste management, mainly in the UK.

Source: Table constructed from information appearing in the annual reports of the five businesses concerned.

everyday commodities for most of us. These businesses were randomly selected, except that each one is high-profile and from a different industry. For each business the major balance sheet items are expressed as a percentage of the total investment by the providers of long-term finance (equity and non-current liabilities).

The totals for current assets are pretty large when compared with the total long-term investment. This is particularly true of Next and Rolls-Royce. The amounts vary considerably from one type of business to the next. When we look at the nature of working capital held we can see that Next, Rolls-Royce and Tesco, which produce and/or sell goods, are the only ones that hold significant amounts of inventories. The other two businesses are service providers and so inventories are not a significant item. We can see from the table that Tesco does not sell a lot on credit and very few of BA's and Severn Trent's sales are on credit as these businesses have little invested in trade receivables. It is interesting to note that Tesco's trade payables are much higher than its inventories. Since most of these payables will be suppliers of inventories, it means that the business is able, on average, to have the cash from a particular sale in the bank before it needs to pay for the goods concerned.

These types of variation in the amounts and types of working capital elements are typical of other businesses.

In the sections that follow, we shall consider each element of working capital separately and how they might be properly managed. It seems from the evidence presented in Real World 12.2 that there is much scope for improvement in working capital management among European businesses.

Real World 12.2

Working capital not working hard enough!

According to a survey of 1,000 of Europe's largest businesses, working capital is not as well managed as it could be. The survey, conducted in 2007 by REL Consultancy Group and CFO Europe, suggests that larger European businesses have €611bn tied up in working capital that could be released through better management of inventories, trade receivables and trade payables. The potential for savings represents a total of 32 per cent of the total working capital invested (excluding automobile businesses). Although this represents an improvement on the results shown by similar surveys undertaken by REL and CFO Europe over each of the previous five years, it seems that reductions in the holding of inventories and receivables were partially offset by a reduction in trade payables, which increased working capital needs.

The total investment in each element of working capital, along with the estimated excess investment in each element, for the top 1,000 European countries is shown in Figure 12.2.

The figure shows that inventories are the working capital element that has potential for most improvement.

Source: 'US and European companies leave billions of dollars, euros untapped in working capital', www.relconsultancy.com 29 August 2007, p. 4. (The survey referred to is the 2007 *Annual Working Capital Survey*, conducted by REL and CFO Europe.)

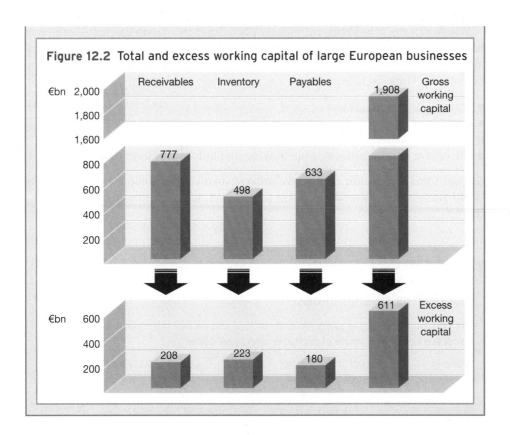

Figure 12.2 Total and excess working capital of large European businesses

Managing inventories

A business may hold inventories for various reasons, the most common of which is to meet the immediate day-to-day requirements of customers and production. However, a business may hold more than is necessary for this purpose if it is believed that future supplies may be interrupted or scarce. Similarly, if the business believes that the cost of inventories will rise in the future, it may decide to stockpile.

For some types of business the inventories held may represent a substantial proportion of the total assets held. For example, a car dealership that rents its premises may have nearly all of its total assets in the form of inventories. Inventories levels of manufacturers tend to be higher than in many other types of business as it is necessary to hold three kinds of inventories: raw materials, work in progress and finished goods. Each form of inventories represents a particular stage in the production cycle. For some types of business, the level of inventories held may vary substantially over the year owing to the seasonal nature of the industry. An example of such a business is a greetings card manufacturer. For other businesses, inventories levels may remain fairly stable throughout the year.

Where a business holds inventories simply to meet the day-to-day requirements of its customers and for production, it will normally seek to minimise the amount of inventories held. This is because there are significant costs associated with holding inventories. These include

- storage and handling costs
- financing costs
- the costs of pilferage and obsolescence
- the cost of opportunities forgone in tying up funds in this form of asset.

To gain some impression of the level of cost involved in holding inventories Real World 12.3 estimates the *financing* cost for four well-known businesses.

Real World 12.3

Inventories financing cost

The cost of holding inventories for each of four well-known businesses, based on their respective opportunity costs of capital, is calculated below.

Business	Type of operations	Cost of capital (a)	Average inventories held* (b)	Cost of holding inventories (a × b)	Profit before tax	Cost as percentage of profit before tax
		%	£m	£m	£m	%
Rolls-Royce	Engineering	12.75	1,378	176	1,391	12.7
Pearson	Media	7.7	364	28	466	6.0
Carphone Warehouse	Mobile phone retailer	6.8	150	10.2	68	15.0
Scottish & Newcastle	Brewer	7.0	223	16.0	222	7.0

* Based on opening and closing inventories for the relevant year.

We can see that for Rolls-Royce and Carphone Warehouse, inventories financing costs are significant in relation to the profits generated. These figures do not take account of other costs of inventories holding mentioned above, such as the cost of providing a secure store for the inventories. Clearly, the efficient management of inventories is an important issue for many businesses.

Source: Annual reports of the companies cited for 2005/2006 or 2006/7.

As we have just seen, the cost of holding inventories can be very large. A business must also recognise, however, that, if the level of inventories held is too low, there will also be associated costs.

Activity 12.2

What costs might a business incur as a result of holding too low a level of inventories? Try to jot down at least three types of cost.

In answering this activity you may have thought of the following costs:

- loss of sales, from being unable to provide the goods required immediately;
- loss of customer goodwill, for being unable to satisfy customer demand;
- high transport costs incurred to ensure that inventories are replenished quickly;
- lost production due to shortages of raw materials;
- inefficient production scheduling due to shortages of raw materials;
- purchasing inventories at a higher price than might otherwise have been possible in order to replenish inventories quickly.

Before we go on to deal with the various approaches that can be taken to managing inventories, Real World 12.4 provides an example of how badly things can go wrong if inventories are not adequately controlled.

Real World 12.4

Pallets lost at Brambles

Brambles Industries plc (BI) is an Anglo-Australian industrial services business, formed in 2001 when the industrial services subsidiary of GKN plc, the UK engineering business, was merged with the Australian business Brambles Ltd.

BI uses 'pallets' on which it delivers its products to customers. These are returnable by customers so BI holds a 'pool' of pallets. Each pallet costs the business about £10. Unfortunately, BI lost 14 million pallets during the year ended in June 2002 as a result of poor control and this led to a significant decline in the business's profits and share price.

At BI's annual general meeting in Sydney, Australia, one of the shareholders was quoted as saying: 'Running a pallet pool is not rocket science. I can teach one of my employees about pallets in 20 minutes.'

Source: Information taken from an article appearing in the *Financial Times*, 27 November 2002.

To try to ensure that the inventories are properly managed, a number of procedures and techniques may be used. These are reviewed below.

Budgeting future demand

One of the best ways to ensure that there will be inventories available to meet future production and sales requirements is to make appropriate plans. The budgets should deal with each product that the business makes and/or sells. It is important that every

attempt is made to ensure that plans are realistic, as they will determine future ordering and production levels.

The budgets may be derived in various ways. They may be developed using statistical techniques such as time series analysis, or they may be based on the judgement
of the sales and marketing staff. We considered inventories budgets and their link to
production and sales budgets in Chapter 9.

Financial ratios

One ratio that can be used to help monitor inventories levels is the average inventories turnover period, which we examined in Chapter 6. As we should recall, this
ratio is calculated as follows:

$$\text{Average inventories turnover period} = \frac{\text{Average inventories held}}{\text{Cost of sales}} \times 365$$

This will provide a picture of the average period for which inventories are held, and
can be useful as a basis for comparison. It is possible to calculate the average inventories turnover period for individual product lines as well as for inventories as a whole.

Recording and reordering systems

The management of inventories in a business of any size requires a sound system of
recording inventories movements. There must be proper procedures for recording
inventories purchases and usages. Periodic inventories checks may be required to
ensure that the amount of physical inventories held is consistent with what is indicated by the inventories records.

There should also be clear procedures for the reordering of inventories.
Authorisation for both the purchase and the issue of inventories should be confined to a few senior staff. This should avoid problems of duplication and lack of
co-ordination. To determine the point at which inventories should be reordered,
 information will be required concerning the lead time (that is, the time between the
placing of an order and the receipt of the goods) and the likely level of demand.

Activity 12.3

An electrical retailer stocks a particular type of light switch. The annual demand for the
light switch is 10,400 units, and the lead time for orders is four weeks. Demand for the
light switch is steady throughout the year. At what quantity of the light switch should
the business reorder, assuming that it is confident of the information given above?

The average weekly demand for the switch is 10,400/52 = 200 units. During the time
between ordering new switches and receiving them, the quantity sold will be 4 × 200 units
= 800 units. So the business should reorder no later than when the level held reaches 800
units, in order to avoid running out of inventories.

In most businesses, there will be some uncertainty surrounding the above factors and so a buffer or safety inventories level may be maintained in case problems occur. The amount of the buffer to be held is really a matter of judgement. This judgement will depend on

- the degree of uncertainty concerning the above factors;
- the likely costs of running out of the item concerned;
- the cost of holding the buffer inventories.

The effect of holding a buffer will be to raise the inventories level (the reorder point) at which an order for new inventories is placed.

Activity 12.4

Assume the same facts as in Activity 12.3. However, we are also told that the business maintains buffer inventories of 300 units. At what level should the business reorder?

Reorder point = expected level of demand during the lead time plus the level of
buffer inventories
= 800 + 300
= 1,100 units

Carrying buffer inventories will increase the cost of holding inventories; however, this must be weighed against the cost of running out of inventories, in terms of lost sales, production problems and so on.

Real World 12.5 provides an example of how small businesses can use technology in inventories reordering to help compete against their larger rivals.

Real World 12.5

Taking on the big boys

The use of technology in inventories recording and reordering may be of vital importance to the survival of small businesses that are being threatened by larger rivals. One such example is that of small independent bookshops. Technology can come to their rescue in two ways. First, electronic point-of-sale (EPOS) systems can record books as they are sold and can constantly update records of inventories held. Thus, books that need to be reordered can be quickly and easily identified. Second, the reordering process can be improved by using web-based technology, which allows books to be ordered in real time. Many large book wholesalers provide free web-based software to their customers for this purpose and try to deliver books ordered during the next working day. This means that a small bookseller, with limited shelf space, may keep one copy only of a particular book but maintain a range of books that competes with that of a large bookseller.

Source: Information taken from 'Small stores keep up with the big boys', *Financial Times*, 5 February 2003, ft.com.

Levels of control

Senior managers must make a commitment to the management of inventories. However, the cost of controlling inventories must be weighed against the potential benefits. It may be possible to have different levels of control according to the nature of the inventories held. The ABC system of inventories control is based on the idea of selective levels of control.

A business may find that it is possible to divide its inventories into three broad categories: A, B and C. Each category will be based on the value of inventories held, as is illustrated in Example 12.1.

Example 12.1

Alascan Products plc makes door handles and door fittings. It makes them in brass, in steel and in plastic. The business finds that brass fittings account for 10 per cent of the physical volume of the finished inventories that it holds, but these represent 65 per cent of its total value. They are treated as Category A inventories. There are sophisticated recording procedures, tight control is exerted over inventories movements and there is a high level of security where the brass inventories are stored. This is economic because the inventories represent a relatively small proportion of the total volume.

The business finds that steel fittings account for 30 per cent of the total volume of finished inventories and represent 25 per cent of its total value. They are treated as Category B inventories, with a lower level of recording and management control being applied.

The remaining 60 per cent of the volume of inventories is plastic fittings, which represent the least valuable items and account for only 10 per cent of the total value of finished inventories held. They are treated as Category C inventories, so the level of recording and management control is lower still. Applying to these inventories the level of control that is applied to Category A or even Category B inventories would be uneconomic.

Categorising inventories in this way seeks to direct management effort to the most important areas, and tries to ensure that the costs of controlling inventories are appropriate to its importance.

Figure 12.3 shows the nature of the ABC approach to inventories control.

Inventories management models

Economic order quantity

It is possible to use decision models to help manage inventories. The economic order quantity (EOQ) model is concerned with answering the question 'How much

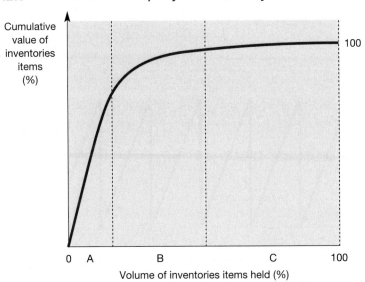

Figure 12.3 ABC method of analysing and controlling inventories

Category A contains inventories that, though relatively few in quantity, account for a large proportion of the total value. Category B consists of those items that are less valuable but more numerous. Category C comprises those items that are very numerous but relatively low in value. Different control rules would be applied to each category. For example, only Category A inventories would attract the more expensive and sophisticated controls.

inventories should be ordered?' In its simplest form, the EOQ model assumes that demand is constant, so that inventories will be depleted evenly over time, and replenished just at the point when they run out. These assumptions would lead to a 'saw-tooth' pattern, as shown in Figure 12.4.

The EOQ model recognises that the key costs associated with inventories management are the cost of holding the inventories and the cost of ordering them. The model can be used to calculate the optimum size of a purchase order by taking account of both of these cost elements. The cost of holding inventories can be substantial, and so management may try to minimise the average amount of inventories held. However, if the level of inventories held, and therefore the holding costs, are reduced, there will be a need to increase the number of orders during the period, and so ordering costs will rise.

Figure 12.5 shows how, as the level of inventories and the size of inventories orders increase, the annual costs of placing orders will decrease because fewer orders will be placed. However, the cost of holding inventories will increase, as there will be higher average inventories levels. The total costs curve, which is based on the sum of holding costs and ordering costs, will fall until point E, which represents the minimum total cost. Thereafter, total costs begin to rise. The EOQ model seeks to identify point

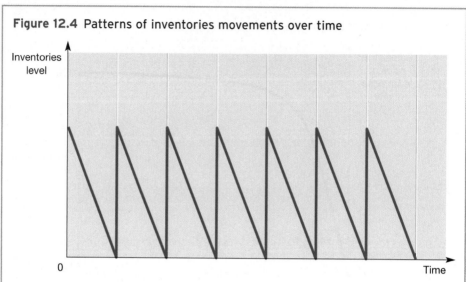

Figure 12.4 Patterns of inventories movements over time

Here we assume that there is a constant rate of usage of the inventories item, and that inventories are reduced to zero just as new inventories arrive. At time 0 there is a full level of inventories. This is steadily used as time passes; and just as it falls to zero it is replaced. This pattern is then repeated.

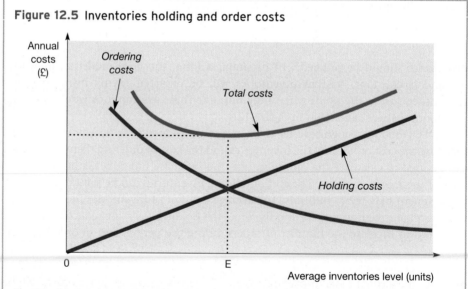

Figure 12.5 Inventories holding and order costs

Small levels of inventories imply frequent reordering and high annual ordering costs. Small levels also imply relatively low holding costs. High levels of inventories imply exactly the opposite. There is, in theory, an optimum order size that will lead to the sum of ordering and holding costs (total costs) being at a minimum.

E at which total costs are minimised. This will represent half of the optimum amount that should be ordered on each occasion. Assuming, as we are doing, that inventories are used evenly over time and that they fall to zero before being replaced, the average inventories level equals half of the order size.

The EOQ model, which can be used to derive the most economic order quantity, is

$$EOQ = \sqrt{\frac{2DC}{H}}$$

where D is the annual demand for the inventories item (expressed in units of the inventories item), C is the cost of placing an order, and H is the cost of holding one unit of inventories for one year.

Activity 12.5

HLA Ltd sells 2,000 bags of cement each year. It has been estimated that the cost of holding one bag of cement for a year is £4. The cost of placing an order for new inventories is estimated at £250.

Calculate the EOQ for bags of cement.

Your answer to this activity should be as follows:

$$EOQ = \sqrt{\frac{2 \times 2,000 \times 250}{4}} = 500 \text{ bags}$$

This will mean that the business will have to order bags of cement four times each year (2,000/500) in batches of 500 bags so that sales demand can be met.

Note that the cost of the inventories concerned, which is the price paid to the supplier, does not directly impact on the EOQ model. The EOQ model is concerned only with the administrative costs of placing each order and the costs of looking after the inventories. Where the business operates an ABC system of inventories control, however, more expensive inventories items will have greater holding costs. For example, Category A inventories would tend to have a lower EOQ than Category B ones. So the cost of the inventories may have an indirect effect on the economic order size that the model recommends.

The basic EOQ model has a number of limiting assumptions. In particular, it assumes that

■ demand for the particular inventories item can be predicted with accuracy;
■ demand is constant over the period and does not fluctuate through seasonality or for other reasons;
■ no 'buffer' inventories are required;
■ there are no discounts for bulk purchasing.

However, the model can be developed to overcome each of these limiting assumptions. Many businesses use this model (or a development of it) to help in the management of inventories.

Materials requirement planning systems

→ A materials requirement planning (MRP) system takes planned sales demand as its starting point. It then uses a computer package to help schedule the timing of deliveries of bought-in parts and materials to coincide with production requirements. It is a co-ordinated approach that links materials and parts deliveries to the scheduled time of their input to the production process. By ordering only those items that are necessary to ensure the flow of production, inventories levels are likely to be reduced. MRP is really a 'top-down' approach to inventories management, which recognises that inventories ordering decisions cannot be viewed as being independent of production decisions. In recent years, this approach has been extended to provide a fully integrated approach to production planning. The approach also takes account of other manufacturing resources such as labour and machine capacity.

Just-in-time inventories management

→ In recent years, many businesses have tried to eliminate the need to hold inventories by adopting just-in-time (JIT) inventories management. This approach was first used in the US defence industry during the Second World War, but was first used on a wide scale by Japanese manufacturing businesses. The essence of JIT is, as the name suggests, to have supplies delivered to the business just in time for them to be used in the production process or in a sale. By adopting this approach the inventories holding costs rest with suppliers rather than with the business itself. On the other hand, a failure by a particular supplier to deliver on time could cause enormous problems and costs to the business. Thus JIT can save cost, but it tends to increase risk.

For JIT to be successful, it is important that the business informs suppliers of its inventories requirements in advance, and that suppliers, in their turn, deliver materials of the right quality at the agreed times. Failure to do so could lead to a dislocation of production or supply to customers and could be very costly. Thus a close relationship is required between the business and its suppliers.

This close relationship enables suppliers to schedule their own production to that of their customers. This should mean that between supplier and customer there will be a net saving in the amount of inventories that need to be held, relative to what would apply were JIT not in operation.

Although a business that applies JIT will not have to hold inventories, there may be other costs associated with this approach. As the suppliers may need to hold inventories for the customer, they may try to recoup this additional cost through increased prices. On the other hand, the close relationship between customer and supplier should enable the supplier to predict its customers' needs for inventories. This means that suppliers can tailor their own production to that of the customer. The close relationship necessary between the business and its suppliers may also prevent the business from taking advantage of cheaper sources of supply if they become available.

Many people view JIT as more than simply an inventories control system. The philosophy underpinning this approach is concerned with eliminating waste and striving for excellence. There is an expectation that suppliers will always deliver inventories on time and that there will be no defects in the items supplied. There is also an expectation that, for manufacturers, the production process will operate at maximum efficiency. This means there will be no production breakdowns and the queuing and storage times of products manufactured will be eliminated, as only that time spent directly on processing the products is seen as adding value. While these expectations may be impossible to achieve, they do help to create a culture that is dedicated to the pursuit of excellence and quality.

Real World 12.6 and Real World 12.7 show how two very well-known businesses operating in the UK (one a retailer, the other a manufacturer) use JIT to advantage.

Real World 12.6

JIT at Boots

The Boots Company plc, the UK's largest healthcare retailer, has improved inventories management at its stores. The business is working towards a JIT system where a delivery from its one central warehouse in Nottingham will be made every day to each retail branch, with nearly all of the inventories lines being placed directly on to the sales shelves, not into a branch inventories store room. The business says that this will bring significant savings of stores staff time and lead to significantly lower levels of inventories being held, without any lessening of the service offered to customers. The new system is expected to lead to major economic benefits for the business.

Source: Information taken from The Boots Company plc Annual Report and Accounts 2005.

Real World 12.7

JIT at Nissan

Nissan Motors UK Limited, the UK manufacturing arm of the world famous Japanese car business, has a plant in Sunderland in the northeast of England. Here it operates a well-developed JIT system.

Sommer supplies carpets and soft interior trim from a factory close to the Nissan plant. It makes deliveries to Nissan once every 20 minutes on average, so as to arrive exactly as they are needed in production. This is fairly typical of all of the 200 suppliers of components and materials to the Nissan plant.

Source: Information taken from Partnership Sourcing Best Practice Case Study, PSL, 2001.

Managing receivables

Selling goods or services on credit will result in costs being incurred by a business. These costs include credit administration costs, bad debts, and opportunities forgone to use the funds for more profitable purposes. However, these costs must be weighed against the benefits of increased sales resulting from the opportunity for customers to delay payment.

Selling on credit is very widespread and is the norm outside the retail industry. When a business offers to sell its goods or services on credit, it must have clear policies concerning

- which customers should receive credit;
- how much credit should be offered;
- what length of credit it is prepared to offer;
- whether discounts will be offered for prompt payment;
- what collection policies should be adopted;
- how the risk of non-payment can be reduced.

In this section, we shall consider each of these issues.

Which customers should receive credit and how much should they be offered?

A business offering credit runs the risk of not receiving payment for goods or services supplied. Thus, care must be taken over the type of customer to whom credit facilities are offered and how much credit is allowed. When considering a proposal from a customer for the supply of goods or services on credit, the business must take a number of factors into account. The following five Cs of credit provide a business with a useful checklist.

- *Capital.* The customer must appear to be financially sound before any credit is extended. Where the customer is a business, its financial statements should be examined. Particular regard should be given to the customer's likely future profitability and liquidity. In addition, any major financial commitments (for example, capital expenditure, contracts with suppliers) must be taken into account.
- *Capacity.* The customer must appear to have the capacity to pay amounts owing. Where possible, the payment record of the customer to date should be examined. If the customer is a business, the type of business operated and the physical resources of the business will be relevant. The value of goods that the customer wishes to buy on credit must be related to the customer's total financial resources.
- *Collateral.* On occasions, it may be necessary to ask for some kind of security for goods supplied on credit. When this occurs, the business must be convinced that the customer is able to offer a satisfactory form of security.
- *Conditions.* The state of the industry in which the customer operates, and the general economic conditions of the particular region or country, may have an important influence on the ability of a customer to pay the amounts outstanding on the due date.
- *Character.* It is important for a business to make some assessment of the customer's character. The willingness to pay will depend on the honesty and integrity of the individual with whom the business is dealing. Where the customer is a limited company this will mean assessing the characters of its directors. The business must feel satisfied that the customer will make every effort to pay any amounts owing.

It is clear from the above that the business will need to gather information concerning the ability and willingness of the customer to pay the amounts owing at the due dates.

Activity 12.6

Assume that you are the credit manager of a business and that a limited company approaches you with a view to buying goods on credit. What sources of information might you decide to use to help assess the financial health of the potential customer?

There are various possibilities. You may have thought of some of the following:

- *Trade references*. Some businesses ask potential customers to supply them with references from other suppliers who have made sales on credit to them. This may be extremely useful provided that the references supplied are truly representative of the opinions of a customer's suppliers. There is a danger that a potential customer will be selective when giving details of other suppliers, in an attempt to create a more favourable impression than is deserved.
- *Bank references*. It is possible to ask the potential customer for a bank reference. Although banks are usually prepared to supply references, the contents of such references are not always very informative. If customers are in financial difficulties, the bank may be unwilling to add to their problems by supplying poor references. It is worth remembering that the bank's loyalty is likely to be with the customer rather than the enquirer. The bank will usually charge a fee for providing a reference.
- *Published financial statements*. A limited company is obliged by law to file a copy of its annual financial statements with the Registrar of Companies. These financial statements are available for public inspection and provide a useful source of information. Apart from the information contained in the financial statements, company law requires public limited companies to state in the directors' report the average time taken to pay suppliers. The annual reports of many companies are available on their own websites or on computer-based information systems (for example, FAME).
- *The customer*. Interviews with the directors of the customer business and visits to its premises may be carried out to gain an impression of the way that the customer conducts its business. Where a significant amount of credit is required, the business may ask the customer for access to internal budgets and other unpublished financial information to help assess the level of risk involved.
- *Credit agencies*. Specialist agencies exist to provide information that can be used to assess the creditworthiness of a potential customer. The information that a credit agency supplies may be gleaned from various sources, including the financial statements of the customer and news items relating to the customer from both published and unpublished sources. The credit agencies may also provide a credit rating for the business. Agencies will charge a fee for their services.
- *Register of County Court Judgments*. Any money judgments given against the business or an individual in a county court will be maintained on the register for six years. This register is available for inspection by any member of the public for a small fee.
- *Other suppliers*. Similar businesses will often be prepared to exchange information concerning slow payers or defaulting customers through an industry credit circle. This can be a reliable and relatively cheap way of obtaining information.

Length of credit period

A business must determine what credit terms it is prepared to offer its customers. The length of credit offered to customers can vary significantly between businesses, and may be influenced by such factors as

- the typical credit terms operating within the industry;
- the degree of competition within the industry;
- the bargaining power of particular customers;
- the risk of non-payment;
- the capacity of the business to offer credit;
- the marketing strategy of the business.

The last point identified may require some explanation. If, for example, a business wishes to increase its market share, it may decide to be more generous in its credit policy in an attempt to stimulate sales. Potential customers may be attracted by the offer of a longer credit period. However, any such change in policy must take account of the likely costs and benefits arising.

To illustrate this point, consider Example 12.2.

Example 12.2

Torrance Ltd produces a new type of golf putter. The business sells the putter to wholesalers and retailers and has an annual turnover of £600,000. The following data relate to each putter produced.

	£
Selling price	40
Variable costs	(20)
Fixed cost apportionment	(6)
Profit	14

The business's cost of capital is estimated at 10 per cent a year.

Torrance Ltd wishes to expand the sales volume of the new putter. It believes that offering a longer credit period can achieve this. The business's average receivables collection period is currently 30 days. It is considering three options in an attempt to increase sales revenue. These are as follows:

	Option 1	Option 2	Option 3
Increase in average collection period (days)	10	20	30
Increase in sales revenue (£)	30,000	45,000	50,000

To enable the business to decide on the best option to adopt, it must weigh the benefits of the options against their respective costs. The benefits arising will be represented by the increase in profit from the sale of additional putters. From the cost data supplied we can see that the contribution (that is, selling price (£40) less variable costs (£20)) is £20 a putter, that is, 50 per cent of the selling price. So, whatever increase there may be in sales revenue, the additional contributions will be half of that figure. The fixed costs can be ignored in our calculations, as they will remain the same whichever option is chosen.

The increase in contribution under each option will therefore be:

	Option 1	Option 2	Option 3
50% of the increase in sales revenue (£)	15,000	22,500	25,000

The increase in trade receivables under each option will be as follows:

	Option 1 £	Option 2 £	Option 3 £
Projected level of trade receivables			
40 × £630,000/365 (Note 1)	69,041		
50 × £645,000/365		88,356	
60 × £650,000/365			106,849
Current level of trade receivables			
30 × £600,000/365	(49,315)	(49,315)	(49,315)
Increase in trade receivables	19,726	39,041	57,534

The increase in receivables that results from each option will mean an additional finance cost to the business.

The net increase in the business's profit arising from the projected change is:

	Option 1 £	Option 2 £	Option 3 £
Increase in contribution (see above)	15,000	22,500	25,000
Increase in finance cost (Note 2)	(1,973)	(3,904)	(5,753)
Net increase in profits	13,027	18,596	19,247

The calculations show that Option 3 will be the most profitable one.

Notes:
1 If the annual sales revenue total £630,000 and 40 days' credit are allowed (both of which will apply under Option 1), the average amount that will be owed to the business by its customers, at any point during the year, will be the daily sales revenue (that is, £630,000/365) multiplied by the number of days that the customers take to pay (that is 40).

Exactly the same logic applies to Options 2 and 3 and to the current level of trade receivables.

2 The increase in the finance cost for Option 1 will be the increase in trade receivables (£19,726) × 10 per cent. The equivalent figures for the other options are derived in a similar way.

Example 12.2 illustrates the way in which a business should assess changes in credit terms. However, if there is a risk that, by extending the length of credit, there will be an increase in bad debts, this should also be taken into account in the calculations, as should any additional trade receivable collection costs that will be incurred.

Real World 12.8 shows how the length of credit taken by some larger UK businesses leads to problems for smaller businesses.

Real World 12.8

Credit where it's due

Late payment to small companies has got progressively worse over the past three years and they need to employ stricter credit management techniques, a survey released today claims.

Siemens Financial Services, a subsidiary of Siemens, the German engineering group, studied the accounts of thousands of UK companies. It found that smaller firms had to wait for 80 days to get paid by customers in 2006, compared with 69 days in 2004.

In contrast, medium-size and large companies have seen their 'days sales outstanding' hold steady over the period at 62 days and 47 days respectively.

Rod Tonna-Barthet, sales director at SFS, said the results showed that 'small firms are suffering' as a result of medium-size and large companies using competitive pressures to extend payment terms.

Source: 'Late payment hits small companies', J. Chisholm, 29 January 2007, ft.com.

An alternative approach to evaluating the credit decision

It is possible to view the credit decision as a capital investment decision. Granting trade credit involves an outlay of resources in the form of cash (which has been temporarily forgone) in the expectation that future cash flows will be increased (through higher sales) as a result. A business will usually have choices concerning the level of investment to be made in trade credit and the period over which it is granted. These choices will result in different returns and different levels of risk. There is no reason in principle why the NPV investment appraisal method, which we considered in Chapter 10, should not be used to evaluate these choices. We have seen that the NPV method takes into account both the time value of money and the level of risk involved.

Approaching the problem as an NPV assessment is not different in principle from the way that we dealt with the decision in Example 12.2. In both approaches the time value of money is considered, but in Example 12.2 we did it by charging interest on the outstanding trade receivables.

Cash discounts

 A business may decide to offer a cash discount (or discount for prompt payment) in an attempt to encourage prompt payment from its credit customers. The size of any discount will be an important influence on whether a customer decides to pay promptly.

From the business's viewpoint, the cost of offering discounts must be weighed against the likely benefits in the form of a reduction both in the cost of financing receivables and in the amount of bad debts.

In practice, there is always the danger that a customer may be slow to pay and yet may still take the discount offered. Where the customer is important to the business it may be difficult to insist on full payment. An alternative to allowing the customer to take discounts by reducing payment is to agree in advance to provide discounts for prompt payment through quarterly credit notes. As credit notes will be given only for those debts paid on time, the customer will often make an effort to qualify for the discount.

? Self-assessment question 12.1

Williams Wholesalers Ltd at present requires payment from its customers by the end of the month after the month of delivery. On average, customers take 70 days to pay. Sales revenue amounts to £4m a year and bad debts to £20,000 a year.

It is planned to offer customers a cash discount of 2 per cent for payment within 30 days. Williams estimates that 50 per cent of customers will accept this facility but that the remaining customers, who tend to be slow payers, will not pay until 80 days after the sale. At present the business has an overdraft facility at an interest rate of 13 per cent a year. If the plan goes ahead, bad debts will be reduced to £10,000 a year and there will be savings in credit administration expenses of £6,000 a year.

Required:
Should Williams Wholesalers Ltd offer the new credit terms to customers? You should support your answer with any calculations and explanations that you consider necessary.

The answer to this question can be found at the back of the book in Appendix B.

Debt factoring and invoice discounting

We saw in Chapter 11 (pages 424–6) that trade receivables can, in effect, be turned into cash by either factoring them or having sales invoices discounted. These both seem to be fairly popular approaches to managing trade receivables.

Collection policies and reducing the risk of non-payment

A business offering credit must ensure that amounts owing are collected as quickly as possible so that the risk of non-payment is minimised. Various steps can be taken to achieve this, including the following:

Develop customer relationships

For major customers it is often useful to cultivate a relationship with the key staff responsible for paying sales invoices. By so doing, the chances of prompt payment may be increased. For less important customers, the business should at least identify key staff responsible for paying invoices, who can be contacted in the event of a payment problem.

Publicise credit terms

The credit terms of the business should be made clear in all relevant correspondence, such as order acknowledgements, invoices and statements. In early negotiations with the prospective customer, credit terms should be openly discussed and an agreement reached.

Issue invoices promptly

An efficient collection policy requires an efficient accounting system. Invoices (bills) must be sent out promptly to customers, as must monthly statements. Reminders must also be dispatched promptly to customers who are late in paying. If a customer fails to respond to a reminder, the accounting system should alert managers so that a stop can be placed on further deliveries.

Monitor outstanding trade receivables

Management can monitor the effectiveness of collection policies in a number of ways. One method is to calculate the average settlement period for trade receivables ratio, which we met in Chapter 6. This ratio, we should recall, is calculated as follows:

$$\text{Average settlement period for trade receivables} = \frac{\text{Average trade receivables}}{\text{Credit sales revenue}} \times 365$$

Although this ratio can be useful, it is important to remember that it produces an *average* figure for the number of days for which trade receivables are outstanding. This average may be badly distorted by a few large customers who are very slow or very fast payers.

Produce an ageing schedule of trade receivables

A more detailed and informative approach to monitoring receivables may be to produce an ageing schedule of trade receivables. Receivables are divided into categories according to the length of time they have been outstanding. An ageing schedule can be produced, on a regular basis, to help managers see the pattern of outstanding receivables. An example of an ageing schedule is set out in Example 12.3.

Example 12.3

Ageing schedule of trade receivables at 31 December

Customer	1 to 30 days £	31 to 60 days £	61 to 90 days £	More than 90 days £	Total £
A Ltd	20,000	10,000	–	–	30,000
B Ltd	–	24,000	–	–	24,000
C Ltd	12,000	13,000	14,000	18,000	57,000
Total	32,000	47,000	14,000	18,000	111,000

Days outstanding

This shows a business's trade receivables figure at 31 December, which totals £111,000. Each customer's balance is analysed according to how long the amount has been outstanding. (This business has just three credit customers.)

Thus we can see from the schedule that A Ltd has £20,000 outstanding for 30 days or fewer (that is, arising from sales during December) and £10,000 outstanding for between 31 and 60 days (arising from November sales). This information can be very useful for credit control purposes.

Many accounting software packages now include this ageing schedule as one of the routine reports available to managers. Such packages often have the facility to put customers 'on hold' when they reach their credit limits. Putting a customer on hold means that no further credit sales will be made to that customer until amounts owing from past sales have been settled.

Answer queries quickly

It is important for relevant staff to deal with customer queries on goods and services supplied quickly and efficiently. Payment is unlikely to be made by customers until their queries have been dealt with.

Deal with slow payers

It is almost inevitably the case that a business making significant sales on credit will be faced with customers who do not pay. When this occurs, there should be agreed procedures for dealing with the situation. However, the cost of any action to be taken against delinquent credit customers must be weighed against the likely returns. For example, there is little point in taking legal action against a customer, incurring large legal expenses, if there is evidence that the customer does not have the necessary resources to pay. Where possible, an estimate of the cost of bad debts should be taken into account when setting prices for products or services.

Real World 12.9 shows that businesses are not always as efficient as they might be with their management of trade receivables.

Real World 12.9

Would you credit it?

According to a 2006 survey of more than 6,500 UK businesses, 44 per cent of businesses leave it a fortnight, or longer, after the due date for payment before sending reminders to their credit customers, while 13 per cent leave it for longer than a month. In other words, many businesses are very slow to react to their customers failing to pay on time.

Intrim Justia UK, who conducted the survey, said: 'A clear credit policy, consistent checks on overdue payments and robust credit management systems are just some of the critical measures that businesses need to adopt.'

Source: Information taken from 'Late reminders lead to late payments', Jonathan Moules, *Financial Times*, 7 January 2006.

As a footnote to our consideration of managing receivables, Real World 12.10 outlines some of the excuses that long-suffering credit managers must listen to when chasing payment for outstanding debt.

It's in the post

Accountants' noses should be growing, if we're to believe a new survey listing the bizarre excuses given by businesses that fail to pay their debts.

'The director's been shot' and 'I'll pay you when God tells me to' are just two of the most outrageous excuses listed in a survey published by the Credit Services Association, the debt collection industry body.

The commercial sector tends to blame financial problems, and excuses such as 'you'll get paid when we do' and 'the finance director is off sick' are common. However, those in the consumer sector apparently feel no shame in citing personal relationship problems as the reason for not paying the bill.

Source: Accountancy, April 2000, p. 18.

Managing cash

Why hold cash?

Most businesses hold a certain amount of cash. The amount of cash held tends to vary considerably between businesses.

Why do you think a business may decide to hold at least some of its assets in the form of cash? (*Hint*: There are broadly three reasons.)

The three reasons are:

1   To meet day-to-day commitments, a business requires a certain amount of cash. Payments for wages, overhead expenses, goods purchased and so on must be made at the due dates. Cash has been described as the lifeblood of a business. Unless it circulates through the business and is available for the payment of claims as they become due, the survival of the business will be at risk. Profitability is not enough; a business must have sufficient cash to pay its debts when they fall due.

2   If future cash flows are uncertain for any reason, it would be prudent to hold a balance of cash. For example, a major customer that owes a large sum to the business may be in financial difficulties. Given this situation, the business can retain its capacity to meet its obligations by holding a cash balance. Similarly, if there is some uncertainty concerning future outlays, a cash balance will be required.

3   A business may decide to hold cash to put itself in a position to exploit profitable opportunities as and when they arise. For example, by holding cash, a business may be able to acquire a competitor's business that suddenly becomes available at an attractive price.

How much cash should be held?

Although cash can be held for each of the reasons identified, doing so may not always be necessary. If a business is able to borrow quickly, the amount of cash it needs to hold can be reduced. Similarly, if the business holds assets that can easily be converted to cash (for example, marketable securities such as shares in Stock Exchange listed businesses or government bonds), the amount of cash held can be reduced.

The decision as to how much cash a particular business should hold is a difficult one. Different businesses will have different views on the subject.

Activity 12.8

What do you think are the major factors that influence how much cash a business will hold? See if you can think of five possible factors.

You may have thought of the following:

- *The nature of the business*. Some businesses, such as utilities (for example, water, electricity and gas suppliers), may have cash flows that are both predictable and reasonably certain. This will enable them to hold lower cash balances. For some businesses, cash balances may vary greatly according to the time of year. A seasonal business may accumulate cash during the high season to enable it to meet commitments during the low season.
- *The opportunity cost of holding cash*. Where there are profitable opportunities it may not be wise to hold a large cash balance.
- *The level of inflation*. Holding cash during a period of rising prices will lead to a loss of purchasing power. The higher the level of inflation, the greater will be this loss.
- *The availability of near-liquid assets*. If a business has marketable securities or inventories that may easily be liquidated, high cash balances may not be necessary.
- *The availability of borrowing*. If a business can borrow easily (and quickly) there is less need to hold cash.
- *The cost of borrowing*. When interest rates are high, the option of borrowing becomes less attractive.
- *Economic conditions*. When the economy is in recession, businesses may prefer to hold cash so that they can be well placed to invest when the economy improves. In addition, during a recession, businesses may experience difficulties in collecting trade receivables. They may therefore hold higher cash balances than usual in order to meet commitments.
- *Relationships with suppliers*. Too little cash may hinder the ability of the business to pay suppliers promptly. This can lead to a loss of goodwill. It may also lead to discounts being forgone.

Controlling the cash balance

Several models have been developed to help control the cash balance of the business. One such model proposes the use of upper and lower control limits for cash balances and the use of a target cash balance. The model assumes that the business will invest in marketable investments that can easily be liquidated. These investments will be purchased or sold, as necessary, in order to keep the cash balance within the control limits.

The model proposes two upper and two lower control limits (see Figure 12.6). If the business exceeds an *outer* limit, the managers must decide whether the cash balance is likely to return to a point within the *inner* control limits set, over the next few days. If this seems likely, then no action is required. If, on the other hand, it does not seem likely, management must change the cash position of the business by either lending or borrowing (or possibly by buying or selling marketable securities).

In Figure 12.6 we can see that the lower outer control limit has been breached for four days. If a four-day period is unacceptable, managers must sell marketable securities to replenish the cash balance.

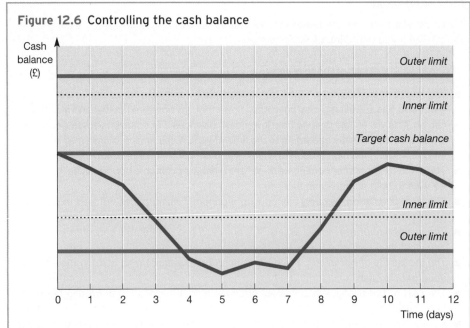

Figure 12.6 Controlling the cash balance

Management sets the upper and lower limits for the business's cash balance. When the balance goes beyond either of these limits, unless it is clear that the balance will return fairly quickly to within the limit, action will need to be taken. If the upper limit is breached, some cash will be placed on deposit or used to buy some marketable securities. If the lower limit is breached, the business will need to borrow some cash or sell some securities.

The model relies heavily on management judgement to determine where the control limits are set and the period within which breaches of the control limits are acceptable. Past experience may be useful in helping managers decide on these issues. There are other models, however, that do not rely on management judgement. Instead, these use quantitative techniques to determine an optimal cash policy. One model proposed, for example, is the cash equivalent of the inventories economic order quantity model, discussed earlier in the chapter.

Cash budgets and managing cash

To manage cash effectively, it is useful for a business to prepare a cash budget. This is a very important tool for both planning and control purposes. Cash budgets were considered in Chapter 9, and so we shall not consider them again in detail. However, it is worth repeating that these statements enable managers to see how planned events are expected to affect the cash balance. The cash budget will identify periods when cash surpluses and cash deficits are expected.

When a cash surplus is expected to arise, managers must decide on the best use of the surplus funds. When a cash deficit is expected, managers must make adequate provision by borrowing, liquidating assets or rescheduling cash payments or receipts to deal with this. Cash budgets are useful in helping to control the cash held. The actual cash flows can be compared with the planned cash flows for the period. If there is a significant divergence between the budgeted and the actual cash flows, explanations must be sought and corrective action taken where necessary.

To refresh your memory on cash budgets, it would probably be worth looking back at Chapter 9, pages 317–20.

Although cash budgets are prepared primarily for internal management purposes, prospective lenders sometimes require them when a loan to a business is being considered.

Operating cash cycle

When managing cash, it is important to be aware of the operating cash cycle (OCC) of the business. For a retailer, for example, this may be defined as the period between the outlay of cash necessary for the purchase of inventories and the ultimate receipt of cash from the sale of the goods. In the case of a business that purchases goods on credit for subsequent resale on credit (for example, a wholesaler), the OCC is as shown in Figure 12.7.

Figure 12.7 shows that payment for inventories acquired on credit occurs some time after those inventories have been purchased and, therefore, no immediate cash outflow arises from the purchase. Similarly, cash receipts from credit customers will occur some time after the sale is made, and so there will be no immediate cash inflow as a result of the sale. The OCC is the period between the payment made to the supplier for goods concerned and the cash received from the credit customer. Although Figure 12.7 depicts the position for a wholesaling business, the precise definition of the OCC can easily be adapted for other types of business.

The OCC is important because it has a significant influence on the financing requirements of the business. Broadly, the longer the cycle, the greater the financing requirements of the business and the greater the financial risks. For this reason, the business is likely to want to reduce the OCC to the minimum possible period.

For the type of business mentioned above, which buys and sells on credit, the OCC can be calculated from the financial statements by the use of certain ratios. It is calculated as shown in Figure 12.8.

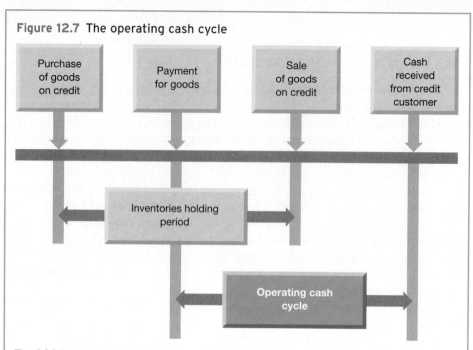

Figure 12.7 The operating cash cycle

The OCC is the time lapse between paying for goods and receiving the cash from the sale of those goods. The length of the OCC has a significant impact on the amount of funds that the business needs to apply to working capital.

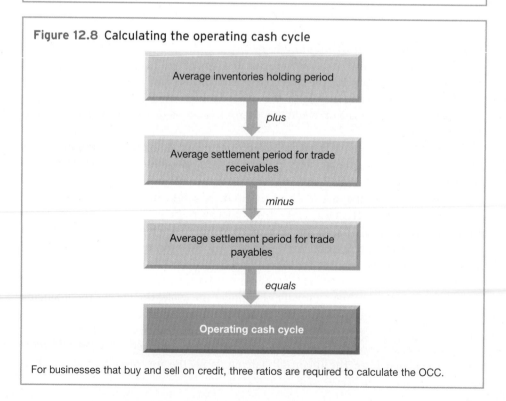

Figure 12.8 Calculating the operating cash cycle

For businesses that buy and sell on credit, three ratios are required to calculate the OCC.

The financial statements of Freezeqwik Ltd, a distributor of frozen foods, for the year ended 31 December last year are set out below.

Income statement for the year ended 31 December last year

	£000	£000
Sales revenue		820
Cost of sales		
Opening inventories	142	
Purchases	568	
	710	
Closing inventories	(166)	544
Gross profit		276
Administration expenses		(120)
Distribution expenses		(95)
Operating profit		61
Financial expenses		(32)
Profit before taxation		29
Taxation		(7)
Profit for the period		22

Balance sheet as at 31 December last year

	£000
Non-current assets	
Property, plant and equipment	
Freehold premises at valuation	180
Fixtures and fittings at cost less depreciation	82
Motor vans at cost less depreciation	102
	364
Current assets	
Inventories	166
Trade receivables	264
Cash	24
	454
Total assets	818
Equity	
Ordinary share capital	300
Share premium account	200
Retained earnings	152
	652
Current liabilities	
Trade payables	159
Taxation	7
	166
	818

→

All purchases and sales are on credit. There has been no change in the level of trade receivables or payables over the period.

Calculate the length of the OCC for the business and go on to suggest how the business may seek to reduce this period.

The OCC may be calculated as follows:

Number of days

Average inventories holding period:

$$\frac{\text{(Opening inventories + Closing inventories)/2}}{\text{Cost of sales}} \times 365 = \frac{(142 + 166)/2}{544} \times 365$$ 103

Average settlement period for trade receivables:

$$\frac{\text{Trade receivables}}{\text{Credit sales}} \times 365 = \frac{264}{820} \times 365$$ 118

Average settlement period for trade payables:

$$\frac{\text{Trade payables}}{\text{Credit purchases}} \times 365 = \frac{159}{568} \times 365$$ (102)

OCC   119

The business can reduce the length of the OCC in a number of ways. The average inventories holding period seems quite long. At present, average inventories held represent more than three months' sales requirements. Lowering the level of inventories held will reduce this. Similarly, the average settlement period for trade receivables seems long, at nearly four months' sales. Imposing tighter credit control, offering discounts, charging interest on overdue accounts and so on may reduce this. However, any policy decisions concerning inventories and trade receivables must take account of current trading conditions.

Extending the period of credit taken to pay suppliers could also reduce the OCC. However, for reasons that will be explained later, this option must be given careful consideration.

Figure 12.9 shows the average operating cash cycle for large European companies and large US companies.

Real World 12.11

Cycling along

The annual survey of working capital by REL Consultancy Group and CFO Europe (see Real World 12.2 above) calculates the average operating cash cycle for the top 1,000 European and top 1,000 US businesses. Comparative figures for five-year period ending in 2006 are shown in Figure 12.9.

We can see that European businesses have a higher average OCC than their US counterparts in each of the five years.

Source: Diagram adapted from diagram in 'US and European companies leave billions of dollars, euros untapped in working capital', www.relconsult.com, 29 August 2007, p. 5.

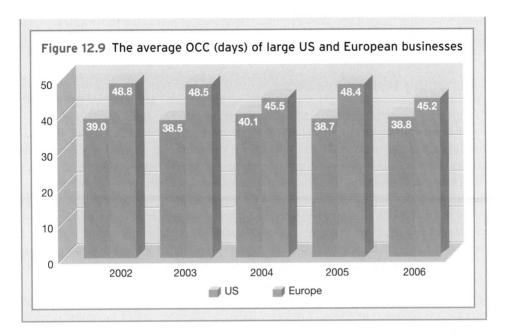

Figure 12.9 The average OCC (days) of large US and European businesses

Cash transmission

A business will normally wish to benefit from receipts from customers at the earliest opportunity. The benefit is immediate where payment is made in cash. However, when payment is made by cheque, there is normally a delay of three to four working days before the cheque can be cleared through the banking system. The business must therefore wait for this period before it can benefit from the amount paid in. In the case of a business that receives large amounts in the form of cheques, the opportunity cost of this delay can be significant.

To avoid this delay, a business could require payments to be made in cash. This is not usually very practical, mainly because of the risk of theft and/or the expense of conveying cash securely. Another option is to ask for payment to be made by standing order or by direct debit from the customer's bank account. This should ensure that the amount owing is always transferred from the bank account of the customer to the bank account of the business on the day that has been agreed.

It is also possible for funds to be transferred directly to a business's bank account. As a result of developments in computer technology, customers can pay for items by using debit cards, which results in the appropriate account being instantly debited and the seller's bank account being instantly credited with the required amount. This method of payment is widely used by large retail businesses, and may well extend to other types of business.

Bank overdrafts

Bank overdrafts are simply bank current accounts that have a negative balance. They are a type of bank loan. We looked at these in Chapter 11 in the context of short-term bank borrowing (page 424). They can be a useful tool in managing the business's cash flow requirements.

Managing trade payables

Trade credit arises from the fact that most businesses buy their goods and service requirements on credit. In effect, suppliers are lending the business money, interest-free, on a short-term basis. Trade payables are the other side of the coin from trade receivables. One business's trade payable is another one's trade receivable, in respect of a particular transaction. Trade payables are an important source of finance for most businesses. They have been described as a 'spontaneous' source, as they tend to increase in line with the increase in the level of activity achieved by a business. Trade credit is widely regarded as a 'free' source of finance and, therefore, a good thing for a business to use. There may be real costs, however, associated with taking trade credit.

First, customers who take credit may not be as well treated as those who pay immediately. For example, when goods are in short supply, credit customers may receive lower priority when allocating the goods available. In addition, credit customers may be less favoured in terms of delivery dates or the provision of technical support services. Sometimes, the goods or services provided may be more costly if credit is required. However, in most industries, trade credit is the norm. As a result, the above costs will not apply except, perhaps, to customers that abuse the credit facilities. A business that purchases supplies on credit will normally have to incur additional administration and accounting costs in dealing with the scrutiny and payment of invoices, maintaining and updating payables' accounts and so on.

These points are not meant to imply that taking credit is a burden to a business. There are, of course, real benefits that can accrue. Provided that trade credit is not abused, it can represent a form of interest-free loan. It can be a much more convenient method of paying for goods and services than paying by cash, and during a period of inflation there will be an economic gain from paying later rather than sooner for goods and services purchased. For most businesses, these benefits will exceed the costs involved.

In some cases, delaying payment to payables can be a sign of financial problems. One such example is given in Real World 12.12.

Real World 12.12

NHS waiting times

The National Health Service is delaying paying bills and cutting orders for supplies as it tries to balance its books, according to the trade associations whose members supply the service with everything from scanners to diagnostic tests.

Ray Hodgkinson, director-general of the British Healthcare Trades Association, said that while the picture was highly variable 'some of our members are having real trouble getting money out of NHS trusts'.

Most had standing orders that said bills should be paid within 30 days, Mr Hodgkinson said. 'But some are not paying for 60 or 90 days and even longer. They are in breach of their standing orders and for a lot of our members who are small businesses this is creating problems with cash flow. There is no doubt there is slow payment on a significant scale.'

Doris-Ann Williams, director-general of the British In-Vitro Diagnostics Association, whose members provide diagnostics supplies and tests, said: 'We are starting to see invoices not being paid and orders not being closed until the start of the new financial year [in April].'

'All sorts of measures are being taken to try not to spend money in this financial year.'

Having seen orders dry up and bills not paid this time last year as the NHS headed for a £500m-plus financial deficit, she added that this was 'starting to seem like an annual event'.

Source: 'NHS paying bills late in struggle to balance books, say suppliers', N. Timmins, *Financial Times*, 13 February 2007, ft.com.

Taking advantage of cash discounts

Where a supplier offers a discount for prompt payment, the business should give careful consideration to the possibility of paying within the discount period. An example may be useful to illustrate the cost of forgoing possible discounts.

Example 12.4

Hassan Ltd takes 70 days to pay for goods from its supplier. To encourage prompt payment, the supplier has offered the business a 2 per cent discount if payment for goods is made within 30 days.

Hassan Ltd is not sure whether it is worth taking the discount offered.

If the discount is taken, payment could be made on the last day of the discount period (that is, the 30th day). However, if the discount is not taken, payment will be made after 70 days. This means that, by not taking the discount, the business will receive an extra 40 (that is, 70 − 30) days' credit. The cost of this extra credit to the business will be the 2 per cent discount forgone. If we annualise the cost of this discount forgone, we have:

$$365/40 \times 2\% = 18.3\%*$$

We can see that the annual cost of forgoing the discount is very high, and so it may be profitable for the business to pay the supplier within the discount period, even if it means that it will have to borrow to enable it to do so.

* This is an approximate annual rate. For the more mathematically minded, the precise rate is:

$$(((1 + 2/98)^{9.125}) - 1) \times 100\% = 20.2\%$$

473

Controlling trade payables

 To help monitor the level of trade credit taken, management can calculate the average settlement period for trade payables. As we saw in Chapter 6, this ratio is:

$$\text{Average settlement period for trade payables} = \frac{\text{Average trade payables}}{\text{Credit purchases}} \times 365$$

Once again, this provides an average figure, which could be misleading. A more informative approach would be to produce an ageing schedule for payables. This would look much the same as the ageing schedule for receivables described earlier.

Summary

The main points of this chapter may be summarised as follows.

Working capital

- Working capital is the difference between current assets and current liabilities.
- That is, working capital = inventories + receivables + cash − payables − bank overdrafts.
- An investment in working capital cannot be avoided in practice – typically large amounts are involved.

Inventories

- There are costs of holding inventories, which include:
  - lost interest
  - storage cost
  - insurance cost
  - obsolescence.
- There are also costs of not holding sufficient inventories, which include:
  - loss of sales and customer goodwill
  - production dislocation
  - loss of flexibility – cannot take advantage of opportunities
  - reorder costs – low inventories imply more frequent ordering.
- Practical points on inventories management include:
  - identify optimum order size – models can help with this
  - set inventories reorder levels
  - use budgets
  - keep reliable inventories records
  - use accounting ratios (for example, inventories turnover period ratio)
  - establish systems for security of inventories and authorisation
  - consider just-in-time (JIT) inventories management.

Trade receivables

- When assessing which customers should receive credit, the five Cs of credit can be used:

  - capital
  - capacity
  - collateral
  - condition
  - character.
- The costs of allowing credit include:
  - lost interest
  - lost purchasing power
  - costs of assessing customer creditworthiness
  - administration cost
  - bad debts
  - cash discounts (for prompt payment).
- The costs of denying credit include:
  - loss of customer goodwill.
- Practical points on receivables management:
  - establish a policy
  - assess and monitor customer creditworthiness
  - establish effective administration of receivables
  - establish a policy on bad debts
  - consider cash discounts
  - use financial ratios (for example, average settlement period for trade receivables ratio)
  - use ageing summaries.

Cash

- The costs of holding cash include:
  - lost interest
  - lost purchasing power.
- The costs of holding insufficient cash include:
  - loss of supplier goodwill if unable to meet commitments on time
  - loss of opportunities
  - inability to claim cash discounts
  - costs of borrowing (should an obligation need to be met at short notice).
- Practical points on cash management:
  - establish a policy
  - plan cash flows
  - make judicious use of bank overdraft finance – it can be cheap and flexible
  - use short-term cash surpluses profitably
  - bank frequently
  - transmit cash promptly.
- An objective of working capital management is to limit the length of the operating cash cycle (OCC), subject to any risks that this may cause:
  - operating cash cycle (for a wholesaler) = length of time from buying inventories to receiving cash from receivables less payables' payment period (in days). →

Trade payables

- The costs of taking credit include:
  - higher price than purchases for immediate cash settlement
  - administrative costs
  - restrictions imposed by seller.
- The costs of not taking credit include:
  - lost interest-free borrowing
  - lost purchasing power
  - inconvenience – paying at the time of purchase can be inconvenient.
- Practical points on payables management:
  - establish a policy
  - exploit free credit as far as possible
  - use accounting ratios (for example, average settlement period for trade payables ratio).

Further reading

If you would like to explore the topics covered in this chapter in more depth, we recommend the following books:

Arnold, G., *Corporate Financial Management* (3rd edn), Financial Times Prentice Hall, 2005, chapter 13.

Brealey, B., Myers, S. and Allen, F., *Corporate Finance* (8th edn), McGraw-Hill, 2005, chapters 30 and 31.

McLaney, E., *Business Finance: Theory and Practice* (8th edn), Financial Times Prentice Hall, 2009, chapter 13.

Pike, R. and Neale, B., *Corporate Finance and Investment* (5th edn), Prentice Hall, 2005, chapters 13 and 14.

? Review questions

Answers to these questions can be found at the back of the book in Appendix C.

12.1 Tariq is the credit manager of Heltex plc. He is concerned that the pattern of monthly cash receipts from credit sales shows that credit collection is poor compared with budget. Heltex's sales director believes that Tariq is to blame for this situation, but Tariq insists that he is not. Why might Tariq not be to blame for the deterioration in the credit collection period?

12.2 How might each of the following affect the level of inventories held by a business?

(a) An increase in the number of production bottlenecks experienced by the business.
(b) A rise in the level of interest rates.
(c) A decision to offer customers a narrower range of products in the future.
(d) A switch of suppliers from an overseas business to a local business.
(e) A deterioration in the quality and reliability of bought-in components.

12.3 What are the reasons for holding inventories? Are these reasons different from the reasons for holding cash?

12.4 Identify the costs of holding:

(a) too little cash;
(b) too much cash.

* Exercises

Exercises 12.4 and 12.5 are more advanced than Exercises 12.1 to 12.3. Those with coloured numbers have answers at the back of the book in Appendix D.

> If you wish to try more exercises, visit MyAccountingLab/

12.1 Hercules Wholesalers Ltd has been particularly concerned with its liquidity position in recent months. The most recent income statement and balance sheet of the business are as follows:

Income statement for the year ended 31 December last year

	£000	£000
Sales revenue		452
Cost of sales		
Opening inventories	125	
Purchases	341	
	466	
Closing inventories	(143)	(323)
Gross profit		129
Expenses		(132)
Loss for the period		(3)

Balance sheet as at 31 December last year

	£000
Non-current assets	
Property, plant and equipment	
Freehold premises at valuation	280
Fixtures and fittings at cost less depreciation	25
Motor vehicles at cost less depreciation	52
	357
Current assets	
Inventories	143
Trade receivables	163
	306
Total assets	663
Equity	
Ordinary share capital	100
Retained earnings	158
	258
Non-current liabilities	
Borrowings – loans	120
Current liabilities	
Trade payables	145
Borrowings – bank overdraft	140
	285
Total equity and liabilities	663

The trade receivables and payables were maintained at a constant level throughout the year.

Required:
(a) Explain why Hercules Wholesalers Ltd is concerned about its liquidity position.
(b) Calculate the operating cash cycle for Hercules Wholesalers Ltd based on the information above. (Assume a 360-day year.)
(c) State what steps may be taken to improve the operating cash cycle of the business.

12.2 International Electric plc at present offers its customers 30 days' credit. Half the customers, by value, pay on time. The other half take an average of 70 days to pay. The business is considering offering a cash discount of 2 per cent to its customers for payment within 30 days.

The credit controller anticipates that half of the customers who now take an average of 70 days to pay (that is, a quarter of all customers) will pay in 30 days. The other half (the final quarter) will still take an average of 70 days to pay. The scheme will also reduce bad debts by £300,000 a year.

Annual sales revenue of £365m is made evenly throughout the year. At present the business has a large overdraft (£60m) with its bank at an interest cost of 12 per cent a year.

Required:
(a) Calculate the approximate equivalent annual percentage cost of a discount of 2 per cent, which reduces the time taken by credit customers to pay from 70 days to 30 days. (*Hint*: This part can be answered without reference to the narrative above.)
(b) Calculate the value of trade receivables outstanding under both the old and new schemes.
(c) How much will the scheme cost the business in discounts?
(d) Should the business go ahead with the scheme? State what other factors, if any, should be taken into account.
(e) Outline the controls and procedures that a business should adopt to manage the level of its trade receivables.

12.3 The managing director of Sparkrite Ltd, a trading business, has just received summary sets of financial statements for last year and this year:

Sparkrite Ltd
Income statements for years ended 30 September last year and this year

	Last year £000	Last year £000	This year £000	This year £000
Sales revenue		1,800		1,920
Cost of sales				
Opening inventories	160		200	
Purchases	1,120		1,175	
	1,280		1,375	
Closing inventories	(200)		(250)	
		(1,080)		(1,125)
Gross profit		720		795
Expenses		(680)		(750)
Profit for the period		40		45

Balance sheets as at 30 September last year and this year

	Last year £000	This year £000
Non-current assets	950	930
Current assets		
Inventories	200	250
Trade receivables	375	480
Bank	4	2
	579	732
Total assets	1,529	1,662
Equity		
Fully paid £1 ordinary shares	825	883
Retained earnings	509	554
	1,334	1,437
Current liabilities	195	225
Total equity and liabilities	1,529	1,662

The finance director has expressed concern at the increase in inventories and trade receivables levels.

Required:
(a) Show, by using the data given, how you would calculate ratios that could be used to measure inventories and trade receivables levels during last year and this year.
(b) Discuss the ways in which the management of Sparkrite Ltd could exercise control over:
   (i) inventories levels;
   (ii) trade receivables levels.

12.4 Mayo Computers Ltd has an annual sales turnover of £20m. Bad debts amount to £0.1m a year. All sales made by the business are on credit, and, at present, credit terms are negotiable by the customer. On average, the settlement period for trade receivables is 60 days. Trade receivables are financed by an overdraft bearing a 14 per cent rate of interest per year. The business is currently reviewing its credit policies to see whether more efficient and profitable methods could be employed. Only one proposal has so far been put forward concerning the management of trade credit.

The credit control department has proposed that customers should be given a 2.5 per cent discount if they pay within 30 days. For those who do not pay within this period, a maximum of 50 days' credit should be given. The credit department believes that 60 per cent of customers will take advantage of the discount by paying at the end of the discount period, and the remainder will pay at the end of 50 days. The credit department believes that bad debts can be effectively eliminated by adopting the above policies and by employing stricter credit investigation procedures, which will cost an additional £20,000 a year. The credit department is confident that these new policies will not result in any reduction in sales revenue.

Required:
Calculate the net annual cost (savings) to the business of abandoning its existing credit policies and adopting the proposals of the credit control department. (*Hint*: To answer this question you must weigh the costs of administration and cash discounts against the savings in bad debts and interest charges.)

12.5 Boswell Enterprises Ltd is reviewing its trade credit policy. The business, which sells all of its goods on credit, has estimated that sales revenue for the forthcoming year will be £3m under the existing policy. Credit customers representing 30 per cent of trade receivables are expected to pay one month after being invoiced and 70 per cent are expected to pay two months after being invoiced. These estimates are in line with previous years' figures.

At present, no cash discounts are offered to customers. However, to encourage prompt payment, the business is considering giving a 2.5 per cent cash discount to credit customers who pay in one month or less. Given this incentive, the business expects credit customers accounting for 60 per cent of trade receivables to pay one month after being invoiced and those accounting for 40 per cent of trade receivables to pay two months after being invoiced. The business believes that the introduction of a cash discount policy will prove attractive to some customers and will lead to a 5 per cent increase in total sales revenue.

Irrespective of the trade credit policy adopted, the gross profit margin of the business will be 20 per cent for the forthcoming year and three months' inventories will be held. Fixed monthly expenses of £15,000 and variable expenses (excluding discounts) equivalent to 10 per cent of sales revenue will be incurred and will be paid one month in arrears. Trade payables will be paid in arrears and will be equal to two months' cost of sales. The business will hold a fixed cash balance of £140,000 throughout the year, whichever trade credit policy is adopted. Ignore taxation.

Required:
(a) Calculate the investment in working capital at the end of the forthcoming year under
   (i) the existing policy;
   (ii) the proposed policy.
(b) Calculate the expected net profit for the forthcoming year under
   (i) the existing policy;
   (ii) the proposed policy.
(c) Advise the business as to whether it should implement the proposed policy.

(*Hint*: The investment in working capital will be made up of inventories, trade receivables and cash, *less* trade payables and any unpaid expenses at the year end.)

ABC *See* Activity-based costing.

ABC system of inventories control A method of applying different levels of inventories control, based on the value of each category of inventories. *p. 450*

Absorption costing A method at costing in which a 'fair share' of all production overhead costs is included when calculating the cost of a particular product or service. *p. 273*

Accounting The process of identifying, measuring and communicating information to permit informed judgements and decisions by users of the information. *p. 3*

Accounting conventions Accounting rules that have evolved over time that deal with practical problems rather than to reflect some theoretical ideal. *p. 52*

Accounting information system The system used within a business to identify, record, analyse and report accounting information. *p. 11*

Accounting period The time span for which a business prepares its financial statements. *p. 72*

Accounting rate of return (ARR) The average profit from an investment, expressed as a percentage of the average investment made. *p. 349*

Accruals accounting The system of accounting that follows the accruals convention. This is the system followed in drawing up the balance sheet and income statement. *p. 86*

Accruals convention The convention of accounting that asserts that profit is the excess of revenue over expenses, not the excess of cash receipts over cash payments. *p. 86*

Accrued expenses Expenses that are outstanding at the end of an accounting period. *p. 82*

Acid test ratio A liquidity ratio that relates the current assets (normally less inventories) to the current liabilities. *p. 203*

Activity-based costing (ABC) A technique for more accurately relating overheads to specific production or provision of a service. It is based on acceptance of the fact that overheads do not just occur but are caused by activities, such as holding products in stores, which 'drive' the costs. *p. 291*

Adverse variance A difference between planned and actual performance, usually where the difference will cause the actual profit to be lower than the budgeted one. *p. 329*

Ageing schedule of trade receivables A report dividing trade receivables into categories, depending on the length of time outstanding. *p. 462*

Allotted share capital *See* Issued share capital.

Alternative Investment Market (AIM) A stock market for the shares of smaller, young and growing businesses. AIM is similar in style to the main London Stock Exchange, but is cheaper for a business to enter and has a lighter regulatory regime. *p. 423*

Asset-based financing A form of financing where assets are used as security for cash advances to the business. Factoring and invoice discounting, where the security is trade receivables, are examples of asset-based financing. *p. 427*

Assets Resources held by a business, that have certain characteristics. *p. 35*

Auditors Professionals whose main duty is to make a report as to whether, in their opinion, the financial statements of a company do what they are supposed to do, namely show a true and fair view and comply with statutory, and financial reporting standard, requirements. *p. 142*

AVCO *See* Weighted average cost.

Average inventories turnover period ratio An efficiency ratio that measures the average period for which inventories are held by a business. *p. 195*

Average settlement period for trade payables The average time taken for a business to pay its trade payables. *pp. 197, 474*

Average settlement period for trade receivables The average time taken for trade receivables to pay the amounts owing. *pp. 196, 462*

Bad debt An amount owed to the business that is considered to be irrecoverable. *p. 101*

Balance sheet A statement of financial position that shows the assets of a business and the claims on those assets. *p. 30*

Bank overdraft A flexible form of borrowing that allows an individual or business to have a negative bank current account balance. *p. 424*

Batch costing A technique for identifying full cost, where the production of many types of goods and services – particularly goods – involves producing in a batch of identical or nearly identical units of output, but where each batch is distinctly different from other batches. *p. 287*

BEP *See* Break-even point.

Bonus issue *See* Bonus shares.

Bonus shares Shares that are created by converting reserves. They are given 'free' to shareholders. *p. 129*

Break-even analysis The activity of deducing the break-even point of some activity through analysing costs and revenue. *p. 239*

Break-even chart A graphical representation of the costs and revenue of some activity, at various levels of output, that enables the break-even point to be identified. *p. 239*

Break-even point (BEP) The level of activity at which total revenue will equal total cost, so that there is neither profit nor loss. *p. 241*

Budget A financial plan for the short term, typically one year or less. *p. 304*

Budget holder An individual responsible for achieving a particular budget. *p. 315*

Budgetary control Using the budget as a yardstick against which the effectiveness of actual performance may be assessed. *p. 333*

Business angel An individual who supplies finance (usually equity finance) and advice to a small business. Usually the amount of finance supplied falls between £10,000 and £100,000. *p 430*

Business entity convention The convention that holds that, for accounting purposes, the business and its owner(s) are treated as quite separate and distinct. *p. 52*

Called-up share capital That part of a company's share capital for which the shareholders have been asked to pay the agreed amount. It is part of the claim of the owners against the business. *p. 131*

Capital reserves Reserves that arise from an unrealised 'capital' profits or gains rather than from normal realised trading activities. *p. 127*

Carrying amount The difference between the cost (or fair value) of a non-current asset and the accumulated depreciation relating to that asset. The carrying value is also referred to as the written-down value (WDV) and the net book value (NBV). *p. 89*

Cash discount A reduction in the amount due for goods or services sold on credit in return for prompt payment. *p. 460*

Cash flow statement A statement that shows the sources and uses of cash for a period. *p. 30*

Claims Obligations on the part of a business to provide cash or some other benefit to outside parties. *p. 35*

Combined Code A code of practice for companies listed on the London Stock Exchange that deals with corporate governance matters. *p. 121*

Common costs Another name for indirect costs or overheads. These are costs that do not relate directly to, and are not measurable in respect of, particular units of output, but relate to all output. *p. 272*

Comparability The requirement that items which are basically the same should be treated in the same manner for measurement and reporting purposes. Lack of comparability will limit the usefulness of accounting information. *p. 6*

Consistency convention The accounting convention that holds that, when a particular method of accounting is selected to deal with a transaction, this method should be applied consistently over time. *p. 100*

Consolidating Reducing the number of shares and increasing their nominal value per share to compensate. *p. 125*

Continual budget   A budgeting system that continually updates budgets so that there is always a budget for a full planning period. (Also known as a rolling budget.) *p. 308*

Contribution per unit   Sales revenue per unit less variable costs per unit. *p. 244*

Control   Compelling events to conform to a plan. *p. 305*

Convertible loan notes   Long-term borrowings that can be converted into equity share capital at the option of the holders. *p. 402*

Corporate governance   Matters concerned with directing and controlling a company. *p. 120*

Corporation tax   Taxation that a limited company is liable to pay on its profits. *p. 119*

Cost behaviour   The manner in which costs alter with changes in the level of activity. *p. 274*

Cost centre   Some area, object, person or activity for which costs are separately collected. *p. 285*

Cost driver   An activity that causes costs. *p. 291*

Cost of sales   The cost of providing the goods or services sold during a period. For a business selling goods, the cost of sales can be derived by adding the opening inventories held to the inventories purchases for the period and then deducting the closing inventories held. *p. 74*

Cost pool   The sum of the overhead costs that are seen as being caused by the same cost driver. *p. 292*

Cost unit   The objective for which the cost is being deduced, usually a product or service. *p. 275*

Creative accounting   Adopting accounting policies to achieve a particular view of performance and position that preparers would like users to see rather than what is a true and fair view. *p. 143*

Current assets   Assets that are held for the short term. They include cash itself and other assets that are held for sale or consumption in the normal course of a business's operating cycle. *p. 44*

Current liabilities   Claims against the business which are expect to be settled within the normal course of the business's operating cycle or within twelve months of the balance sheet date, or which are held primarily for trading purposes, or for which the business does not have the right to defer settlement beyond twelve months of the balance sheet date. *p. 46*

Current ratio   A liquidity ratio that relates the current assets of the business to the current liabilities. *p. 202*

Debt factoring   A service offered by a financial institution (a factor) that involves the factor taking over the management of the trade receivables of the business. The factor is often prepared to make an advance to the business, based on the amount of trade receivables outstanding. *p. 424*

Deep discount bonds   Redeemable loan notes (bonds) offering a rate of interest below the market rate and issued at a discount to their redeemable value. *p. 401*

Depreciation   A measure of that portion of the cost (or fair value) of a non-current asset that has been consumed during an accounting period. *p. 86*

Direct costs   Costs that can be identified with specific cost units, to the extent that the effect of the cost can be measured in respect of each particular unit of output. *p. 271*

Direct method   An approach to deducing the cash flows from operating activities, in a cash flow statement, by analysing the business's cash records. *p. 163*

Director   An individual who is appointed (normally by being elected) to act as the most senior level of management of a company. *p. 120*

Directors' report   A report containing information of a financial and non-financial nature that the directors must produce as part of the annual financial report to shareholders. *p. 142*

Discount factor   The rate applied to future cash flows to derive the present value of those cash flows. *p. 365*

Discretionary budget   A budget based on a sum allocated at the discretion of senior management. *p. 315*

Dividend   The transfer of assets (usually cash) made by a company to its shareholders. *p. 125*

Dividend cover ratio   An investment ratio that relates the earnings available for dividends to the dividend announced, to indicate how many times the former covers the latter. *p. 210*

Dividend payout ratio   An investment ratio that relates the dividends announced for the period to the earnings available for dividends that were generated in that period. *p. 210*

Dividend per share   An investment ratio that relates the dividends announced for a period to the number of shares in issue. *p. 211*

Dividend yield ratio   An investment ratio that relates the cash return from a share to its current market value. *p. 211*

Dual aspect convention   The accounting convention that holds that each transaction has two aspects and that each aspect must be reflected in the financial statements. *p. 55*

Earnings per share (EPS)   An investment ratio that relates the earnings generated by the business during a period, and available to shareholders, to the number of shares in issue. *p. 212*

Economic order quantity (EOQ)   The quantity of inventories that should be bought in each order or manufactured in each batch so as to minimise total costs relating to inventories. *p. 450*

EPS   *See* Earnings per share.

Equity The owners' claim of a business, also known as capital in the case of sole proprietorships and partnerships. For a limited company it is the sum of the ordinary shares and reserves of a company. *p. 38, 123*

Eurobond A form of long-term borrowing where the finance is raised on an international basis. Eurobonds are issued in a currency that is not that of the country in which the bonds are issued. *p. 400*

Expense A measure of the outflow of assets (or increase in liabilities) incurred as a result of generating revenue. *p. 71*

Factoring *See* Debt factoring.

Fair values The values ascribed to assets as an alternative to historic cost. They are usually the current market value (that is, the exchange values in an arm's-length transaction). *p. 59*

Favourable variance A difference between planned and actual performance, where usually the difference will cause the actual profit to be higher than the budgeted one. *p. 329*

Final accounts The income statement, cash flow statement and balance sheet taken together. *p. 34*

Finance The study of how businesses raise funds and select appropriate investments. *p. 3*

Finance lease A financial arrangement where the asset title remains with the owner (the lessor) but the lease agreement transfers virtually all the rewards and risks to the business (the lessee). *p. 405*

Financial accounting The measuring and reporting of accounting information for external users (those users other than the managers of the business). *p. 12*

Financial derivative Any form of financial instrument, based on share capital or borrowings, which can be used by investors either to increase their returns or to decrease their exposure to risk. *p. 404*

Financial gearing The existence of fixed payment-bearing sources of finance (for example, borrowings) in the capital structure of a business. *p. 204*

Financial management A subject area concerned with the financing and investing decisions of businesses. *p. 3*

First in, first out (FIFO) A method of inventories costing which assumes that the earliest acquired inventories are used (in production or sales) first. *p. 97*

Five Cs of credit A checklist of factors to be taken into account when assessing the creditworthiness of a customer. *p. 456*

Fixed costs Costs that stay the same when changes occur to the volume of activity. *p. 234*

Flexible budgets Budgets that are adjusted to reflect the actual levels of output achieved. *p. 328*

Flexing the budget Revising the budget to what it would have been had the planned level of output been different. *p. 327*

Forecast A prediction of future outcomes, or of the future state of the environment. *p. 307*

Full cost The total amount of resources, usually measured in monetary terms, sacrificed to achieve a particular objective. *p. 269*

Full costing Deducing the total direct and indirect (overhead) costs of pursuing some activity or objective. *p. 270*

Fully paid shares Shares on which the shareholders have paid the full issue price. *p. 131*

Gearing ratio A ratio that relates the contribution of finance that required a fixed return (such as borrowings) to the total long-term finance of the business. *p. 206*

Going concern convention The accounting convention that holds that it is assumed that the business will continue operations for the foreseeable future, unless there is reason to believe otherwise. In other words, there is no intention, or need, to liquidate the business. *p. 54*

Gross profit The amount remaining (if positive) after trading expenses (for example, cost of sales) have been deducted from trading revenue. *p. 74*

Gross profit margin ratio A profitability ratio relating the gross profit to the sales revenue for a period. *p. 192*

Hire purchase A method of acquiring an asset by paying the purchase price by instalments over a period. Normally, control of the asset will pass as soon as the hire purchase contract is signed and the first instalment is paid, whereas ownership will pass on payment of the final instalment. *p. 408*

Historic cost convention The accounting convention that holds that assets should be recorded at their historic (acquisition) cost. *p. 52*

Income statement A financial statement (also known as profit and loss account) that measures and reports the profit (or loss) the business has generated during a period. It is derived by deducting from total revenue for a period, the total expenses associated with that revenue. *pp. 30, 72*

Incremental budgeting Constructing budgets on the basis of what happened in the previous period, with some adjustment for expected changes in the forthcoming budget period. *p. 315*

Indirect costs (or overheads) All of those costs that cannot be directly measured in respect of each particular unit of output, that is all costs except direct costs. *p. 271*

Indirect method An approach to deducing the cash flows from operating activities, in a cash flow statement, by analysing the business's financial statements. *p. 163*

Inflation An increase in the general prices of goods and services resulting in a corresponding decline in the purchasing power of money. *p. 361*

Intangible assets   Assets that do not have a physical substance (for example, patents, goodwill and trade receivables). *p. 37*

Interest cover ratio   A gearing ratio that divides the operating profit (that is, profit before interest and taxation) by the interest payable for a period. *p. 207*

Internal rate of return (IRR)   The discount rate for an investment that will have the effect of producing a zero NPV. *p. 368*

International Accounting Standards   *See* International Financial Reporting Standards.

International Financial Reporting Standards   Transnational accounting rules that have been adopted, or developed, by the International Accounting Standards Board and which should be followed in preparing the published financial statements of listed limited companies. *p. 140*

Invoice discounting   A loan provided by a financial institution based on a proportion of the face value of credit sales outstanding. *p. 425*

Issued share capital   That part of the share capital that has been issued to shareholders. Also known as allotted share capital. *p. 131*

Job costing   A technique for identifying the full cost per unit of output, where not all units of output are identical. *p. 272*

Just-in-time (JIT) inventories management   A system of inventories management that aims to have supplies delivered, to production or sales, just in time for their required use. *p. 454*

Last in, first out (LIFO)   A method of inventories costing which assumes that the most recently acquired inventories are used (in production or sales) first. *p. 97*

Lead time   The time lag between placing an order for goods or services and their delivery to the required location. *p. 448*

Liabilities   Claims of individuals and organisations, apart from the owner, that have arisen from past transactions or events such as supplying goods or lending money to the business. *p. 38*

Limited company   An artificial legal person that has an identity separate from that of those who own and manage it. *p. 113*

Limited liability   The restriction of the legal obligation of shareholders to meet all of the company's debts. *p. 116*

Limiting factor   Some aspect of the business (for example, lack of sales demand) that will prevent it achieving its objectives to the maximum extent. *p. 307*

Loan covenant   A condition contained within a loan agreement that is designed to help protect the lenders. *p. 404*

Loan notes   Long-term borrowings usually made by limited companies. *pp. 132, 399*

Loan stock   *See* Loan note.

Management accounting   The measuring and reporting of accounting information for the managers of a business. *p. 12*

Management by exception   A system of control, based on a comparison of planned and actual performance, that allows managers to focus on areas of poor performance rather than dealing with areas where performance is satisfactory. *pp. 000, 312*

Margin of safety   The difference between the actual or planned level of some activity and that activity's break-even point. *p. 244*

Marginal analysis   The activity of decision-making through analysing variable costs and revenues, ignoring fixed costs. *p. 254*

Marginal cost   The additional cost of producing one more unit. This is often the same as the variable cost. *p. 254*

Master budget   A summary of the individual budgets, usually consisting of a budgeted income statement, a budgeted balance sheet and a budgeted cash flow statement. *p. 308*

Matching convention   The accounting convention that holds that, in measuring income, expenses should be matched to revenue which they helped generate in the same accounting period as that in which the revenue was realised. *p. 81*

Materiality   The requirement that material information should be disclosed to users in financial statements. *p. 8*

Materiality convention   The accounting convention that states that, where the amounts involved are immaterial, only what is expedient should be considered. *p. 85*

Materials requirement planning (MRP) system   A computer-based system of inventories control that schedules the timing of deliveries of bought-in parts and materials to coincide with production requirements to meet demand. *p. 454*

Mission statement   A brief statement setting out the aims of the business. *p. 304*

Mortgage   A loan secured on property. *p. 404*

Net book value   *See* Carrying amount.

Net present value (NPV)   A method of investment appraisal based on the present value of all relevant cash flows associated with an investment. *p. 358*

Nominal value   The face value of a share in a company. (Also called par value.) *p. 124*

Non-current (fixed) assets   Assets held that do not meet the criteria of current assets. They are held for the long-term operations of the business rather than continuously circulating within the business. Non-current assets can be seen as the tools of the business. (Also known as fixed assets.) *p. 46*

Non-current liabilities   Those amounts due to other parties that are not current liabilities. *p. 48*

Offer for sale   An issue of shares that involves a public limited company (or its shareholders) selling the shares to a financial institution that will, in turn, sell the shares to the public. *p. 416*

Operating cash cycle (OCC)   The period between the outlay of cash to buy supplies and the ultimate receipt of cash from the sale of goods. *p. 467*

Operating gearing   The relationship between the total fixed and the total variable costs for some activity (also known as operational gearing). *p. 247*

Operating lease   An arrangement where a business hires an asset, usually for a short time. Hiring an asset under an operating lease tends to be seen as an operating, rather than a financing, decision. *p. 406*

Operating profit   The profit achieved during a period after all operating expenses have been deducted from revenues from operations. Financing expenses are deducted after the calculation of operating profit. *p. 74*

Operating profit margin ratio   A profitability ratio relating the operating profit to the sales revenue for the period. *p. 191*

Operational gearing   *See* Operating gearing.

Opportunity cost   The cost incurred when one course of action prevents an opportunity to derive some benefit from another course of action. *p. 373*

Ordinary shares   Shares of a company owned by those who are due the benefits of the company's activities after all other stakeholders have been satisfied. *p. 125*

Outsourcing   Subcontracting activities to (sourcing goods or services from) outside organisations. *p. 258*

Overdraft   *See* Bank overdraft.

Overhead absorption (recovery) rate   The rate at which overheads are charged to cost units (jobs), usually in a job-costing system. *p. 276*

Overheads (or indirect costs)   Any costs except direct costs; costs that cannot be directly measured in respect of particular cost objectives. *p. 271*

Paid-up share capital   That part of the share capital of a company that has been called and paid. *p. 131*

Par value   *See* Nominal value.

Payback period (PP)   The time taken for the initial outlay for an investment to be repaid from its future net cash inflows. *p. 354*

Periodic budget   A budget developed on a one-off basis to cover a particular planning period. *p. 307*

Preference shares   Shares of a company owned by those who are entitled to the first part of any dividend that the company may pay. *p. 126*

Prepaid expenses   Expenses that have been paid in advance at the end of the accounting period. *p. 85*

Price/earnings ratio   An investment ratio that relates the market value of a share to the earnings per share. *p. 212*

Private company   A limited company for which the directors can restrict the ownership of its shares. *p. 117*

Private placing   An issue of shares that involves a limited company arranging for the shares to be sold to the clients of particular issuing houses or stockbrokers, rather than to the general investing public. *p. 416*

Process costing A technique for deriving the full cost per unit of output, where the units of output are the same or it is reasonable to treat them as being so. *p. 211*

Profit The increase in wealth attributable to the owners of a business that arises through business operations. *p. 70*

Profit before taxation The result when all of the appropriately matched expenses of running a business have been deducted from the revenue for the year, but before the taxation charge is deducted. *p. 137*

Profit for the year The result when all of the appropriately matched expenses of running a business have been deducted from the revenue for the year. In the case of a limited company the taxation charge is also deducted. *pp. 74, 137*

Profit-volume (PV) chart A graphical representation of the contributions (revenue less variable costs) of some activity, at various levels, which enables the break-even point and the profits at various activity levels to be identified. *p. 249*

Property, plant and equipment Those non-current assets that have a physical substance; they are tangible non-current assets (for example, plant and machinery, motor vehicles). *p. 58*

Prudence convention The accounting convention that holds that financial statements should err on the side of caution. *p. 53*

Public company A limited company for which the directors cannot restrict the ownership of its shares. *p. 117*

Public issue An issue of shares that involves a public limited company making a direct invitation to the public to buy shares in the company. *p. 416*

Reducing-balance method A method of calculating depreciation that applies a fixed percentage rate of depreciation to the carrying amount of an asset in each period. *p. 90*

Relevance The ability of accounting information to influence decisions; regarded as a key characteristic of useful accounting information. *p. 6*

Relevant cost A cost that is relevant to a particular decision. *p. 373*

Reliability The requirement that accounting information should be free from significant errors or bias and should represent what it purports to represent. Reliability is regarded as a key characteristic of useful accounting information. *p. 6*

Reserves Part of the owners' claim (equity) of a limited company that has arisen from profits and gains, to the extent that these have not been distributed to the shareholders or reduced by losses. *p. 123*

Residual value The amount for which a non-current asset is sold when the business has no further use for it. *p. 88*

Return on capital employed ratio (ROCE) A profitability ratio expressing the relationship between the operating profit (that is, profit before interest and taxation) and the long-term funds (equity and borrowings) invested in the business. *p. 189*

Return on ordinary shareholders' funds ratio (ROSF)   A profitability ratio that compares the amount of profit for the period available to the ordinary shareholders (profit for the year, less any preference dividend) with their stake in the business (equity). *p. 188*

Revenue   A measure of the inflow of assets (for example, cash or amounts owed to a business by credit customers), or a reduction in liabilities, arising as a result of trading operations. *p. 70*

Revenue reserve   Part of the owners' claim (equity) of a company that arises from realised profits and gains, including after-tax trading profits and gains from disposals of non-current assets. *p. 124*

Rights issue   An issue of shares for cash to existing shareholders on the basis of the number of shares already held. *p. 413*

Risk   The extent and likelihood that what is projected to occur will not actually occur. *p. 359*

Risk premium   The additional return required from an investment, owing to a perceived level of risk: the greater the perceived risk, the larger the required risk premium. *p. 360*

Rolling budget   *See* Continual budget.

Sale and leaseback   An agreement to sell an asset (usually property) to another party and simultaneously to lease the asset back in order to continue using the asset. *p. 408*

Sales revenue per employee ratio   An efficiency ratio that relates the sales revenue generated during a period to the average number of employees of the business. *p. 199*

Sales revenue to capital employed ratio   An efficiency ratio that relates the sales revenue generated during a period to the capital employed. *p. 198*

Semi-fixed (semi-variable) cost   A cost that has an element of both fixed and variable cost. *p. 238*

Share premium account   A capital reserve reflecting any amount, above the nominal value of shares, that is paid for those shares when issued by a company. *p. 128*

Shares   Portions of the ownership, or equity, of a company. *p. 113*

Splitting   Dividing the nominal value of the company's shares into smaller values, so that each shareholder has more shares but with the same total nominal value. *p. 125*

Stepped fixed costs   Fixed costs that do not remain fixed over all levels of output but which change in steps as a threshold level of output is reached. *p. 236*

Stock Exchange   A market where 'second-hand' shares may be bought and sold and new capital raised. *p. 417*

Straight-line method   A method of accounting for depreciation that allocates the amount to be depreciated evenly over the useful life of the asset. *p. 89*

Strategic management The process of setting a course to achieve the business's objectives, taking account of the commercial and economic environment in which the business operates. *p. 17*

Tangible assets Those assets that have a physical substance (for example, plant and machinery, motor vehicles). *p. 37*

Tender issue A public issue of shares or loan notes (by a public limited company) where potential investors are invited to place bids for the securities concerned, rather than the company setting the price itself. *p. 416*

Term loan Finance provided by financial institutions, such as banks and insurance companies, under a contract with the borrowing business that indicates the interest rate and dates of payments of interest and repayment of the loan. The loan is not normally transferable from one lender to another. *p. 399*

Total cost The sum of the variable and fixed costs of pursuing some activity. *p. 275*

Understandability The requirement that accounting information should be understood by those for whom the information is primarily provided. Lack of understandability will limit the usefulness of accounting information. *p. 6*

Variable costs Costs that vary according to the volume of activity. *p. 234*

Variance The financial effect, on the budgeted profits of a factor being more or less than budgeted. *p. 329*

Variance analysis Carrying out calculations to find the area of the business's operations that has caused the budgets not to have been met. *p. 331*

Venture capital Long-term finance provided by certain institutions to small and medium-sized businesses to exploit relatively high-risk opportunities. *p. 429*

Warrants Documents giving the holders the right, but not the obligation, to acquire ordinary shares in a company at an agreed price. *p. 403*

Weighted average cost (AVCO) A method of inventories costing which assumes that inventories entering the business lose their separate identity and any issues of inventories reflect the weighted average cost of the inventories held. *p. 97*

Working capital Current assets less current liabilities. *pp. 165, 441*

Written-down value (WDV) *See* Carrying amount.

Zero-base budgeting (ZBB) An approach to budgeting based on the philosophy that all spending needs to be justified annually and that each budget should start as a clean sheet. *p. 316*

Appendix B: Solutions to self-assessment questions

Chapter 2

2.1 Simonson Engineering

The balance sheet you prepare should be set out as follows:

Simonson Engineering
Balance sheet as at 30 September 2008

	£
Non-current assets	
Property, plant and equipment	
Property	72,000
Plant and machinery	25,000
Motor vehicles	15,000
Fixtures and fittings	9,000
	121,000
Current assets	
Inventories	45,000
Trade receivables	48,000
Cash in hand	1,500
	94,500
Total assets	215,500
Equity (owners' claim)	
Opening balance	117,500
Profit	18,000
	135,500
Drawings	(15,000)
	120,500
Non-current liabilities	
Long-term borrowings	51,000
Current liabilities	
Trade payables	18,000
Short-term borrowings	26,000
	44,000
Total equity and liabilities	215,500

Chapter 3

3.1

TT and Co.
Balance sheet as at 31 December 2008

	£
Assets	
Delivery van (12,000 – 2,500)	9,500
Inventories (143,000 + 12,000 – 74,000 – 16,000)	65,000
Trade receivables (152,000 – 132,000 – 400)	19,600
Cash at bank (50,000 – 25,000 – 500 – 1,200	
– 12,000 – 33,500 – 1,650 – 12,000 + 35,000	
+ 132,000 – 121,000 – 9,400)	750
Prepaid expenses (5,000 + 300)	5,300
Total assets	100,150
Claims	
Equity (50,000 + 26,900)	76,900
Trade payables (143,000 – 121,000)	22,000
Accrued expenses (630 + 620)	1,250
Total equity and liabilities	100,150

Income statement for the year ended 31 December 2008

	£
Sales revenue (152,000 + 35,000)	187,000
Cost of goods sold (74,000 + 16,000)	(90,000)
Gross profit	97,000
Rent	(20,000)
Rates (500 + 900)	(1,400)
Wages (33,500 + 630)	(34,130)
Electricity (1,650 + 620)	(2,270)
Bad debts	(400)
Van depreciation ((12,000 – 2,000)/4)	(2,500)
Van expenses	(9,400)
Profit for the year	26,900

The balance sheet could now be rewritten in a more stylish form as follows:

Balance sheet as at 31 December 2008

	£
Non-current assets	
Property, plant and equipment	
Delivery van at cost	12,000
Accumulated depreciation	(2,500)
	9,500
Current assets	
Inventories	65,000
Trade receivables	19,600
Prepaid expenses	5,300
Cash	750
	90,650
Total assets	100,150
Equity (owners' claim)	
Original	50,000
Retained profit	26,900
	76,900

Current liabilities	
Trade payables	22,000
Accrued expenses	1,250
	23,250
Total equity and liabilities	100,150

Chapter 4

4.1

Pear Limited
Balance sheet as at 30 September 2008

	£000
Non-current assets	
Property, plant and equipment	
Cost (1,570 + 30)	1,600
Depreciation (690 + 12)	(702)
	898
Current assets	
Inventory	207
Receivables (182 + 18 − 4)	196
Cash at bank	21
	424
Total assets	1,322
Equity	
Shares capital	300
Share premium account	300
Retained earnings (104 + 41 − 25)	120
	720
Non-current liabilities	
Borrowings − 10% loan (repayable 2009)	300
Current liabilities	
Trade payables	88
Other payables (20 + 30 + 15 + 2)	67
Taxation	17
Dividend approved	25
Borrowings − Bank overdraft	105
	302
Total equity and liabilities	1,322

Income statement for the year ended 30 September 2008

	£000
Revenue (1,456 + 18)	1,474
Cost of sales	(768)
Gross profit	706
Salaries	(220)
Depreciation (249 + 12)	(261)
Other operating costs (131 + (2% × 200) + 2)	(137)
Operating profit	88
Interest payable (15 + 15)	(30)
Profit before taxation	58
Taxation (58 × 30%)	(17)
Profit for the year	41

Chapter 5

5.1

Touchstone plc
Cash flow statement for the year ended 31 December 2008

	£m
Cash flows from operating activities	
Profit before taxation (after interest)	
(see Note 1 below)	60
Adjustments for:	
Depreciation	16
Interest expense (Note 2)	4
	80
Increase in trade receivables (26 – 16)	(10)
Decrease in trade payables (38 – 37)	(1)
Decrease in inventories (25 – 24)	1
Cash generated from operations	70
Interest paid	(4)
Taxation paid (Note 3)	(12)
Dividend paid	(18)
Net cash from operating activities	36
Cash flows from investing activities	
Payments to acquire tangible non-current assets (Note 4)	(41)
Net cash used in investing activities	(41)
Cash flows from financing activities	
Issue of loan notes (40 – 20)	20
Net cash used in financing activities	20
Net increase in cash and cash equivalents	15
Cash and cash equivalents at 1 January 2008	
Cash	4
Cash and cash equivalents at 31 December 2008	
Cash	4
Treasury bills	15
	19

To see how this relates to the cash of the business at the beginning and end of the year it can be useful to provide a reconciliation as follows:

Analysis of cash and cash equivalents during the year ended 31 December 2008

	£m
Cash and cash equivalents at 1 January 2008	4
Net cash inflow	15
Cash and cash equivalents at 31 December 2008	19

Notes:

1 This is simply taken from the income statement for the year.

2 Interest payable expense must be taken out, by adding it back to the profit before taxation figure. We subsequently deduct the cash paid for interest payable during the year. In this case the two figures are identical.

3 Companies pay 50% of their tax during their accounting year and the other 50% in the following year. Thus the 2008 payment would have been half the tax on the 2007 profit (that is, the figure that would have appeared in the current liabilities at the end of 2007), plus half of the 2008 tax charge (that is, $4 + (1/2 \times 16) = 12$).

4 Since there were no disposals, the depreciation charges must be the difference between the start and end of the year's non-current asset values, adjusted by the cost of any additions:

	£m
Carrying amount at 1 January 2008	147
Add Additions (balancing figure)	41
	188
Less Depreciation (6 + 10)	16
Carrying amount at 31 December 2008	172

Chapter 6

6.1 Financial ratios

In answering this question you may have used the following ratios:

	Ali plc	Bhaskar plc
Current ratio	$\frac{853.0}{422.4} = 2.0$	$\frac{816.5}{293.1} = 2.8$
Acid test ratio	$\frac{(853.0 - 592.0)}{422.4} = 0.6$	$\frac{(816.5 - 403.0)}{293.1} = 1.4$
Gearing ratio	$\frac{190}{(687.6 + 190)} \times 100 = 21.6\%$	$\frac{250}{(874.6 + 250)} \times 100 = 22.2\%$
Interest cover ratio	$\frac{151.3}{19.4} = 7.8$ times	$\frac{166.9}{27.5} = 6.1$ times
Dividend payout ratio	$\frac{135.0}{99.9} \times 100 = 135\%$	$\frac{95.0}{104.6} \times 100 = 91\%$
Price/earnings ratio	$\frac{£6.50}{31.2p} = 20.8$ times	$\frac{£8.20}{41.8p} = 19.6$ times

Ali plc has a much lower current ratio and acid test ratio than Bhaskar plc. The reasons for this may be partly due to the fact that Ali plc has a lower average settlement period for receivables. The acid test ratio of Ali plc is substantially below 1.0: this may suggest a liquidity problem.

The gearing ratio of each business is quite similar. Neither business seems to have excessive borrowing. The interest cover ratio for each business is also similar. The ratios indicate that both businesses have good profit coverage for their interest charges.

The dividend payout ratio for each business seems very high. In the case of Ali plc, the dividends announced for the year are considerably higher than the profit for the year that is available for dividend. As a result, part of the dividend was paid out of retained profits from previous years. This is an unusual occurrence; although it is quite legitimate, such action may nevertheless suggest a lack of prudence on the part of the directors.

The P/E ratios for both businesses seem high, which indicates market confidence in their future prospects.

Chapter 7

7.1 Khan Ltd

(a) The break-even point if only the Alpha service were rendered would be:

$$\frac{\text{Fixed costs}}{\text{Sales revenue per unit} - \text{Variable cost per unit}} = \frac{£40,000}{£30 - £(15 + 6)}$$

$$= 4,445 \text{ units (a year)}$$

(Strictly it is 4,444.44 but 4,445 is the smallest number of units of the service that must be rendered to avoid a loss.)

(b)

	Alpha	Beta	Gamma
Selling price (£/unit)	30	39	20
Variable material costs (£/unit)	(15)	(18)	(10)
Variable production costs (£/unit)	(6)	(10)	(5)
Contribution (£/unit)	9	11	5
Staff time (hr/unit)	2	3	1
Contribution/staff hour	£4.50	£3.67	£5.00
Order of priority	2nd	3rd	1st

(c)

	Hours		Contribution £
Render:			
5,000 Gamma using	5,000	generating (that is, 5,000 × £5 =)	25,000
2,500 Alpha using	5,000	generating (that is, 2,500 × £9 =)	22,500
	10,000		47,500
		Less fixed costs	40,000
		Operating profit	7,500

This leaves a demand for 500 units of Alpha and 2,000 units of Beta unsatisfied.

Chapter 8

8.1 Promptprint

(a) The budget may be summarised as:

	£	
Sales revenue	196,000	
Direct materials	(38,000)	
Direct labour	(32,000)	
Total overheads	(77,000)	(2,400 + 3,000 + 27,600 + 36,000 + 8,000)
Operating profit	49,000	

The job may be priced on the basis that both overheads and operating profit should be apportioned to it on the basis of direct labour cost, as follows:

	£	
Direct materials	4,000	
Direct labour	3,600	
Overheads	8,663	(£77,000 × 3,600/32,000)
Operating profit	5,513	(£49,000 × 3,600/32,000)
	21,776	

This answer assumes that variable overheads vary in proportion to direct labour cost. Various other bases of charging overheads and profit loading the job could have been adopted. For example, materials cost could have been included (with direct labour) as the basis for profit loading, or even apportioning overheads.

(b) This part of the question is, in effect, asking for comments on the validity of 'full-cost-plus' pricing. This approach can be useful as an indicator of the effective long-run cost of doing the job. On the other hand, it fails to take account of relevant opportunity costs as well as the state of the market and other external factors. For example, it ignores the price that a competitor printing business may quote.

Chapter 9

9.1 Antonio Ltd

(a) (i) The raw materials inventories budget for the six months ending 31 December (physical quantities) is as follows:

	July Units	Aug Units	Sept Units	Oct Units	Nov Units	Dec Units
Opening inventories						
(current month's production)	500	600	600	700	750	750
Purchases (balance figure)	600	600	700	750	750	750
	1,100	1,200	1,300	1,450	1,500	1,500
Issues to production						
(from question)	(500)	(600)	(600)	(700)	(750)	(750)
Closing inventories						
(next month's production)	600	600	700	750	750	750

The raw materials inventories budget for the six months ending 31 December (in financial terms), that is, the physical quantities × £8, is:

	July £	Aug £	Sept £	Oct £	Nov £	Dec £
Opening inventories	4,000	4,800	4,800	5,600	6,000	6,000
Purchases	4,800	4,800	5,600	6,000	6,000	6,000
	8,800	9,600	10,400	11,600	12,000	12,000
Issues to production	(4,000)	(4,800)	(4,800)	(5,600)	(6,000)	(6,000)
Closing inventories	4,800	4,800	5,600	6,000	6,000	6,000

(ii) The trade payables budget for the six months ending 31 December is:

	July £	Aug £	Sept £	Oct £	Nov £	Dec £
Opening balance						
(current month's payment)	4,000	4,800	4,800	5,600	6,000	6,000
Purchases (from raw						
materials inventories budget)	4,800	4,800	5,600	6,000	6,000	6,000
	8,800	9,600	10,400	11,600	12,000	12,000
Payments	(4,000)	(4,800)	(4,800)	(5,600)	(6,000)	(6,000)
Closing balance						
(next month's payment)	4,800	4,800	5,600	6,000	6,000	6,000

(iii) The cash budget for the six months ending 31 December is:

	July £	Aug £	Sept £	Oct £	Nov £	Dec £
Inflows						
Receipts:						
Trade receivables (40% of sales revenue of two months previous)	2,800	3,200	3,200	4,000	4,800	5,200
Cash sales revenue (60% of current month's revenue)	4,800	6,000	7,200	7,800	8,400	9,600
Total inflows	7,600	9,200	10,400	11,800	13,200	14,800
Outflows						
Trade payables (from trade payables budget)	(4,000)	(4,800)	(4,800)	(5,600)	(6,000)	(6,000)
Direct costs	(3,000)	(3,600)	(3,600)	(4,200)	(4,500)	(4,500)
Advertising	(1,000)	–	–	(1,500)	–	–
Overheads: 80%	(1,280)	(1,280)	(1,280)	(1,280)	(1,600)	(1,600)
20%	(280)	(320)	(320)	(320)	(320)	(400)
New plant	–	–	(2,200)	(2,200)	(2,200)	–
Total outflows	(9,560)	(10,000)	(12,200)	(15,100)	(14,620)	(12,500)
Net inflows (outflows)	(1,960)	(800)	(1,800)	(3,300)	(1,420)	2,300
Balance c/f	5,540	4,740	2,940	(360)	(1,780)	520

The balances carried forward are deduced by deducting the deficit (net outflows) for the month from (or adding the surplus for the month to) the previous month's balance.

Note how budgets are linked; in this case the inventories budget to the trade payables budget and the trade payables budget to the cash budget.

(b) The following are possible means of relieving the cash shortages revealed by the budget:
- Make a higher proportion of sales on a cash basis.
- Collect the money from trade receivables more promptly, for example during the month following the sale.
- Hold lower inventories, both of raw materials and of finished goods.
- Increase the trade payables payment period.
- Delay the payments for advertising.
- Obtain more credit for the overhead costs; at present only 20% are on credit.
- Delay the payments for the new plant.

Chapter 10

10.1 Beacon Chemicals plc

(a) Relevant cash flows are as follows:

	Year 0 £000	Year 1 £000	Year 2 £000	Year 3 £000	Year 4 £000	Year 5 £000
Sales revenue	–	80	120	144	100	64
Loss of contribution		(15)	(15)	(15)	(15)	(15)
Variable costs		(40)	(50)	(48)	(30)	(32)
Fixed costs (Note 1)		(8)	(8)	(8)	(8)	(8)
Operating cash flows		17	47	73	47	9
Working capital	(30)					30
Capital cost	(100)					
Net relevant cash flows	(130)	17	47	73	47	39

Notes:

1 Only the fixed costs that are incremental to the project (existing only because of the project) are relevant. Depreciation is irrelevant because it is not a cash flow.
2 The research and development cost is irrelevant since it has been spent irrespective of the decision on X14 production.

(b) The payback period is as follows:

	Year 0 £000	Year 1 £000	Year 2 £000	Year 3 £000
Cumulative cash flows	(130)	(113)	(66)	7

Thus the equipment will have repaid the initial investment by the end of the third year of operations.

(c) The net present value is as follows:

	Year 0 £000	Year 1 £000	Year 2 £000	Year 3 £000	Year 4 £000	Year 5 £000
Discount factor	1.00	0.926	0.857	0.794	0.735	0.681
Present value	(130)	15.74	40.28	57.96	34.55	26.56
NPV	45.09	(that is, the sum of the present values for years 0 to 5)				

Chapter 11

11.1 Helsim Ltd

(a) The liquidity position may be assessed by using the liquidity ratios discussed in Chapter 6:

$$\text{Current ratio} = \frac{\text{Current assests}}{\text{Current liabilities}}$$

$$= \frac{£7.5m}{£5.4m}$$

$$= 1.4$$

$$\text{Acid test ratio} = \frac{\text{Current assets (excluding inventories)}}{\text{Current liabilities}}$$

$$= \frac{£3.7m}{£5.4m}$$

$$= 0.7$$

These ratios reveal a fairly weak liquidity position. The current ratio seems quite low and the acid test ratio very low. This latter ratio suggests that the business does not have sufficient liquid assets to meet its maturing obligations. It would, however, be useful to have details of the liquidity ratios of similar businesses in the same industry in order to make a more informed judgement. The bank over-draft represents 67% of the current liabilities and 40% of the total liabilities of the business. The continuing support of the bank is therefore important to the ability of the business to meet its commitments.

(b) The finance required to reduce trade payables to an average of 40 days outstanding is calculated as follows:

	£m
Trade payables at balance sheet date	1.80
Trade payables outstanding based on 40 days' credit 40/365 × £8.4m (that is, credit purchases)	(0.92)
Finance required	0.88 (say £0.9m)

(c) The bank may not wish to provide further finance to the business. The increase in overdraft will reduce the level of trade payables but will increase the risk exposure of the bank. The additional finance invested by the bank will not generate further funds and will not therefore be self-liquidating. The question does not make it clear whether the business has sufficient security to offer the bank for the increase in overdraft facility. The profits of the business will be reduced and the interest cover ratio, based on the profits generated last year, would reduce to about 1.6* times if the additional overdraft were granted (based on interest charged at 10% each year). This is very low and means that only a small decline in profits would leave interest charges uncovered.

* Existing bank overdraft (3.6) + extension of overdraft to cover reduction in trade payables (0.9) + loan notes (3.5) = £8.0m. Assuming a 10% interest rate means a yearly

interest payment of £0.8m. The operating profit was £1.3m. Interest cover would be 1.63 (that is, 1.3/0.8).

(d) A number of possible sources of finance might be considered. Four possible sources are as follows:

- *Issue equity shares.* This option may be unattractive to investors. The return on equity is fairly low at 7.9% (that is, profit for the year (0.3)/equity (3.8)) and there is no evidence that the profitability of the business will improve. If profits remain at their current level the effect of issuing more equity will be to reduce further the returns to equity.
- *Make other borrowings.* This option may also prove unattractive to investors. The effect of making further borowings will have a similar effect to that of increasing the overdraft. The profits of the business will be reduced and the interest cover ratio will decrease to a low level. The gearing ratio of the business is already quite high at 48% (that is, loan notes (3.5)/(loan notes + equity (3.5 + 3.8)) and it is not clear what security would be available for the loan. The gearing ratio would be much higher if the overdraft were to be included.
- *Chase trade receivables.* It may be possible to improve cash flows by reducing the level of credit outstanding from customers. At present, the average settlement period is 93 days (that is, (trade receivables (3.6)/sales revenue (14.2)) × 365), which seems quite high. A reduction in the average settlement period by approximately one-quarter would generate the funds required. However, it is not clear what effect this would have on sales.
- *Reduce inventories.* This appears to be the most attractive of the four options. At present, the average inventories holding period is 178 days (that is, (closing inventories (3.8)/cost of sales (7.8)) × 365), which seems very high. A reduction in this period by less than one-quarter would generate the funds required. However, if the business holds a large amount of slow-moving and obsolete items, it may be difficult to reduce inventories levels.

Chapter 12

12.1 Williams Wholesalers Ltd

	£	£
Existing level of trade receivables (£4m × 70/365)		767,123
New level of trade receivables: £2m × 80/365	438,356	
£2m × 30/365	164,384	602,740
Reduction in trade receivables		164,383
Costs and benefits of policy		
Cost of discount (£2m × 2%)		40,000
Less savings		
Interest payable (£164,383* × 13%)	21,370	
Administration costs	6,000	
Bad debts (20,000 – 10,000)	10,000	37,370
Net cost of policy		2,630

* It could be argued that the interest should be based on the amount expected to be received, that is the value of the trade receivables *after* taking account of the discount.

The above calculations reveal that the business will be worse off by offering the discounts.

Chapter 1

1.1   The objective of providing accounting information is to enable users to make more informed decisions and judgements about the organisation concerned. Accounting has no other valid purpose or justification.

1.2

Students	Whether to enrol on a course of study. This would probably involve an assessment of the university's ability to continue to operate and to fulfil students' needs.
Other universities and colleges	How best to compete against the university. This might involve using the university's performance in various aspects as a 'benchmark' when evaluating their own performance.
Employees	Whether to take up or to continue in employment with the university. Employees might assess this by considering the ability of the university to continue to provide employment and to reward employees adequately for their labour.
Government/ funding authority	How efficient and effective the university is in undertaking its various activities.
Local community representatives	Whether to allow/encourage the university to expand its premises. To assess this, the university's ability to continue to provide employment for the community, to use community resources and to help fund environmental improvements might be considered.
Suppliers	Whether to continue to supply the university at all; also whether to supply on credit. This would involve an assessment of the university's ability to pay for any goods and services supplied.
Lenders	Whether to lend money to the university and/or whether to require repayment of any existing loans. To assess this, the university's ability to meet its obligations to pay interest and to repay the principal would be considered.
Board of governors and managers (Faculty deans and so on)	Whether the performance of the university requires improvement. Performance to date would be compared with earlier plans or some other 'benchmark' to decide whether action needs to be taken. Whether there should be a change in the university's future direction. In making such decisions, management will need to look at the university's ability to perform and at the opportunities available to it.

There are clear similarities in the way in which accounting information is used in universities and private-sector businesses.

1.3 Most businesses are far too large and complex for managers to be able to see and assess everything that is going on in their own areas of responsibility merely by personal observation. Managers need information on all aspects within their control. Management accounting reports can provide them with this information, to a greater or lesser extent. These reports can be seen, therefore, as acting as the eyes and ears of the managers, providing insights not necessarily obvious without them.

1.4 Since we can never be sure what is going to happen in the future, the best that we can do is to make judgements on the basis of past experience. Thus information concerning flows of cash and of wealth in the recent past is likely to be a useful source on which to base judgements about possible future outcomes.

Chapter 2

2.1 The confusion arises because the owner seems unaware of the business entity convention in accounting. This convention requires a separation of the business from the owner(s) of the business for accounting purposes. The business is regarded as a separate entity and the balance sheet is prepared from the perspective of the business rather than that of the owner. As a result, funds invested in the business by the owner will be regarded as a claim that the owner has on the business. In the balance sheet, this claim will be shown alongside other claims on the business from outsiders.

2.2 A balance sheet does not show what a business is worth, for two major reasons:

- Only those items which can be measured reliably in monetary terms are shown on the balance sheet. Thus, things of value such as the reputation for product quality, skills of employees and so on will not normally appear in the balance sheet.
- The historic cost convention results in assets being recorded at their outlay cost rather than their current value. In the case of certain assets, the difference between historic cost and current value may be significant.

2.3 The balance sheet equation is simply the relationship between a business's assets, liabilities and equity. For the standard balance sheet layout, it is:

Assets (current and non-current) = Equity + Liabilities (current and non-current)

For the alternative layout mentioned in the chapter, the equation is:

Assets (current and non-current) − Liabilities (current and non-current) = Equity

2.4 Some object to the idea of humans being treated as assets for inclusion on the balance sheet. It can be seen as demeaning for humans to be listed alongside inventories, plant and machinery and other assets. However, others argue that humans are often the most valuable resource of a business and that placing a value on this resource will help bring to the attention of managers the importance of nurturing and developing this 'asset'. There is a saying in management that 'the things that count are the things that get counted'. As the value of the 'human assets' is not stated in the financial statements, there is a danger that managers will treat these 'assets' less favourably than other assets that are on the balance sheet.

Humans are likely to meet the first criterion of an asset listed in the chapter, that is, a probable future benefit exists. There would be little point in employing people if this were not the case. The second criterion concerning exclusive right of control is more problematic. Clearly a business cannot control humans in the same way as most other assets. However, a business can have the exclusive right to the employment services that a person provides. This distinction between control over the services provided and control over the person makes it possible to argue that the second criterion can be met.

Humans normally sign a contract of employment with the business, and so the third criterion is normally met. The difficulty, however, is with the fourth criterion, that is, whether the value of humans (or their services) can be measured with any degree of reliability. To date, none of the measurement methods proposed enjoy widespread acceptance.

Chapter 3

3.1 At the time of preparing the income statement, it is not always possible to determine accurately the expenses that need to be matched to the sales revenue figure for the period. It will only be at some later point in time that the true position becomes clear. However, it is still necessary to try to include all relevant expenses in the income statement and so estimates of the future will have to be made. Examples of estimates that may have to be made include:

- expenses accrued at the end of the period such as the amount of telephone expenses incurred since the last quarter's bill
- the amount of depreciation based on estimates of the life of the non-current asset and future residual value
- the amount of bad and doubtful debts incurred.

3.2 Depreciation attempts to allocate the cost or fair value, less any residual value, of the asset over its useful life. Depreciation does not attempt to measure the fall in value of the asset during the period. Thus, the carrying amount of the asset appearing on the balance sheet normally represents the unexpired cost of the asset rather than its current market value.

3.3 The convention of consistency is designed to provide a degree of uniformity concerning the application of accounting policies. We have seen, that in certain areas, there may be more than one method of accounting for an item, for example inventories. The convention of consistency states that, having decided on a particular accounting policy, a business should continue to apply the policy in successive periods. While this policy helps to ensure that users can make valid comparisons concerning business performance *over time*, it does not ensure that valid comparisons can be made *between businesses*. This is because different businesses may consistently apply different accounting policies.

3.4 An expense is that element of the cost incurred that is used up during the accounting period. An asset is that element of cost which is carried forward on the balance sheet and which will normally be used up in future periods. Thus, both assets and expenses arise from costs being incurred. The major difference between the two is the period over which the benefits (resulting from the costs incurred) accrue.

Chapter 4

4.1 It does not differ. In both cases they are required to meet their debts to the full extent that there are assets available. This means that they both have a liability that is limited to the extent of their assets. This is a particularly important fact for the shareholders of a limited company because they know that those owed money by the company cannot demand that the shareholders contribute additional funds to help meet debts. Thus the liability of the shareholders is limited to the amount that they have paid for their shares, or have agreed to pay in the case of partially unpaid shares. This contrasts with the position of the owner or part owner of an unincorporated (non-company) business. Here all of the individual's assets could be required to meet the unsatisfied liabilities of the business.

4.2 A private limited company may place restrictions on the transfer of its shares, that is, the directors can veto an attempt by a shareholder to sell his or her shares to another person to whom the directors object. Thus, in effect, the majority can avoid having as a shareholder someone that they would prefer not to have. A public company cannot do this.

A public limited company must have authorised share capital of at least £50,000. There is no minimum for a private limited company.

The main advantage of being a public limited company is that the company may offer its shares and loan notes to the general public; a private company cannot make such an offer.

4.3 A reserve is that part of the equity (owners' claim) of a company that is not share capital. Reserves represent gains or surpluses that enhance the claim of the shareholders above the nominal value of their shares. For example, the share premium account is a reserve that represents the excess over the nominal value of shares that is paid for them on a share issue. The retained profit balance is a reserve that arises from ploughed-back profits earned by the company. Revenue reserves arise from realised profits and gains. Capital reserves arise from unrealised profits and gains (for example, the upward revaluation of a non-current asset) or from issuing shares at a premium (share premium).

4.4 A preference share represents part of the ownership of a company. Preference shares entitle their owners to the first part of any dividend paid by the company, up to a maximum amount. The maximum is usually expressed as a percentage of the nominal or par value of the preference shares.

(a) They differ from ordinary shares to the extent that they only entitle their holders to dividends to a predetermined maximum value. Dividends to ordinary shareholders have no predetermined maximum. Usually preference shares attract a maximum payout equal to their nominal value on liquidation, and the ordinary shareholders receive the residue after all other claimants, including the preference shareholders.

(b) They differ from loan notes in that these represent borrowings for the company, where normally holders have a contract with the company that specifies the rate of interest, interest payment dates and redemption date. They are often secured on the company's assets. Preference shareholders have no such contract.

Chapter 5

5.1 People and organisations will not normally accept other than cash in settlement of their claims against the business. If a business wants to employ people it must pay them in cash. If it wants to buy a new non-current asset to exploit a business opportunity, the supplier will normally insist on being paid in cash, normally after a short period of credit. When businesses fail, it is their inability to find the cash to pay claimants that actually drives them under. These factors lead to cash being the pre-eminent business asset and, therefore, the one that analysts and others watch carefully in trying to assess the ability of the business to survive and/or to take advantage of commercial opportunities as they arise.

5.2 With the direct method, the business's cash records are analysed for the period concerned. The analysis reveals the amounts of cash, in total, which have been paid and received in respect of each category of the cash flow statement. This is not difficult in principle, or in practice if it is done by computer as a matter of routine.

The indirect method takes the approach that, while the profit (loss) for the year is not equal to the net inflow (outflow) of cash from operations, they are fairly closely linked to the extent that appropriate adjustment of the profit (loss) for the year figure will produce the correct cash flow one. The adjustment is concerned with depreciation charge for, and movements in relevant working capital items over, the period.

5.3 (a) *Cash flows from operating activities*. This would normally be positive, even for a business with small profits or even losses. The fact that depreciation is not a cash flow tends to lead to positive cash flows in this area in most cases.

(b) *Cash flows from investing activities*. Normally this would be negative in cash flow terms since assets become worn out and need to be replaced in the normal course of business. This means that, typically, old items of property, plant and equipment are generating less cash on their disposal than is having to be paid out to replace them.

(c) *Cash flows from financing activities*. There is a tendency for businesses either to expand or to fail. In either case, this is likely to mean that, over the years, more finance will be raised than will be redeemed or retired.

5.4 There are several reasons for this, including the following:

- Changes in inventories, trade receivables and trade payables. For example, an increase in trade receivables during an accounting period would mean that the cash received from credit sales would be less than the credit sales revenue for the same period.
- Cash may have been spent on new non-current assets or received from disposals of old ones; these would not directly affect profit.
- Cash may have been spent to redeem or repay a financial claim or received as a result of the creation or the increase of a claim. These would not directly affect profit.
- The taxation charged in the income statement would not be the same tax that is paid during the same accounting period.

Chapter 6

6.1 The fact that a business operates on a low operating profit margin indicates that only a small operating profit is being produced for each £1 of sales revenue generated. However, this does not necessarily mean that the ROCE will be low. If the business is able to generate a large amount of sales revenue during a period, the operating profit may be very high even though the operating profit per £1 of sales revenue is low. If the overall operating profit is high, this can lead, in turn, to a high ROCE, since it is the total operating profit that is used as the numerator (top part of the fraction) in this ratio. Many businesses (including supermarkets) pursue a strategy of 'low margin, high turnover'.

6.2 The balance sheet is drawn up at a single point in time – the end of the financial period. As a result, the figures shown on the balance sheet represent the position at that single point in time and may not be representative of the position during the period. Wherever possible, average figures (perhaps based on monthly figures) should be used. However, an external user may only have access to the opening and closing balance sheets for the year and so a simple average based on these figures may be all that it is possible to calculate. Where a business is seasonal in nature or is subject to cyclical changes, this simple averaging may not be sufficient.

6.3 Three possible reasons for a long inventories turnover period are:

- poor inventories controls, leading to excessive investment in inventories;
- inventories hoarding in anticipation of price rises or shortages;
- inventories building in anticipation of increased future sales.

A short inventories turnover period may be due to:

- tight inventories controls, thereby reducing excessive investment in inventories generally and/or the amount of obsolete and slow-moving inventories;
- an inability to finance the required amount of inventories to meet sales demand;
- a difference in the mix of inventories carried by similar businesses (for example, greater investment in perishable goods which are held for a short period only).

6.4 The P/E ratio may vary between businesses within the same industry for the following reasons:

- *Accounting conventions.* Differences in the methods used to compute profit (for example, inventories valuation and depreciation) can lead to different profit figures and, therefore, different P/E ratios.
- *Different prospects.* One business may be regarded as having a much brighter future owing to factors such as the quality of management, the quality of products, and location. This will affect the market price that investors are prepared to pay for the share and hence it will also affect the P/E ratio.
- *Different asset structure.* One business's underlying asset base may be much higher than the other's and this may affect the market price of its shares.

Chapter 7

7.1 A fixed cost is one that is the same irrespective of the level of activity or output. Typical examples of costs that are fixed, irrespective of the level of production or provision of a service, include rent of business premises, salaries of supervisory staff, and electricity charges for heating and lighting.

A variable cost is one that varies with the level of activity or output. Examples include raw materials and labour, where labour is rewarded in proportion to the level of output.

Note particularly that it is relative to the level of activity that costs are fixed or variable. Fixed costs will be affected by inflation and they will be greater for a longer period than for a shorter one.

For a particular product or service, knowing which costs are fixed and which variable enables managers to predict the total cost for any particular level of activity. It also enables them to concentrate only on the variable costs in circumstances where a decision will not alter the fixed costs.

7.2 The break-even point (BEP) is the level of activity, measured either in physical units or in value of sales revenue, at which the sales revenues exactly cover all of the costs, both fixed and variable.

BEP is calculated as:

Fixed costs/(Sales revenue per unit – Variable costs per unit)

which may alternatively be expressed as:

Fixed costs/Contribution per unit

Thus break-even will occur when the contributions for the period are sufficient to cover the fixed costs for the period.

The BEP tends to be useful as a comparison with planned level of activity in an attempt to assess the riskiness of the activity.

7.3 Operating (or operational) gearing refers to the extent of fixed costs relative to variable costs in the total costs of some activity. Where the fixed costs form a relatively high proportion of the total, we say that the activity has high operational gearing.

Typically, high operating gearing is present in environments where there is a relatively high level of mechanisation (that is, capital-intensive environments). This is because such environments tend simultaneously to involve relatively high fixed costs of depreciation, maintenance and so on and relatively low variable costs.

High operating gearing tends to mean that the effects of increases or decreases in the level of activity have an accentuated effect on operating profit. For example, a 20% decrease in output of a particular service will lead to a greater than 20% decrease in operating profit, assuming no cost or price changes.

7.4 In the face of a restricting scarce resource, profit will be maximised by using the scarce resource on output where the contribution per unit of the scarce resource is maximised.

This means that the contribution per unit of the scarce resource (for example, hour of scarce labour, unit of scarce raw material and so on) for each competing product or service needs to be identified. It is then a question of allocating the scarce resource to the product or service that provides the highest contribution per unit of the particular scarce resource.

The logic of this approach is that the scarce resource is allocated to the activity that uses it most effectively in terms of contribution and, therefore, profit.

Chapter 8

8.1 In process costing, the total production costs for a period are divided by the number of completed units of output for the period to deduce the full cost. Where there is work in progress at the beginning and/or the end of the period complications arise.

The problem is that some of the completed output incurred costs in the preceding period. Similarly, some of the costs incurred in the current period lead to completed production in the subsequent period. Account needs to be taken of these facts if reliable full cost information is to be obtained.

8.2 The only reason for distinguishing between direct and indirect costs is to help to deduce the full cost of a unit of output in a job-costing environment. In an environment where all units of output are identical, or can reasonably be regarded as being so, a process-costing approach will be taken. This avoids the need for identifying direct and indirect costs separately.

Direct costs form that part of the total costs of pursuing some activity that can unequivocally be associated with that particular activity. Examples of direct costs in the typical job-costing environment include direct labour and direct materials.

Indirect costs are the remainder of the costs of pursuing some activity. Identifying direct costs reduces the extent to which costs must be related to individual jobs on a more or less arbitrary basis. In practice, knowledge of the direct costs tends to provide the basis used to charge overheads to jobs.

The distinction between direct and indirect costs is irrelevant for any other purpose.

Directness and indirectness is dictated as much by the nature of what is being costed as by the nature of the cost.

8.3 The notion of direct and indirect costs is concerned only with the extent to which particular costs can unequivocally be related to and measured in respect of a particular cost unit, usually a product or service. The distinction between direct and indirect costs is made exclusively for the purpose of deducing the full cost of some cost unit, in an environment where each cost unit is not identical, or close enough to being identical for it to be treated as such. Thus, it is typically in the context of job costing, or some variant of it, that the distinction between direct and indirect costs is usefully made.

The notion of variable and fixed costs is concerned entirely with how costs behave in the face of changes in the volume of output. The value of being able to distinguish between fixed and variable costs is that predictions can be made of what total costs will be at particular levels of volume and/or what reduction or addition to costs will occur if the volume of output is reduced or increased.

Thus the notions of direct and indirect costs, on the one hand, and those of variable and fixed costs, on the other, are not connected with one another. Although it is true that, in most contexts, some direct costs are variable, some direct costs are fixed. Similarly, indirect costs might be fixed or variable.

8.4 The full cost includes all of the costs of pursuing the cost objective, including a 'fair' share of the overheads. Generally the full cost represents an average cost of the various elements, rather than a cost that arises because the business finds itself in a particular situation.

The fact that the full cost reflects all aspects of cost should mean that, were the business to sell its output at a price exactly equal to the full cost, the sales revenue for the period would exactly cover all of the costs and the business would break even, that is, make neither profit nor loss.

Chapter 9

9.1 A budget can be defined as a financial plan for a future period of time. Thus it sets out the intentions which management has for the period concerned. Achieving the budget plans should help to achieve the long-term plans of the business. Achievement of the long-term plans should mean that the business is successfully working towards its objectives.

A budget differs from a forecast in that a forecast is a statement of what is expected to happen without the intervention of management, perhaps because managers cannot intervene (as with a weather forecast). A plan is an intention to achieve.

Normally, management would take account of reliable forecasts when making plans.

9.2 The five uses of budgets are:

■ They tend to promote forward thinking and the possible identification of short-term problems. Managers must plan and the budgeting process tends to force them to do so. In doing so, they are likely to encounter potential problems. If the potential problems can be identified early enough, solutions might be easily found.
■ They can be used to help co-ordination between various sections of the business. It is important that the plans of one area of the business fit in with those of other areas; a lack of co-ordination could have disastrous consequences. Having formal statements of plans for each aspect of the business enables a check to be made that plans are complementary.
■ They can motivate managers to better performance. It is believed that people are motivated by having a target to aim for. Provided that the inherent goals are achievable, budgets can provide an effective motivational device.
■ They can provide a basis for a system of control. Having a plan against which actual performance can be measured provides a potentially useful tool of control.
■ They can provide a system of authorisation. Many managers have 'spending' budgets for research and development, staff training and so on. For these people, the size of their budget defines their authority to spend.

9.3 A variance is the effect on budgeted operating profit of the particular aspect of the business that is being considered. Thus it is the difference between the budgeted operating profit and what the actual operating profit would have been had all other matters, except the one under consideration, gone according to budget. From this it must be the case that budgeted operating profit plus favourable variances less unfavourable variances equals actual operating profit.

The objective of analysing and assessing variances is to identify whether, and if so where, things are not going according to plan. If this can be done, it may be possible to find out the actual cause of things going out of control. If this can be discovered, it may be possible to put things right for the future.

9.4 Where the budgeted and actual volumes of output do not coincide, it is impossible to make a valid comparison of 'allowed' and actual expenses and revenues. Flexing the original budget to reflect the actual output level enables a more informative comparison to be made.

Flexing certainly does not mean that output volume differences do not matter. Flexing will show (as the difference between flexed and original budget operating profits) the effect on operating profit of output volume differences.

Chapter 10

10.1 NPV is usually considered the best method of assessing investment opportunities because it takes account of:

- *The timing of the cash flows.* By *discounting* the various cash flows associated with each project according to when they are expected to arise, the NPV method recognises the fact that cash flows do not all occur simultaneously. Associated with this is the fact that, by discounting, using the opportunity cost of finance (that is, the return that the next best alternative opportunity would generate), the net benefit after financing costs have been met is identified (as the NPV).
- *The whole of the relevant cash flows.* NPV includes all of the relevant cash flows irrespective of when they are expected to occur. It treats them differently according to their date of occurrence, but they are all taken account of in the NPV and they all have, or can have, an influence on the decision.
- *The objectives of the business.* NPV is the only method of appraisal where the output of the analysis has a direct bearing on the wealth of the owners of the business. (Positive NPVs enhance wealth; negative ones reduce it.) Since most private-sector businesses seek to increase their owners' wealth, NPV clearly is the best approach to use.

NPV provides clear decision rules concerning acceptance/rejection of projects and the ranking of projects. It is fairly simple to use, particularly with the availability of modern computer software that takes away the need for routine calculations to be done manually.

10.2 The payback method, in its original form, does not take account of the time value of money. However, it would be possible to modify the payback method to accommodate this requirement. Cash flows arising from a project could be discounted, using the cost of finance as the appropriate discount rate, in the same way as in the NPV and IRR methods. The discounted payback approach is used by some businesses and represents an improvement on the original approach described in the chapter. However, it retains the other flaws of the original payback approach that were discussed. For example, it ignores relevant data after the payback period. Thus, even in its modified form, the PP method cannot be regarded as superior to NPV.

10.3 The IRR method does appear to be preferred to the NPV method among practising managers. The main reasons for this appear to be as follows:

- A preference for a percentage return ratio rather than an absolute figure as a means of expressing the outcome of a project. This preference for a ratio may reflect the fact that other financial goals of the business are often set in terms of ratios, for example return on capital employed.
- A preference for ranking projects in terms of their percentage return. Managers feel that it is easier to rank projects on the basis of percentage returns (though NPV outcomes should be just as easy for them). We saw in the chapter that the IRR method could provide misleading advice on the ranking of projects and that the NPV method was preferable for this purpose.

10.4 Cash flows are preferred to profit flows because cash is the ultimate measure of economic wealth. Cash is used to acquire resources and for distribution to shareholders. When cash is invested in an investment project, an opportunity cost is incurred, as the cash cannot be used in other investment projects. Similarly, when positive cash flows are generated by the project, the cash can be used to reinvest in other investment projects.

Profit, on the other hand, is relevant to reporting the productive effort for a period. This measure of effort may have only a tenuous relationship to cash flows for a period. The conventions of accounting may lead to the recognition of gains and losses in one period and the relevant cash inflows and outflows occurring in another period.

Chapter 11

11.1 Share warrants may be particularly useful for young expanding businesses that wish to attract new investors. They can help provide a 'sweetener' for the issue of loan notes. By attaching warrants it may be possible to agree a lower rate of interest or less restrictive loan covenants. If the business is successful, the warrants will provide a further source of finance. Investors will exercise their option to acquire shares if the market price of the shares exceeds the exercise price of the warrant. However, this will have the effect of diluting the control of existing shareholders.

11.2 A listed business may wish to revert to unlisted status for a number of possible reasons. These include:

- *Cost.* A Stock Exchange listing can be costly, as the business must adhere to certain administrative regulations and financial disclosures.
- *Scrutiny.* Listed companies are subject to close scrutiny by analysts and this may not be welcome if the business is engaged in sensitive negotiations or controversial business activities.
- *Takeover risk.* The shares of the business may be purchased by an unwelcome bidder and this may result in a takeover.

■ *Investor profile*. If the business is dominated by a few investors who wish to retain their interest in the business and do not wish to raise further equity by public issues, the benefits of a listing are few.

11.3 An offer for sale involves an issuing house buying the shares in the business and then, in turn, selling the shares to the public. The issue will be advertised by the publication of a prospectus, which will set out details of the business and the issue price of the shares (or reserve price if a tender issue is being made). The shares issued by the issuing house may be either new shares or shares which have been purchased from existing shareholders. A public issue is where the business undertakes direct responsibility for issuing shares to the public. If an issuing house is employed it will usually be in the role of adviser and administrator of the issue. However, the issuing house may also underwrite the issue. A public issue runs the risk that the shares will not be taken up and is a less popular form of issue for businesses.

11.4 Invoice discounting is a service offered to businesses by a financial institution whereby the institution is prepared to advance a sum equivalent to 75% to 80% of outstanding trade receivables. The amount advanced is usually payable within 60 to 90 days. The business will retain responsibility for collecting the amounts owing from credit customers and the advance must be repaid irrespective of whether the trade receivables have been collected. Factoring is a service that is also offered to businesses by financial institutions. In this case, the factor will take over the business's sales and trade receivables records and will undertake to collect trade receivables on behalf of the client business. The factor will also be prepared to make an advance of 80% to 85% of approved trade receivables that is repayable from the amounts received from customers. The service charge for invoice discounting is up to 0.5% of turnover, whereas the service charge for factoring is up to 3% of turnover. This difference explains, in part, why businesses have shown a preference for invoice discounting rather than factoring in recent years. However, the factor provides additional services, as explained.

Chapter 12

12.1 Although the credit manager is responsible for ensuring that trade receivables pay on time, Tariq may be right in denying blame. Various factors may be responsible for the situation described which are beyond the control of the credit manager. These include:

■ a downturn in the economy leading to financial difficulties among trade receivables;

■ a decision made by other managers to liberalise credit policy in order to stimulate sales;

■ an increase in competition among suppliers offering credit that is being exploited by customers;

■ disputes with customers over the quality of goods or services supplied; and

■ problems in the delivery of goods leading to delays.

You may have thought of others.

12.2 Inventories levels could be affected in the following ways:

(a) An increase in production bottlenecks is likely to result in an increase in raw materials and work in progress being processed within the plant. Therefore, inventories levels should rise.

(b) A rise in interest rates will make the cost of holding inventories more expensive (if they are financed by debt). This may, in turn, lead to a decision to reduce inventories levels.

(c) The decision to reduce the range of products should result in a reduction in the inventories being held. It would no longer be necessary to hold certain items in order to meet customer demand.

(d) Switching to a local supplier may reduce the lead time between ordering an item and receiving it. This should, in turn, reduce the need to carry such high levels of the item.

(e) A deterioration in the quality of bought-in items may result in the purchase of higher quantities of inventories in order to take account of the defective element in inventories acquired and, perhaps, an increase in the inspection time for items received. This would lead to a rise in levels of inventories.

12.3 Inventories are held to meet customer demand, to avoid the problems of running out of supplies and to take advantage of profitable opportunities (for example, buying items that are expected to rise steeply in price in the future). These reasons are similar to the transactionary, precautionary and speculative motives that were used to explain why cash is held by a business.

12.4 (a) The costs of holding too little cash are:

■ failure to meet obligations when they fall due which can damage the reputation of the business and may, in the extreme, lead to the business collapsing;

■ having to borrow and thereby incur interest charges; and

■ an inability to take advantage of profitable opportunities.

(b) The costs of holding too much cash are:

■ failure to use the funds available for more profitable purposes; and

■ loss of value during a period of inflation.

Appendix D: Solutions to selected exercises

Chapter 2

2.1

Paul
Cash flow statement for Thursday

	£
Opening balance (from Wednesday)	59
Cash from sale of wrapping paper	47
Cash paid to purchase wrapping paper	(53)
Closing balance	53

Income statement for Thursday

	£
Sales revenue	47
Cost of goods sold	(33)
Profit	14

Balance sheet as at Thursday evening

	£
Cash	53
Inventories of goods for resale (23 + 53 − 33)	43
Total assets	96
Equity	96

2.2

Helen
Income statement for day 1

	£
Sales revenue (70 × £0.80)	56
Cost of sales (70 × £0.50)	(35)
Profit	21

Cash flow statement for day 1

	£
Opening balance	40
Cash from sales	56
Cash for purchases (80 × £0.50)	(40)
Closing balance	56

Balance sheet as at end of day 1

	£
Cash balance	56
Inventory of unsold goods (10 × £0.50)	5
Total assets	61
Equity	61

Income statement for day 2

	£
Sales revenue (65 × £0.80)	52.0
Cost of sales (65 × £0.50)	(32.5)
Profit	19.5

Cash flow statement for day 2

	£
Opening balance	56.0
Cash from sales	52.0
Cash for purchases (60 × £0.50)	(30.0)
Closing balance	78.0

Balance sheet as at end of day 2

	£
Cash balance	78.0
Inventory of unsold goods (5 × £0.50)	2.5
Total assets	80.5
Equity	80.5

Income statement for day 3

	£
Sales revenue ((20 × £0.80) + (45 × £0.40))	34.0
Cost of sales (65 × £0.50)	(32.5)
Profit	1.5

Cash flow statement for day 3

	£
Opening balance	78.0
Cash from sales	34.0
Cash for purchases (60 × £0.50)	(30.0)
Closing balance	82.0

Balance sheet as at end of day 3

	£
Cash balance	82.0
Inventory of unsold goods	–
Total assets	82.0
Equity	82.0

2.4 Crafty Engineering Ltd

(a)
Crafty Engineering Ltd
Balance sheet as at 30 June last year

	£000
Non-current assets	
Property, plant and equipment	
Property	320
Equipment and tools	207
Motor vehicles	38
	565
Current assets	
Inventories	153
Trade receivables	185
	338
Total assets	903

Equity (Owners' capital, which is the missing figure)	441
Non-current liabilities	
Long-term borrowings (Loan Industrial Finance Co.)	260
Current liabilities	
Trade payables	86
Short-term borrowings	116
	202
Total equity and liabilities	903

(b) The balance sheet reveals a high level of investment in non-current assets. In percentage terms, we can say that more than 60% of the total investment in assets (565/903) has been in non-current assets. The nature of the business may require a heavy investment in non-current assets. The investment in current assets exceeds the current liabilities by a large amount (approximately 1.7 times). As a result, there is no obvious sign of a liquidity problem. However, the balance sheet reveals that the business has no cash balance and is therefore dependent on the continuing support of short-term borrowing in order to meet obligations when they fall due. When considering the long-term financing of the business, we can see that about 37% (that is, 260/(260 + 441)) of the total long-term finance for the business has been supplied by borrowings and about 63% (that is, 441/(260 + 441)) by the owners. This level of long-term borrowing seems quite high but not excessive. However, we would need to know more about the ability of the business to service the borrowing (that is, make interest payments and repayments of the amount borrowed) before a full assessment could be made.

Chapter 3

3.1 (a) Equity does increase as a result of the owners introducing more cash into the business, but it will also increase as a result of introducing other assets (for example, a motor car) and by the business generating revenue by trading. Similarly, equity decreases not only as a result of withdrawals of cash by owners but also by withdrawals of other assets (for example, inventory for the owners' personal use) and through trading expenses being incurred. For the typical business in a typical accounting period, equity will alter much more as a result of trading activities than for any other reason.

(b) An accrued expense is not one that relates to next year. It is one that needs to be matched with the revenue of the accounting period under review, but that has yet to be met in terms of cash payment. As such, it will appear on the balance sheet as a current liability.

(c) The purpose of depreciation is not to provide for asset replacement. Rather, it is an attempt to allocate the cost, or fair value, of the asset (less any residual value) over its useful life. Depreciation is an attempt to provide a measure of the amount of the non-current asset that has been consumed during the period. This amount will then be charged as an expense for the period in deriving the profit figure. Depreciation is a book entry (the outlay of cash occurs when the asset is purchased) and does not normally entail setting aside a separate amount of cash for asset replacement. Even if this were done, there would be no guarantee that sufficient funds would be available at the end of the asset's life for its replacement. Factors such as inflation and technological change may mean that the replacement cost is higher than the original cost of the asset.

(d) In the short term, it is possible for the current value of a non-current asset to exceed its original cost. However, nearly all non-current assets will wear out over time as a result of being used to generate wealth for the business. This will be the case for freehold buildings. As a result, some measure of depreciation should be calculated to take account of the fact that the asset is being consumed. Some businesses revalue their freehold buildings where the current value is significantly different from the original cost. Where this occurs, the depreciation charged should be based on the revalued amount (fair value). This will normally result in higher depreciation charges than if the asset remained at its historic cost.

3.3 The existence of profit and downward movement in cash may be for various reasons, which include the following:

- the purchase of assets for cash during the period (for example, motor cars and inventories), which were not all consumed during the period and are therefore not having as great an effect on expenses as they are on cash
- the payment of an outstanding liability (for example, borrowings), which will have an effect on cash but not on expenses in the income statement
- the withdrawal of cash by the owners from the equity invested, which will not have an effect on the expenses in the income statement
- the generation of revenue on credit where the cash has yet to be received. This will increase the sales revenue for the period but will not have a beneficial effect on the cash balance until a later period.

3.5 WW Associates

WW Associates
Balance sheet as at 31 December 2008

	£
Assets	
Machinery (25,300 + 6,000 + 9,000 − 13,000 + 3,900 − 9,360)	21,840*
Inventories (12,200 + 143,000 + 12,000 − 127,000 − 25,000)	15,200
Trade receivables (21,300 + 211,000 − 198,000)	34,300
Cash at bank (overdraft) (8,300 − 23,000 − 25,000 − 2,000 − 6,000	
− 23,800 − 2,700 − 12,000 + 42,000 + 198,000 − 156,000 − 17,500)	(19,700)
Prepaid expenses (400 − 400 + 5,000 + 500)	5,500
Total assets	57,140

	£
Claims	
Equity (capital) (48,900 − 23,000 + 26,480)	52,380
Trade payables (16,900 + 143,000 − 156,000)	3,900
Accrued expenses (1,700 − 1,700 + 860)	860
Total equity and liabilities	57,140

* Cost less accumulated depreciation at 31 December 2007	25,300
Carrying amount of machine disposed of (£13,000 − £3,900)	(9,100)
Cost of new machine	15,000
Depreciation for 2008 (£31,200 × 30%)	(9,360)
Carrying amount (written-down value) of machine at 31 December 2008	21,840

Income statement for the year ended 31 December 2008

	£
Sales revenue (211,000 + 42,000)	253,000
Cost of goods sold (127,000 + 25,000)	(152,000)
Gross profit	101,000
Rent (20,000)	(20,000)
Rates (400 + 1,500)	(1,900)
Wages (−1,700 + 23,800 + 860)	(22,960)
Electricity (2,700)	(2,700)
Machinery depreciation (9,360)	(9,360)
Loss on disposal of the old machinery (13,000 − 3,900 − 9,000)	(100)
Van expenses (17,500)	(17,500)
Profit for the year	26,480

The loss on disposal of the old machinery is the carrying amount (cost less depreciation) less the disposal proceeds. Since the machinery had only been owned for one year, with a depreciation rate of 30%, the depreciation on it so far is £3,900 (that is, £13,000 × 30%). The effective disposal proceeds were £9,000 because, as a result of trading it in, the business saved £9,000 on the new asset.

The depreciation expense for 2008 is based on the cost less accumulated depreciation of the assets owned at the end of 2008. Accumulated depreciation must be taken into account because the business uses the reducing-balance method.

The balance sheet could now be rewritten in a more stylish form as follows:

WW Associates
Balance sheet as at 31 December 2008

	£
Non-current assets	
Property, plant and equipment	
Machinery at cost less depreciation	21,840
Current assets	
Inventories	15,200
Trade receivables	34,300
Prepaid expenses	5,500
	55,000
Total assets	76,840

	£
Equity (capital)	
Original	48,900
Profit	26,480
Drawings	(23,000)
	52,380
Current liabilities	
Trade payables	3,900
Accrued expenses	860
Borrowings – Bank overdraft	19,700
	24,460
Total equity and liabilities	76,840

Chapter 4

4.1 Limited companies can no more set a limit on the amount of debts they will meet than can human beings. They must meet their debts up to the limit of their assets, just as we as individuals must. In the context of owners' claim, 'reserves' mean part of the owners' claim against the assets of the company. These assets may or may not include cash. The legal ability of the company to pay dividends is not related to the amount of cash that it has.

Preference shares do not carry a guaranteed dividend. They simply guarantee that the preference shareholders have a right to the first slice of any dividend that is paid. Shares of many companies can, in effect, be bought by one investor from another through the Stock Exchange. Such a transaction has no direct effect on the company, however. These are not new shares being offered by the company, but existing shares that are being sold 'second-hand'.

4.2 (a) The first part of the quote is incorrect. Bonus shares should not, of themselves, increase the value of the shareholders' wealth. This is because reserves, belonging to the shareholders, are used to create bonus shares. Thus, each shareholder's stake in the company has not increased.

(b) This statement is incorrect. Shares can be issued at any price, provided that it is not below the nominal value of the shares. Once the company has been trading profitably for a period, the shares will not be worth the same as they were (the nominal value) when the company was first formed. In such circumstances, issuing shares at above their nominal value would not only be legal, but essential to preserve the wealth of the existing shareholders relative to any new ones.

(c) This statement is incorrect. From a legal perspective, the company is limited to a maximum dividend of the current extent of its revenue reserves. This amounts to any after-tax profits or gains realised that have not been eroded through, for example, payments of previous dividends. Legally, cash is not an issue; it would be perfectly legal for a company to borrow the funds to pay a dividend – although whether such an action would be commercially prudent is another question.

(d) This statement is partly incorrect. Companies do indeed have to pay tax on their profits. Depending on their circumstances, shareholders might also have to pay tax on their dividends.

4.4

Chips Limited
Balance sheet as at 30 June 2008

	Cost £000	Depreciation £000	£000
Non-current assets			
Property, plant and equipment			
Buildings	800	(112)	688
Plant and equipment	650	(367)	283
Motor vehicles (102 – 8); (53 – 5 + 19)	94	(67)	27
	1,544	(546)	998
Current assets			
Inventories			950
Trade receivables (420 – 16)			404
Cash at bank (16 + 2)			18
			1,372
Total assets			2,370
Equity			
Ordinary shares of £1, fully paid			800
Reserves at 1 July 2007			248
Retained profit for year			60
			1,108
Non-current liabilities			
Borrowings – secured 10% loan			700
Current liabilities			
Trade payables (361 + 23)			384
Other payables (117 + 35)			152
Taxation			26
			562
Total equity and liabilities			2,370

Income statement for the year ended 30 June 2008

	£000
Revenue (1,850 – 16)	1,834
Cost of sales (1,040 + 23)	(1,063)
Gross profit	771
Depreciation (220 – 2 – 5 + 8 + (94 × 20%))	(240)
Other operating costs	(375)
Operating profit	156
Interest payable (35 + 35)	(70)
Profit before taxation	86
Taxation (86 × 30%)	(26)
Profit for the year	60

Chapter 5

5.1 (a) An increase in the level of inventories would, ultimately, have an adverse effect on cash.

(b) A rights issue of ordinary shares will give rise to a positive cash flow, which will be included in the 'financing' section of the cash flow statement.

(c) A bonus issue of ordinary shares has no cash flow effect.

(d) Writing off some of the value of the inventories has no cash flow effect.

(e) A disposal for cash of a large number of shares by a major shareholder has no cash flow effect as far as the business is concerned.

(f) Depreciation does not involve cash at all. Using the indirect method of deducing cash flows from operating activities involves the depreciation expense in the calculation, but this is simply because we are trying to find out from the profit before taxation (after depreciation) figure what the profit before taxation *and* depreciation must have been.

5.3

Torrent plc
Cash flow statement for the year ended 31 December 2008

	£m
Cash flows from operating activities	
Profit before taxation (after interest) (see Note 1 below)	170
Adjustments for:	
Depreciation (Note 2)	78
Interest expense (Note 3)	26
	274
Decrease in inventories (41 − 35)	6
Increase in trade receivables (145 − 139)	(6)
Decrease in trade payables (54 − 41)	(13)
Cash generated from operations	261
Interest paid	(26)
Taxation paid (Note 4)	(41)
Dividend paid	(60)
Net cash from operating activities	134
Cash flows from investing activities	
Payments to acquire plant and machinery	(67)
Net cash used in investing activities	(67)
Cash flows from financing activities	
Redemption of loan notes (250 − 150) (Note 5)	(100)
Net cash used in financing activities	(100)
Net decrease in cash and cash equivalents	(33)
Cash and cash equivalents at 1 January 2008	
Bank overdraft	(56)
Cash and cash equivalents at 31 December 2008	
Bank overdraft	(89)

To see how this relates to the cash of the business at the beginning and end of the year it can be useful to provide a reconciliation as follows:

Analysis of cash and cash equivalents during the year ended 31 December 2008

	£m
Cash and cash equivalents at 1 January 2008	(56)
Net cash outflow	(33)
Cash and cash equivalents at 31 December 2008	(89)

Notes:

1 This is simply taken from the income statement for the year.
2 Since there were no disposals, the depreciation charges must be the difference between the start and end of the year's plant and machinery values, adjusted by the cost of any additions.

	£m
Carrying amount at 1 January 2008	325
Additions	67
Depreciation (balancing figure)	(78)
Carrying amount at 31 December 2008	314

3 Interest payable expense must be taken out, by adding it back to the profit before taxation figure. We subsequently deduct the cash paid for interest payable during the year. In this case the two figures are identical.
4 Companies pay 50% of their tax during their accounting year and 50% in the following year. Thus the 2008 payment would have been half the tax on the 2007 profit (that is, the figure that appeared in the current liabilities at the end of 2007), plus half of the 2008 tax charge (that is, $23 + (^1/_2 \times 36) = 41$).
5 It is assumed that the cash payment to redeem the loan notes was simply the difference between the two balance sheet figures.

It seems that there was a bonus issue of ordinary shares during the year. These increased by £100m. At the same time, the share premium account balance reduced by £40m (to zero) and the revaluation reserve balance fell by £60m.

5.5

Blackstone plc
Cash flow statement for the year ended 31 March 2008

	£m
Cash flows from operating activities	
Profit before taxation (after interest)	
(see Note 1 below)	1,853
Adjustments for:	
Depreciation (Note 2)	1,289
Interest expense (Note 3)	456
	3,598
Increase in inventories (2,410 – 1,209)	(1,201)
Increase in trade receivables (1,173 – 641)	(532)
Increase in trade payables (1,507 – 931)	576
Cash generated from operations	2,441
Interest paid	(456)
Taxation paid (Note 4)	(300)
Dividend paid	(400)
Net cash from operating activities	1,285
Cash flows from investing activities	
Proceeds of disposals	54
Payment to acquire intangible non-current asset	(700)
Payments to acquire property, plant and equipment	(4,578)
Net cash used in investing activities	(5,224)

Cash flows from financing activities	
Bank borrowings	2,000
Net cash from financing activities	2,000
Net decrease in cash and cash equivalents	(1,939)
Cash and cash equivalents at 1 April 2007	
Cash at bank	123
Cash and cash equivalents at 31 March 2008	
Bank overdraft	(1,816)

To see how this relates to the cash of the business at the beginning and end of the year it can be useful to provide a reconciliation as follows:

Analysis of cash and cash equivalents during the year ended 31 March 2008

	£m
Cash and cash equivalents at 1 April 2007	123
Net cash outflow	(1,939)
Cash and cash equivalents at 31 March 2008	(1,816)

Notes:

1 This is simply taken from the income statement for the year.
2 The full depreciation charge was that stated in Note 2 to the question (£1,251m), plus the deficit on disposal of the non-current assets. According to Note 2, these non-current assets had originally cost £581m and had been depreciated by £489m, that is a net carrying amount of £92m. They were sold for £54m, leading to a deficit on disposal of £38m. Thus the full depreciation expense for the year was £1,289m (that is, £1,251m + £38m).
3 Interest payable expense must be taken out, by adding it back to the profit before taxation figure. We subsequently deduct the cash paid for interest payable during the year. In this case the two figures are identical.
4 Companies pay tax at 50% during their accounting year and the other 50% in the following year. Thus the 2008 payment would have been half the tax on the 2007 profit (that is, the figure that would have appeared in the current liabilities at 31 March 2007), plus half of the 2008 tax charge (that is, $105 + (^1/_2 \times 390) = 300$).

Chapter 6

6.1   I. Jiang (Western) Ltd

The effect of each of the changes on ROCE is not always easy to predict.

1 On the face of it, an increase in the gross profit margin would tend to lead to an increase in ROCE. An increase in the gross profit margin may, however, lead to a decrease in ROCE in particular circumstances. If the increase in the margin resulted from an increase in sales prices, which in turn led to a decrease in sales revenue, a fall in ROCE could occur. A fall in sales revenue can reduce the operating profit (the numerator (top part of the fraction) in ROCE) if the overheads of the business did not decrease correspondingly.

2 A reduction in sales revenue can reduce ROCE for the reasons mentioned above.

3 An increase in overhead expenses will reduce the operating profit and this in turn will result in a reduction in ROCE.

4 An increase in inventories held would increase the amount of capital employed by the business (the denominator (bottom part of the fraction) in ROCE) where long-term funds are employed to finance the inventories. This will, in turn, reduce ROCE.

5 Repayment of the borrowings at the year end will reduce the capital employed and this will increase the ROCE, assuming that the year-end capital employed figure has been used in the calculation. Since the operating profit was earned during a period in which the borrowings existed, there is a strong argument for basing the capital employed figure on what was the position during the year, rather than at the end of it.

6 An increase in the time taken for credit customers to pay will result in an increase in capital employed if long-term funds are employed to finance the trade receivables. This increase in long-term funds will, in turn, reduce ROCE.

6.2 Amsterdam Ltd and Berlin Ltd

The ratios for Amsterdam Ltd and Berlin Ltd reveal that the trade receivables turnover ratio for Amsterdam Ltd is three times that for Berlin Ltd. Berlin Ltd is therefore much quicker in collecting amounts outstanding from customers. On the other hand, there is not much difference between the two businesses in the time taken to pay trade payables.

It is interesting to compare the difference in the trade receivables and payables collection periods for each business. As Amsterdam Ltd allows an average of 63 days' credit to its customers, yet pays suppliers within 50 days, it will require greater investment in working capital than Berlin Ltd, which allows an average of only 21 days to its customers but takes 45 days to pay its suppliers.

Amsterdam Ltd has a much higher gross profit margin than Berlin Ltd. However, the operating profit margin for the two businesses is identical. This suggests that Amsterdam Ltd has much higher overheads (as a percentage of sales revenue) than Berlin Ltd. The inventories turnover period for Amsterdam Ltd is more than twice that of Berlin Ltd. This may be due to the fact that Amsterdam Ltd maintains a wider range of inventories in an attempt to meet customer requirements. The evidence therefore suggests that Amsterdam Ltd is the one that prides itself on personal service. The higher average settlement period for trade receivables is consistent with a more relaxed attitude to credit collection (thereby maintaining customer goodwill) and the high overheads are consistent with incurring the additional costs of satisfying customers' requirements. Amsterdam Ltd's high inventories levels are consistent with maintaining a wide range of inventories, with the aim of satisfying a range of customer needs.

Berlin Ltd has the characteristics of a more price-competitive business. Its gross profit margin is much lower than that of Amsterdam Ltd, that is, it makes a much lower gross profit for each £1 of sales revenue. However, overheads have been kept low, the effect being that the operating percentage is the same as Amsterdam Ltd's. The low inventories turnover period and average collection period for trade receivables are consistent with a business that wishes to minimise investment in current assets, thereby reducing costs.

6.5 Bradbury Ltd

(a)

		2007	2008
1	Operating profit margin	$\dfrac{914}{9{,}482} \times 100\% = 9.6\%$	$\dfrac{1{,}042}{11{,}365} \times 100\% = 9.2\%$
2	ROCE	$\dfrac{914}{11{,}033} \times 100\% = 8.3\%$	$\dfrac{1{,}042}{13{,}943} \times 100\% = 7.5\%$
3	Current ratio	$\dfrac{4{,}926}{1{,}508} = 3.3{:}1$	$\dfrac{7{,}700}{5{,}174} = 1.5{:}1$
4	Gearing ratio	$\dfrac{1{,}220}{11{,}033} \times 100\% = 11.1\%$	$\dfrac{3{,}675}{13{,}943} \times 100\% = 26.4\%$
5	Days trade receivables	$\dfrac{2{,}540}{9{,}482} \times 365 = 98$ days	$\dfrac{4{,}280}{11{,}365} \times 365 = 137$ days
6	Sales revenue to capital employed	$\dfrac{9{,}482}{(9{,}813 + 1{,}220)} = 0.9$ times	$\dfrac{11{,}365}{(10{,}268 + 3{,}675)} = 0.8$ times

(b) The operating profit margin was slightly lower in 2008 than in 2007. Although there was an increase in sales revenue in 2008, this could not prevent a slight fall in ROCE in that year. The lower operating margin and increases in sales revenue may well be due to the new contract. The capital employed by the company increased in 2008 by a larger percentage than the increase in revenue. Hence, the sales revenue to capital employed ratio decreased over the period. The increase in capital during 2008 is largely due to an increase in borrowing. However, the gearing ratio is probably still low in comparison with other businesses. Comparison of the premises and borrowings figures indicates possible unused borrowing (debt) capacity.

The major cause for concern has been the dramatic decline in liquidity during 2008. The current ratio has decreased by more than half during the period. There has also been a similar decrease in the acid test ratio, from 1.7:1 in 2007 to 0.8:1 in 2008. The balance sheet shows that the business now has a large overdraft and the trade payables outstanding have nearly doubled in 2008.

The trade receivables outstanding and inventories have increased much more than appears to be warranted by the increase in sales revenue. This may be due to the terms of the contract that has been negotiated and may be difficult to influence. If this is the case, the business should consider whether it is over-trading. If the conclusion is that it is, increasing its long-term funding may be a sensible policy.

Chapter 7

7.3 Products A, B and C

(a) Total time required on cutting machines is:

$$(2,500 \times 1.0) + (3,400 \times 1.0) + (5,100 \times 0.5) = 8,450 \text{ hours}$$

Total time available on cutting machines is 5,000 hours. Therefore, this is a limiting factor.

Total time required on assembling machines is:

$$(2,500 \times 0.5) + (3,400 \times 1.0) + (5,100 \times 0.5) = 7,200 \text{ hours}$$

Total time available on assembling machines is 8,000 hours. Therefore, this is not a limiting factor.

	A	B	C
Selling price (£/unit)	25	30	18
Variable materials (£/unit)	(12)	(13)	(10)
Variable production costs (£/unit)	(7)	(4)	(3)
Contribution (£/unit)	6	13	5
Time on cutting machines (hours/unit)	1.0 hour	1.0 hour	0.5 hour
Contribution per hour on cutting machines	£6	£13	£10
Order of priority	3rd	1st	2nd

Therefore, produce:

3,400 product B using	3,400 hours
3,200 product C using	1,600 hours
	5,000 hours

(b) Assuming that the business would make no saving in variable production costs by subcontracting, it would be worth paying up to the contribution per unit (£5) for product C, which would therefore be £5 × (5,100 − 3,200) = £9,500 in total.

Similarly it would be worth paying up to £6 per unit for product A, that is, £6 × 2,500 = £15,000 in total.

7.4 Darmor Ltd

(a) Contribution per hour of skilled labour of Product X is:

$$\frac{£(30 - 6 - 2 - 12 - 3)}{(6/12)} = £14$$

Given the scarcity of skilled labour, if the management is to be indifferent between the products, the contribution per skilled-labour-hour must be the same. Thus for product Y the selling price must be:

$$£(14 \times (9/12)) + 9 + 4 + 25 + 7 = £55.50$$

(that is, the contribution plus the variable costs), and for product Z the selling price must be:

$$£(14 \times (3/12)) + 3 + 10 + 14 + 7 = £37.50$$

(b) The business could pay up to £26 an hour (£12 + £14) for additional hours of skilled labour. This is the potential contribution per hour, before taking account of the labour rate of £12 an hour.

7.5 Gandhi Ltd

(a) Given that the spare capacity could not be used by other services, the standard service should continue to be offered. This is because it renders a positive contribution.

(b) The standard service renders a contribution per unit of £15 (that is, £80 – £65), or £30 during the time it would take to render one unit of the nova service. The nova service would provide a contribution of only £25 (that is, £75 – £50). The nova service should, therefore, not replace the standard service.

(c) Under the original plans, the following contributions would be rendered by the basic and standard services:

		£
Basic	11,000 × (£50 – £25) =	275,000
Standard	6,000 × (£80 – £65) =	90,000
		365,000

If the basic were to take the standard's place, 17,000 units (that is, 11,000 + 6,000) of them could be produced in total. To generate the same total contribution, each unit of the standard service would need to provide £21.47 (that is, £365,000/17,000) of contribution. Given the basic's variable cost of £25, this would mean a selling price of £46.47 each (that is £21.47 + £25.00).

Chapter 8

8.1

All three of these costing techniques are means of deducing the full cost of some activity. The distinction between them lies essentially with the difference in the style of the production of the goods or services involved.

- *Job costing* is used where each unit of output or 'job' differs from others produced by the same business. Because the jobs are not identical, it is not normally acceptable to those who are likely to use the cost information to treat the jobs as if they are identical. This means that costs need to be identified, job by job. For this purpose, costs fall into two categories: direct costs and indirect costs (or overheads).

  Direct costs are those that can be measured directly in respect of the specific job, such as the amount of labour that was directly applied to the job or the amount of material that has been incorporated in it. To this must be added a share of the indirect costs. This is usually done by taking the total overheads for the period concerned and charging part of them to the job. This, in turn, is usually done according to some measure of the job's size and importance, relative to the other jobs done during the period. The number of direct labour hours worked on the job is the most commonly used measure of size and/or importance.

  The main problem with job costing tends to be the method of charging indirect costs to jobs. Indirect costs, by definition, cannot be related directly to jobs, yet must, if full cost is to be deduced, be charged on a basis that is more or less arbitrary. If indirect costs accounted for a small proportion of the total, the arbitrariness of charging them would probably not matter. Indirect costs, in many cases, however, form the majority of total costs, so arbitrariness is a problem.

- *Process costing* is the approach taken where all output is of identical units. These can be treated, therefore, as having identical cost. Sometimes a process-costing approach is taken even where the units of output are not strictly identical. This is because process costing is much simpler and cheaper to apply than the only other option, job costing. Provided that users of the cost information are satisfied that treating units as identical when they are not strictly so is acceptable, the additional cost and effort of job costing is not justified.

In process costing, the cost per unit of output is found by dividing total costs for the period by the total number of units produced in the period.

The main problem with process costing tends to be that at the end of any period/beginning of the next period, there will probably be partly completed units of output. An adjustment needs to be made for this work in progress if the resulting figures for cost per unit are not to be distorted.

- *Batch costing* is really an extension of job costing. Batch costing tends to be used where production is in batches. A batch consists of more than one, perhaps many, identical units of output. The units of output differ from one batch to the next. For example, a clothing manufacturing business may produce 500 identical jackets in one batch. This is followed by a batch of 300 identical skirts.

  Each batch is costed, as one job, using a job-costing approach. The full cost of each garment is then found by dividing the cost of the batch by the number of garments in the batch.

  The main problem of batch costing is exactly that of job costing, of which it is an extension. This is the problem of dealing with overheads.

8.4 Kaplan plc

(a) At present, the business makes each model of suitcase in a batch. The direct materials and labour costs will be recorded in respect of each batch. To these costs will be added a share of the overheads of the business for the period in which production of the batch takes place. The basis of the batch absorbing overheads is a matter of managerial judgement. Direct labour hours spent working on the batch, relative to total direct labour hours worked during the period, is a popular method. This is not the 'correct' way, however. There is no correct way. If the activity is capital-intensive, some machine-hour basis of dealing with overheads might be more appropriate, though still not 'correct'. Overheads might be collected, department by department, and charged to the batch as it passes through each department. Alternatively, all of the overheads for the entire production facility might be totalled and the overheads dealt with more globally. It is only in restricted circumstances that overheads charged to batches will be affected by a decision to deal with them departmentally rather than globally.

Once the 'full cost' (direct costs plus a share of indirect costs) has been ascertained for the batch, the cost per suitcase can be established by dividing the batch cost by the number in the batch.

(b) The uses to which full cost information can be put have been identified as follows:
- *Pricing.* Usually the customer will want to know the price in advance of placing the order. Thus, it is not possible to wait until all of the costs have been incurred, and are known, before the price can be deduced. Even where a job is not for an identified customer, the business still needs to have some idea of whether it can produce the good or service at a price that the market will bear. In practice, a luggage manufacturer would be unlikely to be able to base prices on full cost. It would have to compete with others and would probably be a 'price-taker'.

- *Exercising control.* Where the cost of doing something is planned (budgeted), the actual cost of doing it can be compared with the plan and steps taken to get things back on track if there are divergences between plans and actual. Using full costs in this way can lead to managers being held accountable for costs, particularly overheads, over which they have no control. This could weaken the control process.

- *Assessing relative efficiency.* Full costs can also be used to help assess operational efficiency. Comparing costs for the forthcoming period with those of previous periods, or with those of similar businesses, can provide some insight into relative efficiency. This can give misleading information where costs are being derived on different bases; for example overheads might be absorbed on a business-wide basis in one business and on a departmental one in the other.

- *Assessing performance.* Valuing work in progress is an important purpose for which full costs are required. If managers are to benefit fully from accounting information, the costs (including overheads) of generating revenues for a period must be identified. The relatively arbitrary nature of overhead absorption by cost units can weaken the value of the financial reports.

(c) Whereas the traditional approach to dealing with overheads is just to accept that they exist and deal with them in a fairly broad manner, ABC takes a much more enquiring approach. ABC takes the view that overheads do not just 'occur', but that they are caused or 'driven' by 'activities'. It is a matter of finding out which activities are driving the costs and how much cost they are driving.

For example, a significant part of the costs of making suitcases of different sizes might be resetting machinery to cope with a batch of a different size from its predecessor batch. Where a particular model is made in very small batches, because it has only a small market, ABC would advocate that this model is charged directly with its machine-setting costs. The traditional approach would be to treat machine setting as a general overhead that the individual suitcases (irrespective of the model) might bear equally. ABC, it is claimed, leads to more accurate costing and thus to more accurate assessment of profitability.

(d) The other advantage of pursuing an ABC philosophy and identifying cost drivers is that, once the drivers have been identified, costs are likely to become much more susceptible to being controlled. Thus the ability of management to assess the benefit of certain activities against their cost becomes more feasible.

8.5

Offending phrase	Explanation
'Necessary to divide up the business into departments'	This can be done but it will not always be of much benefit. Only in quite restricted circumstances will it give significantly different job costs.
'Fixed costs (or overheads)'	This implies that fixed costs and overheads are the same thing. They are not really connected with one another. 'Fixed' is to do with how costs behave as the level of output is raised or lowered; 'overheads' are to do with the extent to which costs can be directly measured in respect of a particular unit of output. Although it is true that many overheads are fixed, not all are. Also, direct labour is usually a fixed cost. All of the other references to fixed and variable costs are wrong. The person should have referred to indirect and direct costs.
'Usually this is done on the basis of area'	Where overheads are apportioned to departments, they will be apportioned on some logical basis. For certain costs – for example, rent – the floor area may be the most logical; for others, such as machine maintenance costs, the floor area would be totally inappropriate.
'When the total fixed costs for each department have been identified, this will be divided by the number of hours that were worked'	Where overheads are dealt with on a departmental basis, they may be divided by the number of direct labour hours to deduce a recovery rate. However, this is only one basis of applying overheads to jobs. For example, machine hours or some other basis may be more appropriate to the particular circumstances involved.
'It is essential that this approach is taken in order to deduce a selling price'	It is relatively unusual to be able to use the 'job cost' to dictate the price which the manufacturer can charge for its output. For many businesses, the market dictates the price.

Chapter 9

9.3 Nursing Home

(a) The rates per patient for the variable overheads, on the basis of experience during months 1 to 6, are as follows:

Expense	Amount for 2,700 patients £	Amount per patient £
Staffing	59,400	22
Power	27,000	10
Supplies	54,000	20
Other	8,100	3
	148,500	55

Since the expected level of activity for the full year is 6,000, 3,300 (that is, 6,000 – 2,700) is the expected level of activity for the second six months.

Thus the budget for the second six months will be:

	£	
Variable element:		
Staffing	72,600	(3,300 × £22)
Power	33,000	(3,300 × £10)
Supplies	66,000	(3,300 × £20)
Other	9,900	(3,300 × £3)
	181,500	(3,300 × £55)
Fixed element:		
Supervision	60,000	
Depreciation/finance	93,600	6/12 of the values given in the question
Other	32,400	
	186,000	(per patient = £56.36 (= £186,000/3,300))
Total (second six months)	367,500	(per patient = £111.36 (= £56.36 + 55.00))

(b) For the second six months the actual activity was 3,800 patients. For a valid comparison with the actual outcome, the budget will need to be revised to reflect this activity.

	Actual costs	Budget (3,800 patients)	Difference
	£	£	£
Variable element	203,300	209,000 (3,800 × £55)	5,700 (saving)
Fixed element	190,000	186,000	4,000 (overspend)
Total	393,300	395,000	1,700 (saving)

(c) Relative to the budget, there was a saving of nearly 3% on the variable element and an overspend of about 2% on fixed costs. Without further information, it is impossible to deduce much more than this.

The differences between the budget and the actual may be caused by some assumptions made in framing the budget for 3,800 patients in the second part of the year. There may be some element of economies of scale in the variable costs, that is, the costs may not be strictly linear. If this were the case, basing a relatively large activity budget on the experience of a relatively small activity period would tend to overstate the large activity budget. The fixed-cost budget was deduced by dividing the budget for twelve months by two. In fact, there could be seasonal factors or inflationary pressures at work that might make such a crude division of the fixed-cost element unfair.

9.4 Linpet Ltd

(a) Cash budgets are extremely useful for decision-making purposes. They allow managers to see the likely effect on the cash balance of the plans that they have set in place. Cash is an important asset and it is necessary to ensure that it is properly managed. Failure to do so can have disastrous consequences for the business. Where the cash budget indicates a surplus balance, managers must decide whether this balance should be reinvested in the business or distributed to the owners. Where the cash budget indicates a deficit balance, managers must decide how this deficit should be financed or how it might be avoided.

(b) The cash budget to 30 November is:

	June £	July £	Aug £	Sept £	Oct £	Nov £
Receipts						
Cash sales revenue						
(Note 1)	4,000	5,500	7,000	8,500	11,000	11,000
Credit sales revenue						
(Note 2)	–	–	4,000	5,500	7,000	8,500
	4,000	5,500	11,000	14,000	18,000	19,500
Payments						
Purchases (Note 3)	–	29,000	9,250	11,500	13,750	17,500
Overheads	500	500	500	500	650	650
Wages	900	900	900	900	900	900
Commission (Note 4)	–	320	440	560	680	880
Equipment	10,000	–	–	–	–	7,000
Motor vehicle	6,000	–	–	–	–	–
Leasehold	40,000	–	–	–	–	–
	57,400	30,720	11,090	13,460	15,980	26,930
Cash flow	(53,400)	(25,220)	(90)	540	2,020	(7,430)
Opening balance	60,000	6,600	(18,620)	(18,710)	(18,170)	(16,150)
Closing balance	6,600	(18,620)	(18,710)	(18,170)	(16,150)	(23,580)

Notes:
1 50% of the current month's sales revenue.
2 50% of sales revenue of two months previous.
3 To have sufficient inventories to meet each month's sales will require purchases of 75% of the month's sales revenue figures (25% is profit). In addition, each month the business will buy £1,000 more inventories than it will sell. In June, the business will also buy its initial inventories of £22,000. This will be paid for in the following month. For example, June's purchases will be (75% × £8,000) + £1,000 + £22,000 = £29,000, paid for in July.
4 This is 5% of 80% of the month's sales revenue, paid in the following month. For example, June's commission will be 5% × 80% × £8,000 = £320, payable in July.

Appendix D

9.5 Newtake Records Ltd

(a) The inventories budget for the six months to 30 November is:

	June £000	July £000	Aug £000	Sept £000	Oct £000	Nov £000
Opening balance	112	154	104	48	39	33
Inventories purchased	180	142	94	75	66	57
	292	296	198	123	105	90
Cost of inventories sold						
(60% of sales revenue)	(138)	(192)	(150)	(84)	(72)	(66)
Closing balance	154	104	48	39	33	24

(b) The cash budget for the period to 30 November is:

	June £000	July £000	Aug £000	Sept £000	Oct £000	Nov £000
Cash receipts						
Sales (Note 1)	227	315	246	138	118	108
Cash payments						
Administration (Note 2)	(40)	(41)	(38)	(33)	(31)	(30)
Goods purchased	(135)	(180)	(142)	(94)	(75)	(66)
Borrowings repayments	(5)	(5)	(5)	(5)	(5)	(5)
Selling expenses	(22)	(24)	(28)	(26)	(21)	(19)
Taxation paid	–	–	(22)	–	–	–
Shop refurbishment	–	(14)	(18)	(6)	–	–
	(202)	(264)	(253)	(164)	(132)	(120)
Cash surplus (deficit)	25	51	(7)	(26)	(14)	(12)
Opening balance	(35)	(10)	41	34	8	(6)
Closing balance	(10)	41	34	8	(6)	(18)

(c) The budgeted income statement for the six months ending 30 November is:

	£000
Sales revenue	1,170
Cost of goods sold	(702)
Gross profit	468
Selling expenses	(136)
Admin. expenses	(303)
Credit card charges	(18)
Operating profit	11
Interest payable	(6)
Profit for the period	5

Notes:
1 (50% of the current month's sales revenue) + (97% × 50% of that sales revenue). For example, the June cash receipts = (50% × £230,000) + (97% × 50% × £230,000) = £226,550.
2 The administration expenses figure for the month, less £15,000 for depreciation (a non-cash expense).

538

(d) We are told that the business is required to eliminate the bank overdraft by the end of November. However, the cash budget reveals that this will not be achieved. There is a decline in the overdraft of nearly 50% over the period, but this is not enough and ways must be found to comply with the bank's requirements. It may be possible to delay the refurbishment programme that is included in the plans or to obtain an injection of funds from the owners or other investors. It may also be possible to stimulate sales in some way. However, there has been a decline in the sales revenue since the end of July and the November sales revenue is approximately one-third of the July figure. The reasons for this decline should be sought.

The inventories levels will fall below the preferred minimum level for each of the last three months. However, to rectify this situation it will be necessary to purchase more inventories, which will, in turn, exacerbate the cash flow problems of the business.

The budgeted income statement reveals a very low profit for the period. For every £1 of sales revenue, the business is managing to generate only 0.4p in profit. The business should look carefully at its pricing policies and its overhead expenses. The administration expenses, for example, absorb more than one-quarter of the total sales revenue. Any reduction in overhead expenses will have a beneficial effect on cash flows.

Chapter 10

10.1 Mylo Ltd

(a) The annual depreciation of the two projects is:

$$\text{Project 1: } \frac{£100,000 - £7,000}{3} = £31,000$$

$$\text{Project 2: } \frac{£60,000 - £6,000}{3} = £18,000$$

Project 1

(i)

	Year 0 £000	Year 1 £000	Year 2 £000	Year 3 £000
Operating profit/(loss)		29	(1)	2
Depreciation		31	31	31
Capital cost	(100)			
Residual value				7
Net cash flows	(100)	60	30	40
10% discount factor	1.000	0.909	0.826	0.751
Present value	(100.00)	54.54	24.78	30.04
NPV	9.36			

(ii) Clearly the IRR lies above 10%. Try 15%:

15% discount factor	1.000	0.870	0.756	0.658
Present value	(100.00)	52.20	22.68	26.32
NPV	1.20			

Thus the IRR lies a little above 15%, perhaps around 16%.

(iii) To find the payback period, the cumulative cash flows are calculated:

Cumulative cash flows	(100)	(40)	(10)	30

Thus the payback will occur within three years.

Project 2

(i)

	Year 0 £000	Year 1 £000	Year 2 £000	Year 3 £000
Operating profit/(loss)		18	(2)	4
Depreciation		18	18	18
Capital cost	(60)			
Residual value				6
Net cash flows	(60)	36	16	28
10% discount factor	1.000	0.909	0.826	0.751
Present value	(60.00)	32.72	13.22	21.03
NPV	6.97			

(ii) Clearly the IRR lies above 10%. Try 15%:

15% discount factor	1.000	0.870	0.756	0.658
Present value	(60.00)	31.32	12.10	18.42
NPV	1.84			

Thus the IRR lies a little above 15%, perhaps around 17%.

(iii) The cumulative cash flows are:

Cumulative cash flows	(60)	(24)	(8)	20

Thus, the payback will occur within three years.

(b) Assuming that Mylo Ltd is pursuing a wealth-enhancement objective, Project 1 is preferable since it has the higher NPV. The difference between the two NPVs is not significant, however.

(c) NPV is the preferred method of assessing investment opportunities because it fully addresses each of the following:

■ *The timing of the cash flows.* Discounting the various cash flows associated with each project, according to when they are expected to arise, takes account of the fact that cash flows do not all occur simultaneously. Associated with this is the fact that by discounting, using the opportunity cost of finance (namely the return that the next-best alternative opportunity would generate), the net benefit, after financing costs have been met, is identified (as the NPV).

- *The whole of the relevant cash flows.* NPV includes all of the relevant cash flows irrespective of when they are expected to occur. It treats them differently according to their date of occurrence, but they are all taken into account in the calculation of the NPV and they all have, or can have, an influence on the decision.
- *The objectives of the business.* NPV is the only method of appraisal where the output of the analysis has a direct bearing on the wealth of the owners of the business. (Positive NPVs enhance wealth; negative NPVs reduce it.) Since most private-sector businesses seek to increase their owners' wealth, NPV clearly is the best approach to use.

10.4 Newton Electronics Ltd
(a) Option 1

	Year 0 £m	Year 1 £m	Year 2 £m	Year 3 £m	Year 4 £m	Year 5 £m
Plant and equipment	(9.0)	–	–	–	–	1.0
Sales revenue	–	24.0	30.8	39.6	26.4	10.0
Variable costs	–	(11.2)	(19.6)	(25.2)	(16.8)	(7.0)
Fixed costs (ex. dep'n)	–	(0.8)	(0.8)	(0.8)	(0.8)	(0.8)
Working capital	(3.0)	–	–	–	–	3.0
Marketing costs	–	(2.0)	(2.0)	(2.0)	(2.0)	(2.0)
Opportunity costs	–	(0.1)	(0.1)	(0.1)	(0.1)	(0.1)
	(12.0)	9.9	8.3	11.5	6.7	4.1
Discount factor 10%	1.000	0.909	0.826	0.751	0.683	0.621
Present value	(12.0)	9.0	6.9	8.6	4.6	2.5
NPV	19.6					

Option 2

	Year 0 £m	Year 1 £m	Year 2 £m	Year 3 £m	Year 4 £m	Year 5 £m
Royalties	–	4.4	7.7	9.9	6.6	2.8
Discount factor 10%	1.000	0.909	0.826	0.751	0.683	0.621
Present value	–	4.0	6.4	7.4	4.5	1.7
NPV	24.0					

Option 3

	Year 0	Year 2
Instalments	12.0	12.0
Discount factor 10%	1.000	0.826
Present value	12.0	9.9
NPV	21.9	

(b) Before making a final decision, the board should consider the following factors:
- The long-term competitiveness of the business may be affected by the sale of the patents.
- At present, the business is not involved in manufacturing and marketing products. Would a change in direction be desirable?
- The business will probably have to buy in the skills necessary to produce the product itself. This will involve costs, and problems will be incurred. Has this been taken into account?
- How accurate are the forecasts made and how valid are the assumptions on which they are based?

(c) Option 2 has the highest NPV and is therefore the most attractive to share-holders. However, the accuracy of the forecasts should be checked before a final decision is made.

10.5 Chesterfield Wanderers

(a) and (b)
Player option

	Year 0 £000	Year 1 £000	Year 2 £000	Year 3 £000	Year 4 £000	Year 5 £000
Sale of player	2,200					1,000
Purchase of Bazza	(10,000)					
Sponsorship and so on		1,200	1,200	1,200	1,200	1,200
Increased gate receipts		2,500	1,300	1,300	1,300	1,300
Salaries paid		(800)	(800)	(800)	(800)	(1,200)
Salaries saved		400	400	400	400	600
Net cash received (paid)	(7,800)	3,300	2,100	2,100	2,100	2,900
Discount factor 10%	1.000	0.909	0.826	0.751	0.683	0.621
Present values	(7,800)	3,000	1,735	1,577	1,434	1,801
NPV	1,747					

Ground improvement option

	Year 1 £000	Year 2 £000	Year 3 £000	Year 4 £000	Year 5 £000
Ground improvements	(10,000)	–	–	–	–
Increased gate receipts	(1,800)	4,400	4,400	4,400	4,400
	(11,800)	4,400	4,400	4,400	4,400
Discount factor 10%	0.909	0.826	0.751	0.683	0.621
Present values	(10,726)	3,634	3,304	3,005	2,732
NPV	1,949				

(c) The ground improvement option provides the higher NPV and is therefore the preferable option, based on the objective of shareholder wealth maximisation.
(d) A professional football club may not wish to pursue an objective of shareholder wealth enhancement. It may prefer to invest in quality players in an attempt to enjoy future sporting success. If this is the case, the NPV approach will be less appropriate because the club is not pursuing a strict wealth-related objective.

Chapter 11

11.1 H. Brown (Portsmouth) Ltd

(a) The main factors to take into account are:

- *Risk.* If a business borrows, there is a risk that at the maturity date of the loan the business will not have the funds to repay the amount owing and will be unable to find a suitable form of replacement borrowing. With short-term borrowings, the maturity dates will arrive more quickly and the type of risk outlined will occur at more frequent intervals.
- *Matching.* A business may wish to match the life of an asset with the maturity date of the borrowing. In other words, long-term assets will be purchased with long-term borrowed funds. A certain level of current assets, which form part of the long-term asset base of the business, may also be funded by long-term borrowing. Those current assets that fluctuate owing to seasonality and so on will be funded by short-term borrowing. This approach to funding assets will help reduce risks for the business.
- *Cost.* Interest rates for long-term borrowings may be higher than for short-term ones as investors may seek extra compensation for having their funds locked up for a long period. However, issue costs may be higher for short-term borrowings as there will be a need to refund at more frequent intervals.
- *Flexibility.* Short-term borrowings may be more flexible. It may be difficult to repay long-term ones before the maturity period.

(b) When deciding to grant a loan, a lender should consider the following factors:

- security
- purpose of the loan
- ability of the borrower to repay
- loan period
- availability of funds
- character and integrity of the senior managers.

(c) Loan conditions may include:

- the need to obtain permission before issuing further loans
- the need to maintain a certain level of liquidity during the loan period
- a restriction on the level of dividends and directors' pay.

11.2 Carpets Direct plc

(a) The earnings per share (EPS) is:

$$\frac{\text{Profit for the year}}{\text{Number of ordinary shares}} = \frac{£4.5m}{120m} = £0.0375$$

The current market value per share is:

$$\text{Earnings per share} \times \text{P/E} = £0.0375 \times 22 = £0.825$$

The rights issue price will be £0.825, less 20% discount = £0.66.
The theoretical ex-rights price is:

	£
Original shares (4 @ £0.825)	3.30
Rights share (1 @ £0.66)	0.66
Value of five shares following rights issue	3.96

Therefore, the value of one share following the rights issue is:

$$\frac{£3.96}{5} = 79.2p$$

(b) **Value of one share after rights issue**   79.2p

Cost of a rights share	(66.0p)
Value of rights to shareholder	13.2p

(c) (i) *Taking up rights issue*

	£
Shareholding following rights issue ((4,000 + 1,000) × 79.2p)	3,960
Less cost of rights shares (1,000 × 66p)	(660)
Shareholder wealth	3,300

(ii) *Selling the rights*

	£
Shareholding following rights issue (4,000 × 79.2p)	3,168
Add proceeds from sale of rights (1,000 × 13.2p)	132
Shareholder wealth	3,300

(iii) *Doing nothing*

As the rights are neither purchased nor sold, the shareholder wealth following the rights issue will be:

Shareholding (4,000 × 79.2p)	3,168

We can see that the investor will have the same wealth under the first two options. However, by the investor doing nothing, the rights offer will lapse and so the investor will lose the value of the rights and will be worse off.

11.3 Raphael Ltd

The existing credit policies have the following costs:

	£
Cost of investment in trade receivables ((50/365) × £2.4m × 12%)	39,452
Cost of bad debts (1.5% × £2.4m)	36,000
Total cost	75,452

Employing a factor will result in the following costs and savings:

	£
Charges of the factor (2% × £2.4m)	48,000
Interest charges on advance ((30/365) × (80% × £2.4m) × 11%)	17,359
Interest charges on overdraft [(30/365) × (20% × £2.4m) × 12%]	4,734
Total cost	70,093
Less credit control savings	(18,000)
Net cost	52,093

We can see that the net cost of factoring is lower than the existing costs, and so there would be a benefit gained from entering into an agreement with the factor.

Chapter 12

12.1 Hercules Wholesalers Ltd

(a) The liquidity ratios of the business seem low. The current ratio is only 1:1.1 (that is, 306/285) and its acid test ratio is 0.6:1 (that is, 163/285). This latter ratio suggests that the business has insufficient liquid assets to pay its short-term obligations. A cash flow projection for the next period would provide a better insight to the liquidity position of the business. The bank overdraft seems high and it would be useful to know whether the bank is pressing for a reduction and what overdraft limit has been established for the business.

(b) The operating cash cycle can be calculated as follows:

	Number of days
Average inventories holding period:	
$\dfrac{((\text{Opening inventories} + \text{Closing inventories})/2) \times 360}{\text{Cost of sales}} = \dfrac{((125 + 143)/2) \times 360}{323}$	149
Add Average settlement period for trade receivables:	
$\dfrac{\text{Trade receivables} \times 360}{\text{Credit sales revenue}} = \dfrac{163}{452} \times 360$	130
	279
Less Average settlement period for trade payables:	
$\dfrac{\text{Trade payables} \times 360}{\text{Credit purchases}} = \dfrac{145}{341} \times 360$	153
	126

(c) The business can reduce the operating cash cycle in a number of ways. The average inventories holding period seems quite long. At present, average inventories held represent almost five months' sales needs. This period can be shortened by reducing the level of inventories held. Similarly, the average settlement period for trade receivables seems long at more than four months' sales revenue. This may be shortened by imposing tighter credit control, offering discounts, charging interest on overdue accounts and so on. However, any policy decisions concerning inventories and trade receivables must take account of current trading conditions.

The operating cash cycle would also be reduced by extending the period of credit taken to pay suppliers. However, for the reasons mentioned in the chapter, this option must be given careful consideration.

12.4

Mayo Computers Ltd
New proposals from credit control department

	£000	£000
Current level of investment in trade receivables		
(£20m × (60/365))		3,288
Proposed level of investment in trade receivables		
((£20m × 60%) × (30/365))	(986)	
((£20m × 40%) × (50/365))	(1,096)	(2,082)
Reduction in level of investment		1,206

The reduction in overdraft interest as a result of the reduction in the level of investment will be £1,206,000 × 14% = £169,000.

	£000	£000
Cost of cash discounts offered (£20m × 60% × 2.5%)		300
Additional cost of credit administration		20
		320
Bad debt savings	(100)	
Interest charge savings (see above)	(169)	(269)
Net cost of policy each year		51

These calculations show that the business would incur additional annual costs if it implemented this proposal. It would therefore be cheaper to stay with the existing credit policy.

12.5 Boswell Enterprises Ltd

(a) The investment in working capital will be:

	Current policy		New policy	
	£000	£000	£000	£000
Trade receivables				
((£3m × $^1/_{12}$ × 30%) + (£3m × $^2/_{12}$ × 70%))		425.0		
((£3.15m × $^1/_{12}$ × 60%) + (£3.15m × $^2/_{12}$ × 40%))				367.5
Inventories				
((£3m − (£3m × 20%)) × $^3/_{12}$)		600.0		
((£3.15m − (£3.15m × 20%)) × $^3/_{12}$)				630.0
Cash (fixed)		140.0		140.0
		1,165.0		1,137.5
Trade payables				
((£3m − (£3m × 20%)) × $^2/_{12}$)	(400.0)			
((£3.15m − (£3.15m × 20%)) × $^2/_{12}$)			(420.0)	
Accrued variable expenses				
(£3m × $^1/_{12}$ × 10%)	(25.0)			
(£3.15m × $^1/_{12}$ × 10%)			(26.3)	
Accrued fixed expenses	(15.0)	(440.0)	(15.0)	(461.3)
Investment in working capital		725.0		676.2

(b) The forecast planned profit for the year will be:

	Current policy		New policy	
	£000	£000	£000	£000
Sales revenue		3,000.0		3,150.0
Cost of goods sold		(2,400.0)		(2,520.0)
Gross profit (20%)		600.0		630.0
Variable expenses (10%)	(300.0)		(315.0)	
Fixed expenses	(180.0)		(180.0)	
Discounts	–	(480.0)	(47.3)	(542.3)
Operating profit		120.0		87.7

(c) Under the proposed policy we can see that the investment in working capital will be slightly lower than under the current policy. However, profit will be substantially lower as a result of offering discounts. The increase in sales revenue resulting from the discounts will not be sufficient to offset the additional costs of making the discounts to customers. It seems that the business should, therefore, stick with its current policy.

Appendix E: Present value table

Present value of £1, that is, $1/(1 + r)^n$

where r = discount rate

n = number of periods until payment

Periods (n)	Discount rates (r)										
	1%	2%	3%	4%	5%	6%	7%	8%	9%	10%	
1	0.990	0.980	0.971	0.962	0.952	0.943	0.935	0.926	0.917	0.909	1
2	0.980	0.961	0.943	0.925	0.907	0.890	0.873	0.857	0.842	0.826	2
3	0.971	0.942	0.915	0.889	0.864	0.840	0.816	0.794	0.772	0.751	3
4	0.961	0.924	0.888	0.855	0.823	0.792	0.763	0.735	0.708	0.683	4
5	0.951	0.906	0.863	0.822	0.784	0.747	0.713	0.681	0.650	0.621	5
6	0.942	0.888	0.837	0.790	0.746	0.705	0.666	0.630	0.596	0.565	6
7	0.933	0.871	0.813	0.760	0.711	0.665	0.623	0.583	0.547	0.513	7
8	0.923	0.853	0.789	0.731	0.677	0.627	0.582	0.540	0.502	0.467	8
9	0.914	0.837	0.766	0.703	0.645	0.592	0.544	0.500	0.460	0.424	9
10	0.905	0.820	0.744	0.676	0.614	0.558	0.508	0.463	0.422	0.386	10
11	0.896	0.804	0.722	0.650	0.585	0.527	0.475	0.429	0.388	0.350	11
12	0.887	0.788	0.701	0.625	0.557	0.497	0.444	0.397	0.356	0.319	12
13	0.879	0.773	0.681	0.601	0.530	0.469	0.415	0.368	0.326	0.290	13
14	0.870	0.758	0.661	0.577	0.505	0.442	0.388	0.340	0.299	0.263	14
15	0.861	0.743	0.642	0.555	0.481	0.417	0.362	0.315	0.275	0.239	15

	11%	12%	13%	14%	15%	16%	17%	18%	19%	20%	
1	0.901	0.893	0.885	0.877	0.870	0.862	0.855	0.847	0.840	0.833	1
2	0.812	0.797	0.783	0.769	0.756	0.743	0.731	0.718	0.706	0.694	2
3	0.731	0.712	0.693	0.675	0.658	0.641	0.624	0.609	0.593	0.579	3
4	0.659	0.636	0.613	0.592	0.572	0.552	0.534	0.516	0.499	0.482	4
5	0.593	0.567	0.543	0.519	0.497	0.476	0.456	0.437	0.419	0.402	5
6	0.535	0.507	0.480	0.456	0.432	0.410	0.390	0.370	0.352	0.335	6
7	0.482	0.452	0.425	0.400	0.376	0.354	0.333	0.314	0.296	0.279	7
8	0.434	0.404	0.376	0.351	0.327	0.305	0.285	0.266	0.249	0.233	8
9	0.391	0.361	0.333	0.308	0.284	0.263	0.243	0.225	0.209	0.194	9
10	0.352	0.322	0.295	0.270	0.247	0.227	0.208	0.191	0.176	0.162	10
11	0.317	0.287	0.261	0.237	0.215	0.195	0.178	0.162	0.148	0.135	11
12	0.286	0.257	0.231	0.208	0.187	0.168	0.152	0.137	0.124	0.112	12
13	0.258	0.229	0.204	0.182	0.163	0.145	0.130	0.116	0.104	0.093	13
14	0.232	0.205	0.181	0.160	0.141	0.125	0.111	0.099	0.088	0.078	14
15	0.209	0.183	0.160	0.140	0.123	0.108	0.095	0.084	0.074	0.065	15

Index

Note: Page numbers in **bold** indicate highlighted **key terms** and their glossary definitions.

reducing inventory levels 392, 394–5
reducing liabilities *see* revenue
references for credit 457
refunding risk 427
Registrar of Companies 113, 117, 126, 139
regulations 12
relative efficiency, assessing 268
relevance **6**, 6–7, 10, **492**
relevant costs **373**, **492**
reliability **6**, 7, 10, **492**
rent 235–6
replacement of non-current assets 95
reporting dates 12–13
reporting periods *see* accounting periods
reports 12–13
   auditors 142–3
   budgets 334
   directors 141–2
rescue capital 429
reserves **123**, 126–7, **492**
   balance sheets 138
   capital **127**, 133–5, 136, **484**
   general 138
   revenue **124**, 127, 128, 133–5, 136, **493**
   share premium accounts **128–9**, **493**
   transfers to 138
residual values of assets **88**, **492**
resources
   investment decisions and 346
   scarce, most efficient use of 256–8
restricted vision of ratios 221
retained profits 132, 138, 391–3
return, accounting rate of *see* accounting rate
   of return
return, internal rate of *see* internal rate of
   return
return on capital employed (ROCE) **189**,
   189–91, 200–1, 351, **492**
return on ordinary shareholders' funds (ROSF)
   188, 188–9, **493**
returns, balancing risks and 20–1
returns on investments and servicing of
   finance *see* cash flow statements
revenue **70**, **493**
   break-even analysis and 239–44, 250
   equalling costs *see* break-even analyses
   examples 70–1
   and expenses *see* income statements
   forms of 70–1
   recognition 77–81
   reserves *see* reserves
   sales per employee ratios **199**, 199–200,
      493
   sales to capital employed **198**, **493**
rights issues *see* shares

risks **493**
   NPV and 359–60, 361
   premiums **360**, 361, **493**
   refunding 427
   returns and, balancing 20–1
ROCE *see* return on capital employed
rolling budgets **308**, **485**
Rolls-Royce 71, 214, 379–80, 443–4, 446
ROSF *see* return on ordinary shareholders'
   funds
round tripping 144
Royal Bank of Scotland 131
Royal Mail 295
Ryanair 242–3, 246, 397

safety
   inventory levels 449
   margins of **244**, 244–7, **490**
Safeway 11
Sainsbury's 19, 118, 218, 347
sale and leasebacks **408**, **493**
sales
   budgets 308–11
   commission 82–3
   cost of 71, **74–5**, **485**
   on credit *see* credit
   profit–volume charts 250
   revenue per employee ratio **199**, 199–200,
      493
   revenue to capital employed **198**,
      198–200, **493**
   volume variances 328–31
scale of investments 372
scarce resources, most efficient use of
   256–8
Scottish & Newcastle 446
scrip issues *see* bonus issues
secondary market, Stock Exchange as 417
semi-fixed (semi-variable) costs **238**,
   238–9, **493**
service function of accounting 6–8
service industries, ABC in 293
services, revenue recognition 80–1
SES Global 379
settlement periods *see* trade payables; trade
   receivables
Severn Trent 442–4
shareholders 113–14, 119, 121, 142–3
shares **113–42**, **493**
   bonus issues **129**, 129–31, 417, **483**
   capital 125–6, 131, 133–5, 136
   consolidating **125–6**, **484**
   earnings per share (EPS) **212**, **486**
   initial public offerings (IPO) 417–19
   issues 413–17